PRINCIPLES OF MODERN MANAGEMENT

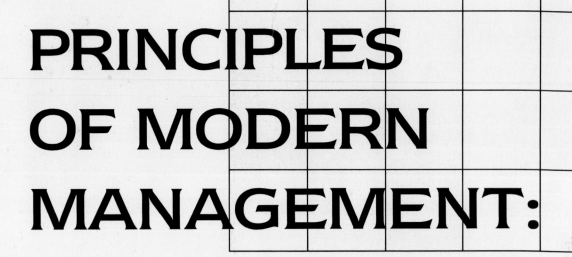

PRINCIPLES OF MODERN MANAGEMENT:

FUNCTIONS AND SYSTEMS

FOURTH EDITION

SAMUEL C. CERTO

Roy E. Crummer Graduate School of Business
Rollins College

Allyn and Bacon
Boston   London   Sydney   Toronto

Series Editor: Jack Peters
Editor-in-Chief: Bill Barke
Special Projects Editor: Diana Murphy
Developmental Editor: Leslie B. G. Goldberg
Cover Administrator: Linda Dickinson
Composition Buyer: Linda Cox
Copy Editor: Jo-Anne Naples
Text Designer: Caliber Design Planning, Inc.
Photo Researcher: Laurel Anderson / Photosynthesis
Cover Designer: Susan Slovinsky
Editorial-Production Administrator: Mary Beth Finch

Library of Congress Cataloging-in-Publication Data

Certo, Samuel C.
    Principles of modern management.

    Includes bibliographies and indexes.
    1. Management.   I. Title.
HD31.C414   1989   658   88-22233
ISBN 0-205-11677-9

Printed in the United States of America.

10 9 8 7 6 5 4 3 2 1   93 92 91 90 89 88

The credits and acknowledgements for figures, tables, boxes, and cases begin on
p. 657. They should be considered an extension of the copyright page.

Photo Credits   Photos pp. xiv, 3, 29, 30, 53, 55, 83, 84, 86, 103, 107, 108, 110, 131, 132, 159, 160, 195, 207, 221, 222, 251, 281, 284, 286, 319, 349, 350, 375, 403, 434, 439, 467, 497, 533, 534, 560, 569, 570, 599, 600, David E. Dempster; pp. xxviii, 192, 530, Lou Jones; p. 4, G. Contorakes/The Stock Market; p. 10, John Curtis, p. 26, Vail Cart Tyler; p. 32, Courtesy of Allen-Bradley; pp. 34, 36, Historical Picture Service; p. 35, Bettmann Archive; pp. 56, 436, 565, Pete Salutos/The Stock Market; p. 63, Ted Horowitz/The Stock Market; p. 77 © Donald L. Miller; p. 78, Michael L. Abramson/Woodfin Camp and Associates; pp. 79, 188, 196, 432, Gabe Palmer/The Stock Market; p. 128, Joseph Kugielsky; p. 140, courtesy of IBM; pp. 155, 162, 320, Ted Cordingley; pp. 218, 494, Andrew Popper/The Picture Group; p. 228, courtesy of Service Master; p. 247, Arthur Grace/SYGMA; p. 252, courtesy of Fairchild Industries; p. 273, 526, SYGMA; p. 292, courtesy of Apple Computer; p. 311, courtesy of GE Plastics; p. 313, Michael Pronzini/FOS Inc.; p. 316, Russ Schliepmann; p. 339, Fredrik D. Bodin; p. 345, Andy Swayne; p. 360, Takeshi Takahara/Photo Researchers; p. 371, J. Barry O'Rourke/The Stock Market; p. 376, courtesy of North American Tool and Die; p. 385, Jim Knowles/The Picture Group; p. 400, George Turner/Photo Researchers; p. 404, Henley & Savage/The Stock Market; p. 440, Doug Menuez/Picture Group; p. 448, Mike Powell/Woodfin Camp and Associates; p. 464, NASA; p. 468, courtesy of Commodore; p. 489, Stuart Franklin/SYGMA; p. 498, Bob O'Shaughnessy/The Stock Market; p. 506, courtesy of CARE; p. 528, Peter A. Simon/The Stock Market; p. 541, Tom McHugh/Photo Researchers; p. 559, courtesy of Martin Marietta; p. 588, William Mitchell/*Time* Magazine; p. 596, courtesy of Nissan Motor Corporation; p. 611, Sepp Seitz/Woodfin Camp and Associates; p. 622, Carolyn Caddes; p. 624, Tom Bean/The Stock Market.

To Mimi, Trevis, Matthew, Sarah, and Brian

My life has been much enriched by my family. By seeing the world through the eyes of the young, I remember how simple truth can be. By viewing an adolescent struggling for identity, I remember how frustrating the challenges of life can be. Through thoughtful conversation with my wife, I remember how important keeping perspective can be.

Note to Students from the Author

Management success is what happens when preparation meets opportunity. Take advantage of this text and this course as a vehicle for preparing for management opportunities that you inevitably will have. Keep this text in your professional library as a *reference book*, which can be used to enhance your preparedness for opportunities throughout various stages of your future management career.

BRIEF CONTENTS

CONTENTS

SECTION 2
PLANNING   80

SECTION 3

ORGANIZING 192

SECTION 4
INFLUENCING   316

SECTION 5
CONTROLLING 436

SECTION 6
TOPICS FOR SPECIAL EMPHASIS   530

APPENDIX:
VIDEO CASES 626

PREFACE

It is difficult to describe the excitement and personal satisfaction I feel in writing this overview. This book reflects a distinctive tradition in management education materials that has evolved in character and scope over several years. For more than a decade, the *Principles of Modern Management* learning package—this text and its related ancillaries—has been popularly used as learning materials for management courses in colleges and universities throughout the United States and several foreign countries.

Many credit the steadily growing popularity of this package to my conviction that appropriate management concepts must be covered and presented clearly and concisely, that learning materials must reflect an empathy for and an enhancement of the student learning process, and that instructional support materials must facilitate the design and conduct of only the highest-quality principles of management courses. Starting with the text, the following sections describe each major component of this newest management learning package and explain how this conviction has become even more pronounced in this newest edition.

TEXT: THEORY OVERVIEW

As with the first three editions, the purpose of this text is straightforward: to prepare students to be managers. The overall approach employed in this book is to emphasize the wisdom of both management scholars and practicing managers. Special emphasis is placed on the careful and thorough explanation of important management theory as well as the discussion of how it can be practically applied to help managers meet the everyday organizational challenges of modern organizations.

Deciding on the management concepts that should be included in a text of this sort and on how they should be covered is probably the most difficult task an author faces. Much insight was gleaned through careful consideration of such materials as (1) reports and opinions of accrediting agencies—for example, the American Assembly of Collegiate Schools of Business (AACSB); (2) trends and issues in management research as highlighted by the work of management scholars; and (3) accounts by practicing managers emphasizing the contemporary organizational problems they face and how to deal with them.

Over all, management theory in this text is divided into six main sections: "Introduction to Management," "Planning," "Organizing," "Influencing," "Controlling," and "Topics for Special Emphasis." Naturally, updates of theory and example have been extensively made throughout each section. More specifically, Section 1, "Introduction to Management," lays the groundwork necessary for studying management. Chapter 1, "Introducing Management and Manage-

The text presents appropriate management theory, enhances student learning, and facilitates the instructional process.

The new edition prepares students to be managers.

Revisions reflect ideas from AACSB, management scholars, and practicing managers.

Theory and example updates are included.

There is a new emphasis on management careers.

xvi

ment Careers," has been renamed and significantly revised in this edition not only to better expose students to what management is but also to give them a better understanding of management careers in organizations. This chapter also highlights Peters and Waterman's *In Search of Excellence,* which provides insights on how to manage a successful organization. Chapter 2, "Approaches to Managing," presents several fundamental but different ways that managers can perceive their jobs. The last chapter in this section, Chapter 3, "Organizational Objectives," discusses the nature of goals that organizations can adopt and the relationship between these goals and the management process.

Section 2, "Planning," elaborates on planning activities as a primary management function. Chapter 4, "Fundamentals of Planning," presents the basics of planning. Chapter 5, "Making Decisions," discusses the decision-making process as a component of the planning process. Chapter 6, "Types of Planning: Strategic and Tactical," has undergone significant revision. Its discussion of environmental analysis as a component of strategy formulation has been extended, and special emphasis has been given to the general, operating, and internal levels of organizational environments. Chapter 7, "Plans and Planning Tools," discusses various managerial planning tools available to help formulate plans.

There is a new emphasis on environmental analysis.

Section 3, "Organizing," discusses organizing activities as a major management function. Chapter 8 presents the fundamentals of organizing, and chapter 9 elaborates on how to organize various worker activities appropriately. Chapter 10, "Providing Appropriate Human Resources for the Organization," discusses obtaining people who will make a desirable contribution to organizational objectives. Lee Iacocca's thoughts from his autobiography are highlighted in this chapter. Chapter 11 has been significantly revised; it is renamed "Organizational Change and Stress." Coverage still focuses on how managers change organizations, but it now includes additional focus on stress-related issues that can accompany such action. The discussion highlights the definition of stress and the importance of studying and managing stress.

There is a new emphasis on stress.

Section 4, "Influencing," discusses how managers should deal with people. The four chapters in this section (chapters 12–15) respectively discuss the fundamentals of influencing and communication, leadership, motivation, and managing groups.

Section 5, "Controlling," analyzes the performance of control activities as another basic management function. Chapter 16, "Principles of Controlling," presents the basics of controlling. Chapter 17, "Fundamentals of Production Management and Control," describes the basics of the production process, robotics, and a number of useful managerial tools for controlling production. Chapter 18, "Information," defines *information* and elaborates on the role it plays in the controlling process. New coverage focuses on computers and decision support systems, which managers can use to improve controlling efforts.

There is new material on decision support systems.

The last section of this text is "Topics for Special Emphasis." Chapter 19, "Social Responsibility: An Emphasis on Ethics," discusses the responsibilities managers have to society, as well as ethics, as a possible rationale for encouraging managers to meet these responsibilities. The focus on ethics is new to this edition. Chapter 20, "International Management," discusses the basics of international and multinational organizations. New coverage in this edition includes more comparative management focus on the study of Japanese management techniques, with special emphasis on just-in-time inventory control. Chapter 21 discusses skills people must possess in order to manage successfully in the future. Current updates including future age distribution of the workforce, growth

There is a new emphasis on ethics.

There is new emphasis on Japanese management: just-in-time (JIT) inventory control.

of the workforce, industry growth, and women in the workforce. These topics lend particular relevance and timeliness to chapter revisions.

TEXT: STUDENT LEARNING AIDS

Several features of this text were designed to make the study of management more efficient, effective, and enjoyable. A list of these features and an explanation of each follow.

LEARNING OBJECTIVES   The opening pages of each chapter contain a set of learning objectives that are intended as guidelines on how to study the chapter.

CHAPTER OUTLINES   The opening pages of each chapter also contain a chapter outline that previews the textual material and helps the reader keep the information in perspective while it is being read.

INTRODUCTORY CASES WITH "FLASHES" BACK TO THE CASE   The opening of each chapter contains a case study that introduces readers to management problems related to chapter content. Detailed "Back to the Case" sections appear throughout each chapter, applying specific areas of management theory discussed in the chapter to the introductory case. Most of these cases involve real companies and highlight contemporary issues in organizations such as McDonald's, Toro, and Hospital Corporation of America.*

There are new and updated end-of-chapter cases.

CONCLUDING CASES   The concluding pages of each chapter contain a real-life case that further applies chapter content to related management situations. Sixteen end-of-chapter cases are new to this edition. The cases cover a wide range of subjects, including recent accounts about business, government, sports, and the like. Among the companies focused on are Frito-Lay, People Express, and Shell Oil.

SECTIONAL CASES   Each of the six major sections of the text ends with a case relating to that section as a whole. These cases provide students with the opportunity to review and apply material from entire sections of the text. All sectional cases are based on real, undisguised situations.

New video cases focus on
1. Management careers.
2. Strategic planning.
3. Ethics.
4. International management.

VIDEO CASE APPENDIX   A very innovative feature of this text, which is new to this edition, is the Video Case Appendix. This appendix is a collection of classroom learning activities specially designed to be used in conjunction with a series of four video tapes. The video cases and their related learning activities were carefully crafted as an integral part of this text to illustrate and extend specific text chapters. The video cases are

Fired: A Focus on Management Careers
Battle of the Blimps: A Focus on Strategic Planning

---

* All real-life materials in this text were chosen because of their special relevance to management concepts discussed in the chapter. However, because changes occur so rapidly in the real world of business and government, certain facts and figures contained in these materials may already be somewhat dated.

The Parable of the Sadhu: A Focus on Ethics
The Colonel Comes to Japan: A Focus on International Management

Extensive instructional materials are available in the Instructor's Resource Manual, and they offer detailed suggestions on how best to use these video case materials. One copy of each of the videos will be provided to every school (in the U.S. only) using the fourth edition of *Principles of Modern Management*.

MARGINAL NOTES   Each chapter contains marginal notes and key words that can be helpful in the initial reading and for review.

"MANAGEMENT IN ACTION"   All chapters contain a short reading that is intended to illustrate how a management concept presented in a chapter relates to an actual company. Eighteen exhibits are new to this edition and emphasize the usefulness of the management concepts discussed. Companies such as Wendy's, Armco, and Johnson & Johnson are highlighted.

New real-world examples of management applications are included.

ACTION SUMMARIES   Each chapter ends with an action-oriented chapter summary. In this summary, students respond to several objective questions that are clearly linked to the learning objectives stated at the beginning of the chapter. Students can check their answers with the answer key at the end of the chapter. This key also lists the pages in the chapter that can be referred to for a fuller explanation of the answers.

INTRODUCTORY CASE WRAP-UP   Each chapter ends with several questions about its introductory case. These questions provide the opportunity to apply chapter concepts directly to the case.

DISCUSSION QUESTIONS   The concluding pages of each chapter contain a set of discussion questions that test the understanding of chapter material and can serve as vehicles for study and for class discussion.

GLOSSARY   Major management terms and their definitions are gathered at the end of the text. They appear in boldface type along with the text pages on which the discussion of each term appears.

ILLUSTRATIONS   Figures, tables, and photographs depicting various management situations are used throughout the text to help bridge the gap between management theory and authentic situations.

New photographs and artwork are included.

COLOR   A quick inspection of this edition will reveal that it is in full color. Color has been used not simply for the sake of color but to help students learn through more engaging text material.

SUPPLEMENTARY MATERIALS

A number of ingredients have been developed to complement the use of *Principles of Modern Management*. Although the text itself was designed to offer a desirable amount of material for a high-quality course in principles of management, special supplements are available to further enrich the learning situation in which the text is used.

EXPERIENCING MODERN MANAGEMENT: A WORKBOOK, FOURTH EDITION

This is a combination study guide and sourcebook of more than sixty experiential exercises and is to be used in conjunction with the text. The fourth edition of this workbook contains several new and modified exercises that correspond to the revised text. Workbook elements that correspond to each text chapter include the following.

AN EXTENDED CHAPTER SUMMARY   Extended summaries are helpful for quick review of text material. Summaries are keyed to chapter learning objectives in the text in order to facilitate student learning.

LEARNING ASSESSMENT ACTIVITIES   For each chapter of the text, the workbook contains a series of twenty-five objective questions that test the understanding of chapter content. Correct answers and the text page numbers on which answers are explained are furnished for all questions.

EXPERIENTIAL EXERCISES, ACTIVITIES, PROJECTS, CASES   A number of diverse in-class and out-of-class learning activities that further illustrate the content of each text chapter are provided. Many exercises are available for larger and smaller classes. A suggested sequence for using the text and the workbook jointly is shown in Figure P.1.

COMPUTER SIMULATIONS IN MANAGEMENT (CSM)

Six computer-assisted experiential exercises are available.

This software contains six computer-assisted experiential exercises designed to help students understand how software application programs can be used in practical management situations. The exercises focus on major sections in the text and are keyed to an introductory case within each section. Topics addressed in these exercises include using decision trees, assessing management style, and computer-assisted scheduling.

WORKOUT: A COMPUTERIZED STUDY GUIDE

There is a new interactive computer study guide.

Workout is designed to help students determine their understanding of the text material by testing their knowledge using a fast, interactive computer program. Workout asks students questions keyed to the learning objectives in the text. This division by learning objectives allows the student to conveniently and logically study a segment of the chapter, thus more easily determining problem areas. The program keeps score of the correct answers given, and a comment is displayed at the end of each objective describing the student's performance. Printed reports may be run at the end of each session.

Workout is available for the IBM PC or the Apple II. It is free to instructors upon adoption.

INSTRUCTIONAL AIDS

In addition to the supplements just described, several other ingredients of the *Principles of Modern Management* learning package also have been designed to enhance the learning environment in which this text is used. These ingredients offer various optional aids to the management instructor.

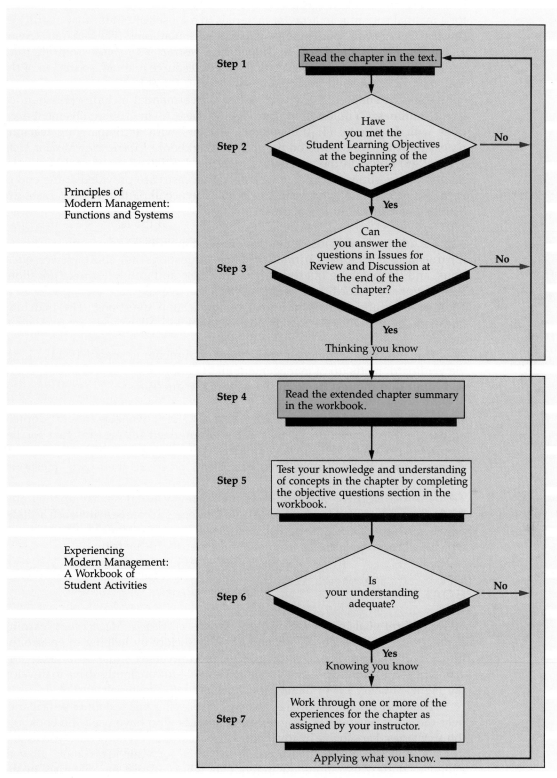

Principles of
Modern Management:
Functions and Systems

Step 1 Read the chapter in the text.

Step 2 Have you met the Student Learning Objectives at the beginning of the chapter? — No

Yes

Step 3 Can you answer the questions in Issues for Review and Discussion at the end of the chapter? — No

Yes

Thinking you know

Experiencing
Modern Management:
A Workbook of
Student Activities

Step 4 Read the extended chapter summary in the workbook.

Step 5 Test your knowledge and understanding of concepts in the chapter by completing the objective questions section in the workbook.

Step 6 Is your understanding adequate? — No

Yes

Knowing you know

Step 7 Work through one or more of the experiences for the chapter as assigned by your instructor.

Applying what you know.

FIGURE P.1
Suggested sequence for using the text and student workbook jointly

The instructional support materials are better organized.

INSTRUCTOR'S RESOURCE MANUAL   This unique and innovative instructor's manual contains an array of materials in a looseleaf binder that instructors can use to organize their lectures and teaching materials. The separate *Lecture Enrichment Kit, Extended Lecture Outline,* and *Instructor's Manual* from the third edition have been incorporated into this new resource manual, so that all of the materials are organized in a chapter-by-chapter format.

For each chapter in the text, the resource manual includes (1) extended lecture outlines; (2) notes on the introductory case; (3) in-class involvement exercises with handouts; (4) transparency masters with accompanying teaching notes; (5) instructor's notes on the student workbook, *Experiencing Modern Management;* (6) notes on the concluding cases; and (7) solutions to end-of-chapter discussion questions. Notes on the integrative cases are provided at the end of each section, and detailed instructor's notes to accompany the video cases are included at the end of the manual.

Revised test bank includes:
1. cases with questions
2. true/false questions
3. multiple-choice questions
4. short-answer questions
5. matching questions

Test instruments reflect the insights of the Test Bank Reviewer Board.

TEST BANK   Testing instruments for the text include (1) cases with questions, (2) true/false questions, (3) multiple choice questions, (4) short-answer questions, and (5) matching questions. The true/false and multiple-choice questions are categorized according to the learning objective they are testing and as to whether they are factual/conceptual or application questions. The matching questions focus exclusively on chapter terminology. All answers are page referenced.

Due to the importance of the testing instruments, a special Test Bank Reviewer Board, made up of management instructors, was established. This board had input into the test bank and reviewed the questions.

There is an improved computerized testing program.

MICROTEST—A COMPUTERIZED TEST BANK   Available free to adopters of 100 copies or more of the text is a computerized testing program for the Apple, IBM PC, and Macintosh computers. This program enables instructors to choose from a bank of questions, edit them, or create their own questions.

There are over 150 transparencies available.

TRANSPARENCIES   Sixty full-color transparency acetates make up the transparency package, with teaching notes and strategies accompanying each acetate. Also available is the Allyn and Bacon Transparencies for Management package, which includes 100 acetates from sources other than this text.

GOAL

My long-term goal in publishing the *Principles of Modern Management* learning package is to make a positive contribution to society by helping to ensure the future management success of the college and university students of today. My action plan for reaching this goal is quite simple—to constantly strive to develop the highest-quality set of management instructional materials available.

The most valuable source of ideas for improving this text and its ancillaries over the years has been colleagues and students who have used the book and the ancillaries. I apologize in advance for any frustrations I may cause you as you use my materials. I also thank you in advance for your ideas about how to eliminate these frustrations for individuals who will use the materials in the future.

ACKNOWLEDGMENTS

Positive comments generated by the *Principles of Modern Management* learning package have been very pleasing. A multitude of people have played significant roles in the design and development of this package. It is with great pleasure that I recognize these individuals and extend to them my gratitude for their insight, expertise, and warm personal support and encouragement.

As with previous editions, Professor Lee A. Graf, Illinois State University, has been a major force behind this text and its accompanying experiential workbook. Professor Graf's conceptual and organizational skills have been critical in improving this learning package to the greatest degree possible.

Several other individuals have provided this text with valuable ancillary materials, and I would like to recognize each of them for their dedication and hard work:

Robert Goldberg and Tricia McConville of Northeastern University for revising the Instructor's Resource Manual.

Philip Weatherford of Embry-Riddle Aeronautical University for revising the Test Bank.

Robert Kemper of Northern Arizona University for contributing the case studies in the Test Bank.

I would also like to thank our Test Bank Advisory board:

William Francis Herlehy, Embry-Riddle Aeronautical University

James Westwater, College of Notre Dame of Maryland

James Moreau, Rock Valley College

Every author appreciates the valuable contribution reviewers make to the development of a text project. Reviewers offer that "different viewpoint" that requires an author to constructively question his or her work. I had an excellent team of reviewers. Thoughtful comments, concern for student learning, and insights regarding instructional implications of the written word characterized the high-quality feedback I received. I am pleased to be able to recognize members of my review team for their valuable contributions to the development of this text:

Billie Allen, University of Southern Mississippi

Dr. Randi Ellis, North Harris Community College

Frederick Sheppard, Sylvia Keyes, and Dr. Chuck England, Bridgewater State College

Dr. Don B. Bradley, University of Central Arkansas

Robert Goldberg, Northeastern University

Valeriano Cantu, Angelo State University

Thomas Goodwin, Johnson and Wales College

Another source of valuable feedback that I used for developing and implementing the revision plan for this edition was an opinion survey. This survey was conducted to expand the breadth of relevant feedback from colleagues about the instructional value of various components of this text as well as the *Principles of Modern Management* learning package as a whole. I would like to personally thank my colleagues who spent the time and the effort to provide data that were critical in defining the character and scope of this text and its ancillaries.

Christopher Aglo-Ostoghile, *Prairie View Agriculture and Technology College*

Milton C. Alderfer, *Miami Dade Community College North*

Arturo Alonzo Jr., *St. Philip's College*

David Anstett, *College of St. Scholastica*

Donald L. Ashbaugh, *University of Northern Iowa*

Jack Ashmore, *Bee County College*

Lorraine Bassette, *Prince George's Community College*

David Baxter, *San Diego Mesa College*

Charles Beavin, *Miami-Dade Community College*

Lee A. Belovarac, *Mercyhurst College*

Jack Blanton, *University of Kentucky*

Pam Braden, *Parkersburg Community College*

Terry H. Brattin, *Texas State Technical University–Harlingen*

William Brichner, *San Jose State University*

Duane Brickner, *Southern Mountain Community College*

John W. Jr. Brown, *SUNY Brockport*

W. Brown, *Berry College*

Robert Bruns, *Central College*

Shirley Bryan, *Pennsylvania State University–Berks*

F. M. Buchanan, *Salisbury State College*

Alison Buck, *Phillips University*

Robert S. Bulls, *J. Sargeant Reynolds Community College*

Ellen Burns, *Phillips University*

Thomas Burns, *Keystone Jr. College*

David T. Bussard, *Susquehanna University*

Dennis G. Butler, *Orange Coast College*

Austin Byron, *Northern Arizona University*

Edward Cahaly, *Stonehill College*

Robert E. Callahan, *Seattle University*

Perry Camingore, *Brazosport College*

Mario Carrillo, *Colorado School of Mines*

Thomas Case, *Georgia Southern University*

Tommy Cates, *University of Tennessee at Martin*

C. Dale Caudill, *Morehead State University*

Herschel Chait, *Indiana State University*

Pamela Chandler, *University of Mary Hardin–Baylor*

John F. Chisholm, *Allegheny Community College*

Daniel W. Churchill, *Mount Ida College*

Robert A. Cisek, *Mercyhurst College*

Joseph Clairmont, *Bay De Noc Community College*

William Clark, *Leeward Community College*

Debra M. Clingerman, *California University of Pennsylvania*

Larry A. Coleman, *Indiana State University*

Terry Comingor, *Brazosport College*

John Coppola, *Cosumnes River College*

Pati Crabb, *Bellarmine University*

D. James Day, *Shawnee State University*

John R. Deegan, *Texas Wesleyan College*

Linda Dell'Osso, *California State Polytechnic University–Pomona*

Sezai Demiral, *Edinboro University of Pennsylvania*

Richard L. Dickinson, *California State University–Sacramento*

Dale L. Dickson, *Mesa College*

Daniel J. Duffy, *Loyola College–Evergreen*

Robert Dunn, *Alexander City State College*

John Eberle, *Embry-Riddle Aeronautical University*

Sidney W. Eckert, *Appalachian State University*

Jeb Egbert, *Ambassador College*

Randi Sue Ellis, *North Harris County Community College*

Mary Sue Ewald, *Missouri Baptist College*

Vincent E. Faherty, *University of Northern Iowa*

Jeffrey W. Fahrenwal, *Central College*

Deborah Fajcak, *Harding Business College*

Jay Felton, *North Harris County Community College*

Judy Field, *Willmar Community College*

Stephen Field, *University of West Florida*

Richard Forsyth, *University of Wisconsin–Green Bay*

Paula S. Funkhouser, *Truckee Meadows Community College*

Dick Gardner, *West Virginia University*

Gerald Garrity, *Anna Maria College*

Carl Gates, *Sauk Valley College*

Pat Gaudette, *Pine Manor College*

Beth Gershon, *University of LaVerne*

Faith Gilroy, *Loyola College–Evergreen*

Carolyn Goad, *Oakland City Community College*

R. Goddard, *Appalachian State University*

Robert Goldberg, *Northeastern University*

David Goldenberg, *Bellarmine University*

Jack N. Grose, *Mars Hill College*

Raymond M. Guydosh, *SUNY Plattsburgh*

Luther Guynes, *Los Angeles City College*

James L. Hall, *University of Santa Clara*

Ed Hammer, *University of Tennessee–Chattanooga*

Kathleen Harcharik, *California State Polytechnic University–Pomona*

James Harvey, *University of West Florida*

D. B. Heide, *California State University–Fullerton*

Wayne Hemberger, *Edinboro University of Pennsylvania*

John W. Henry, *Georgia Southern University*

Bill Herlehy, *Embry-Riddle Aeronautical University*

Irving L. Herman, *California State University–Sacramento*
J. C. Hill, *Appalachian State University*
Robert T. Holland, *Woodbury University*
William Houlihan, *Detroit College of Business*
Fred House, *Northern Arizona University*
Edmund Hunter, *Delaware County Community College*
Warren Imada, *Leeward Community College*
William Jacobs, *Lake City Community College*
Ernest Jaski, *Richard J. Daley College*
David J. Jobson, *Keystone Jr. College*
Alan E. Johnson, *Embry-Riddle Aeronautical University*
Edwin Johnson, *Parkersburg Community College*
Karen R. Johnson, *University of New Hampshire*
Paul W. Joice Sr., *Walla Walla College*
Bette-Jean Jones, *Embry-Riddle Aeronautical University*
Charlie Jones, *East Central Oklahoma University*
Frazier C. Jones, *Montreat-Anderson College*
Frank Kattwinkel, *St. Leo College*
Fred Jeffrey Keil, *J. Sargeant Reynolds Community College*
Robert E. Kemper, *Northern Arizona University*
George Kevorkian, *Northern Virginia Community College*
Scott King, *Sinclair Community College*
Jerome M. Kinskey, *Sinclair Community College*
Barney J. Klecker, *Normandale Community College*
John P. Kohl, *San Jose State University*
Bob Kovacev, *California State University–Fullerton*
Dennis Lee Kovach, *Community College of Allegheny North*
William Lacewell, *Westark Community College*
Patricia Laidler, *Massasoit Community College*
Philip M. Lee, *Campbellsville College*
Jery Lemmons, *State Technical Institute–Memphis*
Charles LePore, *Embry-Riddle Aeronautical University*
Robert Lerosen, *Northern Virginia Community College*
Ardyce S. Lightner, *D'Youville College*
Malcom H. Livick, *Blue Ridge Community College*
Mary Alice Lo Cicero, *Oakland Community College*
Chris Lockwood, *Northern Arizona University*
John F. Logan, *Thiel College*
David J. Lonergan, *Greater Hartford Community College*
David H. Lydick, *St. Leo College*
Robert J. Lyons, *Sweet Briar College*
Willard Machen, *Amarillo College*
Anita Marcellis, *College of St. Elizabeth*
John D. McCurdy, *Embry-Riddle Aeronautical University*
Barbara McDonnell, *College of Notre Dame of Maryland*
Robert L. McElwee, *University of Akron*
James L. McGuigan, *Community College of Allegheny County*
James M. McHugh, *St. Louis Community College–Forest Park*
Pat McLaughlin, *Merrimac College*
Edward Meier, *Concordia College*

Peggy C. Mifflin, *Indiana State University*
Robert A. Moore, *Southern Utah State*
James Moreau, *Rock Valley College*
Bill Morris, *Devry Institute of Technology*
J. B. Mosca, *Monmouth College*
Alexander Mosley, *Miami-Dade Community College*
Bonnie S. Moyers, *Blue Ridge Community College*
Eugene Murkison, *Georgia Southern University*
John E. Murray, *Massasoit Community College*
M. James Nead, *Vincennes University*
Thomas Nist, *La Roche College*
Janet M. Noble, *University of Maryland*
James Nordin, *Coffeyville Community College*
Christopher E. Nussbaumer, *Austin Peay State University*
Erna O'Connor, *Kishwaukee College*
Diana Page, *University of West Florida*
Karl Pape, *Embry-Riddle Aeronautical University*
Michael H. Parson, *Hagerstown Junior College*
John Paxton, *Southwest Missouri State University*
Joseph O. Pecenka, *Northern Illinois University*
Dennis Pennington, *Spartanburg Methodist College*
Shri Penugonda, *Wilkes College*
Joseph Platts, *Miami-Dade Community College*
Sylvia Poster-Keyes, *Bridgewater State University*
Shane Premeux, *McNeese State University*
Rebecca Pyrne, *Wilmington College*
William Racker, *Anoka-Ramsey Community College*
Kenneth J. Radig, *Medaille College*
Harry Ramsden, *University of LaVerne–NAS No. Island*
Richard Raspen, *Wilkes College*
Mary C. Raven, *Mount Mary College*
Wm. R. Rawlinson, *Solano Community College*
Morris Dale Reed, *East Central University*
Harriet Rice, *Los Angeles City College*
Charles A. Rickman, *University of Arts and Sciences*
Robert Roller, *Oral Roberts University*
Peggy Romanelli, *Oral Roberts University*
Stanford H. Rosenberg, *La Roche College*
Greg Runyon, *Trevecca Nazarene College*
Mary Beth Ruthem, *Jefferson Tech College*
Robb Ruyle, *Mesa College*
Madan Saluja, *Lake Superior State College*
Richard D. Sambuco, *West Virginia Northern Community College*
Cheryl Savage, *California State Polytechnic University–Pomona*
Clemmie Saxton, *Howard University*
Dietrich L. Schaupp, *West Virginia University*
Suzanne Seedorf, *Northeast Iowa Technical Institute*
Charles R. Schatzer, *Solano Community College*
David Shepard, *Virginia Western Community College*
Steven Shiring, *Butler County Community College*
Sara Shryock, *Black Hills State College*
Jack Skaggs, *Oklahoma Christian College*

Bonnie Slager, *Rancho Santiago College*
Bob Smoot, *No. Virginia Community College*
Sherwin Snyder, *Ottawa University*
M. S. St. John, *Westmoreland County Community College*
Gary Steedley, *McKendree College*
C. R. Sterrett, *Frostburg State College*
Kathy Stewart, *Prestonburg Community College*
Ken Stewart, *Oral Roberts University*
Bill Strasen, *California State Polytechnic University–Pomona*
Jeff Streiter, *SUNY Brockport*
Assad Tavakoli, *Fayetteville State University*
Bruce E. Textley, *Bethany College*
Stephen Tilley, *Gainesville Jr. College*
Frank Tomassi, *Johnson and Wales College*
Richard F. Tyler, *Anne Arundel Community College*
Steve Vest, *Embry-Riddle Aeronautical University*
William Vicars, *Southern Illinois University*
Dean R. Vickstrom, *Iowa Western Community College*
Phillip A. Weatherford, *Embry-Riddle Aeronautical University*

Warren C. Weber, *California State Polytechnic University–Pomona*
Bernard Weinrich, *St. Louis Community College–Forest Park*
Robert J. Welsh, *Greenfield Community College*
Lee Westerlin, *Cerritos College*
James D. Westwater, *College of Notre Dame of Maryland*
Yvonne Weyrich, *Black Hills State College*
Paula Wilcoxon, *Cleveland Institute of Music*
David A. Wilkerson, *Indiana State University*
William Williams, *Mississippi County Community College*
Fairlee Winfield, *Northern Arizona University*
Alexander Wojtalik, *Edinboro University of Pennsylvania*
Robert Woodin, *Texas Women's University*
Charles L. Wright, *Tarleton State University*
Ignatius Yacoub, *Loma Linda University*
Wayne A. Yerxa, *Mount Vernon Nazarene College*
Mary Rose J. Zink, *Wilmington College*

I would also like to recognize the personal interest and encouragement for this project shown by my colleagues in the Roy E. Crummer Graduate School of Business at Rollins College. The faculty in general has been very supportive of this project. In more specific terms, Dean Martin Schatz has been instrumental in helping me acquire the resources necessary to complete this project. Additionally, James M. Higgins, Theodore T. Herbert, and Max R. Richards, my management colleagues, have all helped me clarify the character and scope of this book. I greatly appreciate the professional orientation of my colleagues at Crummer.

The support that Allyn and Bacon has shown throughout this revision process must not go unnoticed. The attention to detail and book development skills displayed by the special projects team was absolutely critical. Sandi Kirshner, special projects director and director of marketing, Diana Murphy and Nancy Forsyth, special projects managers, and Susan Lewis, special projects assistant, have all made significant contributions. For helping me to deal with everyday publishing issues, Diana Murphy and Mary Beth Finch deserve a special thanks. The patience they showed and the advice they offered me during the development of this text were invaluable. In addition, Bill Barke, editor-in-chief, has provided valuable global insights regarding publishing in general and the management discipline in particular. Clearly, this text and its ancillaries have gotten all the critical care and attention necessary.

Lastly, on more of a personal note, I want to thank my family for encouraging me to strive for excellence in the development of this project. In this regard, the example set by Samuel C. Certo, Sr., my father, and Annette Certo, my mother, will always be a positive influence on my life.

PRINCIPLES OF MODERN MANAGEMENT

INTRODUCTION TO MANAGEMENT

The purpose of this section is to introduce the field of management. In general terms, the introduction will be accomplished through extended discussion on how *management* is defined, on various approaches to management that have evolved over the years, and on organizational objectives. In more specific terms, this section will offer a thorough explanation of the steps of the management process, of managerial effectiveness and efficiency, of the skills needed by managers, and of what can be expected from a management career. The explanation of different ways to perform the manager's job will emphasize the classical, behavioral, management science, contingency, and systems approaches. Lastly, this section will discuss the relationship of management and organizational objectives, individual versus organizational objectives, operational objectives, and management by objectives (MBO).

As you study chapters in this section, keep in mind that this material is extremely important. An understanding of these foundation concepts will significantly influence your ability to understand the material in the remaining sections of the text.

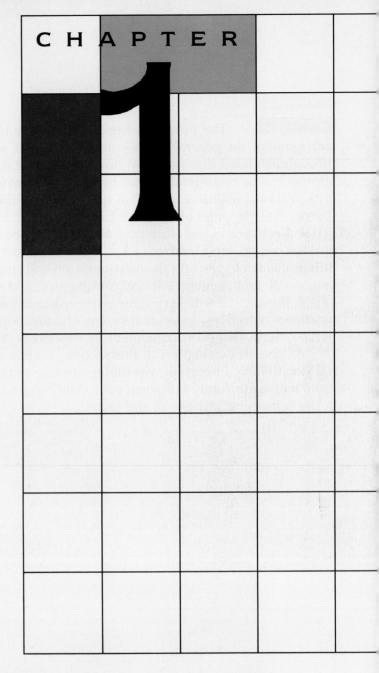

STUDENT LEARNING OBJECTIVES

From studying this chapter, I will attempt to acquire:

1. An understanding of the importance of management to society and individuals.
2. An understanding of the role of management.
3. An ability to define *management* in several different ways.
4. An ability to list and define the basic functions of management.
5. Working definitions of managerial effectiveness and managerial efficiency.
6. An understanding of basic management skills and their relative importance to managers.
7. An understanding of the universality of management.
8. Insights concerning what careers are and how they evolve.

MANAGEMENT AND MANAGEMENT CAREERS

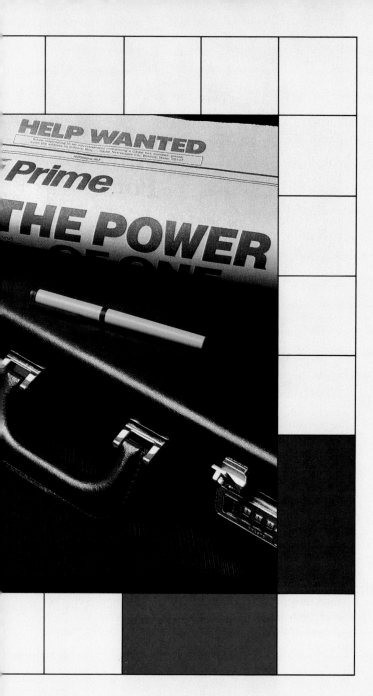

CHAPTER OUTLINE

INEXPERIENCED MANAGERS AT WEIRTON STEEL MILL

John G. Redline approached the microphones at his press conference in Weirton, West Virginia. As president of the Weirton Steel Division of National Steel, he had an important announcement to make. A significant proportion of the audience already knew what Redline was going to say: A deal had been finalized whereby workers at the Weirton plant would buy the steel mill from National Steel. The press conference was simply part of the formality of making this deal final.

The recent financial performance of the Weirton plant had left the parent company little choice. In the previous year, National Steel had lost $60 million at the plant. In addition, since demand for the products manufactured by the Weirton plant was decreasing steadily, National Steel saw little hope for a turnaround in the near future.

National Steel had decided that it had two alternatives. The first was that it could phase out most of the operations of the Weirton plant. This action, of course, would necessitate laying off a significant number of Weirton's 11,500 employees. Since the entire population of Weirton was only 26,000, such a layoff would have had a profound effect on the community's economy. In addition, this action would have been the first step toward finally closing the plant.

National Steel's other alternative was to sell the plant to the workers. Organizing all of the employees and getting them to agree to purchase the plant was an extremely complex task, but eventually a deal was made.

Under the terms of the final agreement, the employees agreed to pay $66 million for the mill and its

equipment and $200 million for the current assets at the mill. They also agreed to assume $85 million worth of long-term debt that the mill had incurred. No payments of principal or interest would be due until after the newly independent mill had been operating five years. The board of directors of the newly formed company would consist of two union representatives, two members of management, and six individuals from outside the organization.

One result of the employee decision to purchase the Weirton plant was that employees would have a much larger part in managing the plant in the future than they had in the past. A number of employees who had been simply line workers at Weirton in the past would undoubtedly be made managers in the future.

What's Ahead

As discussed in the introductory case, the employees purchased the Weirton plant and would have to begin taking an active role in managing it. The information in this chapter is designed to help new managers such as these Weirton employees to understand the basics of management. Management *is defined through (1) a discussion of its importance both to society and to individuals, (2) a description of the management task, and (3) a discussion of its universality.*

⊞ THE IMPORTANCE OF MANAGEMENT

Managers influence all phases of our modern organizations. Plant managers run manufacturing operations that produce our clothes, food, and automobiles. Sales managers maintain a sales force that markets goods. Personnel managers provide organizations with a competent and productive work force. The "jobs available" section in the classified advertisements of any major newspaper describes many different types of management activities and confirms the importance of management (see Figure 1.1 on page 6).

Our society simply could not exist as we know it today or improve its present status without a steady stream of managers to guide its organizations. Peter Drucker makes this point in stating that effective management is quickly becoming the main resource of developed countries and the most needed resource of developing ones.[1] In short, countries desperately need good managers.

Society needs good managers.

In addition to being important to our society as a whole, management is vital to many individuals simply because they earn their living by being managers. Government statistics show that management positions have increased from approximately 10 percent to approximately 18 percent of the work force since 1950.[2] Managers typically come from varying backgrounds and have diverse educational specialties. Many individuals who originally trained to be accountants, teachers, financiers, or even writers eventually make their livelihood from being managers. In the short term, the demand for managers may vary somewhat from year to year.[3] In the long term, managerial positions can yield high salaries, status, interesting work, personal growth, and intense feelings of accomplishment. To illustrate how substantial management salaries can be, Figure 1.2 on page 7 shows how the average chief executive officer (CEO) salary plus bonuses at Fortune 500 companies has changed since 1974. Examples of CEOs whose annual salary plus bonuses is above this average are Edward Telling of Sears, Roebuck ($1,425,000) and William S. Anderson of NCR ($1,075,000).

Management also has much to offer individuals.

5

SR. MANAGEMENT DEVELOPMENT SPECIALIST

We are a major metropolitan service employer of over 5,000 employees seeking a person to join our management development staff. Prospective candidates will be degreed with 5 to 8 years experience in the design, implementation, and evaluation of developmental programs for first line and mid-level management personnel. Additionally, candidates must demonstrate exceptional oral and written communications ability and be skilled in performance analysis, programmed instruction, and the design and the implementation of reinforcement systems.

If you meet these qualifications, please send your resume, including salary history and requirements to:
Box RS-653
An Equal Opportunity Employer

BRANCH MGR—$27,500. Perceptive pro with track record in adm & lending has high visibility with respected firm.
Box PH-165

AVIATION FBO MANAGER NEEDED

Southeast Florida operation catering to corporate aviation. No maintenance or aircraft sales – just fuel and the best service. Must be experienced. Salary plus benefits commensurate with qualifications. Submit complete resume to: **Box LJO-688**

DIVISION CREDIT MANAGER

Major mgf. corporation seeks an experienced, shirt-sleeve credit manager to handle the credit and collection function of its midwest division (Chicago area). Interpersonal skills are important, as is the ability to communicate effectively with senior management. Send resume with current compensation to:
Box NM-43

ACCOUNTING MANAGER

Growth opportunity. Michigan Ave. location. Acctg. degree, capable of supervision. Responsibilities include G/L, financial statements, inventory control, knowledge of systems design for computer applications. Send resume, incl. salary history to:
Box RJM-999
An Equal Opportunity Employer

FINANCIAL MANAGER

CPA/MBA (U of C) with record of success in mngmnt positions. Employed, now seeking greater opportunity. High degree of professionalism, exp. in dealing w/financial inst., strong communication & analytical skills, stability under stress, high energy level, results oriented. Age 34, 1 1 yrs exper. incl. major public acctng, currently 5 years as Financial VP of field leader. Impressive references.**Box LML-666**

MARKET MANAGER

Major lighting manufacturer seeks market manager for decorative outdoor lighting. Position entails establishing and implementing marketing, sales, and new product development programs including coordination of technical publications and related R & D projects. Must locate at Denver headquarters. Send resume to **Box WM-214**
No agencies please.

GENERAL MANAGER

Small industrial service company, privately owned, located in Springfield, Missouri, needs aggressive, skilled person to make company grow in profits and sales. Minimum B.S. in Business, experienced in all facets of small business operations. Must understand profit. Excellent opportunity and rewards. Salary and fringes commensurate with experience and performance. **Box LEM-116**

FOUNDRY SALES MANAGER

Aggressive gray iron foundry located in the Midwest, specializing in 13,000 tons of complex castings yearly with a weight range of 2 to 400 pounds, is seeking experienced dynamic sales manager with sound sales background in our industry. Salary commensurate with experience and excellent benefit package. **Box MO-948**

PERSONNEL MANAGER

Publicly owned, national manufacturer with 12 plants, 700 employees, seeks first corporate personnel director. We want someone to administer programs in:
- Position and rate evaluation
- Employee safety engineering
- Employee training
- Employee communications
- Employee benefits
- Federal compliance

Qualifications: minimum of 3–5 years personnel experience in mfg. company, ability to tactfully deal on shirt-sleeve basis with employees at all levels from all walks of life, free to travel. Position reports to Vice President, Operations. Full range of company benefits, salary $28,000–$35,000. Reply in complete confidence to:
Box JK-236

FIGURE 1.1
The variety of management positions available

BACK TO THE CASE

The information just presented furnishes the employee-owners of Weirton Steel with insights concerning the significance of their decision. Their role in management will be important not only to society as a whole but also to the individual managers. In general, managers make some contribution to creating the standard of living we all enjoy and thereby obtain corresponding rewards. Given the status of the Weirton plant, the societal contributions that this organization will be able to afford will probably be relatively modest in the near future. If the plant becomes successful, however, its contributions will undoubtedly be more significant as time passes.

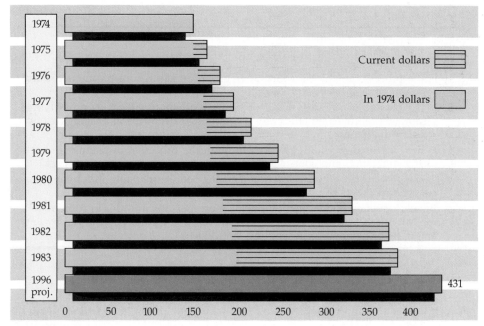

FIGURE 1.2
Average CEO salary plus bonuses at Fortune 500 companies (in thousands of dollars)

THE MANAGEMENT TASK

Besides understanding the significance of being a manager and its related potential benefits, prospective managers should know what the management task entails. The sections that follow introduce the basics of the management task through discussions of the role and definition of management.

Management entails reaching goals.

The Role of Management

Essentially, the role of managers is to guide organizations toward goal accomplishment. All organizations exist for some purpose or goal, and managers have the responsibility for combining and using organizational resources to ensure that the organizations achieve their purpose. Management moves organizations toward purposes or goals by assigning activities that organization members perform. If the activities are designed effectively, the production of each individual worker represents a contribution to the attainment of organizational goals. Management strives to encourage individual activity that will lead to reaching organizational goals and to discourage individual activity that will hinder organizational goal accomplishment. "There is no idea more important to managing than goals. Management has no meaning apart from its goals."[4] Management must keep organizational goals in mind at all times.

Managers guide organizations toward goals.

Defining Management

Students of management should be aware that the term *management* can be and often is used in several different ways.[5] For instance, it can refer simply to the

TABLE 1.1

Contemporary definitions of management

Management—
1. Is the process by which a cooperative group directs actions of others toward common goals (Massie and Douglas)
2. Is the process of working with and through others to effectively achieve organizational objectives by efficiently using limited resources in a changing environment (Kreitner)
3. Is the coordination of all resources through the processes of planning, organizing, directing, and controlling in order to attain stated objectives (Sisk)
4. Is establishing an effective environment for people operating in formal organizational groups (Koontz and O'Donnell)
5. Entails activities undertaken by one or more persons in order to coordinate the activities of others in the pursuit of ends that cannot be achieved by any one person (Donnelly, Gibson, and Ivancevich)

process that managers follow to accomplish organizational goals. It can also be used to refer to a body of knowledge. In this context, it is a cumulative body of information that furnishes insights on how to manage. *Management* also can be the term used to pinpoint the individuals who guide and direct organizations or to designate a career devoted to the task of guiding and directing organizations. An understanding of the various uses and related definitions of the term should help students and practitioners eliminate miscommunication during management-related discussions.

Managers reach goals by working with and through people and other organizational resources.

As used most commonly in this text, **management** is the process of reaching organizational goals by working with and through people and other organizational resources. A comparison of this definition with the definitions offered by several contemporary management thinkers (see Table 1.1) shows that there is some agreement that management has the following three main characteristics: (1) it is a process or series of continuing and related activities, (2) it involves and concentrates on reaching organizational goals, and (3) it reaches these goals by working with and through people and other organizational resources. A discussion of each of these characteristics follows.

The Management Process: Management Functions

The four basic management functions:

The four basic **management functions**—activities that make up the management process—are as follows:

1. Planning.

1. *Planning* Planning involves choosing tasks that must be performed to attain organizational goals, outlining how the tasks must be performed, and indicating when the tasks should be performed. Planning activity focuses on attaining goals. Managers, through their plans, outline exactly what organizations must do to be successful. They are concerned with organizational success in the near future, or short term, as well as in the more distant future, or long term.

2. Organizing.

2. *Organizing* Organizing can be thought of as assigning the tasks developed during planning to various individuals or groups within the organization.

Organizing creates a mechanism to put plans into action. People within the organization are given work assignments that contribute to goal attainment. Tasks are organized so that the output of individuals contributes to the success of departments, which contributes to the success of divisions, which in turn contributes to the overall success of organizations.

3. *Influencing* Influencing is another of the basic functions within the management process. This function—also commonly referred to as motivating, leading, directing, and actuating—is concerned primarily with people within organizations.* *Influencing* can be defined as the process of guiding the activities of organization members in appropriate directions. An appropriate direction is any direction that helps the organization move toward goal attainment. The ultimate purpose of influencing is to increase productivity. Human oriented work situations usually generate higher levels of production over the long term than do work situations that people find distasteful.

3. Influencing.

4. *Controlling* Controlling is the management function for which managers (a) gather information that measures recent performance within the organization; (b) compare present performance to preestablished performance standards; and (c) from this comparison, determine if the organization should be modified to meet preestablished standards. Controlling is an ongoing process. Managers continually gather information, make their comparisons, and then try to find new ways of improving production through organizational modification.

4. Controlling.

Naturally, if managers wish to be successful, they must perform all four of the management functions well. The "Management in Action" feature illustrates this point by describing how Richard Ringoen, chairman of Ball Corporation, uses all of these functions to successfully manage his company. Ringoen maneuvers to meet company goals (planning), automates (organizing), rewards employees (influencing), and compares performance to plans to see if changes are necessary (controlling).

Management Process and Goal Attainment

Although the four functions of management have been discussed individually, planning, organizing, influencing, and controlling are integrally related and cannot be separated. Figure 1.3 on page 11 illustrates this interrelationship and also that managers use these activities solely for the purpose of reaching organizational goals. Basically, these functions are interrelated because the performance of one depends on the performance of the others. To illustrate, organizing is based on well-thought-out plans developed during the planning process, and influencing systems must be tailored to reflect both these plans and the organizational design used to implement them. The fourth function, controlling, proposes possible modifications to existing plans, organizational structure, or the motivation system to develop a more successful effort.

Management functions are integrally related and are used solely to attain organizational goals.

---

* In early management literature, the term *motivating* was more commonly used to signify this people oriented management function. The term *influencing* is used consistently in this text because it is broader and allows more flexibility in discussions of people oriented issues. Later in the text, motivating is discussed as a major part of influencing.

MANAGEMENT FUNCTIONS AT BALL CORPORATION

When it comes to showing steady growth in earnings year after year, Ball Corp. of Muncie, Ind. ($1.1 billion, 1986 revenues) is in a league by itself. Yet with manufacturing activities in everything from mason jars to satellites, the company stood to suffer badly from [the] repeal of the investment tax credit. Net income looked to rise by only 6%, well below its target of 13%.

But was Ball worried? Nope. On Dec. 28 [1986] the company simply sold off a chunk of its passive investment in Dorsey Corp. stock for an aftertax profit of $2.3 million. Combined with another divestiture, the sale allowed Ball to report a 14% gain in net income, continuing a ten-year record of 14% compounded annual increases in net earnings. "I have never seen such incredibly smooth income growth," says Steven Johnson, a professor of accounting at the Columbia Business School.

Such consistency has brought Ball's shareholders rich rewards. While the S&P's 500 has tripled since 1976, Ball's stock, currently selling at 42, has grown tenfold. The writers of *A Passion for Excellence* sought to include Ball in their book—an honor Ball's chairman, Richard Ringoen, turned down. "It's the kiss of death," says he. "Have you looked at what happened to those companies?"

Ball fine-tunes everything as carefully as it does its accounting. The company chooses its eclectic product mix, which ranges from beer cans to atomic clocks, to avoid overlapping industries. With mathematical precision, it rewards employees, down to the level of plant foreman, for hitting targets. Says Ringoen, "You've got to be on top of everything."

Ball's earnings may be fine-tuned, but they are not phony. Cash flow from operations has grown at a compounded 19% annual rate for ten years, even faster than net income. "I think it's in the best interest of the shareholders not to have the stock too volatile," Ringoen says. "You don't want to double your income one year and be down the next. That's stupid."

Ball Corp. was founded 107 years ago by five brothers as a maker of wooden-jacketed tin cans. Today some $500 million of its revenues still comes from beverage cans. To assure product quality, Ball's taste panels meet regularly to sample beer. The panel members claim they can pick up a Budweiser and, on taste alone, tell you where it was brewed.

Satellites are a far cry from mason jars, but Ball has been making them since 1960. It got into the business by mistake, buying a company that manufactured precision weighing devices. Though the business flopped for Ball, the new employees redeemed themselves with a missile guidance system. As revenues from NASA have shrunk, Ball has taken on defense contracts, including Strategic Defense Initiative work.

Other products in the technical products division, which had sales of $188 million [in 1986], include an atomic clock, which measures time to within one second every 3 million years, and an automated visual inspection system, which is being installed in Ball's mason jar lid production lines. An industrial products division turns zinc into copper-plated pennies.

Ringoen reveals his background as an engineer when he compares the company to a servomechanism, a power-control device that continually corrects its own performance. Ball fine-tunes its businesses by measuring performance monthly against plan expectations. Within five days of the month's end, managers know if they need to start cutting costs.

Bonuses for meeting targets are generous. Plant foremen can earn up to 20% of their base salaries by coming in under target for machine downtime. The top five officers of Ball made more money on their stock options last year than on their salaries.

After such a long runup, is Ball stock still a buy? Ball did a secret study of its breakup value and found the firm still undervalued by Wall Street. "I can't really talk about this," says Ringoen. With the company carrying real estate on its books at 19th-century prices, the firm's businesses could indeed command a higher value if they were sold separately.

That study seems to be one reason Ball voted staggered director terms, "poison pill" preferred stock and "fair price" takeover defenses last year. About 54% of Ball is in friendly hands, including 41% owned by 125 descendants of the Ball brothers. But about 30% of Ball's stock is in trusts. At a high enough price, their trustees would have a fiduciary duty to sell.

That would be a shame. If Ball were swallowed up, or broken up, would it lose its passion for consistency? Ringoen hopes that remains an unanswered question.

FIGURE 1.3
Interrelations of the four functions of
management to attain organizational goals

To be effective, a manager must understand how the four management functions must be practiced, not simply how they are defined and related. Thomas J. Peters and Robert H. Waterman, Jr., studied numerous organizations—including Frito-Lay and Maytag—for several years to determine what management characteristics best described excellently run companies. Table 1.2 on pages 12 and 13 contains the list and descriptions of characteristics finally developed by Peters and Waterman and published in their book *In Search of Excellence.* This list implies that planning, organizing, influencing, and controlling should be characterized by a bias for action; a closeness to the customer; autonomy and entrepreneurship; productivity through people; a hands-on, value-driven orientation; sticking to the knitting; a simple form with a lean staff; and simultaneous loose-tight properties.

The information in this section has been only a brief introduction to the four management functions. Later sections are devoted to developing these functions in much more detail.

Management and Organizational Resources

Management must always be aware of the status and use of **organizational resources.** These resources, composed of all assets available for activation during the production process, are of four basic types: (1) human, (2) monetary, (3) raw materials, and (4) capital. As Figure 1.4 on page 12 depicts, organizational resources are combined, used, and transformed into finished products during the production process.

Human resources are the people who work for an organization. The skills they possess and their knowledge of the work system are invaluable to managers. Monetary resources are amounts of money managers use to purchase goods and services for the organization. Raw materials are ingredients acquired to be used directly in the manufacturing of products. For example, rubber is a raw material that a company such as B. F. Goodrich would purchase with its monetary resources and use directly in the manufacturing of tires. Capital resources are the machines an organization uses during the manufacturing process. Modern machines, or equipment, can be a major factor in maintaining desired pro-

Organizational resources include people, money, raw materials, and machines.

TABLE 1.2

Characteristics of excellently run companies

1. *A bias for action*, for getting on with it. Even though these companies may be analytical in their approach to decision making, they are not paralyzed by that fact (as so many others seem to be). In many of these companies, the standard operating procedure is "Do it, fix it, try it." Says a Digital Equipment Corporation senior executive, for example, "When we've got a big problem here, we grab ten senior guys and stick them in a room for a week. They come up with an answer *and* implement it." Moreover, the companies are experimenters supreme. Instead of allowing 250 engineers and marketers to work on a new product in isolation for fifteen months, they form bands of 5 to 25 and test ideas out on a customer, often with inexpensive prototypes, within a matter of weeks. What is striking is the host of practical devices the excellent companies employ to maintain corporate fleetness of foot and counter the stultification that almost inevitably comes with size.

2. *Close to the customer*. These companies learn from the people they serve. They provide unparalleled quality, service, and reliability—things that work and last. They succeed in differentiating—*à la* Frito-Lay (potato chips), Maytag (washers), or Tupperware—the most commoditylike products. IBM's marketing vice president, Francis G. (Buck) Rodgers, says, "It's a shame that, in so many companies, whenever you get good service, it's an exception." Not so at the excellent companies. Everyone gets into the act. Many of the innovative companies got their best product ideas from customers. That comes from listening, intently and regularly.

3. *Autonomy and entrepreneurship*. The innovative companies foster many leaders and many innovators throughout the organization. They are a hive of what we've come to call champions; 3M has been described as "so intent on innovation that its essential atmosphere seems not like that of a large corporation but rather a loose network of laboratories and cubbyholes populated by feverish inventors and dauntless entrepreneurs who let their imaginations fly in all directions." They don't try to hold everyone on so short a rein that he can't be creative. They encourage practical risk taking, and support good tries. They follow Fletcher Byrom's ninth commandment: "Make sure you generate a reasonable number of mistakes."

4. *Productivity through people*. The excellent companies treat the rank and file as the root source of quality and productivity gain. They do not foster we/they labor attitudes or regard capital investment as the fundamental source of efficiency improvement. As Thomas J. Watson, Jr., said of his company, "IBM's philosophy is largely contained in three simple beliefs. I want to begin with what I think is

duction levels; worn-out or antiquated machinery can make it impossible for an organization to keep pace with competitors.

Managerial Effectiveness

As managers use their resources, they must strive to be both effective and efficient. **Managerial effectiveness** is defined in terms of resource utilization in relation to organizational goal attainment. If organizations are using their resources to attain their goals, the managers are effective. In reality, there are degrees of managerial effectiveness. The closer organizations come to achieving

Managerial effectiveness is measured by how closely organizations come to achieving their goals.

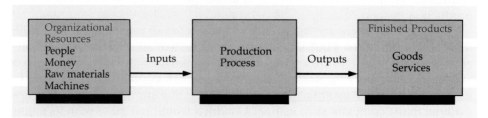

FIGURE 1.4
Transformation of organizational resources into finished products through the production process

TABLE 1.2 cont.

the most important: *our respect for the individual.* This is a simple concept but in IBM it occupies a major portion of management time." Texas Instrument's chairman Mark Shepherd talks about it in terms of every worker being "seen as a source of ideas, not just acting as a pair of hands"; each of his more than *nine thousand* People Involvement Program, or PIP, teams (Texas Instrument's quality circles) does contribute to the company's sparkling productivity record.

5. *Hands-on, value driven.* Thomas Watson, Jr., said that "the basic philosophy of an organization has far more to do with its achievements than do technological or economic resources, organizational structure, innovation, and timing." Watson and Hewlett-Packard's William Hewlett are legendary for walking the plant floors. McDonald's Ray Kroc regularly visit[ed] stores and assess[ed] them on the factors the company holds dear, Q.S.C. & V. (Quality, Service, Cleanliness, and Value.)

6. *Stick to the knitting.* Robert W. Johnson, former Johnson & Johnson chairman, put it this way: "Never acquire a business you don't know how to run." Or as Edward G. Harness, past chief executive at Procter & Gamble, said, "This company has never left its base. We seek to be anything but a conglomerate." While there were a few exceptions, the odds for excellent performance seem strongly

to favor those companies that stay reasonably close to businesses they know.

7. *Simple form, lean staff.* As big as most of the companies we have looked at are, none when we looked at it was formally run with a matrix organization structure, and some which had tried that form had abandoned it. The underlying structural forms and systems in the excellent companies are elegantly simple. Top-level staffs are lean; it is not uncommon to find a corporate staff of fewer than one hundred people running multi-billion-dollar enterprises.

8. *Simultaneous loose-tight properties.* The excellent companies are both centralized and decentralized. For the most part, as we have said, they have pushed autonomy down to the shop floor on product development team. On the other hand, they are fanatic centralists around the few core values they hold dear. 3M is marked by barely organized chaos surrounding its product champions. Yet one analyst argues, "The brainwashed members of an extremist political sect are no more conformist in their central beliefs." At Digital the chaos is so rampant that one executive noted, "Damn few people know who they work for." Yet Digital's fetish for reliability is more rigidly adhered to than any outsider could imagine.

their goals, the more effective the managers are said to be. Managerial effectiveness can be depicted as being on a continuum ranging from ineffective to effective.

Managerial Efficiency

Managerial efficiency is defined in terms of the proportion of total organizational resources that contribute to productivity during the manufacturing process. The higher this proportion, the more efficient the manager. The more resources wasted or unused during the production process, the more inefficient the manager. As with management effectiveness, management efficiency is best described as being on a continuum ranging from inefficient to efficient. *Inefficient* means that a very small proportion of total resources contributes to productivity during the manufacturing process; *efficient* means that a very large proportion contributes.

Managerial efficiency is measured by the proportion of organizational resources used during the production process.

As Figure 1.5 on page 14 shows, the concepts of managerial effectiveness and efficiency are obviously related. A manager could be relatively ineffective, the organization making very little progress toward goal attainment, primarily because of major inefficiencies or poor utilization of resources during the production process. In contrast, a manager could be somewhat effective despite being inefficient. Demand for the finished goods may be so high that the manager can get an extremely high price per unit sold and thus absorb inefficiency costs.

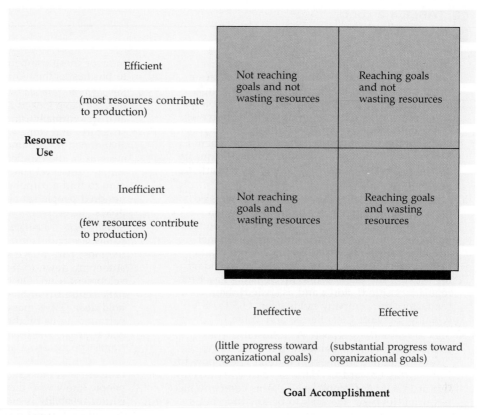

FIGURE 1.5
Various combinations of managerial effectiveness and managerial efficiency

For example, some oil companies in Saudi Arabia could probably absorb many managerial inefficiencies when oil sells at a high price. Management in this situation has a chance to be somewhat effective despite its inefficiency. Thus, a manager can be effective without being efficient and vice versa. To maximize organizational success, however, both effectiveness and efficiency are needed.

BACK TO THE CASE

Weirton employees now have specific information on what management is and what managers do. Employees who actually become managers will have to acquire a clear understanding of company objectives and guide the parts of the organization in which they work toward reaching these objectives. This guidance, of course, will involve working not only with other people at Weirton but also with all other department resources.

The new managers will be heavily involved in planning, organizing, influencing, and controlling. In other words, they will have to outline how jobs must be performed to reach objectives, assign these jobs to appropriate workers, encourage the workers to perform their jobs, and make any changes necessary to ensure reaching company objectives. Also, as the new managers perform these four functions, they will need to remember that the activities themselves are interrelated and must blend together appropriately.

The wise use of organizational resources by these new managers will be imperative. The managers should strive to be both effective and efficient—to reach company goals without wasting company resources.

"Oh, I believe in free enterprise, sir—I'm just not good at it."
Wall Street Journal, *September 17, 1987. From the* Wall Street Journal–*permission, Cartoon Features Syndicate.*

Management Skills

No discussion of organizational resources would be complete without the mention of management skills, perhaps the primary determinant of how effective and efficient managers will be. The cartoon shown here makes the point that certain skills are needed to successfully manage an organization.

According to an article by Robert L. Katz, managerial success depends primarily on performance rather than personality traits.[6] Katz also states that a manager's ability to perform is a result of the managerial skills possessed. A manager with the necessary management skills will probably perform well and be relatively successful. One without the necessary skills will probably perform poorly and be relatively unsuccessful.

Katz indicates that three types of skills are important for successful management performance: technical skills, human skills, and conceptual skills. **Technical skills** involve using specialized knowledge and expertise in executing work related techniques and procedures. Examples of these skills are engineering, computer programming, and accounting. Technical skills are mostly related to working with "things"—processes or physical objects. **Human skills** are skills that build cooperation within the team being led. They involve working with attitudes, communication, individuals and groups, and individual interests—in short, working with people. **Conceptual skills** involve the ability to see the organization as a whole. A manager with conceptual skills is able to understand how various functions of the organization complement one another, how the organization relates to its environment, and how changes in one part of the organization affect the rest of the organization.

> Successful management performance depends on technical skills, human skills, and conceptual skills.

Basically, as one moves from lower-level management to upper-level management, conceptual skills become more important and technical skills less important (see Figure 1.6, p. 16). The supportive rationale is that as managers advance in an organization, they become less involved with the actual production activity or technical areas and more involved with guiding the organization as a whole. Human skills, however, are extremely important to managers at top, middle,[7] and lower (or supervisory) levels.[8] The common denominator of all management levels is people.

> Different management skills are important at different levels of management.

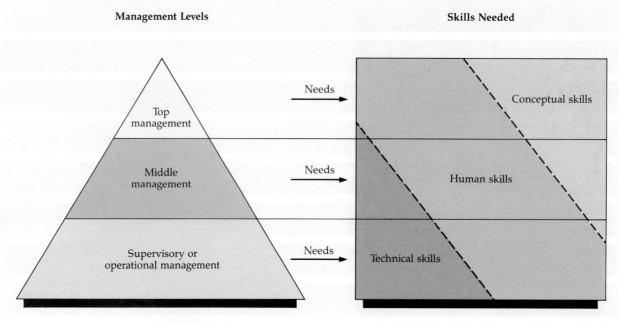

Management Levels   Skills Needed

Top management

Needs →

Conceptual skills

Middle management

Needs →

Human skills

Supervisory or operational management

Needs →

Technical skills

FIGURE 1.6
As a manager moves from the supervisory to the top management level, conceptual skills become more important than technical skills, but human skills remain equally important

THE UNIVERSALITY OF MANAGEMENT

The four basic functions of management can be applied in all organizations.

Management principles are **universal;** that is, they apply to all types of organizations (businesses, churches, sororities, athletic teams, hospitals, and so on) and organizational levels. Naturally, managers' jobs are somewhat different in each of these organizations because each organization requires the use of specialized knowledge, exists in unique working and political environments, and uses different technology. However, job similarities also exist because of the common basic management activities necessary in all organizations: planning, organizing, influencing, and controlling.

Successful managers possess common qualities.

The administrative theorist Henri Fayol stated that all managers should possess certain characteristics, such as positive physical qualities, mental qualities, and special knowledge related to the specific operation.[9] B. C. Forbes, also describing managerial characteristics, has emphasized the importance of certain more personal qualities in successful managers. He has inferred that enthusiasm, earnestness of purpose, confidence, and faith in their worthwhileness are primary characteristics of successful managers. Forbes has described Henry Ford as follows:

> At the base and birth of every great business organization was an enthusiast, a man consumed with earnestness of purpose, with confidence in his powers, with faith in the worthwhileness of his endeavors. The original Henry Ford was the quintessence of enthusiasm. In the days of his difficulties, disappointments, and discouragements, when he was wrestling with his balky motor engine— and wrestling likewise with poverty—only his inexhaustible enthusiasm saved him from defeat.[10]

Fayol and Forbes can describe these desirable characteristics of successful managers only because of the universality concept: the basic ingredients of the successful management situation are applicable to organizations of all types.

◼ BACK TO THE CASE

The new employee-owners of Weirton Steel will be successful as managers only if they possess technical skills, human skills, and conceptual skills. A relatively low-level management position at Weirton would require first human skills, then technical skills, and finally conceptual skills. Of course, as lower-level managers take over middle- and upper-level management positions, this ranking of skill importance would change, and there would be increasing emphasis on conceptual skills.

As Weirton employees gain experience in managing, they probably will find that their cumulative management experience is valuable in whatever management position they assume, whether at Weirton, in some other steel company, or even in some other business altogether. They may also discover that enthusiasm, earnestness, confidence, and faith in their worthwhileness are important personal qualities of successful managers in every organization.

▦ MANAGEMENT CAREERS

Thus far, this chapter has focused on outlining the importance of management to our society, presenting a definition of management and the management process, and explaining the universality of management. Individuals commonly study such topics because they are interested in pursuing a management career. This section presents information that will help students preview what might characterize their own management careers and describes some of the issues they might face in attempting to manage the careers of others within an organization. The specific focus is on career definition, career and life stages and performance, and career promotion.

A Definition of Career

A **career** is an individual's perceived sequence of attitudes and behaviors associated with the performance of work related experiences and activities over the span of the person's working life.[11] This definition implies that a career is cumulative in nature. As individuals accumulate successful experiences in one position, they generally develop abilities and attitudes that qualify them to hold more advanced positions. In general, management positions at one level tend to be stepping-stones to management positions at the next higher level.

Careers involve attitudes and behavior.

Career Stages, Life Stages, and Performance

Careers are generally viewed as evolving through a series of stages. The evolutionary stages—exploration, establishment, maintenance, and decline—appear in Figure 1.7 on page 18. This figure highlights the performance levels and age ranges commonly associated with each stage. The levels and ranges indicate what is likely at each stage, not what is inevitable.

There are four career stages: exploration, establishment, maintenance, and decline.

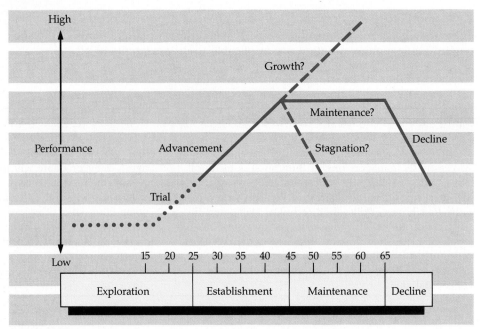

FIGURE 1.7
The relationships among career stages, life stages, and performance

Exploration Stage

In the exploration stage, individuals analyze themselves and explore available jobs.

The first stage in career evolution is the **exploration stage,** which occurs at the beginning of a career and is characterized by self-analysis and the exploration of different types of available jobs. Individuals at this stage are generally about fifteen to twenty-five years old and involved in some type of formal training, such as college or vocational education. They often pursue part-time employment to gain a richer understanding of what it might be like to have a career in a particular organization or industry. Typical jobs held during this stage might include cooking at Burger King, stocking at a Federated Department Store, or being an office assistant at a Nationwide Insurance office.

Establishment Stage

In the establishment stage, individuals become more productive.

The second stage in career evolution is the **establishment stage,** during which individuals who are about twenty-five to forty-five years old typically start to become more productive, or higher performers (as Figure 1.7 indicates by the upturn in the dotted line). Employment sought during this stage is guided by what was learned during the exploration stage. In addition, the jobs sought are usually full-time. Individuals at this stage commonly move to different jobs within the same company, to different companies, or even to different industries.

Maintenance Stage

The maintenance stage involves growth, maintenance, or stagnation.

The third stage in career evolution is the **maintenance stage.** In this stage, individuals who are about forty-five to sixty-five years old show either increased

TABLE 1.3

Aspects of Coca-Cola USA that help enhance career growth of employees

- *Newsmakers* is a monthly publication listing moves within Coca-Cola USA. This gives people information on the kinds and number of internal career moves taking place.
- Job posting and the Exempt Job Opening Listing indicate specific open positions of the lower and mid-level management levels.
- Career opportunities booklets provide a broad overview of each department, as well as specific qualifications for typical positions.
- The 30-page *Career Planning Workbook,* designed specifically for Coca-Cola USA, gives individuals an opportunity to assess their strengths, values, and alternative career directions and provides a structured means of developing a career plan. A worksheet captures all the critical information in one place.
- Career planning can also be explored through a two-day "Career Strategies Workshop." Participants examine themselves, possible career options, and strategies for attaining their goals. A special feature of the program is the opportunity to meet key human resource people representing each functional area in Coca-Cola USA as well as the larger structure of the Coca-Cola Company.
- The company helps employees develop their skills through an extensive in-house training program. The *Employee Training Catalog,* distributed annually with quarterly updates, lists courses offered by Coca-Cola USA by performance factor, such as organizing and planning. Therefore, if a particular skill area is identified during a performance evaluation or a career discussion, the appropriate course can easily be selected.
- A 100 percent reimbursement tuition aid program offers employees the opportunity to return to school to enhance their formal education.
- On- and off-the-job developmental activities are considered primary opportunities for growth. Employees may ask for feedback from their managers, act as an instructor or trainer, take on new projects, participate on a task force or project team, or join professional organizations. All of these activities allow the development of new professional skills and contribute to professional growth.

performance (career growth), stabilized performance (career maintenance), or decreased performance (career stagnation).

From a managerial viewpoint, it is better to have growth than maintenance or stagnation. Some companies, such as IBM, Monsanto, and Brooklyn Union Gas, attempt to eliminate career plateauing.[12] Table 1.3 shows how Coca-Cola USA tries to avoid career maintenance and stagnation by ensuring that employees know where to go for career development guidance, know what jobs are open within the company, and know what avenues are available for self-development.[13]

Decline Stage

The last stage in career evolution is the **decline stage,** which involves people of about sixty-five years and older whose productivity naturally is declining. These individuals are either close to retirement, semiretired, or retired. People at this stage commonly find it difficult to maintain prior performance levels because they begin to lose interest in their careers or fail to keep their job skills up to date. As people live longer and stay healthier, many of them become part-time workers in businesses such as Publix supermarkets and McDonald's and in volunteer groups such as the March of Dimes and the American Heart Association.

The decline stage brings declining performance.

Promoting Your Own Career

Practicing managers[14] and management scholars generally agree that the careful formulation and implementation of appropriate tactics can enhance the success

Career success can be enhanced with appropriate tactics.

TABLE 1.4

Manager and employee roles in enhancing employee career development

Dimension	Professional Employee	Manager
Responsibility	Assumes responsibility for individual career development	Assumes responsibility for employee development
Information	Obtains career information through self-evaluation and data collection: What do I enjoy doing? Where do I want to go?	Provides information by holding up a mirror of reality: How manager views the employee How others view the employee How "things work around here"
Planning	Develops an individual plan to reach objectives	Helps employee assess plan
Follow-through	Invites management support through high performance on the current job by understanding the scope of the job and taking appropriate initiative	Provides coaching and relevant information on opportunities

of management careers.[15] Perhaps the most important tactic is to work for managers who carry out a realistic and constructive role in the career development of their employees.[16] Table 1.4 outlines what career development responsibility, information, planning, and follow-through might include. This figure also contains an example of a complimentary career development role for a professional employee. Table 1.5 lists several additional tactics for enhancing career success.

Success comes with demonstrations of abilities and accomplishments.

To enhance their career success, individuals must be proactive rather than reactive.[17] That is, they must take specific action to demonstrate their abilities and accomplishments. They must also have a clear idea of the next position they are seeking, the skills they must acquire to function appropriately in that posi-

TABLE 1.5

Tips for enhancing your management career

- Remember that good performance that pleases your superiors is the basic foundation of success, but recognize that not all good performance is easily measured. Determine the real criteria by which you are evaluated and be rigorously honest in evaluating your own performance against these criteria.
- Manage your career; be active in influencing decisions, because pure effort is not necessarily rewarded.
- Strive for positions that have high visibility and exposure where you can be a hero observed by higher officials. Check to see that the organization has a formal system of keeping track of young people. Remember that high-risk line jobs tend to offer more visibility than staff positions like corporate planning or personnel, but also that visibility can sometimes be achieved by off-job community activities.

- Develop relations with a mobile senior executive who can be your sponsor. Become a complementary crucial subordinate with different skills than your superior.
- Learn your job as quickly as possible and train a replacement so you can be available to move and broaden your background in different functions.
- Nominate yourself for other positions: modesty is not necessarily a virtue. However, change jobs for more power and influence, not primarily for status or pay. The latter could be a substitute for real opportunity to make things happen.
- Before taking a position, rigorously assess your strengths and weaknesses, what you like and don't like. Don't accept a promotion if it draws on your weaknesses and entails mainly activities that you don't like.

tion, and a plan for how they will acquire those skills. Finally, they need to think about the ultimate position they will want and the sequence of positions they must hold in order to gain the skills and attitudes necessary to qualify for that position.

BACK TO THE CASE

Assume that Martin Plane is a plant manager for Weirton Steel. He is forty-five years old and is considered a member of Weirton's middle management.

As with many individuals, Plane began his career (exploration stage) in college by considering various areas of study and by holding a number of different types of primarily part-time positions. He delivered pizzas for Domino's Pizza and worked for Scott's, a lawn care company. He began college at age eighteen and graduated when he was twenty-two.

Plane then moved into the establishment stage of his career. For a few years immediately after graduation, he held full-time trial positions in the steel industry as well as in the restaurant and retailing industries. What he learned during the career exploration stage helped him choose the types of full-time trial positions to pursue. At the age of twenty-six, he accepted a trial position as an entry-level line worker at Weirton. Through this position, he discovered that he wanted to remain in the steel industry in general and at Weirton in particular. From age twenty-seven

to age forty-five, he held a number of supervisory and middle management positions.

Now Plane is moving into an extremely critical part of his career, the maintenance stage. He could probably remain in his present position and maintain his productivity for several more years. However, he wants to advance his career. Therefore he must emphasize a proactive attitude by formulating and implementing tactics aimed at enhancing his career success, such as seeking training to develop critical skills, or moving to a position that is a prerequisite for other, more advanced positions.

In the future, as Plane approaches sixty-five years of age (the decline stage), it is probable that his productivity at Weirton will decline somewhat. From a career viewpoint, he may want to go from full-time employment to semiretirement. Perhaps he could work for Weirton or another steel company on a part-time advisory basis or even pursue part-time work in another industry. For example, he might be able to teach a management course at a nearby college.

TABLE 1.5 cont.

- Leave at your convenience, but on good terms without parting criticism of the organization. Do not stay under an immobile superior who is not promoted in three to five years.
- Don't be trapped by formal, narrow job descriptions. Move outside them and probe the limits of your influence.
- Accept that responsibility will always somewhat exceed authority and that organizational politics are inevitable. Establish alliances and fight necessary battles, minimizing upward ones to very important issues.
- Get out of management if you can't stand being dependent on others and having them dependent on you.
- Recognize that you will face ethical dilemmas no

matter how moral you try to be. No evidence exists that unethical managers are more successful than ethical ones, but it may well be that those who move faster are less socially conscious. Therefore, from time to time you must examine your personal values and question how much you will sacrifice for the organization.
- Don't automatically accept all tales of managerial perversity that you hear. Attributing others' success to unethical behavior is often an excuse for one's own personal inadequacies. Most of all, don't commit an act which you know to be wrong in the hope that your supervisor will see it as loyalty and reward you for it. Sometimes he will, but he may also sacrifice you when the organization is criticized.

Action Summary

Reread the learning objectives that follow. Each objective is followed by questions. Answering these questions accurately will help you to retain the most important concepts discussed in this chapter. After answering each question, check your answer with the answer key at the end of this chapter. (*Hint:* If you have doubt regarding the correct response, consult the page whose number follows the answer.)

From studying this chapter, I will attempt to acquire:

1. An understanding of the importance of management to society and individuals.

Circle:

T, F

a. Managers constitute less than 1 percent of the U.S. work force.

T, F

b. Management is important to society.

2. An understanding of the role of management.

a, b, c, d, e

a. The role of a manager is: (a) to make workers happy; (b) to satisfy only the manager's needs; (c) to make the most profit; (d) to survive in a highly competitive society; (e) to achieve organizational goals.

T, F

b. Apart from its goals, management has no meaning.

3. An ability to define *management* in several different ways.

a, b, c, d, e

a. Management is: (a) a process; (b) reaching organizational goals; (c) utilizing people and other resources; (d) all of the above; (e) a and b.

T, F

b. Management is the process of working with people and through people.

4. An ability to list and define the basic functions of management.

a, b, c, d, e

a. Which of the following is *not* a function of management: (a) influencing; (b) planning; (c) organizing; (d) directing; (e) controlling.

a, b, c, d, e

b. The process of gathering information and comparing this information to preestablished standards is part of (a) planning; (b) influencing; (c) motivating; (d) controlling; (e) commanding.

5. Working definitions of managerial effectiveness and managerial efficiency.

T, F

a. If an organization is using its resources to attain its goals, the organization's managers are efficient.

T, F

b. A manager who is reaching goals but wasting resources is efficient but ineffective.

6. An understanding of basic management skills and their relative importance to managers.

a, b, c, d, e

a. Conceptual skills require that management view the organization as: (a) a profit center; (b) a decision-making unit; (c) a problem-solving group; (d) a whole; (e) individual contributions.

T, F

b. Managers require fewer and fewer human skills as they move from lower to higher management levels.

7. An understanding of the universality of management.

T, F

a. The statement that management principles are universal means that they apply to all types of organizations and organizational levels.

T, F

b. The universality of management means that management principles are taught the same way in all schools.

8. Insights concerning what management careers are and how they evolve.   T, F
  a. In general, as careers evolve, individuals tend to further develop job skills but show very little or no change in attitude about various job circumstances.
  b. Individuals tend to show the first significant increase in performance during the establishment career stage.   T, F
  c. Tips for enhancing the success of your career should not be seen as too useful over the long run.   T, F

■ INTRODUCTORY CASE WRAP-UP

"Inexperienced Managers at Weirton Steel Mill" (p. 4) and its related back-to-the-case sections were written to help you better understand the management concepts contained in this chapter. Answer the following discussion questions about this introductory case to further enrich your understanding of the chapter content:

1. If you were an employee-owner at the Weirton plant, would you like to become a manager? Explain.
2. What concerns would you have as an employee sharing in the purchase of the Weirton plant?
3. A Weirton employee-owner has just taken a Weirton management position. List and describe five activities that you think this individual must perform as part of the new job.

Issues for Review and Discussion

1. What is the main point illustrated in the introductory case on Weirton Steel?
2. How important is the management function to society?
3. How important is the management function to individuals?
4. What is the basic role of the managers?
5. How is *management* defined in this text? What main themes are contained in this definition?
6. List and define each of the four functions of management.
7. Outline the relationship between the four management functions.
8. List and describe five of Peters and Waterman's characteristics of excellent companies, and explain how each of these characteristics could affect planning, organizing, influencing, and controlling.
9. List and define the basic organizational resources managers have at their disposal.
10. What is the relationship between organizational resources and production?
11. Draw and explain the continuum of managerial effectiveness.
12. Draw and explain the continuum of managerial efficiency.
13. Are managerial effectiveness and managerial efficiency related concepts? If so, how?
14. According to Katz's article, what are the three primary types of skills important to management success? Define each of these types of skills.
15. Describe the relative importance of each of these three types of skills to lower-level, middle-level, and upper-level managers.
16. What is meant by "the universality of management"?
17. What is a career?
18. Discuss the significance of the maintenance career stage.
19. What tips for promoting the success of a career are most valuable to you? Explain.

Sources of Additional Information

Alpander, Guvenc G. "Training First-Line Supervisors to Criticize Constructively." *Personnel Journal* (March 1980): 216–21.

Burack, Elmer H., and Nicholas J. Mathys. *Introduction to Management: A Career Perspective*. New York: Wiley, 1983.

Burgelman, Robert A., and Leonard R. Sayles. *Inside Corporate Innovation*. New York: Free Press, 1986.

Drucker, P. *Management: Tasks, Responsibilities, Practices*. New York: Harper & Row, 1985.

Elliott, Clifford, and Jang H. Yoo. "Innovations in the Japanese Distributive System: Are the Barriers to Entry Being Lifted?" *Akron Business and Economic Review* (Spring 1980): 28–33.

Garfield, Charles A. "The Right Stuff." *Management World* 13 (July 1984): 18–20.

Hamermesh, Richard G. *Making Strategy Work: How Senior Managers Produce Results*. New York: Wiley, 1986.

Hayes, James L. "Making a Professional Manager," *Management Review* 69 (November 1980): 2–3.

Heide, Dorothy. "I Can Improve My Management Skills By:" *Personnel Journal* 63 (June 1984): 52–54.

Kamerschen, David R., Robert J. Paul, and David A. Dilts. "Ownership and Management of the Firm—Another Look," *Business and Society* 25 (Spring 1986): 8–14.

Koontz, Harold, Cyril O'Donnell, and Heinz Weihrich. *Management*, 8th ed. New York: McGraw-Hill, 1984.

Lorsch, Jay W., and Peter F. Mathias. "When Professionals Have to Manage." *Harvard Business Review* (July/August 1987): 78–83.

Molz, Richard. "Entrepreneurial Managers in Large Organizations " *Business Horizons* 27 (September/October 1984): 54–61.

Ozawa, Terutomo. "Japan's Industrial Groups." *MSU Business Topics* (Autumn 1980): 33–41.

Ruch, Richard S., and Ronald Goodman. *Image at the Top*. New York: Free Press, 1983.

Taylor, James W., and Ronald N. Paul. "The Real Meaning of Excellence." *Business* 36 (April/May/June 1986): 27–33.

Veiga, John F. "Do Managers on the Move Get Anywhere?" *Harvard Business Review* (March/April 1981): 20–22, 26–30, 34–38.

Webber, Alan M. "Red Auerbach on Management." *Harvard Business Review* (March/April 1987): 84–91.

Notes

1. Peter F. Drucker, "Management's New Role," *Harvard Business Review* (November/December 1969): 54.

2. U.S. Bureau of the Census, *Statistical Abstract of the United States*, 108th ed. (Washington, D.C.: Government Printing Office, 1987), 230.

3. "Who Are the Unemployed?" *U.S. News & World Report*. November 16, 1970, 54.

4. Robert Albanese, *Management: Toward Accountability for Performance* (Homewood, Ill.: Richard D. Irwin, 1975), 49.

5. For a more detailed description of each of these definitions of management, see Dalton E. McFarland, *Management: Principles and Practice*, 4th ed. (New York: Macmillan, 1974), 6–10.

6. Robert L. Katz, "Skills of an Effective Administrator," *Harvard Business Review* (January/February 1955): 33–41.

7. W. Earl Sasser, Jr., and Frank S. Leonard, "Let First-Level Supervisors Do Their Job," *Harvard Business Review* (March/April 1980): 113–21.

8. Peter D. Couch, "Learning to Be a Middle Manager," *Business Horizons* (February 1979): 33–41.

9. Henri Fayol, *General and Industrial Management* (London: Sir Isaac Pitman & Sons, 1949).

10. B. C. Forbes, *Forbes*, March 15, 1976, 128.

11. Douglas T. Hall, *Careers in Organizations* (Santa Monica, Calif.: Goodyear Publishing, 1976), 4.

12. John W. Slocum, Jr., William L. Cron, and Linda C. Yows, "Whose Career Is Likely to Plateau?" *Business Horizons* (March/April 1987): 31–38.

13. Lynn Slavenski, "Career Development: A Systems Approach," *Training and Development Journal* (February 1987): 56–59.

14. Joseph E. McKendrick, Jr., "What Are You Doing the Rest of Your Life?" *Management World* (September/October 1987): 2.

15. Carl Anderson, *Management: Skills, Functions, and Organization Performance*, Second Edition. (Boston: Allyn and Bacon, 1988).

16. Paul H. Thompson, Robin Zenger Baker, and Norman Smallwood, "Improving Personal Development by Applying the Four-Stage Career Model," *Organizational Dynamics* (Autumn 1986): 49–62.

17. Buck Blessing, "Career Planning: Five Fatal Assumptions," *Training and Development Journal* (September 1986): 49–51.

Action Summary Answer Key

1. a. F, p. 5
   b. T, p. 5
2. a. e, p. 7
   b. T, p. 7
3. a. d, p. 8
   b. F, p. 8
4. a. d, pp. 8–9
   b. d, p. 9
5. a. F, p. 12
   b. F, p. 13

6. a. d, p. 15
   b. F, p. 15
7. a. T, p. 16
   b. F, p. 16
8. a. F, p. 17
   b. T, p. 18
   c. F, p. 20

SHELL'S THE NAME, EFFICIENCY'S THE GAME

The recent history of the oil industry has been characterized by turmoil. Along with the incredible profits of a few years back, when Mobil was earning $6.62 per share, Chevron $7.02, and Texaco $8.75, came overpayment for fashionable diversification. By buying into businesses they knew nothing about, Mobil, Chevron, Exxon, Standard Oil, and Atlantic Richfield wasted much of the profits of a now-vanished prosperity. Losses in the new ventures ran not into the millions but into the hundreds of millions, often billions. The oil companies were trying to compete with corporations as varied as IBM and Sears, Roebuck. On the questionable ground that oil reserves were cheaper on Wall Street than in oil fields, oil companies were seduced into megamergers engineered by investment bankers. For example, Texaco paid $10 billion, a 63 percent premium over market, to buy Getty Oil. Today, the whole of Texaco has a market value of $8 billion.

At Shell Oil, behind chief executive John F. Bookout, the trend has not been the same. In 1976, when Bookout took over, Shell ranked seventh in the industry in net profits. By 1985, with a net $165 billion, it had moved to fourth place—even though its competition had purchased profits in the marketplace through huge acquisitions. Shell, by contrast, generated its earnings increases almost entirely internally.

The measure of whether an oil company is a continuing business or a wasting asset is reserve replacement. As Bookout suggests, Shell has added more oil and gas than it has used up in the last ten years: "In 1976 we had 3.2 billion barrels of reserves. Since then we've used 3.1 billion barrels, and our reserves now stand at 3.9 billion." This is in contrast to U.S. reserves shrinking 11 percent for the industry as a whole.

Considering the financial success of Shell, there would appear to be a lesson to be learned from studying Bookout's techniques. Today, virtually every oil company is restructuring in one way or another. "We have not felt the need for any major restructuring efforts," says Bookout. "We didn't let staff get out of hand during the upswing. We didn't cut like others did in the downswing." One of the reasons for this success is that while other oil companies were growing fat, Bookout kept Shell on a diet.

Bookout remembers, "The first thing I was confronted with by our board was, 'Should Shell Oil diversify?'" "At the end of a year and a half, I was in a position to say we shouldn't diversify." His reasoning: "It had to be almost egotistical to think that Shell could pay a premium to take over a company we knew nothing

about and cause it to perform 2 to 2½ times better than it had been, which would have been necessary to get the return on investment we needed." "We decided we have abundant opportunity in our mainline businesses, and that's where we should stay," he adds. "You have to decide what game you're going to play." "Are you going to play the game that scatters you all over? That means you're playing other people's technology, or their ideas, aren't you?"

"Our strategic plan has been in place virtually unchanged since 1978," says Bookout. "It's been our North Pole. It keeps us on course. It's been through one shock after another—shortages, surpluses, tripling of oil prices, weak markets, high interest rates, falling oil prices—and it's still pointing us in the same direction." If you ask Bookout what direction, he states, "It's efficiency, efficiency, efficiency." According to Bookout, the achievement of low-cost proficiency is the guiding principle. For example, in 1978, Shell began cutting out the less profitable service stations and concentrating on large metropolitan markets, where it could supply the stations more economically and achieve high gasoline volume per station. Shell was a good two years ahead of the competition in implementing this practice. Similarly, Shell was the first in the industry to overhaul refineries. The $1.2 billion refinery upgrading program is credited with allowing Shell's output to be 61 percent in the more profitable products—gasoline and jet fuels—while, for example, competitor Chevron had output of only 40 percent.

Enhanced oil recovery is Shell's special field. The technology involved allows Shell to scour the last drops of oil from a reservoir. Those last drops accounted for 32 percent of Shell's 174 million barrels of oil production last year. Shell's expertise, both geographic and technological, makes the company a highly efficient oil finder. In one of the last exploration frontiers in the United States, offshore waters deeper than 600 feet, Shell has few rivals.

What's ahead for the oil industry and Shell oil? To answer this question, Bookout makes use of two sharpened forecasting tools, or decision-making aids, he calls "risk discounting" and "looking back." Risk discounting is figuring out how many times a given type of project is likely to fail. "Maybe a lot of people risk-discount, but how well you do it depends on how well you've analyzed your business on a look-back basis," suggests Bookout. Looking back, as Bookout describes it, is learning from the past. Results are compared constantly with the results forecasted for a project. If the rate of failure based on the later analysis is, say, one in four, any projections are given a further reduction on the basis of that failure rate. The result is a cautious safeguard against normal human optimism.

Bookout has developed a script on the course of future oil prices. He senses wide swings around $15 a barrel for a year or two, edging up to $20 and above by 1989—possibly earlier if the world economy becomes stronger and oil users get careless again. He also sees OPEC dictating its terms again in the early or mid 1990s.

Considering all the internal and external factors together, what, then, is John Bookout's motto? He says, "With a good strategic plan, adversity doesn't lead to panic, and prosperity doesn't lead to unwise commitments that cannot be sustained."

DISCUSSION ISSUES

1. It is obvious that Shell's John Bookout envisions many benefits from a well-conceived plan of action. Using information from the case, identify as many examples as you can of the planning process in action.
2. Explain how Shell attained corporate efficiency. What role did organizational resources play? How does this efficiency contribute to organizational effectiveness?
3. Which two of the characteristics of excellently run companies, as identified in Table 1.2, relate to Shell's success? Provide examples that show these characteristics.
4. *Influencing* is defined as the process of guiding the activities of organization members in appropriate directions. Explain how Bookout's actions work indirectly as an influence on corporate culture.

STUDENT LEARNING OBJECTIVES

From studying this chapter, I will attempt to acquire:

1. An understanding of the classical approach to management.
2. An appreciation for the work of Frederick W. Taylor, Frank and Lillian Gilbreth, Henry L. Gantt, and Henri Fayol.
3. An understanding of the behavioral approach to management.
4. An understanding of the studies at the Hawthorne Works of the Western Electric Company.
5. An understanding of the management science approach to management.
6. An understanding of how the management science approach has evolved.
7. An understanding of the system approach to management.
8. An understanding of how triangular management and the contingency approach to management are related.

APPROACHES TO MANAGING

CHAPTER OUTLINE

McDONALD'S RECIPE FOR SUCCESS

"Wow, we just had a customer walk out on us!" Jim Delligatti drops his Big Mac in midbite and bolts from the booth, rushing past four rows of customers who make up the noonday rush at the Warrendale McDonald's. Taking a command position behind the counter that stretches the width of the restaurant, Jim Delligatti, by his mere presence, spurs his twelve workers to hustle even faster.

It's not enough that Delligatti has opened forty-seven of the famous hamburger outlets over the past twenty-six years and has become a millionaire in the process. He hates to see anyone leave one of his "stores" unhappy, and his white-suited crews in their white "McNugget Mania" painter's caps know it.

"Production—twelve burgers, six Macs," barks the fresh-faced assistant manager posted behind the warming bin, where wrapped burgers can remain no more than ten minutes before being discarded. "Coming up," says a high school boy, who slaps a handful of frozen patties on the hot, stainless steel grill. Behind him, a young woman takes buns from a toaster and "dresses" them with quick squirts of mustard and ketchup from a silver dispenser. She puts the pickles on by hand, taking care to spread them out so the customer will not get everything in one gulp. At the french-fry station, another young woman shakes salt onto a hot batch of golden-brown potatoes and then scoops the fries into red paper containers. With today's crowd, none will remain in the warming bin over the seven-minute maximum.

The lunchtime whirl all comes together to meet

one goal: to serve the customer within sixty seconds of the order's being placed.

As huge as it is, the McDonald's empire really is built around individual stores, each striving to conform to the company motto of "quality, service, cleanliness, and value." These standards are hammered into new franchisees at McDonald's Hamburger "U" training center in Oak Brook, Illinois. The way the firm sees it, customers should get the same McDonald's quality whether they buy their hamburgers at a McDonald's in Brooklyn, Singapore, or Warrendale, a small community twenty miles north of Pittsburgh.

What's Ahead

A manager such as McDonald's Jim Delligatti knows that there are several ways to analyze management situations and to solve organizational problems. This chapter explains five such approaches to management: (1) the classical approach, (2) the behavioral approach, (3) the management science approach, (4) the contingency approach, and (5) the system approach.

Chapter 1 focused primarily on defining *management*. This chapter presents various approaches to analyzing and reacting to the management situation. Each approach recommends a basically different method of analysis and a different type of action as a result of the analysis.

Over the years, disagreement on exactly how many different approaches to management exist and what each approach entails has been common. In an attempt to organize and condense the various approaches, Donnelly, Gibson, and Ivancevich[1] combined the ideas of Koontz, O'Donnell, and Weihrich[2] and Haynes and Massie[3] and offered these three: (1) the classical approach, (2) the behavioral approach, and (3) the management science approach. They stated that their objective was to simplify the discussion of the field of management without sacrificing significant information.

The following sections build on the work of Donnelly, Gibson, and Ivancevich in presenting the classical approach, the behavioral approach, and the management science approach. The contingency approach is also discussed as a fourth primary approach to analyzing the management task. The fifth approach, the system approach, is presented as a more recent trend in management thinking and is the approach emphasized in this text.

Five approaches to management:

1. The classical approach.

2. The behavioral approach.

3. The management science approach.

4. The contingency approach.

5. The system approach.

THE CLASSICAL APPROACH

The **classical approach to management** resulted from the first significant, concentrated effort to develop a body of management thought. Management writers who participated in this effort are considered the pioneers of management study.

The classical approach emphasizes efficiency.

The classical approach recommends that managers continually strive to increase organizational efficiency to increase production. Although the fundamentals of this approach were developed some time ago, modern managers are just as concerned about finding the "one best way" to get the job done as were their predecessors. One example of their concern is the present-day trend of incorporating robots into the workplace. The "Management in Action" feature for this chapter is an account of how one company, Allen-Bradley, has created a robotics-based production process in attempting to find the "one best way" to manufacture its products.

ROBOTS USED TO ENHANCE PRODUCTION AT THE ALLEN-BRADLEY COMPANY

The oak floor glistens through four coats of polyurethane, reflecting red, blue and yellow blinking lights. The machinery, tenderly adjusted and lubricated and looking like mobile sculpture, whirs and swivels competently behind transparent plastic enclosures. The employees are gung ho, and the most enthusiastic of all is their boss, John Rothwell, 41. "This is my life's dream," he says. "I love it." The atmosphere where they work is electric, suffused with a feeling that what is taking place here, in its boldness and sophistication, is happening nowhere else on earth.

And that could just be true. Because behind the doors on the eighth floor of Allen-Bradley's good gray corporate headquarters near downtown Milwaukee is an operation that may signal a renaissance in U.S. manufacturing. Department 260, as it is known, is the company's innovative and expensive ($15 million) attempt to make its popular lines of sturdy industrial-control devices better and cheaper than those of competing companies in the U.S., Western Europe and Japan.

In stark contrast to Allen-Bradley assembly operations elsewhere in the same building, where some 1,650 workers still put products together largely by hand, Department 260 is run by 14 people. Six of those are white-coated attendants who man the floor's 26 machine stations, clearing equipment jams and feeding the machines' voracious appetites for raw materials. Department 260 is what engineers call a CIM plant, for computer-integrated manufacturing. Computers, from programmable controllers on the floor to a large IBM 3090 Sierra mainframe across the hall, tell the machines how to fashion 600 different varieties of relays and contractors, essentially boxy switches that turn electric motors on and off. Only 14 months old, Department 260's assembly line is not yet running at full speed. But when it does, working at a rate of 600 devices an hour, it will be able to make 4,800 in a single eight-hour shift. If required, it could turn out this volume for orders received the same day.

And yet unlike the overwhelming machines of Charlie Chaplin's *Modern Times*, Department 260's equipment is mostly nonthreatening, with sometimes vexing personalities. *"Mamma mia, ti prego comincia a lavorare!* [Please, start working!]" implores Mechanic Bruno Lockner to one balky contraption. "This machine understands Italian," he jokes. Some machines have names. Clarabelle is a complex wonder that churns out 1,000 crossbar assemblies an hour. It was designed by Allen-Bradley engineers, and is tended by 18-year veteran Employee Cheryl Braddock. Says Braddock: "I talk to her every morning. I pat her on the side. I say, 'It's going to be a good day.'"

For the machines, the day begins just before dawn, when much of Milwaukee's human population is still asleep. All night, orders have been flowing to the IBM from Allen-Bradley distributors in London, Singapore, Hong King, Caracas, Melbourne and 400 locations

in the U.S. From the IBM, they travel silently across hidden cables to Department 260's own network of 29 smaller computers.

At 6:30 a.m., the ceiling lights turn themselves on. At 7:30, on cue from electronic signals speeding through an overhead conduit, the factory goes through its morning calisthenics. The machines begin moving and stretching, flexing conveyor belts, cams, steel-armed grippers, hissing pneumatic tubes, spot welders, laser beams, grinding stones, power drills and screwdrivers. Warning lights, strung like Japanese lanterns across the ceiling, start blinking. Soon the assembly line is running, producing the day's orders.

On the largest scale, the 45,000-sq.-ft. facility is Allen Bradley's bid to stop chasing cheap labor in distant locales. Since 1977 the company has moved manufacturing to Texas, North Carolina and Mexico, resulting in the loss of 1,300 Milwaukee jobs. Now, with Department 260, Allen-Bradley is putting a factory where its skilled work force is. . . .

By the late 1970s, though, [company president C. R. ("Bud")] Whitney and President J. Tracy O'Rourke realized that the marketplace was changing, and Allen-Bradley would have to evolve to survive. The company was too dependent on the machine-tool industry and its biggest customer, Detroit's automakers. Both were reeling from lower-cost foreign competitors. Although Allen-Bradley's domestic sales had not been severely hurt, the day when they would be seemed just around the corner.

What to do? A planning team assembled by Whitney came up with the answer: Allen-Bradley, since its founding a parochial company doing almost all its business in North America, would aggressively expand in Europe, but with a major new twist. Instead of making industrial controls almost exclusively to American standards, the company began designing them to the specifications of the International Electrotechnical Commission, the European arbiter. And instead of buying a foreign company to make the controls, which several competitors had done, it would make them in Milwaukee, in a new facility.

Thus was born the idea for Department 260. Says Whitney: "The light bulb came on." But an unprecedented degree of automation would be required to pull it off. Reason: a representative contactor that sold for $20 in the U.S. sold for just $8 in the highly competitive markets of West Germany and Australia. To make a profit at the lower price, Allen-Bradley had to get costs down. By using automated equipment, the company could produce contactors for 60% less than it could by relying on a manual assembly line. "Labor costs," says Whitney "obviously had to be a nonissue."

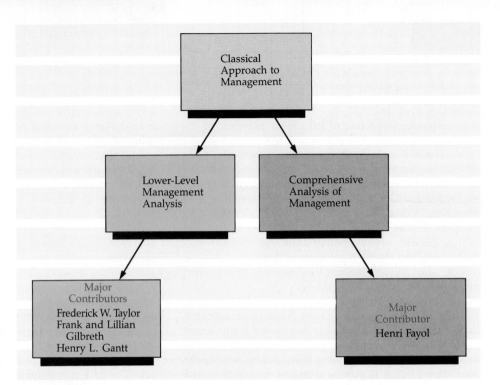

FIGURE 2.1
Division of classical approach to management into two areas and the major contributors to each area

Frederick W. Taylor

For discussion purposes, the classical approach to management breaks into two distinct areas. The first area, lower-level management analysis, consists primarily of the work of Frederick W. Taylor, Frank and Lillian Gilbreth, and Henry L. Gantt. These individuals studied mainly the jobs of workers at lower levels of the organization. The second area, comprehensive analysis of management, concentrates more on the management function as a whole. The primary contributor to this category was Henri Fayol. Figure 2.1 illustrates the two areas in the classical approach.

Lower-Level Management Analysis

Lower-level management analysis concentrates on the "one best way" to perform a task; that is, it asks how a task situation can be structured to get the highest production from workers. The process of finding this "one best way" has become known as the scientific method of management, or simply **scientific management.** Although the techniques of scientific managers could conceivably be applied to all management levels, the research, research applications, and illustrations relate mostly to lower-level managers. The work of Frederick W. Taylor, Frank and Lillian Gilbreth, and Henry L. Gantt is summarized in the sections that follow.

Scientific management involves finding the "one best way" to perform a task.

Frederick W. Taylor (1856—1915)

Because of the significance of his contributions, Frederick W. Taylor is commonly called the father of scientific management. His primary goal was to in-

Taylor, the father of scientific management, reduced jobs to a science.

34

crease worker efficiency by scientifically designing jobs. His basic premise was that there was one best way to do a job and that that way should be discovered and put into operation.

Perhaps the best illustration of Taylor's scientific method and his management philosophy lies in a description of how he modified the job of employees whose sole responsibility was shoveling materials at the Bethlehem Steel Company.[4] During the modification process, Taylor made the assumption that any worker's job could be reduced to a science. To construct the "science of shoveling," he obtained answers—through observation and experimentation—to the following questions:

1. Will a first-class worker do more work per day with a shovelful of five, ten, fifteen, twenty, thirty, or forty pounds?
2. What kinds of shovels work best with which materials?
3. How quickly can a shovel be pushed into a pile of materials and pulled out properly loaded?
4. How much time is required to swing a shovel backward and throw the load a given horizontal distance at a given height?

As Taylor began formulating answers to these types of questions, he developed insights on how to increase the total amount of materials shoveled per day. He increased worker efficiency by matching shovel size with such factors as the size of the men, the weight of the materials, and the height and distance the materials were to be thrown. After the third year that Taylor's shoveling efficiency plan was in operation, records at Bethlehem Steel indicated that the total number of shovelers needed was reduced from about 600 to 140, the average number of tons shoveled per worker per day rose from sixteen to fifty-nine, the average earnings per worker per day rose from $1.15 to $1.88, and the average cost of handling a long ton (2,240 pounds) dropped from $0.072 to $0.033—an impressive application of scientific management to the task of shoveling.

Lillian and Frank Gilbreth

Frank Gilbreth (1868–1924), Lillian Gilbreth (1878–1972)

The Gilbreths were also significant contributors to the scientific method. By definition, therefore, they ascribed to the idea of finding and using the one best way to perform a job. The primary investigative tool in their research was **motion study,** which consisted of reducing each job to the most basic movements possible. Motion analysis was then used to establish job performance standards and to eliminate unnecessary or wasted movement.

During a motion analysis, the Gilbreths considered the work environment, the motion itself, and behavioral variables concerning the workers. Table 2.1 on page 36 lists the primary factors in each of these groups. The analysis of each of the variables in a task situation was obviously a long, involved, and tedious process.

Frank Gilbreth's experience as an apprentice bricklayer led him to do motion studies of bricklaying. He found that bricklayers could increase their output significantly by concentrating on performing some motions and eliminating others. Table 2.2, page 37, shows a portion of the results of one of Gilbreth's bricklaying motion studies. For each bricklaying activity, Gilbreth indicated whether or not it should be omitted for the sake of efficiency and why. He reduced the twelve motions per brick listed under "The Wrong Way" to the two motions per brick listed under "The Right Way." Gilbreth's bricklaying motion studies re-

A motion study reduces a job to its basic movements.

TABLE 2.1

Primary variables considered in analyzing motions

Variables of the Worker	Variables of the Surroundings, Equipment, and Tools	Variables of the Motion
1. Anatomy	1. Appliances	1. Acceleration
2. Brawn	2. Clothes	2. Automaticity
3. Contentment	3. Colors	3. Combination with other motions and sequence
4. Creed	4. Entertainment, music, reading, etc.	4. Cost
5. Earning power	5. Heating, cooling, ventilating	5. Direction
6. Experience	6. Lighting	6. Effectiveness
7. Fatigue	7. Quality of material	7. Foot-pounds of work accomplished
8. Habits	8. Reward and punishment	8. Inertia and momentum overcome
9. Health	9. Size of unit moved	9. Length
10. Mode of living	10. Special fatigue-eliminating devices	10. Necessity
11. Nutrition	11. Surroundings	11. Path
12. Size	12. Tools	12. "Play for position"
13. Skill	13. Union rules	13. Speed
14. Temperament	14. Weight of unit moved	
15. Training		

sulted in reducing the number of motions necessary to lay a brick by approximately 70 percent and tripling bricklaying production.

Lillian Gilbreth, in addition to collaborating with her husband, researched and wrote on motion studies after her husband's death. She applied the scientific method to the role of the homemaker and to the handicapped.

Gantt increased worker efficiency through scheduling innovation and reward innovation.

Henry L. Gantt (1861–1919)

A third major contributor to the area of scientific management was Henry L. Gantt. He, like Taylor and the Gilbreths, was interested in increasing worker efficiency. Gantt attributed unsatisfactory or ineffective tasks and piece rates (incentive pay for each product piece an individual produces) primarily to the fact that they were set on what had been done in the past or on somebody's *opinion* of what could be done. According to Gantt, *exact scientific knowledge* of what could be done should be substituted for opinion. He considered this the role of scientific management.

Gantt's management philosophy is described by his statement that "the essential differences between the best system of today and those of the past are the manner in which tasks are 'scheduled' and the manner in which their performance is rewarded."[5] Following his own rationale, Gantt tried to improve systems or organizations through task scheduling innovation and reward innovation.

Scheduling Innovation
The Gantt chart, the primary scheduling tool that Gantt developed, is still used in many organizations today. Basically, this chart provides managers with an easily understood summary of what work was scheduled for specific time peri-

Henry L. Gantt

TABLE 2.2

Partial results for one of Gilbreth's bricklaying motion studies

Operation No.	The Wrong Way Motions Per Brick $\frac{1}{4}\ \frac{1}{2}\ \frac{3}{4}\ \frac{4}{4}$	The Right Way Motions Per Brick $\frac{1}{4}\ \frac{1}{2}\ \frac{3}{4}\ \frac{4}{4}$	Pick and Dip Method: The Exterior Four Inches (Laying to the Line)
1	Step for mortar	Omit	On the scaffold the inside edge of mortar box should be plumb with inside edge of stock platform. On floor the inside edge of mortar box should be twenty-one in. from wall. Mortar boxes never over four ft. apart.
2	Reach for mortar	$\frac{4}{4}$	Do not bend any more than absolutely necessary to reach mortar with a straight arm.
3	Work up mortar	Omit	Provide mortar of right consistency. Examine sand screen and keep in repair so that no pebbles can get through. Keep tender on scaffold to temper up and keep mortar worked up right.
4	Step for brick	Omit	If tubs are kept four ft. apart, no stepping for brick will be necessary on scaffold. On floor keep brick in a pile not nearer than one ft. nor more than four ft. six ins. from wall.
5	Reach for brick	Included in 2	Brick must be reached for at the same time that the mortar is reached for, and picked up at exactly the same time the mortar is picked up. If it is not picked up at the same time, allowance must be made for operation.
6	Pick up right brick	Omit	Train the leader of the tenders to vary the kind of brick used as much as possible to suit the conditions; that is, to bring the best brick when the men are working on the line.
7	Mortar box to wall	$\frac{4}{4}$	Carry stock from the staging to the wall in the straightest possible line and with an even speed, without pause or hitch. It is important to move the stock with an even speed and not by quick jerks.
8	Brick pile to wall	Included in 7	Brick must be carried from pile to wall at exactly same time as the mortar is carried to the wall, without pause or jerk.
9	Deposit mortar on wall	Included in 7	If a pause is made, this space must be filled out. If no pause is made, it is included in No. 7.
10	Spreading mortar	Omit	The mortar must be thrown so as to require no additional spreading and so that the mortar runs up on the end of the previous brick laid, or else the next two spaces must be filled out.
11	Cutting off mortar	Omit	If the mortar is thrown from the trowel properly, no spreading and no cutting is necessary.
12	Disposing of mortar	Omit	If mortar is not cut off, this space is not filled out. If mortar is cut off, keep it on trowel and carry back on trowel to box, or else butter on end of brick. Do not throw it on mortar box.

ods, how much of this work was completed, and by whom it was done. The Gantt chart is covered in much more detail in chapter 7.

Reward Innovation

Gantt seemed more aware of the human side of production than either Taylor or the Gilbreths. He wrote that "the taskmaster (manager) of the past was practically a slave driver, whose principal function was to force workmen to do that which they had no desire to do, or interest in doing. The task setter of today under any reputable system of managment is not a driver. When he asks the workmen to perform tasks, he makes it to their interest to accomplish them, and is careful not to ask what is impossible or unreasonable."[6]

Gantt believed in encouraging workers to higher levels of production through bonuses.

Whereas Taylor had developed a system that allowed for all workers to be paid at the same rate, Gantt developed a system wherein workers could earn a bonus in addition to the piece rate if they went beyond their daily production quota. Gantt believed that worker compensation needed to correspond not only to production through the piece-rate system but also to overproduction through the bonus system.

BACK TO THE CASE

Jim Delligatti, the owner/manager of forty-seven McDonald's outlets who was discussed in the introductory case, could use a classical approach to management to stress organizational efficiency—the "one best way" to perform jobs at McDonald's—to increase productivity. As a simplified example, Delligatti might want to check whether the silver dispenser used to apply mustard and ketchup is of the appropriate size to require only one squirt or whether more than one squirt is necessary to adequately cover the hamburger bun.

Delligatti also could use motion studies to eliminate unnecessary or wasted motions by his employees. For example, are hamburgers, french fries, and drinks located for easy insertion into customer bags, or must an employee walk unnecessary steps during the sales process? Also, would certain McDonald's employees be more efficient over an entire working day if they sat, rather than stood, while working?

The classical approach to management might also guide Delligatti in scheduling more efficiently. By ensuring that an appropriate number of people with the appropriate skills are scheduled to work during peak hours and that fewer such individuals are scheduled to work during slower hours, Delligatti would maximize the return on his labor costs.

Delligatti also might want to consider offering his employees some sort of bonus if they reach certain work goals. But he should make sure that the goals that he sets are realistic, since unreasonable or impossible goals tend to make workers resentful and unproductive. For example, Delligatti might ask that certain employees reduce errors in filling orders by 50 percent during the next month. If and when these employees reached the goal, Delligatti could give them a free lunch as a bonus.

Comprehensive Analysis of Management

Comprehensive analysis of management involves studying the management function as a whole.

Whereas scientific managers approach the study of management primarily in terms of job design, managers who embrace the comprehensive view—the second area of the classical approach—are concerned with the entire range of managerial performance.

Among the well-known contributors to the comprehensive view were Chester Barnard,[7] Alvin Brown,[8] Henry Dennison,[9] Luther Gulick and Lyndall Urwick,[10] J. D. Mooney and A. C. Reiley,[11] and Oliver Sheldon.[12] Perhaps the most notable of all contributors, however, was Henri Fayol. His book *General and*

Industrial Management presents a management philosophy that many modern managers still look to for advice and guidance.[13]

Henri Fayol (1841—1925)

Because of his writings on the elements of management and the general principles of management, Henri Fayol is usually regarded as the pioneer of administrative theory. The elements of management he outlined—planning, organizing, command, coordination, and control—are still considered worthwhile divisions under which to study, analyze, and put into action the management process. (Note the similarities between Fayol's elements of management and the management functions outlined in chapter 1—planning, organizing, influencing, controlling.)

Fayol suggested five elements of management.

The general principles of management suggested by Fayol also are still considered by most managers to be useful in contemporary management practice. These principles follow in the order developed by Fayol and are accompanied by corresponding definitional themes:[14]

Fayol also suggested fourteen general principles of management.

1. *Division of work* Work should be divided among individuals and groups to ensure that effort and attention are focused on special portions of the task. Fayol presented work specialization as the best way to use the human resources of the organization.
2. *Authority* The concepts of authority and responsibility are closely related. *Authority* was defined by Fayol as the right to give orders and the power to exact obedience. Responsibility involves being accountable and, therefore, is naturally associated with authority. When one assumes authority, one also assumes responsibility.
3. *Discipline* A successful organization requires the common effort of workers. Penalties, however, should be applied judiciously to encourage this common effort.
4. *Unity of command* Workers should receive orders from only one manager.[15]
5. *Unity of direction* The entire organization should be moving toward a common objective, in a common direction.
6. *Subordination of individual interests to the general interests* The interests of one person should not have priority over the interests of the organization as a whole.
7. *Remuneration* Many variables, such as cost of living, supply of qualified personnel, general business conditions, and success of the business, should be considered in determining the rate of pay a worker will receive.
8. *Centralization* Fayol defined *centralization* as lowering the importance of the subordinate role. Decentralization is increasing the same importance. The degree to which centralization or decentralization should be adopted depends on the specific organization in which the manager is working.
9. *Scalar chain* Managers in hierarchies are actually part of a chainlike authority scale. Each manager, from the first-line supervisor to the president, possesses certain amounts of authority. The president possesses the most authority; the first-line supervisor possesses the least authority. The existence of this chain implies that lower-level managers should always keep upper-level managers informed of their work activities. The existence of and adherence to the scalar chain are necessary if organizations are to be successful.
10. *Order* For the sake of efficiency and coordination, all materials and people

related to a specific kind of work should be assigned to the same general location in the organization.

11. *Equity* All employees should be treated as equally as possible.
12. *Stability of tenure of personnel* Retaining productive employees should always be a high priority of management. Recruitment and selection costs, as well as increased reject rates, are usually associated with hiring new workers.
13. *Initiative* Management should take steps to encourage worker initiative, which can be defined as new or additional work activity undertaken through self-direction.
14. *Esprit de corps* Management should encourage harmony and general good feeling among employees.

Fayol's general principles of management cover a broad range of topics, but organizational efficiency, the handling of people, and appropriate management action seem to be the three general themes stressed. With the writings of Fayol, the study of management as a broad comprehensive activity began to receive the attention it deserved.

Limitations of the Classical Approach

Although the classical approach generally improves productivity, people emphasis is inadequate.

Individual contributors to the classical approach were probably encouraged to write about their experiences largely because of the success they enjoyed. Structuring work to be more efficient and defining the manager's role more precisely yielded significant improvement in productivity, which individuals such as Taylor and Fayol were quick to document.

The human variable for the organization, however, may not be adequately emphasized in the classical approach. People today do not seem to be as influenced by bonuses as they were in the nineteenth century. It is generally agreed that critical interpersonal areas, such as conflict, communication, leadership, and motivation, were not emphasized enough in the classical approach.

THE BEHAVIORAL APPROACH

The behavioral approach emphasizes people.

The **behavioral approach to management** emphasizes striving to increase production through an understanding of people. According to proponents of this approach, if managers understand their people and adapt their organizations to them, organizational success usually follows.

The behavioral approach is usually described as beginning with a series of studies conducted between 1924 and 1932. These studies investigated the behavior and attitudes of workers at the Hawthorne (Chicago) Works of the Western Electric Company.[16] Accounts of these studies are usually divided into phases: the relay assembly test room experiments and the bank wiring observation room experiment.

The Relay Assembly Test Room Experiments

The relay assembly test room experiments originally had a scientific management orientation.[17] The experimenters believed that if productivity were studied long enough under different working conditions (including variations in weather conditions, temperature, rest periods, work hours and humidity), the working conditions that maximized production would be found. The purpose of the relay assembly test room experiments was to determine the relationship between intensity of lighting and efficiency of workers, as measured by worker output. Two groups of female employees were used as subjects. The light intensity for one group was varied, while the light intensity for the other group was held constant.

The results of the experiments surprised the researchers. No matter what conditions employees were exposed to, production increased. A consistent relationship between productivity and lighting intensity seemed nonexistent. An extensive interviewing campaign was begun to determine why the subjects continued to increase production. The following are the main reasons, as formulated from the interviews:

1. The subjects found working in the test room enjoyable.
2. The new supervisory relationship during the experiment allowed the subjects to work freely, without fear.
3. The subjects realized that they were taking part in an important and interesting study.
4. The subjects seemed to become friendly as a group.

The experimenters concluded that human factors within organizations could significantly influence production. More research was needed to evaluate the potential impact of this human component in organizations.

Production increased continuously, regardless of working conditions.

The Bank Wiring Observation Room Experiment

The purpose of the bank wiring observation room experiment was to analyze the social relationships in a work group.[18] More specifically, the study focused on the effect of group piecework incentives on a group of men who assembled terminal banks for use in telephone exchanges. The group piecework incentive system dictated that the harder a group worked as a whole, the more pay each member of that group received.

The experimenters believed that the study would find that members of the work group would pressure one another to work harder so that each group member would receive more pay. To the surprise of the researchers, the opposite occurred. The work group pressured the faster workers to slow down their work rate. In essence, the men whose work rate would have increased individual salaries were pressured by the group, rather than the men whose work rate would have decreased individual salaries. Evidently, the men were more interested in preserving the work group than in making more money. The researchers concluded that social groups in organizations could effectively exert enough pressure to influence individuals to disregard monetary incentives.

The experiment showed that social groups in organizations can be preserved even when monetary incentives are offered.

Taken together, the series of studies conducted at the Hawthorne plant gave management thinkers a new direction for research. Obviously, the human variable in the organization needed much more analysis, since it could either increase or decrease production drastically. Managers began to realize that they needed to understand this influence in order to maximize its positive effects and minimize its negative effects. This attempt to understand people is still a major force of today's organizational research. More current behavioral findings and their implications for management are presented in much greater detail in later sections of this text.

BACK TO THE CASE

Comprehensive analysis of management implies that Jim Delligatti might be able to improve his McDonald's restaurants by evaluating the entire range of his managerial performance—especially with regard to organizational efficiency, the handling of people, and appropriate management action. For example, Delligatti should check with his employees to make sure they are receiving orders from only one source—that a manager isn't instructing an employee to man the french fry station while moments later an assistant manager tells the same employee to tend to the grill. Along the same lines, Delligatti might want to verify that all of his employees are being treated equitably—that fry cooks, for example, don't get longer work breaks than order takers.

The behavioral approach to management suggests that Delligatti should consider the people working for him and evaluate the impact of their feelings and relationships on the productivity of his restaurants. He could, for example, try to make the work more enjoyable, perhaps by allowing his employees to work at different stations (grill, beverage, french fry, cash register, etc.) each day. He might also consider creating opportunities for employees to become more friendly with one another, perhaps through company sponsored softball teams. In essence, the behavioral approach to management stresses that Delligatti should recognize the human variable in his restaurants and strive to maximize its positive effects.

THE MANAGEMENT SCIENCE APPROACH

Churchman, Ackoff, and Arnoff define the management science, or operations research (OR), approach as (1) an application for the scientific method to problems arising in the operation of a system and (2) the solving of these problems by the solving of mathematical equations representing the system.[19] The **management science approach** suggests that managers can best improve their organizations by using the scientific method and mathematical techniques to solve operational problems.

The management science approach involves using the scientific method and mathematical techniques.

The Beginning of the Management Science Approach

The management science, or operations research, approach can be traced to World War II. During this era, leading scientists were asked to help solve complex operational problems that existed in the military.[20] The scientists were organized into teams that eventually became known as operations research (OR) groups. One OR group was asked to determine which gunsights would best stop German attacks on the British mainland.

These early OR groups typically included physicists and other "hard" scientists, who used the problem-solving method with which they had the most experience: the scientific method. The **scientific method** dictates that scientists:

The scientific method involves:

1. Observing.

1. Systematically *observe* the system whose behavior must be explained to solve the problem.

2. Constructing a model.

2. Use these specific observations to *construct* a generalized framework (a model) that is consistent with the specific observations and from which consequences of changing the system can be predicted.

3. Use the model to *deduce* how the system will behave under conditions that have not been observed but could be observed if the changes were made.

4. Finally, *test* the model by performing an experiment on the actual system to see if the effects of changes predicted using the model actually occur when the changes are made.[21]

3. Deducing.

4. Testing the model.

The OR groups were very successful in using the scientific method to solve their operational problems.

Management Science Today

After World War II, the world again became interested in manufacturing and selling products. The success of the OR groups had been so obvious in the military that managers were anxious to try management science techniques in an industrial environment. After all, managers also had complicated operational problems.

By 1955, the management science approach to solving industrial problems had proven very effective. Many people found this approach valuable and saw great promise in refining its techniques and analytical tools. Managers and universities alike anxiously began these refinement attempts.

By 1965, the management science approach was being used in many companies and applied to many diverse management problems, such as production scheduling, plant location, and product packaging.[22]

Characteristics of Management Science Applications

Four primary characteristics usually are present in situations in which management science techniques are applied.[23] First, the management problems studied are so complicated that managers need help in analyzing a large number of variables. Management science techniques increase the effectiveness of the managers' decision making. Second, a management science application generally uses economic implications as guidelines for making a particular decision. Perhaps this is because management science techniques are best suited for analyzing quantifiable factors, such as sales, expenses, and units of production. Third, the use of mathematical models to investigate the decision situation is typical in management science applications. Models are constructed to represent reality and then used to determine how the real world situation might be improved. The fourth characteristic of a management science application is the use of computers. The great complexity of managerial problems and the sophisticated mathematical analysis required of problem related information are two factors that make computers very valuable to the management science analyst.

Today, managers are using such management science tools as inventory control models, network models, and probability models as aids in the decision-making process. Later parts of this text will outline some of these models in more detail and illustrate their applications to management decision making. Because management science thought is still evolving, more and more sophisticated analytical techniques can be expected.

Characteristics of management science applications include:

1. Large number of variables.

2. Use of economic implications.

3. Use of mathematical models.

4. Use of a computer.

▦ THE CONTINGENCY APPROACH

With the contingency approach, management action depends on the situation.

In simple terms, the **contingency approach to management** emphasizes that what managers do in practice depends on, or is contingent on, a given set of circumstances—a situation.[24] In essence, this approach emphasizes "if-then" relationships. "If" this situational variable exists, "then" this is the action a manager probably would take. As an example, if a manager has a group of inexperienced subordinates, then the contingency approach would recommend that she lead in a different fashion than if she had an experienced group.

The situation must be perceived accurately, and the best-suited management tactics must be chosen and implemented.

In general, the contingency approach attempts to outline the conditions or situations in which various management methods have the best chance of success.[25] This approach is based on the premise that although there is probably no one best way to solve a management problem in all organizations, there probably is one best way to solve any given management problem in any one organization. Perhaps the main challenges of using the contingency approach are (1) perceiving organizational situations as they actually exist, (2) choosing the management tactics best suited to those situations, and (3) competently implementing those tactics.

Although the notion of a contingency approach to management is not new,[26] the use of the term itself is relatively new. In addition, the contingency approach has become a popular discussion topic for contemporary management writers. The general consensus of their writings seems to indicate that if managers are to apply management concepts, principles, and techniques successfully, they must consider the realities of the specific organizational circumstances they face.[27]

▦ THE SYSTEM APPROACH

Understanding the system as a whole requires understanding the interdependence of its parts.

The **system approach to management** is based on general system theory. Ludwig von Bertalanffy, a scientist who worked mainly in the areas of physics and biology, is recognized as the founder of general system theory.[28] The main premise of the theory is that to understand fully the operation of an entity, the entity must be viewed as a system. A **system** is a number of interdependent parts functioning as a whole for some purpose. For example, according to general system theory, to fully understand the operations of the human body, one must understand the workings of its interdependent parts (ears, eyes, brain, etc.). General system theory integrates the knowledge of various specialized fields so that the system as a whole can be better understood.

Types of Systems

Closed systems: No interaction with environment.

Open systems: Interaction with environment.

According to von Bertalanffy, there are two basic types of systems: closed and open. **Closed systems** are not influenced by and do not interact with their environments. They are mostly mechanical and have necessary predetermined motions or activities that must be performed regardless of the environment. A clock is an example of a closed system. Regardless of its environment, a clock's wheels, gears, and so forth must function in a predetermined way if the clock as a whole is to exist and serve its purpose. The second type of system, the **open**

system, is constantly interacting with its environment. A plant is an example of an open system. Constant interaction with the environment influences the plant's state of existence and its future. In fact, the environment determines whether or not the plant will live.

Systems and "Wholeness"

The concept "wholeness" is very important in general system analysis. The system must be viewed as a whole and modified only through changes in its parts. A thorough knowledge of how each part functions and the interrelationships among the parts must be present before modifications of the parts can be made for the overall benefit of the system. L. Thomas Hopkins suggested six guidelines for system wholeness that should be remembered during system analysis:[29]

1. The whole should be the main focus of analysis, with the parts receiving secondary attention.
2. Integration is the key variable in wholeness analysis. It is defined as the interrelatedness of the many parts within the whole.
3. Possible modifications in each part should be weighed in relation to possible effects on every other part.
4. Each part has some role to perform so that the whole can accomplish its purpose.
5. The nature of the part and its function is determined by its position in the whole.
6. All analysis starts with the existence of the whole. The parts and their interrelationships should then evolve to best suit the purpose of the whole.

Since the system approach to management is based on general system theory, analysis of the management situation as a system is stressed. The following sections present the parts of the management system and recommend information that can be used to analyze the system.

The Management System

As with all systems, the **management system** is composed of a number of parts that function on an interdependent basis to achieve a purpose. The main parts of the management system are organizational input, organizational process, and organizational output. As discussed in chapter 1, these parts consist of organizational resources, the production process, and finished goods respectively. The parts represent a combination that exists to achieve organizational objectives, whatever they may be.

The management system is an open system, one that interacts with its environment (see Figure 2.2, p. 46.). Environmental factors with which the management system interacts include the government, suppliers, customers, and competitors. Each of these represents a potential environmental influence that could significantly change the future of a management system.

Environmental impact on management cannot be overemphasized. As an example, the federal government, through its Occupational Safety and Health

A system is changed by changing its parts.

The management system is open and consists of input, process, and output.

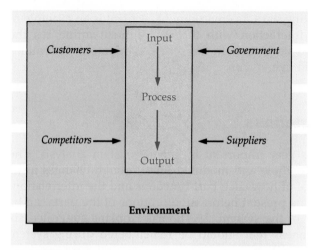

FIGURE 2.2
The open management system

Act (OSHA) of 1970, encourages management to take costly steps to safeguard workers. Many managers are frustrated because they believe the safeguards are not only too expensive but also unnecessary.

Information for Management System Analysis

Environmental factors can impact management systems.

As noted earlier, to better understand a system, general system theory allows for the use of information from many specialized disciplines. This certainly holds true for the management system. Information from any discipline can increase the understanding of management system operations and thereby enhance the success of the system. A broad, sweeping statement such as this, however, presents a problem. Where do managers go to get this information?

Triangular management uses classically based, behaviorally based, and management science based information.

The information used to discuss the management system in the remainder of this text comes from three primary sources: (1) the classical approach to management, (2) the behavioral approach to management, and (3) the management science approach to management. The use of these three sources of information to analyze the management system is referred to as **triangular management.** Figure 2.3 presents the triangular management model. The three sources of information in the model are not meant to represent all the information that can be used to analyze the management system. Rather, they are the three bodies of management related information that probably would be most useful to managers analyzing the management system.

Managers synthesize information.

A synthesis of classically based information, behaviorally based information, and management science based information is critical to effectively managing the management system. This information is integrated and presented in this text in the five remaining parts of the book. These parts discuss management systems and planning (chapters 4–7), organizing (chapters 8–11), influencing (chapters 12–15), controlling (chapters 16–18), and topics for special emphasis (chapters 19–21).[30] In addition, some information in these parts is presented from a contingency viewpoint to give added emphasis to the practical application of management principles.

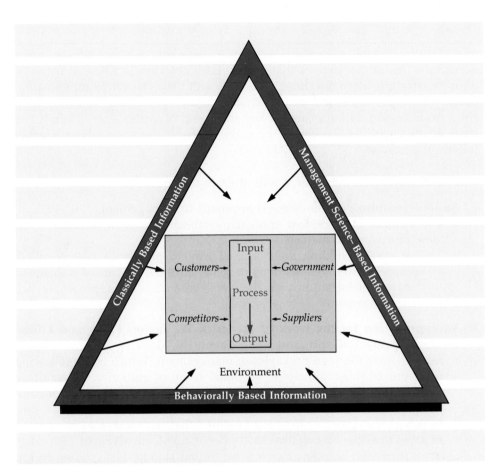

FIGURE 2.3
Triangular management model

BACK TO THE CASE

Jim Delligatti could use the management science approach to solve any operational problems that arose. According to the scientific method, Delligatti would first spend some time observing what takes place in one of his restaurants. Next, he would use these observations to outline exactly how the restaurant operates as a whole, Third, he would apply this understanding of restaurant operations by predicting how various changes might help or hinder the restaurant as a whole. Before implementing possible changes, he would test them on a small scale to see if they actually affected the restaurant as desired.

If Delligatti were to accept the contingency approach to management, his actions as a manager would depend on the situation. For example, *if* some customers hadn't been served within sixty seconds because the deep-fat fryer had unexpectedly broken down, *then* Delligatti probably would not hold his employees responsible. But *if* he knew that the fryer

had broken down because of employee mistreatment or neglect, *then* his reaction to the situation would likely be very different.

Delligatti could also apply the system approach and view each of his restaurants as a system, or a number of interdependent parts that function as a whole to reach restaurant objectives. Naturally, each restaurant would be seen as an open system—a system that exists in and is influenced by its environment. Major factors within the environment of a McDonald's restaurant would include customers, suppliers, competitors, and the government. For example, if one of McDonald's fast-food competitors were to significantly lower its price for hamburgers to a point well below what McDonald's was asking for a hamburger, Delligatti might be forced to consider modifying different parts of his restaurant system in order to meet or beat that price.

Action Summary

Reread the learning objectives that follow. Each objective is followed by questions. Answering these questions accurately will help you retain the most important concepts discussed in this chapter. After answering each question, check your answer with the answer key at the end of this chapter. (*Hint:* If you have doubt regarding the correct response, consult the page whose number follows the answer.)

Circle:

From studying this chapter, I will attempt to acquire:

1. An understanding of the classical approach to management.

T, F   **a.** The classical management approach established what it considered the "one best way" to manage.

a, b, c, d, e   **b.** The process of finding the one best way to perform a task is called: (a) comprehensive analysis of management; (b) the concept of wholeness; (c) the Hawthorne studies; (d) the management science approach; (e) scientific management.

2. An appreciation for the work of Frederick W. Taylor, Frank and Lillian Gilbreth, Henry L. Gantt, and Henri Fayol.

a, b, c, d, e   **a.** Fayol defines fourteen principles of management. Which of the following is *not* one of those principles: (a) scalar chain of authority; (b) esprit de corps; (c) centralization; (d) unity of command; (e) directedness of command.

a, b, c, d, e   **b.** Which of the following theorists assumed that any worker's job could be reduced to a science: (a) Gilbreth; (b) Gantt; (c) Mayo; (d) Fayol; (e) Taylor.

T, F   **c.** Gantt increased worker efficiency by setting standards according to top management's opinion of what maximum performance should be.

3. An understanding of the behavioral approach to management.

T, F   **a.** The behavioral approach to management emphasizes striving to increase production through an understanding of the organization itself.

a, b, c, d, e   **b.** The behavioral approach began with: (a) the Hawthorne studies; (b) the mental revolution; (c) the Industrial Revolution; (d) motion studies; (e) the Bethlehem Steel studies.

4. An understanding of the studies at the Hawthorne Works of the Western Electric Company.

T, F   **a.** The Hawthorne studies showed a direct relationship between lighting and efficiency.

T, F   **b.** The Hawthorne experimenters found that people were more concerned with preserving the work group than with maximizing their pay.

5. An understanding of the management science approach to management.

a, b, c, d, e   **a.** Which of the following is not one of the philosophies of the management science approach; (a) managers can improve the organization by using scientific methods; (b) mathematical techniques can solve organizational problems; (c) models should be used to represent the system; (d) individual work is better than teamwork; (e) observation of the system must take place.

T, F   **b.** In the management science theory, models are used to represent reality and then to determine how the real world situation might be improved.

6. **An understanding of how the management science approach has evolved.**
   a. The management science approach emerged after: (a) World War I; (b) the Civil War; (c) the Korean War; (d) World War II; (e) the 1930 depression.   a, b, c, d, e
   b. Although management science was first applied to military problems, it is now applied by companies to diverse management problems.   T, F

7. **An understanding of the system approach to management.**
   a. An organization that interacts with external forces is: (a) a closed system; (b) a model; (c) an independent entity; (d) an open system; (e) a contingency.   a, b, c, d, e
   b. Which of the following is *not* one of the guidelines proposed by Hopkins in the concept of wholeness: (a) the whole should be the main focus of analysis; (b) all analysis starts with the existence of the whole; (c) the nature of the art is determined by its position in the whole; (d) each part has some role to perform so that the whole can accomplish its purpose; (e) modifications should be made as they occur.   a, b, c, d, e

8. **An understanding of how triangular management and the contingency approach to management are related.**
   a. The contingency approach emphasizes the viewpoint that what managers do in practice depends over all on: (a) the worker; (b) the situation; (c) the task; (d) the environment; (e) the manager's personality.   a, b, c, d, e
   b. The three sources of information in triangular management are: (a) input, process, and output; (b) management science, classically and behaviorally based; (c) mathematics, psychology, and sociology; (d) managers, directors, and stockholders; (e) executives, administrators, and supervisors.   a, b, c, d, e

INTRODUCTORY CASE WRAP-UP

"McDonald's Recipe for Success" (p. 30) and its related back-to-the-case sections were written to help you better understand the management concepts contained in this chapter. Answer the following discussion questions about this introductory case to further enrich your understanding of the chapter content:

1. What problems do you think an individual like Delligatti faces in managing a McDonalds's restaurant?
2. What action(s) do you think a manager like Delligatti would have to take to solve these problems?
3. From what you know about McDonald's restaurants, how easy would it be to hold Delligatti's job? Why?

Issues for Review and Discussion

1. List the five approaches to managing.
2. Define the classical approach to management.
3. Compare and contrast the contributions to the classical approach made by Frederick W. Taylor, Frank and Lillian Gilbreth, and Henry L. Gantt.
4. How does Henri Fayol's contribution to the classical approach differ from those of Taylor, the Gilbreths, and Gantt?
5. What is scientific management?
6. Describe motion study as used by the Gilbreths.
7. Describe Gantt's innovation in the area of worker bonuses.
8. List and define Fayol's general principles of management.
9. What is the primary limitation to the classical approach to management?

10. Define the behavioral approach to management.
11. What is the significance of the studies at the Hawthorne Works of the Western Electric Company?
12. What is the management science approach to management?
13. What are the steps in the scientific method of problem solving?
14. List and explain three characteristics of situations in which management science applications usually are made.

15. Define the contingency approach to management.
16. What is a system?
17. What is the difference between a closed system and an open system?
18. Explain the relationship between system analysis and "wholeness."
19. What are the parts of the management system?
20. What is triangular management?

Sources of Additional Information

Abernathy, William J., Kim B. Clark, and Alan M. Kantrow. "The New Industrial Competition." *Harvard Business Review* (September/October 1981): 68–81.

Boddewyn, J. "Frederick Winslow Taylor Revisited." *Academy of Management Journal* 4 (1961): 100–107.

Boone, Louis E., and Donald D. Bowen. *The Great Writings in Management and Organizational Behavior,* 2d ed. New York: Random House, 1987.

Braddick, Bill, and Denis Boyle. "Business Success in a Changing World." *Personnel Management* 13 (June 1981): 37–39, 48.

Cameron, Kim S., and David A. Whetten. *Organizational Effectiveness.* New York: Academic Press, 1983.

Carey, A. "The Hawthorne Studies: A Radical Criticism." *American Sociological Review* 32 (1967): 403–16.

Davis, R. C. *Industrial Organization and Management,* 2d ed. New York: Harper & Bros., 1940.

———. "A Philosophy of Management." *Academy of Management Journal* 1 (1958): 37–40.

Feulner, Terry, and Brian H. Kleiner. "When Robots Are the Answer." *Personnel Journal* 65 (February 1986): 44.

Franklin, William H., Jr. "What Japanese Managers Know That American Managers Don't." *Administrative Management* 42 (September 1981): 36–39, 51–54, 56.

Gilbreth, F. B. *Motion Study.* New York: Van Nostrand, 1911.

Gilbreth, Lillian M. *The Psychology of Management.* New York: Sturgis and Walton, 1914.

Gilbreth, Lillian M., Orphae Mae Thomas, and Eleanor Clymer. *Management in the Home.* New York: Dodd, Mead, 1954.

Halloran, Jack. *Applied Human Relations: An Organizational Approach,* 2d ed. Englewood Cliffs, N.J.: Prentice-Hall, 1983.

Hayes, James L. *Memos for Management—The Manager's Job.* New York: Amacom, 1983.

Kakar, S. *Frederick Taylor: A Study in Personality and Innovation.* Cambridge, Mass.: MIT Press, 1970.

Kelly, John E. *Scientific Management, Job Redesign and Work Performance.* London: Academic Press, 1982.

Klein, Bruce A., and Pamela A. Posey. "Good Supervisors Are Good Supervisors—Anywhere." *Harvard Business Review* (November/December 1986): 125.

Merrill, H. F., ed. *Classics in Management.* New York: American Management Association, 1960.

Pringle, Charles D. "Managing a Closed System in an Open Systems World." *Business* 36 (October/November/December 1986): 9–16.

Riker, Richard R. "What Makes a Manager Unique?" *Journal of Systems Management* 35 (August 1984): 41.

Rogers, David. "Managing in the Public and Private Sectors: Similarities and Differences." *Management Review* 70 (May 1981): 48–49.

Thomas, Philip S. "Scanning Strategy: Formulation and Implementation." *Managerial Planning* 33 (July/August 1984): 14–20.

Yost, Edna, and Lillian M. Gilbreth. *Normal Lives for the Disabled.* New York: Macmillan, 1944.

Notes

1. James H. Donnelly, Jr., James L. Gibson, and John M. Ivancevich, *Fundamentals of Management* (Plano, Tex.: Business Publications, 1987), 6–8.

2. Harold Koontz, Cyril O'Donnell, and Heinz Weihrich, *Management,* 8th ed. (New York: McGraw-Hill, 1984), 52–69.

3. W. Warren Haynes and Joseph L. Massie, *Management*, 2d ed. (Englewood Cliffs, N.J.: Prentice-Hall, 1969), 4–13.

4. Frederick W. Taylor, *The Principles of Scientific Management* (New York: Harper & Bros., 1947), 66–71.

5. Henry L. Gantt, *Industrial Leadership* (New Haven, Conn.: Yale University Press, 1916), 57.

6. Gantt, *Industrial Leadership*, 85.

7. Chester I. Barnard, *Organization and Management* (Cambridge, Mass.: Harvard University Press, 1952).

8. Alvin Brown, *Organization of Industry* (Englewood Cliffs, N.J.: Prentice-Hall, 1947).

9. Henry S. Dennison, *Organization Engineering* (New York: McGraw-Hill, 1931).

10. Luther Gulick and Lyndall Urwick, eds., *Papers on the Science of Administration* (New York: Institute of Public Administration, 1937).

11. J. D. Mooney and A. C. Reiley, *Onward Industry!* (New York: Harper & Bros., 1931). With some modifications, this book appeared as *The Principles of Organization* (New York: Harper & Bros., 1939).

12. Oliver Sheldon, *The Philosophy of Management* (London: Sir Isaac Pitman and Sons, 1923).

13. Henri Fayol, *General and Industrial Management* (London: Sir Isaac Pitman and Sons, 1949).

14. Fayol, *General and Industrial Management*, 19–42.

15. For a provocative discussion of the principle of unity of command, see James I. Mashburn and Bobby C. Vaught, "Two Heads Are Better than One: The Case for Dual Leadership," *Management Review* (December 1980): 53–56.

16. For detailed summaries of these studies, see *Industrial Worker*, 2 vols. (Cambridge, Mass.: Harvard University Press, 1938); and F. J. Roethlisberger and W. J. Dickson, *Management and the Worker* (Cambridge, Mass.: Harvard University Press, 1939).

17. For additional information, see George C. Homans, *Fatigue of Workers: Its Relation to Industrial Production* (New York: Committee on Work in Industry, National Research Council, Reinhold Publishing, 1941).

18. Homans, *Fatigue of Workers*.

19. C. West Churchman, Russell L. Ackoff, and E. Leonard Arnoff, *Introduction to Operations Research* (New York: Wiley, 1957), 18.

20. Hamdy A. Taha, *Operations Research: An Introduction* (New York: Macmillan, 1988), 1–2.

21. James R. Emshoff, *Analysis of Behavioral Systems* (New York: Macmillan, 1971), 10.

22. C. C. Shumacher and B. E. Smith, "A Sample Survey of Industrial Operations Research Activities II," *Operations Research* 13 (1965): 1023–27.

23. Discussion concerning these factors is adapted from Donnelly, Gibson, and Ivancevich, *Fundamentals of Management*, 302–303; Efraim Turban and Jack R. Meredith, *Fundamentals of Management Science* (Plano, Tex.: Business Publications, 1981), 15–23.

24. Harold Koontz, "The Management Theory Jungle Revisited," *Academy of Management Review* 5 (1980): 175–87.

25. Don Hellriegel, John W. Slocum, and Richard W. Woodman, *Organizational Behavior* (St. Paul, Minn.: West Publishing, 1986), 22.

26. J. W. Lorsch, "Organization Design: A Situational Perspective," *Organizational Dynamics* 6 (1977): 2–4.

27. Louis W. Fry and Deborah A. Smith, "Congruence, Contingency, and Theory Building," *Academy of Management Review* (January 1987): 117–32.

28. For a more detailed development of von Bertalanffy's ideas, see "General System Theory: A New Approach to Unity of Science," *Human Biology* (December 1951): 302–61.

29. L. Thomas Hopkins, *Integration: Its Meaning and Application* (New York: Appleton-Century-Crofts, 1937), 36–49.

30. For a discussion of the value of teaching management through these management functions, see Stephen J. Carroll and Dennis A. Gillen, "Are the Classic Management Functions Useful in Describing Managerial Work?" *Academy of Management Review* (January 1987): 38–51.

Action Summary Answer Key

1. a. T, p. 31
   b. e, p. 34
2. a. e, pp. 39–40
   b. e, p. 35
   c. F, p. 36

3. a. F, p. 40
   b. a, p. 40
4. a. F, pp. 40–41
   b. T, p. 41

5. a. d, pp. 42–43
   b. T, p. 43
6. a. d, pp. 42–43
   b. T, pp. 42–43

7. a. d, pp. 44–45
   b. e, p. 45
8. a. b, p. 44
   b. b, p. 46

JUSTIFYING NEW HANDLING EQUIPMENT AT FRITO-LAY

Efficiency is the factor that will determine, in many instances, whether an operation will succeed or fail. At Frito-Lay, efficiency review and structured cost justification procedures take the concept of efficiency and turn it into solid returns on expenditures for new materials and handling equipment. This success is not surprising to the people at Frito-Lay, because efficiency has been and will remain a standing goal for Frito-Lay's thirty-eight manufacturing and distribution operations in the United States.

The operational review and structured cost justification procedure is central to Frito-Lay's continually improving efficiency and success. This procedure was recently used at the San Antonio plant to improve efficiency in moving palletized loads from the packaging department to short-term storage facilities. A nearly $70,000 expenditure led to a 47.6 percent internal rate of return on new equipment. That equipment included a counterbalanced lift truck, four quick-closing doors, and other types of small-ticket materials handling equipment. The internal rate of return resulted from increased storage space, a reduced number of times loads are handled, and reduced labor costs.

Frito-Lay's efficiency review and cost justification procedure consists of three steps. First, handling efficiency is compared to that at other company facilities. Then, the materials handling activity is rigorously analyzed. Finally, an economic model is used to evaluate the alternatives of buying, leasing, and rebuilding equipment. Mason Harvey, materials manager at the San Antonio plant, suggests that the procedure "may be painful, but it's worth it." Although the procedure is time-consuming and challenging, the benefits overshadow the increased costs.

San Antonio's previous handling system used pallet jacks to move palletized loads from a packaging line through two doors and into a staging area. Each load stayed in this area for only a few hours before a counterbalanced lift truck transported it either to a bulk storage area, for shipment within five days, or to a pick line for immediate shipment. Three workers constituted the first and second shifts, whereas two made up the lower-volume third shift. Until recently, management considered this procedure adequate. However, with increased volume, warehousing space was getting tight. Managers therefore decided to implement their efficiency review and cost justification procedures to see if the efficiency of handling practices could be improved.

Harvey explains, "There's a whole culture at Frito-Lay that encourages materials managers to compare operational efficiencies between locations, and share ideas for improvement." "There's also a friendly competitiveness between facilities." When the San Antonio materials management team reviewed its pounds of product moved per labor hour, a common company measure of efficiency, it discovered it was solidly in the middle tier of the company. Yet, even with a more than adequate efficiency level, the team was not satisfied; so it established a goal to improve handling efficiency while maximizing space utilization. It generated alternative solutions by considering layout and materials handling procedures used in plants similar to the San Antonio plant.

Of the alternatives given serious consideration, one looked more promising than the others. It called for the elimination of all pallet jacks and the purchase of an additonal counterbalanced lift truck. Furthermore, it appeared that significantly expanded storage capacity, without an increase in total warehouse space, would result from the elimination of the staging area and the addition of ten new pallet racks. Two more door openings would expedite materials flow; cooling costs could also be reduced by the inclusion of quick-closing doors on all four openings. In addition, this alternative sug-

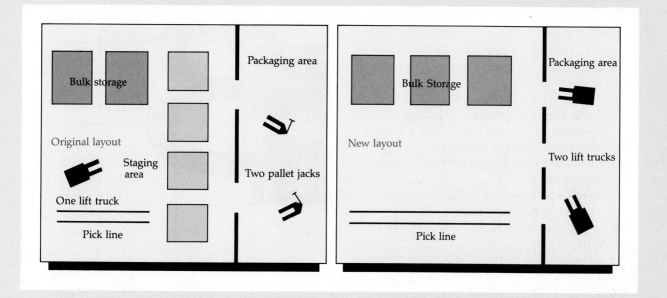

gested that work crews on each shift coud be reduced by one. Thus, the new system promised substantial labor savings.

Although the selected alternative was supported by a trial run using equipment loaned by a local lift truck dealer, the toughest test was still to come—the official corporate economic justification procedure. The first step of this procedure was a materials handling activity analysis. This analysis evaluated the amount of time needed by the old system versus the new one to move an equal number of pallets. These results would allow staffing and equipment levels to be compared. To conduct the analysis, the team broke the duties of each work crew into small jobs. These jobs included such things as travel to the pallet, lifting the pallet, and documenting the inventory. After a number of time trials for each job, an average or standard time required to perform the various jobs could be determined. The team totaled the average times for all jobs to determine the cumulative time needed for an individual to move a single pallet. It determined the total number of labor hours needed by multiplying the average time required to move a pallet by the average number of pallets handled daily. "From this study alone, we were pretty sure we had a winner," recalls Harvey.

A computer program was then used to determine costs for specific components, the first step in building an economic model for the justification step of the pro-cess. Using this data, the team evaluated the economic alternatives of rebuilding, leasing, and buying the various components. As anticipated, the project surpassed all economic model criteria, primarily because of labor savings. On the basis of this evaluation, the materials management team prepared a capital appropriations request and obtained quick approval of the project.

DISCUSSION ISSUES
1. Explain the three steps of Frito-Lay's operational review and structured cost justification procedure in terms of triangular management. In your explanation, use concepts borrowed from classical, behavioral, and management science approaches.
2. Is there anything in the case that could cause one to believe that, from a behavioral perspective, the impact of the change may not have been fully considered? What human reaction might one expect when the change was announced?
3. How is Frito-Lay's materials/handling activity analysis similar to the Gilbreths' motion study? List possible variables in Frito-Lay's analysis.
4. The contingency approach to management attempts to outline the conditions or situations in which various management methods have the best chance of being successful. Outline the internal and external contingencies that may be considered in this process.

STUDENT LEARNING OBJECTIVES

From studying this chapter, I will attempt to acquire:

1. An understanding of organizational objectives.
2. An appreciation for the importance of organizational objectives.
3. An ability to tell the difference between organizational objectives and individual objectives.
4. A knowledge of the areas in which managers should set organizational objectives.
5. An understanding of the development of organizational objectives.
6. Some facility in writing good objectives.
7. An awareness of how managers use organizational objectives and help others to attain the objectives.
8. An appreciation for the potential of a management by objectives (MBO) program.

ORGANIZATIONAL OBJECTIVES

CHAPTER OUTLINE

THE DIRECTION OF FLOW GENERAL

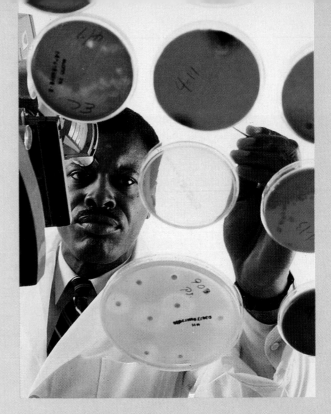

In the early 1980s, Flow General, Inc., seemed destined for great things as a company. Its basic businesses related to the areas of cell biology and defense consulting, and business was booming. Over a three-year period, Flow General's earnings more than tripled, from approximately $2 million to slightly over $7 million. The company seemed to be in excellent financial shape and poised for significant growth.

However, to the surprise of many outside observers as well as company employees, within two years Flow General had shifted from making slightly over $7 million to losing approximately $4 million. It was obvious that there was a problem that had to be discovered and solved as quickly as possible.

A longtime Flow General employee expressed the opinion that company losses were closely related to the fact that few people within the company seemed to clearly understand the direction in which the company was moving. According to this employee, Flow General's former president and chief executive officer, Joseph E. Hall, "had a tendency to go off on a whim." Over recent years, the company had moved further and further away from its basic business and closer and closer to more "glamorous" research on artificial skin and interferon, a protein that has shown promise in fighting viruses and cancer.

Hall, however, disagreed with the assessment that the company lacked a clear direction during his term. In his opinion, he and other top executives had a "preconceived notion" as to where the company should go. Furthermore, Hall believed the company was definitely moving in this direction when he departed from Flow General.

Even if Flow General had such clear direction, there apparently was some disagreement concerning whether Hall's proposed direction was the most appropriate for the company. Chris Price, a company re-searcher, indicated that it was no secret that the professional scientists disagreed with the corporate objectives set during Hall's tenure. According to these scientists, Hall's objectives necessitated unrealistic timetables within which research projects had to be completed.

After Hall's departure, the emphasis at Flow General was placed on developing and implementing a more concrete strategy for organizational success. This strategy included reducing investments in glamorous, high-risk projects and concentrating organizational resources in the company's basic and successful products. For example, the focus on interferon-related research was reduced to enable the biomedical division to concentrate more on the mechanics of growing cell cultures.

It is hard to measure the exact extent to which past leadership at Flow General provided a clear direction for the company. Present company leadership, however, seems determined to furnish the company with a direction that all employees understand.

What's Ahead

Managers such as Joseph E. Hall, the former president and chief executive officer of Flow General, must recognize that organizational objectives are important guidelines and should be used purposefully. This chapter discusses (1) the general nature of organizational objectives, (2) different types of organizational objectives, (3) various areas in which organizational objectives should be set, (4) how managers actually work with organizational objectives, and (5) management by objectives (MBO).

GENERAL NATURE OF ORGANIZATIONAL OBJECTIVES

Definition of Organizational Objectives

Organizational objectives are the targets toward which the open management system is directed. Organizational input, process, and output, discussed in chapter 2, all exist to reach organizational objectives (see Figure 3.1). Properly

Organizational objectives flow from organizational purpose.

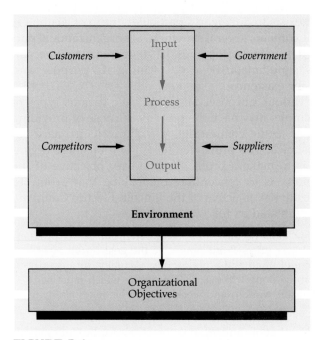

FIGURE 3.1
Existence of open management system to reach organizational objectives

TABLE 3.1

Examples of statements of organizational purpose

Organization Name	Organizational Purpose
DuPont	DuPont is a multinational high-technology company that manufactures and markets chemically related products. It services a diversified group of markets in which proprietary technology provides the competing edge.
Polaroid	Polaroid manufactures and sells photographic products based on its inventions in the field of one-step instant photography and light-polarizing products. Utilizing its inventions in the field of polarized light, the company considers itself to be engaged in one line of business.
Central Soya	The basic mission of Central Soya is to be a leading producer and merchandiser of products for the world-wide agribusiness and food industry.
General Portland Cement	It has long been a business philosophy of General Portland that "we manufacture and sell cement, but we market concrete." The company sees its job as manufacturing top-quality cement and working with customers to develop new applications for concrete while expanding current uses.

developed organizational objectives reflect the purpose of the organization; that is, they flow naturally from the organizational purpose. The **organizational purpose** is what the organization exists to do, given a particular group of customers and customer needs. Table 3.1 contains several statements of organizational purpose, or mission, as developed by actual companies. If an organization is accomplishing its objectives, it is simultaneously accomplishing its purpose and thereby justifying its reason for existence.

Organizations exist for various purposes.

Organizations exist for various purposes and thus have various types of objectives. A hospital, for example, may have the primary purpose of providing high-quality medical assistance to the community. Therefore, its primary objective is furnishing this assistance. The primary purpose of a business organization, in contrast, usually is to make a profit. The primary objective of the business organization, therefore, is to concentrate on making that profit. To illustrate, the primary organizational objective of the Lincoln Electric Company is profit oriented and has been stated as follows:

> The goal of the organization must be this—to make a better and better product to be sold at a lower and lower price. Profit cannot be the goal. Profit must be a by-product. This is a state of mind and a philosophy. Actually, an organization doing this job as it can be done will make large profits which must be properly divided between user, worker, and stockholder. This takes ability and character.[1]

John F. Mee has suggested that organizational objectives for businesses can be summarized in three points:

1. Profit is the motivating force for managers.
2. Service to customers by the provision of desired economic values (goods and services) justifies the existence of the business.
3. Social responsibilities do exist for managers in accordance with ethical and moral codes established by the society in which the industry resides.[2]

Importance of Organizational Objectives

Marshall E. Dimock stresses that "fixing your objective is like identifying the North Star—you sight your compass on it and then use it as the means of getting back on track when you tend to stray."[3] Organizational objectives give managers and all other organization members important guidelines for action in such areas as decision making, organizational efficiency, organizational consistency, and performance evaluation.

Organizational objectives are guidelines for:

Guide for Decision Making

A significant portion of managerial responsibility involves making decisions that inevitably influence the everyday operation and existence of the organization and of organization members. Once managers have a clear understanding of organizational objectives, they know the direction in which the organization must move. It then becomes their responsibility to make decisions that move the organization toward the achievement of its objectives.

1. Decision making.

Guide for Organizational Efficiency

Since inefficiency results in a costly waste of human effort and resources, managers strive to increase organizational efficiency whenever possible. Efficiency is defined in terms of the total amount of human effort and resources an organization uses to move itself toward the attainment of organizational goals. Therefore, before organizational efficiency can improve, managers must have a clear understanding of organizational goals. Only then are they able to use the limited resources at their disposal as efficiently as possible.

2. Increasing efficiency.

Guide for Organizational Consistency

Organization members often need work related directives. If organizational objectives are used as the basis for these directives, the objectives serve as a guide to consistent encouragement of such things as productive activity, quality decision making, and effective planning.

3. Establishing consistency.

Guide for Performance Evaluation

Periodically, the performance of all organization members is evaluated to assess individual productivity and to determine what might be done to increase it.

4. Making performance evaluations useful.

Organizational goals are the guidelines or criteria that should be used as the basis for these evaluations. The individuals who contribute most to the attainment of organizational goals should be considered the most productive. Specific recommendations for increasing productivity should include suggestions about what individuals can do to help the organization move toward goal attainment.

BACK TO THE CASE

The discussion of organizational objectives gives managers such as Hall, the past president of Flow General, useful insights on how a company can be put and kept on the right track. The introductory case revealed that Flow General had moved away from its basic business and concentrated instead on research in artificial skin and interferon. This change in emphasis apparently occurred either without a redefinition of the purpose of the organization and formulation of related objectives or without communication and agreement about organizational purpose and objectives. Communication and agreement would help managers to guide the company appropriately, to make better decisions, to assess the level of company efficiency, to be consistent, and to evaluate employee performance.

TYPES OF OBJECTIVES IN ORGANIZATIONS

Objectives can be separated into two categories: organizational and individual. Recognizing the two categories and reacting appropriately to each is a challenge for all modern managers.

TABLE 3.2

Types of organizational objectives and organizations using each type

Type of Objective	Number of Companies Studied Having Objective Type	Percentage of Companies Studied Having Objective Type*
Profitability	73	89
Growth	67	82
Market share	54	66
Social responsibility	53	65
Employee welfare	51	62
Product quality and service	49	60
Research and development	44	54
Diversification	42	31
Efficiency	41	50
Financial stability	40	49
Resource conservation	32	39
Management development	29	35
Multinational enterprise	24	29
Consolidation	14	17
Miscellaneous other goals	15	18

* Adds to more than 100 percent because most companies have more than one goal.

Organizational Objectives

Organizational objectives are the formal targets of the organization and are set to help the organization accomplish its purpose. They concern such areas as organizational efficiency, productivity, and profit maximization.

Y. K. Shetty conducted a study to determine the nature and pattern of corporate objectives as they actually exist in organizations. Shetty analyzed 193 companies in four basic industrial groups: (1) chemicals and drugs, (2) packaging materials, (3) electricity and electronics, and (4) food processing.[4] The results of his study, shown in Table 3.2, indicate that the most common organizational objectives relate to profitability, growth, and market share. Social responsibility and employee welfare objectives are also common and probably reflect a change in managerial attitude over a period of years. The types of objectives shown in the table certainly do not reflect the only areas in which organizational objectives are made, but they probably indicate the most common ones.

Organizational objectives commonly focus on profitability, growth, and market share.

Individual Objectives

Individual objectives, which also exist within organizations, are the personal goals each organization member would like to reach through activity within the organization. These objectives might include high salary, personal growth and development, peer recognition, and societal recognition.

Individual objectives are one's personal goals within the organization.

A management problem arises when organizational objectives and individual objectives are not compatible.[5] For example, a professor may have an individual goal of working at a university primarily to gain peer recognition. Perhaps she pursues this recognition primarily by channeling most of her energies into research. This professor's individual objective could make a significant contribution to the attainment of organizational objectives if she were at a university whose organizational objectives emphasized research. Her individual objective might contribute little or nothing to organizational goal attainment, however, if she were employed at a teaching oriented university. Rather than improving her general teaching ability and the quality of her courses, as the university goals would suggest, she would be secluded in the library writing research articles.

When organizational objectives and individual objectives are not compatible, managers should strive for goal integration.

One alternative managers have in situations of this type is to structure the organization so that individuals have the opportunity to accomplish individual objectives while contributing to organizational goal attainment. For example, the teaching oriented university could take steps to ensure that good teachers received peer recognition—for example, by offering an "excellence in teaching" award. In this way, professors could strive for their personal peer recognition goal while also contributing to the university's organizational objective of good teaching.

An objective, or goal, integration model can assist managers trying to understand and solve problems related to conflict between organizational and individual objectives. Jon Barrett's model, presented in Figure 3.2 on page 62, depicts a situation in which the objectives in area C are the only individual ones (area A) compatible with organizational ones (area B). Area C represents the extent of **goal integration.**

Goal integration occurs when organizational and individual objectives are the same.

Managers should keep two things in mind about the situation depicted in

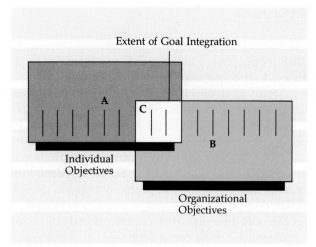

FIGURE 3.2
Goal integration model

this figure: The individual will tend to work for goals in area C without much managerial encouragement, because the attainment of these goals will result in some type of reward the individual considers valuable. And the individual will usually not work for goals outside area A without some significant type of managerial encouragement, because the attainment of these goals holds little promise of any reward the individual considers valuable. Barrett suggests that "significant types of managerial encouragement" could be (1) modifications to existing pay schedules, (2) considerate treatment from superiors, and (3) additional opportunities to engage in informal social relationships with peers.

BACK TO THE CASE

Finding a common ground between organizational objectives and individual objectives often is no easy task, and conflict between these two types of objectives can spell trouble for the organization. Perhaps part of the problem at Flow General was a conflict between organizational and individual objectives. For example, Hall, the past president of Flow General, could have had individual objectives of peer recognition and societal recognition that led him into glamorous, high-risk projects. While the projects had merit in their own right, they might have been in conflict with Flow General's long-standing organizational objective of concentrating on its basic business. In this type of situation, it would have been to both Hall's and Flow General's advantage to seek out areas of goal integration.

The "Management in Action" feature for this chapter discusses John Scheel, an employee of Armco, Inc. Scheel's personal objectives seem to include the attainment of peer and societal recognition through the accomplishment of such activities as coaxing workers to accept new technologies, increasing production, and producing goods more cheaply than before. The level of goal integration between Scheel's objectives and Armco's is undoubtedly high.

GOAL INTEGRATION FOR JOHN SCHEEL AND ARMCO, INC.

Armed with a shovel, John Scheel is banging away at a gummed-up ore dumper at the Armco sinter plant, which processes iron ore. The air is thick with fine red ore dust, and clouds of it swirl up each time he whacks the dumper. Soon he will be covered in the dust, which he will blow out of his nose for days because he won't wear a face mask.

This is an unlikely place for a 32-year-old, who, in addition to an engineering degree has an M.B.A. in finance and international business and fancies himself an amateur poet. "With his background and ability, John could be working in several places other than a steel mill," says Glenn D. Easterling, one of Mr. Scheel's supervisors. "He's not a normal steel man."

But his single-minded devotion to the blast furnace, named Amanda, enables him to make a difference in basic industry. Photographs of Amanda adorn the walls of his apartment and the local restaurant and bar he owns a stake in.

Some of that attachment goes back to 1963, when Mr. Scheel's father brought the family along for the summer while he helped build the furnace. Mr. Sheel's life revolves around its 24-hour cycle. He works at least 12-hour days but can often be found at the furnace at odd hours of the night; he was there at 2 a.m. last Christmas, for instance.

LEADING THE ORCHESTRA

He likens his work to "being an orchestra conductor." He is engrossed with the computer system he created, monitoring the complex chemical makeup of iron coming from the blast furnace. Then he is on the phone tracking down a late coal shipment. ("Grace, Grace, Grace," he intones to a supplier on the other end of the phone line in Lexington, Ky. "This is really no way to treat a good customer.")

"The process runs you, you don't run the process," he tells a visitor during a tour. "When the furnace has to cast, it's got to cast. When you have trouble, you have to fix it right then."

Suddenly, there is trouble in the boiler house, where the great thrusts of air are generated to power the blast furnace. Mr. Scheel is told Amanda has been decreasing "the wind," thereby lowering production. He suspects the problem is a worn tuyere, one of several nozzles through which air is forced into the furnace. He hurries to the furnace. He confirms on a computer termi-

nal that some iron has dripped onto a tuyere, causing a leak. He dispatches several workers to change it.

That Mr. Scheel could identify the worn tuyere before it became a serious problem reflects his abilities; he devised the computer warning system that pinpoints a leaking tuyere before the damage is even visible.

Mr. Scheel also integrates technology into the mill, a crucial mission in a domestic industry that must modernize to survive. Besides the computer-monitoring system, he has developed a way to accurately measure and regulate the amount of coal slurry—a mix of pulverized coal and coal slurry going into the furnace. The company has since patented the process and sells it to other steelmakers.

"Now everybody understands that you've got to run it like a Porsche instead of an old beat-up Chevy," he says. Although such efforts are important to the survival of the mill, they also can generate enemies among workers who fear that Mr. Scheel is putting them out of a job.

As a result, Mr. Scheel, who is paid about $40,000 a year, also must be part psychologist, coaxing workers to accept new technologies. "The whole trick is to make better quality, more production and make it cheaper," he tells them. "The fellows are hardheaded sometimes because they're afraid for their jobs. That's really sad," he says, "but in the long run if you don't make a profit, then there's no jobs at all."

⊞ AREAS FOR ORGANIZATIONAL OBJECTIVES

Peter F. Drucker, one of the most influential management writers of modern times, indicates that the very survival of a management system may be endangered if managers emphasize only a profit objective. This single-objective emphasis encourages managers to take action that will make money today with little regard for how a profit will be made tomorrow.[6]

In practice, managers should strive to develop and attain a variety of objectives in all management system areas where activity is critical to the operation and success of the system. Following are the eight key areas in which Drucker advises managers to set management system objectives:

In addition to profitability, there are seven other key areas in which an organization should specify goals.

1. *Market standing* Management should set objectives indicating where it would like to be in relation to its competitors.
2. *Innovation* Management should set objectives outlining its commitment to the development of new methods of operation.
3. *Productivity* Management should set objectives outlining the target levels of production.
4. *Physical and financial resources* Management should set objectives with regard to the use, acquisition, and maintenance of capital and monetary resources.
5. *Profitability* Management should set objectives that specify the profit the company would like to generate.
6. *Managerial performance and development* Management should set objectives that specify rates and levels of managerial productivity and growth.
7. *Worker performance and attitude* Management should set objectives that specify rates of worker productivity as well as the attitudes workers possess.
8. *Public responsibility* Management should set objectives that indicate the company's responsibilities to its customers and society and the extent to which the company intends to live up to those responsibilities.

According to Drucker, since the first five goal areas relate to tangible, impersonal characteristics of organizational operation, most managers would not dispute their designation as key areas. Designating the last three as key areas could arouse some managerial opposition, however, since these areas are more personal and subjective. Regardless of potential opposition, an organization should have objectives in all eight areas to maximize its probability of success.

⊞ WORKING WITH ORGANIZATIONAL OBJECTIVES

Appropriate objectives are fundamental to the success of any organization. Theodore Levitt states that some leading industries may be on the verge of facing the same financial disaster as did the railroads, because their objectives are inappropriate for their organizations.[7] Managers, therefore, should approach the development, use, and modification of organizational objectives with utmost seriousness. In general, an organization should have (1) **short-term objectives** (targets to be achieved in one year or less), (2) **intermediate-term objectives** (targets to be achieved in one to five years), and (3) **long-term objectives** (targets to be achieved in five to seven years).

An organization should have short-term, intermediate-term, and long-term objectives.

The Mister Boffo cartoon illustrates that long-term objectives may not be

Reprinted by permission: Tribune Media Services.

useful for every individual. From a management viewpoint, however, their development and use are critical factors in maintaining long-term viability.

The necessity of predetermining appropriate organizational objectives has led to the development of what is called the **principle of the objective.** The principle is that before managers initiate any action, organizational objectives should be clearly determined, understood, and stated.[8]

Establishing Organizational Objectives

The three main steps that managers must take to develop a set of working organizational objectives are (1) determining the existence of any environmental trends that could significantly influence the operation of the organization, (2) developing a set of objectives for the organization as a whole, and (3) developing a hierarchy of organizational objectives. These three steps are interrelated and usually require input from several people at different levels and operational sections of the organization. Each step is further developed in the paragraphs that follow.

> Managers take three interrelated steps in developing organizational objectives.

Analyzing Trends

The first step in setting organizational objectives is to list major trends that have existed in the organizational environment over the past five years and to determine if these trends have had a noticeable impact on organizational success. Conceivably, the trends could include such factors as marketing innovations of competitors, government controls, and social trends, such as decreasing family size. Management should then decide which present and future trends are likely to affect organizational success over the next five years. This decision will determine what kinds of objectives are set at various levels of the organization.

> The first step involves analyzing environmental trends.

Developing Objectives for the Organization as a Whole

After analyzing environmental trends, management should develop objectives that reflect this analysis for the organization as a whole. For example, the analysis may show that a major competitor has been continually improving its products over the past five years and, as a result, is gaining an increasingly larger share of the market. In reaction to this trend, management should set a product improvement objective in an effort to keep up with competitors. This objective

> The second step requires developing objectives for the organization as a whole.

would result directly from identification of a trend within the organizational environment and from the organizational purpose of profit. The paragraphs that follow illustrate how management might set financial objectives, product-market mix objectives, and functional objectives for the organization as a whole.

Establishing Financial Objectives

Financial objectives are organizational targets relating to monetary issues. In some organizations, government regulations guide management's setting of these objectives. Managers of public utility organizations, for example, have definite guidelines for the types of financial objectives they are allowed to set. In organizations free from government constraints, the setting of financial objectives is influenced mainly by return on investment and financial comparisons with competitors.

Return on investment is the amount of money an organization earns in relation to the amount of money invested to keep the organization in operation.[9] Figure 3.3 shows how to use earnings of $50,000 and an investment of $500,000 to calculate a return on investment. If the calculated return is too low, managers can set an overall objective to modify the organization's rate of return.

Information on organizational competition is available through published indexes, such as Dun & Bradstreet's *Ratios for Selected Industries*. These ratios reflect industry averages for key financial areas. Comparing company figures with the industrial averages should tell management about the areas in which new financial objectives probably should be set or the ways in which existing objectives should be modified.

Establishing Product-Market Mix Objectives

Product-market mix objectives outline which products—and the relative number or mix of these products—the organization will attempt to sell. Granger suggests the following five steps in formulating product-market mix objectives:[10]

1. Examination of key trends in the business environments of the product-market areas.
2. Examination of growth trends (both market and volume) and profit trends (for the industry and for the company) in the individual product-mix areas.
3. Separation of product-market areas into those that are going to pull ahead and those that are going to drag. For promising areas, these questions need to be asked: How can these areas be made to flourish? Should additional injec-

Financial objectives are influenced by return on investment and financial comparison with competitors.

Product-market mix objectives outline the relative number or mix of products an organization will attempt to sell.

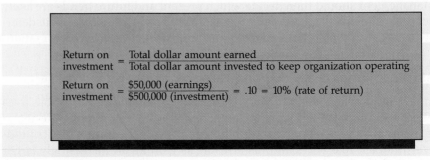

$$\text{Return on investment} = \frac{\text{Total dollar amount earned}}{\text{Total dollar amount invested to keep organization operating}}$$

$$\text{Return on investment} = \frac{\$50,000 \text{ (earnings)}}{\$500,000 \text{ (investment)}} = .10 = 10\% \text{ (rate of return)}$$

FIGURE 3.3
Calculations for return on investment

tions of capital, marketing effort, technology, management talent, or the like be used? For the less promising areas, these questions are pertinent: Why is the product lagging? How can this be corrected? If it cannot be corrected, should the product be milked for whatever can be regained, or should it be withdrawn from the market?

4. Consideration of the need or desirability of adding new products or market areas to the mix. In this regard, management should ask these questions: Is there a profit gap to be filled? Based on the criteria of profit opportunity, compatibility, and feasibility of entry, what are possible new areas of interest in order of priority? What sort of programs (acquisitions or internal development) does the company need to develop the desired level of business in these areas?

5. Derivation of an optimum yet realistic product-market mix profile based on the conclusions reached in steps 1–4. This profile embodies the product-market mix objectives, which should be consistent with the organization's financial objectives. Interaction while setting these two kinds of objectives is advisable.

Establishing Functional Objectives

Functional objectives are targets relating to key organizational functions, including marketing, accounting, production, and personnel. Functional objectives that are consistent with the financial and product-market mix objectives should be developed for these areas. People in the organization should perform their functions in a way that helps the organization attain its other objectives.[11]

Functional objectives should be consistent with financial and product-market mix objectives.

BACK TO THE CASE

The information just presented implies that managers such as Hall should set objectives in addition to profit objectives. These other objectives should be set in such areas as market standing, innovation, productivity, physical and financial resources, managerial performance and development, worker performance and attitude, and public responsibility. Naturally, they should probably be set for the short, intermediate, and long term.

Before developing such objectives, however, managers should pinpoint any environmental trends that could influence company operations. Objectives that reflect the environmental trends could then be set for the organization as a whole. They normally would include financial, product-market mix, and functional objectives.

Developing a Hierarchy of Objectives

In practice, an organizational objective must be broken down into subobjectives so that individuals of different levels and sections of the organization know what they must do to help reach the overall organizational objective.[12] An organizational objective is attained only after the subobjectives have been reached.

The overall organizational objective and the subobjectives assigned to the various people or units of the organization are referred to as a **hierarchy of objectives.** Figure 3.4 presents a sample hierarchy of objectives for a medium-sized company.

Suboptimization exists when subobjectives are conflicting or not directly aimed at accomplishing the overall organizational objective. Figure 3.4 shows

The third step in establishing organizational objectives involves developing a hierarchy of organizational objectives and subobjectives.

Conflicting subobjectives produce suboptimization.

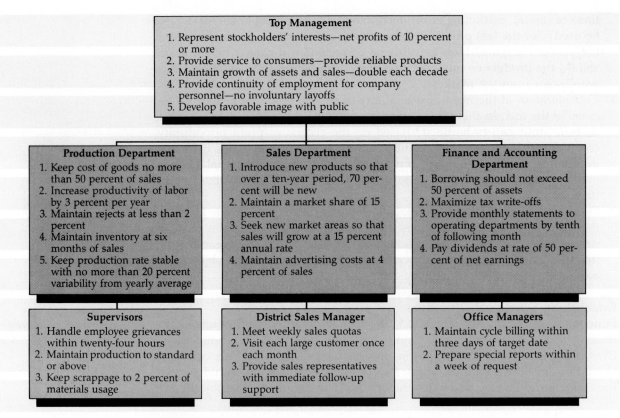

FIGURE 3.4
Hierarchy of objectives for a medium-sized organization

that suboptimization could exist within this company between the first subobjective for the finance and accounting department and the second subobjective for the supervisors. Suboptimization would result if supervisors needed new equipment to maintain production and the finance and accounting department couldn't approve the loan without the company's borrowing surpassing 50 percent of company assets. In this situation, established subobjectives would be aimed in different directions. A manager would have to choose which subobjective would best contribute to obtaining overall objectives and should therefore take precedence.

Controlling suboptimization in organizations is part of a manager's job. Suboptimization can be minimized by developing a thorough understanding of how various parts of the organization relate to one another and by making sure that subobjectives properly reflect these relations.

Guidelines for Establishing Quality Objectives

Managers should follow these eight guidelines for making objectives effective.

As with all humanly developed commodities, the quality of goal statements can vary drastically. Managers can increase the quality of their objectives, however, by following some general guidelines:

1. *Managers should allow the people responsible for attaining the objectives to have a voice in setting them* Often, the people responsible for attaining the objectives know their job situation better than the managers do and can help to make

the objectives more realistic. (They will also be more motivated to achieve them.) Work related problems that these people face should be thoroughly considered when meaningful objectives are being developed.

2. *Managers should state objectives as specifically as possible* Precise statements minimize confusion and misunderstanding and ensure that employees have explicit directions for what they should do.

3. *Managers should relate objectives to specific actions whenever necessary* In this way, employees do not have to infer what they should do to accomplish their goals.

4. *Managers should pinpoint expected results* Employees should know exactly how managers will determine whether or not an objective has been reached.

5. *Managers should set goals high enough that employees will have to strive to meet them but not so high that employees give up trying to meet them* Managers want employees to work hard but not to be frustrated.

6. *Managers should specify when goals are expected to be achieved* Employees must know the time frame for accomplishing their objectives. They then can be somewhat flexible and pace themselves accordingly.

7. *Managers should set objectives only in relation to other organizational objectives* In this way, conflicting objectives and suboptimization can be kept to a minimum.

8. *Managers should state objectives clearly and simply* The written or spoken word should not get in the way of communicating a goal to organization members.

Guidelines for Making Objectives Operational

Objectives must be stated in operational terms. That is, if an organization has **operational objectives,** managers should be able to tell if the objectives are being attained by comparing the actual results with the goal statements.

Operational objectives specify the activities or operations needed to attain them.

For example, assume that a physical education instructor has set the following objectives for his students:

1. Each student will strive to develop a sense of balance.
2. Each student will attempt to become flexible.
3. Each student will try to become agile.

TABLE 3.3 On quiz

Nonoperational objectives versus operational objectives

Nonoperational Objectives	Operational Objectives
1. Improve product quality	1. Reduce quality rejects to 2 percent
2. Improve communications	2. Hold weekly staff meetings and initiate a newsletter to improve communications
3. Improve social responsibility	3. Hire fifty hard-core unemployed each year
4. Issue monthly accounting reports on a more timely basis	4. Issue monthly accounting reports so they are received three days following the close of the accounting period

4. Each student will try to become strong.
5. Each student will work on becoming powerful.
6. Each student will strive to become durable.

These objectives are not operational because the activities and operations a student must perform to attain them are not specified. Additional information, however, could easily make the objectives operational. For example, the fifth physical education objective could be replaced with: Each student will strive to develop the power to do standing broad jumps the distance of his or her height plus one foot. Table 3.3 on page 69 lists four basically nonoperational objectives and then shows how each can be made operational.

BACK TO THE CASE

Once managers have set overall objectives for their organizations, their next step is to develop a company hierarchy of objectives. The development of this hierarchy entails breaking down the organization's overall objectives into subobjectives so that all organization members know what they must do to help the company reach its overall objectives. At Flow General, this hierarchy of objectives may have been confusing, since, as the introductory case indicates, most employees did not seem to understand the company's overall objectives and thus probably were unclear as to their individual roles in helping the company attain these objectives.

In establishing a hierarchy of objectives, managers must be careful not to suboptimize, or establish subobjectives that conflict with one another. Suboptimization also may have been a problem at Flow General, since confusion about organizational objectives and subobjectives would have made it difficult for managers to recognize when subobjectives were in conflict.

Other guidelines for establishing quality objectives include making the objectives clear, consistent, challenging, and specific. Perhaps most important of all, organizational objectives should be operational. At Flow General, allowing workers such as Chris Price to participate in establishing organizational objectives would have helped ensure that company objectives were realistic and that organization members were committed to reaching them.

Attainment of Objectives

The attainment of organizational objectives is the obvious goal of all conscientious managers. Managers quickly discover, however, that moving the organization toward goal attainment requires taking appropriate actions within the organization to reach the desired ends. This process is called means-ends analysis.

Organizational goals are attained by managers taking appropriate means to reach desired ends.

Basically, **means-ends analysis** entails "(1) starting with the general goal to be achieved; (2) discovering a set of means, very generally specified, for accomplishing this goal; and (3) taking each of these means, in turn, as a new subgoal and discovering a more detailed means for achieving it."[13]

Table 3.4 illustrates means-ends analysis for three sample goals for a hotel: increased market share, financial stability, and owner satisfaction. The goal of increased market share includes two means: good service and employee morale and loyalty. These two means are subgoals that the hotel manager must focus on attaining in order to reach the goal of increased market share. The last column of the table lists the measures that can be taken to operationalize the subgoals.

Effective managers are aware of the importance of not only setting organizational objectives but also clearly outlining the means by which these objectives can be attained. They know that means-ends analysis is important for guiding

■ TABLE 3.4

Sample goals, means, and measures for a hotel

Goals	Means	Measures
Increased market share	Good service	Ratio of repeat business Occupancy Informal feedback
	Employee morale and loyalty	Turnover Absenteeism Informal feedback
Financial stability	Image in financial markets	Prince-earnings ratio Share price
	Profitability	Earnings per share Gross operating profit Cost trends Cash flow
	Strength of management team	Turnover Divisional profit Rate of promotion Informal feedback
Owner satisfaction	Adequate cash flow	Occupancy Sales Gross operating profit Departmental profit

their own activities as well as those of their subordinates. The better everyone within the organization understands the means by which goals are to be attained, the greater the probability that the goals actually will be reached.

How to Use Objectives

As stated previously, organizational objectives flow naturally from organizational purpose and reflect the organization's environment. Managers must have a firm understanding of the influences that mold organizational objectives, because as these influences change, the objectives themselves must change. Objectives are not unchangeable directives. In fact, a significant managerial responsibility is to help the organization change objectives when necessary.

⊞ MANAGEMENT BY OBJECTIVES (MBO)

Some managers find organizational objectives such an important and fundamental part of management that they use a management approach based exclusively on them. This management approach, called **management by objectives (MBO),** has been popularized mainly through the writings of Peter Drucker.[14] It has three basic characteristics:

1. All individuals within an organization are assigned a specialized set of objectives that they try to reach during a normal operating period. These objectives are mutually set and agreed upon by individuals and their managers.[15]

2. Performance reviews are conducted periodically to determine how close individuals are to attaining their objectives.
3. Rewards are given to individuals on the basis of how close they come to reaching their goals.[16]

Factors Necessary for a Successful MBO Program

Management by objectives: Management and subordinates work together to develop and achieve goals.

Certain key factors are necessary for an MBO program to be successful.[17] First, appropriate goals must be set by top managers of the organization. All individual MBO goals are based on these overall objectives. If overall objectives are inappropriate, individual MBO objectives also are inappropriate; and the related individual work activity is nonproductive. Second, managers and subordinates together must develop and agree on each individual's goals. Both managers and subordinates must feel that the individual objectives are just and appropriate if each party is to use them seriously as a guide for action. Third, employee performance should be conscientiously evaluated on the basis of established objectives. This evaluation helps determine if the objectives are fair and if appropriate means are being used to attain them. Fourth, management must follow through on the employee performance evaluations and reward employees accordingly.[18]

MBO Programs: Advantages and Disadvantages

Experienced MBO managers say that there are two advantages to this approach. First, MBO programs continually emphasize what should be done in an organization to achieve organizational goals. Second, the MBO process secures employee commitment to attaining organizational goals. Because managers and subordinates have developed objectives together, both parties are more interested in working to reach those goals.

Managers also admit that MBO programs have disadvantages.[19] One disadvantage is that, because organization members develop objectives together, they actually have less time in which to do their work. Also, elaborate written goals, careful communication of goals, and detailed performance evaluations naturally increase the volume of paperwork in an organization.

Most managers seem to think, however, that MBO's advantages outweigh its disadvantages. Over all, they find MBO programs beneficial.[20]

■ BACK TO THE CASE

In addition to making sure that an appropriate set of objectives has been developed for an organization, management must also clearly outline for employees the means by which these objectives can be attained. Flow General leadership was striving to accomplish this.

Flow General management might want to consider clarifying company objectives for employees through a management by objectives program. If it did so, each employee would develop with her or his manager a set of mutually agreed upon objectives. Performance reviews would give employees feedback on their progress in reaching their objectives, and rewards would be given to the employees who made the most progress.

Action Summary

Reread the learning objectives that follow. Each objective is followed by questions. Answering these questions accurately will help you retain the most important concepts discussed in this chapter. After answering each question, check your answer with the answer key at the end of this chapter. (*Hint:* If you have doubt regarding the correct response, consult the page whose number follows the answer.)

From studying this chapter, I will attempt to acquire: **Circle:**

1. **An understanding of organizational objectives.**
   a. Organizational objectives should reflect the organization's purpose.   T, F
   b. The targets toward which an open management system is directed are referred to as: (a) functional objectives; (b) organizational objectives; (c) operational objectives; (d) courses of action; (e) individual objectives.   a, b, c, d, e

2. **An appreciation for the importance of organizational objectives.**
   a. Organizational objectives serve important functions in all of the following areas except: (a) making performance evaluations useful; (b) establishing consistency; (c) increasing efficiency; (d) improving wages; (e) decision making that influences everyday operations.   a, b, c, d, e
   b. Implied within organizational objectives are hints on how to define the most productive workers in the organization.   T, F

3. **An ability to tell the difference between organizational objectives and individual objectives.**
   a. Which of the following is considered to be an individual objective: (a) peer recognition; (b) financial security; (c) personal growth; (d) b and c; (e) all of the above.   a, b, c, d, e
   b. When goal integration exists: (a) there is a positive situation, desired by management; (b) managers will not see conflict between organizational and personal objectives; (c) the individual will work for goals without much managerial encouragement; (d) additional opportunities to engage in informal social relationships with peers will not be necessary to encourage the individual; (e) all of the above.   a, b, c, d, e

4. **A knowledge of the areas in which managers should set organizational objectives.**
   a. The eight key areas in which Peter F. Drucker advises managers to set objectives include all of the following except: (a) market standing; (b) productivity; (c) public responsibility; (d) inventory control; (e) manager performance and development.   a, b, c, d, e
   b. Long-term objectives are defined as targets to be achieved in one to five years.   T, F

5. **An understanding of the development of organizational objectives.**
   a. Which of the following factors would not be considered in analyzing trends: (a) marketing innovations of competitors; (b) projections for society; (c) government controls; (d) known existing and projected future events; (e) product-market mix.   a, b, c, d, e
   b. Which of the following factors would not be considered in the "developing objectives for the organization as a whole" stage of setting organizational objectives: (a) establishing a hierarchy of objectives; (b) establishing   a, b, c, d, e

product-market mix objectives; (c) establishing financial objectives; (d) establishing return on investment objectives; (e) establishing functional objectives.

6. **Some facility in writing good objectives.**

a, b, c, d, e
    a. Which of the following is an objective stated in nonoperational terms: (a) reduce customer complaints by 9 percent; (b) make great progress in new product development; (c) develop a new customer; (d) increase profit before taxes by 10 percent; (e) reduce quality rejects by 2 percent.

T, F
    b. An example of a good operational objective is: "Each student in this class will try to learn how to manage."

7. **An awareness of how managers use organizational objectives and help others to attain the objectives.**

T, F
    a. Means-ends analysis implies that the manager is results-oriented and discovers a set of means for accomplishing a goal.

a, b, c, d, e
    b. Which of the following guidelines should managers use in changing objectives: (a) objectives should not be changed; (b) adapt objectives when the organization's environmental influences change; (c) change objectives to create suboptimization as needed; (d) adapt objectives so that they are nonoperational; (e) all of the above are valid guidelines.

8. **An appreciation for the potential of a management by objectives (MBO) program.**

T, F
    a. Both performance evaluations and employee rewards should be tied to objectives assigned to individuals when the firm is using MBO.

a, b, c, d, e
    b. A method under which a manager is given specific objectives to achieve and is evaluated according to the accomplishment of these objectives is: (a) means-ends analysis; (b) operational objectives; (c) individual objectives; (d) management by objectives; (e) management by exception.

INTRODUCTORY CASE WRAP-UP

"The Direction of Flow General" (p. 56) and its related back-to-the-case sections were written to help you better understand the management concepts contained in this chapter. Answer the following discussion questions about this introductory case to further enrich your understanding of the chapter content:

1. Should Flow General employees have clearly understood Joseph E. Hall's objectives or where the organization was going? Why?

2. What is the significance of Chris Price's saying that objectives necessitated unrealistic research timetables? Explain fully.

3. Assuming that you were able to give Hall advice about how to improve himself as a manager, what would you say?

Issues for Review and Discussion

1. What are organizational objectives and how do they relate to organizational purpose?
2. Explain why objectives are important to an organization.
3. List four areas in which organizational objectives can act as important guidelines for performance.
4. Explain the difference between organizational objectives and individual objectives.
5. What is meant by goal integration?

6. List and define eight key areas in which organizational objectives should be set.
7. How do environmental trends affect the process of establishing organizational objectives?
8. How does return on investment relate to setting financial objectives?
9. Define *product-market mix objectives*. What process should a manager go through to establish them?
10. What are functional objectives?
11. What is a hierarchy of objectives?
12. Explain the purpose of a hierarchy of objectives.
13. How does suboptimization relate to a hierarchy of objectives?
14. List eight guidelines a manager should follow to establish quality organizational objectives.
15. How does a manager make objectives operational?
16. Explain the concept of means-ends analysis.
17. Should a manager ever modify or change existing organizational objectives? If no, why? If yes, when?
18. Define *MBO* and describe its main characteristics.
19. List and describe the factors necessary for an MBO program to be successful.
20. Discuss the advantages and disadvantages of MBO.

Sources of Additional Information

Buller, Paul F., and Cecil H. Bell, Jr. "Effects of Team Building and Goal Setting on Productivity: A Field Experiment." *Academy of Management Journal* 29 (June 1986): 305–28.

Chung, Kae H. *Critical Success Factions in Management.* New York: Allyn & Bacon, 1987.

Dowst, Somerby (C.P.M.). "Classify Your Objectives." *Purchasing* 25 (April 1979): 38.

Drucker, Peter. *Managing for Results.* New York: Harper & Row, 1964.

Frisbie, Gilbert, and Vincent A. Mabert. "Crystal Ball vs. System: The Forecasting Dilemma." *Business Horizons* 24 (September/October 1981): 72–76.

Godiwalla, Yezdi M., Wayne A. Meinhart, and William A. Warde. "General Management and Corporate Strategy." *Managerial Planning* 30 (September/October 1981): 17–23.

Hughes, Charles L. *Goal Setting.* New York: American Management Association, 1965.

Kizilos, Tolly, and Roger P. Heinisch. "Special Report: How a Management Team Selects Managers." *Harvard Business Review* (September–October 1986): 6–13.

Nash, Michael. *Managing Organizational Performance.* San Francisco: Jossey-Bass, 1983.

Odiorne, George S. *Management by Objectives.* Belmont, Calif.: Pitman, 1965.

Odiorne, George S. *Management Decision by Objectives.* Englewood Cliffs, N.J.: Prentice-Hall, 1982.

Patten, Thomas H., Jr. *A Manager's Guide to Performance Appraisal.* New York: Free Press, 1982.

Scanlan, Burt K. "Maintaining Organizational Effectiveness—A Prescription for Good Health." *Personnel Journal* 59 (May 1980): 381, 422.

Smith, August W. *Management Systems: Analyses and Applications.* Chicago: Dryden Press, 1982.

Steers, Richard M. *Introduction to Organizational Behavior.* Pacific Palisades, Calif.: Goodyear Publishing, 1981.

Stewart, John, Jr. *Managing a Successful Business Turnaround.* New York: Amacom, 1984.

Stone, W. Robert, and Donald F. Heany. "Dealing with a Corporate Identity Crisis." *Long-Range Planning* 17 (February 1984): 10–18.

Wright, Norman B. "Rekindling Managerial Innovativeness." *Business Quarterly* 51 (Summer 1986): 38–40.

Notes

1. James F. Lincoln, "Intelligent Selfishness and Manufacturing," Bulletin 434 (New York: Lincoln Electric Company).
2. John F. Mee, "Management Philosophy for Professional Executives," *Business Horizons* (December 1956): 7.
3. Marshall E. Dimock, *The Executive in Action* (New York: Harper & Bros., 1945), 54. For more on objectives as the central driving force of organizations, see F. G. Harmon and G. Jacobs, "Company Personality: The Heart of the Matter," *Management Review* (October 1985): 36–40.

4. Y. K. Shetty, "New Look at Corporate Goals," *California Management Review* 22 (Winter 1979): 71–79.

5. Thomas J. Murray, "The Unseen Corporate 'War,'" *Dun's Review* (June 1980): 110–14.

6. Peter F. Drucker, *The Practice of Management* (New York: Harper & Bros., 1954), 62–65, 126–29. For a worthwhile discussion about the constituencies that organizational objectives must serve, see Hal B. Pickle and Royce L. Abrahamson, *Small Business Management* (New York: Wiley, 1986), 211–12.

7. Theodore Levitt, "Marketing Myopia," *Harvard Business Review* (July/August 1960): 45.

8. Mee, "Management Philosophy for Professional Executives," 7.

9. Joseph G. Louderback and George E. Manners, Jr., "Integrating ROI and CVP," *Management Accounting* (April 1981): 33–39. For a related discussion of financial objectives, see Gordon Donaldson, "Financial Goals and Strategic Consequences," *Harvard Business Review* (May/June 1985): 56–66.

10. Adapted, by permission of the publisher, from "How to Set Company Objectives," by Charles H. Granger, *Management Review*, July 1970. © 1970 by American Management Association, Inc. All rights reserved. See also Max D. Richards, *Setting Goals and Objectives* (St. Paul, Minn.: West Publishing, 1986).

11. Granger, "How to Set Company Objectives," 7.

12. Charles H. Granger, "The Hierarchy of Objectives," *Harvard Business Review* (May/June 1964): 64–74. See also Heinz Weihrich, *Management Excellence: Productivity through MBO* (New York: McGraw-Hill, 1985), 65–84.

13. James G. March and Herbert A. Simon, *Organizations* (New York: Wiley, 1958), 191.

14. Drucker, *The Practice of Management*; also Peter Drucker, Harold Smiddy, and Ronald G. Greenwood, "Management by Objectives," *Academy of Management Review* 6 (April 1981): 225.

15. "Tailor MBO to Fit the Person," *Training* (September 1985): 58–60.

16. Robert L. Mathis and John H. Jackson, *Personnel: Human Resource Management* (St. Paul, Minn.: West Publishing, 1985), 353–55.

17. For characteristics that usually make an MBO program unsuccessful, see Dale D. McConkey, "Twenty Ways to Kill Management by Objectives," *Management Review* (October 1972): 4–13.

18. William H. Franklin, Jr., "Create an Atmosphere of Positive Expectations," *Administrative Management* (April 1980): 32–34.

19. Charles H. Ford, "Manage by Decisions, Not by Objectives," *Business Horizons* (February 1980): 7–18.

20. E. J. Seyna, "MBO: The Fad That Changed Management," *Long-Range Planning* (December 1986): 116–23.

Action Summary Answer Key

1. a. T, p. 58
   b. b, p. 57
2. a. d, p. 59
   b. T, pp. 59–60
3. a. e, p. 61
   b. e, pp. 61–62
4. a. d, p. 64
   b. F, p. 64
5. a. e, p. 65
   b. a, pp. 65–67
6. a. b, pp. 69–70
   b. F, pp. 69–70
7. a. T, pp. 70–72
   b. b, p. 71
8. a. T, p. 72
   b. d, pp. 71–72

MAKING MBO WORK AT ALCAN ALUMINUM

Roy A. Gentles, president and chief executive officer of Alcan Aluminum Corporation, is the first to laud the contributions that a modified version of the management by objectives (MBO) process has made to Alcan's overall effectiveness. Yet Gentles is quick to point out two calamitous pitfalls that must be avoided in the implementation of MBO.

According to Gentles, the first MBO snare into which a company can fall is an overemphasis on technicalities. Gentles suggests that in the early stages of developing an MBO program, it is easy to become mesmerized by the complexities of measurement. How does one set objectives so an individual's performance in achieving them can be measured? How does one differentiate between the providential factors and those over which one has some degree of influence? How does one account for an individual's performance in achieving an objective when the individual's ability to do so is partially dependent on others? Gentles intimates that one must not be discouraged when such difficult questions are encountered and simple answers are not readily available.

The Alcan experience also has convinced Gentles that there is a limit to the number of objectives that can be specified. Although some have argued that the number should be limited to three or, at the most, four, Gentles is convinced that if the program is properly designed, individuals in an MBO system can cope with up to ten objectives. Furthermore, he suggests that top management should initiate a significant effort to assure that there is a satisfactory balance between long- and short-term objectives. According to Gentles, "At Alcan, we compensate for the ramifications of including longer-term objectives in an individual's annual performance evaluation by limiting their attainment of objectives to 50 percent of a person's annual rating. The other half depends on how the person has carried out his or her principal accountabilities or performed overall."

An even more dangerous pitfall encountered in MBO programs, suggests Gentles, involves developing a program without ensuring that formal linkages exist between all having a role related to the accomplishment of a particular individual or corporate objective. Each year, Gentles, in conjunction with his management group, develops a list of corporate objectives. This process begins as divisional and functional heads, considering the "integrative link" principle and the primary strategies with which they are directly involved, perform a needs analysis that results in a draft of no more than ten potential objectives. From this draft, the two or three objectives deemed the most important from a corporate perspective are selected. The two or three selected objectives from each division or function are then combined to form a composite corporate list. This list generally contains thirty to thirty-five objective statements. The eight to ten most important objectives are then chosen in a management meeting, with the need for balance from both a functional and a time standpoint kept in mind.

The most important objectives become the basis for all objective settings. Once these objectives are identified, they are "cascaded" down to the appropriate divisional or functional heads. Further, where the attainment of an objective is equally dependent on the efforts of two or more managers, such as a functional head and the president of a division, or two division presidents, Gentles indicates that it is critical that the shared responsibility is understood and accepted by all involved.

According to Gentles, the success of an MBO program is directly proportional to the effectiveness with which the *cascading* and the *shared* processes are carried out. For certain key objectives, it is not uncommon to have the corporate objectives cascading in one form or another through several layers of management, both in the divisions and in one or more of the functional areas.

Finally, suggests Gentles, to have a successful MBO program, not only must objectives be clearly set so that they can be fairly measured and thoroughly cascaded, but it also is essential that there be constructive and effective performance evaluation. An Alcan employee survey indicated that evaluations are considered by *all* employee groups to be the most important form of feedback.

DISCUSSION ISSUES

1. Compare Gentles's objective-setting approach at Alcan with the three-step approach to establishing organizational objectives outlined in the chapter.
2. How closely does Gentles's modified MBO approach match the three main MBO characteristics described in the chapter? Explain.
3. Gentles indicates that the success of MBO at Alcan is almost directly proportional to the effectiveness with which the *cascading* and *shared* processes are carried out. What do you think Gentles means by "cascading" and "shared" processes? Do you find any text terminology with similar meaning to the word *cascading*? Explain.

A MIDLIFE CRISIS AT PLAYBOY ENTERPRISES

Christie Hefner

After many years of losses and difficulties, 1987 appears to be a money-making year for Playboy Enterprises, Inc. Newsstand sales of *Playboy* magazine, which were drastically reduced by 7-Eleven's 1986 decision to stop selling the magazine, are showing signs of recovery. The first Chinese edition of the magazine sold out in Hong Kong within hours of reaching the market. Company profits from twelve other foreign editions are up 88 percent over 1986. Franchise clubs in smaller markets such as Des Moines, Omaha, and Wichita remain profitable. And four clubs have opened in Japan and the Philippines. Playboy's video cassette business is booming. And Playboy's licensing division sells more designer underwear than Calvin Klein. As a result, the company's stock price has nearly doubled, from $8 to $14 a share. The restructuring efforts of president Christie Hefner appear to be paying off.

Christie Hefner is a thirty-four-year-old Phi Beta Kappa and summa cum laude graduate of Brandeis University. She was appointed president of the company in 1975 by her father, Hugh Hefner, Playboy's founder and chairman. Despite her limited experience and lack of formal business training, she seemed to have a zest for turning up facts and for reshaping the organization. Unlike her father, she was willing to look closely at balance sheets and income statements. She hired and fired without the indecision that was characteristic of her father. It did not, therefore, take her long to develop a reputation as a no-nonsense manager.

By the early 1980s, Christie Hefner had concluded that the company was small enough not to need a group of corporate number-crunchers. She therefore began shifting power away from the corporate staff and back to individual businesses. She eliminated a five-man team that analyzed the divisions' financial data for top management and required each division to report directly to her. She also fired numerous vice-presidents and slashed overhead by $8 million a year.

Despite her efforts and the company's recent improvement in performance, however, her problems are far from over. Today, her greatest challenges lie in dealing with the drastic change in public attitudes toward sex, redefining Playboy's "entertainment for men" credo, and creating a new image for Playboy—one that will distance the company from the pornography industry. Christie Hefner's current strategic responses to these challenges have two basic themes. First, she plans to remold Playboy into a smaller, more profitable company by focusing on three key areas: publishing (which accounted for 79 percent of 1986's sales) video (13 per-

cent), and licensing and merchandising of the Playboy line of such items as underwear and cologne (7 percent). The second theme in her strategic responses involves steering Playboy away from its traditional focus on sex related issues and repositioning it as a leisure oriented company attuned to the tastes and values of the 1980s. In at least two key business areas—the Playboy Channel and *Playboy* magazine—Christie Hefner seems to have concluded that sex alone does not sell as well as it used to.

Consistent with the outlined strategies, Playboy's money-losing Atlantic City casino was recently sold (for $37.9 million) and its trouble-plagued casino in London and clubs in New York, Chicago, and Los Angeles were written off. *Game* magazine was sold to a private partnership. The company's flagship product, *Playboy* magazine, hired Ron Reagan, Jr., as a correspondent and has been devoting more editorial attention to political issues, social causes, and entertainment in order to differentiate itself from more sexually explicit competitors. Finally, the Playboy Channel's programming was broadened beyond standard sex fare in order to boost the channel's subscriber base. It now features major studio and classic films without sexual themes.

Although some of the these actions have contributed to Playboy's recent performance improvement, some analysts believe that the company's repositioning attempt will create a new problem. As a leading cable industry consultant put it: "The question is, can you call an apple an orange and get away with it? Playboy wants to be known as the Playboy channel for the name recognition but is afraid that being known as Playboy will keep their [subscriber] base down because the name suggests a hard-core programming mix."

Whether the new strategies will prove successful in the long term, therefore, will depend ultimately on just how quickly and how well Christie Hefner can manage to deal with the "split personality" prevailing throughout her company.

DISCUSSION ISSUES

1. Given Christie Hefner's lack of formal management training, does it appear that she has a clear understanding of the role of management? Explain.

2. Which of the functions of the management process does it appear that she is concentrating most of her efforts on? Explain.

3. Does it appear that she is effectively managing all of the organizational resources at her disposal? Explain. How would you assess her efficiency as president of Playboy Enterprises? Explain.

4. How closely does Playboy Enterprises, under Christie Hefner's guidance, match up with the eight characteristics of excellently run companies? (See Table 1.2.) Explain.

5. How would you assess Christie's management skills? Does she appear to be utilizing the skills that are important for success at her level as Playboy's president? Explain.

6. Which of the bases of the triangular management model appear to be the primary moving forces at Playboy Enterprises? Explain.

7. Do you find any evidence in the case that suggests a profit motive at Playboy Enterprises? A service objective? A social objective? Explain. What other types of objectives appear to be targets for Playboy Enterprises? (Refer to Table 3.1.)

8. Does information in the case allow you to identify Christie Hefner's personal (individual) objectives? Explain.

PLANNING

The purpose of this section is to provide a thorough explanation of planning. Section 1 ended with a discussion of organizational objectives. Planning is the next section because, according to generally accepted management theory, after managers have developed organizational objectives, they are ready to plan.

In general terms, the topic of planning is covered through extended discussion of the fundamentals of planning, the decision-making process, strategic and tactical planning, and the various plans and planning tools available to managers. In more specific terms, the section offers the following planning fundamentals: a definition of *planning*, the steps of the planning process, the relationship between planning and the chief executive, the qualifications and duties of planners, and the evaluation of planners. The material on decision making will emphasize the definition of *decision*, important elements of the decision situation, and the use of probability theory and decision trees as tools for making decisions involving risk. The strategic and tactical planning material will include strategies themselves, strategy formulation, and environmental analysis. It will also include information about the tools that managers can use to develop organizational strategy: critical question analysis, SWOT, and business portfolio analysis. Plans and planning tool sections will cover such topics as the dimensions of a plan, why plans fail, plant facilities planning, human resource planning, forecasting, and scheduling.

As with the previous section, the material here will be challenging. As you study this section, think about how planning concepts relate to the material you read about in section 1. Also remember that an understanding of this new information is important to the comprehension of the material in the remaining sections of the text.

STUDENT LEARNING OBJECTIVES

From studying this chapter, I will attempt to acquire:

1. A definition of planning and an understanding of the purposes of planning.
2. A knowledge of the advantages and potential disadvantages of planning.
3. Insights on how the major steps of the planning process are related.
4. An understanding of the planning subsystem.
5. A knowledge of how the chief executive relates to the planning process.
6. An understanding of the qualifications and duties of planners and how planners are evaluated.
7. Guidelines on how to get the greatest return from the planning process.

C H A P T E R

4

FUNDAMENTALS OF PLANNING

RALPH AND HARVEY MOSS MUST PLAN

Ralph Moss was facing the most challenging task of his business career. His brother, Louis, had died, leaving Ralph to be the chief executive officer of John Nageldinger & Sons, Inc. The company, located in Westbury, New York, had been founded and run by Ralph's family for the last ninety-seven years. The company was in the business of manufacturing and selling compressed-gas regulators and portable oxygen equipment.

Ralph's business experience within the company was what made his new position such a challenge. For almost forty years, Ralph had worked primarily in the manufacturing area of the company. His experience was limited to supervising the machine operators who manufactured company products. Most other responsibilities had been left to Louis.

As the new chief executive officer, Ralph was struggling to solve one company problem after another, but his lack of experience made it very difficult. The longer Ralph functioned as Nageldinger & Sons' chief executive, the more frustrated he became. Finally, he realized that he was unable to manage the company alone.

Ralph convinced his thirty-nine-year-old son, Harvey, to move from California to Westbury to help manage the family business. Although Harvey had recently begun his career as a management consultant, he decided to try to help his father.

One of the first things Harvey did upon arriving at Nageldinger & Sons was to tour the Long Island plant, a modest one-story concrete-and-brick building stashed in the far corner of a dead-end street. Although Harvey had worked at Nageldinger & Sons several years earlier and knew some of what to expect on his tour, he was depressed with what he found.

Over all, the company's manufacturing operation hadn't changed in a long time. The company was using

machinery and operators that had been there thirty-five to forty years. In addition, the company was still marketing its products with a catalog that Harvey had helped design while attending college, in 1960. Given this situation, it was not hard for Harvey to believe that Nageldinger & Sons had not made a profit for the last three years.

It was clear to Harvey that changes had to be made if Nageldinger & Sons was to be successful. A carefully developed plan would have to be designed and implemented.

What's Ahead

The introductory case ends with Harvey Moss resolving to do a better job of planning at Nageldinger & Sons. The fundamentals of planning are described in this chapter. Specifically, this chapter (1) outlines the general characteristics of planning, (2) discusses steps in the planning process, (3) describes the planning subsystem, (4) elaborates upon the relationship between planning and the chief executive, (5) summarizes the qualifications and duties of planners and explains how planners are evaluated, and (6) explains how to maximize the effectiveness of the planning process.

 GENERAL CHARACTERISTICS OF PLANNING

Defining Planning

Planning is the process of determining how the organization can get where it wants to go. Chapter 3 emphasized the importance of organizational objectives and explained how to develop them. Planning is the process of determining exactly what the organization will do to accomplish its objectives. In more formal terms, planning is "the systematic development of action programs aimed at reaching agreed business objectives by the process of analyzing, evaluating, and selecting among the opportunities which are foreseen."[1]

> Planning determines how the organization can get where it wants to go.

The "Management in Action" feature for this chapter is an excerpt from a letter to stockholders in a Wendy's International annual report. It illustrates how Wendy's formulated plans to reach the objective of reversing the negative trend in sales and profits that the company was experiencing.

Purposes of Planning

Over the years, management writers have presented several different purposes of planning. For example, C. W. Roney indicates that organizational planning has two purposes: protective and affirmative. The protective purpose of planning is to minimize risk by reducing the uncertainties surrounding business conditions and clarifying the consequences of related management action. The affirmative purpose is to increase the degree of organizational success.[2] Still another purpose of planning is to establish a coordinated effort within the organization. An absence of planning is usually accompanied by an absence of coordination and, therefore, usually contributes to organizational inefficiency.

The fundamental purpose of planning, however, is to help the organization reach its objectives. As stated by Koontz and O'Donnell, the primary purpose of planning is to "facilitate the accomplishment of enterprise and objectives."[3] All other purposes of planning are simply spin-offs of this fundamental purpose.

> The fundamental purpose of planning is to help the organization reach its objectives.

WENDY'S PLANS TO REACH OBJECTIVES

TO OUR SHAREHOLDERS:

There is no doubt about it, 1986 results were far below those expected at the beginning of the year. In the face of both external and internal challenges, we made some difficult decisions and took decisive action. Year-to-year sales comparisons reached a low during the month of June. Since then, those comparisons have improved significantly. Even so, we have entered 1987 with our work cut out for us, but with confidence that we are positioning Wendy's for a recovery in operating performance.

MAJOR DEVELOPMENTS

The Wendy's Big Classic was just one of several major developments that resulted from a plan formulated to reverse the negative trend in sales and profits. Others include:

- The appointment of a new President and Chief Operating Officer, Jim Near. Jim is a hands-on operator with over 30 years of restaurant experience and a direct focus on operations and customer satisfaction. He has been associated with Wendy's since 1974. As a Wendy's franchisee, Jim developed 40 restaurants in just three years. In 1981, he became president of our Sisters Restaurants and has also served on our Board of Directors since that time.
- A realignment plan, which anticipates the franchising of the vast majority of 120 under-performing domestic company-owned Wendy's restaurants. Forty-four others, comprising 26 international Wendy's units and 18 Sisters Restaurants, are being disposed of. Although it resulted in a $75 million pretax charge in the third quarter, this program should enhance our royalty income. Return on investment, as well as return on equity, should also improve. . . .
- A renewed commitment to people-oriented programs that will include significant improvements to our training for manager trainees and crew members. Our action plan also calls for upgrading the "quality of life" of our store managers. We believe recognizing the importance of our people in these ways is a major step toward reducing turnover, an industry-wide problem.
- A strategy to attract more of the family market, including testing of a number of new menu items with lower prices than currently on the menu.
- Selection of a new national advertising agency, Dick Rich, Inc. We encourage you to watch for a new campaign in 1987 from this creator of the highly successful "Hot 'n Juicy" commericals of the late 1970's.

- Reemphasis on research and development as we continue to reevaluate our present menu; reformulating existing products, as well as looking for additional items to satisfy customer demand.
- Real progress toward lowering the cost of investment in new Wendy's restaurants to promote profitable unit growth and improve the sales-to-investment ratio for both the company and our franchisees.
- A reorganization to put the corporate support departments closer to restaurant operations, the heart of our business. The result: improved support of the restaurants and better communication. We have also eliminated some levels of reporting in operations, giving more authority to those charged with actually running the restaurants.

THE FUTURE

In 1986, for the sixth year in a row, consumers voted Wendy's the most popular hamburger restaurant, according to "Restaurants & Institutions" seventh annual Tastes of America survey. In fact, with the exception of one non-hamburger chain, Wendy's has the highest satisfaction rating for food quality among all fast-food concepts.

Clearly, our strategy of building upon our quality reputation is sound and our emphasis on serving the quality hamburger is right. Our customers are coming to Wendy's for high-quality food and now, more than ever before, we are working to make sure that is exactly what we deliver.

The company has weathered difficult periods before and we have emerged stronger each time. We believe that we can do it again by laying a firm foundation for the future—not by quick fixes. We enter 1987 with a renewed determination toward long-term success.

Planning: Advantages and Potential Disadvantages

A vigorous planning program has many advantages. One is that it helps managers to be future oriented. They are forced to look beyond their normal everyday problems to project what may face them in the future. Decision coordination is a second advantage of a sound planning program. A decision should not be made today without some idea of how it will affect a decision that will have to be made tomorrow. The planning function assists managers in their efforts to coordinate their decisions. A third advantage to planning is that it emphasizes organizational objectives. Since organizational objectives are the starting points for planning, managers are constantly reminded of exactly what their organization is trying to accomplish.

As a group, managers believe that planning is extremely advantageous to the organization. In a study by Stieglitz, 280 managers were asked to assess the relative importance of such functions as public relations, organizational meetings, organizational planning, and organizational control. Over 65 percent of these managers ranked planning as the most important function.[4]

If the planning function is not well executed within the organization, however, planning can have several disadvantages. For example, an overemphasized planning program can take up too much managerial time. Managers must strike an appropriate balance between time spent on planning and time spent on organizing, influencing, and controlling. If they don't, some activities that are extremely important to the success of the organization may be neglected. Usually, the disadvantages of planning result from the planning function being used incorrectly.[5] Over all, the advantages of planning generally outweigh the disadvantages.

> Planning emphasizes the future, helps to coordinate decisions, and keeps the focus on objectives.

> If done incorrectly or excessively, planning can be disadvantageous.

Primacy of Planning

Planning is the primary management function—the function that precedes and is the foundation for the organizing, influencing, and controlling functions of managers. Only after managers have developed their plans can they determine

> Planning is the foundation function.

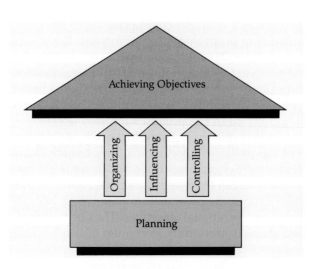

FIGURE 4.1
Planning as the foundation for organizing, influencing, and controlling

how they want to structure their organization, place their people, and establish organizational controls. As discussed in chapter 1, planning, organizing, influencing, and controlling are interrelated. Planning is the foundation function and the first function to be performed. Organizing, influencing, and controlling are interrelated and based upon the results of planning. Figure 4.1 on page 87 shows this relationship.

BACK TO THE CASE

It is obvious from the introductory case that little planning has occurred at Nageldinger & Sons in recent years. Harvey Moss, however, realizes that planning is the process of determining what Nageldinger & Sons should do to reach its objectives.

Because of the many related benefits of planning, Ralph Moss should encourage Harvey to pursue his resolution to plan more at Nageldinger & Sons. One particularly notable benefit is the probability of increased profits. To gain the benefits of planning,

however, Ralph and Harvey must be careful that the planning function is well executed and not overemphasized.

They should also keep in mind that planning is the primary management function. Thus, as managers, they should not begin to organize, influence, or control until the planning process is complete. Planning is the foundation management function upon which all other functions at Nageldinger & Sons should be based.

STEPS IN THE PLANNING PROCESS

The planning process contains the following six steps:

The six steps of the planning process are

1. Stating objectives.

1. *Stating organizational objectives* A clear statement of organizational objectives is necessary for planning to begin, since planning focuses on how the management system will reach those objectives.[6] Chapter 3 discusses how the objectives themselves are developed.

2. Listing alternatives.

2. *Listing alternative ways of reaching objectives* Once organizational objectives have been clearly stated, a manager should list as many available alternatives as possible for reaching those objectives.

3. Developing premises.

3. *Developing premises upon which each alternative is based* To a large extent, the feasibility of using any one alternative to reach organizational objectives is determined by the **premises,** or assumptions, upon which the alternative is based. For example, two alternatives a manager could generate to reach the organizational objective of increasing profit might be: (1) increase the sale of products presently being produced, or (2) produce and sell a completely new product. Alternative 1 would be based on the premise that the organization could get a larger share of an existing market. Alternative 2 would be based on the premise that a new product would capture a significant portion of a new market. A manager should list all of the premises for each alternative.

4. Choosing alternatives.

4. *Choosing the best alternative for reaching objectives* An evaluation of alternatives must include an evaluation of the premises upon which the alternatives are based. A manager usually finds that the premises upon which some alternatives are based are unreasonable and can therefore be excluded from further consideration. This elimination process helps in determining which alternative would be best to accomplish organizational objectives. The decision making required for this step is discussed more fully in chapter 5.

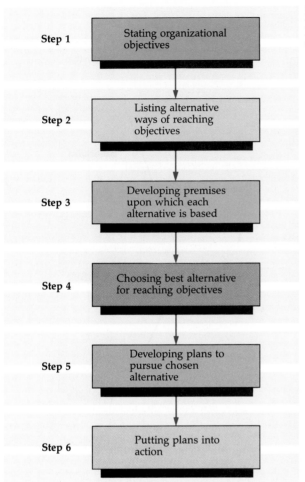

FIGURE 4.2
Elements of the planning
process

Step 1 — Stating organizational objectives

Step 2 — Listing alternative ways of reaching objectives

Step 3 — Developing premises upon which each alternative is based

Step 4 — Choosing best alternative for reaching objectives

Step 5 — Developing plans to pursue chosen alternative

Step 6 — Putting plans into action

5. *Developing plans to pursue the chosen alternative* After an alternative has been chosen, a manager begins to develop strategic (long-range) and tactical (short-range) plans.[7] More information about strategic and tactical planning is presented in chapter 6.

6. *Putting the plans into action* Once plans have been developed, they are ready to be put into action. The plans should furnish the organization with both long-range and short-range direction for activity. Obviously, the organization does not directly benefit from the planning process until this step is performed.

Figure 4.2 shows how the six steps of the planning process relate to one another.

THE PLANNING SUBSYSTEM

Once managers understand the basics of planning, they can take steps to implement the planning process in their organization. This implementation is the key

5. Developing plans.

6. Taking action.

Implementation of the planning process is the key to success.

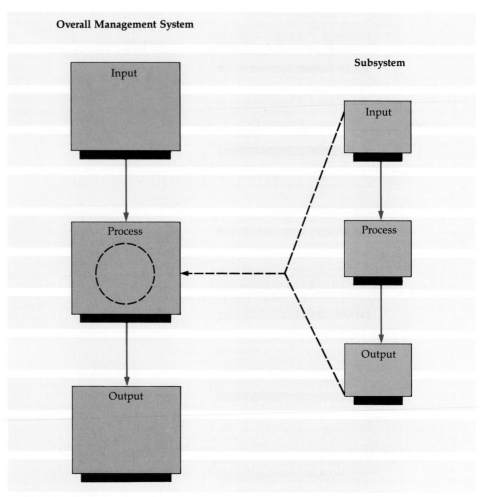

FIGURE 4.3
Relationship between overall management system and subsystem

to a successful planning process. Even though managers might be experts on facts related to planning and the planning process, if they cannot transform this understanding into appropriate action, they are not able to generate useful organizational plans.

One way of approaching this implementation is to view planning activities as an organizational subsystem. A **subsystem** is a system created as part of the process of the overall management system. Figure 4.3 illustrates this relationship between the overall management system and a subsystem. Subsystems help managers organize the overall system and enhance its success.

Figure 4.4 presents the elements of the planning subsystem. The purpose of this subsystem is to increase the effectiveness of the overall management system through more effective planning. The planning subsystem helps managers to identify planning activities within the overall system and, therefore, to guide and direct these activities.

Obviously, only a portion of organizational resources are used as input in

The planning subsystem increases the effectiveness of the overall management system.

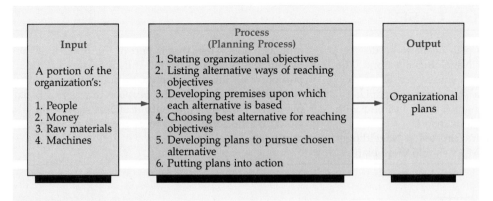

FIGURE 4.4
The planning subsystem

the planning subsystem. This input is allocated to the planning subsystem and transformed into output through the steps of the planning process.

How planning subsystems are organized in the industrial world can be exemplified by the more informal planning subsystem at the Quaker Oats Company and the more formal planning subsystem at the Sun Oil Company.[8]

Quaker Oats Company

At Quaker Oats, speculations about the future are conducted, for the most part, on an informal basis. To help anticipate particular social changes, the company has opened communication lines with various groups believed to be the harbingers of change. To spearhead this activity, the company has organized a "noncommittee" whose members represent a diversity of orientations. They listen to what is going on—monitor social changes—and thus augment the company's understanding of social change.

Quaker Oats plans on an informal basis.

Sun Oil Company

Several groups within Sun Oil Company are engaged in formal business planning and forecasting. Operational planning with a five-year horizon is done annually. The planning activity with the longest time horizon exists within the Sun Oil Company of Pennsylvania, the corporation's refining, transportation, and marketing arm. A centralized planning group, reporting to the vice-president of development and planning, is responsible for assisting top management in setting the company's long-term objectives, developing plans to achieve these objectives, and identifying likely consumer needs and market developments of the future that might indicate business areas for diversification. Current efforts are focused on discussions of a series of long-range issues with the executive committee, a planning process designed to generate a restatement of long-term objectives.

Sun Oil plans on a formal basis.

BACK TO THE CASE

Harvey Moss believes that a plan needs to be designed and implemented for Nageldinger & Sons. The process of developing this plan should consist of six steps. It should begin with a statement of organizational objectives for Nageldinger & Sons and end with putting organizational plans into action.

To implement a planning process at Nageldinger & Sons, Ralph and Harvey Moss should view planning as a subsystem that is part of the process of the overall management system. Thus they should use a portion of all the organizational resources available at Nageldinger & Sons for the purpose of organizational planning. Naturally, the output of this subsystem would be the actual plans to be used in managing the company.

⊞ PLANNING AND THE CHIEF EXECUTIVE

Chief executives have many roles.

Henry Mintzberg has pointed out that the top managers—the chief executives—of organizations have many different roles to perform.[9] As organizational figureheads, they must represent their organizations in a variety of social, legal, and ceremonial matters. As leaders, they must ensure that organization members are properly guided in relation to organizational goals. As liaisons, they must establish themselves as links between their organizations and factors outside their organizations. As monitors, they must assess organizational progress. As disturbance handlers, they must settle disputes between organization members. And as resource allocators, they must determine where resources will be placed to benefit their organizations best.

Chief executives also are responsible for planning.

In addition to these many and varied roles, chief executives have the final responsibility for organizational planning. As the scope of planning broadens to include a larger portion of the management system, it becomes increasingly important for chief executives to become more involved in the planning process.

As planners, chief executives seek answers to the following broad questions:

1. In what direction should the organization be going?
2. In what direction is the organization going now?
3. Should something be done to change this direction?
4. Is the organization continuing in an appropriate direction?[10]

Keeping informed about social, political, and scientific trends is of utmost importance in helping chief executives to answer these questions.

Many chief executives obtain planning assistance from organization planners.

Given the importance of top management's participating in organizational planning and performing other time-consuming roles, more and more top managers obtain planning assistance by establishing a position for an organization planner.[11] Just as managers can ask others for help and advice in making decisions, they can involve others in formulating organizational plans.

Chief executives of most substantial organizations need help to plan.[12] The remainder of this chapter, therefore, assumes that the organization planner is an individual who is not the chief executive of the organization. The planner is presented as a manager responsible for giving assistance to the chief executive on organizational planning issues. If, by chance, the planner and the chief executive are the same person in a particular organization, the following discussion relating to the planner can be modified slightly to relate also to the chief executive.

⊞ THE PLANNER

Perhaps the most important input in the planning subsystem is the planner. This individual combines all other input and influences the subsystem process so that effective organizational plans become subsystem output. The planner is responsible not only for the plans that are developed but also for advising management about what action should be taken in relation to those plans. Regardless of who actually does the planning or of the organization in which the planning is being done, the qualifications and duties of planners and how planners are evaluated are very important considerations in increasing the effectiveness of the planning subsystem.

Qualifications of Planners

Planners should have four primary qualifications. First, they should have considerable practical experience within their organization. Preferably, they should have been executives in one or more of the organization's major departments. This experience will help them develop plans that are both practical and tailor-made for the organization.

Planners should be able to apply organizational experience,

Second, planners should be able to replace any narrow view of the organization (probably acquired while holding other organizational positions) with an understanding of the organization as a whole. They must know how all parts of the organization function and interrelate. In other words, they must possess an abundance of the conceptual skills mentioned in chapter 1.

see the organization as a whole,

Third, planners should have some knowledge of and interest in the social, political, technical, and economic trends that could affect the future of the organization. They must be skillful in defining these trends and have the expertise to determine how the organization should react to the trends to maximize success. This particular qualification cannot be overemphasized.

detect and react to trends, and

The fourth and last qualification is that planners should be able to work well with others. They inevitably will work closely with several key members of the organization and should possess personal characteristics that are helpful in collaborating and advising effectively. The ability to communicate clearly, both orally and in writing, is one of the most important of these characteristics.[13]

get along with others.

Duties of Planners

Organizational planners have at least three general duties to perform: (1) overseeing the planning process, (2) evaluating developed plans, and (3) solving planning problems.[14]

Overseeing the Planning Process

First, and perhaps foremost, planners must see that planning gets done. To this end, they establish rules, guidelines, and planning objectives that apply to themselves and others involved in the planning process. In essence, planners must develop a plan for planning.

Simply described, a **plan for planning** is a listing of all of the steps that must be taken to plan for an organization. It generally includes such activities as

A plan for planning ensures that planning gets done.

evaluating an organization's present planning process in an effort to improve it, determining how much benefit an organization can gain as a result of planning, and developing a planning timetable to ensure that all of the steps necessary to plan for a particular organization are performed by some specified date.

Evaluating Developed Plans

Planners evaluate developed plans to see if they require modification.

The second general duty of planners is to evaluate plans that have been developed. Planners must decide if plans are sufficiently challenging for the organization, if they are complete, and if they are consistent with organizational objectives. If the developed plans do not fulfill these three requirements, they should be modified appropriately.

Solving Planning Problems

Planners recognize a problem, gather information, and then suggest solutions.

Planners also have the duty to gather information that will help solve planning problems. Sometimes, they may find it necessary to conduct special studies within the organization to obtain this information. They can then recommend what the organization should do in the future to deal with planning problems and forecast how the organization might benefit from related opportunities.

For example, a planner may observe that production objectives set by the organization are not being met. This is a symptom of a planning problem. The problem causing this symptom might be that objectives are unrealistically high or that plans developed to achieve production objectives are inappropriate. The planner must gather information pertinent to the problem and suggest to management how the organization can solve its problem and become more successful. King and Cleland have presented the relationships among problems, symptoms, and opportunities in Figure 4.5.

A planner advises management on what should be done in the future.

The three duties of planners just discussed—overseeing the planning process, evaluating developed plans, and solving planning problems—are general comments on planners' activities. Table 4.1 lists the specific responsibilities of an organization planner at a large manufacturing company. As this list implies, the main focus of the planner's activities is to advise management on what should be done in the future. The planner assists management not only in determining appropriate future action but also in ensuring that the timing of that action is appropriate. In the end, the possibility always exists that the manager may not accept the planner's recommendations.

FIGURE 4.5
Relationships among symptoms, problems, and opportunities that face the planner

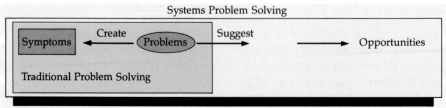

TABLE 4.1

Responsibilities of an organization planner

The planner has the responsibility to—

1. Provide information to assist management in formulating long- and short-range goals and plans of the company. Also assist in the updating of these goals plus general monitoring of attainment.
2. Coordinate activities and prepare special studies centering on acquisition, disposals, joint endeavors, manufacturing rights, and patents.
3. Serve as resource for determining the acquisition, disposal, and movement of physical properties.
4. Encourage the stimulation of ideas from management toward broadening company operations; extract these ideas and follow up on possibilities.
5. Develop, recommend, and obtain management approval of plans, procedures, and policies to be followed in implementing diversification program.
6. Perform basic research on diversification, using such sources as the American Management Association, National Industrial Conference Board, Research Institute of America, and others.
7. Perform internal and external economic studies to secure necessary information for overall planning.
8. Utilize staff service personnel plus line and committee persons in accumulating and evaluating data.
9. Analyze the company's physical properties and personnel capabilities to determine production spans.
10. In conjunction with staff services, periodically survey performance capabilities of sales, engineering, manufacturing, and service components of the company.
11. Conduct an initial survey of the manufacturing organization's physical properties (facilities, equipment, and tools) and keep information current.
12. Investigate and determine possibilities of other significant use for basic products.
13. Assist in communicating and implementing the diversification decisions of management during transition periods.
14. Prepare necessary reports to keep management informed.

Evaluation of Planners

As with all other organization members, the performance of planners must be evaluated against the contribution they make toward helping the organization achieve its objectives. The quality and appropriateness of the system for planning and the plans that the planners develop for the organization should be the primary considerations in this evaluation. Because the organizing, influencing, and controlling functions of the manager are based on the fundamental planning function, the evaluation of planners becomes critically important.

Although the assessment of planners is somewhat subjective, a number of objective indicators do exist. For example, the use of appropriate techniques is one objective indicator. If a planner is using appropriate techniques, it is probable that the planner is doing an acceptable job. The degree of objectivity displayed by the planner is another indicator. To a great extent, the planner's advice should be based on a rational analysis of appropriate information.[15] This is not to say that subjectivity and judgment should be excluded by the

Evaluation of planners should be based on both objective and subjective appraisals of performance.

planner. Typically, however, they should be based on specific and appropriate information.

Malik suggests that objective evidence that a planner is doing a reputable job exists if:

1. The organizational plan is in writing.
2. The plan is the result of all elements of the management team working together.
3. The plan defines present and possible future business of the organization.
4. The plan specifically mentions organizational objectives.
5. The plan includes future opportunities and suggestions on how to take advantage of them.
6. The plan emphasizes both internal and external environments.
7. The plan describes the attainment of objectives in operational terms when possible.
8. The plan includes both long- and short-term recommendations.[16]

These eight points furnish managers with some objective guidelines for evaluating the performance of planners. This evaluation, however, should never be completely objective. More subjective considerations include how well planners get along with key members of the organization, the amount of organizational loyalty they display, and their perceived potential.

BACK TO THE CASE

Technically, as chief executive officer of Nageldinger & Sons, Ralph Moss is responsible for organizational planning and for performing such related time-consuming functions as keeping abreast of internal and external trends that could affect the future of the company. Because planning requires so much time, and because the chief executive officer of Nageldinger & Sons has many other responsibilities within the company, Ralph might want to consider appointing a director of planning.

The organization planner at Nageldinger & Sons would need certain qualities. Ideally, the planner should have some experience at Nageldinger & Sons, be able to see the company as an entire organization, have some ability to gauge and react to major trends that probably will affect the company's future, and be able to work well with others. Ralph's son, Harvey, might be an ideal candidate.

If Harvey were to take over planning responsibilities at Nageldinger & Sons, he would be expected to oversee the planning process, evaluate developed plans, and solve planning problems. Perhaps the first problem he would have to tackle would be the development of plans for updating the company's manufacturing operations and for pointing Nageldinger & Sons in a profit oriented direction.

An evaluation of Harvey as an organization planner would be based on both objective and subjective appraisals of his performance.

⊞ MAXIMIZING THE EFFECTIVENESS OF THE PLANNING PROCESS

Success in implementing a planning subsystem is not easily attainable. As the size of the organization increases, the planning task becomes more complicated, requiring more people, more information, and more complicated decisions.[17] Several safeguards, however, can ensure the success of an organizational planning effort. These safeguards include (1) top management support, (2) an effective and efficient planning organization, (3) an implementation focused planning orientation, and (4) inclusion of the right people.

Top Management Support

Top management in an organization must support the planning effort, or other organization members may not take the planning effort seriously.[18] Whenever possible, top management should actively help to guide and participate in planning activities. Furnishing the planner with whatever resources are needed to structure the planning organization, encouraging planning as a continuing process (not as a once-a-year activity), and preparing people for the changes that usually result from planning are clear signs that top management is solidly behind the planning effort. The chief executive must give continual and obvious attention to the planning process if it is to be successful.[19] He or she must not be so concerned about other matters that planning is not given the emphasis it deserves.[20]

All organization members should be aware that top management supports the planning effort.

An Effective and Efficient Planning Organization

A well-designed planning organization is the primary vehicle by which planning is accomplished and planning effectiveness is determined. The planner must take the time to design as efficient and effective a planning organization as possible.

The planning organization should have three built-in characteristics. First, it should be designed to use established management systems within the company. As expressed by Paul J. Stonich:

The planning organization should:

> Many organizations separate formal planning systems from the rest of the management systems that include organization, communication, reporting, evaluating, and performance review. These systems must not be viewed as separate from formal planning systems. Complex organizations need a comprehensive and coordinated set of management systems, including formal planning systems to help them toward their goals.[21]

1. Use established systems.

Second, the planning organization should be simple, yet complex enough to ensure a coordinated effort of all planning participants. Planning can be a complicated process requiring a somewhat large planning organization. The planner should strive to simplify the planning organization and make its complex facets as clearly understood as possible.

2. Be simple yet complex.

Lastly, the planning organization should be flexible and adaptable. Planning conditions are constantly changing, and the planning organization must be able to respond to these changing conditions.

3. Be flexible and adaptable.

An Implementation Focused Planning Orientation

Because the end result of the planning process is some type of action that will help achieve stated organizational objectives, planning should be aimed at implementation.[22] As Peter Drucker points out, a plan is effective only if its implementation helps attain organizational objectives.[23] Plans should be developed and scrutinized after the planner has looked ahead to when they are to be implemented.[24] Ease of implementation is a positive feature of a plan that should be built in whenever possible.

Planning should be aimed at implementation.

The marketing plan for the Edsel automobile introduced by Ford in the 1950s is an example of how a sound plan can become unsuccessful simply because of ineffective implementation.[25] The rationale behind the Edsel was complete, logical, and defensible. Three consumer trends at that time solidly justified the automobile's introduction: (1) a trend toward the purchase of higher-priced cars, (2) a general income increase that resulted in all income groups purchasing higher-priced cars, and (3) owners of lower-priced Fords trading them in on Buicks, Oldsmobiles, or Pontiacs after they became more affluent. Conceptually, these trends were so significant that Ford's plan to introduce the larger and more expensive Edsel appeared virtually risk-free.

Two factors in the implementation of this plan, however, turned the entire Edsel situation into a financial disaster. First, the network of controllers, dealers, marketing managers, and industrial relations managers created within Ford to get the Edsel to the consumer became very complicated and inefficient. Second, because Ford pushed as many Edsels as possible onto the road immediately after introduction, the quality of the Edsel suffered; and consumers were buying poorly manufactured products. Although the plan to make and market the Edsel was defensible, the long-run influence of the organization and manufacturing processes created to implement the plan doomed it to failure.

Inclusion of the Right People

Planning must include the right people.[26] Whenever possible, planners should obtain input from the managers of the functional areas for which they are planning. These managers are close to the everyday activity of their segments of the organization and can provide planners with invaluable information. They probably also will be involved in implementing whatever plan develops and will be able to furnish the planner with feedback on how easily various plans are being implemented.

Input from individuals who will be directly affected by the plans also can be helpful to planners. The individuals who do the work in the organization can give opinions on how various plans will influence work flow. Although it is extremely important that planners involve others in the planning process, not all organization members can or should be involved. Stonich offers the following advice on the involvement of organization members in the planning process:

> In many corporations, the wrong sets of people participate in particular planning activities. Planning requires not only generation of information for making decisions, but decision making itself. The kinds of decisions and types of data needed should dictate the choice of who is involved in what aspects of planning within an organization.[27]

BACK TO THE CASE

Regardless of who actually ends up having primary responsibility for planning at Nageldinger & Sons, a number of safeguards can be taken to ensure that the planning efforts of this person will be successful. First, Ralph Moss and other top executives of the company should actively encourage planning activities and show support of the planning process. Second, the planning organization designed to implement the planning process should use established systems at Nageldinger & Sons, be simple yet complex, and be flexible and adaptable. Third, the entire planning process should be oriented toward easing the implementation of generated plans. Finally, all key people at Nageldinger & Sons should be included in the planning process.

Action Summary

Reread the learning objectives that follow. Each objective is followed by questions. Answering these questions accurately will help you retain the most important concepts discussed in this chapter. After answering each question, check your answer with the answer key at the end of this chapter. (*Hint:* If you have doubt regarding the correct response, consult the page whose number follows the answer.)

From studying this chapter, I will attempt to acquire: **Circle:**

1. **A definition of planning and an understanding of the purposes of planning.**
   a. The affirmative purpose of planning is to increase the degree of organizational success.   T, F
   b. Which of the following is not one of the purposes of planning: (a) systematic; (b) protective; (c) affirmative; (d) coordination; (e) fundamental.   a, b, c, d, e

2. **A knowledge of the advantages and potential disadvantages of planning.**
   a. The advantages of planning include all of the following except: (a) helping managers to be future oriented; (b) helping coordinate decisions; (c) requiring proper time allocation; (d) emphasizing organizational objectives; (e) all of the above are advantages of planning.   a, b, c, d, e
   b. The following is a potential disadvantage of planning: (a) too much time may be spent on planning; (b) an inappropriate balance between planning and other managerial functions may occur; (c) some important activities may be neglected; (d) incorrect use of the planning function could work to the detriment of the organization; (e) all of the above.   a, b, c, d, e

3. **Insights on how the major steps of the planning process are related.**
   a. The first major step in the planning process, according to the text, is: (a) developing premises; (b) listing alternative ways of reaching organizational objectives; (c) stating organizational objectives; (d) developing plans to pursue chosen alternatives; (e) putting plans into action.   a, b, c, d, e
   b. The assumptions on which alternatives are based are usually referred to as: (a) objectives; (b) premises; (c) tactics; (d) strategies; (e) probabilities.   a, b, c, d, e

4. **An understanding of the planning subsystem.**
   a. A subsystem is a system created as part of the process of the overall management system.   T, F
   b. The purpose of the planning subsystem is to increase the effectiveness of the overall management system through which of the following: (a) systematizing the planning function; (b) more effective planning; (c) formalizing the planning process; (d) integrating the planning process; (e) none of the above.   a, b, c, d, e

5. **A knowledge of how the chief executive relates to the planning process.**
   a. The responsibility for organizational planning rests with middle management.   T, F
   b. The final responsibility for organizational planning rests with: (a) the planning department; (b) the chief executive; (c) departmental supervisors; (d) the organizational planner; (e) the entire organization.   a, b, c, d, e

6. **An understanding of the qualifications and duties of planners and how planners are evaluated.**
   a. The performance of planners should be evaluated with respect to the con-   T, F

tribution they make toward helping the organization achieve its objectives.

a, b, c, d, e
   b. The organizational planner's full responsibilities are: (a) developing plans only; (b) advising about action that should be taken relative to the plans that the chief executive developed; (c) advising about action that should be taken relative to the plans of the board of directors; (d) selecting the person who will oversee the planning process; (e) none of the above.

7. Guidelines on how to get the greatest return from the planning process.

T, F
   a. Top management should encourage planning as an annual activity.

a, b, c, d, e
   b. Which of the following is not a built-in characteristic of an effective and efficient planning organization: (a) it should be designed to use established systems within a company; (b) it should be simple, yet complex enough to ensure coordinated effort; (c) it should cover an operating cycle of not more than one year; (d) it should be flexible and adaptive; (e) all of the above are characteristics of an effective and efficient planning organization.

INTRODUCTORY CASE WRAP-UP

"Ralph and Harvey Moss Must Plan" (p. 84) and its related back-to-the-case sections were written to help you better understand the management concepts contained in this chapter. Answer the following discussion questions about this introductory case to further enrich your understanding of chapter content:

1. Do you think that Nageldinger & Sons has emphasized planning over the years? Explain.

2. What problems will Ralph and Harvey face in trying to make their company more of a planning organization?
3. Who would make a better planner for this organization—Ralph or Harvey? Explain.

Issues for Review and Discussion

1. What is planning?
2. What is the main purpose of planning?
3. List and explain the advantages of planning.
4. Why are the disadvantages of planning called *potential* disadvantages?
5. Explain the phrase *primacy of planning.*
6. List the six steps in the planning process.
7. Outline the relationships between the six steps in the planning process.
8. What is an organizational subsystem?
9. List the elements of the planning subsystem.
10. How do the many roles of a chief executive relate to his or her role as organization planner?
11. Explain the basic qualifications of an organization planner.
12. Give a detailed description of the general duties an organization planner must perform.
13. How would you evaluate the performance of an organization planner?
14. How can top management show its support of the planning process?
15. Describe the characteristics of an effective and efficient planning organization.
16. Why should the planning process emphasize the implementation of organizational plans?
17. Explain why the Edsel automobile failed to generate consumer acceptance.
18. Which people in an organization typically should be included in the planning process? Why?

Sources of Additional Information

Aguilar, F. J. *Scanning the Business Environment.* New York: Macmillan, 1967.

Alpander, Guvenc G. *Human Resources Management Planning.* New York: Amacom, 1982.

Belohlav, James A. "Long-Range Planning: Some Common Misconceptions." *Managerial Planning* 30 (September/October 1981): 41–43.

Belohlav, James A., and Herman A. Waggener. "Keeping the 'Strategic' in Your Strategic Planning." *Managerial Planning* (March/April 1980): 23–25.

Dilenschneider, R. L., and Richard C. Hyde. "Crisis Communications: Planning for the Unplanned." *Business Horizons* (January/February 1985): 35–41.

Donnelly, Robert M. *Guidebook to Planning: Strategic Planning and Budgeting Basics for the Growing Firm.* New York: Van Nostrand Reinhold, 1984.

Dyson, R. G., and M. J. Foster. "Making Planning More Effective." *Long-Range Planning* 16 (1983): 68–73.

Emery, J. C. *Organizational Planning and Control Systems.* New York: Macmillan, 1971.

Gluck, Frederick W., Stephen P. Kaufman, and A. Steven Walleck. "Strategic Management for Competitive Advantage." *Harvard Business Review* (July/August 1980): 154–61.

Hall, William K. "Survival Strategies in a Hostile Environment." *Harvard Business Review* (September/October 1980): 75–85.

Kaplan, Eileen E., and Jack M. Kaplan. "Career Planning: Gaining Managerial Commitment to the Planning Process." *Managerial Planning* 33 (July/August 1984): 48–50.

McConkey, Dale D. "If It's Not Broke—Fix It Anyway!" *Business Quarterly* 51 (Spring 1986): 50–52.

Naor, Jacob. "How to Make Strategic Planning Work for Small Business." *S.A.M. Advanced Management Journal* (Winter 1980): 35–39.

Nutt, Paul C. "Tactics of Implementation." *Academy of Management Journal* 29 (June 1986): 230–61.

Shim, Jae K., and Randy McGlade. "Current Trends in the Use of Corporate Planning Models." *Journal of Systems Management* 35 (September 1984): 24–31.

Steiner, G. A. *Managerial Long-Range Planning.* New York: McGraw-Hill, 1963.

Van Voorhis, Kenneth R. *Entrepreneurship and Small Business Management.* New York: Allyn & Bacon, 1980.

Yavitz, Boris, and William H. Newman. *Strategy in Action: The Execution, Policy, and Payoff of Business Planning,* New York: Free Press, 1984.

Notes

1. Harry Jones, *Preparing Company Plans: A Workbook for Effective Corporate Planning* (New York: Wiley, 1974), 3.
2. C. W. Roney, "The Two Purposes of Business Planning," *Managerial Planning* (November/December 1976): 1–6.
3. Harold Koontz and Cyril O'Donnell, *Management: A Systems and Contingency Analysis of Management Functions* (New York: McGraw-Hill, 1976), 130.
4. H. Stieglitz, *The Chief Executive and His Job,* Personnel Policy Study No. 214 (New York: National Industrial Conference Board, 1969).
5. For a discussion of several of these disadvantages, see George R. Terry, *Principles of Management* (Homewood, Ill.: Irwin, 1972), 198–200.
6. George C. Sawyer, "The Hazards of Goal Conflict in Strategic Planning," *Managerial Planning* (May/June 1980): 11–13, 27.
7. For more detailed information on how strategic planning takes place, see Richard F. Vancil and Peter Lorange, "Strategic Planning in Diversified Companies," *Harvard Business Review* (January/February 1975): 81–90; and William R. King and David I. Cle-

land, "A New Method for Strategic Systems Planning," *Business Horizons* (August 1975): 55–64.
8. Excerpted, by permission of the publisher, from *1974–75 Exploratory Planning Briefs: Planning for the Future by Corporations and Agencies, Domestic and International,* by William A. Simmons, © 1975 by AMACOM, a division of American Management Associations, pp. 10–11. All rights reserved.
9. Henry Mintzberg, "A New Look at the Chief Executive's Job," *Organizational Dynamics* (Winter 1973): 20–40.
10. Adapted from J. F. R. Perrin, *Focus on the Future* (London: Management Publications, 1971).
11. James M. Hardy, *Corporate Planning for Nonprofit Organizations* (New York: Association Press, 1972), 37.
12. Milton Leontiades, "The Dimensions of Planning in Large Industrialized Organizations," *California Management Review* 22 (Summer 1980): 82–86.
13. The section "Qualifications of Planners" is adapted from John Argenti, *Systematic Corporate Planning* (New York: Wiley, 1974), 126.
14. These three duties are adapted from Walter B. Schaf-

fir, "What Have We Learned about Corporate Planning?" *Management Review* (August 1973): 19–26.

15. Edward J. Green, *Workbook for Corporate Planning* (New York: American Management Association, 1970).

16. Z. A. Malik, "Formal Long-Range Planning and Organizational Performance" (Ph.D. diss., Rensselaer Polytechnic Institute, 1974).

17. James Brian Quinn, "Managing Strategic Change," *Sloan Management Review* 21 (Summer 1980): 3–20.

18. Kamal E. Said and Robert E. Seiler, "An Empirical Study of Long-Range Planning Systems: Strengths—Weaknesses—Outlook." *Managerial Planning* 28 (July/August 1979): 24–28.

19. George A. Steiner, "The Critical Role of Management in Long-Range Planning," *Arizona Review,* April 1966.

20. Myles L. Mace, "The President and Corporate Planning," *Harvard Business Review* (January/February 1965): 49–62.

21. Paul J. Stonich, "Formal Planning Pitfalls and How to Avoid Them," *Management Review* (June 1975): 5–6.

22. Thomas A. Ratcliffe and David J. Logsdon, "The Business Planning Process—A Behavioral Perspective," *Managerial Planning* (March/April 1980): 32–37.

23. Peter F. Drucker, *Management: Tasks, Responsibilities, Practices* (New York: Harper & Row, 1973).

24. Bernard W. Taylor, III, and K. Roscoe David, "Implementing an Action Program via Organizational Change," *Journal of Economics and Business* (Spring/Summer 1976): 203–208.

25. William H. Reynolds, "The Edsel: Faulty Execution of a Sound Marketing Plan," *Business Horizons* (Fall 1967): 39–46,

26. To see how various management positions are typically involved in U.S. human resource planning, see Guvenc G. Alpander, "Human Resource Planning in U.S. Corporations," *California Management Review* 22 (Spring 1980): 24–32.

27. Stonich, "Formal Planning Pitfalls and How to Avoid Them," 5.

Action Summary Answer Key

1. a. T, p. 85	3. a. c, p. 88	5. a. F, p. 92	7. a. F, p. 97
b. a, p. 85	b. b, p. 88	b. b, p. 92	b. c, p. 97
2. a. c, p. 87	4. a. T, p. 90	6. a. T, pp. 95–96	
b. e, p. 87	b. b, p. 92	b. e, p. 95	

DO "REAL" ENTREPRENEURS PLAN?

Walter R. Lovejoy is a man who believes strongly in the value of planning. He learned at a small business, then moved on to do the planning for a huge conglomerate. In the late 1960s, Lovejoy was running A-1 Tool Company. There were so many tool-and-die shops fighting for work at that time that careful planning was a necessity. Developing new tools for making new products while simultaneously keeping tabs on pricing, costs, and competitors became a way of life for Walter Lovejoy at A-1.

In 1969 the $4 million company was sold to Beatrice Foods and Lovejoy went along for the ride. At Beatrice, however, Lovejoy soon learned how meaningless planning was to many managers. As head of the metal-products division and later as the man in charge of 30-odd industrial companies within the conglomerate's industrial division, he came to recognize that there are two distinct types of nonplanners: successful entrepreneurs who "keep everything in their heads," and business school–trained professionals who "think planning is an exercise on their calculators."

How could he get his nonplanning managers to plan? Through a close examination of numerous planning approaches being used by such solid companies as General Electric and Westinghouse Electric Corporation, Lovejoy became convinced that a new, less mechanical approach might work. However, it was during a series of conversations with business guru Peter Drucker that the answer came to him: the planning process should be one built around questions, not numbers. While a screw-machine operation is completely different from a water-treatment business, many of the questions that need to be asked are very much the same.

"I wanted to create an environment where key people in each of the businesses would get together and talk about what was happening. What should they be doing, for example, to reduce their costs? And should they be thinking about new products?" stated Lovejoy. The system that he developed revolved around a 39-page manual and nearly 40 pages of worksheets. Managers of each business were expected to review the questions, answer the relevant ones, and focus on priorities. The questions were designed to stimulate serious thinking before any numbers got written down. The goal, said Lovejoy, was "to get people to question the validity of their (planning) assumptions."

How did subordinate managers respond to this new approach? Many, especially those entrepreneurial

types who were nearing retirement, thought this method, as well as all other approaches, were nothing but a "pain in the neck." Others, however, began to spot money-losing areas and redundancies that they had not recognized before. Lovejoy left Beatrice in 1982, but he still uses the same basic approach to planning at his own company, Lovejoy Industries Inc., a more than $75-million miniconglomerate.

Many other chief executive officers in smaller companies also use a broad question approach to planning to keep their organizations on-track or to get them back on-track. This "broad question" planning process begins with questions such as: How fast should we grow? What is our risk exposure? What business are we in? What business do we want to be in? Why do our customers buy from us? Who is our competition? What are we doing right?

When George Patterson, co-founder of City Gardens Inc., asked himself what business he was in, he discovered that, deep down, he really wasn't sure. He and his partners had begun the Boston-area business in the mid 1970s. But by 1983, the original focus—selling and maintaining plants for offices—had changed, a result of opening a retail flower store, a garden center in Washington, D.C., and a branch office in Atlanta. "We lost a lot of money and we were going nowhere," said Patterson. "Until we wrote things down, we were tempted by little and big opportunities whenever they appeared." What business *were* they in? "Plants" seemed to be the only real way to describe it. What business *should* they be in? The answer, they finally decided, was interior landscaping. "Our edge was knowledge of the local market," concluded Patterson. So they got rid of operations outside of this niche, and in other locations, and consolidated their position.

Until recently, Everette Jewell, founder and CEO of Jewell Building Systems Inc., in Dallas, North Carolina, assumed that customers purchased his prefabricated steel buildings because of their low price. He was soon to discover that it is hard to effectively plan when one does not know why people buy a product. For nine years, selling small structures at relatively low prices had been a very profitable niche. Recently, however, Jewell's customers began letting him know that prices are a lot less important than they had been previously. Reliability of a supplier had replaced price as the primary factor in many purchase decisions. "People will even pay a premium to get rid of headaches. We're at a point where we don't just sell buildings. We sell solutions to problems," comments Jewell. Jewell Building Systems is now getting increasing numbers of orders for larger, more expensive structures; Jewell is planning for his company's future accordingly.

DISCUSSION ISSUES

1. From comments in the case, do you see a difference in the purpose for planning at Beatrice, City Gardens, and Jewell Building Systems? Explain.
2. Your text suggests that there are numerous advantages to planning. Which were mentioned or implied in the case?
3. Which step in the planning process is Walter Lovejoy trying to get subordinate managers to concentrate on? Which step seems to be providing the focus at City Gardens? At Jewell Building Systems? Explain.

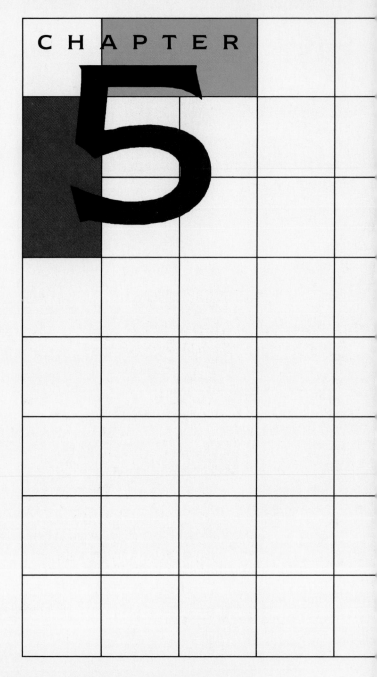

CHAPTER

5

MAKING DECISIONS

CHAPTER OUTLINE

IMPORTANT DECISIONS AT TORO

Nearly everyone recognizes the name Toro. The Toro Company, based in Minneapolis, is a leading manufacturer of outdoor power equipment. Toro's product line includes lawn mowers, tillers, snowblowers, and chain saws. Since the company sells lawn mowers in the summer and snow removal equipment in the winter, it is usually considered to have an ideal product line.

However, two mild winters in a row reduced Toro's snowblower sales from $130 million to $6 million during a two-year period. Naturally, this drastic sales reduction trapped many retail outlets with excessive inventories of Toro snow related equipment.

Ken Melrose, Toro's president, admitted that some of the decisions made to overcome this undesirable financial situation were not the best. For example, Toro attempted to open up new sales avenues by extending its distribution of products to mass merchandisers such as J. C. Penney and Zayre. This move, however, antagonized Toro's long-established independent distributors and dealers rather than opening up new sales avenues. As another example, Toro decided to bring out a new, less expensive lawn mower whose sales could help make up for the drop in sales of snow related products. The quality of this mower turned out to be inferior to that of Toro's usual products, however. For that reason, the mower posed a real danger to Toro, since Toro customers rely on the firm's product quality.

Finally, in response to the continued weakening demand for Toro's products and the worsening financial condition of the company, Melrose decided to cut operating expenses. He reduced Toro's work force from 4,000 to 1,700 employees and temporarily closed the company's six snowblower and lawn mower plants. This

cost-cutting tactic contributed significantly to Toro's first profit in nearly three years.

The future undoubtedly will challenge Melrose further by requiring him to make complicated decisions of the following sort: If weather conditions change so that demand for snow related equipment skyrockets, how will Toro increase its manufacturing capability? If government regulations require new safety devices on Toro products, how will Toro handle the increased cost of these devices relative to product pricing? How will Toro best handle increasing competition from such companies as Emerson Electric, Sears, and Honda?

With the many factors that could affect the manufacturing of outdoor power equipment in the future, it is certain that Melrose will have to make difficult decisions in his effort to improve Toro's product quality and profitability.

What's Ahead

The introductory case ends with the comment that Ken Melrose will undoubtedly have many difficult decisions to make at Toro. The purpose of this chapter is to assist individuals such as Melrose by discussing (1) the fundamentals of decisions, (2) the elements of the decision situation, (3) the decision-making process, (4) various decision-making conditions, and (5) decision-making tools. These topics are critical to managers and other individuals who make decisions.

 FUNDAMENTALS OF DECISIONS

Definition of a Decision

A **decision** is a choice made between two or more available alternatives. Choosing the best alternative for reaching objectives—the fourth step of the planning process (presented in chapter 4)—is, strictly speaking, making a decision. Although decision making is covered in the planning section of this text, a manager also must make decisions when performing the other three managerial functions: organizing, controlling, and influencing.

Everyone is faced with decision situations each day. A decision situation may involve simply choosing among studying, swimming, or golfing as ways of spending the day. It does not matter which alternative is chosen, only that a choice is actually made.[1]

A practicing manager must make numerous decisions every day.[2] Not all of them are of equal significance to the organization. Some affect a large number of organization members, cost much money to carry out, or have a long-term effect on the organization. These significant decisions can have a major impact not only on the management system itself but also on the career of the manager. Other decisions are fairly insignificant, affecting only a small number of organization members, costing little to carry out, and having only a short-term effect on the organization.

Types of Decisions

Decisions can be categorized by how much time a manager must spend in making them, what proportion of the organization must be involved in making them, and the organizational functions on which they focus.[3] Probably the most generally accepted method of categorizing decisions, however, is based on computer language and divides the decisions into two basic types: programmed and nonprogrammed.[4]

Programmed decisions are routine and repetitive, and the organization typically develops specific ways to handle them. A programmed decision might involve determining how products will be arranged on the shelves of a supermarket. This is a routine and repetitive problem for the organization, and standard arrangement decisions typically are made according to established management guidelines.

A decision is a choice between alternatives.

Programmed decisions are routine and repetitive.

109

TABLE 5.1

Traditional and modern ways of handling programmed and nonprogrammed decisions

Types of Decisions	Decision-Making Techniques	
	Traditional	**Modern**

Programmed:
Routine, repetitive decisions
Organization develops specific processes for handling them
	1. Habit
	2. Clerical routine:
	  Standard operating procedures
	3. Organization structure:
	  Common expectations
	  A system of subgoals
	  Well-defined information channels
		1. Operations research:
		  Mathematical analysis
		  Models
		  Computer simulation
		2. Electronic data processing

Nonprogrammed: One-shot, ill-structured, novel policy decisions Handled by general problem-solving processes	1. Judgment, intuition, and creativity 2. Rules of thumb 3. Selection and training of executives	Heuristic problem-solving techniques applied to: Training human decision makers Constructing heuristic computer programs

Nonprogrammed decisions are one-shot occurrences.

Nonprogrammed decisions, in contrast, typically are one-shot occurrences and are usually less structured than programmed decisions. A nonprogrammed decision might involve whether or not a supermarket should carry an additional type of bread. In making this decision, the manager must consider whether the new bread will stabilize bread sales by competing with existing bread carried in the store or increase bread sales by offering a choice of breads to customers who have never before bought bread in the store. These types of issues must be dealt with before the manager can finally decide whether or not to offer the new bread. Table 5.1 shows traditional and modern ways of handling programmed and nonprogrammed decisions.

Programmed and nonprogrammed decisions should be thought of as being at opposite ends of a programming continuum, as shown in Figure 5.1. The continuum also indicates that some decisions may not clearly be either programmed or nonprogrammed, but some combination of the two.

The "Management in Action" feature for this chapter illustrates a highly publicized nonprogrammed decision that James Burke, a top manager at Johnson & Johnson, had to make. He decided that his company would no longer sell any of its over-the-counter drugs in capsule form. As a result of the decision, Johnson & Johnson incurred costs estimated as high as $150 million to recall its capsules and scrap their production.

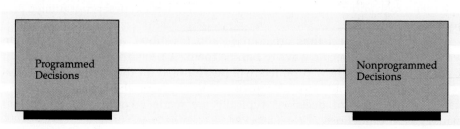

FIGURE 5.1
Continuum of extent of decision programming

JAMES BURKE MAKES A NONPROGRAMMED DECISION AT JOHNSON & JOHNSON

Johnson & Johnson Chairman James Burke is not one to back away from trouble. Appearing last week on the *Donahue* television program to answer questions about the Tylenol poisoning earlier this month, Burke reacted swiftly when one caller denounced the culprit as a terrorist. In a gesture that was rare for a buttoned-down businessman, he clenched his fist and pumped it in the air, as if to say, ''Right on. I agree.''

It was a fitting symbol of the drug manufacturer's dramatic response to the tragedy. Only the day before, Burke had announced that Johnson & Johnson would no longer sell any of its over-the-counter drugs in capsule form. The pharmaceuticals maker saw the move as the best hope of preventing a recurrence of the still unsolved poisoning of Diane Elsroth, 23, of Peekskill, N.Y., who died Feb. 8, after swallowing two Extra-Strength Tylenol capsules laced with potassium cyanide. Said Burke at a press conference: ''We take this action with great reluctance and a heavy heart. But since we can't control random tampering with capsules after they leave our plant, we feel we owe it to consumers to remove capsules from the market.''

The decision will cost Johnson & Johnson as much as $150 million to recall its capsules and scrap their production. In addition to Tylenol, Johnson & Johnson made and sold capsule forms of Sine-Aid, a remedy for sinus congestion, and Dimensyn, a medicine for the relief of menstrual pain. The capsule form of Tylenol amounted to about 30% of the pain reliever's estimated 1985 sales of $525 million. To make up for its loss, the company last week began promoting Tylenol in the form of caplets, which are the smooth, elongated tablets that Johnson & Johnson began producing in 1983, after seven people in the Chicago area were poisoned by tainted Tylenol capsules. The caplets, far more difficult to adulterate, already make up about 15% of all Tylenol sales.

Johnson & Johnson's sudden decision prompted the pharmaceutical industry to re-examine its widespread use of over-the-counter capsules, which now include dozens of preparations ranging from Contac decongestant to Dexatrim diet formula. But as the industry sent its packaging experts to Washington last week for an emergency meeting with Food and Drug Administration officials, most companies said that they would keep on using capsules.

A huge consumer demand for capsules still exists

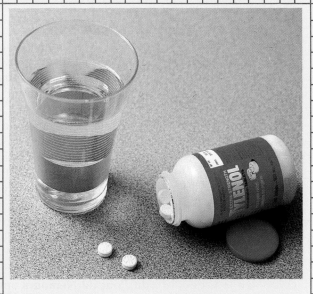

despite the Tylenol scare. Many people find the gelatin-cased medicine easier to swallow and less bitter than tablets. The bright color combinations of capsules also make them more readily identifiable. Moreover, because so many prescription medicines come in capsule form, a common—but false—impression has arisen that capsules are more effective than tablets.

After the Chicago poisonings, which caused Tylenol's share of the pain-killer market to plunge from 35% to 7%, Johnson & Johnson staged what industry experts called a ''miracle'' comeback. The company spent an estimated $300 million to recall 31 million old packages of Tylenol capsules and promote new ones that were ''triple sealed'' to resist tampering. Now the company must restore confidence yet again. It will not be easy: the poisoned woman's mother described the plan to withdraw capsules from the market as ''three years too late.''

Even so, many consumers feel sympathy for the manufacturer, and investors have been impressed by the company's decisiveness. Said Robert Benezra, who follows the drug industry for the investment firm Alex Brown & Sons: ''Johnson & Johnson acted responsibly in the interest of the public's safety. That's how the consumers see it.'' The company's stock price went up 1½ points last week, to 49, in contrast to a fall of 5¾ during the week after the poisoning. Investors generally believe that Johnson & Johnson (1985 revenues: $6.4 billion) has the financial wherewithal to preserve Tylenol's position as the best-selling nonprescription pain reliever. During 1985, the brand held a 34% share of the $1.6 billion market. The company's debts are low, and it holds a cash reserve of some $800 million.

The Responsibility for Making Organizational Decisions

Many different kinds of decisions must be made within an organization—such as how to manufacture a product, how to maintain machines, how to ensure product quality, and how to establish advantageous relationships with customers. With varied decisions of this sort, some type of rationale must be developed to stipulate who within the organization has the responsibility for making which decisions.

One such rationale is based primarily on two factors: the scope of the decision to be made and the levels of management. The **scope of the decision** is the proportion of the total management system that the decision will affect. The greater this proportion, the broader the scope of the decision is said to be. *Levels of management* are simply lower-level management, middle-level management, and upper-level management. The rationale for designating who makes which decisions is this: The broader the scope of a decision, the higher the level of the manager responsible for making that decision. Figure 5.2 illustrates this rationale.

One example of this decision-making rationale is the manner in which E. I. du Pont de Nemours and Company handles decisions related to the research and development function.[5] As Figure 5.3, shows, this organization makes rela-

The broader the scope of a decision, the higher the level of the manager responsible for making that decision.

FIGURE 5.2
Level of managers responsible for making decisions as decision scope increases from *A* to *B* to *C*

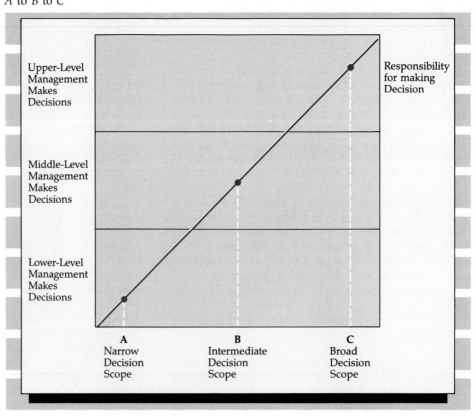

FIGURE 5.3
How scope of decision affects management level making decision at du Pont

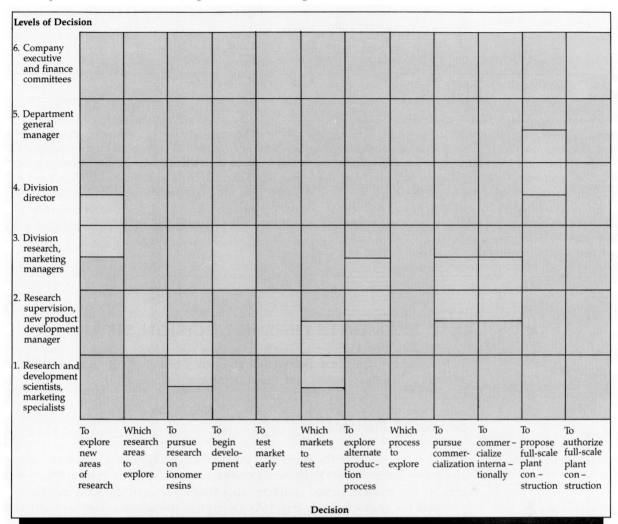

tively narrow-scope research and development decisions, such as "which markets to test" (made by lower-level managers), and relatively broad-scope research and development decisions, such as "authorize full-scale plant construction" (made by upper-level managers).

Even the manager who has the responsibility for making a particular decision can ask the advice of other managers or subordinates. In fact, some managers advise having groups make certain decisions.

Consensus is one method a manager can use in getting a group to arrive at a particular decision.[6] **Consensus** is agreement on a decision by all the individuals involved in making the decision. It usually occurs after lengthy deliberation and discussion by members of the decision group, who may be either all managers or a mixture of managers and subordinates.

Decisions through consensus have both advantages and disadvantages. One advantage is that managers can focus "several heads" on the decision.

Decisions through consensus: Everyone agrees.

Another is that individuals in the decision group are more likely to be committed to implementing a decision if they helped make it. The main disadvantage to decisions through consensus is that discussions relating to the decisions tend to be lengthy and therefore costly.

▌ BACK TO THE CASE

If Ken Melrose, president of Toro Company, was forced to confront an issue such as increasing Toro's manufacturing capability for snow related equipment, he would definitely be faced with a formal decision situation, a situation requiring him to pick one of a number of solutions. Melrose would need to scrutinize this decision carefully because of its significance to the organization and to Melrose himself. Technically, this decision would be nonprogrammed in nature and therefore would be characterized more by judgment than by simple quantitative data.

As the president of Toro, Melrose would probably have the ultimate responsibility for making such a broad-scope decision. This does not mean, however, that Melrose would have to make the decision by himself. He could ask for advice from other Toro employees and perhaps even appoint a group of managers/employees to arrive at a consensus on which decision alternative should be implemented.

▦ ELEMENTS OF THE DECISION SITUATION

Wilson and Alexis have indicated that there are six basic elements in the decision situation.[7] These elements and their definitions follow.

State of Nature

Environmental characteristics influence decision makers.

State of nature refers to the aspects of the decision maker's environment that can affect the choice. Robert B. Duncan conducted a study in which he attempted to identify the environmental characteristics that influenced decision makers. He grouped the characteristics into two categories: the internal environment and the external environment (see Table 5.2).[8]

The Decision Makers

Decision makers are the individuals or groups who actually make the choice among alternatives. According to Dale, weak decision makers can have four different orientations: receptive, exploitation, hoarding, and marketing.[9]

Decision makers who have a receptive orientation believe that the source of all good is outside themselves, and therefore they rely heavily on suggestions from other organization members. Basically, they like others to make their decisions for them.

Decision makers with an exploitation orientation also believe that good is outside themselves, and they are willing to take ethical or unethical steps to steal ideas necessary to make good decisions. They build their organization on the ideas of others and typically extend little or no credit for the ideas to anyone but themselves.

TABLE 5.2

Environmental factors that can influence managerial decision making

Internal Environment	External Environment

1. Organizational personnel component
  a. Educational and technological background and skills
  b. Previous technological and managerial skill
  c. Individual member's involvement and commitment to attaining system's goals
  d. Interpersonal behavior styles
  e. Availability of human resources for utilization within the system
2. Organizational functional and staff units component
  a. Technological characteristics of organizational units
  b. Interdependence of organizational units in carrying out their objectives
  c. Intraunit conflict among organizational functional and staff units
  d. Interunit conflict among organizational functional and staff units
3. Organizational level component
  a. Organizational objectives and goals
  b. Integrative process integrating individuals and groups into contributing maximally to attaining organizational goals
  c. Nature of the organization's product service
	4. Customer component
	  a. Distributors of product or service
	  b. Actual users of product or service
	5. Supplier component
	  a. New materials suppliers
	  b. Equipment suppliers
	  c. Product parts suppliers
	  d. Labor supply
	6. Competitor component
	  a. Competitors for suppliers
	  b. Competitors for customers
	7. Sociopolitical component
	  a. Government regulatory control over the industry
	  b. Public political attitude toward industry and its particular product
	  c. Relationship with trade unions with jurisdiction in the organization
	8. Technological component
	  a. Meeting new technological requirements of own industry and related industries in production of product or service
	  b. Improving and developing new products by implementing new technological advances in the industry

The hoarding orientation is characterized by decision makers who preserve the status quo as much as possible. They accept little outside help, isolate themselves from others, and are extremely self-reliant. These decision makers emphasize maintaining their present existence.

Marketing oriented decision makers consider themselves commodities that are only as valuable as the decisions they make. They try to make decisions that will enhance their value and are therefore conscious of what others think of their decisions.

The ideal decision-making orientation is one that emphasizes trying to realize the potential of the organization as well as of the decision maker. Ideal decision makers try to use all of their talents and are influenced mainly by reason and sound judgment. They do not possess the qualities of the four undesirable decision-making orientations just described.

Ideal decision makers emphasize reason and sound judgment.

Goals to Be Served

The goals that decision makers seek to attain are another element of the decision situation. In the case of managers, these goals should most often be organizational objectives. (Chapter 3 contains specifics about organizational objectives.)

Goals are usually organizational objectives.

Relevant Alternatives

Relevant alternatives can be implemented to solve an existing problem.

The decision situation is usually composed of at least two relevant alternatives. A **relevant alternative** is one that is considered feasible for implementation and for solving an existing problem. Alternatives that cannot be implemented or will not solve an existing problem are irrelevant alternatives and should be excluded from the decision-making situation.

Ordering of Alternatives

Decision makers rank alternatives.

The decision situation must have a process or mechanism that ranks alternatives from most desirable to least desirable. The process can be subjective, objective, or some combination of the two. Past experience of the decision maker is an example of a subjective process, and the rate of output per machine is an example of an objective process.

Choice of Alternatives

The chosen alternative maximizes long-term return.

The last element of the decision situation is an actual choice between available alternatives. This choice establishes the fact that a decision is made. Typically, managers choose the alternative that maximizes long-term return for the organization.

BACK TO THE CASE

If Ken Melrose had to make a decision about whether or not to increase Toro's manufacturing capability for snow related equipment, he would need to be aware of all the elements in the decision situation. Both the internal and external environments of Toro would be one focus of Melrose's analysis. For example, internally, does Toro have the human resources and equipment to increase its manufacturing capability? Externally, is there a customer market for snow related equipment? Reason and sound judgment would need to characterize Melrose's orientation as a decision maker. Also, Melrose would have to keep Toro's organizational objectives in mind and list relevant alternatives to the increase in manufacturing capability of snow related equipment. For example, one relevant alternative might be to increase Toro's manufacturing capability of lawn mowers. In addition, Melrose would need to list relevant alternatives in some order of desirability before choosing an alternative to implement.

THE DECISION-MAKING PROCESS

The decision-making process makes three assumptions.

A decision is a choice of one alternative from a set of available alternatives. The **decision-making process** is the steps the decision maker takes to actually choose this alternative. The evaluation of a decision should be at least partially based on the process used to make the decision.[10]

A model of the decision-making process is presented in Figure 5.4. In order of occurrence, the decision-making steps this model suggests are (1) identifying an existing problem, (2) listing possible alternatives to solve the problem, (3) selecting the most beneficial of these alternatives, (4) putting the selected alternative into action, and (5) gathering feedback to find out if the implemented alter-

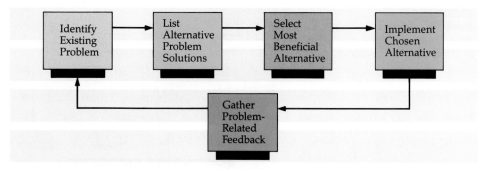

FIGURE 5.4
Model of the decision-making process

native is solving the identified problem. The paragraphs that follow elaborate upon each of these steps and explain their interrelationships.

This model of the decision-making process is based on three primary assumptions.[11] First, the model assumes that humans are economic beings with the objective of maximizing satisfaction or return. Second, it assumes that within the decision-making situation all alternatives and their possible consequences are known. The last assumption is that decision makers have some priority system that allows them to rank the desirability of each alternative. If each of these assumptions is met in the decision-making situation, decision makers probably will make the best possible decision for the organization. In reality, one or more of the assumptions usually are not met, and related decisions, therefore, are usually something less than the best possible for the organization.

Problems are barriers to goal attainment and must be identified.

Identifying an Existing Problem

Decision making is essentially a problem-solving process that involves eliminating barriers to organizational goal attainment. Naturally, the first step in this elimination process is identifying exactly what the problems or barriers are. Only after the barriers have been adequately identified can management take steps to eliminate them. Chester Barnard has stated that organizational problems are brought to the attention of managers mainly through (1) orders issued by managers' supervisors, (2) situations relayed to managers by their subordinates, and (3) the normal activity of the managers themselves.[12]

Listing Alternative Problem Solutions

Once a problem has been identified, managers should list the various possible solutions. Very few organizational problems can be solved in only one way. Managers must search out the many alternative solutions that exist for most organizational problems.

A manager's decision alternatives are limited by various factors.

Before searching for solutions, managers must be aware of five limitations on the number of problem-solving alternatives available: (1) authority factors (for example, a manager's superior may have told the manager that the alternative was feasible); (2) biological or human factors (for example, human factors within the organization may be inappropriate for implementing the alternatives); (3) physical factors (for example, the physical facilities of the organization

FIGURE 5.5
Additional factors that limit a manager's number of acceptable alternatives

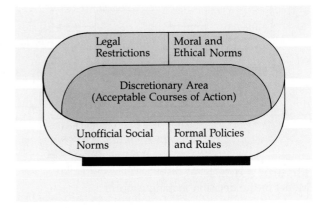

may be inappropriate for certain alternatives to be seriously considered); (4) technological factors (for example, the level of organizational technology may be inadequate for certain alternatives); and (5) economic factors (for example, certain alternatives may be too costly for the organization).[13]

Figure 5.5 presents additional factors that can limit managers' decision alternatives. This figure uses the term *discretionary area* to designate feasible alternatives available to managers. Factors that limit this area are legal restrictions, moral and ethical norms, formal policies and rules, and unofficial social norms.[14]

Selecting the Most Beneficial Alternative

Each alternative should undergo a three-step evaluation.

Decision makers can select the most beneficial solution only after they have evaluated each alternative very carefully. This evaluation should consist of three steps. First, decision makers should list, as accurately as possible, the potential effects of each alternative as if the alternative had already been chosen and implemented. Second, a probability factor should be assigned to each of the potential effects. This would indicate how probable the occurrence of the effect would be if the alternative were implemented. Third, keeping organizational goals in mind, decision makers should compare each alternative's expected effects and their respective probabilities. The alternative that seems to be most advantageous to the organization should be chosen for implementation.

Implementing the Chosen Alternative

The next step is to actually put the chosen alternative into action. Decisions must be supported by appropriate action if they are to have a chance of being successful.

Gathering Problem-Related Feedback

Decision action is evaluated through feedback.

After the chosen alternative has been implemented, decision makers must gather feedback to determine the effect of the implemented alternative on the identified problem. If the identified problem is not being solved, managers need to search out and implement some other alternative.

BACK TO THE CASE

If Ken Melrose were facing a decision such as how to increase product safety, he would first need to identify the problem. For example, he would need to find out if customer injury was the result of faulty parts, inadequate safety devices, or poor operating instructions. Once he identified the problem, he would have to list all possible problem solutions—for example: Can the quality of parts be improved? Would better operating instructions reduce the risk of injury? Can additional safety devices be invented?

After eliminating infeasible solutions, Melrose would have to evaluate all remaining solutions, select one, and implement it. If operating instructions were unreliable because of customer error or if better-quality parts were too expensive to manufacture, the best alternative might be to create new safety devices for Toro products. Melrose would then have to instruct his employees to design and manufacture such devices. Problem related feedback would be extremely important once the safety devices were added. Melrose would need to find out if the new devices did, in fact, reduce customer injury. If they did not, he would need to decide what additional action should be taken to improve product safety.

DECISION-MAKING CONDITIONS

In most instances, it is impossible for decision makers to be sure of exactly what the future consequences of an implemented alternative will be. The word *future* is the key in discussing decision-making conditions. For all practical purposes, because organizations and their environments are constantly changing, future consequences of implemented decisions are not perfectly predictable.

In general, there are three different conditions under which decisions are made. Each of these conditions is based on the degree to which the future outcome of a decision alternative is predictable. These conditions are (1) complete certainty, (2) complete uncertainty, and (3) risk.[15] Figure 5.6 shows these three conditions on a continuum of predictability of the organizational environment, with complete certainty at one end and complete uncertainty at the other.

> The future is not perfectly predictable.

Complete Certainty Condition

The **complete certainty condition** exists when decision makers know exactly what the results of an implemented alternative will be. In this condition, managers have complete knowledge about a decision. All they have to do is list outcomes for alternatives and then pick the outcome with the highest payoff for the organization. For example, the outcome of an investment alternative based on buying government bonds is, for all practical purposes, completely predictable because of established government interest rates. Deciding to implement this

> Complete certainty condition: Results of alternative are known.

FIGURE 5.6
Continuum of decision-making conditions

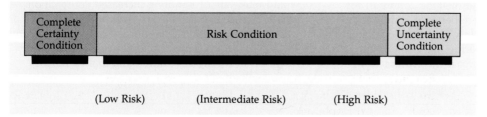

alternative essentially would be making a decision in a complete certainty situation. Unfortunately, most organizational decisions are made outside the complete certainty situation.

Complete Uncertainty Condition

The **complete uncertainty condition** exists when decision makers have absolutely no idea what the results of an implemented alternative will be. The complete uncertainty condition would exist, for example, if there were no historical data on which to base a decision. Not knowing what happened in the past makes it difficult to predict what will happen in the future. In this situation, decision makers usually find that sound decisions are merely a matter of chance. An example of a decision made in a complete uncertainty situation would be choosing to pull the candy machine lever labeled "Surprise of the Day" rather than the lever that would deliver a candy bar that looks delicious. It is fortunate that few organizational decisions are made in the complete uncertainty condition.

Risk Condition

The primary characteristic of the **risk condition** is that decision makers have only enough information about the outcome of each alternative to estimate how probable the outcome will be if the alternative is implemented. Obviously, the risk condition is somewhere between complete certainty and complete uncertainty. The manager who hires two extra salespeople to increase annual organizational sales is deciding in a risk situation. He may believe that the probability is high that these two new salespeople will increase total sales, but it is impossible for him to know for sure. Some risk is associated with this decision.

In reality, *degrees* of risk can be associated with decisions made in the risk situation. The lower the quality of information related to the outcome of an alternative, the closer the situation is to complete uncertainty and the higher the risk of choosing that alternative is. Most decisions made in organizations have some amount of risk associated with them.

■ BACK TO THE CASE

The introductory case reveals that in the future, Ken Melrose probably will have to make a decision regarding how to handle increased competition from other companies. Melrose's decision-making condition for such a situation is somewhere between complete certainty and complete uncertainty about the outcome of his alternatives. He could decide, for example, to lower Toro's prices or to increase advertising to fight off the competition, but he has no guarantee that such measures would produce the desired results. He *does* know, however, what has worked in the past to stop competitors, and thus he is not dealing with a complete unknown. Therefore, any decision Melrose would make about handling increased competition would be made under the risk condition. In other words, Melrose would have to determine the outcome probability for each of his alternatives and base his decision on the alternative that looked most advantageous.

"That, at any rate, is the situation as my coolly analytical left brain sees it. Now let me communicate, if I can, my right brain's gut reaction."

Reprinted by permission of J. B. Handelsman, Harvard Business Review *(September/October 1986).*

⊞ DECISION-MAKING TOOLS

Although some writers indicate that subjective tools, such as extrasensory perception (ESP),[16] can be important to decision making, most managers tend to emphasize more objective decision-making tools, such as linear programming, queuing or waiting-line methods, and game theory.[17] (The cartoon illustrates that some situations can be influenced by both subjective and objective decision tools.) Perhaps the two most widely used of the objective decision-making tools are probability theory and decision trees.

Probability Theory

Probability theory is a decision-making tool used in risk situations—situations wherein decision makers are not completely sure of the outcome of an implemented alternative. Probability refers to the likelihood that an event or outcome will actually occur and allows decision makers to calculate an expected value for each alternative. The **expected value (EV)** for an alternative is the income (I) it would produce multiplied by its probability of making that income (P). In formula form, $EV = I \times P$. Decision makers generally choose and implement the alternative with the highest expected value.

An example will clarify the relationship of probability, income, and expected value. A manager is trying to decide where to open a store that specializes in renting surfboards. She is considering three possible locations (A, B, and C), all of which seem feasible. For the first year of operation, the manager has projected that, under ideal conditions, she would earn $90,000 in Location A, $75,000 in Location B, and $60,000 in Location C. After studying historical weather patterns, however, she has determined that there is only a 20 percent chance, or a .2 probability, of ideal conditions during the first year of operation in Location A. Locations B and C have a .4 and a .8 probability, respectively, for

Probability theory is a decision-making tool for risk situations.

$EV = I \times P$

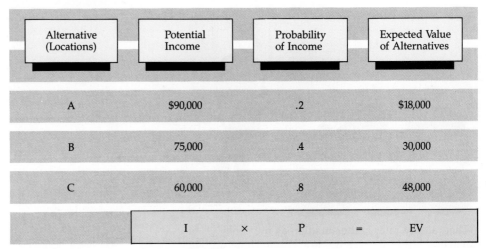

Alternative (Locations)	Potential Income	Probability of Income	Expected Value of Alternatives
A	$90,000	.2	$18,000
B	75,000	.4	30,000
C	60,000	.8	48,000
	I ×	P =	EV

FIGURE 5.7
Expected values for locating surfboard rental store in each of three possible locations

ideal conditions during the first year. Expected values for each of these locations are as follows: Location A—$18,000; Location B—$30,000; Location C—$48,000. Figure 5.7 shows the situation this decision maker is faced with. According to her probability analysis, she should open a store in Location C, the alternative with the highest expected value.

Decision Trees

In the previous section, probability theory was applied to a relatively simple decision situation. Some decisions, however, are more complicated and involve a series of steps. These steps are interdependent; that is, each step is influenced by the step that precedes it. A **decision tree** is a graphic decision-making tool typically used to evaluate decisions containing a series of steps.[18]

A decision tree is a graphic decision-making tool for more complicated decisions.

John F. Magee has developed a classic illustration that outlines how decision trees can be applied to a production decision.[19] In his illustration (see Figure 5.8), the Stygian Chemical Company must decide whether to build a small or a large plant to manufacture a new product with an expected life of ten years. This figure clearly shows that mangement must decide whether to build a small plant or a large one (Decision Point 1). If the choice is to build a large plant, the company could face high or low average product demand or high initial and then low demand. If, however, the choice is to build a small plant, the company could face either initially high or initially low product demand. If the small plant is built and high product demand exists during an initial two-year period, management could then choose whether or not to expand the plant (Decision Point 2). Whether the decision is made to expand or not to expand, management could then face either high or low product demand.

Now that various possible alternatives related to this decision have been outlined, the financial consequence of each different course of action must be compared. To adequately compare these consequences, management must (1) study estimates of investment amounts necessary for building a large plant, for building a small plant, and for expanding a small plant; (2) weigh the proba-

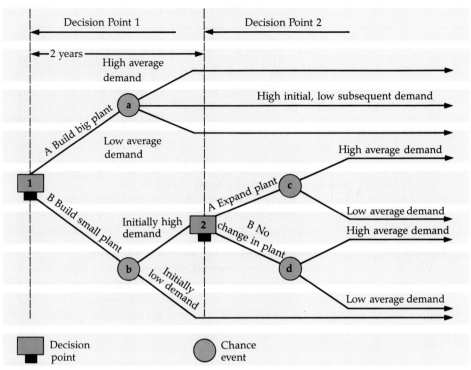

FIGURE 5.8
A basic decision tree illustrating the decision facing Stygian management

bilities of facing different product demand levels for various decision alternatives; and (3) consider projected income yields for each decision alternative.

Analysis of the expected values and net expected gain for each decision alternative helps management to decide on an appropriate choice. *Net expected gain* is defined in this situation as the expected value of an alternative minus the investment cost. For example, if building a large plant yields the highest net expected gain, Stygian management should decide to build the large plant.

BACK TO THE CASE

Ken Melrose has two tools he can use to make better decisions at Toro. First, he can use probability theory to obtain an expected value for various decision alternatives—and then implement the alternative with the highest expected value. For example, Melrose may need to decide whether to devote more of the company's resources to manufacturing snow removal or lawn equipment, a decision that would depend on such factors as manufacturing costs and expected weather conditions.

Second, with decisions that involve a series of steps related to each of several alternatives, Melrose could use a decision tree to assist him in picturing

and evaluating each alternative. For example, he could choose to design a new product or devote more resources to the improvement of existing products. Each of these alternatives would lead to different decision-making steps.

Melrose must remember, however, that business judgment is an essential adjunct to the effective use of any decision-making tool. The purpose of the tool is to improve the quality of the judgment, not to replace it.[20] In other words, Melrose must not only choose alternatives based on probability theory and decision trees, but he must also use his own good judgment in deciding what is best for Toro.

Action Summary

Reread the learning objectives that follow. Each objective is followed by questions. Answering those questions accurately will help you retain the most important concepts discussed in this chapter. After answering each question, check your answer with the answer key at the end of this chapter. (*Hint:* If you have doubt regarding the correct response, consult the page whose number follows the answer.)

From studying this chapter, I will attempt to acquire:

Circle:

T, F
a, b, c, d, e

1. **A fundamental understanding of the term** *decision.*
   a. A decision is a choice made between two or more alternatives.
   b. Decision making is involved in which of the following functions: (a) planning; (b) organizing; (c) controlling; (d) influencing; (e) all of the above.

2. **An understanding of each element of the decision situation.**

a, b, c, d, e
   a. Which type of decision-making orientation involves the belief that the source of all good is outside oneself and that, therefore, one must rely heavily on suggestions from other organizational members: (a) exploitation; (b) hoarding; (c) marketing; (d) natural; (e) receptive.

a, b, c, d, e
   b. According to Wilson and Alexis, all of the following are elements of the decision situation except: (a) the state or nature of the decision environment; (b) the decision makers; (c) the goals to be served; (d) the timeliness of the decision; (e) the relevant alternatives.

3. **An ability to use the decision-making process.**

a, b, c, d, e
   a. After identifying an existing problem, the next major step in the decision-making process is: (a) defining the terminology in the problem statement; (b) listing possible alternatives to solve the problem; (c) investigating possible alternatives to determine their effect on the problem; (d) determining what parties will participate in the problem-solving process; (e) identifying sources of alternatives to solve the problem.

a, b, c, d, e
   b. After going through the decision-making process, if the identified problem is not being solved as a result of the implemented alternative, the manager should: (a) attempt to redefine the problem; (b) turn attention to another problem; (c) search out and implement some other alternative; (d) attempt to implement the alternative until the problem is solved; (e) accept the fact that the problem cannot be solved.

4. **An appreciation for the various situations in which decisions are made.**

T, F
   a. The risk condition exists when decision makers have absolutely no idea of what the results of an implemented alternative will be.

T, F
   b. When operating under the complete uncertainty condition, decision makers usually find that sound decisions are a matter of chance.

5. **An understanding of probability theory and decision trees as decision-making tools.**

a, b, c, d, e
   a. Expected value is determined by using the formula: (a) $EV = I \times P$; (b) $EV = I/P$; (c) $EV = I + P$; (d) $EV = P - I$; (e) $EV = 2P \times I$.

a, b, c, d, e
   b. In the case of the Stygian Chemical Company, the problem was solved through the use of: (a) executive experience; (b) decision tree technique; (c) queuing theory; (d) linear programming; (e) demand probability.

INTRODUCTORY CASE WRAP-UP

"Important Decisions at Toro" (p. 108) and its related back-to-the-case sections were written to help you better understand the management concepts contained in this chapter. Answer the following discussion questions about this introductory case to further enrich your understanding of chapter content:

1. List three alternatives that Melrose might want to consider before making a decision about increasing Toro's manufacturing capability.
2. What information would Melrose need to evaluate these three alternatives?
3. Do you think that you would enjoy making the kinds of decisions at Toro that Melrose must make? Explain.

Issues for Review and Discussion

1. What is a decision?
2. Describe the difference between a significant decision and an insignificant decision. Which would you rather make? Why?
3. List three programmed and three nonprogrammed decisions that the manager of a nightclub would probably have to make.
4. Explain the rationale for determining which managers in the organization are responsible for making which decisions.
5. What is the consensus method of making decisions? When would you use it?
6. List and define the six basic elements of the decision-making situation.
7. How does the receptive orientation for decision making differ from the ideal orientation for decision making?
8. List as many undesirable traits of a decision maker as possible. (They are implied within the explanations of the receptive, exploitation, hoarding, and marketing orientations to decision making.)
9. What is a relevant alternative? An irrelevant alternative?
10. Draw and describe in words the decision-making process presented in this chapter.
11. What is meant by the term *discretionary area*?
12. List the three assumptions on which the decision-making process presented in this chapter is based.
13. Explain the difference between the complete certainty and complete uncertainty decision-making situations.
14. What is the risk decision-making situation?
15. Are there degrees of risk associated with various decisions? Why?
16. How do decision makers use probability theory? Be sure to discuss expected value in your answer.
17. What is a decision tree?
18. Under what conditions are decision trees usually used as decision-making tools?

Sources of Additional Information

Albert, Kenneth J. *Handbook of Business Problem Solving.* New York: McGraw-Hill, 1980.

Baker, Alan J. *Business Decision Making.* New York: St. Martin's Press, 1981.

Byrd, Jack, and L. Ted Moore. *Decision Models for Management.* New York: McGraw-Hill, 1982.

Cohen, Herb. "How You Can Get What You Want by Negotiation." *Nation's Business* 69 (May 1981): 87–90.

Einhorn, Hillel J., and Robin M. Hogarth. "Decision Making: Going Forward in Reverse." *Harvard Business Review* (January/February 1987): 66–70.

Einhorn, Hillel J., and Robin M. Hogarth. "Decision Making under Ambiguity." *Journal of Business* 59 (October 1986): S225–50.

Fox, Harold W. "The Frontiers of Strategic Planning: Intuition or Formal Models?" *Management Review* 70 (April 1981): 8–14.

Goldstein, Marilyn, David Scholthauer, and Brian H. Kleiner. "Management on the Right Side of the Brain." *Personnel Journal* 64 (November 1985): 40.

Heyel, Carl. *The Manager's Bible/How to Resolve 127 Classic Management Dilemmas.* New York: Free Press, 1981.

Kepner, Charles, and Benjamin Tregoe. *The Rational Manager.* New York: McGraw-Hill, 1965.

Mustafi, Chandan Kumar. *Statistical Methods in Managerial Decisions.* Delhi, India: Macmillan India Limited, 1981.

Pickle, Hal B., and Royce L. Abrahamson. *Small Business Management,* 4th ed. New York: Wiley, 1986.

Qubein, Nido R. "How to Make Decisions—Fast." *Management World* 14 (September 1985): 16–17.

Shull, Fremont, Andre Delbecq, and L. L. Cummings. *Organizational Decision Making.* New York: McGraw-Hill, 1970.

Simon, Herbert. *Administrative Behavior.* 3d ed. New York: Free Press, 1976.

Stephenson, Blair Y., and Stephen G. Franklin. "Better Decision Making for a 'Real World' Environment." *Administrative Management* 42 (July 1981): 24–26, 36, 38.

White, Kathy Brittain. "Dynamic Decision Support Teams." *Journal of Systems Management* 35 (June 1984): 26–31.

Wind, Yoram, and Vijay Mahajan. "Designing Product and Business Portfolios." *Harvard Business Review* (January/February 1981): 155–65.

Notes

1. Jack W. Duncan, *Decision Making and Social Issues* (Hinsdale, Ill.: Dryden Press, 1973), 1.
2. S. M. Perrone, "Understanding the Decision Process," *Administrative Management* (May 1968): 88–92.
3. Mervin Kohn, *Dynamic Managing: Principles, Process, Practice* (Menlo Park, Calif.: Cummings, 1977), 58–62.
4. Herbert A. Simon, *The New Science of Management Decision* (New York: Harper & Bros., 1960), 5–8.
5. *The D of Research and Development* (Wilmington, Del.: du Pont, 1966), 28–29.
6. Jack J. Holder, Jr., "Decision Making by Consensus," *Business Horizons* (April 1972): 47–54.
7. Charles Wilson and Marcus Alexis, "Basic Frameworks for Decision," *Academy of Management Journal* 5 (August 1962): 151–64.
8. Robert B. Duncan, "Characteristics of Organizational Environments and Perceived Environmental Uncertainty," *Administrative Science Quarterly* 17 (September 1972): 313–27.
9. See Ernest Dale, *Management: Theory and Practice* (New York: McGraw-Hill, 1973), 548–49. This section of Dale's test is based on Erich Fromm, *Man for Himself* (New York: Holt, Rinehart & Winston, 1947), 62–117.
10. Douglas R. Emery and Francis D. Tuggle, "On the Evaluation of Decisions," *MSU Business Topics* (Spring 1976): 40–48.
11. These assumptions are adapted from James G. March and Herbert A. Simon, *Organizations* (New York: Wiley, 1958), 137–38.
12. Chester I. Barnard, *The Function of the Executive* (Cambridge, Mass.: Harvard University Press, 1938).
13. For further elaboration on these factors, see Robert Tannenbaum, Irving R. Weschler, and Fred Massarik, *Leadership and Organization: A Behavioral Science Approach* (New York: McGraw-Hill, 1961), 277–78.
14. For more discussion of these factors, see F. A. Shull, Jr., A. L. Delbecq, and L. L. Cummings, *Organizational Decision Making* (New York: McGraw-Hill, 1970).
15. F. E. Kast and J. E. Rosenzweig, *Organization and Management: A Systems Approach* (New York: McGraw-Hill, 1970), 385.
16. John Mihalasky, "ESP in Decision Making," *Management Review* (April 1975): 32–37.
17. The scope of this text does not permit elaboration on these three decision-making tools. However, for an excellent discussion on how they are used in decision making, see Richard M. Hodgetts, *Management: Theory, Process and Practice* (Philadelphia: Saunders, 1975), 254–66.
18. William A. Spurr and Charles P. Bonini, *Statistical Analysis for Business Decisions* (Homewood, Ill.: Irwin, 1967), 202–17.
19. John F. Magee, "Decision Trees for Decision Making," *Harvard Business Review* (July/August 1964).
20. Charles H. Lang, "Decision Making," *Manage,* August 1959.

Action Summary Answer Key

1. a. T, p. 109
   b. e, p. 109
2. a. e, p. 114
   b. d, pp. 114–116
3. a. b, p. 117
   b. c, p. 118

4. a. F, p. 120
   b. T, p. 120
5. a. a, p. 121
   b. b, pp. 122–123

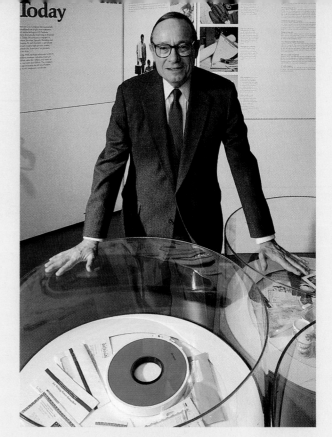

TOUGH DECISIONS AT ROLM AND AMERICAN CAN

Co-founder Kenneth Oshman, 44, of Rolm Corp.—a classic Silicon Valley success, acquired [in 1984] by IBM for $1.9 billion—believes a chief executive's job is to peer intently three to five years into the future, looking for problems. In 1971 the first flicker of an adverse change in Rolm's environment galvanized him into furious activity. Rolm was then a fast-growing $1.5-million-a-year maker of heavy-duty computers, 60% of which were sold to the military—"not a totally rational customer," Oshman recalls. That year, as he began to worry that the market for his specialized product would soon be saturated at around $15 million in annual sales, the Navy announced plans to use only one standard computer design, with specifications identical to a machine made by Sperry Univac. Oshman scrambled to find a second, related product line.

Well, remarked two employees, there's always the computerized telephone business, though that's now grinding up our former employer, Arcata Communications Inc., which distributes such gear. Oshman decided to investigate. Surely, he thought, the Federal Communications Commission's 1968 decision to let non-Bell equipment be hooked up to the phone company's network must create a major opportunity. Six months of research produced a disappointing conclusion: to gain a worthwhile share of the potentially giant market, you'd have to stride in as a full-blown manufacturing, sales, and service behemoth, a task far beyond Rolm's capacity. "But we didn't have a strong enough gut feeling that anything else was right for us," says Oshman. "So we decided to see how we could turn this into a business." After more months of sounding out skeptical telephone experts, he called in reinforcements by hiring a technical expert and a marketing veteran, making Rolm's top management feel even more committed to the decision.

Oshman believed Rolm could develop digital switching equipment much more sophisticated than the equipment AT&T and a handful of competitors were supplying to businesses. What big companies really wanted, Rolm's talks with potential customers found, was a phone system that would route calls over the cheapest available lines, monitor phone use to control costs, and make it easy to let employees keep the same phone number when they changed offices—tasks made to order for a computer-controlled system. The same system could solve Rolm's service problem by having a built-in diagnostic capability that would pinpoint malfunctions on its own.

"As the Boston Consulting Group would tell you," says marketing vice president Richard Moley, 45, "the last thing you ever do is go into a new market with a completely new product." That's true—if you don't want to take the risk of building a giant new business. In this case the product worked, customers bought it, and in nine years Rolm grew at an annual compound rate of 57% to the $660 million in annual sales it reached just before IBM acquired it.

And the premises that set this whole beautifully logical process in motion turned out to be completely wrong. The military-specification computer market did not stop at $15 million a year but grew to an estimated $200 million of which Rolm today has around half. And the Navy began to loosen its single computer standard in 1976 . . .

Sometimes a chief executive's gutsy decision is clearly more a response than a preemptive strike. American Can Co.'s chief, William Woodside, thought he was well in control of a changing world when suddenly that world changed with a vengeance. Company officers had for a decade seen the can business slowly leaking away into new containers. They had steadily been diverting cash from the can business to buy more promising businesses. In the late Seventies, however, high interest rates, inflation, and overcapacity in the company's can and paper operations stopped this process dead. Says Woodside, 63, "We could see ourselves going downhill. We had to free up a lot of cash at one time so that we could then begin to invest in growing businesses."

Woodside told subordinates that the company would have to decide to do something big. But how big is big? What options were thinkable? "You gradually start with the easy stuff and then work up to the things that are unthinkable," Woodside says. "You sort of ratchet yourself along by having a picture of the future that gradually changes as you learn more facts and add more pieces to it."

Early on he looked at the plan of the paper division—which constituted a quarter of the company—to sell one mill and to enter into a joint venture with another. But dramatic as this streamlining seemed to the division, he found that it would make virtually no difference to the corporation—the paper business would still need $1 billion of investment over five years just to keep its share of a hotly competitive market. So he told the division to go back and consider every possible scenario, including selling the business.

By this time Woodside had established a "strategic work group" of half a dozen officers to help him study the alternatives, which the group discussed every week or two with everyone in top management. As is typical of the information-sifting phase of megadecision-making, this procedure had two purposes. First, it really did help Woodside make up his mind, step by step, that only the sale of a big chunk of the company would do; that the can business probably wasn't easily salable; that the paper unit, though the better business, was thus the only candidate.

And as Woodside's senior vice president for strategic planning, Robert Abramson, 42, says, "The process itself was part of the selling of the decision." Observes Woodside, "You must allow all senior managers to get a fair hearing, so you'll end up making a decision that not everybody will agree to, but all will carry out." Those who disagreed, often for fear of losing power, got a chance to see Woodside was unshakeably determined to make big changes and that they'd serve their careers better by helping to shape the future rather than opposing it. Woodside listened patiently at the big meetings to suggestions and challenges: in his own mind he was way ahead of the group on the decision to sell the paper unit—which he finally did in 1982—and half a step ahead on deciding what kind of acquisition he wanted.

Chance and circumstance are as much movers of big decisions as logic, as American Can's ultimate acquisition choice makes clear. Just when Woodside had narrowed the field to three service businesses, an unexpected opportunity arose to acquire the Associated Madison insurance company and its redoubtable chief, Gerald Tsai. An American Can officer, learning that Tsai's bid to build his own financial services empire had suddenly collapsed, rushed to get him together with Woodside. The two men struck a deal. Woodside's company bought Tsai's operation, and the Wall Street veteran joined American Can in 1982; at 56, he is now vice chairman and is considered a strong candidate to succeed Woodside.

DISCUSSION ISSUES

1. Would you categorize the decisions made at Rolm and American Can as programmed or nonprogrammed? Were the techniques used by Oshman and Woodside more traditional or modern (see Figure 5.1)? Explain.
2. Which environmental factors (see Figure 5.5) did Oshman and Woodside consider in the process of making their decisions?
3. Which decision making steps are evident in the Oshman and Woodside decisions? State specific examples.
4. What specific actions did Oshman and Woodside take to reduce the risk associated with their decisions?

STUDENT LEARNING OBJECTIVES

From studying this chapter, I will attempt to acquire:

1. Definitions of both strategic planning and strategy.
2. An understanding of the strategy management process.
3. A knowledge of the impact of environmental analysis on strategy formulation.
4. Insights on how to use critical question analysis and SWOT analysis to formulate strategy.
5. An understanding of how to use business portfolio analysis to formulate strategy.
6. Insights on what tactical planning is and on how strategic and tactical planning should be coordinated.

C H A P T E R

6

TYPES OF PLANNING: STRATEGIC AND TACTICAL

CHAPTER OUTLINE

PLANNING FOR HOSPITAL CORPORATION OF AMERICA

Many changes are taking place in the health-care industry. Improvements in medical technology, surgical procedures, and hospital facilities are obvious examples. One change, however, may be apparent to neither the casual observer nor the hospital patient. More and more hospitals have changed from being operated as nonprofit community organizations to being operated for profit.

The giant in this "hospitals for profit" movement is Hospital Corporation of America (HCA). It owns and manages approximately 400 hospital facilities throughout the world, cares for about 5 million patients a day, and has over 350,000 physicians affiliated with it. HCA has made outstanding progress since its founding in 1968. In 1982 its revenues rose nearly 50 percent, and in 1987 they reached $4.7 billion.

HCA is operated by Dr. Thomas Frist, Jr., the son of one of the cofounders. Although a surgeon by training, Dr. Frist sees himself more as a professional manager than as a physician. His professional reading probably focuses more on the latest management techniques than on the latest surgical techniques.

Profit oriented hospitals and nonprofit hospitals are presently at war. Profit oriented hospitals have begun taking some nontraditional steps to compete for patient dollars. For example, some give birthday parties for babies born in their hospitals as a way of encouraging patients to return for future treatment. Others offer partial reductions on hospital bills if nurses do not respond to patient "call signals" within allotted amounts of time.

Nonprofit hospitals, however, are putting up a

good fight. Some are developing satellite treatment centers—small medical facilities in which physicians can perform minor surgery and deliver babies. Since these treatment centers do not require the full resources of the hospital, patient costs can be cut nearly in half.

Although Dr. Frist and HCA have been successful in recent years, the nonprofit hospitals' promise of substantially cutting medical costs through satellite centers will undoubtedly draw a number of patients. It is difficult to forecast just how many patients might be lured away from HCA-run hospitals by these satellite centers. However, it certainly would seem advisable for Dr. Frist to develop a plan that would enable HCA to compete successfully with them.

What's Ahead

Dr. Thomas Frist, Jr., the head of Hospital Corporation of America in the introductory case, is faced with developing a plan that will help his corporation compete with nonprofit satellite treatment centers. The material in this chapter suggests that Dr. Frist's efforts to meet this planning challenge should focus on the two basic types of organizational planning: strategic and tactical.

⊞ STRATEGIC PLANNING

For managers to be successful strategic planners, they must understand the fundamentals of strategic planning and how to formulate strategic plans.

Fundamentals of Strategic Planning

Defining Strategic Planning

Strategic planning is long-range planning that focuses on the organization as a whole.[1] Managers consider the organization as a total unit and ask themselves what must be done in the long term to attain organizational goals. *Long range* is usually defined as a period of time extending about three to five years into the future. Hence, in strategic planning, managers try to determine what their organization should do to be successful at some point three to five years in the future.

Managers may have a problem trying to decide exactly how far into the future they should extend their strategic planning. As a general rule, they should follow the **commitment principle,** which states that managers should commit funds for planning only if they can anticipate, in the foreseeable future, a return on planning expenses as a result of the long-range planning analysis. Realistically, planning costs are an investment and therefore should not be incurred unless a reasonable return on that investment is anticipated.

Strategic planning is long-range planning for the attainment of organizational goals.

Defining Strategy

Strategy is defined as a broad and general plan developed to reach long-range objectives. Organizational strategy can, and generally does, focus on many different organizational areas,[2] such as marketing, finance, production, research and development, personnel,[3] and public relations.[4]

Actually, strategy is the end result of strategic planning. Although larger organizations tend to be more precise in their development of organizational strategy than smaller organizations,[5] every organization should have a strategy of some sort.[6] For a strategy to be worthwhile, however, it must be consistent with organizational objectives, which in turn must be consistent with organizational purpose. Table 6.1 illustrates this relationship between organizational objectives and strategy by presenting sample organizational objectives and strategies for three well-known business organizations.

Strategy is the end result of strategic planning.

It must be consistent with organizational goals and purpose.

TABLE 6.1

Examples of organizational objectives and related strategies for three organizations in different business areas

Company	Type of Business	Sample Organization Objectives	Strategy to Accomplish Objectives
(a)	Automobile manufacturing	1. Regain market share recently lost to General Motors 2. Regain quality reputation that was damaged because of Pinto gas tank explosions	1. Resize and down-size present models 2. Continue to produce sub-compact, intermediate, standard, and luxury cars 3. Emphasize use of program-med combustion engines instead of diesel engines
(b)	Fast food	Increase productivity	1. Increase people efficiency 2. Increase machine efficiency
(c)	Transportation	1. Continue company growth 2. Continue company profits	1. Modernize 2. Develop valuable real estate holdings 3. Complete an appropriate railroad merger

Strategy Management

Strategy management is the process of ensuring that an organization possesses and benefits from the use of an appropriate organizational strategy. Within this definition, an appropriate strategy is a strategy best suited to the needs of an organization at a particular time.

The process of strategy management is generally thought to consist of four sequential and continuing steps: (1) strategy formulation, (2) strategy implementation, (3) strategy results measurement, and (4) strategy evaluation. The relationships and definitions of these steps are presented in Figure 6.1.

Perhaps the most important lesson to be learned from the figure is that the making of a strategy is only one of four important steps in strategy management. For an organization to get maximum benefit from a strategy, the strategy must be implemented, or put into action, constantly watched to see what effect it is having on the organization, and evaluated, or examined, to see if it is having the effect management desires. If the effect is desirable, perhaps the strategy could remain as is, with strategy results measurement and strategy evaluation continuing so as to determine if change will be necessary in the future. If the effect of

Strategy manage-
ment consists of
1. Strategy formula-
tion.
2. Strategy imple-
mentation.
3. Strategy results
measurement.
4. Strategy evalua-
tion.

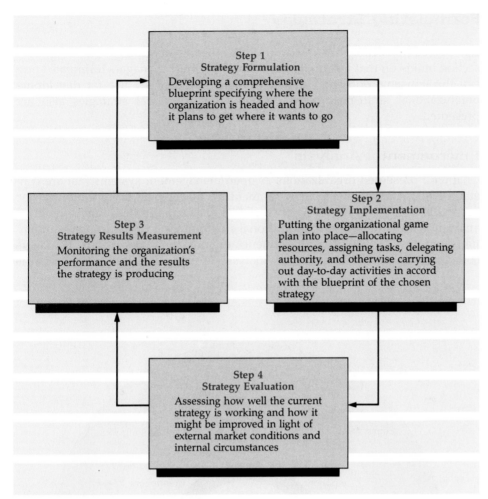

FIGURE 6.1
The process of strategy management

a strategy is undesirable, however, management would probably start the entire strategy management process over again.

In developing a plan to compete with the nonprofit satellite treatment centers, Dr. Thomas Frist, Jr., Hospital Corporation of America manager, should probably begin by thinking strategically. That is, he should try to determine what can be done to ensure that HCA will be successful at some point three to five years in the future. Naturally, combating the satellite treatment centers will be a crucial part of this strategic focus. Dr. Frist must be careful, however, to spend funds on strategic planning only if he can anticipate a return on these expenses in the foreseeable future.

The end result of Dr. Frist's strategic planning will be a strategy—a broad plan that outlines what must be done to reach long-range objectives and carry out the organizational purpose of HCA. This strategy will focus on many organizational areas, one of which will be competing with satellite treatment centers. Once the strategy has been formulated, Dr. Frist must conscientiously carry out the remaining steps of the strategy management process: strategy implementation, strategy results measurement, and strategy evaluation.

Formulating Strategies

The preceding section discussed the fundamentals of strategic planning. This section builds on that information by explaining how managers formulate strategy through environmental analysis and what tools they use for developing organizational strategies. Several sample organizational strategies also are presented.

Environmental Analysis

Chapter 2 presented organizations as open management systems that are constantly interacting with their environment. In essence, an organization can be successful only if it is appropriately matched to its environment. **Environmental analysis** is the study of the organizational environment to pinpoint environmental factors that can significantly influence organizational operations. Managers commonly perform environmental analyses to help them understand what is

Environmental analysis pinpoints factors that can influence operations.

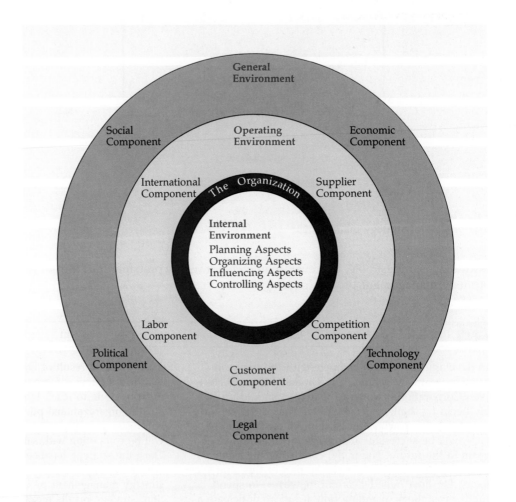

FIGURE 6.2
The organization, the levels of its environment, and the components of those levels

happening both inside and outside their organization and to increase the probability that the organizational strategies they develop will appropriately reflect the organizational environment.

In order to perform an environmental analysis efficiently and effectively, a manager must thoroughly understand how organizational environments are structured.[7] For purposes of environmental analysis, the environment of an organization is generally divided into three distinct levels: the general environment, the operating environment, and the internal environment.[8] Figure 6.2 illustrates the relative positions of these levels to one another and to the organization; it also shows the important components of each level. Over all, managers must be aware of these three environmental levels, understand how each level affects organizational performance, and then formulate organizational strategies in response to this understanding.

The three levels of the organizational environment are general, operating, and internal.

The General Environment

The level of an organization's external environment that contains components normally having broad long-term implications for managing the organization is the **general environment.** The components normally considered part of the general environment are economic, social, political, legal, and technological.

The general environment has broad long-term management implications; its components are economic, social, political, legal, and technological.

The *economic component* is the part of the general environment that indicates how resources are being distributed and used within the environment. This component is based on **economics,** the science that focuses on understanding how people of a particular community or nation produce, distribute, and use various goods and services. Important issues considered in an economic analysis of an environment generally include the wages paid to labor, the taxes paid by labor and businesses, the cost of materials used during the production process, and the prices at which produced goods and services are sold to customers.[9]

Wages, taxes, costs, and prices are examined in an economic analysis.

Economic issues such as these can significantly influence the environment in which a company operates and the ease or difficulty the organization experiences in attempting to reach its objectives. For example, it should be somewhat easier for an organization to sell its products at higher prices if potential consumers in the environment are earning relatively high wages and paying relatively low taxes than if these same potential customers are earning relatively low wages and have significantly fewer after-tax dollars to spend.

Economic issues can have an impact on attainment of objectives.

Naturally, organizational strategy should reflect the economic issues in the organization's environment. To build on the preceding example, if the total amount of after-tax income that potential customers earn has significantly declined, an appropriate organizational strategy might be to lower the price of goods or services to make them more affordable. Such a strategy should be evaluated carefully, however, since it could have a serious impact on organizational profits.

Organizational strategy should reflect economic issues.

The *social component* is the part of the general environment that describes the characteristics of the society in which the organization exists. Two important features of a society commonly studied during environmental analysis are demographics and social values.[10]

Demographics are the statistical characteristics of a population. The characteristics include changes in number of people and income distribution among various population segments. These changes can influence the reception of goods and services within the organization's environment and thus should be reflected in organizational strategy.

Organizational strategy should reflect demographics.

For example, the demand for retirement housing probably would increase dramatically if both the number and the income of retirees in a particular market area doubled. Effective organizational strategy would include a mechanism for dealing with such a probable increase in demand within the organization's environment.

Demographics should also affect recruitment strategy.

An understanding of demographics also can be helpful in developing a strategy aimed at recruiting new employees to fill certain positions within an organization. Knowing that only a small number of people have a certain type of educational background, for example, would indicate to an organization that it should compete more intensely to attract these people. To formulate a recruitment strategy, managers need a clear understanding of the demographics of the groups from which employees eventually will be hired.

Social values are the relative degrees of worth that society places on the ways in which it exists and functions. Over time, social values can change dramatically, causing obvious changes in the way people live. Table 6.2 offers several brief examples of how changes in social values can cause changes in the way people live; these changes alter the organizational environment and, as a result, have an impact on organizational strategy. It is important for managers to re-

TABLE 6.2

Examples of how social values can affect strategy

- For many years, people were opposed to gambling. This has changed in some places, such as Las Vegas and Atlantic City. And a number of states have legalized state-run lotteries. But legalized gambling was voted down in Miami, Florida. This value has special relevance for such firms as Resorts International and Holiday Inns.
- At one time, it was thought that families should have two to four children. Today, not all accept this norm, and the new standards have a big impact on P&G (Pampers), Gerber (baby food), builders (houses versus condominiums), Mattel (toys), and others.
- It used to be common for retired people, single people, widows, and widowers to live with relatives. Now there is a trend toward living alone, and this has a big impact on builders, appliance manufacturers, food packers, magazine publishers, and others.
- For years, most married women stayed home. Now, most work. This has caused problems for firms that sold door-to-door (Avon and Fuller Brush) and has increased business for a variety of firms, such as nursery schools, prepared food firms, restaurants (two-employee families eat out more frequently), and home security systems, to name a few.
- At one time, people lived in one place all their lives. Now, there are thousands of people who are nomads. They live in campers and motor homes and move from place to place as jobs open up or as the spirit moves them. This provides opportunities for and threats to firms.
- Increased education has led to new attitudes on the part of employees about how many hours they wish to work, the quality of life they expect at work, and the kind of supervisory style they expect, which can affect how strategies are developed and implemented. New benefits programs are also needed for new life-styles.
- After the Three Mile Island nuclear plant incident, more people started to question the safety of nuclear power. New plant construction and uranium mining in Canada, the United States, and Australia have been cut drastically, while coal operators are seeing new opportunities.

member that although changes in the values of a particular society may come either slowly or quickly, they are inevitable.[11]

The *political component* is the part of the general environment that contains the elements related to government affairs. Examples include the type of government in existence, the government's attitude toward various industries, lobbying efforts by interest groups, progress on the passage of laws, and political party platforms and candidates.

The *legal component* is the part of the general environment that contains passed legislation. Simply stated, this component is the rules or laws that society's members must follow. Some examples of legislation specifically aimed at the operation of organizations are the Clean Air Act of 1963, the Air Quality Act of 1967, the Occupational Safety and Health Act of 1970, the Consumer Product Safety Act of 1972, and the Energy Policy and Conservation Act of 1975. Naturally, over time, new laws are passed and some old ones are eliminated.

The *technology component* is the part of the general environment that includes new approaches to producing goods and services. These approaches can include new procedures as well as new equipment. The trend toward exploiting robots to improve productivity is an example of the technology component. The increasing use of robots in the next decade should vastly improve the efficiency of U.S. industry. Installation of these computer-controlled machines is expected to grow at an annual rate of 35 to 45 percent within the next ten years.[12]

The Operating Environment

The level of an organization's external environment that contains components normally having relatively specific and more immediate implications for managing the organization is the **operating environment**. As Figure 6.2 shows, major components of this environmental level are generally thought to include customers, competition, labor, suppliers, and international issues.

The *customer component* is the operating environment segment that is composed of factors relating to those who buy goods and services provided by the organization. Profiles—detailed descriptions—of those who buy organizational products are commonly created by businesses. Developing such profiles helps management generate ideas for improving customer acceptance of organizational goods and services. The "Management in Action" feature for this chapter illustrates how John Akers, the chief executive officer at International Business Machines (IBM) has included customer feedback as part of the strategic management process.

The *competition component* is the operating environment segment that is composed of those with whom an organization must battle in order to obtain resources. Since understanding competitors is a key factor in developing effective strategy, understanding the competitive environment is a fundamental challenge to management. Basically, the purpose of competitive analysis is to help management understand the strengths, weaknesses, capabilities, and likely strategies of existing and potential competitors.[13]

The *labor component* is the operating environment segment that is composed of factors influencing the supply of workers available to perform needed organizational tasks. Issues such as skill levels, trainability, desired wage rates, and average age of potential workers are important to the operation of the organization. Another important but often overlooked issue is the potential workers' desire to work for a particular organization.

Margin notes:

Organizational strategy should reflect social values.

The political component is related to government affairs.

The legal component involves passed legislation.

The technology component includes new approaches to production.

The operating environment includes relatively specific issues with more immediate implications.

Buyers of goods and services are profiled by organizations.

The organization must battle others to obtain resources.

CUSTOMER FEEDBACK IN STRATEGIC MANAGEMENT AT IBM

John Akers had done the unthinkable. When his senior managers filed into a top-secret strategy conference last fall, they found six *outsiders*, all invited by Akers. The aliens were customers, and their mission was to tell IBM why it had just suffered through two of its worst years ever.

For two days Akers sat in the back of the room, asking questions and taking notes. Then, in rapid order, he summarized every comment the customers had made and reeled off details of the actions Big Blue would take to answer their criticisms. The visitors were astonished. Says one: "Nobody realized the extent to which he was listening."

The unorthodox meeting was vintage Akers: direct, decisive, and with all the bases covered. At 52 he is handsome, charming, articulate, and supremely self-confident, a chief executive from central casting. Critics say Akers is not as smart as some of his predecessors. But they give him high marks for sharp instincts, sure grasp of the big picture, and undoubted ability to lead. At one session in January he declared to his executives, "It's time for you and me to take a trip to the woodshed," then chewed them out for their errors. They gave him a standing ovation.

Akers is relentlessly self-disciplined. Says his high school buddy and Yale College roommate, Don Riley: "In the dormitory, John would even schedule time for playing cards." His desk was neat, his laundry sorted, his papers in on time (he earned mostly Bs). As a manager, subordinates say, Akers is "unusually balanced" and superb at delegation. He wheels his brown Mercedes out of the parking lot most days by 5:30 P.M. and never works weekends. When he's off, he's *off*—playing golf or bridge, relaxing with his wife and three children at home in Connecticut, or renovating his summer house on Nantucket.

Like most of IBM's chief executives, Akers rose from sales and marketing. In 1971 he became administrative assistant to Frank Cary, then an executive vice president. Within ten months of Akers' arrival, Cary

John Akers

became chairman and CEO. From then on Akers was a serious contender for the top spot.

Akers was made chief executive in 1984, only to find a mixed legacy. In the late 1970s, IBM had launched a big expansion, spending close to $50 billion on plant, equipment, and R&D. Then demand for computers unexpectedly diminished. Net earnings flattened to $6.5 billion in 1985 and dropped to $4.8 billion last year. Return on equity, which peaked in 1984 at 26.5%, fell to 14.4% in 1986.

Having cut costs by $700 million last year, Akers is striving to take the company "back to basics," as he puts it. IBM has told salesmen, who were spending only 30% of their time with customers and the rest in the office, to reverse those percentages. Akers has rousted 6,800 employees from plant, lab, and staff positions to IBM's marketing offices. Says Stephen P. Cohen, a former IBMer now at Gartner Securities, which analyzes computer stocks: "Marketing is back in the driver's seat."

The *supplier component* is the operating environment segment that entails all variables related to the individuals or agencies that provide organizations with resources needed to produce goods or services. The individuals or agencies are called **suppliers.** Issues such as how many suppliers offer specified resources for sale, the relative quality of the materials offered by suppliers, the reliability of supplier deliveries, and the credit terms offered by suppliers all become important in managing an organization effectively and efficiently.

The supply of workers is influenced by skill, trainability, wages, and age.

Suppliers are providers of organizational resources.

The *international component* is the operating environment segment that is composed of all the factors relating to the international implications of organizational operations. Although not all organizations must deal with international issues, the number is increasing dramatically and continually. Significant factors in the international component include other countries' laws, culture, economics, and politics.[14] Important variables within each of these four categories are presented in Table 6.3.

International implications for organizations include other countries' laws, culture, economics, and politics.

The Internal Environment

The level of an organization's environment that exists inside the organization and normally has immediate and specific implications for managing the organization is the **internal environment.** In broad terms, the internal environment includes marketing, finance, and accounting. From a more specifically management viewpoint, it includes planning, organizing, influencing, and controlling

The internal environment includes specific issues with immediate implications.

TABLE 6.3

Important aspects of the international component of the organization's operating environment

Legal Environment	*Cultural Environment*
Legal tradition	Customs, norms, values, beliefs
Effectiveness of legal system	Language
Treaties with foreign nations	Attitudes
Patent and trademark laws	Motivations
Laws affecting business firms	Social institutions
	Status symbols
	Religious beliefs
Economic Environment	*Political System*
Level of economic development	Form of government
Population	Political ideology
Gross national product	Stability of government
Per capita income	Strength of opposition parties and groups
Literacy level	Social unrest
Social infrastructure	Political strife and insurgency
Natural resources	Government attitude toward foreign firms
Climate	Foreign policy
Membership in regional economic blocks (EEC, LAFTA, etc.)	
Monetary and fiscal policies	
Nature of competition	
Currency convertability	
Inflation	
Taxation system	
Interest rates	
Wage and salary levels	

TABLE 6.4

Several management-specific aspects of an organization's internal environment and questions related to exploring them

Planning Aspects
- Are organizational plans clearly linked to organizational goals?
- Is the sequencing for the performance of specific tasks appropriate?
- Are plans developed for both the short term and the long term?

Organizing Aspects
- Are tasks assigned to the right people?
- Do organizing efforts put plans into action?
- Are tasks appropriately assigned to either individuals or groups?

Influencing Aspects
- Do the rewards offered employees actually motivate them?
- Are organization members encouraged to do work that actually contributes to organizational goal attainment?
- Is communication within the organization effective and efficient?

Controlling Aspects
- Is information gathered to measure recent performance?
- Is present performance compared to preestablished standards?
- Are organizational characteristics modified when necessary to ensure that preestablished standards are met?

within the organization. Table 6.4 contains these more management-specific factors in the internal environment and sample questions that managers can ask in exploring them.

BACK TO THE CASE

As part of his strategy development process, Dr. Frist should spend time analyzing the environment in which Hospital Corporation of America exists. Naturally, he should focus on his company's general, operating, and internal environments. Environmental factors that probably would be important for him to consider as he pursues strategic planning include levels of income and medical insurance possessed by potential patients in various areas, ages of potential patients within these areas, and social values regarding such issues as obtaining medical care in a traditional hospital versus a nontraditional satellite treatment center. Obtaining information about environmental issues such as these will increase the probability that any strategy developed for HCA will be appropriate for the environment in which the firm operates and that the firm will be successful in the long term.

Tools for Developing Organizational Strategies

Strategy development tools include critical question analysis, SWOT analysis, and business portfolio analysis.

The preceding material emphasized that, since an organization must be well suited to its environment, the development of organizational strategy should include an environmental analysis. This section focuses on the special tools and techniques used to systematically develop organizational strategy that is based on the results of environmental analysis. These tools are (1) critical question analysis, (2) SWOT analysis, and (3) business portfolio analysis.

The three strategy development tools are related but distinct. Managers should use whichever one tool or combination of tools that seem most appropriate for them and their organizations.

Critical Question Analysis

A synthesis of the ideas of several contemporary management writers suggests that formulating appropriate organizational strategy is a process of **critical question analysis**—answering the following four basic questions:[15]

What are the purposes and objectives of the organization? The answer to this question states where the organization wants to go. As indicated earlier, appropriate strategy reflects organizational purpose and objectives. By answering this question during strategy formulation, managers are likely to remember this important point and thereby minimize inconsistencies among purposes, objectives, and strategies.

Where is the organization presently going? The answer to this question can tell managers if an organization is achieving organizational goals and, if so, whether the level of such progress is satisfactory. Whereas the first question focuses on where the organization wants to go, this one focuses on where the organization is actually going.

In what kind of environment does the organization now exist? Both internal and external environments—factors both inside and outside the organization—are covered in this question. For example, assume that a poorly trained middle-management team and a sudden influx of competitors in a market are factors that exist respectively in the internal and external environments of an organization. Any strategy formulated, if it is to be appropriate, probably should deal with these factors.

What can be done to better achieve organizational objectives in the future? The answer to this question actually results in the strategy of the organization. The question should be answered, however, only after managers have had adequate opportunity to reflect on the answers to the previous three questions. In other words, managers can develop appropriate organizational strategy only if they have a clear understanding of where the organization wants to go, where the organization is going, and in what environment the organization exists.

SWOT Analysis

SWOT analysis is a strategic planning tool that matches internal organizational strengths and weaknesses with external opportunities and threats.[16] (SWOT is an acronym for a firm's S̲trengths and W̲eaknesses and its environmental O̲pportunities and T̲hreats.) SWOT analysis is based on the assumption that if managers carefully review such strengths, weaknesses, opportunities, and threats, a useful strategy for ensuring organizational success will become evident. Table 6.5 contains several key considerations that managers should cover in performing a SWOT analysis.

Business Portfolio Analysis

Another strategy development tool that has gained wide acceptance is **business portfolio analysis,** the development of business related strategy that is based

Margin notes:

Answering questions about

where the organization wants to go,

where the organization is going,

and the environment in which the organization exists

results in strategy.

SWOT analysis involves reviewing strengths, weaknesses, opportunities, and threats.

Business portfolio analysis is based primarily on market share and market growth rate.

TABLE 6.5
Important considerations for SWOT analysis

Internal

Strengths	*Weaknesses*
A distinctive competence?	No clear strategic direction?
Adequate financial resources?	A deteriorating competitive position?
Good competitive skills?	Obsolete facilities?
Well thought of by buyers?	Subpar profitability because . . . ?
An acknowledged market leader?	Lack of managerial depth and talent?
Well-conceived functional area strategies?	Missing key skills or competences?
Access to economies of scale?	Poor track record in implementing strategy?
Insulated (at least somewhat) from strong competitive pressures?	Plagued with internal operating problems?
Proprietary technology?	Vulnerable to competitive pressures?
Cost advantages?	Falling behind in R&D?
Competitive advantages?	Too narrow a product line?
Product innovation abilities?	Weak market image?
Proven management?	Competitive disadvantages?
Other?	Below-average marketing skills?
	Inability to finance needed changes in strategy?
	Other?

External

Opportunities	*Threats*
Enter new markets or segments?	Likely entry of new competitors?
Add to product line?	Rising sales of substitute products?
Diversify into related products?	Slower market growth?
Add complementary products?	Adverse government policies?
Integrate vertically?	Growing competitive pressures?
Able to move to better strategic group?	Vulnerability to business cycles?
Complacency among rival firms?	Growing bargaining power of customers or suppliers?
Faster market growth?	Changing buyer needs and tastes?
Other?	Adverse demographic changes?
	Other?

primarily on market share of businesses and the growth of markets in which businesses exist.[17] The philosophy on which business portfolio analysis is based is that organizations should develop strategy much as they handle investment portfolios. Just as sound investments should be supported and unsound ones discarded, sound organizational activities should be emphasized and unsound ones deemphasized.

The first step in performing a business portfolio analysis is identifying strategic business units (SBUs) that exist within an organization. A **strategic business unit** is a significant organization segment that is analyzed to develop organizational strategy aimed at generating future business or revenue. Exactly what constitutes an SBU varies from organization to organization. In larger organizations, an SBU could be a company division, a single product, or a complete product line. In smaller organizations, it might be the entire company. Although

Strategic business units (SBUs) vary in form but have four common characteristics.

SBUs vary drastically in form, each has the characteristics of (1) being a single business or collection or related businesses, (2) having its own competitors, (3) having a manager who is accountable for its operation, and (4) being an area that can be independently planned for within the organization.[18]

After SBUs have been identified for a particular organization, the next step in a business portfolio analysis is to categorize them as being within one of the following four quadrants of the business portfolio matrix (see Figure 6.3):

1. *Stars* SBUs that are "stars" have a high share of a high-growth market and typically need large amounts of cash to support their rapid and significant growth. Stars also generate large amounts of cash for the organization and are usually areas in which management can make additional investments and earn attractive returns.

2. *Cash cows* SBUs that are "cash cows" have a large share of a market that is growing only slightly. Naturally, these SBUs provide the organization with large amounts of cash. Since the market is not growing significantly, however, the cash is generally used to meet the financial demands of the organization in other areas, such as in the expansion of a star SBU.

3. *Question marks* SBUs that are "question marks" have a small share of a high-growth market. They are called "question marks" because it is uncertain whether management should invest more cash in them to get a larger share of the market or should deemphasize or eliminate them because such an investment would be ineffective. Naturally, through further investment, management attempts to turn question marks into stars.

4. *Dogs* SBUs that are "dogs" have a relatively small share of a low-growth market. They may barely support themselves, or they may even drain cash resources that other SBUs have generated. Examples of dogs are buggy whips and slide rules.

Companies such as General Electric, Westinghouse, and Shell Oil have used business portfolio analysis in their strategy management processes. There are, however, some possible pitfalls in this technique. For example, business

SBUs are categorized as:

1. "Stars"— high-growth market, high market share.

2. "Cash cows"— low-growth market, high market share.

3. "Question marks"—high-growth market, small market share.

4. "Dogs"— low-growth market, low market share.

Various factors must be weighed carefully when using business portfolio analysis.

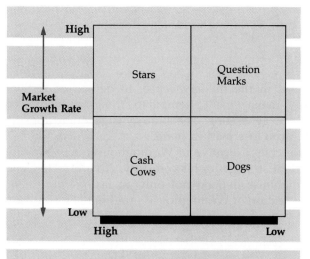

FIGURE 6.3
The business portfolio matrix

portfolio analysis does not consider such factors as (1) various types of risk associated with product development, (2) threats that inflation and other economic conditions can create in the future, and (3) social, political, and ecological pressures.[19] Managers must remember to weigh such factors carefully when designing organizational strategy based on this model.

Sample Organizational Strategies

Analyzing the organizational environment and applying one or more of the strategy tools—critical question analysis, SWOT analysis, and business portfolio analysis—give managers a foundation on which to formulate an organizational strategy. Four of the organizational strategies that can evolve are growth, stability, retrenchment, and divestiture. The discussion of sample organizational strategies will feature business portfolio analysis as the tool used to arrive at the strategy, but the same strategies could also result from critical question analysis or SWOT analysis.

Growth

Growth is a strategy to increase business.

Growth is a strategy adopted by management to increase the amount of business that an SBU is currently generating. The growth strategy is generally applied to star SBUs or question mark SBUs that hold the potential of becoming stars. Management generally invests substantial amounts of money to implement this strategy and may even sacrifice short-term profit to build long-term gain.[20]

Managers can also encourage growth by purchasing an SBU from another organization. For example, Black & Decker, not satisfied with being an international power in power tools, purchased General Electric's small-appliance business. Through this purchase, Black & Decker hoped that the amount of business it did would grow significantly over the long term.[21]

Stability

Stability is a strategy to maintain or slightly improve business.

Stability is a strategy adopted by management to maintain or slightly improve the amount of business that an SBU is generating. This strategy is generally applied to cash cows, since these SBUs are already in an advantageous position. Management must be careful, however, that the strategy doesn't turn cash cows into dogs.

Retrenchment

Retrenchment is a strategy to strengthen or protect business.

In this section, *retrench* is used in the military sense: to defend or fortify. Through **retrenchment** strategy, management attempts to strengthen or protect the amount of business an SBU is generating. The strategy is generally applied to cash cows or stars that begin to lose market share.

Douglas D. Danforth, the chief executive of Westinghouse, is convinced that retrenchment is an important strategy for his company. According to Danforth, bigger profits at Westinghouse depend not only on fast-growing new products but also on the revitalization of Westinghouse's traditional businesses of manufacturing motors and gears.[22]

Divestiture

Divestiture is a strategy adopted to eliminate an SBU.

Divestiture is a strategy generally adopted to eliminate an SBU that is not generating a satisfactory amount of business and that has little hope of doing so in the near future. In essence, the organization sells or closes down the SBU in ques-

"Divestiture is completed, sir."

Wall Street Journal, *March 27, 1984. From the* Wall Street Journal–*Permission, Cartoon Feature Syndicate.*

tion. This strategy is generally applied to SBUs that are dogs or question marks that have failed to increase market share but still require significant amounts of cash. The cartoon illustrates that divestiture means discarding or getting rid of something.

BACK TO THE CASE

Dr. Frist has several tools available to assist him in formulating strategy for Hospital Corporation of America. If they are to be effective, however, he must use them in conjunction with environmental analysis.

One of the tools, critical question analysis, would require Dr. Frist to analyze the purpose of HCA, the direction in which the organization is going, the environment in which it exists, and how its goals might be better achieved.

SWOT analysis, another strategy development tool, would require Dr. Frist to generate information regarding the internal strengths and weaknesses of HCA as well as the opportunities and threats that exist within HCA's environment. He probably would classify the satellite treatment centers as an environmental threat and a significant factor to be considered in his strategy development process.

Business portfolio analysis would require Dr. Frist to classify each SBU as a star, cash cow, question mark, or dog, depending on the growth rate of the market in which the SBU exists and the market share the SBU possesses. Dr. Frist could decide, for example, to consider each of his hospitals an SBU and categorize them according to the four classifications. As a result of this categorization process, he could develop growth, stability, retrenchment, or divestiture strategies.

Dr. Frist should use whichever strategy development tools he thinks would be most useful to him. His objective, of course, is to develop an appropriate strategy for HCA.

TACTICAL PLANNING

Tactical planning is short-range planning that emphasizes the current operations of various parts of the organization. *Short range* is defined as a period of

Tactical planning is short-range planning.

time extending only about one year or less into the future. Managers use tactical planning to outline what the various parts of the organization must do for the organization to be successful at some point one year or less into the future.[23] Tactical plans usually are developed for organizations in the areas of production, marketing, personnel, finance, and plant facilities.

COMPARING AND COORDINATING STRATEGIC AND TACTICAL PLANNING

Tactical planning should reflect strategic planning.

In striving to implement successful planning systems within organizations, managers must remember several basic differences between strategic planning and tactical planning. First, since upper-level managers generally have a better understanding of the organization as a whole than do lower-level managers, and since lower-level managers generally have a better understanding of the day-to-day organizational operations than do upper-level managers, strategic plans usually are developed by upper-level management and tactical plans by lower-level management. Second, since strategic planning emphasizes analyzing the future and tactical planning emphasizes analyzing the everyday functioning of the organization, facts on which to base strategic plans are usually more difficult to gather than are facts on which to base tactical plans.

A third difference between strategic and tactical planning involves the amount of detail in the final plans. Since strategic plans are based primarily on a prediction of the future and tactical plans on known circumstances that exist within the organization, strategic plans generally are less detailed than tactical plans. Lastly, since strategic planning focuses on the long term and tactical planning on the short term, strategic plans cover a relatively long period of time while tactical plans cover a relatively short period of time. All of these major differences between strategic and tactical planning are summarized in Table 6.6.

In spite of their differences, tactical and strategic planning are integrally related. As Russell L. Ackoff states:

> In general, strategic planning is concerned with the longest period worth considering; tactical planning is concerned with the shortest period worth considering. Both types of planning are necessary. They complement each other. They

TABLE 6.6

Major differences between strategic and tactical planning

Area of Difference	Strategic Planning	Tactical Planning
Individuals involved	Developed mainly by upper-level management	Developed mainly by lower-level management
Facts on which to base planning	Facts are relatively difficult to gather	Facts are relatively easy to gather
Amount of detail in plans	Plans contain relatively little detail	Plans contain substantial amounts of detail
Length of time plans cover	Plans cover long periods of time	Plans cover short periods of time

are like the head and tail of a coin. We can look at them separately, even discuss them separately, but we cannot separate them in fact.[24]

In other words, managers need both tactical and strategic planning programs, but these programs must be closely related to be successful. Tactical planning should focus on what to do in the short term to help the organization achieve the long-term objectives determined by strategic planning.

PLANNING AND LEVELS OF MANAGEMENT

Top management of an organization has the primary responsibility for seeing that the planning function is carried out. Although all levels of management typically are involved in the planning process, upper-level managers usually spend more time planning than do lower-level managers. Lower-level managers are highly involved with the everyday operations of the organization and therefore normally have less time to contribute to planning than does top management. Middle-level managers usually spend more time planning than lower-level managers but less time than upper-level managers. Figure 6.4 shows the increase in planning time spent as managers move from lower-level to upper-level management positions. In small as well as large organizations, deciding on the amount and nature of the work that managers should personally handle is extremely important.[25]

As managers move up in the organization, the time they spend on planning increases.

The type of planning managers do also changes as the managers move up in the organization. Typically, lower-level managers plan for the short term, middle-level managers plan for a somewhat longer term, and upper-level managers plan for an even longer term. The expertise of lower-level managers in everyday operations makes them the best planners for what can be done in the short term to reach organizational objectives—in other words, tactical planning. Upper-level managers usually have the best understanding of the organizational situation as a whole and are therefore better equipped to plan for the long term—or to develop strategic plans. Figure 6.5 shows that as managers move from lower to upper management, they spend more time on strategic planning and

As managers move up in the organization, the scope of their planning broadens.

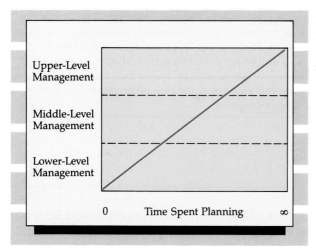

FIGURE 6.4
Increase in planning time as manager moves from lower-level to upper-level management positions

	Today	One Week Ahead	One Month Ahead	Three to Six Months Ahead	One Year Ahead	Two Years Ahead	Three to Four Years Ahead	Five to Ten Years Ahead
President	1%	2%	5%	17%	15%	25%	30%	5%
Vice-President	2%	4%	10%	29%	20%	20%	13%	2%
Works Manager	4%	8%	15%	38%	20%	10%	5%	
Superintendent	6%	10%	20%	43%	10%	9%	2%	
Department Manager	10%	10%	25%	39%	10%	5%	1%	
Section Supervisor	15%	20%	25%	37%	3%			
Group Supervisor	38%	40%	15%	5%	2%			

FIGURE 6.5
Movement of planning activities from a short-range to a long-range emphasis as a manager moves from a lower-level to an upper-level management position

less time on tactical planning. The total amount of time spent on strategic planning by lower-level managers, however, has been increasing.[26]

BACK TO THE CASE

In addition to developing strategic plans for Hospital Corporation of America, Dr. Frist should consider tactical, or short-range, plans that would complement the strategic plans. Tactical plans for HCA should emphasize what can be done within approximately the next year to reach the organization's three-to-five-year objectives and to stem competition from non-profit satellite treatment centers. For example, Dr. Frist could devote more resources to aggressive, short-range marketing campaigns, or he could increase his hospital's staff in order to provide more personalized, immediate care for patients.

In addition, Dr. Frist must closely coordinate strategic and tactical planning within HCA. He must keep in mind that strategic planning and tactical planning are different types of activities that may involve different people within the organization and result in plans with different degrees of detail. Yet he must also remember that these two types of plans are interrelated. While lower-level managers would be mostly responsible for developing tactical plans, upper-level managers would mainly spend time on long-range planning and developing strategic plans that reflect company growth.

Action Summary

Reread the learning objectives that follow. Each objective is followed by questions. Answering these questions accurately will help you retain the most important concepts discussed in this chapter. After answering each question, check your answer with the answer key at the end of this chapter. (*Hint:* If you have doubt regarding the correct response, consult the page whose number follows the answer.)

From studying this chapter, I will attempt to acquire:	**Circle:**

1. Definitions of both strategic planning and strategy.

   a. Strategic planning is long-range planning that focuses on the organization as a whole.   T, F

   b. Strategy (a) is a specific, narrow plan designed to achieve tactical planning; (b) is designed to be the end result of tactical planning; (c) is a plan designed to reach long-range objectives; (d) is timeless, and the same strategy can meet organizational needs anytime; (e) is independent of organizational objectives and therefore need not be consistent with them.   a, b, c, d, e

2. An understanding of the strategy management process.

   a. Which of the following is not one of the steps in strategy management: (a) strategy formulation; (b) strategy implementation; (c) strategy results measurement; (d) strategy evaluation; (e) all of the above are steps.   a, b, c, d, e

   b. Strategy evaluation includes: (a) looking at current strategy relative to market conditions; (b) allocating resources; (c) measuring results; (d) assigning tasks; (e) developing goals.   a, b, c, d, e

3. A knowledge of the impact of environmental analysis on strategy formulation.

   a. Environmental analysis is the strategy used to change an organization's environment to satisfy the needs of the organization.   T, F

   b. All of the following are factors to be considered in environmental analysis except: (a) suppliers; (b) economic issues; (c) demographics; (d) social values; (e) none of the above.   a, b, c, d, e

4. Insights on how to use critical question analysis and SWOT analysis to formulate strategy.

   a. Which of the following is *not* one of the four basic questions used in critical question analysis: (a) Where has the organization been? (b) Where is the organization presently going? (c) What are the purposes and objectives of the organization? (d) In what kind of environment does the organization now exist? (e) What can be done to better achieve organizational objectives in the future?   a, b, c, d, e

   b. SWOT is an acronym for "Strengths and Weaknesses, Objectives and Tactics."   T, F

5. An understanding of how to use business portfolio analysis to formulate strategy.

   a. Business portfolio analysis considers which of the following factors: (a) types of risk associated with product development; (b) threats that economic conditions can create in the future; (c) social factors; (d) market shares and growth of markets in which products are selling; (e) political pressures.   a, b, c, d, e

   b. Products that capture a high share of a rapidly growing market are sometimes known as: (a) cash cows; (b) milk products; (c) sweepstakes products; (d) stars; (e) dog products.   a, b, c, d, e

   c. General Electric's sale of its small appliance business to Black & Decker is an example of which of the following types of organizational strategies for General Electric: (a) growth; (b) stability; (c) retrenchment; (d) divestiture; (e) none of the above.   a, b, c, d, e

6. **Insights on what tactical planning is and on how strategic and tactical planning should be coordinated.**

T, F

a. Tactical plans generally are developed for one year or less and usually contain fewer details than strategic plans.

a, b, c, d, e

b. Which of the following best describes strategic planning: (a) facts are difficult to gather, and plans cover short periods of time; (b) facts are difficult to gather, and plans cover long periods of time; (c) facts are difficult to gather, and plans are developed mainly by lower-level managers; (d) facts are easy to gather, and plans are developed mainly by upper-level managers; (e) facts are easy to gather, and plans are developed mainly by lower-level managers.

INTRODUCTORY CASE WRAP-UP

"Planning for Hospital Corporation of America" (p. 132) and its related back-to-the-case sections were written to help you better understand the management concepts contained in this chapter. Answer the following discussion questions about this introductory case to further enrich your understanding of chapter content:

1. Will Dr. Frist have to worry about competing with the satellite treatment centers in the short term or in the long term? Explain.

2. Assuming that Dr. Frist must do short-range and long-range planning to compete with the satellite treatment centers, which of these two types of planning must he do first? Explain.

3. How might patients' attitudes toward medical care enhance or diminish the success rate of the new satellite treatment centers?

Issues for Review and Discussion

1. What is strategic planning?
2. How does the commitment principle relate to strategic planning?
3. Define *strategy* and discuss its relationship with organizational objectives.
4. What are the major steps in the strategy management process? Discuss each step fully.
5. Why is environmental analysis an important part of strategy formulation?
6. List one major factor from each environmental level that could have significant impact on specific strategies developed for an organization. How could the specific strategies be affected by each factor?
7. Discuss the significance of the questions answered during critical question analysis.
8. Explain in detail how SWOT analysis can be used to formulate strategy.
9. What is business portfolio analysis?

10. Discuss the philosophy on which business portfolio analysis is based.
11. What is an SBU?
12. Draw and explain the business portfolio matrix.
13. What potential pitfalls must managers avoid in using business portfolio analysis?
14. List and define four sample strategies that can be developed for organizations.
15. How do the strategies that you listed in Question 14 relate to dogs, question marks, cash cows, and stars?
16. What is tactical planning?
17. How do strategic and tactical planning differ?
18. What is the relationship between strategic and tactical planning?
19. How do time spent planning and scope of planning vary as management level varies?

Sources of Additional Information

Certo, Samuel C., and J. Paul Peter. *Strategic Management: Concepts and Applications*. New York: Random House, 1988.

Christopher, William F. "Is the Annual Planning Cycle Really Necessary?" *Management Review* 70 (August 1981): 38–42.

Cotton, Donald B. *Organizing for Companywide Planning*. New York: Macmillan, 1969.

Feinberg, Mortimer R. "Preparing Contingency Plans." *Restaurant Business* 80 (May 1981): 3–8, 16.

Fennell, Mary L., and Jeffrey A. Alexander. "Organizational Boundary Spanning in Institutionalized Environments." *Academy of Management Journal* 30 (September 1987): 456–76.

Hall, George E. "Reflections on Running a Diversified Company." *Harvard Business Review* (January/February 1987): 84–92.

Heroux, Richard L. "How Effective Is Your Planning?" *Managerial Planning* 30 (September/October 1980): 3–8ff.

Hutchinson, J. D. *Management Strategy and Tactics*. New York: Holt, Rinehart & Winston, 1971.

Naylor, Thomas H. "Organizing for Strategic Planning." *Managerial Planning* 28 (July/August 1979): 3–9, 17.

Paul, Ronald N., and James W. Taylor. "The State of Strategic Planning." *Business* 36 (January/February/March 1986): 37.

Payne, B. *Planning for Company Growth*. New York: McGraw-Hill, 1963.

Pruchansky, Neal R., and William C. Scott. "Managing Strategy through an Interactionist Perspective." *Managerial Planning* (September/October 1984): 40–44, 50.

Ross, Joel E., and Michael J. Kami. *Corporate Management in Crisis: Why the Mighty Fall*. Englewood Cliffs, N.J.: Prentice-Hall, 1973.

Sawyer, George C. "The Hazards of Goal Conflict in Strategic Planning." *Managerial Planning* 28 (May/June 1980): 11–13, 27.

Scarborough, Norman M., and Thomas W. Zimmerer. "Strategic Planning for the Small Business." *Business* 37 (April/May/June 1987): 11–20.

Sord, Burnard H., and Glen A. Welsch. *Managerial Planning and Control*. Austin, Tex.: University of Texas, Bureau of Business Research, 1964.

Sweet, F. H. *Strategic Planning*. Austin, Tex.: University of Texas, Bureau of Business Research, 1964.

Warren, E. K. *Long-Range Planning: The Executive Viewpoint*. Englewood Cliffs, N.J.: Prentice-Hall, 1966.

Wortman, Leon A. *Successful Small Business Management*. New York: American Management Association, 1976.

Notes

1. Donald F. Harvey, *Strategic Management* (Columbus, Ohio: Merrill, 1982), 19.

2. Lawrence R. Jauch and Richard N. Osborn, "Toward an Integrated Theory of Strategy," *Academy of Management Review* 6 (July 1981): 491–98.

3. Charles R. Greer, "Counter-Cyclical Hiring as a Staffing Strategy for Managerial and Professional Personnel: Some Considerations and Issues," *Academy of Management Review* 9 (April, 1984): 324–30.

4. Yedzi M. Godiwalla, Wayne A. Meinhart, and William D. Warde, "How CEOs Form Corporate Strategy," *Management World* (May 1981): 28–29, 44.

5. Richard B. Robinson, Jr., and John A. Pearce II, "Research Thrusts in Small Firm Strategic Planning," *Academy of Management Review* 9 (January 1984): 128–37.

6. George Sawyer, "Elements of Strategy," *Managerial Planning* (May/June 1981): 3–59.

7. Samuel C. Certo and J. Paul Peter, *Strategic Management: Concepts and Applications* (New York: Random House, 1988).

8. Philip S. Thomas, "Environment Analysis for Corporate Planning," *Business Horizons* (October 1974): 27–38.

9. For more information about several of these examples, see Abraham Katz, "Evaluating the Environment: Economic and Technological Factors," in *Handbook of Business Strategy*, ed. William D. Guth (Boston: Warren, Gorham & Lamont, 1985), 2–9.

10. This section is based on William F. Glueck and Lawrence R. Jauch, *Business Policy and Strategic Management* (New York: McGraw-Hill, 1984), 99–110.

11. D. Stanley Eitzen, *Social Structure and Social Problems in America* (Boston: Allyn & Bacon, 1974), 12–14.

12. "Robots for Greater Efficiency," *U.S. News & World Report*, September 5, 1983.

13. R. S. Wilson, "Managing in the Competitive Environment," *Long-Range Planning* 17 (1984): 50–63.

14. Peter Wright, "MNC—Third World Business Unit Performance: Application of Strategic Elements," *Strategic Management Journal* 5 (1984): 231–40.

15. Discussion in this section is based primarily on Thomas H. Naylor and Kristin Neva, "Design of a Strategic Planning Process," *Managerial Planning* (January/February 1980): 2–7; Donald W. Mitchell, "Pursuing Strategic Potential," *Managerial Planning* (May/June 1980): 6–10; Benton E. Gup, "Begin Strategic Planning by Asking Three Questions," *Managerial Planning* (November/December 1979): 28–31, 35; L. V. Gerstner, Jr., "Can Strategic Planning Pay Off?" *Business Horizons* 15 (1972): 5–16.

16. This section is based on Arthur A. Thompson and A. J. Strickland III, *Strategy Formulation and Implementation* (Plano, Tex.: Business Publications, 1983), 277–91.

17. Bruce D. Henderson, *Henderson on Corporate Strategy* (Cambridge, Mass.: ABT Books, 1979).

18. Philip Kotler, *Marketing Management: Analysis, Planning and Control*, 4th ed. (Englewood Cliffs, N.J.: Prentice-Hall, 1980), 76.

19. Harold W. Fox, "The Frontiers of Strategic Planning: Intuition or Formal Models?" *Management Review* (April 1981): 8–14.

20. Ian C. MacMillan, Donald C. Hambrick, and Diana L. Day, "The Product Portfolio and Profitability—A PIMS-Based Analysis of Industrial-Product Businesses," *Academy of Management Journal* (December 1982): 733–55.

21. Bill Saporito, "Black & Decker's Gamble on Globalization," *Fortune*, May 14, 1984, 40–48.

22. Doron P. Levin, "Westinghouse's New Chief Aims to Push New Lines, Revitalize Traditional Ones," *Wall Street Journal*, November 28, 1983, 10.

23. For a detailed discussion of the characteristics of strategic and tactical planning, see George A. Steiner, *Top Management Planning* (Toronto, Canada: Collier-Macmillan, 1969), 37–39.

24. Russell L. Ackoff, *A Concept of Corporate Planning* (New York: Wiley, 1970), 4.

25. G. E. Tibbits, "Small Business Management: A Normative Approach," *MSU Business Topics* (Autumn 1979): 5–12.

26. "The New Breed of Strategic Planner," *Business Week*, September 17, 1984, 62–67.

Action Summary Answer Key

1. a. T, p. 133
   b. c, p. 133
2. a. e, p. 134
   b. a, p. 134
3. a. F, p. 136
   b. e, pp. 136–137

4. a. a, p. 143
   b. F, p. 143
5. a. d, pp. 143–144
   b. d, p. 145
   c. d, p. 146

6. a. F, pp. 147–148
   b. b, p. 148

ZAYRE: COURTING THE LOW END OF THE MARKET

It is 8:45 Sunday morning, and Maurice Segall is not reading his local newspaper. Instead, he is engrossed in a phone conversation with an executive vice-president about weekly sales volume for the 845 stores he runs. As chief executive officer of Zayre retail chains, Segall took the Framingham, Massachusetts, headquartered corporation from deep trouble to prosperity in a little over six years. An economist by training, a manager by preference, Segall was pirated away from American Express by Zayre chairman Sumner Feldberg.

Profits, at Segall's entrance, were only 1 percent of $1.3 billion in sales; and year-end long-term debt, at $188 million, was nearly 60 percent of capital. The Feldberg family's one-third ownership in Zayre stock had diminished in value to around $9 million, a $51 million drop from its value a few years earlier. Furthermore, the appearance of most Zayre stores would be called, at best, shabby.

Today, long-term debt is only 30 percent of a much larger capital base, and profits are up from $12 million to about $70 million. At 18 percent, return on equity is twice what it was, and the Feldberg family's 2.5 million shares are now worth close to $110 million.

This about-face is remarkable indeed if one considers Zayre's market niche. Zayre discount stores cater primarily to blue-collar workers earning less than $20,000 annually.

During the years that Segall was turning the company around, rival discounters catering to the same market were, one by one, going under. What strategy did Segall employ that bygones Woolco, Korvettes, Two Guys, and Mammoth Mart overlooked?

According to Segall, the formula for success included hard work, clear thinking, and tough decisions that were ruthlessly executed. Unpromising operations were closed, and $75 million was poured into renovating and expanding Zayre stores and stocking them with more desirable merchandise, such as lower-priced sweaters, jackets, housewares, and toys. In short, Zayre's assets were redeployed in a more efficient way.

This retrenchment was to a great extent based on Segall's belief that lower-income shoppers attach considerable weight to the treatment they are given, just as do high-income shoppers. He advertised this service philosophy in newspapers by pledging to open a cash register every time a checkout line grew to three people. He promised a 10 percent discount if an advertised item was out of stock and had to be ordered. More importantly,

he kept his promises. He even upgraded store layouts and improved the appearance of the surroundings. As Segall indicates, lower-income people appreciate attractive surroundings just as much as do affluent people.

All of this is now paying off on the bottom line. Zayre's gross profit margin per square foot comes to $5.85, as compared with K mart's $5.55. With Segall at the helm, it is predicted that the gross profit margin per square foot will rise to over $9 in three to four years, putting Zayre in hailing distance of industry leader Wal-Mart's $10 per square foot.

Segall is running deliberately counter to trendy, modern merchandising that suggests that the up-market is the place to be. As Segall has stated, "We are one of the few large retailers still actively catering to minorities, and we've proved we can do it profitably. Blacks and Hispanics constitute rapidly growing populations, which offer us a major market opportunity." At first, Segall, concentrating on upgrading, opened only ten new stores each year. Now, ribbon cuttings occur twenty to twenty-five times each year.

On the up-market side, Segall inherited two retail operations that he has revived. T. J. Maxx, a small, off-priced family apparel retailing subsidiary, included only 12 stores when he took over. Now it has 155, and 35 are being added each year. The Maxx stores carry cut-priced, brand name merchandise of such firms as Calvin Klein, Gloria Vanderbilt, and Liz Claiborne. They cater to those who are snobby enough to want brand names but who are unwilling to pay full price for them. Despite

155

increasing competition among discounters, Segall expected T. J. Maxx to ring up nearly $1 billion in sales in 1986.

Hit or Miss, the second struggling retail operation, was missing more than hitting when Segall took over. His first action was to close 110 of the 260 lower-priced junior apparel retail stores. Segall then shifted the merchandising emphasis to the career woman, featuring brand name sportswear, ready-to-wear, and accessories. Today, there are more than 400 Hit or Miss Stores.

Segall also undertook two other retailing ventures. One was an off-priced women's apparel mail-order catalog operation called Chadwick's of Boston. It was expected to be slightly in the black by the end of 1984. Later, Segall opened three 100,000-square-foot warehouse operations called BJ's Wholesale Club, patterned after Price Club and Sam's Club.

With the newer ventures looking promising, with T. J. Maxx and Hit or Miss hitting, and with the basic Zayre stores still growing in number, Segall budgets earning growth at better than 20 percent a year for the next five years. If he achieves his target, Zayre will be netting almost $8 a share by 1989. He also expects Zayre's revenues to be approaching $7 billion by then.

DISCUSSION ISSUES

1. What appear to be the objectives that guided Maurice Segall in strategy development? Explain.
2. What was Segall's primary strategy for turning Zayre around? Explain.
3. What tactics did he use to carry out his strategy? Explain.

STUDENT LEARNING OBJECTIVES

From studying this chapter, I will attempt to acquire:

1. A complete definition of a plan.
2. Insights regarding various dimensions of plans.
3. An understanding of various types of plans.
4. Insights on why plans fail.
5. A knowledge of various planning areas within an organization.
6. A definition of forecasting.
7. An ability to see the advantages and disadvantages of various methods of sales forecasting.
8. A definition of scheduling.
9. An understanding of Gantt charts and PERT.

CHAPTER 7

PLANS AND PLANNING TOOLS

CHAPTER OUTLINE

A PLANNING INCIDENT

Jane and Paul were partners in a small machine shop that did jobbing (contract) work predominantly for machine tool manufacturers. Because of a transportation strike, the shop was virtually shut down for a few days. The partners came in every day, of course, and one morning Jane mentioned that it had been months since both of them had sat down to discuss their business in general terms. The daily routine had kept them so busy that there hardly had been time to say, "good morning."

Paul agreed and suggested that they get at it right then and there. During the next two hours, they discussed everything from how old their machines were to putting in new vending machines for coffee and sandwiches. What seemed to concern the partners most, however, was that most of their equipment was quite old, dating back to World War II days in many instances. This situation made matching the competition's quality and speed of output difficult.

Finally, Jane leaned back in her chair. "Paul, we've got to get our costs down. We can't do it overnight, but we can make that one of our major goals over the next few years. If we don't, we're just going to lose out on the bidding on new contracts."

Paul nodded his assent. "You're right, and there's something else too. For a long time, we've been preaching quality to our people, but it's really difficult for them with the equipment they've got to work with. We could lower costs and emphasize quality successfully if we could get some modern machinery in here. From what I've learned in the trade journals, with new machine tools, we could drop our costs 10 to 20 percent over the next five years."

What's Ahead

Chapter 5 focused on the decision-making, or evaluation-of-alternatives, phase of the planning process. Chapter 6 examined the two basic types of organizational planning—strategic and tactical. This chapter continues the discussion of the planning process by emphasizing additional fundamental issues about the plans that managers develop. Jane and Paul, the partners in the introductory case, need to formulate plans for their organization. The chapter presents basic facts about plans and about tools that managers can use to develop them.

⊞ PLANS

The first half of the chapter covers the basic facts about plans. It (1) defines what a plan is, (2) outlines the dimensions of a plan, (3) lists various types of plans, (4) discusses why plans fail, and (5) explains two major organizational areas in which planning usually takes place.

Plans: A Definition

A **plan** is a specific action proposed to help the organization achieve its objectives. According to Sisk, "planning, the process of evaluating all relevant information and the assessment of probable future developments, results in the statement of a recommended course of action—a plan."[1] Regardless of how important experience related intuition may be to managers, successful management actions and strategies typically are based on reason. Rational managers are extremely important to the development of an organizational plan.[2] The "Management in Action" feature for this chapter illustrates how management at Dominion Bankshares incorporated five years of study in emphasizing the rational approach to planning for a child-care center.

A plan is a statement of recommended action.

Dimensions of Plans

Kast and Rosenzweig have indicated that a plan has four major dimensions: (1) repetitiveness, (2) time, (3) scope, and (4) level.[3] Each dimension is an independent characteristic of a plan and should be considered during plan development.[4]

The **repetitiveness dimension** describes the extent to which a plan is used time after time. Some plans are specially designed for one situation that is relatively short term in nature. Plans of this sort are essentially nonrepetitive. Other plans, however, are designed to be used time after time for situations that continue to occur over the long term. These plans are basically repetitive in nature.

In planning, managers should consider:

the degree to which the plan is to be used over and over again,

161

PLANNING FOR A DAY-CARE CENTER AT DOMINION BANKSHARES

ROANOKE, Va.—Warner Dalhouse, the president of Dominion Bankshares Corp., ate lunch at his operations center here the other day. The meal was baked fish, broccoli and gingerbread. His dining companions took pains not to spill their milk.

The occasion was an executive visit to Dominions's child-care center; the CEO's lunchmates were four-year-olds. The chairs and table were Lilliputian. A guinea pig named Chicago lurked watchfully nearby. Before Mr. Dalhouse left, he held high-level discussions with the staff—over the repair of a stuffed elephant's ear.

A bit cute, perhaps, but Dominion treats its child-care center as serious business. "There are no altruistic motivations," Mr. Dalhouse says. "We do everything we do with the objective of profit." And enhancing earnings is precisely what the bank holding company believes the day-care center will do—by lowering turnover and absenteeism, improving productivity and morale, and attracting the best workers. . . .

A NEW GENERATION

Dominion's center is part of a new generation of corporate day-care programs, says Dana Friedman, a senior research associate with the Work and Family Information Center of the Conference Board, an industry research group. While the first centers often were set up largely out of a sense of social responsibility, some companies now find that such programs can aid the bottom line as well.

Employers will have an increasing incentive to provide child-care assistance in coming years as tight labor markets make it more difficult to replace experienced female workers who leave jobs to start families, say Martin O'Connell of the U.S. Census Bureau and David Bloom of Harvard University, who studied the issue for the Population Reference Bureau, a nonprofit research group. They say most employers will need coaxing by government to adopt progressive child-care policies, "even though such actions might actually serve their own interests by improving employee loyalty and job satisfaction."

A program such as Dominion's might not be suited to every company. Costs can be high, some employees without young children might find it unfair, and others don't want to commute with kids. Each employer must "shape a solution that fits" it workers' needs, says Ellen Galinsky, the project director of work and family-

life studies at Bank Street College of Education, in New York. But where on-site care works, she says, "it's wonderful." . . .

FIVE YEARS OF STUDY

Dominion's painstakingly planned program provides a glimpse of the problems faced by corporations confronting the child-care quandary, and suggests some of the reasons why the project has been a success. "One of the reasons this place is so good is because we were chicken," Mr. Dalhouse says. "We were protecting ourselves against doing a bad job."

Before starting the center, Dominion spent five years, on and off, studying the idea. It researched how other companies were handling such programs, and conducted two in-house surveys of employees at its Roanoke Valley facilities.

The polls showed employees were having enormous problems balancing their families with work. More than half of those with children under six said they would probably use an on-site center. Parents were having difficulty arranging quality child care—and as a result there was more absenteeism in the workplace, more turnover and more stress.

Indeed, more than a quarter of Dominion's working mothers had considered quitting because of child-care problems. Barbara Martinet, age 37, a vice president, had lost three child-care providers, for various reasons, in two years. "The third time, I just sat in my office and cried," she recalls. She began to wonder "whether the stress was worth the satisfaction of work." She considers Dominion's center "manna from heaven."

Company officials considered the risks and benefits from every angle. Among their concerns were potential costs, the acceptability of the idea to Dominion's directors, and possible feelings of inequitable treatment among childless employees or those working in other areas at offices without on-site centers. Still, Dominion received only four comments from employees raising questions about fairness.

The path nevertheless took some rocky turns. The project was almost shelved when Dominion went through some less profitable times. Directors worried about the center's effect on profits, though they subsequently supported the project. And skeptics sent Mr.

Dalhouse newspaper clippings about child abuse and other problems at day-care centers. In the end, Mr. Dalhouse says, the project "got done because I wanted it done."

Ann Francis, the center's executive director, was first hired as a consultant and then persuaded to leave her job running a hospital's day-care center. Ms. Francis, who has a master's degree in child development, helped plan Dominion's center—even ordering architects to sit on the floor so that they could see the room from a child's perspective.

She and her staff of 18 are all Dominion employees with salary and benefits, an arrangement Dominion likes because it allows control over personnel and operations. Firms with on-site centers often hire established day-care operators or consultants to run the operations independently, but Dominion officials say they can better ensure quality if they are in charge.

the length of time the plan covers,

The **time dimension** of a plan is the length of the time period the plan covers. In chapter 6, strategic planning was defined as being long term in nature and tactical planning was defined as being short term. It follows, then, that strategic plans cover relatively long periods of time and tactical plans cover relatively short periods of time.

the parts of the management system on which the plan focuses,

The **scope dimension** describes the portion of the total management system at which the plan is aimed. Some plans are designed to cover the entire open management system: the organizational environment, inputs, process, and outputs. A plan for the management system as a whole is often referred to as a master plan. Other plans, however, are developed to cover only a portion of the management system. An example would be a plan developed to cover the recruitment of new workers—a portion of the organizational input segment of the management system. The greater the portion of the management system that a plan covers, the broader the scope of the plan is said to be.

and the organizational level at which the plan is aimed.

The **level dimension** of a plan indicates the level of the organization at which the plan is aimed. Top-level plans are those designed for the top-management level of the organization, while middle-level and lower-level plans are designed for middle-level and lower-level management, respectively. Because all parts of the management system are interdependent, however, plans for any level of the organization have some effect on all other levels.

Figure 7.1 illustrates the four dimensions of an organizational plan. This

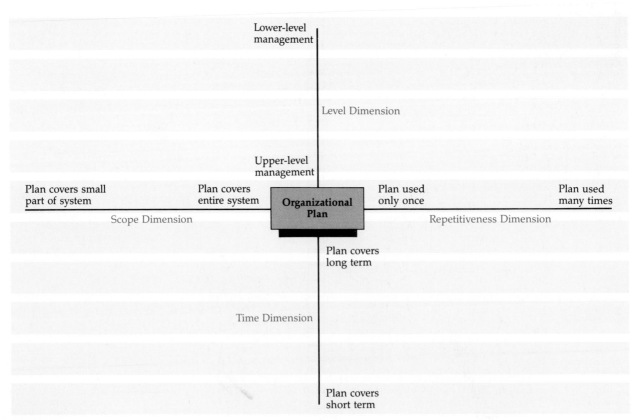

FIGURE 7.1
Four major dimensions to consider when developing a plan

figure stresses that when managers develop a plan, they should consider the degree to which it will be used over and over again, the period of time it will cover, the parts of the management system on which it focuses, and the organizational level at which it is aimed.

■ BACK TO THE CASE

Before Jane and Paul, the partners in the introductory case, develop plans for cutting costs and improving quality, they should understand that plans are recommendations for future actions and therefore should be action oriented. Their plans should state precisely what they are going to do in order to achieve their goals.

In developing the plans, they should consider how often the plans will be used and the length of time they will cover. Will a plan be implemented only once, for a year, to address the quality issue, or to be used on a long-term basis to handle the ongoing issue of quality control?

In addition, Jane and Paul should consider what part of the machine shop the plans will be aimed at and what level the plans will focus on. In other words, a plan to cut costs may encompass all shop operations, whereas a plan to improve quality may affect only one part of the production process. Similarly, a plan to cut costs may be aimed at top-level management, whereas a quality-control plan may be aimed toward lower-level management and the machine operators themselves. Of course, Jane and Paul must realize that since management systems are interdependent, any plans they implement will affect the system as a whole.

Types of Plans

With the repetitiveness dimension as a guide, organizational plans usually are divided into two types: standing and single-use. **Standing plans** are used over and over again, because they focus on organizational situations that occur repeatedly. **Single-use plans** are used only once or several times, because they focus on relatively unique situations within the organization. Figure 7.2 illustrates that standing plans can be subdivided into policies, procedures, and rules and that single-use plans can be subdivided into programs and budgets.[5]

Standing plans are used repeatedly; single-use plans are used only once or several times.

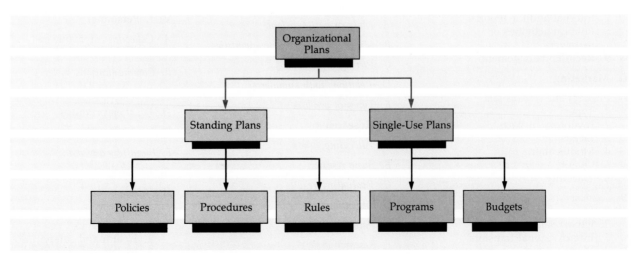

FIGURE 7.2
Standing plans and single-use plans

TABLE 7.1

Organizational areas in which policy statements usually are written

I. General Management

A. *Divisions and functional staffs*
1. Authority and responsibilities of divisions concerning pricing, capital authorization, interdivisional transfers, product areas, and authority retained in central headquarters
2. Functional staff relationships at headquarters and authority in divisions

B. *Growth*
1. Sales rate
2. Profit rate
3. Acquisitions

C. *Planning*
1. Budgets
2. Company basic lines of business
3. Comprehensive planning
4. Organization

D. *Policy authority and statements*

E. *Miscellaneous*
1. Acceptance of gifts or services by employees
2. Answering correspondence
3. Computer procurement
4. Disaster control
5. Employment of consultants
6. Gifts and gratuities to government and company personnel
7. Internal auditor reports
8. Political activities of managers
9. Records management

II. Marketing

A. *Products and services sold*
1. Types
2. Inventory of parts
3. Licensing
4. Modification
5. Quality
6. Warranty

B. *Customers*
1. Contract clearance
2. Export sales
3. Interdivisional transfers
4. Market areas
5. Market channels
6. Relations with customers, including dealers and distributors
7. Service for customers
8. Size of customers

C. *Pricing*
1. Authority to price
2. Compliance with antitrust laws
3. Discounting
4. Resale price maintenance
5. Timing of price change

D. *Sales promotion*
1. Advertising media
2. Product publicity

III. Production

A. *Assignments of products to divisions*

B. *Contracting*

C. *Manufacturing methods*

D. *Production control*

E. *Production planning*

F. *Quality control*

G. *Safety*

H. *Shipping*

I. *Size of production runs*

J. *Stabilization of production*

K. *Tooling*

IV. Procurement

A. *Make-or-buy decisions*

B. *Minimum procurement quantities*

C. *Purchasing channels*

D. *Relations with suppliers*

E. *Types of vendors*

V. Research

A. *Allocating funds*

B. *Basic research*

C. *Evaluating results*

D. *Inventions*

E. *Patents*

F. *Research areas*

G. *Research records*

H. *Trademarks*

VI. Finance

A. *Audit*

B. *Budget*
1. Developing
2. Controlling

C. *Credit*
1. Customers
2. Employees

D. *Dividend policy*
1. Size relative to profit
2. Stabilizing

E. *Expenditures*
1. Authority to spend company money
2. Contributions and donations

F. *Protecting capital*
1. Insurance
2. Reserves

G. *Structure*
1. Debt rations
2. Long-term financing
3. Short-term financing

VII. Facilities

A. *Decision-making process for expenditure*

B. *Location*

C. *Maintenance*

D. *Replacement*

VIII. Personnel

A. *Collective bargaining and union relations*

B. *Communications systems*

C. *Employment and recruiting*

D. *Equal opportunities*

E. *Hours of work*

F. *Incentives and bonuses*

G. *Pensions*

H. *Selection*

I. *Services*
1. Food service
2. Health and safety
3. Insurance
4. Recreational and educational activities

TABLE 7.1 cont.

5. Retirement
6. Sick leave
7. Transportation and parking

J. *Training and education*

K. *Wages and salaries*

L. *Working conditions*

IX. Public Relations

A. *Community*

B. *Conflicts of interest*

C. *Contributions*

D. *Determining contents of communications*

E. *Extent of function*

F. *Role of executives*

G. *Selecting media for communications*

X. Legal

A. *Clearance of contracts*

B. *Compliance with law*

C. *Patents for employee inventors*

D. *Protection of proprietary rights*

E. *Reservation of rights and interests*

F. *Real property leases*

Standing Plans: Policies, Procedures, and Rules

A **policy** is a standing plan that furnishes broad, general guidelines for channeling management thinking toward taking action consistent with reaching organizational objectives. For example, an organizational policy relating to personnel might be worded as follows: Our organization will strive to recruit only the most talented employees. This policy statement is very broad, giving managers only a general idea of what to do in the area of employment. The policy is intended to display the extreme importance management has attached to hiring competent employees and to guiding action accordingly. Other organizational areas in which policy statements usually are written are listed in Table 7.1.

A **procedure** is a standing plan that outlines a series of related actions that must be taken to accomplish a particular task. In general, procedures outline

Policies are broad, general guidelines for action.

Procedures outline specific actions to be performed sequentially.

"In this organization, Challis, middle management uses only blue highlighting markers."

Wall Street Journal, *June 17, 1987. From the* Wall Street Journal—*permission, Cartoon Features Syndicate.*

more specific actions than do policies. Organizations usually have many different sets of procedures covering the various tasks to be accomplished. The sample procedure in Table 7.2 lists the series of steps that recruiters take to interview prospective academic employees at Indiana State University.

Rules designate specific, mandatory action.

A **rule** is a standing plan that designates specific required action. In essence, a rule indicates what an organization member should or should not do and allows no room for interpretation. An example of a rule is: All students must

---

TABLE 7.2

Procedure for interviewing prospective academic employees at Indiana State University

---

1. Any candidate brought to campus for an interview should be a best prospect of at least three qualified persons whose credentials have been examined. Personnel supply in an academic field may reduce the number of possible candidates.

2. Before an invitation is extended to a candidate who must travel a distance greater than five hundred miles to reach Terre Haute, the department chairperson should:
   a. ascertain the existence of the vacancy or authorization by a call to the assistant vice-president for academic affairs.
   b. forward to the dean and assistant vice-president credentials which should include, if possible, parts d, e, f, and g, Item 6, below.

3. Any administrative person who is scheduled to interview a candidate should be forwarded credentials for the candidate prior to the interview.

4. Interviews with administrative personnel should be scheduled as follows:
   A candidate whose probable academic rank will be instructor or assistant professor should talk with the dean prior to the assistant vice-president. A candidate whose academic rank should probably be associate professor, in addition to the dean and assistant vice-president, should be scheduled for an interview with the vice-president for academic affairs. In addition to the above, a candidate for appointment as professor or department chairperson should also be scheduled for a meeting with the president.

5. Although courtesy to the candidate may demand that the interview schedule be maintained, the vice-president, at his or her discretion or in agreement with the suggestion by the chairperson, dean, or assistant vice-president, may cancel the interview for the candidate with the president.

6. A recommendation for appointment should contain the following:
   a. a letter from the department chairperson (or dean) setting forth the recommendation and proposing the academic rank and salary.
   b. a statement from the dean if the recommenda-

tion letter is prepared by the department chairperson.
   c. the completed university resume form. This can be completed by the candidate when on campus or returned to the chairperson by mail later, but must be included.
   d. vitae information.
   e. placement papers.
   f. official transcripts (especially important if placement papers are not current or prepared by a university bureau).
   g. as many as three letters of recommendation, one or two of these reflecting the candidate's current assignment. These letters are necessary if the placement materials have not been updated to contain current recommendations.
   h. a written report on any telephone conversations concerning the candidate made by the department chairperson.

7. Because of the difficulty in arranging interviews on Saturday, campus visits should occur during the week.

8. Whenever possible, accommodations at the Hulman Center should be limited to one overnight. The university cannot accept any charge for hotel accommodations other than at the Hulman Center. "Hotel accommodations" are defined to be lodging only, and not food, telephone, or other personal services.

9. Travel can be reimbursed in one of the following ways:
   a. a candidate traveling in-state will have mileage paid, at the rate of eight cents per mile. The official Indiana map is used to compute mileage rather than a speedometer reading.
   b. a candidate traveling from out-of-state can claim the cost of airfare (tourist class) or train fare (coach class).
   c. a candidate who may choose to drive from out-of-state cannot be paid a mileage cost. Instead, airfare and train-fare amounts are determined and the lesser of the two is paid as an automobile mileage reimbursement.

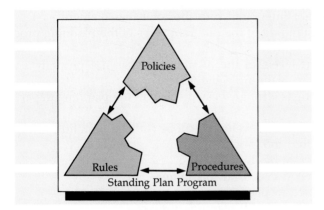

FIGURE 7.3
A successful standing plan program with mutually supportive policies, procedures, and rules

be seated in silence immediately after the bell rings. The concept of rules may become clearer if one thinks about the purpose and nature of rules in such games as Scrabble and Monopoly. Some organizations have too many rules, as the cartoon on page 167 suggests.

Although policies, procedures, and rules are all standing plans, they are different from one another and have different purposes within the organization. As Figure 7.3 illustrates, however, for the standing plans of an organization to be effective, policies, procedures, and rules must be consistent and mutually supportive.

Single-Use Plans: Programs and Budgets

A **program** is a single-use plan designed to carry out a special project within an organization. The project itself typically is not intended to be in existence over the entire life of the organization. However, the program exists to achieve some purpose that, if accomplished, will contribute to the organization's long-term success.

Programs aid success indirectly.

A common example is the management development program found in many organizations. This program exists to raise the skill levels of managers in regard to one or more of the skills mentioned in chapter 1: technical skills, conceptual skills, or human skills. Increasing the skill levels, however, is not an end in itself. The purpose of the program is to produce competent managers who are equipped to help the organization be successful over the long term. Once managerial skills have been raised to a desired level, the management development program can be deemphasized.

A **budget** is a single-use financial plan that covers a specified length of time. It details how funds will be spent on labor, raw materials, capital goods, and so on, as well as how the funds will be obtained.[6] Although budgets are planning devices, they are also strategies for organizational control. They are covered in more detail in chapter 17.

Budgets are financial plans.

Why Plans Fail

If managers know why plans fail, they can take steps to eliminate the factors that cause failure and thereby increase the probability that their plans will be successful. A study by K. A. Ringbakk indicates that plans fail when:[7]

1. Corporate planning is not integrated into the total management system.
2. There is a lack of understanding of the different steps of the planning process.
3. Management at different levels in the organization has not properly engaged in or contributed to planning activities.
4. Responsibility for planning is wrongly vested solely in the planning department.
5. Management expects that plans developed will be realized with little effort.
6. In starting formal planning, too much is attempted at once.
7. Management fails to operate by the plan.
8. Financial projections are confused with planning.
9. Inadequate inputs are used in planning.
10. Management fails to see the overall planning process.

Planning Areas: Input Planning

As discussed earlier, organizational inputs, process, outputs, and environment are major factors in determining how successful a management system will be. Naturally, a comprehensive organizational plan should focus on each of these factors. The following two sections cover planning in two areas normally associated with the input factor: plant facilities planning and human resource planning. Planning in areas such as these normally is called **input planning**—the development of proposed action that will furnish sufficient and appropriate organizational resources for reaching established organizational objectives.

Input planning: Plans to provide organizational resources.

Plant Facilities Planning

Plant facilities planning involves determining the type of buildings and equipment an organization needs to reach its objectives. A major part of this determination is called **site selection**—deciding where a plant facility should be located. Table 7.3 shows several major areas to be considered in plant site selection, and it gives sample questions that can be asked when these areas are to be explored. Naturally, the specifics of site selection vary from organization to organization.

One facet of plant facilities planning is site selection.

One factor that can significantly influence site selection is whether a site is being selected in a foreign country. In a foreign country, management may face such issues as foreign governments taking different amounts of time to approve site purchases and political pressures slowing down or preventing the purchase of a site.

Many organizations use a weighting process to compare site differences among foreign countries. Basically, this process involves (1) deciding on a set of variables that are critical to obtaining an appropriate site; (2) assigning each of these variables a weight, or rank, of relative importance; and (3) ranking alternative sites, depending on how they reflect these different variables.

Site selection may involve a weighting process to compare site differences.

As an example, Table 7.4 shows the results of such a weighting process for seven site variables and six countries. In this table, "living conditions" are worth 100 points and are the most important variable; "effect on company reputation" is worth 35 points and is the least important variable. Also in this table, various countries are given a number of points for each variable, depending on the importance of the variable and how it exists within the country. The illustration

TABLE 7.3

Major areas of consideration when selecting a plant site and sample exploratory questions

Major Areas For Consideration in Site Selection	Sample Question to Begin Exploring Major Areas
Profit	
Market location	Where are our customers in relation to the site?
Competition	What competitive situation exists at the site?
Operating costs	
Suppliers	Are materials available near the site at reasonable cost?
Utilities	What are utility rates at the site? Are utilities available in sufficient amounts?
Wages	What wage rates are paid in comparable organizations near the site?
Taxes	What are tax rates on income, sales, property, etc. for the site?
Investment costs	
Land/development	How expensive is land and construction at the site?
Others	
Transportation	Are airlines, railroads, highways, etc. available to the site?
Laws	What laws exist related to zoning, pollution, etc. that influence operations if the site is chosen?
Labor	Does an adequate labor supply exist around the site?
Unionization	What degree of unionization exists in the site area?
Living conditions	Are housing, schools, etc. appropriate around the site?
Community relations	Is the community supportive of the organization moving into the area?

TABLE 7.4

Results of weighing seven site variables for six countries

Criteria	Maximum Value Assigned	Sites					
		Japan	Chile	Jamaica	Australia	Mexico	France
Living conditions	100	70	40	45	50	60	60
Accessibility	75	55	35	20	60	70	70
Industrialization	60	40	50	55	35	35	30
Labor availability	35	30	10	10	30	35	35
Economics	35	15	15	15	15	25	25
Community capability and attitude	30	25	20	10	15	25	15
Effect on company reputation	35	25	20	10	15	25	15
Total	370	260	190	165	220	275	250

shows that given the established set of weighted criteria, Japan, Mexico, and France received more points and therefore are more desirable sites than Chile, Jamaica, and Australia.

Human Resource Planning

The human resource planning process involves determining net human resource needs and finding people to meet those needs.

Human resources are another area with which input planners usually are concerned. Organizational objectives cannot be attained without appropriate personnel. Future needs for human resources are influenced mainly by employee turnover, the nature of the present work force, and the rate of growth of the organization.[8]

Personnel planners should try to answer such questions as: (1) What types of people does the organization need to reach its objectives? (2) How many of each type are needed? (3) What steps for the recruitment and selection of these people should the organization take? (4) Can present employees be further trained to fill future needed positions? (5) At what rate are employees lost to

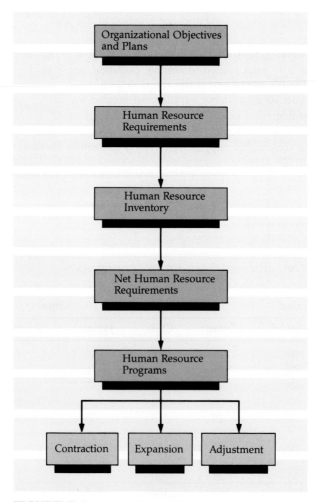

FIGURE 7.4
The human resource planning process

other organizations? These are not the only questions personnel planners should ask, but they are representative.

Figure 7.4 shows the human resource planning process developed by Bruce Coleman. According to his model, **human resource planning** involves reflecting on organizational objectives to determine overall human resource needs, comparing these needs to the existing human resource inventory to determine net human resource needs, and, finally, seeking appropriate organization members to meet the net human resource needs.

BACK TO THE CASE

Jane and Paul probably should develop both standing plans and single-use plans for their machine shop. Standing plans include policies, procedures, and rules and should be developed for situations that occur repeatedly. For example, one policy Jane and Paul could develop might focus on the product quality they want to emphasize with employees.

Single-use plans include programs and budgets and should be developed to help manage less repetitive situations. For example, Jane and Paul might want to work on a budget that would allow them to purchase new machine tools. They also should become thoroughly aware of the reasons that plans fail and should take steps to avoid these pitfalls.

Plant facilities planning and human resource planning are two additional areas Jane and Paul might want to discuss. Plant facilities planning entails developing the type of plant facility Jane and Paul would need to reach company objectives. Since they already have an operating plant, plan site location as part of plant facilities planning probably is not too important to them. Modernization of equipment as part of plant facilities planning, however, probably would be very interesting to them, since they need to update their machinery to keep up with competitors. Human resource planning involves obtaining or developing the personnel the organization needs to reach its objectives. In this area, for example, Jane and Paul might want to discuss additional skills their employees would need to run new machinery.

 PLANNING TOOLS

Planning tools are techniques managers can use to help develop plans. The remainder of this chapter discusses forecasting and scheduling, two of the most important of these tools.

Forecasting

Forecasting is the process of predicting future environmental happenings that will influence the operation of the organization. Although sophisticated forecasting techniques have been developed only rather recently, the concept of forecasting can be traced at least as far back in the management literature as Fayol.[9] The importance of forecasting lies in its ability to help managers understand the future makeup of the organizational environment, which in turn helps them formulate more effective plans.

William C. House, in describing the Insect Control Services Company, has developed an excellent illustration of how forecasting works. Table 7.5 lists the primary factors the company attempts to measure in developing its forecast. In general, Insect Control Services forecasts by attempting to:[10]

1. Establish relationships between industry sales and national economic and social indicators.

Forecasting involves predicting the future organizational environment.

2. Determine the impact of government restrictions concerning the use of chemical pesticides on the growth of chemical, biological, and electromagnetic energy pest control markets.
3. Evaluate sales growth potential, profitability, resources required, and risks involved in each of its market areas (commercial, industrial, institutional, governmental, and residential).
4. Evaluate the potential for expansion of marketing efforts in geographical areas of the United States as well as foreign countries.
5. Determine the likelihood of technological breakthroughs that would make existing product lines obsolete.

In addition to the more general process of organizational forecasting illustrated by Insect Control Services are specialized types of forecasting, such as economic forecasting, technological forecasting, social trends forecasting, and sales forecasting. Although a complete organizational forecasting process can and usually should include all of these types of forecasting, sales forecasting is typically cited as the key organizational forecast. A *sales forecast* is a prediction of how high or how low sales will be over the period of time under consideration. It is the key forecast because it serves as the fundamental guideline for planning within the organization. Once the sales forecast has been completed, managers can decide, for example, if more salespeople should be hired, if more money for

Sales forecasting is the key organizational forecast.

TABLE 7.5

Primary factors measured during Insect Control Services' forecasting process

---

Gross National Product
Measure of total dollars available for industrial, commercial, institutional, and residential purchases of insect control units.

Personal Consumption Expenditures
Measure of dollars available for consumer purchases of:
1. *Services*—affect potential contract insect control services.
2. *Durables*—affect market potential for residential units.
3. *Nondurables*—affect sales of food, drugs, and other products that influence expansion of industrial and commercial users of insect control equipment.

Governmental Purchases of Goods, Services
Measure of spending for hospitals, government food services, other institutions that purchase insect control equipment.

Gross Private Domestic Investment in New Plant and Equipment
A measure of business expansion that indicates the size and nature of market potential for industrial and commercial purchases of insect control units in new or expanded existing establishments.

Industrial Production for Selected Industries
Measure of expansion of industrial output for industries that are users, potential users of insect control units, or materials suppliers for insect control services. Such expansion (or contraction) of output will likely affect:
1. Industrial and commercial purchases of insect control units.
2. Availability of materials used to manufacture insect control units.

Employment and Unemployment Levels
Indicates availability or scarcity of human resources available to augment Insect Control Services human resources pool.

Consumer, Wholesale Prices
Measure of ability, willingness of homeowners to purchase residential units, and availability and cost of raw materials and component parts.

Corporate Profits
Indicates how trends in prices, unit labor costs, and productivity affect corporate profits. Size of total corporate profits indicates profit margins in present and potential markets and funds available for expansion.

Business Borrowings, Interest Rates
Measures of the availability and cost of borrowed funds needed to finance working capital needs and plant and equipment expansion.

plant expansion must be borrowed, or if layoffs are upcoming and cutbacks in certain areas are necessary. The following section outlines various methods of sales forecasting.

Methods of Sales Forecasting

Jury of Executive Opinion Method

The **jury of executive opinion method** of sales forecasting is straightforward. A group of managers within the organization assemble to discuss their opinions on what will happen to sales in the future. Since these discussion sessions usually revolve around the hunches or experienced guesses of each of the managers, the resulting forecast is a blend of expressed opinions.

Jury of executive opinion: Executives predict sales.

A more recently developed forecasting method, similar to the jury of executive opinion method, is called the *delphi method*.[11] This method also gathers, evaluates, and summarizes expert opinions as the basis for a forecast.[12] The basic delphi method employs the following steps:

The delphi method of forecasting requires six steps.

Step 1 Various experts are asked to answer independently, in writing, a series of questions about the future of sales or whatever other area is being forecasted.

Step 2 A summary of all the answers is then prepared. No expert knows how any other expert answered the questions.

Step 3 Copies of the summary are given to the individual experts with the request that they modify their original answers if they think they should.

Step 4 Another summary is made of these modifications, and copies again are distributed to the experts. This time, however, expert opinions that deviate significantly from the norm must be justified in writing.

Step 5 A third summary is made of the opinions and justifications, and copies are distributed to the experts. Justification for all answers is now required in writing.

Step 6 The forecast is generated from all of the opinions and justifications that arise from step 5.

Sales Force Estimation Method

The **sales force estimation method** requires the solicitation of the opinions of company salespeople instead of company managers. Salespeople interact with customers and can use this interacton as a basis for predicting future sales. As with the jury of executive opinion method, the resulting forecast generally is a blend of the views of the salespeople as a group.

Sales force estimation: Salespeople predict sales.

Times Series Analysis Method

The **time series analysis method** predicts future sales by analyzing the historical relationship between sales and time. Information showing the relationship between sales and time typically is presented on a graph, as in Figure 7.5 on page 176. This presentation clearly displays past trends, which can be used to predict future sales.

Time series analysis: Past sales predict future sales.

The time series analysis in the figure indicates steadily increasing sales over time. However, since, in the long term, products generally go through what is called a product life cycle, the predicted increase probably is overly optimistic. A **product life cycle** is the five stages through which most new products and services pass. The stages are introduction, growth, maturity, saturation, and decline.

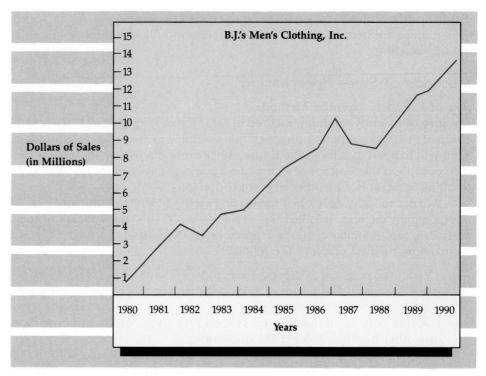

FIGURE 7.5
Time series analysis method

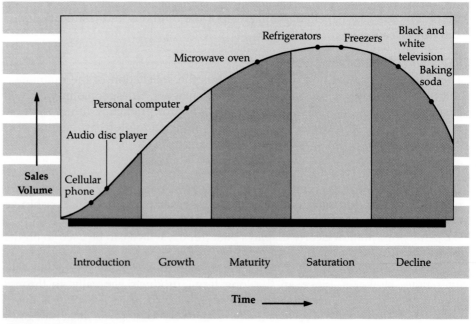

FIGURE 7.6
Stages of the product life cycle

Figure 7.6 shows how these five stages are related to product sales over a period of time. In the introduction stage, a product is brand-new, and sales are just beginning to build. In the growth stage, because the product has been in the marketplace for some time and is now becoming more accepted, product sales continue to climb. During the maturity stage, competitors enter the market; and while sales are still climbing, they normally climb at a slower rate than in the

Most new products and services go through a five-stage life cycle.

TABLE 7.6

Advantages and disadvantages of three methods of sales forecasting

Sales Forecasting Method	Advantages	Disadvantages
Jury of executive opinion	1. Can provide forecasts easily and quickly 2. May not require the preparation of elaborate statistics 3. Pools a variety of specialized viewpoints for experience and judgment 4. May be the only feasible means of forecasting, especially in the absence of adequate data	1. Is inferior to a more factual basis of forecasting, since it is based so heavily on opinion 2. Requires costly executive time 3. Is not necessarily more accurate, because opinion is averaged 4. Disperses responsibility for accurate forecasting 5. Presents difficulties in making breakdowns by products, time intervals, or markets for operating purposes
Sales force estimation	1. Uses specialized knowledge of people closest to the market 2. Places responsibility for the forecast in the hands of those who must produce the results 3. Gives sales force greater confidence in quotas developed from forecasts 4. Tends to give results greater stability because of the magnitude of the sample 5. Lends itself to the easy development of product, territory, customer, or sales representatives' breakdowns	1. Sales representatives of some firms may be poor estimators, being either more optimistic or more pessimistic than conditions warrant 2. If estimates are used as a basis for setting quotas, sales representatives are inclined to understate the demand to make the goal easier to achieve 3. Sales representatives are often unaware of the broad economic patterns shaping future sales and are thus incapable of forecasting trends for extended periods 4. Since sales forecasting is a subsidiary function of the sales force, sufficient time may not be made available for it 5. Requires an extensive expenditure of time by executives and sales force 6. Elaborate schemes are sometimes necessary to keep estimates realistic and free from bias
Time series analysis	1. Forces the forecaster to consider the underlying trend, cycle, and seasonal elements in the sales series 2. Takes into account the particular repetitive or continuing patterns exhibited by the sales in the past 3. Provides a systematic means of making quantitative projections	1. Assumes the continuation of historical patterns of change in sales components without considering outside influences that may affect sales in the forecast period 2. Is often unsatisfactory for short-term forecasting, since, for example, the pinpointing of cyclical turning points by mechanical projections is seldom possible 3. May be difficult to apply in cases where erratic, irregular forces disrupt or hide the regularity of component patterns within a sales series 4. Requires technical skill, experience, and judgment

growth stage. After the maturity stage comes the saturation stage, when nearly everyone who wanted the product has it. Sales during the saturation stage typically are due to replacements of a worn-out product or to population growth. The last product life cycle stage—decline—finds the product being replaced by a competing product.

Managers may be able to keep some products out of the decline stage through high-quality product improvements. Other products, such as scissors, may never reach this last stage because of the lack of competing products.

Evaluating Sales Forecasting Methods

The sales forecasting methods just described are not the only ones available to managers. Other more complex methods include the statistical correlation method and the computer simulation method.[13] The methods just discussed, however, do provide a basic foundation for understanding sales forecasting.

The sales forecasting method should be logical and adaptable and fit the organization's needs.

In practice, managers find that each sales forecasting method has advantages and disadvantages, as shown in Table 7.6, p. 177. Before deciding to use a particular sales forecasting method, a manager must carefully weigh the advantages and disadvantages as they relate to a particular organization. The decision may be to use a combination of methods rather than just one. Whatever method is finally adopted, the framework should be logical, fit the needs of the organization, and be capable of adaptation to changes in the environment.[14]

■ BACK TO THE CASE

One of the planning tools available to Jane and Paul is forecasting, which involves predicting future environmental events that could influence the operation of their machine shop. Although various specific types of forecasting—such as economic, technological, and social trends forecasting—are available to them, Jane and Paul would probably use sales forecasting as their key forecast since it will predict for them how high or low their sales will be during the time period they are considering. Such a prediction can help Jane and Paul make decisions concerning hiring more employees, expanding the shop, and ordering the correct amount of raw materials.

In order to forecast sales, Jane and Paul could follow the jury of executive opinion method by discussing their opinions of future sales. Although this method would be quick and easy for them, it may not be as good as other methods because, in this case, it relies heavily on the opinions of only two people.

Jane and Paul could also ask their small sales force for opinions on predicted sales. Although the opinions of sales representatives may not be completely reliable, these people are closest to the market and must ultimately make the sales.

Finally, Jane and Paul could use the time series analysis method by analyzing the relationship between sales and time. Although this method takes into account the cyclical patterns and past history of sales, it also assumes the continuation of these patterns in the future without considering outside influences that could cause the patterns to change.

Since each sales forecasting method has both advantages and disadvantages, Jane and Paul should carefully analyze each of them before deciding which method or combination of methods should be used in their company.

Scheduling

Scheduling involves listing activities for reaching an objective.

Basically, **scheduling** is the process of formulating a detailed listing of activities that must be accomplished to attain an objective. This listing is an integral part of an organizational plan. Two scheduling techniques are Gantt charts and the program evaluation and review technique (PERT).

Gantt Charts

The **Gantt chart,** a scheduling device developed by Henry L. Gantt, is essentially a bar graph with time on the horizontal axis and the resource to be scheduled on the vertical axis. Possible resources to be scheduled include management system inputs, such as human resources and machines.

The Gantt chart schedules resources.

Figure 7.7 shows a completed Gantt chart for a work period entitled "Workweek 28." The resources scheduled over the five workdays on this chart were human resources: Wendy Reese and Peter Thomas. During this workweek, both Reese and Thomas were scheduled to produce ten units a day for five days. Actual units produced, however, show a deviation from this planned production. There were days when each of the two workers produced more than ten units, as well as days when each produced fewer then ten units. Cumulative production on the chart shows that Reese produced forty units and Thomas produced forty-five units over the five days.

Although the Gantt chart may seem quite simple, it has many valuable uses for managers. First, managers can use the chart as a summary overview of how organizational resources are being used. From this summary, they can detect such facts as which resources are consistently contributing to productivity. Second, mangers can use the Gantt chart to help coordinate organizational resources. The chart can show which resources are not being used during specific periods, thereby allowing the resources to be scheduled for work on other production efforts. Third, the chart can be used to establish realistic worker output standards. For example, if workers are completing scheduled work too quickly, output standards may need to be raised so that workers are scheduled for more work per time period.

Gantt charts have many valuable uses.

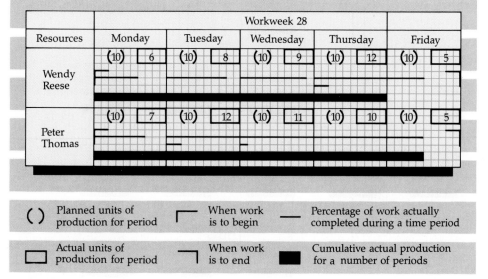

FIGURE 7.7
Completed Gantt chart

Program Evaluation and Review Technique (PERT)

PERT emphasizes the interrelationship of tasks.

The main weakness of the Gantt chart is that it does not contain any information about the interrelationship of tasks to be performed. All tasks to be performed are listed on the chart, but there is no way of telling if one task must be performed before another can be completed. The program evaluation and review technique (PERT), a technique that evolved in part from the Gantt chart, is a scheduling tool designed to emphasize the interrelationship of tasks.

Defining PERT

PERT networks show both time estimates and sequential relationships.

PERT is a network of project activities showing both the estimates of time necessary to complete each activity within the project and the sequential relationships among activities that must be followed to complete the project. PERT was developed in 1958 for use in designing the Polaris submarine weapon system.[15] The individuals involved in managing this project found Gantt charts and other existing scheduling tools of little use because of the complicated nature of the Polaris project and the interdependence of its tasks.[16]

Activities and events are the primary elements of a PERT network.

The PERT network contains two primary elements: activities and events. **Activities** are specified sets of behavior within a project, and **events** are the completions of major project tasks. Within the PERT network, each event is assigned corresponding activities that must be performed before the event can materialize.[17]

A sample PERT network designed for the building of a house is presented

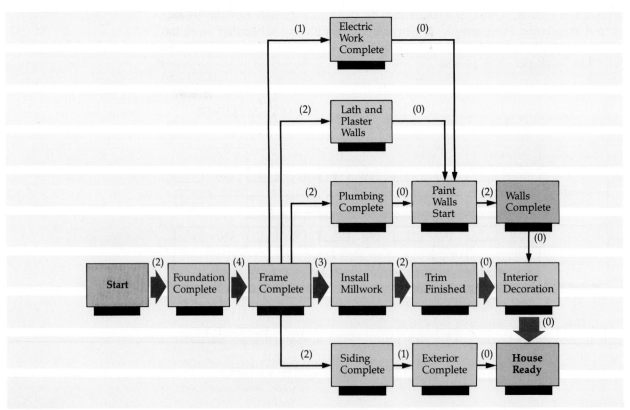

FIGURE 7.8
PERT network designed for building a house

in Figure 7.8. In this figure, events are symbolized by circles and activities are symbolized by arrows. To illustrate, the figure indicates that after the event "Foundation Complete" (represented by a circle) has materialized, certain activities (represented by an arrow) must be performed before the event "Frame Complete" (represented by another circle) can materialize.

Two other features of the network shown here also should be emphasized. First, the left-to-right presentation of events shows how the events interrelate or the sequence in which they should be performed. Second, the numbers in parentheses above each arrow indicate the units of time necessary to complete each activity. These two features should help managers ensure that only necessary work is being done on a project and that no project activities are taking too long.

Critical Path

Close attention should be paid to the **critical path** of a PERT network—the sequence of events and activities requiring the longest period of time to complete. The path is called the critical path because a delay in the time necessary to complete this sequence results in a delay for the completion of the entire project. The critical path in Figure 7.8 is indicated by thick arrows; all other paths are indicated by thin arrows. Managers try to control a project by keeping it within the time designated by the critical path.

The critical path is the sequence requiring the longest period of time.

Steps in Designing a PERT Network

When designing a PERT network, managers should follow four primary steps:

Step 1 List all the activities/events that must be accomplished for the project and the sequence in which these activities/events should be performed.

Step 2 Determine how much time will be needed to complete each activity/event.

Step 3 Design a PERT network that reflects all of the information contained in Steps 1 and 2.

Step 4 Identify the critical path.

▮ BACK TO THE CASE

Scheduling is another planning tool available to Jane and Paul. It involves the detailed listing of activities that must be accomplished to reach an objective. For example, if Jane and Paul's goal is to have all of their employees working proficiently on new equipment within two years, they need to schedule activities such as installing the equipment, training the employees, and establishing new output standards.

Two scheduling techniques Jane and Paul could use are Gantt charts and PERT. To schedule their employee production output they might want to use Gantt charts—bar graphs with time on the horizontal axis and the resource to be scheduled on the vertical axis. They might also find these charts helpful for evaluating worker performance and setting new production standards.

If Jane and Paul want to see the relationship between tasks, they could use PERT to develop a flowchart showing activities, events, and the amount of time necessary to complete each task. For example, a PERT network would be helpful in scheduling the installation of new machines, since this type of schedule would allow Jane and Paul to see which equipment needed to be installed first, the amount of time each installation would require, and how other activities in the shop would be affected before the installation was completed.

PERT would also indicate to Jane and Paul the critical path they must follow for successful installation. This path represents the sequence of activities and events requiring the longest amount of time to complete, and it indicates the total time the project will take to finish. If new welding machinery takes longer to install than other types of equipment, Jane and Paul should target the completion of the entire equipment installation on the basis of this equipment's installation time.

Action Summary

Reread the learning objectives that follow. Each objective is followed by questions. Answering these questions accurately will help you retain the most important concepts discussed in this chapter. After answering each question, check your answer with the answer key at the end of this chapter. (*Hint:* If you have doubt regarding the correct response, consult the page whose number follows the answer.)

Circle:

From studying this chapter, I will attempt to acquire:

1. **A complete definition of a plan.**

a, b, c, d, e
   a. A plan is: (a) the company's buildings and fixtures; (b) a specific action proposed to help the company achieve its objectives; (c) a policy meeting; (d) a projection of future sales; (e) an experiment to determine the optimal distribution system.

a, b, c, d, e
   b. Which of the following is generally *not* an important component of a plan: (a) the evaluation of relevant information; (b) the assessment of probable future developments; (c) a statement of a recommended course of action; (d) a statement of manager intuition; (e) strategy based on reason or rationality.

2. **Insights regarding various dimensions of plans.**

T, F
   a. Most plans affect top management only.

a, b, c, d, e
   b. Which of the following is one of the four major dimensions of a plan: (a) repetitiveness; (b) organization; (c) time; (d) a and c; (e) b and c.

3. **An understanding of various types of plans.**

a, b, c, d, e
   a. Standing plans that furnish broad guidelines for channeling management thinking in specified directions are called: (a) procedures; (b) programs; (c) single-use plans; (d) policies; (e) rules.

a, b, c, d, e
   b. Programs and budgets are examples of: (a) single-use plans; (b) standing rules; (c) procedures; (d) Gantt chart components; (e) critical paths.

4. **Insights on why plans fail.**

a, b, c, d, e
   a. Which of the following is a reason that plans fail: (a) adequate inputs are used in planning; (b) corporate planning is integrated into the total management system; (c) management expects that plans developed will be realized with little effort; (d) management operates by the plan; (e) responsibility for planning is vested in more than just the planning department.

T, F
   b. The confusion of planning with financial projections will have no effect on the success of the plans.

5. **A knowledge of various planning areas within an organization.**

T, F
   a. Input planning includes only site selection planning.

a, b, c, d, e
   b. Personnel planners who reflect on organizational objectives to determine overall human resource needs and compare needs to existing human resource inventory are engaging in a type of planning called: (a) process layout; (b) plant facilities; (c) input; (d) life cycle; (e) delphi.

6. **A definition of forecasting.**

T, F
   a. Forecasting is the process of setting objectives and scheduling activities.

a, b, c, d, e
   b. According to the text, which of the following products is in the growth stage of the product life cycle: (a) microwave oven; (b) cellular phone; (c) black and white television; (d) personal computer; (e) refrigerator.

7. **An ability to see the advantages and disadvantages of various methods of sales forecasting.**

   a. The sales forecasting technique that utilizes specialized knowledge based on interaction with customers is: (a) jury of executive opinion; (b) sales force estimation; (c) time series analysis; (d) a and b; (e) b and c.   a, b, c, d, e

   b. One of the advantages of the jury of executive opinion method of forecasting sales is that it may be the only feasible means of forecasting, especially in the absence of adequate data.   T, F

8. **A definition of scheduling.**

   a. Scheduling can best be described as: (a) the evaluation of alternative courses of action; (b) the process of formulating goals and objectives; (c) the process of formulating a detailed listing of activities; (d) the calculation of the breakeven point; (e) the process of defining policies.   a, b, c, d, e

   b. Scheduling is the process of predicting future environmental happenings that will influence the operations of the organization.   T, F

9. **An understanding of Gantt charts and PERT.**

   a. Which of the following is not an acceptable use of a Gantt chart: (a) as a summary overview of how organizational resources are being used; (b) to help coordinate organizational resources; (c) to establish realistic worker output standards; (d) to determine which resources are consistently contributing to productivity; (e) none of the above (all are acceptable uses of Gantt charts).   a, b, c, d, e

   b. In a PERT network, the sequence of events and activities requiring the longest period of time to complete is: (a) called the network; (b) indicated by thin arrows; (c) the path that managers avoid; (d) the critical path; (e) eliminated from the rest of the project so the project will not take too long.   a, b, c, d, e

INTRODUCTORY CASE WRAP-UP

"A Planning Incident" (p. 160) and its related back-to-the-case sections were written to help you better understand the management concepts contained in this chapter. Answer the following discussion questions about this introductory case to further enrich your understanding of chapter content:

1. Given Jane and Paul's situation, list the kinds of plans they probably need.

2. Write some sample plans that could be developed, given the planning needs you listed in number 1.
3. What kind of information would Jane and Paul need to actually develop the plans you have written?

Issues for Review and Discussion

1. What is a plan?
2. List and describe the basic dimensions of a plan.
3. What is the difference between standing plans and single-use plans?

4. Compare and contrast policies, procedures, and rules.
5. What are the two main types of single-use plans?
6. Why do organizations have programs?

7. Of what use is a budget to managers?
8. Summarize the ten factors that cause plans to fail.
9. What is input planning?
10. Evaluate the importance of plant facilities planning to the organization.
11. What major factors should be involved in site selection?
12. Describe the human resource planning process.
13. What is a planning tool?
14. Describe the measurements usually employed in forecasting. Why are they taken?
15. Draw and explain the product life cycle.
16. Discuss the advantages and disadvantages of three methods of sales forecasting.
17. Elaborate on the statement that all managers should spend some time scheduling.
18. What is a Gantt chart? Draw a simple chart to assist you in your explanation.
19. How can information related to the Gantt chart be used by managers?
20. How is PERT a scheduling tool?
21. How is the critical path related to PERT?
22. List the steps necessary to design a PERT network.

Sources of Additional Information

Allen, Louis A. "Managerial Planning: Back to Basics." *Management Review* (April 1981): 15–20.

Anderholm, Fred, III, James Gaertner, and Ken Milani. "The Utilization of PERT in the Preparation of Marketing Budgets." *Managerial Planning* 30 (July/August 1981): 18–23.

Brady, F. Neil. "Rules for Making Exceptions to Rules." *Academy of Management Review* 12 (July 1987): 436–44.

Cartwright, T. J. "The Lost Art of Planning." *Long-Range Planning* 20 (April 1987): 92–99.

Clark, Thomas B., Walter E. Riggs, and Richard H. Deane. "Guidelines to Compressing Projects for Profit." *Business* 35 (January/February/March 1985): 16–21.

Diven, David L. "Organizational Planning: The Neglected Factor in Merger and Acquisition Strategy." *Managerial Planning* 33 (July/August 1984): 4–8.

Germane, Gayton E. *The Executive Course: What Every Manager Needs to Know about the Essentials of Business.* Reading, Mass.: Addison-Wesley, 1986.

Levin, R. I., and C. A. Kirkpatrick. *Planning and Control with PERT/CPM.* New York: McGraw-Hill, 1966.

Lyneis, James M. *Corporate Planning and Policy Design: A System Dynamics Approach.* Cambridge, Mass.: MIT Press, 1980.

McLaughlin, Harold J. *Building Your Business Plan: A Step-by-Step Approach.* New York: Wiley, 1985.

Naylor, Thomas H. "Strategic Planning Models." *Managerial Planning* 30 (July/August 1981): 3–11.

Newman, William H., and James P. Logan. *Strategy, Policy, and Central Management,* 9th ed. Cincinnati: South-Western, 1985.

Rubin, Leonard R. "Planning Trees: A CEO's Guide through the Corporate Planning Maze." *Business Horizons* 27 (September/October 1984): 66–70.

Scott, Mel, and Richard Bruce. "Five Stages of Growth in Small Business." *Long-Range Planning* 20 (June 1987): 45–52.

Tagiuri, Renato. "Planning: Desirable and Undesirable." *Human Resource Management* (Spring 1980): 11–14.

Thompson, Stewart. *How Companies Plan.* New York: American Management Association, 1962.

Webb, Stan G. "Productivity through Practical Planning." *Administrative Management* 42 (August 1981): 47–50.

Welch, Jonathan B. "Strategic Planning Could Improve Your Share Price." *Long-Range Planning* 17 (April 1984): 144–47.

Notes

1. Henry L. Sisk, *Management and Organization* (Cincinnati: South-Western, 1973), 101.
2. Stewart Thompson, "What Planning Involves," American Management Association Research Study no. 54, 1962.
3. Fremont E. Kast and James E. Rosenzweig, *Organization and Management: A Systems Approach* (New York: McGraw-Hill, 1970), 443–49.
4. For discussion on expanding this list of four characteristics to thirteen, see P. LeBreton and D. A. Hen-

ning, *Planning Theory* (Englewood Cliffs, N.J.: Prentice-Hall, 1961), 320–44. These authors list the dimensions of a plan as (1) complexity, (2) significance, (3) comprehensiveness, (4) time, (5) specificity, (6) completeness, (7) flexibility, (8) frequency, (9) formality, (10) confidential nature, (11) authorization, (12) ease of implementation, and (13) ease of control.

5. For further discussion on each type of plan, see Herbert G. Hicks and C. Ray Gullett, *The Management of Organizations* (New York: McGraw-Hill, 1976), 271–78.

6. J. Fred Weston and Eugene F. Brigham, *Essentials of Managerial Finance* (New York: Holt, Rinehart & Winston, 1971), 107.

7. Kjell A. Ringbakk, "Why Planning Fails," *European Business*, July 1970.

8. Dale S. Beach, *Personnel: The Management of People at Work* (New York: Macmillan, 1975), 220.

9. Henri Fayol, *General and Industrial Management* (New York: Pitman, 1949).

10. William C. House, "Environmental Analysis: Key to More Effective Dynamic Planning," *Managerial Planning* (January/February 1977): 25–29.

11. Olfa Hemler, "The Uses of Delphi Techniques in Problems of Educational Innovations," no. 3499, RAND Corporation, December 1966.

12. A. R. Fusfeld and R. N. Foster, "The Delphi Technique: Survey and Comment," *Business Horizons* 14 (1971): 63–74.

13. For elaboration on these methods, see George A. Steiner, *Top Management Planning* (London: Collier-Macmillan, 1969), 223–27.

14. Gilbert Frisbie and Vincent A. Mabert, "Crystal Ball vs. System: The Forecasting Dilemma,"*Business Horizons* 24 (September/October 1981): 72–76.

15. Willard Fazar, "The Origin of PERT," *The Controller*, December 1962.

16. Harold L. Wattel, *Network Scheduling and Control Systems CAP/PERT* (Hempstead, N.J.: Hofstra University, 1964).

17. R. J. Schonberger, "Custom-Tailored PERT/CPM Systems," *Business Horizons* 15 (1972): 64–66.

Action Summary Answer Key

1. a. b, p. 161
   b. d, p. 161
2. a. F, pp. 161, 164
   b. d, pp. 161, 164
3. a. d, p. 165
   b. a, p. 169
4. a. c, pp. 169–170
   b. F, pp. 169–170
5. a. F, p. 170
   b. c, pp. 172–173
6. a. F, p. 173
   b. d, p. 176
7. a. b, pp. 175–177
   b. T, p. 177
8. a. c, pp. 178–179
   b. F, pp. 178–179
9. a. e, p. 179
   b. d, p. 181

ARO PLANS TO STREAMLINE OPERATIONS

"We categorically reject the idea that we can't compete by manufacturing in this country," said L. David Black, president and chief executive officer of the Aro Corporation. This comment relates to his company's commitment to strengthen its competitive position. "Clearly we have to do things differently. It is not just a price situation we want to go after. We want to greatly improve quality of product and quality of service. We should make [foreign producers] compete on our terms. All of this argues for a different way of doing things."

These comments reflect the philosophy behind the Bryant, Ohio, company's "Quality Thru Excellence" program, a venture aimed at improving all operations: sales and marketing, office operations, product design, and manufacturing. The Aro Corporation is a major international manufacturer of air-powered industrial equipment in four broad categories—air tools, hoists, and self-feed drills; fluid handling pumps, adhesive application systems, and lubrication systems; fluid power cylinders, valves, and logic controls; and air system filters, lubricators, regulators, and quick-disconnect couplers—plus aeronautical life support systems and package integrity testing equipment.

To carry out its program, Aro has developed a formal master plan for improving quality and cutting costs in manufacturing. Black and his management team are committed to becoming the undisputed leaders in their market. Their strategy includes three key points: getting more purchase orders (marketing and sales), reducing operating costs (all departments), and stabilizing employment levels and minimizing large swings in manpower.

"Embarking on the master plan will be like going on a journey as opposed to doing a project," Black told employees. Although projects are normally seen as having start and end points, the various activities of the master plan will be ongoing. Changes and adjustments made as time goes on will be based on inputs from involved parties and on technological innovation.

The company-developed master plan grew out of an idea triggered by guest speakers at a company technology conference for plant managers and engineers. Although the master plan idea is new, cell manufacturing and group manufacturing concepts, major elements of the master plan, had been applied in the company for the past decade. Because of the size of the overall master plan, a number of departments will have to be involved in its development while attending to their regular duties. However, to minimize confusion, Gene Casebere, director of materials, was selected to live with the plan and run it. Four planners, officially titled the manufacturing research and development team, were scheduled to work full time on the master plan under Casebere's direction, but actual implementation was to take place through existing functional areas. Once gross relationships studies were completed and targets and budgets for all functional areas were established, departmental cost-of-sales committees would be formed to begin developing more specific plans and reporting progress.

The planning groups' first major task was to come up with the overall direction. It was quickly agreed that the best design was a rod and tube cell arrangement. A manufacturing cell groups dissimilar machines producing similar parts, rather than grouping similar machines producing dissimilar parts. But where should the rod and tube cell be positioned? Before this decision could be reached, an even more basic issue had to be resolved. Would a new plating facility be incorporated into the design? The old plating equipment was wearing out; in addition, to stay in the plating business, the Environmental Protection Agency (EPA) would require the company to install a wastewater treatment plant. After analyzing the in-house and farm-out options, the planning groups decided to stay in the plating business, which would require a $1 million investment.

With this decision behind them came a whole host of others. Where should the plating equipment be located? was the next "biggie." Although it had been situated along the outside wall, it was used in a batch-type operation that would need to interface with many other processes. The groups finally decided that it belonged in the center of the facility. Many other cells were then designed to radiate out from this centralized plating station.

The rod line (1974) and the rotor and spindle line (1979) had been Aro's early entry into cell development. The rod cell was a group of screw machines, drilling machines, mills, and some cleaning and finishing equipment used to produce 380 parts in thirty families. Throughput for these parts went from an average of twenty-four days down to eight days. The rotor and spindle cell produced 60 rotor shapes and 50 spindle shapes. Operations were reduced from 141 to 16 for rotors and from 118 to 18 for spindles. The cell concept increased throughput, improved quality, cut costs, and reduced inventory. Operators became rotor and spindle makers rather than machine operators.

As of April 9, 1987, the master plan at Aro included the installation of a new plating system (scheduled for startup at the end of December); realignment of the pump assembly department and the diaphragm pump cell; relocation of the service department, the machine repair department, the pick center and ship-

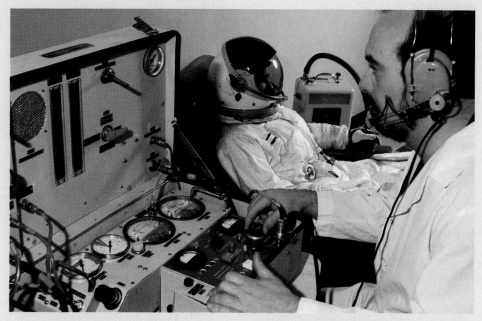

Portable test unit for pre-flight check on full pressure suit.

ping office, and the receiving department; and realignment of the lube assembly department and the fluid handling customer order picking department. Of course, the purpose of the master plan was to integrate these cells.

According to Paul Jones, plant manager, although the master plan provides great benefit, it "makes it very hard to run the store." In Aro's case, almost every piece of equipment in the plant will have to be moved. Offices will be moved. Even material handling equipment is going to change, with fewer lift trucks and concentration on special baskets and carts.

Although master plan implementation is putting a good deal of strain on the entire company, it has been especially hectic for those in maintenance (the department that must carry out the moves). Even though Paul Nowak, manager of maintenance, put together a "move team" to look into all aspects of each operation beforehand, many small but nagging details continue to surface. For example, the shifting of department locations has drastically changed utility requirements. Three of the plant's six electrical load centers have to be moved and upgraded, and a 300 horsepower compressor, a 150 horsepower compressor, and several receivers have to be added to the compressed air distribution system.

It is too early to say just how successful the project will be, but Aro is keeping track of the impact of each phase of master plan implementation. On the financial side, a spreadsheet is used to track budgeted costs and savings of the master plan development, capital expenditures, and impact on plant operations for every master plan task. On the physical side, the moving of equipment has increased plant floor space by 30 percent. On the psychological side, employees have renewed vigor. "I'm as enthused about manufacturing," says Dan Moore, vice-president of manufacturing, "as I have ever been in my life because there are some things happening here that represent real breakthroughs and not just the same old thing of cranking it out every month and trying to keep the costs under control."

DISCUSSION ISSUES

1. What are the dimensions of the master plan as outlined in the case? Explain.
2. What examples of standing and single-use plans are mentioned in the case?
3. K. A. Ringbakk lists ten reasons that plans fail. Identify specific statements from the case that suggest that the Aro Corporation has taken or plans to take steps to eliminate factors that could cause failure in the carrying out of its master plan (streamlining of operations). Give specific examples.

MORE EFFECTIVE PLANNING FOR THE CALIFORNIA SOCIETY OF CPAs

The California Society of Certified Public Accountants (CPAs) has fourteen chapters throughout the state, a membership approaching twenty-five thousand, and a paid staff of approximately seventy-five persons. Sixty percent of the membership is employed in public practice, with the remaining 40 percent in private industry, government, or academe. While meeting the needs of this diverse group was one significant reason for undertaking long-range planning, the more compelling reason was a recognition that, in today's rapidly changing social and economic environment, nonprofit professional service organizations face a tough challenge. Slow reaction time, infrequent meetings of decision-making bodies, built-in lack of continuity stemming from the annual turnover of elected volunteer leadership groups, and frustration of paid staff because of seemingly conflicting instructions issued from frequently changing officers all point to a need for a longer-range viewpoint and a more adaptive structure.

To initiate the planning process, the California Society of CPAs established a standing planning committee. The committee's objectives were to extend the society's perspective beyond the short term by identifying significant long-range opportunities that needed addressing and to enhance the society's understanding of the implications of current decision making. Nine persons seasoned in society affairs were selected to serve as the planning committee. This group was to act as a freethinking body and not bias its deliberations with perceived implementation difficulties. Implementation of plans remained the principal responsibility of the society's paid staff. The planning committee's charge was to oversee and maintain a planning process that provided for an ongoing assessment of the environment; identification of emerging problems, opportunities, and needs; and development of strategies to deal with these problems, opportunities, and needs.

One of the first official acts of the planning committee was to conduct a "horizon-planning session" with a selected cross section of the society's leaders. The session represented a free-form discussion of problems, opportunities, and trends within the profession's economic, political, and social environment. While many far-reaching issues were identified, one primary outgrowth of this session was a decision to conduct a "needs assessment survey" of the membership to obtain a better picture of member and firm problems and concerns. The anticipated result of the project was to restate the society's objectives in terms of current needs.

Utilizing the data obtained from the survey, the planning committee began the task of revising the society's mission statement. The mission statement articulating the society's fundamental purpose for being, had not been revised since the society's founding in 1909. As it turns out, this task became one of the most time-consuming parts of the entire planning process. Countless drafts were considered, rejected, and redrafted. The final version was as follows:

> The California Society of Certified Public Accountants is a voluntary association of certified public accountants in public practice, industry, government, education, and other occupations. The mission of the society is to enhance the California CPA profession and to promote the well-being of its members.

The operative words *enhance* and *promote* are especially noteworthy in that all future activities of the society are to be tested against these purposes.

Having agreed on a mission statement, the planning committee initiated action to develop related objectives, goals, strategies, and action plans. However, it became immediately apparent that before such actions could be successfully carried out, a uniform understanding of the meaning of those terms would have to be reached. The agreed-upon definitions are set forth in the accountants' definitions. Once the terminology was accepted, the society staff drew up an illustrative set of objectives and goals for the committee's consideration and prepared a "grocery list" of issues the society would be facing over the upcoming two years. These were ex-

Term	Definition and Purpose	Characteristics	Time Frame
Mission	The mission of an organization is its focus. The mission provides: • the vision of what the organization can be. • the "why" of organizational existence. • the organization's philosophical operational base. • the ultimate target of decision making.	Abstract Ideal	Infinite
Objective	An objective is a highly desirable ambition toward which an organization works. It provides more specificity than the organization's mission but may not be attainable within a planning period.	Believable Desirable Stable	Long-term
Goal	A goal is a milestone along the path toward an objective. Its attainment is planned within the planning period. It provides definitive direction.	Flexible Achievable Definitive Relevant	3 to 5 years
Strategy	A strategy is a plan of action that leads to major organizational commitments. It provides the framework for action.	Flexible Achievable Controllable Relevant	1 to 5 years
Action plan	An action plan is a plan to achieve a specific outcome. It provides the specific means to accomplish the outcomes required to achieve the organization's goals.	Realistic Controllable Tactical Measurable	Up to 12 months

tracted from the horizon-planning session referred to previously. The final product was a listing of six basic objectives having an aggregate of twenty-three separate goals; priorities were assigned to twenty-seven specific issues.

The planning committee then focused attention on the formulation of *strategic* goals. These were to be specific, high priority goals that could be attained by society committees, chapters, and divisions. About forty separate strategic goals were identified. A two-year cycle was adopted to provide sufficient time in which to develop and implement action plans.

Up to this point, the planning process had involved only the planning committee and the top echelon of society leaders and staff. It was now time to expose the plan to a wider segment of the membership. The mission, objectives, goals, and strategic goals were circulated to all chapter presidents, state committee chairpersons, and staff division heads. These people were asked to review the plans and then respond to three questions. They first were asked to specify the results they would achieve to assist the society in accomplishing specific strategic goals by the end of the two-year planning cycle. Next, they were asked to identify the specific programs or activities they would undertake to accomplish these results. Finally, they were asked to specify the new and continuing objectives, programs, and activities they would undertake during the two-year planning cycle. Worksheets were supplied to help

the respondents brainstorm on how to achieve objectives and develop new program ideas. Respondents were asked to specify anticipated results in the past tense and in specific and measurable terms. Society staff analyzed the responses, eliminated duplications, and classified the responses according to the original listing of strategic goals.

One sample of output from the entire process was as follows:

Objective: To assure the vitality of the CPA profession
Goal: To develop future leaders of the CPA profession
Action Plans: To develop and present a leadership training course for existing emerging society leaders; prepare a curriculum of other appropriate leadership courses; and develop a training plan for the society's management staff.

If the society had had unlimited funds, the planning process could have been terminated at this point. Unfortunately, even for the best new programs, resources are scarce. The task of linking desirable programs with the budgeting process is a difficult but indispensable aspect of planning. To a great extent, successes in this effort hinged on the society's ability to estimate the cost of each program with reasonable accuracy. The society decided to produce its cost estimates on the basis of three levels of funding. The first level represented the minimum commitment of resources necessary to support a viable program. The second level reflected incremental costs associated with maintaining the program at a normal (historical) level of activity. The third level was a projection showing the cost required to operate the program at the highest practical level. In addition to costs, narrative descriptions of the activities envisioned were provided for each level of funding.

DISCUSSION ISSUES

1. Compare the planning process implemented by the California Society of CPAs and the six-step planning process outlined in chapter 4.
2. Evaluate the effectiveness of the society's planning committee by comparing the committee's efforts to Malik's eight guidelines to assessing planner effectiveness outlined in chapter 4.
3. Do most of the planning committee's decisions appear to be of a programmed or nonprogrammed nature? Explain.
4. According to Dale, decision makers can have four different orientations: a receptive orientation, an exploitation orientation, a hoarding orientation, or a marketing orientation. What type of decisional orientation does the planning committee appear to be displaying? Explain. Does this orientation seem appropriate for a voluntary, nonprofit organization such as the California Society of CPAs? Explain.
5. You may have noticed that the sample of output (objective, goal, action plans) appearing near the end of the case does not include a strategy or strategic goal statement. Develop this strategic goal statement. Explain your logic.
6. Several specific environmental factors have been identified in chapter 6 as being extremely important for managers to consider when developing organizational strategies. In developing its strategy, has the planning committee omitted from consideration any of these environmental factors? Explain.
7. Does information in the case suggest that the society's planning committee employed a modified version of critical question analysis? SWOT analysis? Explain.
8. Is the "action planning" terminology used in the case the same as "tactical planning"? Explain.

3

ORGANIZING

This section discusses the second major management function—organizing. Organizing naturally follows planning, discussed in the previous section, because it is the primary mechanism by which managers put plans into action.

In general, the section covers the fundamentals of organizing, organizing the activity of individuals, the process of providing appropriate human resources within the organization, and organizational change and stress. More specifically, it covers several organizing fundamentals, including the definition of *organizing*, the five main steps involved in organizing, and the classical principles that influence the organizing process.

The material on organizing the activity of individuals will focus on responsibility as a fundamental ingredient in the organizing process and will indicate that delegating authority is an important component of organizing. In addition, the section will explain that an organization can be centralized or decentralized, depending on the amount of authority its management delegates. The discussion of providing appropriate human resources will emphasize the tasks of furnishing the organization with people who will make desirable contributions toward the attainment of organizational objectives and the tasks of utilizing the processes of recruitment, selection, training, and performance evaluation. Finally, the section will explain that organizational change is often necessary in order to increase organizational effectiveness and that the success of a particular change is based on the collective influence of such issues as how and what type of changes are made. This discussion also will address the relationship between stress and organizational change and will emphasize the importance of studying and managing stress.

One important point to remember is that organizing naturally follows planning. Organizing concepts discussed here will be challenging and relate to concepts discussed in previous sections. Understanding organizing is important to understanding the remainder of the text.

STUDENT LEARNING OBJECTIVES

From studying this chapter, I will attempt to acquire:

1. An understanding of the organizing function.
2. An appreciation for the complications of determining appropriate organizational structure.
3. Insights on the advantages and disadvantages of division of labor.
4. A working knowledge of the relationship between division of labor and coordination.
5. An understanding of span of management and the factors that influence its appropriateness.
6. An understanding of scalar relationships.

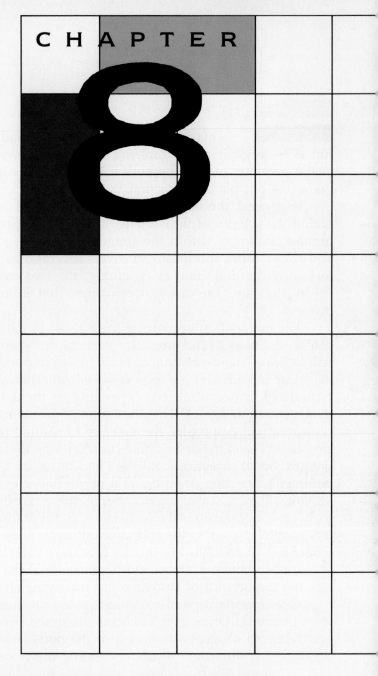

FUNDAMENTALS OF ORGANIZING

CHAPTER OUTLINE

CONSOLIDATING BAKERIES

Dianne Elmort, a management consultant in Baltimore, is in a meeting with a client. The telephone rings and Elmort's secretary tells her that she has a long-distance call from Los Angeles. The individual placing the call is Ralph Zacarachy, the owner of a bakery. Elmort excuses herself for a moment and accepts the call privately. The following conversation takes place:

ELMORT: Hello, this is Dianne Elmort speaking.

ZACARACHY: Ms. Elmort, this is Ralph Zacarachy. A friend of mine, James Earl, suggested that I call you for advice concerning a management problem I am presently facing. As you may recall, Jim was one of your past clients.

ELMORT: Yes, I remember Jim very well. He was trying to reorganize the departments in his housewares store and do some long-term planning. As I recall, we were able to solve his problem with minimum difficulty, and we also developed a very good working relationship. I'm glad you called. Is your situation similar to Jim's?

ZACARACHY: No. I wish it were. My problem is a lot more difficult, or so it seems to me. You see, for several years I've owned a bakery in downtown Los Angeles. I've been doing well downtown, and I recently decided to purchase another bakery in a suburban shopping center.

Now I'm faced with the problem of trying to organize the two bakeries. I don't really have a formal structure in either bakery. And since I've been a baker all my life, not a manager, I don't know how to coordinate the activities in the bakeries or organize my employees. I need to know what kinds of departments I should set up and how to divide up my employees' tasks. Also, it's difficult for me to manage both bakeries, since I obviously can't be in two places at once. I need the bakeries to be well organized, with their own managers, so they can function without me.

I'd really appreciate it if you could help me develop an organizing strategy. Do you think you can help?

ELMORT: Your situation is not all that difficult, though I'm sure it seems confusing to you right now. I've had experience handling this type of consolidation problem and would be happy to help you. Don't worry about the fee. I'm sure we can arrive at some mutually agreeable figure.

I have a list of standard questions regarding organizing that I usually ask clients with your kind of problem. Actually, these questions will only lay the rough groundwork for solving your problem. After you answer the questions, I should spend approximately a week thinking about your answers and then fly to Los Angeles to spend a couple days with you to finalize your organizing strategy.

Since I am in a meeting right now, it would be difficult for me to talk too much longer. If you want, I'll call you back this afternoon to ask you these questions.

ZACARACHY: Your suggestion sounds fine, and I'm pleased you'll be able to work with me. I'll be in the downtown bakery all afternoon, so call at your convenience.

What's Ahead

The ending of the introductory case leaves Ralph Zacarachy, a bakery owner, waiting for a call from Dianne Elmort, a management consultant. Elmort will be calling to ask Zacarachy some questions. Zacarachy's answers will provide the basis for organizing his old bakery and a new one that he just purchased. For these questions to be worthwhile, they must focus on the organizing function and furnish information that will help Elmort recommend a specific organizing strategy for Zacarachy's situation. The material in this chapter emphasizes both a definition of organizing and principles of classical organizing theory so the types of questions Elmort should ask will be better understood.

A DEFINITION OF ORGANIZING

Organizing is the process of establishing orderly uses for all resources within the management system. These uses emphasize the attainment of management system objectives and assist managers not only in making objectives apparent but also in clarifying which resources will be used to attain them.[1] *Organization* refers to the result of the organizing process.

In essence, each organizational resource represents an investment from which the management system must get a return. Appropriate organization of these resources increases the efficiency and effectiveness of their use. Henri Fayol developed sixteen general guidelines for organizing resources:[2]

1. Judiciously prepare and execute the operating plan.
2. Organize the human and material facets so that they are consistent with objectives, resources, and requirements of the concern.
3. Establish a single competent, energetic guiding authority (formal management structure).
4. Coordinate all activities and efforts.
5. Formulate clear, distinct, and precise decisions.
6. Arrange for efficient selection so that each department is headed by a competent, energetic manager and all employees are placed where they can render the greatest service.
7. Define duties.
8. Encourage initiative and responsibility.
9. Offer fair and suitable rewards for services rendered.
10. Make use of sanctions against faults and errors.
11. Maintain discipline.
12. Ensure that individual interests are consistent with the general interests of the organization.
13. Recognize the unity of command.
14. Promote both material and human coordination.
15. Institute and effect controls.
16. Avoid regulations, red tape, and paperwork.

The Importance of Organizing

The organizing function is extremely important to the management system, because it is the primary mechanism with which managers activate plans. Organizing creates and maintains relationships between all organizational resources by

Organizing is establishing orderly uses for all management system resources.

The organizing function is the mechanism to activate plans.

indicating which resources are to be used for specified activities and when, where, and how they are to be used. A thorough organizing effort helps managers to minimize costly weaknesses, such as duplication of effort and idle organizational resources.

Some management theorists consider the organizing function so important that they advocate the creation of an organizing department within the management system.[3] Typical responsibilities of this department would include developing (1) reorganization plans that make the management system more effective and efficient, (2) plans to improve managerial skills to fit current management system needs, and (3) an advantageous organizational climate within the management system.[4]

The Organizing Process

The five-step organizing process should be continually repeated so feedback will indicate potential improvements.

The five main steps of the organizing process, as presented in Figure 8.1, are (1) reflecting on plans and objectives, (2) establishing major tasks, (3) dividing major tasks into subtasks, (4) allocating resources and directives for subtasks, and (5) evaluating the results of implemented organizing strategy. As the figure implies, managers should continually repeat these steps. Through repetition, they obtain feedback that will help them improve the existing organization.

The management of a restaurant can illustrate how the organizing process might work. The first step the manager would take to initiate the organizing process would be to reflect on the restaurant's plans and objectives. Since planning involves determining how the restaurant will attain its objectives, and organizing involves determining how the restaurant's resources will be used to activate plans, the restaurant manager must start to organize by understanding planning.

The second and third steps of the organizing process focus on tasks to be performed within the management system. The manager must designate major tasks or jobs to be performed within the restaurant. Two such tasks might be waiting on customers and cooking food. Then the tasks must be divided into subtasks. For example, the manager might decide that waiting on customers includes the subtasks of taking orders and clearing tables.

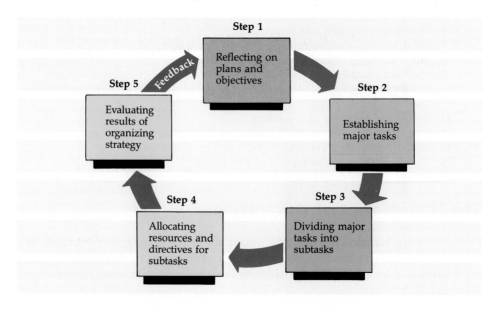

FIGURE 8.1
Five main steps of the organizing process

The fourth organizing step is determining who will take orders, who will clear the tables, and what the details of the relationship between these individuals will be. The type of tables and the type of silverware also are factors to be considered at this point.

In the fifth step, evaluating the results of a particular organizing strategy, the manager gathers feedback on how well the implemented organizing strategy is working. This feedback should furnish information that can be used to improve the existing organization. For example, the manager may find that a particular type of table is not large enough and that larger ones must be purchased if the restaurant is to attain its goals.

The Organizing Subsystem

The organizing function, like the planning function, can be visualized as a subsystem of the overall management system (see Figure 8.2). The primary purpose of the organizing subsystem is to enhance the goal attainment of the general management system by providing a rational approach for using organizational resources. Figure 8.3 on page 200 presents the specific ingredients of the orga-

The output of the organizing subsystem is organization.

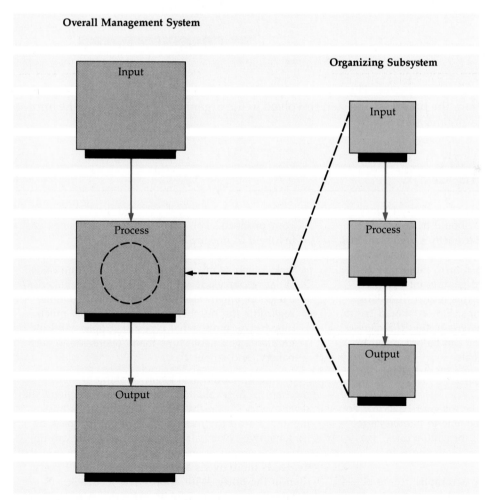

FIGURE 8.2
Relationships between overall management system and organizing subsystem

FIGURE 8.3
Organizing subsystem

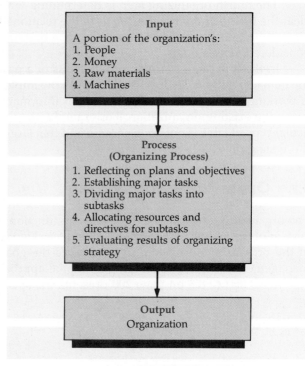

nizing subsystem. The input is a portion of the total resources of the organization, the process is the steps involved in the organizing function, and the output is organization.

■ BACK TO THE CASE

Elmort's questions to Zacarachy in the introductory case "Consolidating Bakeries" should be aimed at establishing an orderly use of Zacarachy's organizational resources. Since these resources represent an investment on which he must get a return, Elmort's questions should be geared toward gaining information that will be used to maximize this return. In asking Zacarachy preliminary questions, Elmort should try to pinpoint exactly what Zacarachy is trying to accomplish with his bakeries, so they can be organized in the best way to achieve his goals.

   Some preliminary questions Elmort could ask are as follows:

1. What objectives do you have for your bakeries? For example, do you want to be able to handle large orders in addition to small, individual ones? Do you want to be able to open more shops in the future?
2. What plans do you have to accomplish these objectives? Are you going to open more shops? Hire more employees?

3. What are the major tasks you go through to bake your products? For example, how many steps are involved in making cakes to order?
4. Can these steps be broken down into smaller tasks, such as mixing batter and decorating cakes?
5. What resources do you have to run your bakeries? I need as much information as you can give me regarding the number of employees, how much money you have, what types of supplies and ingredients you need, how many ovens are in each bakery, and so on.

   Elmort should also begin thinking of some mechanism for evaluating the organizing strategy she develops for Zacarachy. Once the strategy is implemented, Zacarachy must be able to get feedback on how his two bakeries are functioning, so he can improve the organization. For example, he may find that he needs more ovens and employees in one bakery than in the other. With appropriate feedback, Zacarachy can continually improve the existing organizational system.

⊞ CLASSICAL ORGANIZING THEORY

Classical organizing theory is the cumulative insights of early management writers on how organizational resources can best be used to enhance goal attainment. The writer who had perhaps the most profound influence on classical organizing theory was Max Weber.[5] According to Weber, the main components of an organizing effort are detailed procedures and rules, a clearly outlined organizational hierarchy, and, mainly, impersonal relationships among organization members.

Weber used the term **bureaucracy** to label the management system that contains these components. Although Weber firmly believed in the bureaucratic approach to organizing, he became concerned when managers seemed to overemphasize the merits of a bureaucracy.[6] He cautioned that a bureaucracy is not an end in itself but a means to the end of management system goal attainment. The main criticism of Weber's bureaucracy, as well as the concepts of other classical organizing theorists, is the obvious lack of concern for the human variable within the organization.[7] Considerable discussion on this variable is presented in section 4 ("Influencing") of this text.

The rest of this chapter summarizes four main considerations of classical organizing theory that all modern managers should include in their organizing efforts. They are (1) structure, (2) division of labor, (3) span of management, and (4) scalar relationships.[8]

Weber's organizing efforts contained detailed procedures and rules, an organizational hierarchy, and interpersonal relationships.

Structure

In any organizing effort, managers must choose an appropriate structure.[9] **Structure** refers to designated relationships among resources of the management system. Its purpose is to facilitate the use of each resource, individually and collectively, as the management system attempts to attain its objectives.[10]

Structure is designated relationships among organizational resources.

Organization structure is represented primarily by means of a graphic illustration called an **organization chart.** Traditionally, an organization chart is constructed in pyramid form, with individuals toward the top of the pyramid having more authority and responsibility than individuals toward the bottom.[11] The relative positioning of individuals within boxes on the chart indicates broad working relationships, and lines between boxes designate formal lines of communication between individuals.

An organization chart is a graphic illustration of authority and responsibility designations within the organization.

Figure 8.4 on page 202 is an example of an organization chart. Its dotted line is not part of the organization chart but has been added to illustrate the pyramid shape of the chart. The positions close to the restaurant manager's involve more authority and responsibility; the positions farther away involve less authority and responsibility. The locations of positions also indicate broad working relationships. For example, the positioning of the head chef over the three other chefs indicates that the head chef has authority over them and is responsible for their productivity. The lines between the individual chefs and the restaurant manager indicate that formal communication from chef 1 to the restaurant manager must go through the head chef.

Formal and Informal Structure

In reality, two basic types of structure exist within management systems: formal and informal. **Formal structure** is defined as the relationships among organiza-

Formal structure: Relationships outlined by management.

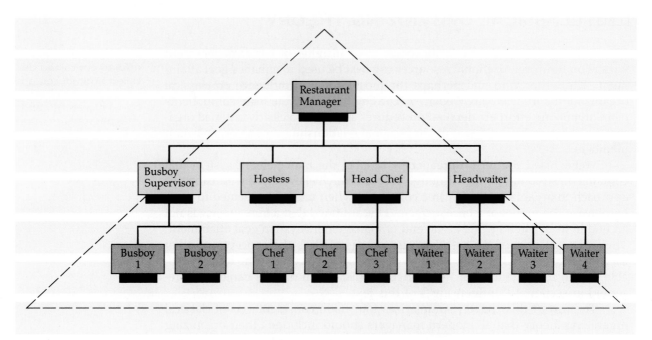

FIGURE 8.4
Sample organization chart for small restaurant

tional resources as outlined by management. It is represented primarily by the organization chart.

Informal structure: Informal relationships that develop among organization members.

Informal structure is defined as the patterns of relationships that develop because of the informal activities of organization members. It evolves naturally and tends to be molded by individual norms, values, or social relationships. Informal structure coexists with formal structure and sometimes resembles it.[12] The primary focus of this chapter is formal structure. More details on informal structure are presented in chapter 15.

Departmentalization and Formal Structure: A Contingency Viewpoint

Departmentalization establishes formal relationships between resources.

The most common method of instituting formal relationships among resources is by establishing departments. Basically, a **department** is a unique group of resources established by management to perform some organizational task. The process of establishing departments within the management system is called **departmentalization.** These departments typically are based on, or contingent on, such situational factors as the work functions being performed, the product being assembled, the territory being covered, the customer being targeted, and the process designed for manufacturing the product. (For a quick review of the contingency approach to management, see p. 365.)

Organizational design is contingent on:

the type of activity,

Perhaps the most widely used base for establishing departments within the formal structure is the type of *work functions* (activities) being performed within the management system.[13] The major categories into which the functions typically are divided are marketing, production, and finance. Figure 8.5 is an organization chart showing structure based primarily on function for a hypothetical organization, Greene Furniture Company.

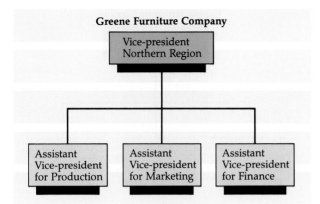

FIGURE 8.5
Organization structure based primarily on function

Organization structure based primarily on *product* departmentalizes resources according to the products being manufactured. As more and more products are manufactured, it becomes increasingly difficult to coordinate activities across them. Organizing according to product allows managers to logically group the resources necessary to produce each product. Figure 8.6 is a Greene Furniture Company organization chart showing structure based primarily on product.

Structure based primarily on *territory* departmentalizes according to the place where the work is being done or the geographic market area on which the management system is focusing. As market areas and work locations expand, the physical distance between places can make the management task extremely cumbersome. The distances can range from a relatively short span between two points in the same city to a relatively long span between two points in the same state or different states.[14] To minimize the effects of distances, resources can be departmentalized according to territory. Figure 8.7 on page 204 is a Greene Furniture Company organization chart based primarily on territory.

Structure based primarily on the *customer* establishes departments in response to the organization's major customers. This structure, of course, assumes that major customers can be identified and divided into logical categories. Figure 8.8 is a Greene Furniture Company organization chart based primarily on customers. Greene Furniture obviously can clearly identify its customers and divide them into logical categories.

the goods produced,

work or market locations,

who buys the products,

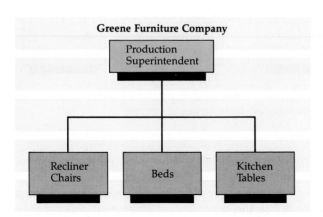

FIGURE 8.6
Organization structure based primarily on product

FIGURE 8.7
Organization structure based
primarily on territory

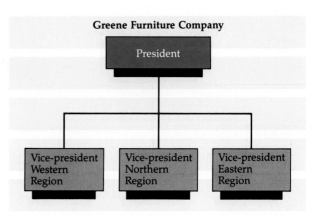

FIGURE 8.8
Organization structure based primarily on customers

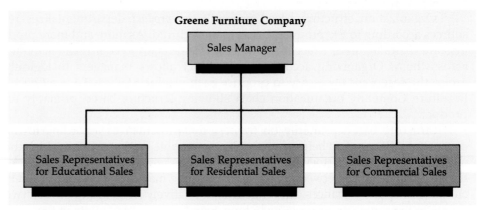

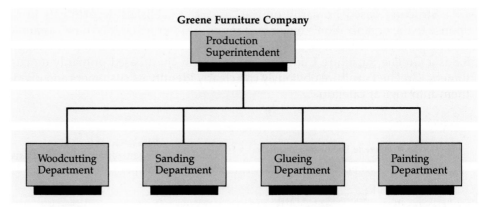

FIGURE 8.9
Organization structure based primarily on manufacturing process

and how the products
are made.

Structure based primarily on *manufacturing process* departmentalizes according to the major phases of the process used to manufacture products. In the case of Greene Furniture Company, the major phases are woodcutting, sanding, glueing, and painting. Figure 8.9 is the organization chart that reflects these phases.

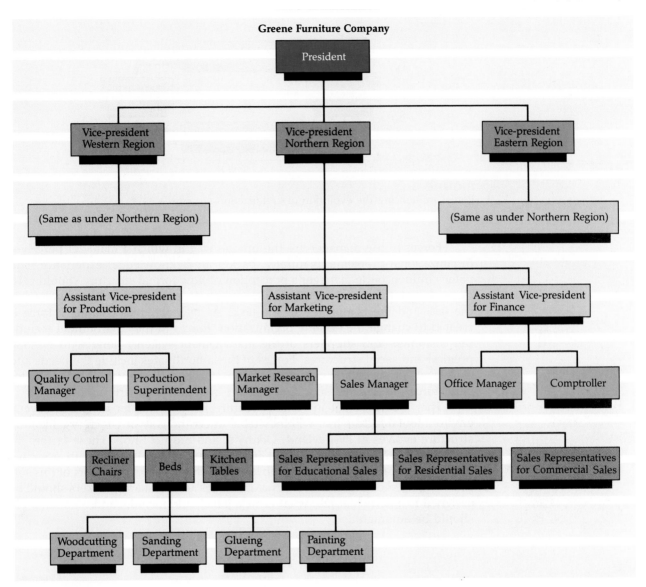

FIGURE 8.10
Organization structure based primarily on function, product, territory, customers, and manufacturing process

If the situation warrants it, individual organization charts can be combined to show all five of these factors. Figure 8.10 shows how all the factors are included on the same organization chart for Greene Furniture Company.

Forces Influencing Formal Structure

According to Shetty and Carlisle, the formal structure of a management system is continually evolving. Four primary forces influence this evolution: (1) forces in the manager, (2) forces in the task, (3) forces in the environment, and (4) forces in the subordinates.[15] The evolution of a particular organization is actually the result of a complex and dynamic interaction among these forces, as Figure 8.11 on page 206 illustrates.

Forces in the manager, the task, the environment, and the subordinates influence the evolution of organizational structure.

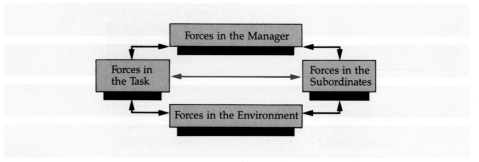

FIGURE 8.11
Forces influencing the evolution of organization structure

Forces in the manager are the unique way in which a manager perceives organizational problems. Naturally, background, knowledge, experience, and values influence the manager's perception of how formal structure should exist or be changed. Forces in the task include the degree of technology involved in the task and the complexity of the task. As task activities change, a force is created to change the existing organization. Forces in the environment include the customers and suppliers of the management system, along with existing political and social structures. Forces in the subordinates include the needs and skill levels of subordinates. Obviously, as the environment and subordinates vary, forces are created simultaneously to change the organization.

The "Management in Action" feature for this chapter discusses several environmental factors that will inevitably affect the way in which organization structure evolves at Disneyland, Denny's, and Stop & Shop. These factors include low birthrates, which result in a low supply of labor and in potential workers who cannot commute to job locations. Environmental factors of this sort can bring up such organization structure issues as how many workers should be assigned to a particular job, what tasks a job should include, and whether a job should be automated.

BACK TO THE CASE

In order to help Zacarachy organize his bakeries, Elmort must take classical organizing theory into consideration and base her questions on its four major elements—the first of which is structure. Elmort's questions about structure should be aimed at creating working relationships among all bakery employees. In order to develop an effective organizational structure, Elmort should analyze situational factors in the bakeries, such as functions, products, geographic locations, customers, and processes involved in making the baked goods.

For example, Elmort could create departments in the bakery on the basis of the types of functions or activities the bakery workers perform, such as waiting on customers, baking for the store, and baking to customers' orders. Elmort could also structure the bakeries on the basis of product, dividing them into the bread department, cookie department, cake department, and so on. Of course, the bakeries could also be organized using a combination of these structures.

Regardless of the structure Elmort develops, she could present and explain the departments to Zacarachy with an organization chart. This chart will allow him to see the line of authority and responsibility in his bakeries and to understand the broad working relationships among his employees.

ENVIRONMENTAL FACTORS AT DISNEYLAND, DENNY'S, AND STOP & SHOP

Disneyland has sent "presentation teams" to Los Angeles–area schools to tout the advantages of summer jobs at the giant amusement park. The teams have plenty to offer: wages of $4.25 an hour or more, well above the $3.35 minimum wage; free entry to the park during non-working hours; the right to request or occasionally refuse specific shifts. And any employee who refers another gets to enter a monthly raffle for a free TV set. Even so, as of last week 200 of Disneyland's 2,000 or so summer jobs were still unfilled.

Across the continent in Hyannis, Mass., Denny's Restaurant closed before the start of what should have been its peak season. It needed at least 70 employees to serve the summer crowds flocking to Cape Cod, but was able to hire only 13. A nearby Stop & Shop Supermarket found six cashiers only by recruiting in New Bedford, Mass., 40 miles away. The store will send a van to pick up the six every morning and drive them back at night, and the company will pay the employees time and a half for their two hours of daily travel.

Similar stories abound around the country, illustrating a disturbing trend in the labor market. In the U.S. economy's fifth year of steady expansion, the coexistence of spotty labor shortages and relatively high unemployment rates (6.1% nationally in June) is no longer news. But it is not just those seeking engineers, accountants, computer systems analysts and other highly skilled workers who are having trouble finding help. Employers seeking to fill seasonal and entry-level jobs demanding no experience and little skill—dishwasher, store clerk, hotel maid, gas-station attendant, farmhand, to name just a few—are often having just as much difficulty or more.

One reason is simple: such jobs traditionally are taken by young people eager to get their first taste of the work. But because of the low birth rates of the late 1960s and early 1970s, there are a lot fewer such youths than there used to be. The number of people ages 16 to 24 dropped from 37 million in 1980 to 34 million in 1986. While the economy has grown at a 3% rate since July 1986, the number of young people in the summer labor force has stayed the same: about 26 million. Says Louis Masotti, a political scientist at Northwestern University: "What we have is a burgeoning service economy that has walked right into the face of a declining demography."

But isn't unemployment among youths frighteningly high? It is indeed: 15.9% among teenagers generally, 33.3% for black teenagers. Unfortunately, many of the jobless youngsters are stuck in central-city ghettos. They have no way of getting to the fast-growing suburban areas where jobs in stores, hotels, fast-food restaurants and the like go begging; public transportation out to the suburbs is often nonexistent. They also do not have easy access to the resort areas, where the summer-worker crunch is particularly severe.

Better-off youngsters who live in the suburbs are equally inaccessible to many employers who are desperately trying to fill entry-level jobs, though for a different reason. Says Oscar Ornati, professor of manpower management at the New York University Graduate School of Business Administration: "Kids in Hastings-on-Hudson [a community in wealthy Westchester County, north of New York City] don't get jobs wrapping fast food. They get jobs as summer paralegals or interns at corporations." . . .

Employers are coming up with other lures, such as flexible hours for students and working mothers and medical-benefit programs for jobs that never had them before. McDonald's and other companies are recruiting retired people for jobs usually held by youths. But the most ambitious efforts are those that try to resolve the labor mismatch by searching in city ghettos for workers who can be brought to the available work. Universal Studios worked with two Los Angeles County high schools to select 400 mostly black and Hispanic students and put them through six hours of "employability" classes where they were taught how to dress and behave in job interviews. It hired 209 for summer jobs at up to $4.15 an hour serving tourists who visit the movie studios in Universal City; the new employees arrive in school buses donated by the county.

Such efforts so far are all too rare, but they are likely to expand. The pool of youths about to start their first jobs will go on shrinking into the early 1990s, and the suburbanization of the economy seems an irreversible trend. At least until the next recession, the days when employers could pick and choose among hundreds of youths lined up outside their doors seeking low-paying jobs appear to be over.

Division of Labor

Division of labor calls for specialization.

The second main consideration of any organizing effort is how to divide labor. The **division of labor** is the assignment of various portions of a particular task among a number of organization members. Rather than one individual doing the entire job, several individuals perform different parts of it. Production is divided into a number of steps, with the responsibility for completion of various steps assigned to specific individuals.[16] In essence, individuals specialize in doing part of the task rather than the entire task.

A commonly used illustration of division of labor is the automobile production line. Rather than one individual assembling an entire car, specific portions of the car are assembled by various individuals. The following sections discuss the advantages and disadvantages of division of labor and the relationship between division of labor and coordination.

Advantages and Disadvantages of Division of Labor

Division of labor may be efficient and have economic benefits.

Several generally accepted explanations have been offered for why division of labor should be employed. First, since workers specialize in a particular task, their skill for performing that task tends to increase. Second, workers do not lose valuable time in moving from one task to another. Since they typically have one job and one place in which to do it, time is not lost changing tools or locations. Third, because workers concentrate on performing only one job, they naturally try to make the job easier and more efficient. Last, division of labor creates a situation in which workers need to know only how to perform their part of the work task rather than the process for the entire product. The task of understanding their work, therefore, typically does not become too much of a burden.

However, overspecialization is boring and may depress production rates.

Arguments also have been presented, however, to discourage the use of extreme division of labor.[17] Over all, these arguments stress that the advantages of division of labor focus solely on efficiency and economic benefit and overlook the human variable. Work that is extremely specialized tends to be boring and therefore usually causes production rates to go down. Clearly, some type of balance is needed between specialization and human motivation. How to arrive at this balance is discussed further in chapter 14.

Division of Labor and Coordination

Coordination involves encouraging the completion of individual portions of a task in an appropriate, synchronized order.

In a division of labor situation with different individuals doing portions of a task, the importance of effective coordination becomes obvious. Mooney has defined **coordination** as "the orderly arrangement of group effort to provide unity of action in the pursuit of a common purpose."[18] Coordination involves encouraging the completion of individual portions of a task in a synchronized order that is appropriate for the overall task. For example, part of the synchronized order for assembling an automobile entails installing seats only after the floor has been installed. Adhering to this order of installation is coordination.

Establishing and maintaining coordination may, but does not always, involve close supervision of employees. Managers can also establish and maintain coordination through bargaining, formulating a common purpose, or improving on specific problem solutions.[19] Each of these efforts is considered a specific management tool. Managers should try to break away from the idea that coordination is achieved only through close employee supervision.

Mary Parker Follett has furnished concerned managers with valuable advice on how to establish and maintain coordination within the organization. First, Follett has indicated that coordination can be attained with the least difficulty through direct horizontal relationships and personal communications. When a coordination problem arises, speaking with peer workers may be the best way to solve it. Second, Follett has suggested that coordination be a discussion topic throughout the planning process. In essence, managers should plan for coordination. Third, maintaining coordination is a continuing process and should be treated as such. Managers cannot assume that because their management system shows coordination today it will show coordination tomorrow. Follett also has noted that managers should not leave the existence of coordination to chance. Coordination can be achieved only through purposeful managerial action. Last, according to Follett, the importance of the human element and the communication process should be considered in any attempt to encourage coordination. Employee skill levels and motivation levels are primary considerations, as is the effectiveness of the human communication process used during coordination activities.[20]

■ BACK TO THE CASE

To help Zacarachy organize his employees, Elmort should make use of the second major element in classical organizing theory—division of labor. Elmort could propose that instead of one person doing all the work involved in making cakes or bread, the labor could be divided so that for each product, one person mixes dough, one person decorates or braids, and one person watches the ovens. In this way, employees can work more quickly and can specialize in one area of the baking process, such as cake decorating or bread braiding.

When Elmort makes suggestions for the division of labor, she should also consider a mechanism for enhancing coordination. Her questions to Zacarachy should allow her to gain a thorough understanding of how the baking process occurs, so she can divide the tasks and maintain coordination within the departments. If, for example, the frosting on cakes must be a certain temperature before the cakes are decorated, Elmort must coordinate the frosting and decorating tasks so the cakes are frosted and chilled before the decorator is ready for them.

Elmort should stress to Zacarachy that precise coordination will require him to communicate with his employees. He will also need to continually plan for and take action toward maintaining such coordination.

Span of Management

The third main consideration of any organizing effort is **span of management**—the number of individuals a manager supervises. The more individuals a manager supervises, the greater the span of management. Conversely, the fewer individuals a manager supervises, the smaller the span of management. Span of management is also called span of control, span of authority, span of supervision, and span of responsibility.

The central concern of span of management is a determination of how many individuals a manager can supervise effectively.[21] To use human resources effectively, managers should supervise as many individuals as they can best guide toward production quotas. If they are supervising too few individuals, they are wasting a portion of their productive capacity. If they are supervising too many, they lose part of their effectiveness.

Span of management: How many individuals can one manager supervise effectively?

Designing Span of Management: A Contingency Viewpoint

As reported by Harold Koontz, several important situational factors influence the appropriateness of the size of an individual's span of management:[22]

The appropriate span of management is contingent on: similarity of subordinates' jobs,

Similarity of functions The degree to which activities performed by supervised individuals are similar or dissimilar. As the similarity of subordinates' activities increases, the span of management appropriate for the situation becomes wider. The converse is also generally accurate.

closeness of subordinates' jobs,

Geographic contiguity The degree to which subordinates are physically separated. In general, the closer subordinates are physically, the more of them managers can supervise effectively.

difficulty of subordinates' jobs,

Complexity of functions The degree to which workers' activities are difficult and involved. The more difficult and involved the activities are, the more difficult it is to manage a large number of individuals effectively.

interdependence of subordinates' jobs,

Coordination The amount of time managers must spend to synchronize the activities of their subordinates with the activities of other workers. The greater the amount of time managers must spend on coordination, the smaller their span of management should be.

and planning required for subordinates' jobs.

Planning The amount of time managers must spend developing management system objectives and plans and integrating them with the activities of their subordinates. The more time managers must spend on planning activities, the fewer individuals they can manage effectively.

Table 8.1 summarizes the factors that tend to increase and decrease span of management.

Graicunas and Span of Management

Graicunas's formula determines the number of possible relationships between a manager and subordinates.

Perhaps the best-known contribution to span of management literature was made by V. A. Graicunas, a management consultant.[23] His contribution was the development of a formula for determining the number of *possible* relationships between a manager and subordinates when the number of subordinates is known. **Graicunas's formula** is as follows:

$$C = n\left(\frac{2^n}{2} + n - 1\right)$$

TABLE 8.1

Major factors that influence the span of management

Factor	Factor Has Tendency to Increase Span of Management When—	Factor Has Tendency to Decrease Span of Management When—
1. Similarity of functions	1. Subordinates have similar functions	1. Subordinates have different functions
2. Geographic contiguity	2. Subordinates are physically close	2. Subordinates are physically distant
3. Complexity of functions	3. Subordinates have simple tasks	3. Subordinates have complex tasks
4. Coordination	4. Work of subordinates needs little coordination	4. Work of subordinates needs much coordination
5. Planning	5. Manager spends little time planning	5. Manager spends much time planning

TABLE 8.2

Geometric increase of
possible management-
subordinate relationships

Number of Subordinates	Number of Relationships
1	1
2	6
3	18
4	44
5	100
6	222
7	490
8	1,080
9	2,376
10	5,210
11	11,374
12	24,708
18	2,359,602

C is the total number of possible relationships between manager and subordinates, and n is the known number of subordinates. Table 8.2 shows what happens to the total possible number of manager-subordinate relationships as the number of subordinates increases from 1 to 18. As the number of subordinates increases arithmetically, the number of possible relationships between the manager and those subordinates increases geometrically. Figure 8.12 (p. 212) illustrates the six possible relationships between a manager and two subordinates.

A number of criticisms have been leveled at Graicunas's work. Arguments that Graicunas did not take into account a manager's relationships outside the organization and that he considered only potential relationships rather than actual relationships have some validity. The real significance of Graicunas's work, however, does not lie within the realm of these criticisms. His main contribution was pointing out that span of management is an important consideration that can have far-reaching organizational impact.[24]

Height of Organization Chart

A definite relationship exists between span of management and the height of an organization chart. Normally, the greater the height of the organization chart, the smaller the span of management. It also follows that the lower the height of the organization chart, the greater the span of management. Organization charts with little height are usually referred to as **flat;** those with much height are usually referred to as **tall.**

Figure 8.13 on page 212 is a simple example of the relationship between organization chart height and span of management. Organization chart A has a span of management of six, and organization chart B has a span of management of two. As a result, chart A is flatter than chart B. Both charts have the same number of individuals below the top manager. The larger span of management in A is reduced in B simply by adding a level to B's organization chart.

A broad span of management indicates a flat organization chart; a narrow span indicates a tall organization chart.

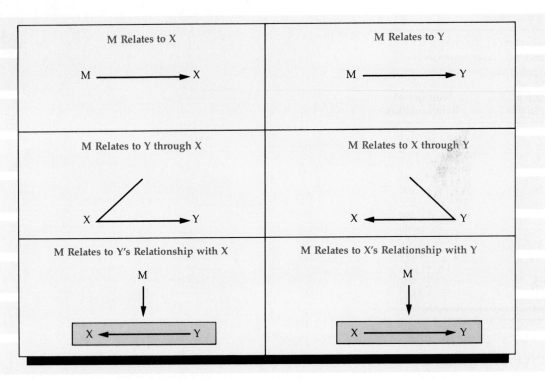

FIGURE 8.12
Six possible relationships between manager M and two subordinates, X and Y

Scalar Relationships

The fourth main consideration of any organizing effort is **scalar relationships**—the chain of command. Organization is built on the premise that the individual at the top possesses the most authority and that other individuals' authority is scaled downward according to their relative position on the organization chart. The lower an individual's position on the organization chart, the less authority possessed.

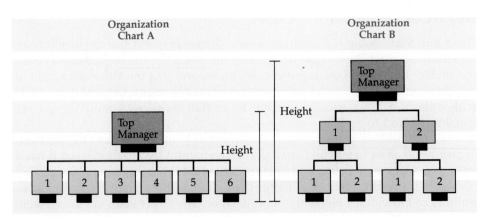

FIGURE 8.13
Relationship between organization chart height and span of management

The scalar relationship, or chain of command, is related to the unity of command. **Unity of command** means that an individual should have only one boss. If too many bosses give orders, the probable result is confusion, contradiction, and frustration, a situation that usually results in ineffectiveness and inefficiency.

Fayol has indicated that strict adherence to the chain of command is not always advisable.[25] Figure 8.14 serves to explain Fayol's rationale. If individual F needs information from individual G and follows the concept of chain of command, F has to go through individuals D, B, A, C, and E before reaching G. The information would get back to F only by going from G through E, C, A, B, and D. Obviously, this long and involved process can be very expensive for the organization in terms of time spent getting the information.

To decrease this expense, Fayol has recommended that in some situations a bridge, or **gangplank,** be used to allow F to go directly to G for information. This bridge is represented in Figure 8.14 by the dotted line that goes directly from F to G. Managers should use these organizational bridges with great care, however, because although F might get the information from G more quickly and cheaply, individuals D, B, A, C, and E are left out of the communication channel. The lack of information caused by Fayol's bridge might be more costly in the long term than would going through the established chain of command. If managers do use an organizational bridge, they must be extremely careful to inform all other appropriate individuals within the organization of the information they received.

Unity of command means having only one boss.

Use of Fayol's gangplank may be quicker, but it could be costly in the long term.

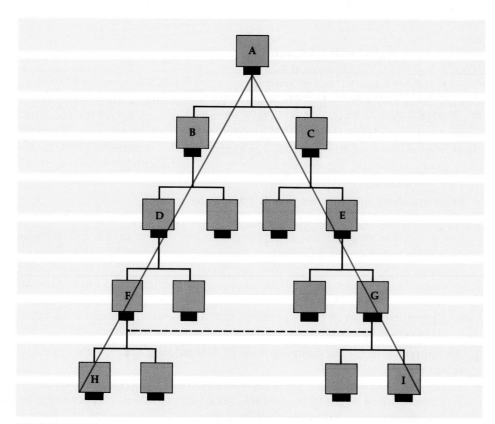

FIGURE 8.14
Sample organization chart showing that always adhering to the chain of command is not advisable

BACK TO THE CASE

The last two major elements in classical organizing theory are span of management and scalar relationships. Span of management is another of Elmort's major areas of recommendation to Zacarachy. It focuses on the number of subordinates managers can supervise in the bakeries. Elmort's questions to Zacarachy about span of management should cover several important situational factors, such as similarities among baking activities, the extent to which bakery workers are physically separated, and the complexity of baking functions.

For example, Elmort should know that baking cookies is fairly simple but baking bread is much more difficult. Therefore, the span of management for the bread department should generally be smaller than that for the cookie department. Other important factors Elmort should consider are the amount of time managers must spend coordinating bakery workers' activities and the amount of time managers spend planning. With all of this information, Elmort can suggest appropriate spans of management for the managers in Zacarachy's bakeries.

Elmort's recommendations should also relate to designating scalar relationships within the bakeries, such as determining that the manager of each department reports to the general manager of each bakery, who in turn reports to Zacarachy. Elmort must also consider when, if ever, this proposed chain of command should be bridged. For example, a bread baker who runs out of sugar and needs to borrow some from another department should be able to go directly to that department, rather than going through the chain of command. However, if sugar supplies in both departments are to be maintained, others in the chain of command, such as the bakery manager, would need to know, so more sugar could be ordered. Therefore, in making her recommendations to Zacarachy, it is important for Elmort to understand the relationships among the tasks being performed in the bakery and when it is necessary for an individual within the chain to know what others are doing.

Action Summary

Reread the learning objectives that follow. Each objective is followed by questions. Answering these questions accurately will help you retain the most important concepts discussed in this chapter. After answering each question, check your answer with the answer key at the end of this chapter. (*Hint:* If you have doubt regarding the correct response, consult the page whose number follows the answer.)

Circle:

From studying this chapter, I will attempt to acquire:

1. **An understanding of the organizing function.**

a, b, c, d, e
    a. Of the five steps in the organizing process, which of the following is grossly out of order: (a) reflect on plans and objectives; (b) establish major tasks; (c) allocate resources and directives for subtasks; (d) divide major tasks into subtasks; (e) evaluate results of the implemented organizational strategy.

T, F
    b. Proper execution of the organizing function normally results in minimal duplication of effort.

2. **An appreciation for the complications of determining appropriate organizational structure.**

a, b, c, d, e
    a. The XYZ Corporation is organized as follows: it has (1) a president, (2) a vice-president in charge of finance, (3) a vice-president in charge of marketing, and (4) a vice-president in charge of human resources management. This firm is organized on the: (a) functional basis; (b) manufacturing process basis; (c) customer basis; (d) territorial basis; (e) production basis.

b. All of the following forces are influences on the evolution of formal struc- a, b, c, d, e
ture except: (a) forces in the manager; (b) forces in subordinates; (c) forces
in the environment; (d) forces in the division of labor; (e) forces in the task.

3. Insights on the advantages and disadvantages of division of labor.

a. Extreme division of labor tends to result in: (a) human motivation; (b) bor- a, b, c, d, e
ing jobs; (c) nonspecialized work; (d) decreased work skill; (e) all of the
above.

b. Which of the following is *not* a generally accepted advantage of division of a, b, c, d, e
labor within an organization: (a) workers' skills in performing their jobs
tend to increase; (b) workers need to know only how to perform their
specific work tasks; (c) workers do not waste time in moving from one task
to another; (d) workers naturally tend to try to make their individual tasks
easier and more efficient; (e) none of the above (all are advantages of the
division of labor).

**4. A working knowledge of the relationship between division of labor and
coordination.**

a. Effective coordination is best achieved through close employee supervi- T, F
sion.

b. Mary Parker Follett has contended that managers should plan for coordi- T, F
nation.

**5. An understanding of span of management and the factors that influence its
appropriateness.**

a. Of the factors listed, which one would have a tendency to increase (ex- a, b, c, d, e
pand) the span of management: (a) subordinates are physically distant;
(b) subordinates have similar functions; (c) subordinates have complex
tasks; (d) subordinates' work needs close coordination; (e) manager spends
much time in planning.

b. The concept of span of management concerns: (a) seeing that managers at a, b, c, d, e
the same level have equal numbers of subordinates; (b) employee skill and
motivation levels; (c) supervision of one less than the known number of
subordinates; (d) a determination of the number of individuals a manager
can effectively supervise; (e) a and d.

6. An understanding of scalar relationships.

a. The management concept that recommends that employees should have a, b, c, d, e
one and only one boss is termed: (a) departmentalization; (b) function;
(c) unity of command; (d) scalar relationship; (e) none of the above.

b. According to Fayol, under no circumstances should a "gangplank" be T, F
used in organizations.

INTRODUCTORY CASE WRAP-UP

"Consolidating Bakeries" (p. 196) and its related
back-to-the-case sections were written to help you better understand the management concepts contained in
this chapter. Answer the following discussion questions about this introductory case to further enrich
your understanding of the chapter content:

1. How would you define *organizing*?
2. List as many questions as you can that you think

Elmort will ask Zacarachy in order to lay the foundation for solving the organizing problem in the
case.
3. Explain why it would be important for Elmort to
ask each of the questions you listed.

Issues for Review and Discussion

1. What is organizing?
2. Explain the significance of organizing to the management system.
3. List the steps in the organizing process. Why should managers continually repeat these steps?
4. Can the organizing function be thought of as a subsystem? Explain.
5. Fully describe what Max Weber meant by the term *bureaucracy*.
6. Compare and contrast formal structure with informal structure.
7. List and explain three factors that management structure is based on, or contingent on. Draw three sample portions of organization charts that illustrate the factors you listed.
8. Describe the forces that influence formal structure. How do these forces collectively influence structure?
9. What is division of labor?
10. What are the advantages and disadvantages of employing division of labor within a management system?
11. Define coordination.
12. Does division of labor increase the need for coordination? Explain.
13. Summarize Mary Parker Follett's thoughts on how to establish and maintain coordination.
14. Is span of management an important management concept? Explain.
15. Do you think that similarity of functions, geographic contiguity, complexity of functions, coordination, and planning influence appropriate span of control in all management systems? Explain.
16. Summarize and evaluate Graicunas's contribution to span of management literature.
17. What is the relationship between span of management and *flat* and *tall* organizations?
18. What are scalar relationships?
19. Explain the rationale behind Fayol's position that always adhering to the chain of command is not necessarily advisable.
20. What caution should managers exercise when they use the gangplank Fayol described?

Sources of Additional Information

Allen, Louis A. "Managerial Planning: Back to Basics." *Management Review*, no. 4 (April 1981): 15–20.

Argyris, C. *Integrating the Individual and the Organization*. New York: Wiley, 1964.

Arnold, Mark R. "Unleashing Middle Managers." *Management Review*, no. 5 (May 1981): 58.

Brown, A. *Organization*. New York: Hibbert, 1945.

Chamberlain, Neil W. *Social Strategy and Corporate Structure*. New York: Macmillan, 1982.

Etzioni, A. *A Comparative Analysis of Complex Organizations*. Glencoe, Ill.: Free Press, 1961.

Fink, Stephen L., R. Stephen Jenks, and Robin D. Willits. *Designing and Managing Organizations*. Homewood, Ill.: Richard D. Irwin, 1983.

Ford, Jeffrey D., and David A. Baucus. "Organizational Adaptation to Performance Downturns: An Interpretation-Based Perspective." *Academy of Management Review* 12 (April 1987): 366–80.

Giblin, Edward J. "Differentiating Organizational Problems." *Business Horizons* 24 (May/June 1981): 60–64.

Goddard, Robert W. "The Rise of the New Organization." *Management World* 14 (January 1985): 7–11.

Jelinek, Mariann, Joseph A. Litterer, and Raymond E. Miles. *Organizations by Design: Theory and Practice*, 2d ed. Plano, Tex.: Business Publications, 1986.

Lorsch, J. W., and John J. Morse. *Organizations and Their Members: A Contingency Approach*. New York: Harper & Row, 1974.

Mintzberg, Henry. "Organization Design: Fashion or Fit?" *Harvard Business Review* (January/February 1981): 103–16.

Mitroff, Ian I. *Stakeholders of the Organizational Mind*. San Francisco: Jossey-Bass, 1983.

Mondy, R. Wayne, and Robert M. Noe III. *The Management of Human Resources*, 3d ed. Boston: Allyn & Bacon, 1987.

Putnam, Linda L., and Michael E. Pacanowsky. *Communication and Organizations: An Interpretive Approach*. Beverly Hills, Calif.: Sage, 1983.

Ritchie, J. B., and Paul Thompson. *Organization and People: Readings, Cases, and Exercises in Organizational Behavior*, 3d ed. St. Paul, Minn.: West Publishing, 1984.

Robbins, Stephen P. *Organization Theory: The Structure*

and Design of Organizations. Englewood Cliffs, N.J.: Prentice-Hall, 1983.

Skibbins, Gerald J. *Organizational Evolution.* Seaside, Calif.: Intersystems Publications, 1981.

Notes

1. Douglas S. Sherwin, "Management of Objectives," *Harvard Business Review* (May/June 1976): 149–60.
2. Henri Fayol, *General and Industrial Management* (London: Sir Isaac Pitman and Sons, 1949), 53–54.
3. William F. Glueck, "Who Needs an Organization Department?" *California Management Review* 4 (Winter 1972): 77–82.
4. Burt K. Scanlan, "Managerial Leadership in Perspective: Getting Back to Basics," *Personnel Journal* (March 1979): 168–70.
5. Max Weber, *Theory of Social and Economic Organization,* trans. and ed. A. M. Henderson and Talcott Parsons (London: Oxford University Press, 1947).
6. Richard Bendix, *Max Weber: An Intellectual Portrait* (New York: Doubleday, 1960).
7. Charles Perrow, "The Short and Glorious History of Organizational Theory," *Organizational Dynamics* (Summer 1973): 2–15.
8. William G. Scott, "Organization Theory: An Overview and Appraisal," *Academy of Management Journal* (April 1961): 7–26.
9. George H. Rice, Jr., "A Set of Organizational Models," *Human Resource Management* 19 (Summer 1980): 21.
10. Lyndall Urwich, *Notes on the Theory of Organization* (New York: American Management Association, 1952).
11. For an interesting discussion of a nontraditional organization structure, see Pamela M. Banks and David W. Ewing, "It's Not Lonely Upstairs," *Harvard Business Review* (November/December 1980): 111–32.
12. Fred A. Katz, "Explaining Informal Work Groups in Complex Organizations: The Case for Autonomy of Structure," *Administrative Science Quarterly* 10 (September 1965): 204–23.
13. Gerald C. Werner, "Organizing for Innovation: Does a Product Group Structure Inhibit Technological Developments?" *Management Review* (March 1981): 47–51.
14. For information regarding steps to handle international organizing problems, see Gilbert H. Clee and Wilber M. Sachtjen, "Organizing a Worldwide Business," *Harvard Business Review* (November/December 1964): 55–67.
15. Y. K. Shetty and Howard M. Carlisle, "A Contingency Model of Organization Design," *California Management Review* 15 (1972): 38–45.
16. Adam Smith, *The Wealth of Nations* (New York: Random House, 1937).
17. C. R. Walker and R. H. Guest, *The Man on the Assembly Line* (Cambridge, Mass.: Harvard University Press, 1952).
18. J. Mooney, "The Principles of Organization," in *Ideas and Issues in Public Administration,* ed. D. Waldo (New York: McGraw-Hill, 1953), 86.
19. George D. Greenberg, "The Coordinating Roles of Management," *Midwest Review of Public Administration* 10 (1976): 66–76.
20. Henry C. Metcalf and Lyndall F. Urwich, eds., *Dynamic Administration: The Collected Papers of Mary Parker Follett* (New York: Harper & Bros., 1942), 297–99.
21. Gerald G. Fisch, "Stretching the Span of Management," *Harvard Business Review,* no. 5 (1963): 74–85.
22. Harold Koontz, "Making Theory Operational: The Span of Management," *Journal of Management Studies* (October 1966): 229–43.
23. V. A. Graicunas, "Relationships in Organization." *Bulletin of International Management Institute* (March 1933): 183–87. For more on the life of Graicunas, see Arthur C. Bedeian, "Vytautas Andrius Graicunas: A Biographical Note," *Academy of Management Journal* 17 (June 1974): 347–49.
24. L. F. Urwick, "V. A. Graicunas and the Span of Control," *Academy of Management Journal* 17 (June 1974): 349–54.
25. Henri Fayol, *General and Industrial Administration* (Belmont, Calif.: Pitman, 1949).

Action Summary Answer Key

1. a. c, p. 198–199
   b. T, pp. 197–198
2. a. a, pp. 202–204
   b. d, pp. 205–206
3. a. b, p. 208
   b. e, p. 208
4. a. F, pp. 208–209
   b. T, p. 209
5. a. b, p. 210
   b. d, pp. 209–210
6. a. c, p. 213
   b. F, p. 213

PEOPLE EXPRESS—
A ONCE EMULATED
ORGANIZATION

Back in 1981, Donald C. Burr created an innovative new airline: People Express. Based at a little-used airport in Newark, New Jersey, it opened up air travel to a huge segment of society by charging the equivalent of bus fares. This was when the company served only a limited number of cities as a no-frills, low-priced carrier.

In those early years, Burr created quite a mystique at People Express. The company was characterized by minimal bureaucracy, group organization of workers, salaries tied to profits, rotation of staff through jobs, and "manager" titles for all. No employee was more than three levels away from Burr or a managing director, so problems could be dealt with in person. Employees moved from job to job, sometimes daily. It was not uncommon to find pilots taking tickets and tending computer operations or flight attendants tracking lost bags. Burr titled this "cross-utilization," a way for employees to understand all aspects of their business. In addition, People Express employees were required to be shareholders—to purchase a minimum number of shares before beginning work. This was intended to give every employee a personal stake in the company.

In its early days, this maverick approach to organization inspired admiration and emulation. Executives, consultants, and even academics swarmed to the airline, seeking insight into the methods that had stirred the company's initial success. When People Express served only a limited number of cities, this no-bureaucracy, little hierarchy system seemed to work.

However, the initial prosperity was followed by rapid growth. People Express began challenging the airline giants by flying to Chicago and Dallas. It also went on a buying spree, acquiring Provincetown-Boston Airline and Britt Airways, both commuter carriers, and Frontier Airlines, a major regional carrier based in Denver. In addition, it began flying larger planes, such as jumbo Boeing 747s and 727s. And through all this expansion and change, the board of directors, made up of five members, met only four times.

By late 1984, People Express's revenues approached $1 billion a year and employees numbered near 3,500. In an attempt to overshadow the effects of a slumping economy and the plunging value of People's stock, and to regain some of the enthusiasm associated with the intimacy of the earlier days, Burr decided to initiate a few organizational changes. Eleven new managing officers were selected, and employees were directed to join one of the eleven new operating groups.

Each team contained about 300 people—100 pilots and 200 flight attendants—who all would work on the same type of aircraft, say Boeing 747s. Groups were to function semiautonomously and were assigned suites at headquarters to give them a place for reading, talking, and relaxing. Videocassette players were provided to employees to keep them informed on what was going on in the airline. Burr's hope was that each group would view itself as its own little family, a return to one of his founding precepts.

But the changes were not adequate. Burr's measures were far less elaborate than were needed to run smoothly and profitably what was now a big airline. The company was hit hard in one of the most important areas for airlines: service. Maintenance problems were causing flight delays, the lack of sophisticated computers contributed to overbooking and ticket problems, and the lack of a good luggage handling system caused thousands of bags to be lost. Many customers became disgruntled former customers.

Statistics compiled by the U.S. Department of Transportation (DOT) for the first quarter of 1986 showed that People Express had shot to the top of the charts in number of passenger complaints filed. At 10.3 per 100,000 passengers, the numbers showed People to be more than three times worse than Eastern Airlines, whose score was considered average, and seventeen times worse than Delta, whose score was considered one of the best. Furthermore, DOT statistics show that a major cause for complaints was overbooking. In November through January, a busy holiday traveling period,

People Express overbooked and denied boarding to 29,600 passengers, a figure nearly triple of that of Eastern, a much bigger carrier. In addition, People had enormous baggage handling problems. Outside contractors hired to sort and load bags managed to lose 14,000 bags a month. These problems caused People Express to attain the title of "People Distress."

With all of these troubles becoming more apparent, the board was forced into taking a more active role in company affairs. In May 1986, People Express hired outsider Robert Norris as chief accounting officer. But by June 23, the numbers looked so bad that People announced it was ready to sell all or part of itself. With Frontier's $58 million net loss in the first quarter of 1986, People soon agreed to sell Frontier to United.

In addition, the investment firm of Morgan Stanley was engaged to help in planning new strategies. One of its first suggestions was to develop a new management team. People Express went for a total makeover, tightening up its much publicized "democratic" organizational culture. Burr had been criticized for resisting delegation of authority and keeping tight reign on a few overworked officers. In the shakeup, Burr remained the chairman, president, and chief executive; but much power was delegated to others in an attempt to set up some formal management structures. David McElroy, a longtime People executive, was named chief operating officer, coordinating marketing, operations, and finance. Norris became the main financial officer.

An internal memo from Burr, highlighting major points made in a July 1986 presentation to employees, reflected the changed emphasis at People Express. The several themes included references to the fact that executives had been spread too thinly and would need to narrow their focus, that specific goals should be pursued, and that special attention should be devoted to a new program for cost control.

Unfortunately, the shakeup came too late. In December 1986, with a reported loss of $300 million for that year, shareholders of People Express approved the airline's acquisition by Texas Air Corporation, the country's largest airline holding company. The name People Express was to be dropped by February 4, 1987. As for Burr, he was assigned the position of executive vice-president at Texas Air. He held that post for only two months before resigning. His plans included writing a book about his experiences at People Express.

DISCUSSION ISSUES

1. Does Donald Burr's "cross-utilization" concept violate any of the four fundamental organizing considerations from classical organization theory? Explain.

2. In the early days at People Express, what was the maximum length of the chain of command, or scalar chain? After Burr's reorganization attempt in late 1984, what was the span of management for each of the eleven new managing directors? Does this information hint at a reason for the eventual demise of People Express? Explain.

3. After Burr's 1984 reorganization, what was the primary basis of the departmentation used at People Express? Did the basis change with the 1986 board-initiated reorganization? Explain.

STUDENT LEARNING OBJECTIVES

From studying this chapter, I will attempt to acquire:

1. An understanding of the relationship of responsibility, authority, and delegation.
2. Information on how to divide and clarify job activities of individuals within an organization.
3. Knowledge of the differences among line authority, staff authority, and functional authority.
4. An appreciation for the issues that can cause conflict in line and staff relationships.
5. Insights on the value of accountability to the organization.
6. An understanding of how to delegate.
7. A strategy for eliminating various barriers to delegation.
8. A working knowledge of when and how an organization should be decentralized.

ORGANIZING THE ACTIVITY OF INDIVIDUALS

CHAPTER OUTLINE

REDESIGNING JOB ACTIVITIES

Leo Mercer recently was appointed manager of the student employment department in the financial aids division of Athens University. The purpose of the student employment department is to help students who need part-time work to compete effectively in the community labor market. This help includes such activities as assistance in finding a position, guidance in writing résumés, and suggestions on how to interview. Mercer graduated from the school of business and administration at Central University six months ago.

During his first week on the job, Mercer's only official responsibility was reading a policy manual that familiarized him with the student financial aids division. According to this manual, Mercer was under the direct supervision of the manager of the student financial aids division and at the same level as the manager of student loans and the manager of scholarships and grants. The formal relationship between these four individuals is presented in Case Figure 9.1.

On the first day of Mercer's second week on the job, he called a meeting with his eight subordinates to introduce himself and to begin orienting himself to his new position. During the meeting, Mercer admitted that to do his job well he would have to become familiar with the job each individual was performing, the relationship of the student employment department to other depart-

ments in the student financial aids division, and the student employment situation within the community.

The meeting ended with Mercer stressing that his first priority was to learn how the student employment department operated. To this end, Mercer asked all of the people at the meeting to submit within two weeks a detailed written summary of their activities during a normal workweek.

At the end of two weeks, Mercer was pleased to discover that all eight performance summaries had been submitted. After analyzing the summaries, however, he was somewhat puzzled that no one was responsible for performing certain job activities that seemed fundamental to a student employment department. For example, no one from the student employment department ever followed up to see how well a student performed in a job. Mercer reasoned that this follow-up could be of significant help in convincing certain employers of the value of student employees. If the follow-up and the other neglected fundamental activities that Mercer found were to be added to the present normal operation of the student employment department, however, some individuals within the department would have an increased work load.

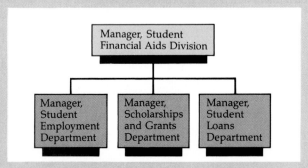

CASE FIGURE 9.1
The formal relationship of managers in the financial aids division

What's Ahead

Leo Mercer, the lower-level manager in the introductory case, is faced with the task of modifying the job activities of certain individuals within the student employment department. In essence, Mercer must change the way in which his department operates. The information in this chapter should be of great value to Mercer or to anyone confronted with a similar task, since organizing the job activities of individuals within an organization is the principal topic of the chapter. Three major elements of organizing are presented: (1) responsibility, (2) authority, and (3) delegation.

Chapter 8 dealt with using principles of organizational structure, division of labor, span of management, and scalar relationships to establish an orderly use of resources within the management system. Productivity within any management system, however, results from specific activities performed by various individuals within the organization. An effective organizing effort therefore includes not only a rationale for the orderly use of management system resources but also three other elements of organizing that specifically channel the activities of organization members. These three elements are responsibility, authority, and delegation.

⊞ RESPONSIBILITY

Perhaps the most fundamental method of channeling the activity of individuals within an organization, **responsibility** is the obligation to perform assigned activities. It is the self-assumed commitment to handle a job to the best of one's ability. The source of responsibility lies within the individual. A person who accepts a job agrees to carry out a series of duties or activities or to see that someone else carries them out. The act of accepting the job means that the person is obligated to a superior to see that job activities are successfully completed. Since responsibility is an obligation that a person *accepts*, there is no way it can be delegated or passed on to a subordinate.

> Responsibility is the obligation to complete assigned activities.

A summary of an individual's job activities within an organization is usually in a formal statement called a **job description**—a listing of specific activities that must be performed by whoever holds the position. Unclear job descriptions can confuse employees and may cause them to lose interest in their jobs.[1]

> A job description summarizes a person's job activities.

Job activities, of course, are delegated by management to enhance the accomplishment of management system objectives. Management analyzes its objectives and assigns specific duties that will lead to reaching those objectives. A sound organizing strategy includes specific job activities for each individual within the organization. As objectives and other conditions within the manage-

> Job activities are related to organizational objectives.

ment system change, however, individual job activities within the organization may have to be changed.

Three areas related to responsibility are (1) dividing job activities, (2) clarifying job activities of managers, and (3) being responsible. Each of these topics is discussed in the sections that follow.

Dividing Job Activities

Since, typically, many individuals work within a given managment system, organizing necessarily involves dividing job activities among a number of people. One individual cannot be obligated or responsible for performing all of the activities within an organization. Some method of distributing job activities and thereby channeling the activities of several individuals is needed.

Functional similarity
method: Four interrelated, sequential
steps for dividing job
activities.

The phrase *functional similarity* refers to what many management theorists believe to be the most basic method of dividing job activities. Stated simply, the **functional similarity method** suggests that management should take four basic interrelated steps to divide job activities. These steps, in the sequence in which they should be taken, are (1) management examines management system objectives, (2) management designates appropriate activities that must be performed to reach those objectives, (3) management designs specific jobs by grouping similar activities, and (4) management makes specific individuals responsible for performing those jobs. Figure 9.1 illustrates the sequence of activities suggested by the functional similarity method.

In dividing job activities, managers should
avoid overlapping responsibility, responsibility gaps, and job
activities that do not
enhance goal attainment.

Thierauf, Klekamp, and Geeding have indicated that at least three additional guides can be used to supplement the functional similarity method.[2] The first of these supplemental guides suggests that overlapping responsibility should be avoided in making job activity divisions. **Overlapping responsibility** exists when more than one individual is responsible for the same activity. Generally speaking, only one individual should be responsible for completing any one activity. The second supplemental guide is to avoid responsibility gaps. A **responsibility gap** exists when certain tasks are not included in the responsibility area of any individual. In essence, a responsibility gap creates a situation in which nobody within the organization is obligated to perform certain necessary activities. The third supplemental guide is to avoid creating job activities for accomplishing tasks that do not enhance goal attainment. Organization members should be obligated to perform only those activities that lead to goal attainment.

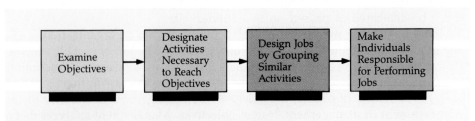

FIGURE 9.1
Sequence of activities for the functional similarity method of dividing responsibility

BACK TO THE CASE

Leo Mercer in the introductory case is faced with modifying the required activities of various individuals within the student employment department. These activity modifications should help his department become more successful if he derives them directly from student employment objectives. Mercer's specific steps to make these modifications should include the analysis of departmental objectives, the outlining of specific student employment activities that must be performed to reach those objectives, the designing of student employment jobs by the grouping of similar activities, and the assigning of these jobs to student employment personnel. To supplement these steps, Mercer must be careful not to create overlapping responsibilities, responsibility gaps, or responsibilities for activities that do not lead directly to goal attainment.

Clarifying Job Activities of Managers

Clarification of the job activities of managers is as important as, if not more important than, dividing the job activities of nonmanagers, since managers affect greater portions of resources within the management system. Hence, such factors as responsibility gaps usually have a more significant impact on the management system when they relate to managers as opposed to nonmanagers.

One process used to clarify management job activities "enables each manager to actively participate with his or her superiors, peers, and subordinates in systematically describing the managerial job to be done and then clarifying the role each manager plays in relationship to his or her work group and to the organization."[3] The purpose of this interaction is to assure that no overlaps or gaps in perceived management responsibilities exist and that managers are performing only the activities that lead to the attainment of management system objectives. Although this process typically has been used to clarify the responsibilities of managers, it may also be effective in clarifying the responsibilities of nonmanagers.

TABLE 9.1

Seven responsibility relationships among managers, as used in the management responsibility guide

1. *General Responsibility*—The individual guides and directs the execution of the function through the person accepting operating responsibility
2. *Operating Responsibility*—The individual is directly responsible for the execution of the function
3. *Specific Responsibility*—The individual is responsible for executing a specific or limited portion of the function
4. *Must Be Consulted*—The individual, if the decision affects his or her area, must be called upon before any decision is made or approval is granted, to render advice or relate information, but not to make the decision or grant approval
5. *May Be Consulted*—The individual may be called upon to relate information, render advice, or make recommendations
6. *Must Be Notified*—The individual must be notified of action that has been taken
7. *Must Approve*—The individual (other than persons holding general and operating responsibility) must approve or disapprove

Sample page of management responsibility guide for division of aerospace company

Number	Function	Vice-president Aerospace	Vice-president Manufacturing	Director Engineering	Manager Industrial Technology	Manager Quality Assurance	Manager Marketing	Manager Contracts	Manager Master Scheduling	Manager Financial Services
101	Coordinate division budgeting and financial planning activities and communicate financial information to division management	A	E-F	E-F	E-F	E-F	E-F	E-F	E	B
		A-F	D-F	E	F	F	E-F	E-F	D	
102	Develop project and program schedule requirements; establish, coordinate, and control schedules and report on status	A	E-F	E-F	E-F	E-F	E-F	E-F	B	
		A	D	D	D-F	C	D	D		F
103	Direct contract activities and evaluate and approve contract provisions of all division sales proposals and contract documents	A				E-F	B	E-F	F	
		A		E		D		D-F	C	
104	Plan and coordinate divisional marketing activities so as to secure the business necessary to maximize division's capabilities	A	E-F	E-F	E-F		B	D-F	E-F	F
		A-D	F			E		C-G	C-D	F
105	Develop and design new and improve existing electronic and electromechanical aerospace products and processes	A	F	B			E			
		A-F	E		E		D-G			
106	Secure materials and tools, coordinate human resources, and manufacture products to specified quantity, quality, time, and cost requirements	A	B			F		E-F		E-F
		A		E	E	C-D		E	F	E
107	Establish quality assurance policies, procedures, and controls to ensure that products meet applicable standards and specifications	A	D-F	D-F	E	B	F	E-F	E-F	
		A	D-G	E-F	E		E	D		F
108	Develop and design propriety products and processes utilizing proven technology specifically adapted to industrial automation	A	D-F	C	B	E	E	D	F	F
		A-F	E-F	B	D-F			E	E	F
		A	E					E-F	D-F	F

Relationship Code

A — General Responsibility

B — Operating Responsibility

C — Specific Responsibility

D — Must Be Consulted

E — May Be Consulted

F — Must Be Notified

G — Must Approve

Organization identification Aerospace Aerospace division	Number 200	Management responsibility guide Approval	Date	Page No. 1 of 1

FIGURE 9.2
Sample page of management responsibility guide for division of aerospace company

The job activities of managers can be clarified with a management responsibility guide.

A specific tool developed to implement this interaction process is the **management responsibility guide**.[4] This guide, some version of which is used in most organizations, assists organization members in describing the various responsibility relationships that exist in their organization and summarizing how

226

the responsibilities of various managers within their organization relate to one another.

The seven main organizational responsibility relationships described by this tool are listed in Table 9.1. Once organization members decide which of these relationships exist within their organization, they define the relationships between these responsibilities.

Figure 9.2 is a sample completed management responsibility guide for a division of an aerospace company. It summarizes existing management responsibility relationships within the division and shows how these relationships complement one another. The actual members of the aerospace division, of course, were the individuals who completed the management responsibility guide.

Being Responsible

Managers can be described as responsible if they perform the activities they are obligated to perform.[5] Since managers typically have more impact on an organization than nonmanagers, responsible managers are a prerequisite for management system success. Several studies have shown that responsible management behavior is highly valued by top executives, because the responsible manager guides many other individuals within the organization in performing their duties appropriately.

Performance of obligated activities is a measure of managerial responsibleness.

The degree of responsibleness that managers possess can be determined by analysis of managers' (1) attitude toward and conduct with subordinates, (2) behavior with upper management, (3) behavior with other groups, and (4) personal attitudes and values. Table 9.2 summarizes what each of these dimensions includes for the responsible manager.

The "Management in Action" feature for this chapter emphasizes the importance of managers being responsible in their attitude toward and conduct with subordinates. The responsible treatment of subordinates by managers at ServiceMaster has resulted in high-quality services being offered to customers.

TABLE 9.2

Four key dimensions of responsible management behavior

Behavior with Subordinates	Behavior with Upper Management	Behavior with Other Groups	Personal Attitudes and Values
Responsible managers— 1. Take complete charge of their work groups 2. Pass praise and credit along to subordinates 3. Stay close to problems and activities 4. Take action to maintain productivity and are willing to terminate poor performers if necessary	Responsible managers— 1. Accept criticism for mistakes and buffer their groups from excessive criticism 2. Ensure that their groups meet management expectations and objectives	Responsible managers make sure that any gaps between their areas and those of other managers are securely filled	Responsible managers— 1. Identify with the group 2. Put organizational goals ahead of personal desires or activities 3. Perform tasks for which there is no immediate reward but which help subordinates, the company, or both 4. Conserve corporate resources as if the resources were their own

RESPONSIBLE TREATMENT OF SUBORDINATES AT SERVICEMASTER

The U.S. "service economy" is in big trouble. The reason: The quality of much service today, like the quality of many manufactured goods 15 years ago, stinks. When you do encounter the rare, high-quality service, the experience stands in stark and lonely contrast to the undifferentiated mass of miserable service. . . .

Why is the quality of service so lousy? Executives blame the poor quality of people who are willing to work in lower-paying service jobs. But this argument does not explain why higher-paying manufacturing jobs turned out poor-quality goods for many years. High pay does not equal good service, and, as McDonald's has shown, low pay need not result in poor service. . . .

There are two explanations that are more compelling. First, too many providers do not understand the nature of a service. Most are intangible: You cannot see a lawyer's advice nor take home a waiter's behavior. Services are generally consumed when provided: Unlike a defective car that can be recalled, you cannot recall a blundered heart operation or a demeaning comment to a customer.

The second and more powerful explanation for poor service is management. Service providers treat customers similar to the way they, as employees, are treated by management. In many such organizations management treats employees as unvalued and unintelligent. The employees in turn convey the identical message to the customer. If management treats employees' concerns with indifference, then employees will not care about the customers' complaints. It is a rare employee who can rise above the effects of such poor management.

In poorly managed organizations, a pecking order exists. The boss gets the most respect and receives the widest degree of tolerance for less-than-social behavior. If the top executive treats a middle manager with rudeness and disrespect, then that manager mimics the executive by acting similarly toward his subordinate. This process continues until the last person in the organizational chain has no one to dump on. And that person is usually the airline ticket agent, the order taker at the fast-food chain, the bank teller or the nurse's aide. Since he has no one to abuse inside the organization, he treats customers as if they were the ones on the next rung down.

If managers want to improve service quality they must treat employees the same way they want employees to treat customers. Managers are the servants of the employees, not just the bosses. They must provide services to the employees in a friendly, helpful and efficient manner that will enable those employees to better serve the customers. Customers thus become the beneficiaries of high-quality service that mirrors the organization's inner working.

ServiceMaster Co., an Illinois-based provider of support services in housekeeping and food service, exemplifies this approach. Employee illiteracy in these jobs is high. ServiceMaster understands that illiteracy handicaps their employees' job performance and self-image, resulting in poorer-quality service to the clients. The company offers education programs; develops pictorial, color-coded instructional material to improve job productivity; and provides performance-based promotion opportunities to improve self-respect and upward mobility. The results: low turnover in these traditionally high turnover jobs; productivity levels higher than industry averages; and an average of 30% return on equity after taxes from 1973 to 1985. Most important, clients are pleased. A company with a billon dollars in annual revenue, ServiceMaster now exports its services—its customers include 15 hospitals in Japan.

BACK TO THE CASE

Mercer must recognize that his own job activities within the student employment department, as well as those of his subordinates, are a major factor in departmental success. Because Mercer's actions have an impact on all personnel within the student employment department, his job activities must be well defined. From the viewpoint of the student financial aids division as a whole, Mercer's job activities should be coordinated with those of the manager of scholar-

ships and grants and the manager of student loans. Perhaps the manager of the student financial aids division could use the management responsibility guide process to achieve this coordination of responsibilities.

Over all, for Mercer to be a responsible manager, he must perform the activities he is obligated to perform. He must also respond appropriately to his subordinates, the manager of the student financial aids division, and his peer managers.

 **AUTHORITY**

Individuals are assigned job activities to channel their behavior appropriately. Once they have been given the assignments, however, they also must be given a commensurate amount of authority to perform the obligations.

Authority is the right to perform or command. It allows its holders to act in certain designated ways and to directly influence the actions of others through orders.

The following example illustrates the relationship between job activities and authority. Two primary tasks for which a particular service station manager is responsible are pumping gasoline and repairing automobiles. The manager has the complete authority necessary to perform either of these tasks. If he chooses, however, he can delegate the activity of automobile repair to the assistant manager. Along with the activity of repairing, however, the assistant also should be delegated the authority to order parts, to command certain attendants to help, and to do anything else necessary to perform the obligated repair jobs. Without this authority, the assistant manager may find it impossible to complete the delegated job activities.

Practically speaking, authority is a factor that only increases the probability that a specific command will be obeyed.[6] The following excerpt emphasizes that authority does not always exact obedience:

> People who have never exercised power have all kinds of curious ideas about it. The popular notion of top leadership is a fantasy of capricious power: the top man presses a button and something remarkable happens; he gives an order as the whim strikes him, and it is obeyed. Actually, the capricious use of power is relatively rare except in some large dictatorships and some small family firms. Most leaders are hedged around by constraints—tradition, constitutional limitations, the realities of the external situation, rights and privileges of followers, the requirements of team work, and most of all, the inexorable demands of large-scale organization, which does not operate on capriciousness. In short, most power is wielded circumspectly.[7]

As chapter 8 showed, the positioning of individuals on an organization chart indicates the relative amount of authority delegated to each individual. Individuals toward the top of the chart possess more authority than individuals toward the bottom. Chester Barnard writes, however, that in reality the source of authority is determined not by decree from the formal organization but by

Authority is the right to perform or command.

Authority must reflect responsibility.

Commands may not be obeyed.

For commands to be obeyed, authority must be accepted.

whether or not authority is accepted by those existing under it. According to Barnard, authority exists and will exact obedience only if it is accepted.

In line with this rationale, Barnard defines *authority* as the character of communication by which an order is accepted by an individual as governing the actions the individual takes within the system. Barnard indicates that authority will be accepted only if the individual (1) can understand the order being communicated, (2) believes the order is consistent with the purpose of the organization, (3) sees the order as compatible with personal interests, and (4) is mentally and physically able to comply with the order. The fewer of these four conditions that exist, the smaller the probability that authority will be accepted and that obedience will be exacted.

Barnard also offers some guidance on what action managers can take to raise the odds that their commands will be accepted and obeyed. According to Barnard, more and more of a manager's commands will be accepted over the long term if:[8]

1. Formal channels of communication are used by the manager and are familiar to all organization members.
2. Each organization member has an assigned formal communication channel through which orders are received.
3. The line of communication between manager and subordinate is as direct as possible.
4. The complete chain of command is used to issue orders.
5. Managers possess adequate communication skills.
6. Managers use formal communication lines only for organizational business.
7. A command is authenticated as coming from a manager.

Acceptance of authority can be increased if managers follow certain guidelines.

BACK TO THE CASE

Mercer must be sure that any individuals within the student employment department who are delegated additional job activities also are delegated a commensurate amount of authority to give related orders and to accomplish their obligated activities. Student employment personnel must recognize, however, that authority must be accepted if obedience is to be exacted. To increase the probability of acceptance, care should be taken to ensure that individuals understand internal orders, see orders as being consistent with the objectives of both the student employment department and the student financial aids division, perceive orders as being compatible with their individual interests, and see themselves as being mentally and physically able to follow the orders.

Types of Authority

Three main types of authority can exist within an organization: (1) line authority, (2) staff authority, and (3) functional authority. Each type exists only to enable individuals to carry out the different types of responsibilities with which they have been charged.

Line and Staff Authority

Line authority reflects existing superior-subordinate relationships.

Line authority, the most fundamental authority within an organization, reflects existing superior-subordinate relationships. It is the right to make decisions and to give orders concerning the production-, sales-, or finance-related behavior of subordinates. Over all, line authority pertains to matters directly involving management system production, sales, and finance and, as a result, the attainment of objectives. Individuals directly responsible for these areas within the organization are delegated line authority to assist them in performing their obligated activities.

Whereas line authority involves giving orders concerning production activities, **staff authority** is the right to advise or assist those who possess line authority and other staff personnel. Staff authority exists to enable those responsible for improving the effectiveness of line personnel to perform their required tasks.

> Staff authority is the right to advise or assist those with line authority.

TABLE 9.3

Basic relationships of line and staff personnel in most organizations

1. The units that are designated as line have ultimate responsibility for successful operation of the company. Therefore, the line must also be responsible for operating decisions.
2. Staff elements contribute by providing advice and service to the line in accomplishing the objectives of the enterprise.
3. Staff is responsible for providing advice and service to appropriate line elements when requested to do so. However, staff also has the responsibility of proffering advice and service where it is not requested, but where it believes it is needed.
4. The solicitation of advice and the acceptance of suggestions and counsel is usually at the option of the line organization. However, in some cases, it must be recognized that only the top level of the line organization has this option and that its decision on the use of staff advice or service is binding throughout lower levels. In these cases, subordinate levels in the line may have no option in the use of specialized staff services, but may be required to use them.

   For example, the engineering department may analyze the use of machines, tools, jigs, and fixtures and present recommendations to the line. The operating line organization does not ask for this advisory service. Higher management provides it as a means of improving operations by bringing to the problem the most highly skilled and best informed specialists.

   In this case, it is the line managers' responsibility to make most effective use of this advice. If they disagree with it, they should have the opportunity to appeal to higher authority.

   The same holds true with certain services. Because line managers cannot possibly equip themselves to perform highly specialized parts of their job, staff units may perform these services for them. For example, the services of cost accountants are provided to help line managers determine their costs. If the line managers disagree with the methods of collecting this data or with the figures themselves, they may appeal to higher authority. But since they are not equipped to gather and analyze this data themselves, and since cost standards are necessary to effective operation, they must use the services of the accountants.
5. Line should give serious consideration to offers of advice and service made by staff units and should follow it if it is to the company's best interest to do so. However, except in those cases where the use of staff advice and service is compulsory and subject only to appeal to higher authority, it is not mandatory that the advice of staff should be followed unfailingly. Except as noted above, line managers have the authority to modify, reject, or accept such advice.
6. Both line and staff should have the right of appeal to higher authority in case of disagreement as to whether staff recommendation should be followed. However, this right to appeal should not be permitted to supersede the line's responsibility for making immediate decisions when they are required by the operating situation.

Examples of organization members with staff authority are members of accounting and personnel departments. Obviously, line and staff personnel must work closely together to maintain the efficiency and effectiveness of the organization. The relationship that exists between line and staff personnel in most organizations is presented in Table 9.3 on page 231.

The need for staff personnel is greater in large organizations.

Size is perhaps the most significant factor in determining whether or not staff personnel are used within an organization. Generally, the larger the organization, the greater the need for staff personnel. As an organization grows, management generally finds a greater need for more expertise in more diversified areas. Although small organizations may also need this expertise, they may find that hiring part-time consultants when a need arises may be more practical than hiring a full-time staff individual who may not always be kept busy.

Figure 9.3 shows how line-staff relationships can be presented on an organization chart. The plant manager on this chart has line authority over each immediate subordinate—personnel manager, production manager, and sales manager. The personnel manager also has staff authority in relation to the plant manager. This simply means that the personnel manager possesses the right to advise the plant manager on personnel matters. Final decisions concerning personnel matters, however, are in the hands of the plant manager, the individual holding line authority. Similar relationships exist between the sales manager and the sales research specialist, as well as between the production manager and the quality control manager. To carry the example of the personnel manager's staff authority one step further, Table 9.4 contains a detailed listing of the types of decision areas over which a personnel manager generally has jurisdiction. These decision areas are not directly related to production but could ultimately have a favorable influence on it.

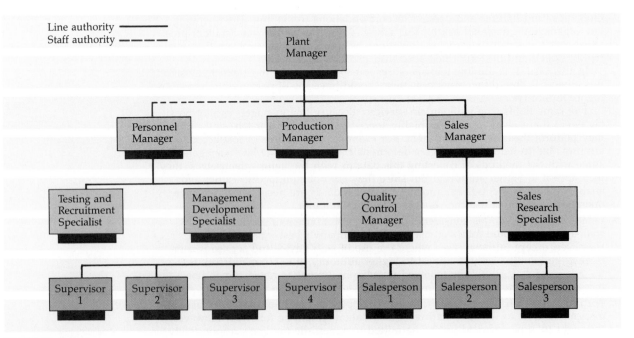

FIGURE 9.3
Possible line-staff relationships in selected organizational areas

TABLE 9.4

Typical decision areas for a personnel director

Personnel records/reports
Personnel research
Insurance benefits administration
Unemployment compensation administration
EEO compliance/affirmative action

Wage/salary/administration
Workers' compensation administration
Tuition aid/scholarships
Job evaluation
Health/medical services

Retirement preparation programs
Pre-employment testing
Vacation/leave processing
Induction/orientation
Promotion/transfer/separation processing

Counseling/employee assistance programs
Pension/profit-sharing plan administration
College recruiting
Recreation/social/recognition programs
Recruiting/interviewing/hiring

Attitude surveys
Union/labor relations
Complaint/disciplinary procedures
Relocation services administration
Supervisory training

Employee communications/publications
Executive compensation administration
Human resource planning
Safety programs/OSHA compliance
Management development

Food services
Performance evaluation, nonmanagement
Community relations/fund drives
Suggestion systems
Thrift/savings plan administration

Security/plant protection
Organization development
Management appraisal/MBO
Stock plan administration
Skill training, nonmanagement

Public relations
Administrative services (mail, PBX, phone, messengers, etc.)
Payroll processing
Travel/transportation services administration
Library
Maintenance/janitorial services

Roles of Staff Personnel

Harold Stieglitz has pinpointed the following three roles that staff personnel typically perform to assist line personnel:[9]

1. *The advisory or counseling role* The professional expertise of staff personnel in this role is aimed at solving organizational problems. The staff personnel are seen as internal consultants, with the relationship between line and staff being similar to that between a professional and a client. An example of this role might be the staff quality control manager who advises the line production manager on possible technical modifications to the production process that will help maintain the quality of products produced.
2. *The service role* Staff personnel in this role provide services that can more efficiently and effectively be provided by a single centralized staff group than by many individuals within the organization attempting to provide the services themselves. This role can probably best be understood by our viewing staff personnel as suppliers and line personnel as customers. For example, members of a personnel department recruit, employ, and train workers for all organizational departments. In essence, they are the suppliers of workers; and the various organizational departments needing workers are their customers.
3. *The control role* In this role, staff personnel help establish a mechanism for evaluating the effectiveness of organizational plans. Staff personnel exercising this role are seen as representatives, or agents, of top management.

The staff relationship to the line can be as three roles:

1. Professional to client.

2. Supplier to customer.

3. Agent of top management.

These three are not the only roles performed by staff personnel within organizations, but they are the main ones. In the final analysis, the role of staff personnel in any organization should be specially designed to best meet the needs inherent within that organization. It is entirely possible that to meet the needs of a particular organization, staff personnel must perform some combination of the three main roles.

Conflict in Line-Staff Relationships

Conflicts arise between line and staff personnel for many reasons.

Most management practitioners readily admit that a noticeable amount of conflict usually centers around line-staff relationships.[10] From the viewpoint of line personnel, conflict is created between line and staff personnel because staff personnel tend to assume line authority, do not give sound advice, steal credit for success, do not keep line personnel informed, and do not see the whole picture. From the viewpoint of staff personnel, conflict is created between line and staff personnel because line personnel do not make proper use of staff personnel, resist new ideas, and do not give staff personnel enough authority.

Overcoming these conflicts requires a serious and continuous effort.

To overcome these potential conflicts, staff personnel must strive to emphasize the objectives of the organization as a whole, encourage and educate line personnel in the appropriate use of staff personnel, obtain needed skill if it is not already possessed, and deal with resistance to change rather than view this resistance as an immovable barrier. Line personnel's effort in minimizing line-staff conflict should include using staff personnel wherever possible, making proper use of the abilities of staff personnel, and keeping staff personnel appropriately informed.[11]

BACK TO THE CASE

Assuming that the main objective of the student employment department is to help students compete more effectively in the community labor market, student employment personnel who are directly responsible for achieving this objective must possess line authority to perform their responsibilities. For example, individuals responsible for contacting prospective employers must be given the right to do everything necessary to develop these contacts to the best benefit of students.

Although the student employment department is relatively small, it may be possible that at least one individual is charged with the responsibility of assisting the line in a staff position. Perhaps this individual is responsible for advising Mercer on various surveys that could be conducted to convince prospective employers that university students make good part-time workers. Any individuals responsible for advising the line should be delegated appropriate staff authority.

As in all organizations, the potential for conflict between student employment line and staff personnel probably would be significant. Mercer should be aware of this potential and encourage both line and staff personnel to minimize it.

Functional Authority

Functional authority allows an individual to exert control in areas of the organization where this person usually has no authority.

Functional authority is the right to give orders within a segment of the organization in which this right is normally nonexistent. This authority usually is assigned to individuals to complement the line or staff authority already possessed. Functional authority generally covers only specific task areas and is operational for only designated amounts of time. It typically is possessed by indi-

TABLE 9.5

Advantages and disadvantages of line authority, staff authority and functional authority

Advantages	Disadvantages
Line Authority	
Maintains simplicity	Neglects specialists in planning
Makes clear division of authority	Overworks key people
Encourages speedy action	Depends on retention of a few key people
Staff Authority	
Enables specialists to give expert advice	Confuses organization if functions are not clear
Frees line executive of detailed analysis	Reduces power of experts to put recommendations into action
Affords young specialists a means of training	Tends toward centralization of organization
Functional Authority	
Relieves line executives of routine specialized decisions	Makes relationships more complex
Provides framework for applying expert knowledge	Makes limits of authority of each specialist a difficult coordination problem
Relieves pressure of need for large numbers of well-rounded executives	Tends toward centralization of organization

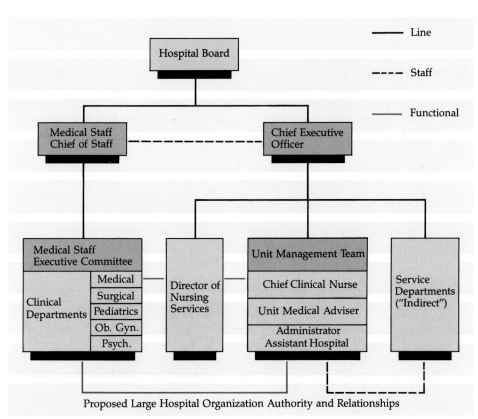

Proposed Large Hospital Organization Authority and Relationships

FIGURE 9.4
Proposed design for incorporating three types of authority in a hospital

viduals who, in order to meet their responsibilities, must be able to exercise some control over organization members in other areas.

The vice-president for finance in a particular organization is an example of someone with functional authority. Among her basic responsibilities, she is obligated to monitor the financial situation within the management system. To accomplish this monitoring, however, she must have appropriate financial information continually flowing to her from various segments of the organization. The vice-president for finance usually is delegated the functional authority to order various departments to furnish her with the kinds and amounts of information she needs to perform her analysis. In reality, the functional authority she possesses allows her to give orders to personnel within departments in which she normally cannot give orders.

Line, staff, and functional authority can be combined for the overall benefit of the organization.

From the previous discussion on line authority, staff authority, and functional authority, it is reasonable to conclude that although authority can exist within an organization in various forms, these forms should be used in a combination that will best enable individuals to carry out their assigned responsibilities and thereby best help the management system accomplish its objectives. When trying to decide what authority combination is best for a particular organization, managers must keep in mind that the use of each type of authority naturally has both advantages and disadvantages (see Table 9.5 on page 235). Figure 9.4 is an organization chart that shows how the three types of authority could be combined for the overall benefit of a hospital management system.

Accountability

The accountability concept implies rewards and punishments.

Accountability is the management philosophy whereby individuals are held liable, or accountable, for how well they use their authority and live up to their responsibility of performing predetermined activities.[12] The concept of accountability implies that if predetermined activities are not performed, some type of penalty, or punishment, is justifiably forthcoming.[13] One company executive has summed up the punishment theme of accountability with the statement, "Individuals who do not perform well simply will not be around too long."[14] Also implied in the accountability concept, however, is the notion that some kind of reward follows if predetermined activities are performed well.

■ BACK TO THE CASE

Functional authority and accountability are two additional factors that Leo Mercer must consider when modifying responsibilities within the student employment department. Some student employment personnel may have to be delegated functional authority to supplement the line or staff authority already possessed. The staff person who advises Mercer on conducting possible surveys to support the hiring of students may need information from various student

employment personnel on what types of students seem to be performing well in certain kinds of jobs. Functional authority would enable this staff individual to command that this information be channeled to him.

Student employment personnel also should understand the accountability concept—that living up to assigned responsibilities brings rewards and not living up to them brings punishments.

 # DELEGATION

Previous sections of this chapter have discussed responsibility and authority as complementary factors that channel activity within the organization. **Delegation** is the actual process of assigning job activities and corresponding authority to specific individuals within the organization. This section focuses on (1) steps in the delegation process, (2) obstacles to the delegation process, (3) elimination of obstacles to the delegation process, and (4) centralization and decentralization.

> Delegation is assigning jobs and authority to others.

Steps in the Delegation Process

According to Newman and Warren, there are three steps in the delegation process, any of which may be either observable or implied.[15] The first of the three steps is assigning specific duties to the individual. In all cases, the manager must be sure that the subordinate has a clear understanding of what these duties entail. Whenever possible, the activities should be stated in operational terms so the subordinate knows exactly what action must be taken to perform the assigned duties. The second step of the delegation process involves granting appropriate authority to the subordinate. The subordinate must be given the right and power within the organization to accomplish the duties assigned. The last step of the delegation process involves creating the obligation for the subordinate to perform the duties assigned. The subordinate must be aware of the responsibility to complete the duties assigned and must accept that responsibility. Table 9.6 offers several suggestions that managers can follow to ensure the success of the delegation process.

> The three-step delegation process involves assigning duties, granting authority, and creating an obligation.

Obstacles to the Delegation Process

Obstacles that can make delegation within an organization difficult or even impossible can be classified in three general categories: (1) obstacles related to the

---

TABLE 9.6

Guidelines for making delegation effective

- Give employees freedom to pursue tasks in their own way
- Establish mutually agreed-upon results and performance standards related to delegated tasks
- Encourage an active role on the part of employees in defining, implementing, and communicating progress on tasks
- Entrust employees with completion of whole projects or tasks whenever possible
- Explain relevance of delegated tasks to larger projects or to department or organization goals
- Give employees the authority necessary to accomplish tasks
- Allow employees the not ordinarily available access to information, people, and departments necessary to perform delegated task
- Provide training and guidance necessary for employees to complete delegated tasks satisfactorily
- When possible, delegate tasks on basis of employee interests

"I hate to fire people, so I'm ordering you two to fire each other."

Wall Street Journal, *September 11, 1987. From the* Wall Street Journal–*permission, Cartoon Features Syndicate.*

supervisor, (2) obstacles related to subordinates, and (3) obstacles related to organizations.

Some obstacles to delegation are supervisor-related.

One supervisor-related obstacle to delegation is that some supervisors resist delegating their authority to subordinates because they find using their authority very satisfying. Two other such obstacles are that supervisors may be afraid that their subordinates will not do a job well or that surrendering some of their authority may be seen by others as a sign of weakness. Also, if supervisors are insecure in their job or see specific activities as being extremely important to their personal success, they may find it difficult to put the performance of these activities into the hands of others. The supervisor in the cartoon has no trouble delegating: The problem is the task he is choosing to delegate. Dislike of a task is not a sufficient reason for delegating it.

Some obstacles are subordinate-related.

Even if supervisors wish to delegate to subordinates, they may encounter several subordinate-related roadblocks. First, subordinates may be reluctant to accept delegated authority for fear of failure or because of a lack of self-confidence. These two obstacles probably will be especially apparent if subordinates have not experienced the use of delegated authority previously. Other obstacles include the feeling that the supervisor will not be available for guidance once the delegation is made or that being a recipient of additional authority may complicate comfortable working relationships.

Some obstacles are organization-related.

Characteristics of the organization itself also may make delegation difficult. For example, a very small organization may present the supervisor with only a minimal number of activities to be delegated. In addition, if few job activities and little authority have been delegated over the history of the organization, an attempt to initiate the delegation process could make individuals reluctant and apprehensive. In essence, the supervisor would be introducing a change in procedure that some members of the organization might resist very strongly.[16]

Eliminating Obstacles to the Delegation Process

Since delegation usually results in several organizational advantages, the elimination of obstacles to delegation is important to managers. Advantages of delegation include improved subordinate involvement and interest, more free time for the supervisor to accomplish tasks, and, as the organization gets larger, assistance from subordinates in completing tasks the manager simply wouldn't have time for otherwise. Although delegation also has potential disadvantages, such as the possibility of the manager losing track of the progress of a task once it has been delegated,[17] the potential advantages of some degree of delegation generally outweigh the potential disadvantages.

What can managers do to eliminate obstacles to the delegation process? First of all, they must continually strive to uncover any obstacles to delegation that exist in their organization. Next, they should approach specific action to eliminate these obstacles with the understanding that the obstacles may be deeply ingrained and may therefore require long-term time and effort. Specific managerial actions usually necessary to overcome obstacles include building subordinate confidence in the use of delegated authority, minimizing the impact of delegated authority on established working relationships, and helping the delegatee with problems whenever necessary.

Koontz, O'Donnell, and Weihrich imply that for mangers to overcome the obstacles to delegation, they also must possess certain critical characteristics. These characteristics include the willingness to consider seriously the ideas of others, the insight to allow subordinates the free rein necessary to carry out their responsibilities, trust in the abilities of subordinates, and the ability to allow people to learn from their mistakes without suffering unreasonable penalties for making them.[18]

Good delegators uncover obstacles to delegation and take specific action to minimize them.

BACK TO THE CASE

To delegate effectively within the student employment department, Mercer must assign specific duties to individuals, grant corresponding authority to these individuals, and create the awareness within these individuals that they are obligated to perform these activities.

Mercer also must be aware that obstacles to delegation may exist within himself, his subordinates, or the student employment department. Discovering which obstacles exist and then taking steps to eliminate them is a prerequisite for successful delegation. If Mercer is to be a successful delegator, he also must be willing to consider the ideas of his subordinates, allow them the free rein necessary to perform their assigned tasks, trust them, and help them learn from their mistakes without suffering unreasonable penalties.

Centralization and Decentralization

Noticeable differences exist in the relative number of job activities and the relative amount of authority delegated to subordinates from organization to organization. In practice, it is not a case of delegation either existing or not existing within an organization. Delegation exists in most organizations but in varying degrees.

The terms **centralization** and **decentralization** describe the general degree to which delegation exists within an organization. These terms can be visualized at opposite ends of a delegation continuum (see Figure 9.5 on page 240). From this figure, it is apparent that centralization implies that a minimal number of job activities and a minimal amount of authority have been delegated to subordinates by management, whereas decentralization implies the opposite.

The problems that practicing managers usually face are determining whether to further decentralize an organization and deciding how to decentral-

Centralization implies minimal delegation; decentralization implies maximum delegation.

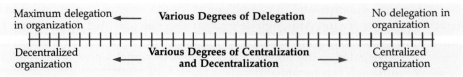

FIGURE 9.5
Centralized and decentralized organizations on delegation continuum

ize if that course of action is advisable. The section that follows contains practical suggestions on whether an organization should be decentralized and how decentralization should take place.

Decentralizing an Organization: A Contingency Viewpoint

The amount of decentralization is determined by the following:

The degree of decentralization managers should employ depends on, or is contingent on, their own unique organizational situation. Specific questions to determine the amount of decentralization appropriate for a situation include:

1. The size of the organization.

1. *What is the present size of the organization?* As indicated earlier, the larger the organization, the greater the likelihood that decentralization will be advantageous. As an organization increases in size, managers have to assume more and more responsibility and different types of tasks. Delegation is typically an effective means of helping managers keep up with this increased work load.

2. The locations of customers.

2. *Where are the organization's customers located?* As a general rule, the more physically separated the organization's customers are, the more viable a significant amount of decentralization is. Decentralization places appropriate management resources close to the customers and thereby allows for quick customer service. J. C. Penney, for example, decentralized its purchasing activities to give managers the ability to buy merchandise best suited to customers of their individual stores.[19]

3. The homogeneity of the product line.

3. *How homogeneous is the product line of the organization?* As the product line becomes more heterogeneous, or diversified, the appropriateness of decentralization generally increases. Different kinds of decisions, talents, and resources are needed to manufacture different products. Decentralization usually minimizes the potential confusion that can result from diversification by separating organizational resources by product and keeping pertinent decision making close to the manufacturing process.

4. The locations of suppliers.

4. *Where are organizational suppliers?* The location of raw materials from which the organization's products are manufactured is another important consideration. Time loss and perhaps even transportation costs associated with shipping raw materials over great distances from supplier to manufacturer could support the need for decentralizing certain functions.

   For example, the wood necessary to manufacture a certain type of bedroom set may be available only from tree growers in certain northern states. If the bedroom set is an important enough product line for a furniture company and if the costs of transporting the lumber are substantial, a sound basis for a decision to decentralize probably exists. The effect of this decision might be the building of a plant that produces only bedroom sets in a northern state close to where the necessary wood is readily available. The advantages of such a costly decision, of course, would accrue to the organization only over the long term.

5. *Is there a need for quick decisions in the organization?* If there is a need for speedy decision making within the organization, a considerable amount of decentralization is probably in order. Decentralization avoids red tape and allows the subordinate to whom authority has been delegated to make on-the-spot decisions if necessary.[20] This delegation is advisable only if the potential delegatees have the ability to make sound decisions. If they don't, the increased decision-making speed via delegation has no advantage. Quick or slow, a decision cannot reap benefits for the organization if it is unsound.

6. *Is creativity a desirable feature of the organization?* If creativity is desirable, then some decentralization probably is advisable. Decentralization allows delegatees the freedom to find better ways of doing things. The mere existence of this freedom can encourage the incorporation of new and more creative techniques within the task process.[21]

> 5. The need for quick decisions.
>
> 6. The desire for creativity.

BACK TO THE CASE

Centralization implies that few job activities and little authority have been delegated to subordinates; decentralization implies that many job activities and much authority have been delegated. Mercer will have to determine the best degree of delegation for the student employment department. For guidelines, he can use the rules of thumb that greater degrees of delegation probably will be appropriate for the student employment department as the department becomes larger, as potential employers and student clients become more dispersed and diversified, and as the needs for quick decision making and creativity increase.

Decentralization at Massey-Ferguson

Positive decentralization is decentralization that is advantageous for the organization in which it is being implemented; negative decentralization is the opposite. One way to ascertain how an organization should be decentralized is to study the efforts of an organization with positive decentralization: Massey-Ferguson.[22]

Massey-Ferguson is a worldwide farm equipment manufacturer that has enjoyed noticeable success with decentralization over the past several years.[23] The company has three guidelines for determining the degree of decentralization of decision making that is appropriate for a situation:[24]

> Positive decentralization is advantageous; negative decentralization is not.
>
> Massey-Ferguson follows guidelines for decentralizing decision making.

1. The competence to make decisions must be possessed by the person to whom authority is delegated. A derivative of this is that the superior must have confidence in the subordinate to whom authority is delegated.
2. Adequate and reliable information pertinent to the decision is required by the person making the decision. Decision-making authority therefore cannot be pushed below the point at which all information bearing on the decision is available.
3. If a decision affects more than one unit of the enterprise, the authority to make the decision must rest with the manager accountable for the most units affected by the decision.

Massey-Ferguson also encourages a definite attitude toward decentralization. The company's organization manual indicates that delegation is not delegation in name only but a frame of mind that includes both what a supervisor says to subordinates and the way the supervisor acts toward them. Managers at Massey-Ferguson are encouraged to allow subordinates to make a reasonable number of mistakes and to help subordinates learn from these mistakes.

Another feature of the positive decentralization at Massey-Ferguson is that decentralization is complemented by centralization:

At Massey-Ferguson, centralization complements decentralization.

> The organization plan that best serves our total requirements is a blend of centralized and decentralized elements. Marketing and manufacturing responsibilities, together with supporting service functions, are located as close as possible to local markets. Activities that determine the long-range character of the company, such as the planning and control of the product line, the planning and control of facilities and money, and the planning of the strategy to react to changes in the patterns of international trade, are highly centralized.[25]

Massey-Ferguson management recognizes that decentralization is not necessarily an either/or decision and uses the strengths of both centralization and decentralization to its advantage.

Some activities at Massey-Ferguson cannot be delegated.

Not all activities at Massey-Ferguson, however, are eligible for decentralization consideration. Only management is allowed to follow through on the following responsibilities:[26]

1. The responsibility for determining the overall objectives of the enterprise.
2. The responsibility for formulating the policies that guide the enterprise.
3. The final responsibility for the control of the business within the total range of the objectives and policies, including control over any changes in the nature of the business.
4. The responsibility for product design where a product decision affects more than one area of accountability.
5. The responsibility for planning for the achievement of overall objectives and for measuring actual performance against those plans.
6. The final approval of corporate plans or budgets.
7. The decisions pertaining to the availability and the application of general company funds.
8. The responsibility for capital investment plans.

BACK TO THE CASE

The Massey-Ferguson decentralization situation could give Mercer many valuable insights on what characteristics the decentralization process in the student employment department should assume. First, Mercer should use definite guidelines to decide whether his situation warrants added decentralization. In general, additional delegation probably is warranted in the student employment department as the competence of subordinates increases, as Mercer's confidence in the subordinates increases, and as more adequate and reliable decision-making information becomes available to subordinates. For delegation to be advantageous for the student employment department, Mercer also must help subordinates learn from their mistakes; and he may want to consider supplementing decentralization with centralization.

Action Summary

Reread the learning objectives that follow. Each objective is followed by questions. Answering these questions accurately will help you retain the most important concepts discussed in this chapter. After answering each question, check your answer with the answer key at the end of this chapter. (*Hint:* If you have doubt regarding the correct response, consult the page whose number follows the answer.)

From studying this chapter, I will attempt to acquire:	Circle:

1. **An understanding of the relationship of responsibility, authority, and delegation.**
   a. Responsibility is a person's self-assumed commitment to handle a job to the best of his or her ability.   T, F
   b. Which of the following elements is *not* an integral part of an effective organizing effort: (a) rationale for the orderly use of management system resources; (b) responsibility; (c) authority; (d) delegation; (e) none of the above (they are all important).   a, b, c, d, e

2. **Information on how to divide and clarify job activities of individuals within an organization.**
   a. Which of the following is *not* one of the four basic steps for dividing responsibility by the functional similarity method: (a) designing specific jobs by grouping similar activities; (b) examining management system objectives; (c) formulating management system objectives; (d) designating appropriate activities that must be performed to reach objectives; (e) making specific individuals responsible for performing activities.   a, b, c, d, e
   b. A management responsibility guide can assist organization members in which of the following ways: (a) by describing the various responsibility relationships that exist in their organization; (b) by summarizing how the responsibilities of various managers within the organization relate to one another; (c) by identifying manager work experience; (d) a and b; (e) none of the above.   a, b, c, d, e

3. **Knowledge of the differences among line authority, staff authority, and functional authority.**
   a. The production manager has mainly: (a) functional authority; (b) staff authority; (c) line authority; (d) a and c; (e) all of the above.   a, b, c, d, e
   b. An example of functional authority is the vice-president of finance being delegated the authority to order various departments to furnish her or him with the kinds and amounts of information needed to perform an analysis.   T, F

4. **An appreciation for the issues that can cause conflict in line and staff relationships.**
   a. From the viewpoint of staff personnel, one reason for line-staff conflict is that line personnel: (a) do not make proper use of staff personnel; (b) resist new ideas; (c) do not give staff personnel enough authority; (d) a and c; (e) all of the above.   a, b, c, d, e
   b. From the viewpoint of line personnel, conflicts between line and staff can occur for which of the following reasons: (a) staff may assume line authority; (b) staff may not offer sound advice; (c) staff may steal credit for success; (d) staff may fail to keep line informed; (e) all of the above.   a, b, c, d, e

5. **Insights on the value of accountability to the organization.**
   a. Accountability is how well individuals live up to their responsibility for performing predetermined activities.   T, F
   b. Rewarding employees for good performance is most closely related to: (a) simplicity; (b) a clear division of authority; (c) centralization; (d) decentralization; (e) accountability.   a, b, c, d, e

T, F

6. An understanding of how to delegate.
   a. The correct ordering of the steps in the delegation process is the assignment of duties, the creation of responsibility, and the granting of authority.

a, b, c, d, e
   b. Which of the following are obstacles to the delegation process: (a) obstacles related to supervisors; (b) obstacles related to subordinates; (c) obstacles related to the organization; (d) all of the above; (e) none of the above.

7. A strategy for eliminating various barriers to delegation.

a, b, c, d, e
   a. Eliminating obstacles to delegation usually results in which of the following advantages: (a) improved subordinate involvement and interest; (b) more free time for supervisor; (c) assistance for the supervisor to accomplish tasks he or she wouldn't be able to do otherwise; (d) all of the above; (e) none of the above.

T, F
   b. Generally, the potential advantages of some degree of delegating outweigh the disadvantages.

8. A working knowledge of when and how an organization should be decentralized.

a, b, c, d, e
   a. A high degree of centralization within an organization would be most advisable under which of the following conditions: (a) the organization is relatively small; (b) the organization is relatively large; (c) creativity is important to the firm's success; (d) the delegatees have the ability to make sound decisions; (e) the product line is diversified.

T, F
   b. According to the management philosophy that exists at Massey-Ferguson, the responsibility for formulating the policies that guide the organization should be highly decentralized.

INTRODUCTORY CASE WRAP-UP

''Redesigning Job Activities'' (p. 222) and its related back-to-the-case sections were written to help you better understand the management concepts contained in this chapter. Answer the following discussion questions about this introductory case to further enrich your understanding of the chapter content:

1. The introductory case ends with Mercer discovering that certain basic job activities are not covered in his department. What should he do now?
2. Assuming that certain fundamental functions have been excluded from the present job activities of the subordinates, what mistakes probably were made by the previous manager that allowed such exclusions to exist?

Issues for Review and Discussion

1. What is responsibility, and why does it exist in organizations?
2. Explain the process a manager would go through to divide responsibility within an organization.
3. What is a management responsibility guide, and how is it used?
4. List and summarize the four main dimensions of responsible management behavior.
5. What is authority, and why does it exist in organizations?
6. Describe the relationship between responsibility and authority.

7. Explain Barnard's notion of authority and acceptance.

8. What steps can managers take to increase the probability that subordinates will accept their authority? Be sure to explain how each of these steps increases the probability.

9. Summarize the relationship that generally exists between line and staff personnel.

10. Explain three roles that staff personnel can perform in organizations.

11. List five possible causes of conflict in line-staff relationships and suggest appropriate action to minimize the effect of these causes.

12. What is functional authority?

13. Give an example of how functional authority actually works in an organization.

14. Compare the relative advantages and disadvantages of line, staff, and functional authority.

15. What is accountability?

16. Define *delegation* and list the steps of the delegation process.

17. List three obstacles to the delegation process and suggest action for eliminating them.

18. What is the relationship between delegation and decentralization?

19. What is the difference between decentralization and centralization?

Sources of Additional Information

Chandler, A. D., Jr. *Strategy and Structure*. Garden City, New York: Anchor Books, Doubleday, 1966.

Clark, P. A. *Organizational Design: Theory and Practice*. London: Tavistock, 1972.

Fotilas, Panagiotis N. "Semi-Autonomous Work Groups: An Alternative in Organizing Production Work?" *Management Review* 70 (July 1981): 50–54.

Griffin, Ricky W. *Task Design: An Integrative Approach*. Glenview, Ill.: Scott, Foresman, 1982.

Hage, Jerald. *Theories of Organizations/Form, Process, and Transformation*. New York: Wiley, 1980.

Hutton, Thomas J. "Human Resources or Management Resources?" *Personnel Administrator* 32 (January 1987): 66–79.

Janz, Tom, Lowell Hellervik, and David C. Gilmore. *Behavior Description Interviewing*. Boston: Allyn and Bacon, 1986.

Kelly, Marcia M. "Exploring the Potentials of Decentralized Work Settings." *Personnel Administrator* 29 (February 1984): 48–52.

Leana, Carrie R. "Predictors and Consequences of Delegation." *Academy of Management Journal* 29 (December 1986): 715–26.

Leavitt, Harold J., Willian R. Dill, and Henry B. Eyring. *The Organizational World*. New York: Harcourt Brace Jovanovich, 1973.

Levinson, Robert E. *The Decentralized Company*. New York: Amacom, 1983.

Reich, Robert B. "The Team as Hero." *Harvard Business Review* (May/June 1987): 77–83.

Roos, Leslie L., Jr., and Roger I. Hall. "Influence Diagrams and Organizational Power." *Administrative Science Quarterly* 25 (March 1980): 57–71.

Sabl, Robert J. "Succession Planning—A Blueprint for Your Company's Future." *Personnel Administrator* 32 (September 1987): 101–108.

Scott, William G., and Terence R. Mitchell. *Organization Theory*, 4th ed. Homewood, Ill.: Richard D. Irwin, 1981.

Shrode, William A., and Dan Voich, Jr. *Organization and Management: Basic Systems Concepts*. Homewood, Ill.: Richard D. Irwin, 1974.

Smith, Howard R. "The Uphill Struggle for Job Enrichment." *California Management Review* 23 (Summer 1981): 33–38.

Tavernier, Gerard. "'Awakening a Sleeping Giant': Ford's Employee Involvement Program." *Management Review* 70 (June 1981): 15–20.

Notes

1. Stephen X. Doyle and Benson P. Shapiro, "What Counts Most in Motivating Your Sales Force?" *Harvard Business Review* (May/June 1980): 133–40. See also G. F. Scollard, "Dynamic Descriptions: Job Descriptions Should Work for You," *Management World* (May 1985): 34–35.

2. Robert J. Theirauf, Robert C. Klekamp, and Daniel W. Geeding, *Management Principles and Practices: A*

Contingency and Questionnaire Approach (New York: Wiley, 1977), 334.

3. Robert D. Melcher, "Roles and Relationships: Clarifying the Manager's Job," *Personnel* 44 (May/June 1967): 34–41.

4. For more information on management responsibility guides, see Melcher, "Roles and Relationships."

5. This section is based primarily on John H. Zenger, "Responsible Behavior: Stamp of the Effective Manager," *Supervisory Management* (July 1976): 18–24.

6. Max Weber, "The Three Types of Legitimate Rule," trans. Hans Gerth, *Berkeley Journal of Sociology* 4 (1953): 1–11.

7. John Gardner, "The Anti-Leadership Vaccine," *Carnegie Foundation Annual Report*, 1965.

8. Chester I. Barnard, *The Functions of the Executive* (Cambridge, Mass.: Harvard University Press, 1938).

9. Harold Stieglitz, "On Concepts of Corporate Structure," *Conference Board Record* 11 (February 1974): 7–13.

10. For a classic discussion of this area, see Louis A. Allen, "Developing Sound Line and Staff Relationships," in *Studies in Personnel Policy*, no. 153, National Industrial Conference Board, 1956, 70–80. See also Wendell L. French, *The Personnel Management Process: Human Resource Administration and Development* (Boston: Houghton Mifflin, 1987), 66–68.

11. Derek Sheane, "When and How to Intervene in Conflict," *Personnel Management* (November 1979): 32–36; John M. Ivancevich and Michael T. Matteson, "Intergroup Behavior and Conflict," in their *Organizational Behavior and Management* (Plano, Tex.: Business Publications, 1987), 305–45. For additional information on how to handle conflict, see Andrew K. Hoh, "Consensus Building: A Creative Approach to Resolving Conflicts," *Management Review* (March 1981): 52–54.

12. Robert Albanese, *Management* (Cincinnati: South-Western Publishing, 1988), 313.

13. For an excellent review of the punishment literature, see Henry P. Sims, Jr., "Further Thoughts on Punishment in Organizations," *Academy of Management Review* 5 (January 1980): 133.

14. "How Ylvisaker Makes 'Produce or Else' Work," *Business Week*, October 27, 1973, 112.

15. William H. Newman and E. Kirby Warren, *The Process of Management: Concepts, Behavior, and Practice*, 4th ed. (Englewood Cliffs, N.J.: Prentice-Hall, 1977), 39–40.

16. For organizational barriers unique to a family business, see Louis B. Barnes and Simon A. Hershon, "Transferring Power in the Family Business," *Harvard Business Review* (July/August 1976): 105–14.

17. Ted Pollock, "You Must Delegate . . . but You're Still Responsible," *Industrial Supervision* (February 1976): 10–11.

18. Harold Koontz, Cyril O'Donnell, and Heinz Weihrich, *Essentials of Management*, 8th ed. (New York: McGraw-Hill, 1986), 231–33.

19. H. Gilman, "J. C. Penney Decentralizes Its Purchasing," *Wall Street Journal*, May 8, 1986, 6.

20. Ernest Dale, "Centralization versus Decentralization," *Advanced Management Journal* (June 1955): 11–16.

21. Donald O. Harper, "Project Management as a Control and Planning Tool in the Decentralized Company," *Management Accounting* (November 1968): 29–33.

22. For further discussion on positive and negative centralization and decentralization, see Terence R. Mitchell and James R. Larson, Jr., *People in Organizations* (New York: McGraw-Hill, 1987), 49–50.

23. Information for this section is mainly from John G. Staiger, "What Cannot Be Decentralized," *Management Record* 25 (January 1963): 19–21. At the time the article was written, Staiger was vice-president of administration, North American Operations, Massey-Ferguson, Limited.

24. Staiger, "What Cannot Be Decentralized," 19.

25. Staiger, "What Cannot Be Decentralized," 21.

26. Staiger, "What Cannot Be Decentralized," 21.

Action Summary Answer Key

1. a. T, p. 223
   b. e, pp. 223–224
2. a. c, p. 224
   b. d, pp. 226–227
3. a. c, pp. 230–231
   b. T, pp. 234–236
4. a. e, p. 234
   b. e, p. 234
5. a. F, p. 236
   b. e, p. 236
6. a. F, p. 237
   b. d, pp. 237–238
7. a. d, pp. 238–239
   b. T, p. 239
8. a. a, pp. 240–241
   b. F, pp. 241–242

MANAGEMENT LESSONS OF IRANGATE

The policy decisions that led to "Irangate" have been proved by hindsight to have been mistakes. But the management methods that turned Irangate into a scandal should have been seen from the beginning as likely—indeed almost certain—to lead to trouble, if not to disaster. They were violations of well-known and amply tested management principles. The Reagan administration violated not just one of these principles—it violated four.

First—in one of the most common but also most unforgivable management mistakes—it confused delegation of authority with abdication of responsibility. A chief executive officer must delegate. Otherwise, he'll end up like Gulliver in Lilliput, ineffectual and ensnared in details, as were Lyndon Johnson and Jimmy Carter. But delegation requires greater accountability and tighter control. Delegation requires clear assignment of a specific task, clear definition of the expected results and a deadline. Above all it requires that the subordinate to whom a task is delegated keep the boss fully informed. It is the subordinate's job to alert the boss immediately to any possible "surprise"—rather than to try to "protect" the boss against surprises, as Mr. Reagan's subordinates apparently did. If they keep surprises away from the boss, they invariably will end up making him look incompetent or not in control or a liar—or all three.

The greatest delegator in recent American political history was not Ronald Reagan; he is apparently quite immersed in all kinds of operational matters. The greatest delegator was Franklin D. Roosevelt, who "did" an absolute minimum. Yet FDR always delegated a specific task, defined the desired results, and stipulated when and how the subordinate—a cabinet member as a rule—would report back. And he demanded upward responsibility from his subordinates. In particular, they had to inform him immediately if the project deviated from the plan even in the smallest detail. He knew, as every chief executive officer learns sooner or later, that there are no "pleasant surprises."

INCOMPATIBLE ROLES

The second major management lesson of Irangate is not to confuse, as the Reagan administration did (and apparently still does), two different and actually incompatible roles—that of the chief operating officer and that of the chief of staff.

Whether a chief operating officer can work in the American constitutional system is by no means clear. The system centralizes all executive authority in the

president, after all. None of the cabinet ministers, for instance, have any political or constitutional authority of their own as they have in a cabinet-government, like that of Britain. And the concept of chief operating officer has never worked when tried in Washington. It always gets the president in trouble.

It did not work when Franklin D. Roosevelt put in James Byrnes as the chief domestic operating officer during World War II. And Dwight Eisenhower did not become an effective president until a scandal forced him to get rid of Sherman Adams, his chief operating officer. But if there is a chief operating officer, the chief executive must retain some direct operating responsibility. Otherwise he soon becomes isolated, and loses "feel" and "touch."

FDR, for all his delegating, never relinquished direct, day-to-day control of congressional relations or of relations with the press. Alfred Sloan at General Motors always had a president and chief operating officer. But he himself kept day-to-day operating responsibilities for what he considered the two true "controls" of the corporation: personnel decisions down four levels—that is, for all appointments to a senior management position even in the smallest accessory division; and allocation of capital, with the chief financial officer reporting directly to him. Both Harry Truman and John F. Kennedy trusted their respective secretaries of state. But both kept day-to-day control of foreign affairs.

It will be argued that Donald Regan was not "chief operating officer"; he was "chief of staff." If so, he was set up to do exactly what a chief of staff must never do: to keep information from the president. The first job of a chief of staff is to make sure that the chief executive officer gets all dissents, conflicting points of view, and alternatives. To do this, he must not himself be a "part of the problem," must not himself represent one of the contending interests or ideologies, and must, above all, not be in the "line of command." In the military the chief of staff is never allowed to get between the senior commander and his subordinate commanders—they always outrank the chief of staff. His job is to make sure that the boss gets all the information he needs to make a decision, rather than only what the chief of staff thinks the boss should hear.

If the two roles are mixed, the chief of staff invariably cuts the boss off from vital information, invariably tries to monopolize access to the boss, invariably ends up making the boss look out of touch. And he also encourages subordinates to do what President Reagan's subordinates at the National Security Council apparently did: keep information away from "upstairs" and bootleg their own policies.

Confusing delegation and abdication, and the chief operating officer with the chief of staff, are structural mistakes. But the Reagan administration also made two elementary mistakes in how it did things. It asked Vice Adm. John Poindexter and Lt. Col. Oliver North to carry out the official policy toward Nicaragua sanctioned by Congress—which was not to give additional aid to the contras. At the same time, these two men also apparently were charged to raise private money for the contras. It does not matter that this hypocrisy was exactly what most members of Congress clearly wanted (including, probably, many who had voted against aid to the contras). If for whatever reason two conflicting policies have to be carried out at the same time—and that, of course, does happen—they must be carried out by different people and in separate organizations. The right hand must not know what the left hand is doing, if the two are working at cross-purposes. Otherwise there will always be a scandal and both policies will miscarry, as they did in Nicaragua.

WRONG SIGNALS

Finally, the Reagan administration violated the simplest rule: There ain't no secrets. If more than one person knows it, it won't stay a secret. And then the only thing to do with bad news—such as the miscarriage of the McFarlane-Poindexter mission to Tehran—is for the executive himself to make it public. This way he has control. If he tries to cover up, he will make sure only that the "secret" is published at the worst possible moment, by someone who tries to hurt him, and in a form that gives it the worst possible interpretation.

American presidents in this century have tended toward secret actions in foreign affairs. Only one of these worked: the Kissinger-Nixon rapprochement with China. The other three ended in disaster. President Wilson, in 1916, sent his personal confidant, Colonel House, to Berlin to get the Germans to stop sinking civilian shipping. House succeeded only in convincing the Germans that Wilson was profoundly isolationist and would never go to war—which then encouraged them, after Wilson's reelection a year later, to launch the unrestricted submarine warfare that forced America into World War I.

President Roosevelt sent Col. Charles Lindbergh to Berlin 20 years later to "establish contact with Nazi moderates." Lindbergh convinced the Germans only that the U.S. was unprepared, and could not mobilize fast enough to turn the balance in Europe. And the McFarlane-Poindexter mission to Tehran clearly also sent the wrong signals to the Iranians.

Yet, the dilemma created by kidnapping and hostage-taking is a real one, and if—a big if, of course—the mission had resulted in the release of the remaining hostages, President Reagan would have been a hero. But when such an endeavor fails, then one does what Franklin D. Roosevelt was particularly good at: make sure that the news is leaked by the president (or, in a business, the chief executive officer), and in a form in which it deflects blame to someone who is sympathetic. But above all one makes sure that there is no secret—for the only secret no one pays any attention to (as Edgar Allen Poe showed 150 years ago in "The Purloined Letter") is something that is out in the open.

These are elementary lessons, and obvious ones. But it is not only the politicians in Washington who seem not to know them. There are far too many chief executives in American business who make the same mistakes. Let's hope that they will learn the management lessons of Irangate.

DISCUSSION ISSUES

1. What is meant by the statement "it [the Reagan Administration] confused delegation of authority with abdication of responsibility"? Explain.
2. Using the terminology of chapter 9, explain the statement indicating that the Reagan administration had confused two different and incompatible roles: that of the chief operating officer and that of the chief of staff.
3. According to the case, as a delegator, Franklin D. Roosevelt "did an absolute minimum." What management terminology is used to reflect an absolute minimum of delegation? Explain.

STUDENT LEARNING OBJECTIVES

From studying this chapter, I will attempt to acquire:

1. An overall understanding of how appropriate human resources can be provided for the organization.
2. An appreciation for the relationship among recruitment efforts, an open position, sources of human resources, and the law.
3. Insights on the use of tests and assessment centers in employee selection.
4. An understanding of how the training process operates.
5. A concept of what performance appraisals are and how they best can be conducted.
6. An appreciation for the complex situation involving women who are working in nontraditional jobs.

PROVIDING APPROPRIATE HUMAN RESOURCES

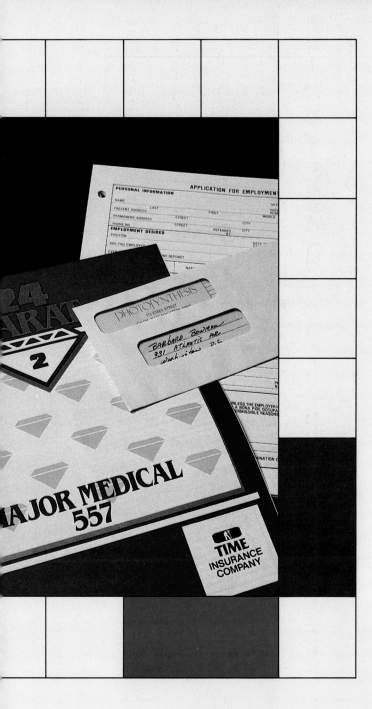

CHAPTER OUTLINE

SPECIAL TRAINING AT FAIRCHILD INDUSTRIES

Charlie Collis still gets hot under the collar when he describes the worst mistake of his thirty-six-year career at Fairchild Industries. Collis, who had retired as executive vice-president one year earlier, was talking about the incident with younger managers at Fairchild who were still on the job.

According to Collis, his big mistake occurred when he was president of Fairchild Republic, the company's airplane manufacturing division. Fairchild Republic had just won a government contract to build the A-10 Thunderbolt attack plane. This contract was especially important to the company because the Thunderbolt project would catapult Fairchild into being a billion-dollar-a-year corporation.

All seemed well with the Thunderbolt project until an Air Force analyst began pressuring Collis. The analyst wanted Collis to move all work other than the Thunderbolt out of the Fairchild plant in Farmingdale, New York, and into a Fairchild plant in Hagerstown, Maryland. The analyst believed that, over the long term, this move would lower the manufacturing costs of the Thunderbolt project.

At the time, Collis resisted the pressure. He believed the Air Force was going well beyond its limits by trying to tell him how to run his business. Because of Collis's uncooperativeness in this area, the Air Force analyst informed his supervisor that Fairchild was not willing to take the steps necessary to carry out the Thunderbolt project appropriately. Quickly, several Air Force investigators were "swarming" all over the company.

The A-10 attack plane

Collis admitted that he made a mistake: "I got mad and didn't organize the problem. I had to go." As a result of this friction with the Air Force, Edward G. Uhl, Fairchild's no-nonsense president, yanked Collis back to corporate headquarters and named a new president of Fairchild Republic.

Collis's frank discussion of his mistake was taking place at company headquarters as part of a special training program through which the retired Collis was expected to pass his accumulated wisdom along to the next generation of Fairchild managers. Fairchild Industries believes that retired executives who are free from corporate politics and pressure on the job can impart some of their experience to present managers, thereby helping them become better corporate leaders in the future.

What's Ahead

Charlie Collis, the retired manager in the introductory case, was assisting Fairchild Industries in one facet of the process of providing appropriate human resources for the organization—training. This chapter focuses on the complete process of providing appropriate human resources by first defining appropriate human resources and then examining the steps to be followed in providing them.

The emphasis in chapter 9 was on organizing the activity of individuals within the management system. To this end, responsibility, authority, and delegation were discussed in detail. This chapter continues to explore the relationship between individuals and organizing by discussing how appropriate human resources can be provided for the organization.

DEFINING APPROPRIATE HUMAN RESOURCES

The phrase **appropriate human resources** refers to the individuals within the organization who make a valuable contribution to management system goal attainment. This contribution, of course, is a result of productivity in the positions they hold. The phrase *inappropriate human resources* refers to organization members who do not make a valuable contribution to the attainment of management system objectives. In essence, these individuals are ineffective in their jobs.

Productivity in all organizations is determined by how human resources interact and combine to use all other management system resources. Such factors as background, age, job related experience, and level of formal education all have some role in determining the degree of appropriateness of the individual to the organization. Although the process of providing appropriate human resources for the organization is involved and somewhat subjective, the following section offers insights on how to increase the success of this process.

Appropriate human resources are the individuals who contribute to the attainment of management system objectives.

STEPS IN PROVIDING APPROPRIATE HUMAN RESOURCES

To provide appropriate human resources to fill either managerial or nonmanagerial openings, managers follow four sequential steps: (1) recruitment, (2) selection, (3) training, and (4) performance appraisal. Figure 10.1 illustrates these steps.

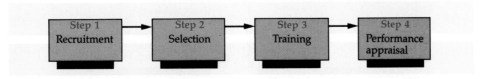

FIGURE 10.1
Four sequential steps to provide appropriate human resources for an organization

253

Recruitment

Recruitment is the initial screening of prospective employees.

Recruitment is the initial screening of the total supply of prospective human resources available to fill a position. Its purpose is to narrow a large field of prospective employees to a relatively small group of individuals from which someone eventually will be hired. To be effective, recruiters must know (1) the job they are trying to fill, (2) where potential human resources can be located, and (3) how the law influences recruiting efforts.

Knowing the Job

Recruitment activities must begin with a thorough understanding of the position to be filled so the broad range of potential employees can be narrowed intelligently. **Job analysis** is a technique commonly used to gain an understanding of a position. Basically, job analysis is aimed at determining a **job description** (the activities a job entails) and a **job specification** (the characteristics of the individual who should be hired for the job). Figure 10.2 shows the relationship of job analysis to job description and job specification.

Job analysis entails determining a job description and a job specification.

The U.S. Civil Service Commission has developed a procedure for performing a job analysis (see Table 10.1).[1] As with all job analysis procedures, the Civil Service procedure uses information gathering as the primary means of determining what workers do and how and why they do it. This information is used to develop both a job description and a job specification.

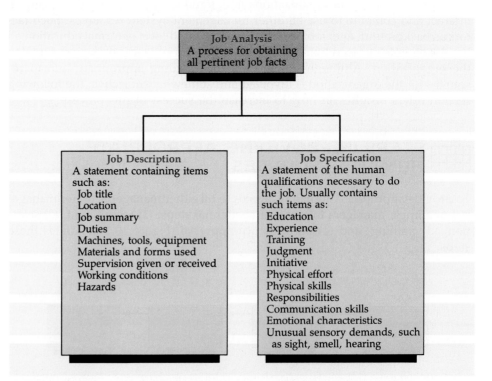

FIGURE 10.2
Relationship of job analysis, job description, and job specification

■ **TABLE 10.1**

■ Information to obtain when performing a job analysis

Identifying Information (such as):
    Name of incumbent
    Organization/unit
    Title and series
    Date
    Interviewer

Brief Summary of Job:
    (This statement will include the primary duties of the job. It may be prepared in advance from class specifications, job descriptions, or other sources. However, it should be checked for accuracy using the task statements resulting from the analysis.)

Job Tasks:
    What does the worker do? How does the worker do it? Why? What output is produced?
    What tools, procedures, aids are involved? How much time does it take to do the task?
    How often does the worker perform the task in a day, week, month, or year?

Knowledge, Skills, and Abilities Required:
    What does it take to perform each task in terms of the following?
    1. Knowledge required
       a. What subject matter areas are covered by the task?
       b. What facts or principles must the worker have an acquaintance with or understand in these subject matter areas?
       c. Describe the level, degree, and breadth of knowledge required in these areas or subjects.
    2. Skills required
       a. What activities must the worker perform with ease and precision?
       b. What are the manual skills required to operate machines, vehicles, equipment, or to use tools?
    3. Abilities required
       a. What is the nature and level of language ability, written or oral, required of the worker on the job?
          Are there complex oral or written ideas involved in performing the task, or simple instructional materials?
       b. What mathematical ability must the worker have? Will the worker use simple arithmetic, complex algebra?
       c. What reasoning or problem-solving ability must the worker have?
       d. What instructions must the worker follow? Are they simple, detailed, involved, abstract?
       e. What interpersonal abilities are required? What supervisory or managing abilities are required?
       f. What physical abilities such as strength, coordination, visual acuity must the worker have?

Physical Activities:
    Describe the frequency and degree to which the incumbent is engaged in such activities as: pulling, pushing, throwing, carrying, kneeling, sitting, running, crawling, reaching, climbing.

Environmental Conditions:
    Describe the frequency and degree to which the incumbent will encounter working under such conditions as these: cramped quarters, moving objects, vibration, inadequate ventilation.

Typical Work Incidents:
    1. Situations involving the interpretation of feelings, ideas, or facts in terms of personal viewpoint.
    2. Influencing people in their opinions, attitudes, or judgments about ideas or things.
                                                  (Continued)

▮ **TABLE 10.1**

▮ Continued

Typical Work Incidents: (Continued)
    3. Working with people beyond giving and receiving instructions.
    4. Performing repetitive work, or continuously performing the same work.
    5. Performing under stress when confronted with emergency, critical, unusual, or dangerous situations; or in situations in which work speed and sustained attention are make-and-break aspects of the job.
    6. Performing a variety of duties, often changing from one task to another of a different nature without loss of efficiency or composure.
    7. Working under hazardous conditions that may result in: violence, loss of bodily members, burns, bruises, cuts, impairment of senses, collapse, fractures, electric shock.

Worker Interest Areas:
    Identify, from the list below, the preferences for work activities suggested by each task.
    A preference for activities:
     1. Dealing with things and objects.
     2. Concerning the communication of data.
     3. Involving business contact with people.
     4. Involving work of a scientific and technical nature.
     5. Involving work of a routine, concrete, organized nature.
     6. Involving work of an abstract and creative nature.
     7. Involving work for the presumed good of people.
     8. Relating to process, machine, and technique.
     9. Resulting in prestige or the esteem of others.
    10. Resulting in tangible, productive satisfaction.

BACK TO THE CASE

In the training session at Fairchild Industries in the introductory case, Charlie Collis was using his knowledge and experience as a manager to help the current managers at Fairchild understand that they must be concerned with obtaining appropriate human resources—the people who will make a valuable contribution to the attainment of Fairchild's organizational objectives. During the Thunderbolt project, for example, Collis should have considered hiring people to work solely on the attack plane in order to meet Fairchild's goal of producing attack planes for the Air Force. In finding appropriate human resources, Collis would have had to follow four basic steps: (1) recruitment, (2) selection, (3) training, and (4) performance appraisal.

Basically, recruitment would entail the initial screening of individuals available to fill open positions at Fairchild. For recruitment efforts to be successful at Fairchild, recruiters would have to know the jobs they were trying to fill, where potential human resources could be located, and how the law influenced recruiting efforts.

Recruiters could acquire an understanding of an open position at Fairchild by performing a job analysis. The job analysis would force them to determine the job description of the open position—the activities of a draftsman, engineer, maintenance supervisor, or accountant, for example—and the job specification of the position, including the type of individual who should be hired to fill that position.

Knowing Sources of Human Resources

The labor supply is constantly in flux.

Besides a thorough knowledge of the position the organization is trying to fill, recruiters must be able to pinpoint sources of human resources. A barrier to this pinpointing is the fact that the supply of individuals from which to choose is continually changing; there are times when finding appropriate human resources is much harder than at other times. For example, an article that appeared over twenty years ago indicated that organizations should prepare for a frantic scramble to obtain managers from a very low supply in the labor market.[2]

In discussing the same managerial recruitment issue, however, a much more recent article indicated that the situation had changed dramatically: "For the past couple of years, a few thoughtful observers of new business trends have been warning that a glut of corporate executives is imminent. The reason, of course, is the U.S. baby boom of the late 1940s and 1950s."[3] Over all, sources of human resources available to fill a position can be categorized in two ways: (1) sources inside the organization and (2) sources outside the organization.

Sources inside the Organization

The existing pool of employees in an organization is one source of human resources. Individuals already in an organization may be well qualified for an open position. Although existing personnel sometimes are moved laterally within an organization, most internal movements are usually promotions. Promotion from within typically has the advantages of building morale, encouraging employees to work harder in hopes of being promoted, and making individuals inclined to

Promoting from within has a number of advantages.

Name Murray, Mel	Age 47	Employed 1977
Present Position Manager, sales (House Fans Division)		On Job 6 years
Present Performance Outstanding—exceeded sales goal in spite of stiffer competition		
Strengths Good planner—motivates subordinates very well—excellent communication.		
Weaknesses Still does not always delegate as much as situation requires. Sometimes does not understand production problems.		
Efforts to Improve Has greatly improved in delegating in last two years; also has organized more effectively after taking a management course on own time and initiative.		
Could Move to Vice-president, Marketing		**When** 1989
Training Needed More exposure to problems of other divisions (attend top staff conference?). Perhaps university program stressing staff role of corporate marketing versus line sales.		
Could Move to Manager, House or Industrial Fans Division		**When** 1990 1991
Training Needed Course in production management; some project working with production people; perhaps a good business game somewhere.		

FIGURE 10.3
Management inventory card

stay with a particular organization because of possible future promotions.[4] Companies such as Exxon and General Electric find it very rewarding to train managers themselves for upward movement within the organization.[5]

Some type of **human resource inventory** usually is helpful to a company to keep current with possibilities for filling a position from within. The inventory should indicate which individuals in the organization would be appropriate for filling a position if it became available. Walter S. Wikstrom has suggested three types of records that can be combined to maintain a useful human resource inventory in an organization.[6] Although Wikstrom focuses on filling managerial positions, slight modifications to his inventory forms would make his records equally applicable to nonmanagerial positions.

The management inventory card contains people-centered information.

The first of Wikstrom's three record-keeping forms for a human resource inventory is a **management inventory card** (see Figure 10.3 on page 257). The card in the figure has been completed for a fictional manager named Mel Murray. It indicates Murray's age, year of employment, present position and length of time it has been held, performance ratings, strengths and weaknesses, the positions to which Murray might move, when he would be ready to assume these positions, and additional training he would need to fill the positions. In short, this card is both an organizational history of Murray and an explanation of how he might be used in the future.

The position replacement form contains job-centered information.

Figure 10.4 shows Wikstrom's second human resource inventory form—a **position replacement form.** This form focuses on maintaining position-centered information, rather than the people-centered information on the management inventory card. The form in the figure indicates little about Murray as a person but much about individuals who could replace him. The position replacement form is helpful in determining what would happen to Murray's present position

Position	Manager, Sales (House Fans Division)		
Performance Outstanding	**Incumbent** Mel Murray	**Salary** $44,500	**May Move** 1 Year
Replacement 1 Earl Renfrew		**Salary** $39,500	**Age** 39
Present Position Field Sales Manager, House Fans		**Employed:** Present Job 3 years	Company 10 years
Training Needed Special assignment to study market potential for air conditioners to provide forecasting experience.			**When ready** now
Replacement 2 Bernard Storey		**Salary** $38,500	**Age** 36
Present Position Promotion Manager, House Fans		**Employed:** Present Job 4 years	Company 7 years
Training Needed Rotation to field sales. Marketing conference in fall 1989.			**When ready** 2 years

FIGURE 10.4
Position replacement form

if Murray were selected to be moved within the organization or if he left the organization altogether.

Wikstrom's third human resource inventory form is called a **management manpower replacement chart** (see Figure 10.5). This chart presents a composite view of the individuals who management considers significant for human resource planning. The performance rating and promotion potential of Murray can easily be compared with those of other employees when the company is trying to determine which individual would most appropriately fill a particular position.

A management manpower replacement chart compares individuals who might be considered for promotion.

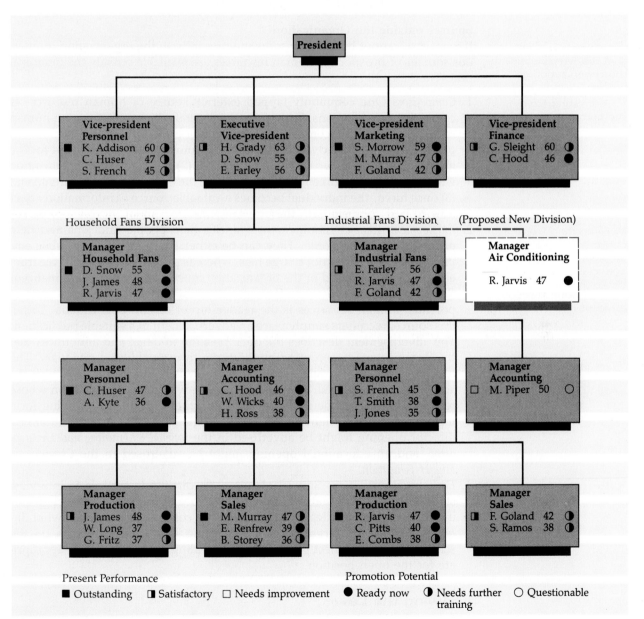

FIGURE 10.5
Management manpower replacement chart

The management inventory card, the position replacement form, and the management manpower replacement chart are three separate record-keeping devices for a human resource inventory. Each form furnishes different data on which to base a hiring-from-within decision. The questions these forms help answer are (1) What is the organizational history of an individual, and what potential does the person possess (management inventory card)? (2) If a position becomes vacant, who might be eligible to fill it (position replacement form)? (3) What are the relative merits of one individual filling the position as compared to another (management manpower replacement chart)? Considering the answers to these three questions collectively should help to ensure the success of hiring-from-within decisions.

Sources outside the Organization

If a position cannot be filled by someone presently in the organization, numerous sources of prospective human resources are available outside the organization. They include:

1. *Competitors* One commonly tapped external source of human resources is competing organizations. Since there are several advantages to luring human resources away from competitors, this type of piracy has become a common practice. Among the advantages are (1) the competitor will have paid for the individual's training up to the time of hire, (2) the competing organization will probably be weakened somewhat by the loss of the individual, and (3) once hired, the individual becomes a valuable source of information about how to best compete with the other organization.

2. *Employment agencies* Employment agencies help people find jobs and help organizations find people. They can be either public or private. Public employment agencies do not charge fees, whereas private ones collect a fee from either the person hired or the organization, once a hiring has been finalized.

3. *Readers of certain publications* Perhaps the most widely addressed source of potential human resources is the readership of certain publications. To tap this source, recruiters simply place an advertisement in a suitable publication. The advertisement describes the open position in detail and announces that the organization is accepting applications from qualified individuals. The type of position to be filled determines the type of publication in which the advertisement is placed. The objective is to advertise in a publication whose readers are likely to be interested in filling the position. An opening for a top-level executive might be advertised in the *Wall Street Journal*, a training director opening might be advertised in the *Journal of Training and Development*, and an educational opening might be advertised in the *Chronicle of Higher Education*.

4. *Educational institutions* Several recruiters go directly to schools to interview students close to graduation. Liberal arts schools, business schools, engineering schools, junior colleges, and community colleges all have somewhat different human resources to offer. Recruiting efforts should focus on the schools with the highest probability of providing human resources appropriate for the open position.

Knowing the Law

Modern legislation has a major impact on organizational recruitment practices, and a recruitment effort must reflect the laws that govern it. The Civil Rights Act

---

Obtaining human resources from outside the organization involves:

1. Recruiting from the competition.

2. Recruiting from public and private employment agencies.

3. Recruiting through advertising.

4. Recruiting of new graduates.

Laws regulate recruiting practices.

passed in 1964 and amended in 1972 created the **Equal Employment Opportunity Commission (EEOC)** to enforce the laws established to prohibit discrimination on the basis of race, color, religion, sex, and national origin in recruitment, hiring, firing, layoffs, and all other employment practices. The EEOC report was amended in 1978 to include the Pregnancy Discrimination Act, which required employees to treat pregnancy as any other form of medical disability, as far as leave and insurance.

Equal opportunity legislation protects the right of a citizen to work and to get a fair wage based primarily on merit and performance. The EEOC seeks to maintain the existence of this right by holding labor unions, private employers, educational institutions, and government bodies responsible for its continuance. The four steps usually followed by the EEOC to hold organizations accountable are presented in Table 10.2.

In response to equal opportunity legislation, many organizations have **affirmative action programs.** Translated literally, *affirmative action* can be defined as positive movement. "In the area of equal employment opportunity, the basic purpose of positive movement or affirmative action is to eliminate barriers and increase opportunities for the purpose of increasing the utilization of under-utilized and/or disadvantaged individuals."[7] The organization can judge how well it is eliminating these barriers by (1) determining how many minority and disadvantaged individuals it presently employs, (2) determining how many minority and disadvantaged individuals it should employ according to EEOC guidelines, and (3) comparing the numbers obtained in steps 1 and 2.[8] If the two numbers are close to the same, employment practices within the organization probably should be maintained; if the numbers are not about the same, employment practices should be modified accordingly.

Affirmative action programs stress the hiring of minority and disadvantaged individuals.

TABLE 10.2

Four steps followed by the EEOC to uphold equal opportunity legislation

1. The EEOC receives a charge alleging employment discrimination. Such a charge can be filed by an individual, by a group on behalf of an individual, or by any of the EEOC commissioners. Primary consideration for processing the charge is given to an approved state or local employment practices agency, if one exists. This agency has 60 days in which to act on the charge (120 days if the agency has been in operation less than a year). In the absence of such an agency, the EEOC is responsible for processing the charge. If neither the local agency nor the EEOC has brought suit within 180 days of the official filing date, the charging party may request a right-to-sue letter by which to initiate private civil action.

2. The EEOC investigates the charge to gather sufficient facts to determine the precise nature of the employer or union practice. If these facts show *probable cause* to believe that discrimination exists, the EEOC initiates step 3.

3. The EEOC conciliates or attempts to persuade the employer to voluntarily eliminate the discrimination. In this regard, the EEOC will provide extensive technical aid to any employer or union in voluntary compliance with the law. If conciliation fails, the EEOC initiates step 4.

4. The EEOC files suit in federal court (or the aggrieved parties may initiate their own private civil action). Court-ordered compliance with Title VII usually results in large expenses for the employer, often exceeding the cost of voluntary affirmative action.

BACK TO THE CASE

A successful recruitment effort at Fairchild Industries would require recruiters to know where to locate the available human resources to fill open Fairchild positions. These sources may be both within Fairchild and outside it.

While handling the Thunderbolt project, Charlie Collis should have recognized that he needed to allocate more human resources to the project in order to satisfy the Air Force. To do this, Collis could have kept current on the possibilities of filling positions from within by maintaining some type of human resource inventory. This inventory would have helped him organize information about (1) the organizational histories and potential of various Fairchild employees, (2) the employees at Fairchild who might be eligible to fill the positions needed to complete the Thunder-

bolt project, and (3) the relative abilities of various Fairchild employees to fill the necessary openings. Some of the sources of potential human resources outside Fairchild that Collis should have been aware of were competitors, public and private employment agencies, the reader of industry related publications, and various types of educational institutions.

In the training session, Collis should have made the current Fairchild managers aware of how the law influences their recruitment efforts. Basically, the law says that Fairchild recruitment practices cannot discriminate on the basis of race, color, religion, sex, or national origin. If recruitment practices at Fairchild are found to be discriminatory, the company is subject to prosecution by the Equal Employment Opportunity Commission.

Selection

Selection follows recruitment.

The second major step involved in furnishing appropriate human resources for the organization is **selection**—choosing an individual to hire from all those who have been recruited. Hence, selection is dependent on and follows recruitment. As the cartoon shows, however, providing appropriate human resources involves more than just selecting what are thought to be the best people.

The selection process typically is represented as a series of stages through which prospective employees must pass to be hired.[9] Each stage reduces the total group of prospective employees until, finally, one individual is hired. Fig-

"I pick the best people I can find, and I don't try to second-guess them."

Reprinted by permission of James Stevenson from Harvard Business Review *(September/October 1987).*

ure 10.6 lists the specific stages of the selection process, indicates reasons for eliminating prospective employees at each stage, and illustrates how the group of potential employees is narrowed down to the individual who ultimately becomes the employee. Two tools often used in the selection process are testing and assessment centers.

Testing

Testing is examining human resources for qualities relevant to performing available jobs.[10] Although many different kinds of tests are available for organizational use, they generally can be divided into four categories:[11]

Tests are used to measure the following:

1. Potential.

2. Skill level.

3. Vocational interests.

4. Personality.

1. *Aptitude tests* Tests of aptitude measure the potential of an individual to perform a task. Some aptitude tests measure general intelligence, and others measure special abilities, such as mechanical, clerical, or visual abilities. Table 10.3 on page 264 describes the eleven information areas covered by one aptitude test, the Wechsler Adult Intelligence Scale.
2. *Achievement tests* Tests that measure the level of skill or knowledge an individual possesses in a certain area are called achievement tests. This skill or knowledge may have been acquired through various training activities or through experience in the area.
3. *Vocational interest tests* Tests of vocational interest attempt to measure an individual's interest in performing various kinds of jobs and are administered on the assumption that certain people perform jobs well because the job activities are interesting to them. The basic purpose of this type of test is to help select the individuals who find certain aspects of an open position interesting.
4. *Personality tests* Personality tests attempt to describe an individual's personality dimensions in such areas as emotional maturity, subjectivity, and objectivity. Personality tests can be used advantageously if the personality

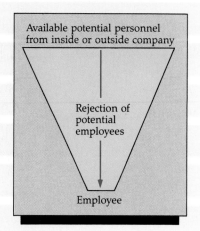

Stages of the Selection Process	Reasons for Elimination	
Preliminary screening from records, data sheets, etc.	Lack of adequate educational and performance record	Available potential personnel from inside or outside company
Preliminary interview	Obvious misfit from outward appearance and conduct	
Intelligence tests	Failure to meet minimum standards	
Aptitude tests	Failure to have minimum necessary aptitude	
Personality tests	Negative aspects of personality	Rejection of potential employees
Performance references	Unfavorable or negative reports on past performance	
Diagnostic interview	Lack of necessary innate ability, ambition, or other qualities	
Physical examination	Physically unfit for job	
Personal judgment	Remaining candidate placed in available position	Employee

FIGURE 10.6
Summary of major factors involved in the selection process

TABLE 10.3

The eleven information areas covered by the Wechsler Adult Intelligence Scale

Verbal

1. Information. A series of open-ended questions dealing with the kinds of factual data people normally pick up in their ordinary contacts.
2. Comprehension. Another series of open-ended questions covering the individual's understanding of the need for social rules.
3. Arithmetic. All the questions are of the story or problem type. Scoring is for correctness of solutions and time to respond.
4. Digit Span. A group of numbers is read and the subject repeats them from memory, sometimes backward.
5. Similarities. Pairs of terms are read and a common property or characteristic must be abstracted.
6. Vocabulary. A series of words must be defined in the subject's own terms.

Performance

7. Picture Completion. A number of pictures are presented in which the subject must identify the missing component.
8. Picture Arrangement. Items require that a series of pictures be arranged as rapidly as possible in the order that makes the most sense.
9. Object Assembly. Jigsaw puzzles must be put together within a given time limit.
10. Block Design. Working with a set of small blocks having red, white, or red and white faces, the subject attempts to duplicate various printed designs as quickly as possible.
11. Digit Symbol. The subject is given a series of paired symbols and numbers as a code. The subject is then to write as many correct numbers as he or she can for each of a series of scrambled symbols within a set time period.

characteristics needed to do well in a particular job are well defined and if individuals possessing those characteristics can be pinpointed and selected.

Tests must be used correctly.

Several guidelines should be observed when tests are used as part of the selection process. First, care should be taken to ensure that the test being used is both valid and reliable. A test is valid if it measures what it is designed to measure and reliable if it measures similarly time after time. Second, test results should not be used as the sole source of information to determine whether to hire someone. People change over time, and someone who doesn't score well on a particular test might still develop into a productive employee. Such factors as potential and desire to obtain a position should be assessed subjectively along with test scores in the final selection decision. A third guideline is that care should be taken to determine that the tests used are nondiscriminatory in nature; "many tests contain language or cultural biases which may discriminate against minorities."[12] This third guideline is especially important in that the EEOC has the authority to prosecute organizations that use discriminatory testing practices.

Assessment Centers

Another tool often used to help increase the success of employee selection is the assessment center. Although the assessment center concept is discussed in this chapter primarily as an aid to selection, it also has been used as an aid in such areas as human resource training and organization development. The first industrial use of the assessment center is usually credited to AT&T.[13] Since

AT&T's initial efforts, the assessment center concept has been growing quickly and has been adopted by such companies as Merrill Lynch, Pierce, Fenner & Smith; Prudential Life Insurance; IBM; General Electric; and the J.C. Penney Company.[14]

"An **assessment center** is a program, not a place, in which participants engage in a number of individual and group exercises constructed to simulate important activities at the levels to which participants aspire."[15] These exercises might include such activities as participating in leaderless discussions, giving oral presentations, or leading a group in solving some assigned problem. Individuals performing the activities are observed by managers or trained observers who evaluate both their ability and their potential.[16] In general, participants are assessed on the basis of (1) leadership, (2) organizing and planning ability, (3) decision making, (4) oral and written communication skills, (5) initiative, (6) energy, (7) analytical ability, (8) resistance to stress, (9) use of delegation, (10) behavior flexibility, (11) human relations competence, (12) originality, (13) controlling, (14) self-direction, and (15) overall potential.[17]

Assessment centers simulate tasks to be performed at specific levels of the organization.

■ BACK TO THE CASE

After the initial screening of potential human resources, Fairchild Industries will be faced with the task of selecting the individuals to be hired from those who have been screened. Two tools that Charlie Collis could suggest to help in this selection process are testing and assessment centers.

For example, after screening potential employees for positions on the Thunderbolt project, Collis could have used aptitude tests, achievement tests, vocational interest tests, or personality tests to see if any of the individuals he had screened had the qualities necessary to work on the attack plane project. In using these tests, however, Collis would have had to make sure that the tests were both valid and reliable, that they were not the sole basis on which his selection decision was made, and that they were nondiscriminatory.

Collis also could have used assessment centers to simulate the tasks necessary to build the Thunderbolt attack plane. Individuals who performed well on these tasks would probably be more appropriate for the project than would those who did poorly.

Over all, in the training session, Charlie Collis should encourage Fairchild managers to use testing and assessment centers in selecting individuals for open positions.

Training

After recruitment and selection, the next step in providing appropriate human resources for the organization is training. **Training** is the process of developing qualities in human resources that ultimately will enable them to be more productive and, thus, to contribute more to organizational goal attainment. Hence, the purpose of training is to increase the productivity of individuals in their jobs by influencing their behavior. "Governmental agencies, industrial firms, volunteer organizations, educational institutions, and other segments of our society are placing more and more emphasis on the need to train human resources."[18] Table 10.4 on page 266 provides an overview of the types and popularity of training being offered by organizations.

Training is developing productive abilities.

The training of individuals is essentially a four-step process: (1) determining training needs, (2) designing the training program, (3) administering the training program, and (4) evaluating the training program. These steps are presented in Figure 10.7 on page 267. Each of these steps is described in more detail in the sections that follow.

TABLE 10.4

Types and popularity of training offered by organizations

Types of Training	Percentage of Surveyed Companies That Offer This Type of Training
1. Management skills and development	74.3
2. Supervisory skills	73.4
3. Technical skills/knowledge updating	72.7
4. Communication skills	66.8
5. Customer relations/services	63.8
6. Executive development	56.8
7. New methods/procedures	56.5
8. Sales skills	54.1
9. Clerical/secretarial skills	52.9
10. Personal growth	51.9
11. Computer literacy/basic computer skills	48.2
12. Employee/labor relations	44.9
13. Disease prevention/health promotion	38.9
14. Customer education	35.7
15. Remedial basic education	18.0

Copyright © 1985, Lakewood Publications Inc., Minneapolis, MN.

Determining Training Needs

Training needs are the areas that require further development to increase productivity.

The first step of the training process is determining the organization's training needs. **Training needs** are the information or skill areas of an individual or group that require further development to increase the organizational productivity of that individual or group. Only if training focuses on these needs can it be of some productive benefit to the organization.

The training of organization members is typically a continuing activity. Even individuals who have been with an organization for some time and who have undergone initial orientation and skills training need continued training to improve skills.

Training needs can be determined through evaluation of the production process, requests for employee feedback, and looking into the future.

Several methods of determining which skills to focus on for more established human resources are available. The first method is evaluating the production process within the organization. Such factors as excessive rejected products, deadlines that are not met, and high labor costs are clues to existing levels of production related expertise. Another method for determining training needs is direct feedback from employees on what they believe are the organization's training needs. Organization members may be able to verbalize clearly and accurately exactly what types of training they need to help them do a better job. A third way of determining training needs involves looking into the future. If the manufacture of new products or the use of newly purchased equipment is foreseen, some type of corresponding training almost certainly will be needed.

Designing the Training Program

Training ingredients must be assembled.

Once training needs have been determined, a training program aimed at meeting those needs must be designed. Basically, designing a program entails assembling various types of facts and activities that will meet the established training

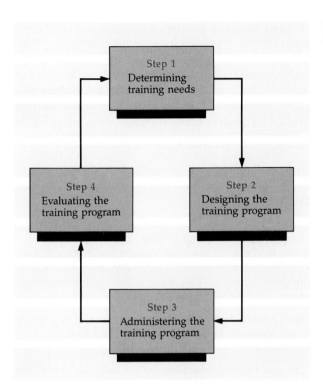

FIGURE 10.7
Steps of the training process

needs. Obviously, as training needs vary, the facts and activities designed to meet those needs vary.

BACK TO THE CASE

After hiring, Fairchild Industries must train new employees to be productive organization members. To train effectively, Fairchild must determine training needs, design a corresponding training program, and administer and evaluate the training program.

Designing a training program requires that Fairchild assemble facts and activities that address specific company training needs. These needs are simply information or skill areas that need to be further developed in Fairchild employees to make them more pro-ductive. Over the long term, training at Fairchild should focus on more established employees as well as newly hired employees.

Charlie Collis, the retired Fairchild manager discussed in the introductory case, was conducting a training session for upwardly mobile managers at Fairchild. The company has determined that training by such an instructor helps managers become "more appropriate"—better able to help Fairchild achieve its objectives.

Administering the Training Program

The next step of the training process is administering the training program, or actually training the individuals. Various techniques exist for both transmitting necessary information and developing needed skills in training programs. Several of these techniques are discussed in the sections that follow.

Techniques for Transmitting Information
Two techniques for transmitting information in training programs are lectures and programmed learning. Although it probably could be argued that these

techniques develop some skills in individuals as well as transmit information to them, they are primarily devices for the dissemination of information.

Lectures involve one-way communication.

Lectures. Perhaps the most widely used technique for transmitting information in training programs is the lecture. Bass and Vaughn define the **lecture** as a primarily one-way communication situation in which an instructor presents information to a group of listeners.[19] The instructor typically does most of the talking in this type of training situation. Trainees participate primarily through listening and note taking.

Lectures have both advantages and disadvantages.

An advantage of the lecture is that it allows the instructor to expose trainees to a maximum amount of information within a given time period. The lecture, however, also has its disadvantages:

> The lecture generally consists of a one-way communication: the instructor presents information to the group of passive listeners. Thus, little or no opportunity exists to clarify meanings, to check on whether trainees really understand the lecture material, or to handle the wide diversity of ability, attitude, and interest that may prevail among the trainees. Also, there is little or no opportunity for practice, reinforcement, knowledge of results, or overlearning.

> Ideally, the competent lecturer should make the material meaningful and intrinsically motivating to his or her listeners. However, whether most lectures achieve this goal is a moot question.

> These limitations, in turn, impose further limitations on the lecture's actual content. A skillful lecture may be fairly successful in transmitting conceptual knowledge to a group of trainees who are ready to receive it; however, all the evidence available indicates that the nature of the lecture situation makes it of minimal value in promoting attitudinal or behavioral change.[20]

Programmed learning is learning independently.

Programmed Learning. Another commonly used technique for transmitting information in training programs is called programmed learning. According to Silvern, **programmed learning** is a technique for instructing without the presence or intervention of a human instructor.[21] Small parts of information that necessitate related responses are presented to individual trainees. The trainees can determine from the accuracy of their responses whether their understanding of the obtained information is accurate. The types of responses required of trainees vary from situation to situation but usually are multiple-choice, true-false, or fill-in-the-blank. Figure 10.8 shows a portion of a programmed learning training package that could be used to familiarize trainees with PERT (program evaluation and review technique).

It has advantages and disadvantages.

As with the lecture method, programmed learning has both advantages and disadvantages. Among the advantages are that students can learn at their own pace, know immediately if they are right or wrong, and participate actively. The primary disadvantage of this method is that there is nobody to answer questions for the learner.

Techniques for Developing Skills

On-the-job techniques include coaching, position rotation, and special project committees.

Techniques for developing skills in training programs can be divided into two broad categories: on-the-job and classroom. Techniques for developing skills on the job usually are referred to as **on-the-job training.** These techniques reflect a blend of job related knowledge and experience and include coaching, position rotation, and special project committees. Coaching is direct critiquing of how well an individual is performing a job. Position rotation involves moving an individual from job to job to enable the person to obtain an understanding of the

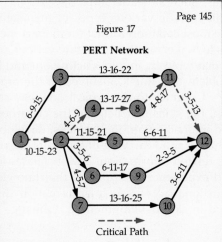

Frame 3[24]

Program evaluation and review technique, PERT, is performed on a set of time-related activities and events which must be accomplished to reach an objective. The evaluation gives the expected completion time and the probability of completing the total work within that time. By means of PERT, it is possible not only to know the exact schedule, but also to control the various activities on a daily basis. Overlapping and related activities are reviewed. PERT is more practical for jobs involving a one-time effort than for repeat jobs. It is a planning-controlling medium designed to: (1) focus attention on key components, (2) reveal potential problem areas, (3) provide a prompt reporting on accomplishments, and (4) facilitate decision making.

The time-related activities and events are set forth by means of a PERT network (see figure 17). In this illustration, the circles represent events that are sequential accomplishment points; the arrows represent activities or the time-consuming elements of the program. In this type of network, an arrow always connects two activities. All of the activities and events must be accomplished before the end objective can be attained. The three numbers shown for each arrow or activity represent its estimated times, respectively, for the optimistic, most likely, and pessimistic times. The program starts with event no. 1 and ends with event no. 12. From calculations for the time required for each path from no. 1 to no. 12,

Page 145

Figure 17

PERT Network

it is found that path 1-2-4-8-11-12 requires the *longest time* and, hence, is the *critical path* because it controls the time required to complete the program. Toward it, managers would direct their attention in order to: (1) ensure that no breakdowns occur in it; (2) better the current times required, if possible; and (3) trade off time from the non-critical paths to the critical path, if the net effect is to reduce total time of the critical path.

Indicate whether each of the following statements is true or false by writing "T" or "F" in the space provided.
_____ 1. PERT centers its attention on social constraints.
_____ 2. PERT is best applied to assembly-line operations.
_____ 3. In PERT, the *critical path* is the path that requires the longest time.
_____ 4. In the PERT network, circles represent events and the arrows represent activities.

Now turn to Answer Frame 3[24], page 146.

Page 146

Answer frame 3[24]

1. False. PERT centers its attention on *time* constraints.
2. False. PERT is more practical for jobs involving a one-time effort than for repeat jobs.
3. True. In PERT, the critical path is the path that requires the *longest* time. If this path can be shortened, the program can be completed in a shorter time period.
4. True. Circles represent events that are sequential accomplishment points, and arrows represent activities or the time-consuming elements for the program.

You have completed chapter 24. Now turn to chapter 25.

FIGURE 10.8
Portion of a programmed learning training package emphasizing PERT

organization as a whole. Special project committees involve assigning a particular task to an individual to furnish the person with experience in a designated area.[22]

Classroom techniques for developing skills also reflect a blend of job related knowledge and experience. The skills addressed through these techniques

Classroom techniques include management games and role-playing activities.

can range from technical skills, such as computer programming, to interpersonal skills, such as leadership. Specific classroom techniques aimed at developing skills include various types of management games and role-playing activities. The most common format for management games requires small groups of trainees to make and then evaluate various management decisions. The role-playing format typically involves acting out and then reflecting on some people oriented problem that must be solved in the organization.

Contrary to the typical one-way communication role in the lecture situation, the skills instructor in the classroom encourages high levels of discussion and interaction among trainees, develops a climate in which trainees learn new behavior from carrying out various activities, acts as a resource person in clarifying related information, and facilitates learning through job related knowledge and experience in applying that knowledge.[23] The difference between the instructional role used in information dissemination and the instructional role used in skill development is dramatic.[24]

Evaluating the Training Program

Successful training programs show a reasonable return.

After the training program has been completed, management should evaluate its effectiveness. Because training programs represent a cost investment—costs include materials, trainer time, and production loss while the individuals are being trained rather than doing their jobs—a reasonable return is required.

Basically, management must evaluate the training program to determine if it meets the needs for which it was designed. Answers to questions such as the following help determine training program effectiveness:

1. Has the excessive reject rate declined?
2. Are deadlines being met more regularly?
3. Are labor costs per unit produced decreasing?

If the answer to such questions is yes, the training program is at least somewhat successful; but perhaps its effectiveness could be enhanced through certain selective changes. If the answer is no, some significant modification to the training program is warranted.

BACK TO THE CASE

After training needs at Fairchild Industries have been determined and programs have been designed to meet those needs, the programs must be administered and evaluated.

Charlie Collis was participating in a training program involving the lecture technique; Fairchild Industries could also use the programmed learning technique for transmitting information to trainees. For actually developing skills in trainees, Fairchild could use on-the-job training methods, such as coaching, position rotation, or special project committees. For developing skills in a classroom setting, it could use instructional techniques, such as role-playing activities. For example, lower-level Fairchild supervisors could be asked to act out the roles of managers han-

dling various kinds of employee problems. These situations then could be analyzed from the viewpoint of how to improve supervisor-worker relationships.

Once a Fairchild training program has been completed, it must be evaluated to determine if it met the training need for which it was designed. Training programs aimed at specific motor skills such as typing would be much easier to evaluate than would training programs such as the one Charlie Collis was conducting, which was aimed at developing managerial decision-making skills. The evaluation of any training program at Fairchild, of course, should emphasize how to improve the program the next time it is implemented.

Performance Appraisal

Even after individuals have been recruited, selected, and trained, the task of making them productive within the organization is not finished. The fourth step in the process of providing appropriate human resources for the organization is **performance appraisal**—the process of reviewing individuals' past productive activity to evaluate the contribution they have made toward attaining management system objectives. As with training, performance appraisal is a continuing activity that focuses on the more established human resources within the organization as well as on the relatively new ones. A main purpose is to furnish feedback to organization members about how they can become more productive. Performance appraisal also has been called performance review and performance evaluation. Table 10.5 describes several methods of performance appraisal.

Performance appraisals evaluate individuals' contributions to the attainment of management system objectives.

Why Use Performance Appraisals?

Most firms in the United States use some type of performance appraisal system.[25] Douglas McGregor has suggested the following three reasons for using performance appraisals in an organization:[26]

1. They provide systematic judgments to support salary increases, promotions, transfers, and sometimes demotions or terminations.
2. They are a means of telling subordinates how they are doing and of suggesting needed changes in behavior, attitudes, skills, or job knowledge; they let subordinates know where they stand with the boss.
3. They also are being used increasingly as a basis for the coaching and counseling of individuals by superiors.

TABLE 10.5

Descriptions of several methods of performance appraisal

Name of Appraisal Method	Description
Rating scale	Individuals appraising performance use a form containing several employee qualities and characteristics to be evaluated (e.g., dependability, initiative, leadership). Each evaluated factor is rated on a continuum or scale ranging, for example, from one to seven or more points.
Employee comparisons	Appraisers rank employees according to such factors as job performance and value to the organization. Only one employee can occupy a particular ranking.
Free-form essay	Appraisers simply write down their impressions of employees in paragraph form.
Critical-form essay	Appraisers write down particularly good or bad events involving employees as these events occur. Records of all documented events for any one employee are used to evaluate that person's performance.

Handling Performance Appraisals

If performance appraisals are not handled well, their benefit to the organization is minimized. Several guidelines can assist in increasing the appropriateness with which the appraisals are conducted.[27] The first guideline is that performance appraisals should stress both the performance within the position the individual holds and the success with which the individual is attaining objectives. Performance and objectives should become inseparable topics of discussion during performance appraisals. The second guideline is that appraisals should emphasize the individual in the job, not the evaluator's impression of observed work habits. In other words, emphasis should be more on an objective analysis of performance than on a subjective evaluation of habits. The third guideline is that the appraisal should be acceptable to both the evaluator and the evaluatee. Both individuals should agree that the appraisal can be of some benefit to the organization and to the worker. The fourth, and last, guideline is that performance appraisals should be used as the basis for improving individuals' productivity within the organization[28] by making them better equipped to produce.[29]

The "Management in Action" feature summarizes Lee Iacocca's thoughts in his best-selling autobiography about how performance appraisals should be handled. Iacocca achieved national prominence as a manager by turning the failing Chrysler Corporation into a profitably run business.

Potential Weaknesses of Performance Appraisals

To maximize the potential payoff of performance appraisals to the organization, managers must avoid several potential weaknesses of the appraisal process. As indicated by George A. Rider, these potential weaknesses are that (1) individuals involved in performance appraisals could view them as a reward-punishment situation, (2) the emphasis of performance appraisal could be put on completing paperwork rather than on critiquing individual performance, and (3) some type of negative reaction from a subordinate could be generated when the evaluator offers any unfavorable comments.[30]

To avoid these potential weaknesses, supervisors and employees should view the performance appraisal process as an opportunity to increase the worth of the individual through constructive feedback, not as a means of rewarding or punishing individuals through positive or negative comments. Paperwork should be seen only as an aid in providing this feedback, not as an end in itself. Also, care should be taken to make appraisal feedback as tactful and objective as possible to help minimize any negative reactions of the evaluatee.[31]

INTEGRATING WOMEN IN NONTRADITIONAL JOBS

Women are being hired in increasing numbers to fill positions in organizations that, traditionally, they have not held.[32] These nontraditional jobs include lower-level positions in construction as well as upper-level positions in plant management. One reason women desire to fill such jobs is that the pay for performing them is typically well above the pay for performing jobs more traditionally held by women. Naturally, organizations are increasing their hiring of

HOW LEE IACOCCA APPRAISES PERFORMANCE

At the age of thirty-six, I was the general manager of the biggest division in the world's second largest company. At the same time, I was virtually unknown. Half the people at Ford didn't know who I was. The other half couldn't pronounce my name. . . .

One of my first ideas came from Wall Street. The Ford Motor Company had finally gone public only four years earlier, in 1956. Now we were owned by a large group of stockholders, who were keenly interested in our health and productivity. Like other publicly-held corporations, we sent those stockholders a detailed financial report every three months. Four times a year they kept tabs on us through these quarterly reports, and four times a year we paid them a dividend out of our earnings.

If our stockholders had a quarterly review system, why shouldn't our executives? I asked myself. I began to develop the management system I still use today. Over the years, I've regularly asked my key people—and I've had them ask *their* key people, and so on down the line—a few basic questions: "What are your objectives for the next ninety days? What are your plans, your priorities, your hopes? And how do you intend to go about achieving them?"

On the surface, this procedure may seem like little more than a tough-minded way to make employees accountable to their boss. It is that, of course, but it's also much more, because the quarterly review system makes employees accountable to *themselves*. Not only does it force each manager to consider his own goals, but it's also an effective way to remind people not to lose sight of their dreams.

Every three months, each manager sits down with his immediate superior to review the manager's past accomplishments and to chart his goals for the next term. Once there is agreement on these goals, the manager puts them in writing and the supervisor signs off on it. As I'd learned from McNamara, the discipline of writing something down is the first step toward making it happen. In conversation, you can get away with all kinds of vagueness and nonsense, often without even realizing it. But there's something about putting your thoughts on paper that forces you to get down to specifics. That way, it's harder to deceive yourself—or anybody else.

The quarterly review system sounds almost too simple—except that it works. And it works for several

Lee Iacocca

reasons. First, it allows a man to be his own boss and to set his own goals. Second, it makes him more productive and gets him motivated on his own. Third, it helps new ideas bubble to the top. The quarterly review forces managers to pause and consider what they've accomplished, what they expect to accomplish next, and how they intend to go about it. I've never found a better way to stimulate fresh approaches to problem solving.

Another advantage of the quarterly review system—especially in a big company—is that it keeps people from getting buried. It's very hard to get lost in the system if you're reviewed every quarter by your superior and, indirectly, by his boss and his boss's boss. This way, good guys don't get passed over. And equally important, bad guys don't get to hide.

Finally, and this is perhaps most important of all, the quarterly review system forces a dialogue between a manager and his boss. In an ideal world, you wouldn't need to institute a special structure just to make sure that kind of interaction takes place. But if a manager and his boss don't get along very well, at least four times a year they still have to sit down to decide what they're going to accomplish together in the months ahead. There's no way they can avoid this meeting, and over time, as they gradually come to know each other better, their working relationship usually improves.

During these quarterly meetings, it's the boss's responsibility to respond to each manager's plan. The boss might say: "Listen, I think you're shooting a little high, but if you think you can do all that in the next ninety days, why not give it a shot?" Or: "This plan makes good sense, but there are some priorities here that I don't agree with. Let's talk it over." Whatever the nature of the discussion, the boss's role begins to shift. Gradually, he becomes less of an authority figure and more of an adviser and senior colleague.

If I'm Dave's supervisor, I might begin by asking Dave what he hopes to get done in the next three months. He might tell me he wants to raise our market penetration by half a point. At that point, I'll say: "Fine. Now, how do you intend to do that?"

Before I ask that question, Dave and I have to agree on the specific goal he's working for. But that's rarely a problem. If there's any conflict between us, it's much more likely to center on *how* rather than on *what*. Most managers are reluctant to let their people run with the ball. But you'd be surprised how fast an informed and motivated guy can run.

The more Dave feels he has set his own goals, the more likely it is that he'll go right through a brick wall in order to reach them. After all, he's decided on them himself, *and* he has the boss's stamp of approval. And because Dave wants to do things his own way, he'll do his utmost to prove his way makes good sense.

The quarterly review system works equally well when Dave doesn't measure up. At that point, the boss usually doesn't have to say anything. More often than not, Dave will bring it up himself, because his failure is so painfully obvious.

In my experience, after the ninety days are up, the guy who hasn't succeeded will usually come in an explain apologetically that he didn't make his goal before the boss says anything. If that happens for several quarters in a row, the guy begins to doubt himself. He comes to realize that this is *his* problem—and not the boss's fault.

Even then, there's usually still time to take some constructive action. Often, the guy himself will say: "Look, I can't handle my job. I'm in over my head. Can you move me somewhere else?"

It's far better for everybody when an employee comes to this decision on his own. Every company has lost good people who have simply been in the wrong job and who might have found more satisfaction as well as greater success if they could have been moved to another area instead of being fired. Obviously, the earlier you can detect this kind of problem, the better your chances of solving, it.

Without a regular system of review, a manager who isn't working out in a particular area may build up resentment against his boss. Or the manager may imagine that the reason he failed to reach his target is that the boss holds a grudge against him. I've seen too many cases where somebody was in the wrong job for years. More often than not, there was no way for management to find that out until it was too late.

women to fill such positions for many reasons. One, for example, is that the Office of Federal Contract Compliance Programs has set a mandatory guideline that requires that a proportion of women must work on all federally financed construction projects.[33]

Regardless of the reasons for this emerging movement of women working in jobs that traditionally were held by men, managers must cope with the problem of how to integrate women workers successfully into the organization. According to Nancy R. Brunner, a program aimed at handling this problem should include two primary phases: prehire preparation and posthire activities.[34]

> Programs that integrate women holding nontraditional jobs into the organization should include both prehire preparation and posthire activities.

Prehire Preparation

Prehire preparation involves getting the women ready to come into the organization as well as making the organization ready for the women's entry. Included in this preparation are the following:[35]

> Prehire activities get women and organizations ready for each other.

Job analysis To define job responsibilities clearly, identify specific training needs, and develop job-proficiency guides. The guides outline expected increases in performance competence and the skills that must be demonstrated at each successive level of improvement.

Interview/selection training To prepare managers for involvement in the selection of women and enable them to help define the job related dimensions that candidates capable of performance and growth in the organization should have.

Workshops for the male supervisors as well as peers To begin to dispel myths about women workers and develop positive solutions for overcoming barriers.

Preselection counseling and tour for women candidates To familiarize women with the specific nature of the work, to show them the areas in which they would be working, and to provide them an opportunity for self-assessment of their readiness for entering the positions.

Planning for technical training and follow-up To provide women with structured training experiences as soon as they report to work and to prepare to offer them needed support services.

Posthire Activities

Phase 2 of Brunner's program to integrate women workers successfully into the organization—posthire activities—is aimed at helping newly hired women workers adapt to their new environment. Management designs these activities and requires the involvement of both men and women from various organizational positions and levels. The activities include:[36]

> Posthire activities help the newly hired women adapt to the environment.

Orientation for women selected To orient them to the job environment, connect them with women already in nontraditional work, and acquaint them with available support services (such as counseling).

General technical training To enable the women to meet basic job requirements.

On-the-job training To facilitate the development of task-specific job skills needed to improve performance at each stage or skill level.

Periodic counseling for the women To monitor the progress of their entry into the workplace and to provide guidance as needed.

Follow-up sessions with the men To monitor the adaptation of men workers to having women on board and to provide guidance as needed.

Rap sessions with both men and women To discuss and reduce possible tensions between men and women workers and to solve other problems as needed.

Periodic management discussions with the women, their trainers, and their supervisors To monitor individual and group progress and to demonstrate ongoing support.

Periodic evaluation and revision To measure results and identify program elements that need to be changed or strengthened.

The main focus of this chapter has been on explaining the generally accepted steps in providing appropriate human resources for the organization: (1) recruitment, (2) selection, (3) training, and (4) performance appraisals. This section implies that managers periodically face special human resource problems, such as integrating women workers into nontraditional jobs, that force them to complement these steps with additional activities.

BACK TO THE CASE

The last step in providing appropriate human resources at Fairchild Industries is performance appraisal. This means that the contributions that Fairchild employees make to the attainment of management system objectives must be evaluated. As with the training effort, performance appraisal at Fairchild should focus on more established employees as well as on new employees.

Charlie Collis probably would have benefited from a performance appraisal from company president Edward Uhl during the Thunderbolt project. Collis's appraisal would have stressed his activities on the job and his effectiveness in accomplishing job objectives, namely building the Thunderbolt attack plane to the Air Force's satisfaction. An objective appraisal would have provided Collis with tactful, constructive criticism that might have helped increase his productivity. Handled properly, Collis's appraisal would have been not a reward or a punishment but rather an opportunity to make him more valuable to Fairchild. Had Collis been given an objective, productive analysis of his performance, he might have been able to complete the Thunderbolt contract to the satisfaction of Fairchild and the Air Force, rather than being taken off the project.

In addition to giving performance appraisals to their employees as a means of maintaining appropriate human resources, Fairchild Industries will probably have to take special prehire and posthire steps to achieve maximum organizational benefits from women workers in nontraditional jobs. If Fairchild addresses these issues, as well as following the generally accepted steps of recruitment, selection and training discussed earlier, they will be better able to provide appropriate human resources within the company.

Action Summary

Reread the learning objectives that follow. Each objective is followed by questions. Answering these questions accurately will help you retain the most important concepts discussed in this chapter. After answering each question, check your answer with the answer key at the end of this chapter. (*Hint:* If you have doubt regarding the correct response, consult the page whose number follows the answer.)

From studying this chapter, I will attempt to acquire:

1. **An overall understanding of how appropriate human resources can be provided for the organization.**

    a. An appropriate human resource is an individual whose qualifications are matched to job specifications.

    b. The term *appropriate human resources* refers to: (1) finding the right number of people to fill positions; (2) individuals being satisfied with their jobs; (3) individuals who help the organization achieve management system objectives; (4) individuals who are ineffective; (5) none of the above.

2. **An appreciation for the relationship among recruitment efforts, an open position, sources of human resources, and the law.**

    a. The process of narrowing a large number of candidates to a smaller field is: (a) rushing; (b) recruitment; (c) selection; (d) enlistment; (e) enrollment.

    b. The characteristics of the individual who should be hired for the job are indicated by the: (a) job analysis; (b) job specification; (c) job description; (d) job review; (e) job identification.

3. **Insights on the use of tests and assessment centers in employee selection.**

    a. The level of skill or knowledge an individual possesses in a particular area is measured by: (a) aptitude tests; (b) achievement tests; (c) acuity tests; (d) assessment tests; (e) vocational interest tests.

    b. Which of the following guidelines does *not* apply when tests are being used in selecting potential employees: (a) the tests should be both valid and reliable; (b) the tests should be nondiscriminatory in nature; (c) the tests should not be the sole source of information for determining whether someone is to be hired; (d) such factors as potential and desire to obtain a position should not be assessed subjectively; (e) none of the above—all are important guidelines.

4. **An understanding of how the training process operates.**

    a. Four steps involved in training individuals are: (1) designing the training program, (2) evaluating the training program, (3) determining training needs, (4) administering the training program. The correct sequence for these steps is:
       (a) 1, 3, 2, 4
       (b) 3, 4, 1, 2
       (c) 2, 1, 3, 4
       (d) 3, 1, 4, 2
       (e) none of the above

    b. The lecture offers learners an excellent opportunity to clarify meanings and ask questions, since communication is two-way.

5. **A concept of what performance appraisals are and how they best can be conducted.**

    a. Performance appraisals are important in an organization because they: (a) provide systematic judgments to support promotions; (b) provide a basis for coaching; (c) provide a basis for counseling; (d) let subordinates know where they stand with the boss; (e) all of the above.

    b. To achieve the maximum benefit from performance evaluations, a manager should: (a) focus only on the negative aspects of performance; (b) punish the worker with negative feedback; (c) be as subjective as possible; (d) focus only on the positive aspects of performance; (e) use only constructive feedback.

Circle:

T, F

a, b, c, d, e

a, b, c, d, e

a, b, c, d, e

a, b, c, d, e

a, b, c, d, e

a, b, c, d, e

T, F

a, b, c, d, e

a, b, c, d, e

6. **An appreciation for the complex situation involving women who are working in nontraditional jobs.**

T, F   a. Prehire preparation focuses on helping women workers in traditional jobs to adapt to their new environment.

a, b, c, d, e   b. One of the steps in phase 2 of the program to integrate women workers into the organization successfully is: (a) planning for technical training and follow-up; (b) interview/selection training; (c) rap sessions with both men and women; (d) job analysis; (e) none of the above.

INTRODUCTORY CASE WRAP-UP

"Special Training at Fairchild Industries" (p. 252) and its related back-to-the-case sections were written to help you better understand the management concepts contained in this chapter. Answer the following discussion questions about this introductory case to further enrich your understanding of chapter content:

1. How important is the training of employees to an organization such as Fairchild Industries? Explain.
2. What actions besides training must an organization such as Fairchild take to make employees as productive as possible?
3. How easy would it be to evaluate the effectiveness of the training program that Charles Collis was conducting at Fairchild Industries? Explain.

Issues for Review and Discussion

1. What is the difference between appropriate and inappropriate human resources?
2. List and define the four major steps in providing appropriate human resources for the organization.
3. What is the purpose of recruitment?
4. How are job analysis, job description, and job specification related?
5. List the advantages of promotion from within.
6. Compare and contrast the management inventory card, the position replacement form, and the management manpower replacement chart.
7. List three sources of human resources outside the organization. How can these sources be tapped?
8. Does the law influence organizational recruitment practices? If so, how?
9. Describe the role of the Equal Employment Opportunity Commission.
10. Can affirmative action programs be useful in recruitment? Explain.
11. Define *selection*.
12. What is the difference between aptitude tests and achievement tests?

13. Discuss three guidelines for using tests in the selection process.
14. What are assessment centers?
15. List and define the four main steps of the training process.
16. Explain two possible ways of determining organizational training needs.
17. What are the differences between the lecture and programmed learning as alternative methods of transmitting information in the training program?
18. On-the-job training methods include coaching, position rotation, and special project committees. Explain how each of these methods works.
19. What are performance appraisals, and why should they be used?
20. If someone asked your advice on how to conduct performance appraisals, describe in detail what you would say.
21. What prehire preparation and posthire activities can be performed to integrate women workers holding nontraditional jobs into the organization?

Sources of Additional Information

Alpander, Guvenc G. *Human Resources Management Planning*. New York: Amacom, 1982.

Brinkerhoff, Derick W., and Rosabeth Moss Kanter. "Appraising the Performance of Performance Appraisal." *Sloan Management Review* (Spring 1980): 3–16.

Chan, Dr. K. H. "Decision Support System for Human Resource Management." *Journal of Systems Management* 35 (April 1984): 17–25.

Cummings, William Theodore, and Mark R. Edwards. "How to Evaluate Your Sales Force." *Business* 34 (April/May/June 1984): 30–36.

Drucker, Peter F. *The Effective Executive*. New York: Harper & Row, 1985.

Franklin, William H., Jr. "Why Training Fails." *Administrative Management* 42 (July 1981): 42–43, 72–74.

Friedman, Martin G. "Ten Steps to Objective Appraisals." *Personnel Journal* 65 (June 1986): 66–71.

Gordon, Judith R. *Human Resource Management: A Practical Approach*. Boston: Allyn and Bacon, 1986.

Hollmann, Robert W., and Mary Ellen Campbell. "Communications Strategies for Improving HRM Effectiveness." *Personnel Administrator* 29 (July 1984): 93–98.

Lebreton, Preston. "The Management Awareness Concept: A Missing Link in the Evolving Science of Management." *Managerial Planning* 30 (July/August 1981): 12–17.

Lopez, Felix M., Jr. *Personnel Interviewing: Theory and Practice*. New York: McGraw-Hill, 1965.

Lowe, Terry R. "Eight Ways to Ruin a Performance Review." *Personnel Journal* 65 (January 1986): 60.

O'Callaghan, John C., Jr. "Human Resource Development." *Managerial Planning* 30 (July/August 1981): 38–42.

Phillips, Stephen R. "The New Time Management." *Training and Development Journal* 42 (April 1988): 73–80.

"Regaining the Competitive Edge." *Personnel Administrator* 31 (July 1986): 34–45.

Regel, Roy W., and Robert W. Hollmann. "Gauging Performance Objectively." *Personnel Administrator* 32 (June 1987): 74–81.

Rowland, Kendrith M., Gerald R. Ferris, and Jay L. Sherman. *Current Issues in Personnel Management*. Boston: Allyn and Bacon, 1983.

Teel, Kenneth S. "Performance Appraisal: Current Trends, Persistent Progress." *Personnel Journal* (April 1980): 296–301, 316.

Thomas, William G. "Training and Development Do Make Better Managers." *Personnel* 65 (January 1988): 52–53.

Wallace, Marc J. *Administering Human Resources*. New York: Random House, 1982.

Wexley, Kenneth N., and Gary A. Yukl. *Organizational Behavior and Personnel Psychology*. Homewood, Ill.: Richard D. Irwin, 1984.

Notes

1. "Job Analysis," *Bureau of Intergovernmental Personnel Programs* (December 1973): 135–52.

2. Arch Patton, "The Coming Scramble for Executive Talent," *Harvard Business Review* (May/June 1967): 155–71.

3. Thomas J. Murray, "The Coming Glut in Executives," *Dun's Review* (May 1977): 64. An even more recent article pointing out this trend is "Slackening in Executive Demand," *Personnel Management* 17 (September 1985): 74.

4. Fred K. Foulkes, "How Top Nonunion Companies Manage Employees," *Harvard Business Review* (September/October 1981): 90.

5. John Perham, "Management Succession: A Hard Game to Play," *Dun's Review* (April 1981): 54–55, 58.

6. Walter S. Wikstrom, "Developing Managerial Competence: Concepts, Emerging Practices," *Studies in Personnel Policy*, no. 189, National Industrial Conference Board (1964), 95–105.

7. Ray H. Hodges, "Developing an Effective Affirmative Action Program," *Journal of Intergroup Relations* 5 (November 1976): 13.

8. James M. Higgins, "The Complicated Process of Establishing Goals for Equal Employment," *Personnel Journal* (December 1975): 631–37.

9. For more discussion on the stages of the selection process, see David J. Cherrington, *Personnel Management: The Management of Human Resources* (Dubuque, Iowa: Wm. C. Brown Publishers, 1987), 186–231.

10. This section is based on Andrew F. Sikula, *Personnel*

Administration and Human Resource Management (New York: Wiley, 1976), 188–90.

11. For information on various tests available, see O. K. Buros, ed., *The 8th Mental Measurements Yearbook* (Highland Park, N.J.: Gryphon Press, 1978).

12. Gene E. Burton, Dev S. Pathak, and David B. Burton, "Recruiting, Testing and Selecting: Delicate EEOC Areas," *Management World* (October 1976): 30.

13. D. W. Bray and, D. L. Grant, "The Assessment Center in the Measurement of Potential for Business Management," *Psychological Monographs* 80, no. 17 (1966): 1–27.

14. James C. Hyatt, "More Concerns Use 'Assessment Centers' to Gauge Employees' Managerial Abilities," *Wall Street Journal*, January 3, 1974, 15.

15. Barry M. Cohen, "Assessment Centers," *Supervisory Management* (June 1975): 30. See also T. J. Hanson and J. C. Balestreri-Sepro, "An Alternative to Interviews: Pre-employment Assessment Process," *Personnel Journal* (June 1985): 114.

16. For information about strengths and weaknesses of assessment centers, see C. W. Millard and Sheldon Pinsky, "Assessing the Assessment Center," *Personnel Administrator* (May 1980): 85–88.

17. Ann Howard, "An Assessment of Assessment Centers," *Academy of Management Journal* 17 (March 1974): 117.

18. Gordon L. Lippitt, "Criteria for Evaluating Human Resource Development," *Training and Development Journal* (October 1976): 3.

19. Bernard Bass and James Vaughn, *Training in Industry: The Management of Learning* (Belmont, Calif.: Wadsworth, 1966).

20. Bass and Vaughn, *Training in Industry*.

21. Leonard Silvern, "Training: Man-Man and Man-Machine Communications," in *Systems Psychology*, ed. Kenyon DeGreen (New York: McGraw-Hill, 1970), 383–405.

22. For more information on training techniques, see Cherrington, *Personnel Management*, 304–36.

23. Samuel C. Certo, "The Experiential Exercise Situation: A Comment on Instructional Role and Pedagogy Evaluation," *Academy of Management Review* (July 1976): 113–16.

24. For more information on instructional roles in various situations, see Bernard Keys, "The Management of Learning Grid for Management Development," *Academy of Management Review* (April 1977): 289–97.

25. For more information on the performance appraisal process, see Robert L. Mathis and John H. Jackson, "Appraisal of Human Resources," in their *Personnel: Human Resource Management* (St. Paul, Minn.: West Publishing, 1985), 337–66.

26. Douglas McGregor, "An Uneasy Look at Performance Appraisal," *Harvard Business Review* (September/October 1972): 133–34.

27. Harold Koontz, "Making Managerial Appraisal Effective," *California Management Review* 15 (Winter 1972): 46–55.

28. Thomas L. Whisler, "Appraisal as a Management Tool," in *Performance Appraisal: Research and Practice*, ed. Thomas L. Whisler and Shirley F. Harper (New York: Holt, Rinehart & Winston, 1962).

29. William J. Birch, "Performance Appraisal: One Company's Experience," *Personnel Journal* (June 1981): 456–60.

30. George A. Rider, "Performance Review: A Mixed Bag," *Harvard Business Review* (July/August 1973): 61–67.

31. John D. Colby and Ronald L. Wallace, "The Art of Leveling with Subordinates about Their Performance," *Supervisory Management* (December 1975): 26–29.

32. Women's Bureau, New York City, U.S. Department of Labor, 1980.

33. "The Hardships That Blue-Collar Women Face," *Business Week*, August 14, 1978, 88.

34. The remainder of this section is based primarily on Nancy R. Brunner, "Blue-Collar Women," *Personnel Journal* (April 1981): 279–82.

35. Brunner, "Blue-Collar Women."

36. Brunner, "Blue-Collar Women."

Action Summary Answer Key

1. a. F, p. 253
   b. c, p. 253
2. a. b, p. 254
   b. b, p. 254
3. a. b, pp. 263–264
   b. d, p. 264
4. a. d, p. 265
   b. F, p. 268
5. a. e, p. 271
   b. e, p. 272
6. a. F, p. 275
   b. c, pp. 275–276

MMI'S OLYMPIC GAMES AND PRODUCTIVITY

"We won. We smeared 'em," says Avanell Hurst, a member of the winning bed-making team. Hurst, a veteran maid at the airport Holiday Inn in Jacksonville, Florida, was competing in the Mississippi Management Inc. (MMI) Employee Olympic Games. Other events included drink mixing, key sorting, sheet and towel folding, directory search, housekeeping cart relay, egg cracking, table busing, wine relay, and commode seat change. MMI, a company that owns or manages fourteen assorted resorts, hotels, and motels in the Southeast, spent about $150,000 on the games.

Although the MMI olympics is not an annual event, the privately held company, with headquarters in Jackson, Mississippi, does expend nearly $100,000 each year on employee training of one variety or another. For example, each property is permitted to send two housekeepers (room maids) to overnight seminars, with all room, transportation, meal, and entertainment expenses paid. Cooks, front-desk clerks, and supervisors are supported in similar fashion.

Furthermore, cash awards are given to five- and ten-year employees, watches to those with fifteen years, and trip awards to employees with twenty or thirty years of service; $34,600 dropped out of MMI's pretax profits one year to cover such awards. MMI's overall human resource budget totaled a respectable $376,000 that year. But what was MMI really getting for its money?

MMI's managers—chief executive officer Earle Jones, seven senior corporate staff people, and two senior operational vice-presidents, Joe Morgan and Dean MaKinster—meeting in a room at the company's Lake City, Florida, Holiday Inn were pondering just this question as they hashed over the next year's budget. Jim Hart, MMI's human resource vice-president, had just requested a 20 percent increase over the prior year's $376,000—a whopping $450,000. "What if you'd rather turn in a 32% [gross operating profit] instead? Do maids *have* to go to seminars *every* year? My people keep asking me, 'How is this, or this, going to improve my GOP [gross operating profit]?' " argued Morgan. Although no one was there simply to object to Hart's programs, the group was meeting to discuss the impact of such programs on GOP. Measured in dollars, GOP had risen, but as a percent of revenues it had fallen from its high of 33.8 percent a few years earlier to a current 24.7 percent.

Jones blamed MMI's disappointing statistics on overbuilding in the industry, lower demand for commercial hotel rooms in the Mississippi-Louisiana division's energy-depressed market, and the resulting

pressure to keep room rates low. If Jones's presumptions are right, MMI should be diligently cutting costs wherever possible to ease the pressure on profits, not increasing human resource spending.

Cutting Hart's budget surely was tempting that Sunday afternoon, but the way MMI runs its human resource programs doesn't require accountants' formulas to judge the value of human resource spending. Instead, the company uses informed common sense plus a good deal of sensitivity to sort out the worthwhile from the wasteful. The people running MMI don't pursue human resource programs only for the sake of corporate culture. They won't approve a program, retain a benefit, or expand a perk unless there's a solid business reason for doing so. What, then, provides the impetus for spending more and more for training under less than favorable conditions? A few examples follow.

At the annual seminar for housekeepers, corporate trainer Colleen Maloney was setting the stage for MMI's version of "The Price Is Right." Two teams were positioned in front of two tables. Displayed on the first table were a dozen items that housekeepers use in their work, including bars of soap. On the second sat twelve price tags. The first team was to match prices to products. The second team could win by correcting the first team's errors. As enthusiasm in the competition was increasing, Maloney stopped the debate and made her point. "Let's see," she said, "what the cost of soap is for a 200-room property in a year. One vanity bar and one bath bar. Let's multiply by 200. That's so much per day.

281

Now let's multiply by 365." "If you walk it through with them," she explained, "they're very comfortable. It ends up being $10,000 and something. 'Wow,' they say. Later I'll ask them, 'How much was that vanity soap?' 'Four cents,' they'll say. They wouldn't remember if I had just told them."

Approximately a quarter of MMI's thirteen hundred employees go through one of these training seminars annually. Employees also see Maloney at ad hoc sessions, such as the three-day program held for Radisson Walthall Hotel's dining-room workers. After the first of two role-playing sessions, Maloney spoke directly to a waitress, crowding closer and closer to the young woman's face. The waitress, uncomfortable with the situation, retreated into her chair back, an action that led to a discussion of body language.

Is this just foolishness? MMI's managers say no. The link between training and service is very obvious to Radisson general manager Ron Stull, an eleven-year MMI veteran. As is the case with other general managers, Stull takes more than an academic interest in the amount of time his employees spend in training. Payroll charges come out of his budget, the short-term costs in lowered productivity show up on his performance reports, and both affect his year-end bonus.

According to Claude Collins, general manager at Jacksonville, there really isn't much difference between employee training and employee motivation: "It isn't so much the education as the experience. What I gain is two or three maids being shown how special it is being a guest."

"How do you motivate somebody to change a toilet seat the fastest?" asks Craig Michelet, food and beverage manager at the Radisson Walthall. "Not by telling him to do it, but by motivating him to be the best." This, presumably, is exactly what the MMI Employee Olympic Games are all about. "It allows some everyday people to be stars in a large organization," says Collins. "Braggin' rights," said Ron Caimano, general manager of MMI's Embassy Suites Hotel in Orlando, after his division took Olympic honors. "That's what we won. We can talk about this until next time."

About half of MMI's human resource budget goes to corporate overhead, covering Hart's and Maloney's salaries and their office and travel expenses. The other half covers seminar costs, award trips, department-of-the-year awards, and other awards; it is allocated among the individual hotels. These charges appear as a cost above the general manager's bottom line, the gross operating profit. Interestingly, it is this GOP that determines, in large part, the general manager's annual bonus. Needless to say, general managers don't happily accept human resource costs unless they see offsetting benefits.

If such benefits were not accruing, one can be sure

that senior operations vice-president Joe Morgan would be hearing loud complaining. This is one way MMI holds human resource spending in check and ensures that human resource programs are directed at operational needs. Under these conditions, what Hart, Morgan, and other executives can settle on Sunday afternoon as a reasonable human resource budget is probably as good a measure of the program's effectiveness an any accounting device might yield.

Yet, assessing the benefits of training and other programs at MMI is not all done by feel. There are measures that MMI uses to determine if it is doing something right, even if what is measured does not always relate to an identifiable cost or specific program. The guest comment card, for example, provides insight into the quality of service rendered by MMI employees. Compared with all Holiday Inns as a group, MMI properties receive 25 percent fewer guest complaints. In addition, such measures as gross operating profit and occupancy rates tell the organization something about how well it is performing in its market environment.

Of course, even though such information paints a very helpful picture, it says little about why the company is performing well or poorly. If the problem is that room prices are depressed, MMI executives know that this issue will not be resolved by eliminating training programs, especially if they have good reason to believe that such programs actually help hold costs down. Other performance measures that have been used to assess the effects of human resource spending include total labor hours per occupied room and employee turnover rates today as compared to those of previous periods.

When the final budget was put together, Hart's request for additional human resource spending remained intact. Jones and his crew believed that to cut it would be a false economy. MMI's experience suggests that wise human resource spending is a way to shave costs, not raise them.

DISCUSSION ISSUES

1. What approach or approaches does MMI use to assess its training needs? Explain.
2. What are the primary training techniques used at MMI? Would other techniques yield greater benefits? Explain.
3. MMI officials intimate that they cannot directly place a dollar value on the benefits derived from their training programs. How, then, do they assess the benefits derived from the programs? Do you believe the benefits derived from training at MMI outweigh the costs associated with such training? Explain.
4. Do you see a link between effective training and employee motivation? Explain.

STUDENT LEARNING OBJECTIVES

From studying this chapter, I will attempt to acquire:

1. A working definition of *changing an organization*.
2. An understanding of the relative importance of change and stability to an organization.
3. Some ability to know what type of change should be made within an organization.
4. An appreciation for why individuals affected by a change should be considered when the change is being made.
5. Some facility in evaluating change.
6. An understanding of how organizational change and stress are related.

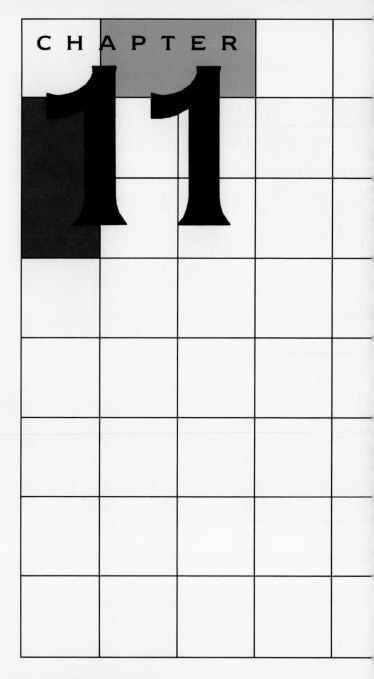

ORGANIZATIONAL CHANGE AND STRESS

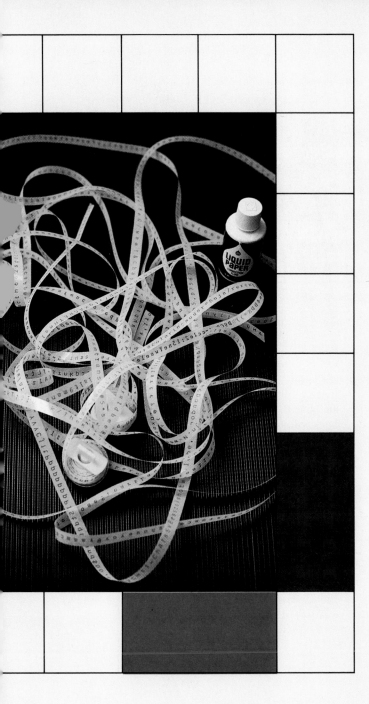

CHAPTER OUTLINE

GM'S GREAT DIVIDE

Roger B. Smith got off to a rocky start in his first year as the chairman of General Motors Corporation. Early in his reign, GM made some strategic goofs in crucial labor negotiations with the United Auto Workers, and Smith himself alienated a number of company VIPs by attempting to limit an annual shareholders' meeting to only three hours. On the positive side, however, Smith guided the giant automaker through a bruising recession and in recent years has helped the company reach profits of over $3.5 billion.

Soon, however, the soft-spoken Smith is expected to make a move even more stunning that his company's recent record profits. He will propose the most revolutionary change in the way GM runs its business since the company was restructured in the 1920s by organizational genius Alfred P. Sloan.

At an upcoming meeting in New York, Smith will ask the GM board of directors to approve a carefully crafted proposal to reduce the company's five famous car divisions—Chevrolet, Pontiac, Oldsmobile, Buick, and Cadillac—to only two, each larger than either the Ford Motor Company or the Chrysler Corporation. Smith's idea calls for the new Chevrolet-Pontiac division to produce and sell only GM's smaller cars and the Buick-Oldsmobile-Cadillac division to handle the larger models.

Beyond this merging of names for the new divisions, Smith's proposal will change the corporate face of General Motors in other important ways. Since the early 1920s, such key activities as design, engineering, and marketing were directed essentially by staffs at the top

corporate level. Under Smith's new proposal, these activities will be handled by separate and independent staffs at the two new divisions. For each division, the buck will stop at the two new executive vice-presidents— the individuals who will head each divison and be strictly accountable to GM's top brass for the division's profits and performance.

Smith's proposal calls for these organizational changes to be implemented over a three-year period. If the proposed organizational structure is adopted, most experts agree, the "new" General Motors will be a leaner, tougher competitor in a domestic market that it already dominates. This would be bad news not only to Ford and Chrysler but to Japan as well.

What's Ahead

Roger B. Smith, the General Motors chairman in the introductory case, has the main role in deciding what changes to make within his company. Smith also is held accountable for implementing changes successfully. In this regard, Smith and other managers facing the task of modifying an organization could use the information in this chapter on the fundamentals of changing an organization, the factors to consider when changing the organization, and organizational change and stress.

FUNDAMENTALS OF CHANGING AN ORGANIZATION

Thus far, discussion in this "Organizing" section of the text has centered on the fundamentals of organizing, furnishing appropriate human resources for the organization, authority, delegation, and responsibility. This chapter focuses on changing an organization.

Defining "Changing an Organization"

Changing an organization is the process of modifying an existing organization. The purpose of organizational modifications is to increase organizational effectiveness—that is, the extent to which an organization accomplishes its objectives. These modifications can involve virtually any organizational segment and typically include changing the lines of organizational authority, the levels of responsibility held by various organization members, and the established lines of organizational communication.

Most managers agree that if an organization is to be successful, it must change continually in response to significant developments, such as customer needs, technological breakthroughs, and government regulations. The study of organizational change is extremely important because all managers at all organizational levels are faced throughout their careers with the task of changing their organization. According to a study by Ronald Daniel, large American manufacturers make major changes in their organizations approximately once every two years.[1] Managers who can make changes successfully are highly valued in organizations of all types.[2]

Many managers consider change to be so critical to the success of the organization that they encourage employees to continually search for areas in which beneficial organizational change can be made. General Motors, for example, provides employees with a "think list" to encourage them to develop ideas for organizational change and to remind them that change is important to the continued success of GM. The think list contains the following questions:[3]

1. Can a machine be used to do a better or faster job?
2. Can the fixture now in use be improved?

Existing organizations are often modified to increase organizational effectiveness.

Organizations must change continually.

Employees can provide ideas for change.

3. Can materials handling for the machine be improved?
4. Can a special tool be used to combine the operations?
5. Can the quality of the part being produced be improved by changing the sequence of the operation?
6. Can the material used be cut or trimmed differently for greater economy or efficiency?
7. Can the operation be made safer?
8. Can paperwork regarding this job be eliminated?
9. Can established procedures be simplified?

Change versus Stability

Stability should complement change.

In addition to organizational change, some degree of stability is a prerequisite for long-term organizational success. Figure 11.1 presents a model developed by Hellriegel and Slocum that shows the relative importance of change and stability to organizational survival. Although these authors use the word *adaptation* in their model rather than *change*, the two terms are essentially synonymous. This model stresses that the greatest probability of organizational survival and growth exists when both stability and adaptation are high within the organization (number 3 on the model). The organization without stability to complement or supplement change is at a definite disadvantage. When stability is low, the probability for organizational survival and growth declines. Change after change without stability typically results in confusion and employee stress.[4]

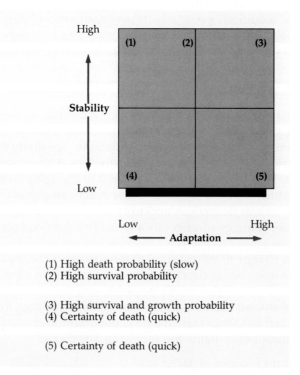

(1) High death probability (slow)
(2) High survival probability

(3) High survival and growth probability
(4) Certainty of death (quick)

(5) Certainty of death (quick)

FIGURE 11.1
Adaptation, stability, and organizational survival

BACK TO THE CASE

If Roger Smith, in his deliberations on changing General Motors, followed the recommendations made in this first section of the chapter, he considered only the modifications that would further facilitate the accomplishment of GM's objectives. Smith probably realized that if GM was to have continued success, he would have to modify the organization a number of times over the long term. In fact, appropriate change is so important to GM that Smith may have considered initiating some type of program that would encourage employees to submit their ideas on increasing the effectiveness of the company. When considering possible changes, however, Smith undoubtedly realized that some level of stability was also necessary if his company was to survive and grow over the long term.

FACTORS TO CONSIDER WHEN CHANGING AN ORGANIZATION

How managers deal with the major factors to be considered when changing an organization determines to a great extent how successful an organizational change will be. These factors are (1) the change agent, (2) determining what should be changed, (3) the type of change to make, (4) individuals affected by the change, and (5) evaluation of change. Although the following sections discuss each of these factors individually, Figure 11.2 makes the point that their collective influence ultimately determines the success of a change.

The Change Agent

Perhaps the most important factor to be considered by managers when changing an organization is determining who will be the **change agent**—anyone inside or

A change agent is an individual inside or outside the organization who tries to effect change.

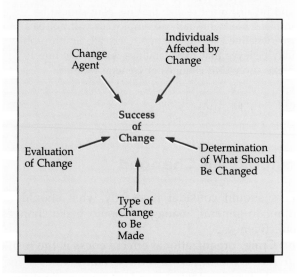

FIGURE 11.2
The collective influence of five major factors on the success of changing an organization

outside the organization who tries to effect change.[5] The change agent might be a self-designated manager within the organization or possibly an outside consultant hired because of a special expertise in a particular area. Although in reality the change agent may not be a manager, the terms *manager* and *change agent* are used synonymously throughout this chapter.

A change agent needs special skills to be successful.

Several special skills are necessary for success as a change agent, including the ability to determine how a change should be made, to solve change related problems, and to use behavioral science tools to influence people appropriately during the change. Perhaps the most overlooked skill of successful change agents is the ability to determine how much change employees can withstand. As indicated by the following excerpt, too much change can be very disturbing:

> Millions of psychologically normal people will experience an abrupt collision with the future when they fall victim to tomorrow's most menacing malady—the disease of change. Unable to keep up with the supercharged pace of change, brought to the edge of breakdown by insistent demands to adapt to novelty, many will plunge into future shock. For them, the future will arrive too soon.[6]

Over all, managers should choose change agents who possess the most expertise in the areas suggested by the necessary special skills. A potentially beneficial change for the organization might not result in any advantages if the wrong person is designated to make the change.

BACK TO THE CASE

Since Roger Smith has the main role in deciding what changes to make at General Motors as well as actually implementing these changes, he is a change agent. Smith probably designated himself change agent because of his abilitiy to determine how the particular type of change within his company should be made and how to solve organizational problems that could arise as a result of it. In order to implement his plan, Smith must recognize that one thing he needs to do is form new, independent departments to handle design, engineering, and marketing. He also must realize that he will need to deal with problems that arise when the two new divisions, each with its own executives, are formed.

As change agent, Smith also has the ability to use behavioral science tools to influene organization members during the change and to determine how much change these members can withstand. Smith should know how to influence his staff so its members learn to work together in their new divisions, and he also must realize that his plan should be implemented gradually so employees will not be overwhelmed by the change. Over all, Smith probably believes that these abilities will enable him to make successful changes at General Motors.

Determining What Should Be Changed

Another major factor managers should consider is exactly what should be changed within the organization. In general, managers should make changes that increase organizational effectiveness.

People, structural, and technological factors must be appropriately matched to maximize organizational effectiveness.

According to Giegold and Craig, organizational effectiveness is the result primarily of organizational activities centering around three main classes of factors: (1) people, (2) structure, and (3) technology.[7] **People factors** are attitudes, leadership skills, communication skills, and all other characteristics of the human resources within the organization. Organizational controls, such as policies and procedures, constitute **structural factors**. And **technological factors** are any types of equipment or processes that assist organization members in the performance of their jobs.

The "Management in Action" feature for this chapter focuses on structural factors at Apple Computer. More specifically, the feature discusses how chairman John Sculley has changed structural factors at Apple in order to make it a more traditional company with a strong emphasis on net profit.

For an organization to maximize effectiveness, appropriate people must be matched with appropriate technology and appropriate structure. Thus, people factors, technological factors, and structural factors are not independent determinants of organizational effectiveness. Instead, as Figure 11.3 shows, organizational effectiveness is determined by the relationship of these three factors.

The Type of Change to Make

The type of change to make is a third major factor that managers should consider when changing an organization. Although managers can choose to change an organization in many different ways, most changes can be categorized as one of three types: (1) technological change, (2) structural change, or (3) people change. These three types obviously correspond to the three main determinants of organizational effectiveness. Each type of change is named for the one determinant that the change emphasizes over the other two.

People change, structural change, and technological change are three types of organizational changes.

For example, **technological change** emphasizes modifying the level of technology within a management system. Since technological change often involves outside experts and highly technical language, structural change and people change are the two types discussed in more detail here.

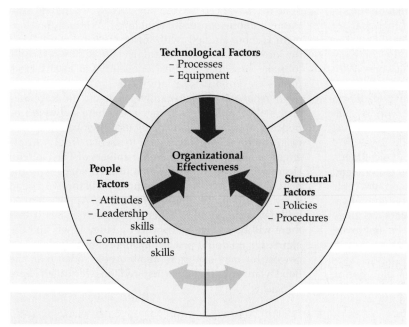

FIGURE 11.3
Determination of organizational effectiveness by the relationship of people, technological, and structural factors

CHANGING STRUCTURAL FACTORS AT APPLE COMPUTER

May you build a ladder to the stars,
And climb on every rung,
And may you stay,
Forever young.

Bob Dylan

Eternal youth is tough to pull off—no less for companies than for folk singers. As Apple Computer Inc. celebrates its 10th birthday, the effects of turning a two-man startup into a $2 billion company with 5,000 employees are starting to show. Workers still call Apple's Cupertino (Calif.) headquarters The Campus, and the atmosphere is still informal. But the original Apple, where founders Steven P. Jobs and Stephen Wozniak spent millions on spur-of-the-moment decisions and staff factions toiled over competing projects until the wee hours, may be gone for good. Chairman John Sculley has created in its place a more traditional company with a strong affection for the bottom line.

"The vision is still intact," insists Sculley, recalling Jobs's goal of putting a computer in every person's hands and thus changing the world in a million unpredictable ways. But the means for reaching that goal are turning out to be different from what Jobs imagined. The change started when Sculley restructured the company in 1985, rolling three separate divisions into one. With that came rules. Strict financial controls. Formal reporting procedures. Tough product-development deadlines.

Sculley says these are tempered with a still-unusual appreciation for imagination. "We didn't just want good financial results this year," he says. "We wanted to hold on to the soul of Apple." But old-timers, now in their 30s, say he's failed. "Now you either blend in or you're history," says Peter Quinn, a former Apple II design engineer. "The real heavy rewards and motivations for doing anything beyond normal work are gone. Why bother? You're a cog in a wheel." As an employer, others add, Apple now appeals to a different crowd. "It's looking for a lot more MBAs these days," says one former engineer. "It's just another big, boring company."

John Sculley (at right)

BEER AND POPCORN

If that's true, it's hard to say if it's bad. Jobs "could take an idea and cut corners to make it happen, and some people miss that," says Lawrence G. Tesler, vice-president for advanced technology. "Now we have to go through more consensus-building." Product development is more studied, with fewer "fits and starts." But the idea isn't to avoid "radical new ideas," he says—it's to make sure that the best ones survive. In any case, profits are up, and sales are rising.

Whatever the substantive changes, the trappings of the old Apple are still in place. There's always free popcorn and, on Fridays, beer busts. Just before Christmas, employees were bused off to see *Star Trek IV*. Apple engineers recently entertained members of The Grateful Dead, who now compose some of their songs with the help of Macintosh. And the company still throws a good party. The halls are abuzz with talk of Apple's Jan. 17 birthday bash. Among other things, rumor has it that there will be a surprise concert by Huey Lewis and the News. It's no doubt just a coincidence, but Huey Lewis' newest hit may say more about Apple today than the Bob Dylan lyrics that once inspired Jobs. It's called *Hip to Be Square*.

Structural Change

Structural change emphasizes increasing organizational effectiveness by changing controls that influence organization members during the performance of their jobs. The following sections further describe this approach and discuss matrix organizations (organizations modified to complete a special project) as an example of structural change.

Describing Structural Change

Structural change is change aimed at increasing organizational effectiveness through modifications to the existing organizational structure. These modifications can take several forms: (1) clarifying and defining jobs; (2) modifying organizational structure to fit the communication needs of the organization; and (3) decentralizing the organization to reduce the cost of coordination, increase the controllability of subunits, increase motivation, and gain greater flexibility.[8] Although structural change must include some consideration of people and technology to be successful, its primary focus is obviously on changing organizational structure, In general, managers choose to make structural changes within the organization if information they have gathered indicates that the present organizational structure is the main cause of organizational ineffectiveness. The precise structural change managers make varies from situation to situation, of course.

Structural change focuses on modifying organizational structure.

Matrix Organizations

Matrix organizations provide a good illustration of structural change. According to C. J. Middleton, a **matrix organization** is a more traditional organization that is modified primarily for the purpose of completing some type of special proj-

Matrix organizations are created to complete special projects.

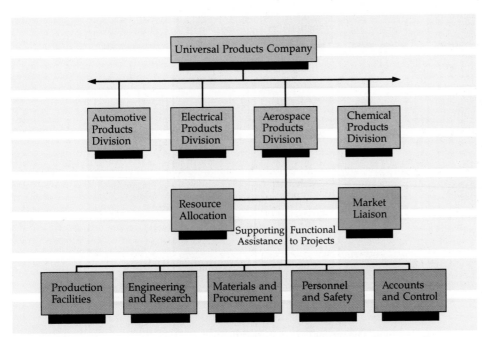

FIGURE 11.4

Portion of a traditional organizational structure based primarily on product

ect.[9] For this reason, matrix organizations are also called project organizations. The project itself may be either long term or short term, with employees needed to complete the project borrowed from various organizational segments.

John F. Mee has developed an excellent example showing how a more traditional organization can be changed into a matrix organization.[10] Figure 11.4 on p. 293 presents a portion of a traditional organizational structure divided primarily according to product line. Although this design could be generally

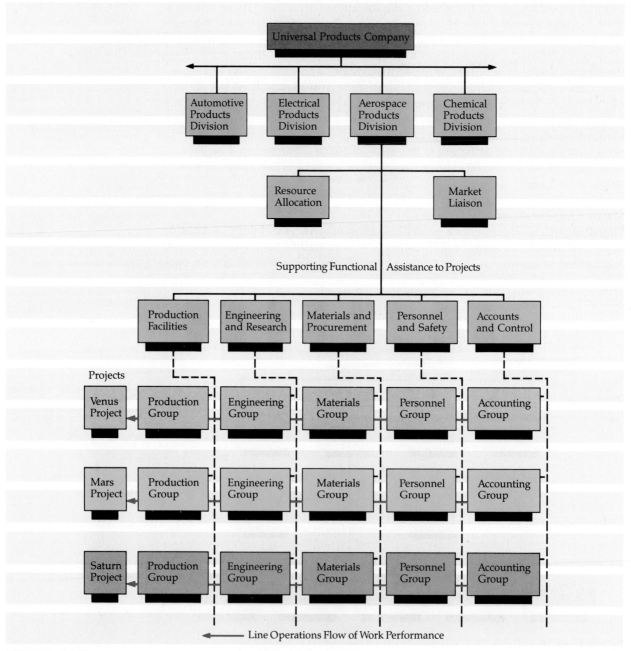

FIGURE 11.5
Traditional organization chart transformed into matrix organization

useful, managers might learn that it makes it impossible for organization members to give adequate attention to three government projects of extreme importance to long-term organizational success.

Figure 11.5 presents one way of changing this more traditional organizational structure into a matrix organization to facilitate completion of the three government projects. A manager would be appointed for each of the three projects and allocated personnel with appropriate skills to complete the project. The three project managers would have authority over the employees assigned to them and be accountable for the performance of those people. Each of the three project managers would be placed on the chart in the figure in one of the three boxes labeled Venus Project, Mars Project, and Saturn Project. As a result, work flow related to each project would go from right to left on the chart. After the projects were completed, the organization chart could be changed back to its original design, if that design is more advantageous.

There are several advantages and disadvantages to making structural changes such as those reflected by the matrix organization. Among the major advantages are that such structural changes generally result in better control of a project, better customer relations, shorter project development time, and lower project costs. Accompanying these advantages, however, are the disadvantages that such structural changes also generally create more complex internal operations, encourage inconsistency in the application of company policy, and result in a more difficult situation to manage.[11] One point, however, is clear. For a matrix organization to be effective and efficient, organization members must be willing to learn and execute somewhat different organizational roles.[12] The significance of the advantages and disadvantages relative to the success of changing a specific organization obviously vary from situation to situation.

> The significance of the advantages and disadvantages of matrix organizations varies from situation to situation.

BACK TO THE CASE

In researching his proposal to restructure General Motors, Roger Smith probably considered changing technological factors, people factors, and structural factors at GM that could increase organizational effectiveness. He must have decided that the needed change concerned primarily structural factors. As a result, he decided to propose to GM's board of directors that the company's five divisions be reduced to two. In addition, Smith's thoughts probably included placing such key functions as design, engineering, and marketing at the divisional level rather than at the corporate level, where they had been in the past. In essence, the executive vice-presidents for each division would be accountable for divisional profits. Smith's proposal called for these changes to be made over a three-year period.

People Change

Although successful people change also involves some consideration of structure and technology, the primary emphasis is on people. The following sections discuss people change and examine grid organization development, one commonly used means of attempting to change organization members.

Describing People Change
People change emphasizes increasing organizational effectiveness by changing certain aspects of organization members. The focus of this type of change is on such factors as employees' attitudes and leadership skills. In general, managers

> Organizational effectiveness can be increased by changing people's attitudes and leadership skills.

Organization develop-
ment is the process
of people change.

should attempt to make this type of change when human resources are shown to be the main cause of organizational ineffectiveness.

The process of people change can be referred to as **organization development (OD).** Although OD focuses mainly on changing certain aspects of people, these changes are based on an overview of structure, technology, and all other organizational ingredients.[13] Figure 11.6 demonstrates this organizational overview approach by showing both overt and covert organizational components considered during OD efforts. Overt factors are generally easily detectable and pictured as the tip of an organizational iceberg; covert factors are usually more difficult to assess and therefore are displayed as the part of the organizational iceberg that is "under water."

Grid OD

Grid OD focuses on
encouraging manag-
ers to adopt the 9,9
management style.

One commonly used OD technique for changing people in organizations is called **grid OD.**[14] The **managerial grid** is a basic model describing various managerial styles; it is used as the foundation for grid OD. The managerial grid is

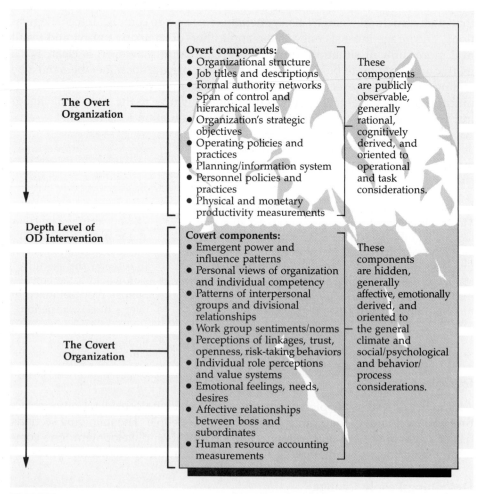

FIGURE 11.6
The organizational iceberg

based on the premise that various managerial styles can be described by means of two primary attitudes of the manager: concern for people and concern for production. Within this model, each attitude is placed on an axis, which is scaled 1 through 9, and is used to generate five managerial styles. Figure 11.7 shows the managerial grid, its five managerial styles, and the factors that characterize each of these styles.

The central theme of this managerial grid is that 9,9 management (as shown on the grid) is the ideal managerial style. Managers using this style have high concern for both people and production. Managers using any other style have lesser degrees of concern for people or production and are thought to reduce organizational success accordingly. The purpose of grid OD is to change organization managers so they will use the 9,9 management style.

How is a grid OD program conducted? The program has six main training phases for all managers within the organization. The first two phases focus on acquainting managers with the managerial grid concept and assisting them in determining which managerial style they most commonly use. The last four phases of the grid OD program concentrate on encouraging managers to adopt the 9,9 management style and showing them how to use this style within their

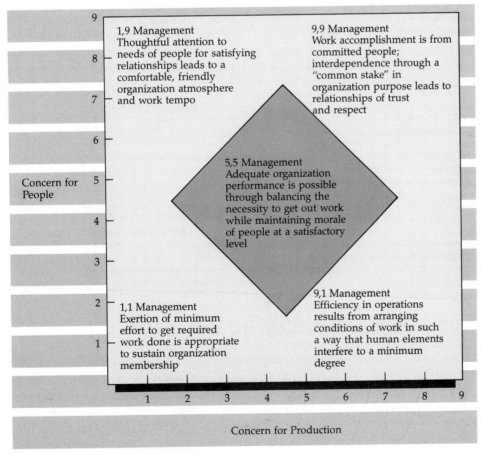

FIGURE 11.7
The managerial grid

specific job situation. Emphasis throughout the program is on developing team-work within the organization.

Some evidence suggests that grid OD is useful because it is effective in enhancing profit, positively changing managerial behavior, and positively influencing managerial attitudes and values.[15] Grid OD probably will have to undergo more rigorous testing for an extended period of time, however, before conclusive statements about it can be made.[16]

The Status of Organization Development

If the entire OD area is taken into consideration, changes that emphasize both people and the organization as a whole seem to have inherent strength. There are, however, several commonly voiced weaknesses of OD efforts. These weaknesses indicate that (1) the effectiveness of an OD program is difficult to evaluate, (2) OD programs are generally too time-consuming, (3) OD objectives are commonly too vague, (4) the total costs of an OD program are difficult to pinpoint at the time the program starts; and (5) OD programs are generally too expensive.[17]

Despite these weaknesses, however, the use of OD techniques probably will grow in the future.[18] Therefore, these weaknesses should not eliminate OD but should indicate areas to perfect within it. Managers can improve the quality of OD efforts by (1) systematically tailoring OD programs to meet the specific needs of the organization, (2) continually demonstrating as part of the program exactly how people should change their behavior, and (3) conscientiously changing organizational reward systems so organization members who change their behavior as suggested by the OD program are rewarded.[19]

BACK TO THE CASE

If the General Motors board of directors approves Roger Smith's plan, the changes he will implement will not be classified as people change. Although the people involved in the change must be considered to some extent, the main emphasis of the proposed change is on structural change.

If, however, Smith had found that problems with human resources were the main cause of organizational ineffectiveness, he might have proposed organization development rather than structural change. In fact, Smith may find that later on that he needs to use a grid OD in order to modify management styles and produce more cooperative team effort once the proposed structural changes are implemented.

Individuals Affected by the Change

A fourth major factor to be considered by managers when changing an organization is the people affected by the change. A good assessment of what to change and how to make the change probably will be wasted if organization members do not support the change. To increase the chances of employee support, managers should be aware of (1) the usual employee resistance to change, (2) how this resistance can be reduced, and (3) the three phases usually present when behavioral change occurs.

Resistance to Change

Resistance to change within an organization is as common as the need for change. After managers decide on making some organizational change, they typically meet with employee resistance aimed at preventing the change from occurring. This resistance generally exists because organization members fear some personal loss, such as a reduction in personal prestige, a disturbance of established social and working relationships, and personal failure because of an inability to carry out new job responsibilities.

Resistance to change is often based on feared personal loss.

Reducing Resistance to Change

Since resistance typically accompanies proposed change, managers must be able to reduce the effects of this resistance to ensure the success of needed modifications. Resistance usually can be reduced by means of the following guidelines:[20]

Resistance to change can be reduced if managers:

1. *Avoid surprises* People need time to evaluate a proposed change before management implements it. Elimination of this time to evaluate how the change may affect individual situations usually results in automatic opposition to it. Whenever possible, individuals who will be affected by a change should be kept informed of the type of change being considered and the probability that the change will be adopted.

   1. Avoid surprises.

2. *Promote real understanding* When fear of personal loss related to a proposed change is reduced, opposition to the change is reduced.[21] Most managers would agree that having organization members thoroughly understand a proposed change is a major step in reducing this fear. This understanding may even generate support for the change by focusing attention on possible individual gains that could materialize as a result of it. Individuals should receive information that will help them answer the following change related questions that invariably will be asked:

   2. Promote under-standing.

   - Will I lose my job?
   - Will my old skills become obsolete?
   - Am I capable of producing effectively under the new system?
   - Will my power and prestige decline?
   - Will I be given more responsibility than I care to assume?
   - Will I have to work longer hours?
   - Will it force me to betray or desert my good friends?[22]

3. *Set the stage for change* Perhaps the most powerful tool for reducing resistance to change is management's positive attitude toward change. This attitude should be displayed openly by top and middle management as well as by lower management. In essence, management should demonstrate its appreciation for change as one of the basic prerequisites for a successful organization. Management also should strive to be seen as encouraging change only to increase organizational effectiveness, not just for the sake of trying something new. To emphasize this attitude toward change, some portion of organizational rewards should be earmarked for the organization members who are most instrumental in implementing constructive change.

   3. Present a positive attitude toward change.

4. *Make tentative change* Resistance to change also can be reduced by making changes on a tentative basis. This approach establishes a trial period during

   4. Implement change on a tentative basis.

which organization members spend some time working under a proposed change before voicing support or nonsupport of it. Tentative change is based on the assumption that a trial period during which organization members live under a change is the best way of reducing feared personal loss. Judson has summarized the benefits of using the tentative approach:

- Those involved are able to test their reactions to the new situation before committing themselves irrevocably.
- Those involved are able to acquire more facts on which to base their attitudes and behavior toward the change.
- Those involved with strong preconceptions are in a better position to regard the change with greater objectivity. Consequently, they could review their preconceptions and perhaps modify some of them.
- Those involved are less likely to regard the change as a threat.
- Management is better able to evaluate the method of change and make any necessary modifications before carrying it out more fully.[23]

The Behavioral Side of Change

Almost any change requires that organization members modify the way in which they are accustomed to behaving or working. Therefore, managers must not only be able to decide on the best people-structure-technology relationship for the organization but also to make corresponding changes in such a way that related human behavior is changed most effectively. Positive results of any change will materialize only if organization members change their behavior as necessitated by the change.

Kurt Lewin, a German social scientist, pioneered the study of field theory. According to Lewin, behavioral change is caused by three distinct but related conditions experienced by an individual: (1) unfreezing, (2) changing, and (3) refreezing.[24]

The first condition, **unfreezing,** is the state in which individuals become ready to acquire or learn new behaviors—they experience the ineffectiveness of their present mode of behavior and are ready to attempt to learn new behavior that will make them more effective. It may be especially difficult for individuals to "thaw out" because of positive attitudes they traditionally associate with their past behavior.

Changing, the second of Lewin's conditions, is the situation in which individuals, now unfrozen, begin experimenting with new behaviors. They try the new behaviors they hope will increase their effectiveness. According to Schein, this changing is best effected if it involves both identification and internalization.[25] *Identification* is the process in which individuals performing new behaviors pattern themselves after someone who already has expertise in those behaviors; that is, individuals model themselves after an expert. *Internalization* is the process in which individuals performing new behaviors attempt to use those behaviors as part of their normal behavioral pattern. In other words, individuals consistently try to make the new behaviors useful over an extended period of time.

Refreezing, the third of Lewin's conditions, is the situation in which individuals see that the new behavior they have experimented with during "changing" is now part of themselves. They have developed attitudes consistent with performing the new behavior and see that behavior as part of their normal mode

---

Unfreezing is the state in which people are ready to change.

Changing is the state in which people experiment with new behaviors.

Refreezing is the state in which people see their new behavior as part of themselves.

of operations. The rewards individuals receive as a result of performing the new behavior are instrumental in refreezing.

For managers to increase their success as change agents, they must be able to make their changes in such a way that individuals who will be required to modify their behavior as a result of the change live through Lewin's three conditions. Here is an example.

A middle-level manager named Sara Clark has gathered information indicating that Terry Lacey, a lower-level manager, must change his technique for transmitting memos. Clark knows that Lacey firmly believes he can save time and effort by writing out his intracompany memos rather than having them typed, proofread, corrected if necessary, and then sent out. Lacey also believes that an added benefit to this strategy is the fact that it frees his secretary to do other kinds of tasks.

Clark, however, has been getting several requests for help in reading Lacey's sometimes illegible handwriting and knows that some of Lacey's memos are written so poorly that words and sentences are misinterpreted. Obviously, some change is necessary. As Lacey's superior, Clark could simply mandate change by telling Lacey to write more clearly or to have his memos typed. This strategy, however, might not have enough impact to cause a lasting behavioral change and could conceivably result in the additional problem of personal friction between the two managers.

Clark could increase the probability of Lacey's changing his behavior in a more lasting way if she helps Lacey experience unfreezing, changing, and refreezing. To encourage unfreezing, Clark could direct all questions she receives about Lacey's memos back to Lacey himself and make sure that Lacey is aware of all misinterpretations and resulting mistakes. This should demonstrate to Lacey that there is some need for change.

Once Lacey recognizes the need for changing the way in which he writes his memos, he will be ready to try alternative memo-writing methods. Clark could then suggest methods to Lacey, taking special care to give him examples of what others do to write intracompany memos (identification). Over time, Clark could also help Lacey develop the method of transmitting memos that best suits his talents (internalization).

After Lacey has developed an effective method of writing memos, Clark should take steps to ensure that positive feedback about his memo writing reaches Lacey. This feedback, of course, will be instrumental in refreezing Lacey's new method. The feedback can come from Clark, from Lacey's subordinates and peers, and from Lacey's own observations.

Evaluation of Change

As with all other actions, managers should spend some time evaluating the changes they make. The purpose of this evaluation is not only to gain insights into how the change itself might be modified to further increase organizational effectiveness but also to determine if the steps taken to make the change can be modified to increase organizational effectiveness the next time they are used.

Evaluating change may increase the organizational benefit from the change.

According to Margulies and Wallace, making this evaluation may be difficult, because data from individual change programs may be unreliable.[26] Regardless of the difficulty, however, managers must do their best to evaluate change to increase the organizational benefit from the change.

Certain symptoms may indicate that further change is warranted.

Evaluation of change often involves watching for symptoms that indicate that further change is necessary. For example, if organization members continue to be oriented more to the past than to the future, if they recognize the obligations of rituals more than the challenges of current problems, or if they owe allegiance more to departmental goals than to overall company objectives, the probability is relatively high that further change is necessary.[27]

A word of caution, however, is needed at this point. Although symptoms such as those listed in the preceding paragraph generally indicate that further change is warranted, this is not always the case. The decision to make additional changes should not be made solely on the basis of symptoms; more objective information also should be considered. In general, additional change is justified if it (1) further improves the means for satisfying someone's economic wants, (2) increases profitability, (3) promotes human work for human beings, or (4) contributes to individual satisfaction and social well-being.[28]

BACK TO THE CASE

Roger Smith must realize that even though he has formulated a change that would be beneficial to General Motors, his attempt to implement this change could prove unsuccessful if he does not appropriately consider the people affected by the change. For example, because Smith is proposing a reduction of the number of GM divisions from five to two, many organization members may fear that this change will eliminate their jobs. As a result, they may subtly resist the change.

To overcome this resistance, Smith could use such strategies as giving affected employees enough time to fully evaluate and understand the change, presenting a positive attitude about the change, and, if resistance is very strong, suggesting that the pro-posed change will be tentative until it is fully evaluated. In addition, Smith probably would find Lewin's unfreezing-changing-refreezing theory helpful in implementing the proposed change.

Smith's proposed change at GM needs to be evaluated after implementation to discover if further organizational change is necessary and if the process used by Smith to make the change might be improved for future use. This evaluation process could result, for example, in a suggestion that marketing should be moved from the divisional level back to the company level or that implementation of future changes should put more emphasis on assisting individuals affected by the change to experience unfreezing, changing, and refreezing.

CHANGE AND STRESS

Change can cause stress.

This chapter focuses on changing an organization to make it more effective, efficient, and successful. When managers implement changes, however, they should be concerned about the stress they may be creating. Such stress could be significant enough to eliminate the improvement that was intended to be the result of the change. In fact, stress could result in the organization being less effective than it was before the change was attempted. This section defines stress and discusses the importance of studying and managing stress.

Defining Stress

Stress is strain.

The bodily strain that an individual experiences as a result of coping with some environmental factor is **stress.** Hans Selye, perhaps the most well-known authority on this subject, says that stress is simply the rate of wear and tear on the body.[29] In organizations, this wear and tear is caused primarily by the body's unconscious mobilization of energy when an individual is confronted with organizational or work demands.[30]

The Importance of Studying Stress

There are at least three sound reasons for studying stress.[31] First, stress can have damaging psychological and physiological effects on employees' health and on employees' contributions to the effectiveness of the organization. It can cause heart disease, and it can keep employees from being able to concentrate or to make decisions. A second important reason to study stress is that it is a major cause of employee absenteeism and turnover. Certainly, such factors severely limit the potential success of an organization. The third reason it is important to study stress is that stress experienced by an employee can affect the safety of other workers or even the public. For example, the stress felt by commercial airline pilots represents a potential danger not only to the copilots and attendants but also to the passengers.

Stress should be studied because it can harm employees, cause absenteeism and turnover, and affect safety.

Managing Stress in Organizations

Since stress is felt by virtually all employees in all organizations, insights about managing stress are valuable to all managers. This section is built on the assumption that in order to appropriately manage stress in organizations, managers must (1) understand how stress influences worker performance, (2) identify where unhealthy stress exists in organizations, and (3) help employees handle stress.

Understanding How Stress Influences Worker Performance

To deal with stress in an organization, managers must understand the relationship between the amount of stress felt by a worker and the worker's performance. This relationship is shown in Figure 11.8 on p. 304. According to this figure, extremely high and extremely low levels of stress tend to have negative effects on production. Additionally, increasing stress tends to increase performance up to some point (Point A in the figure). If the level of stress increases beyond this point, performance will begin to deteriorate. In sum, from a performance viewpoint, having individuals experience some stress is generally considered advantageous because it tends to increase production. However, having individuals feel too much or too little stress is generally considered disadvantageous because it tends to decrease production.

Stress can be too high or too low.

Identifying Unhealthy Stress in Organizations

After managers understand the impact of stress on performance, they must be able to identify where stress exists within the organization. Once the existence of stress is pinpointed, the managers must determine if the stress is at an appropri-

High stress causes more organizational problems than low stress.

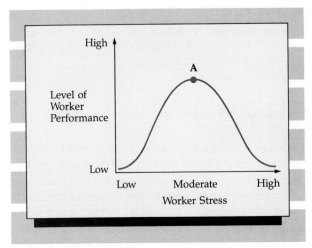

FIGURE 11.8
The relationship between worker stress and the level
of worker performance

ate level or if it is too high or too low. Since most stress related organizational problems involve too much stress, rather than too little, the remainder of this section focuses on undesirably high levels of stress.

Stress can be hard to detect.

It can be difficult for managers to identify the people in the organization who are experiencing detrimentally high levels of stress. Part of the difficulty is that people often respond to high stress in different ways. Another part of the difficulty is that physiological reactions to stress are hard, if not impossible, for managers to observe and monitor. Such reactions include high blood pressure, pounding heart, and gastrointestinal disorders.

Despite the difficulty, there are several observable symptoms of undesirably high stress levels that managers can look for.[32] (The cartoon shows one very obvious—though unlikely—symptom.) These symptoms are as follows:[33]

- Constant fatigue.
- Low energy.
- Moodiness.
- Increased aggression.
- Excessive use of alcohol.
- Temper outbursts.
- Compulsive eating.
- High levels of anxiety.
- Chronic worrying.

Managers who observe one or more of these symptoms in employees should investigate further to determine if employees exhibiting the symptoms are indeed under too much stress. If so, the managers should attempt to help the employees reduce or handle their stress.

Helping Employees Handle Stress

Stressors are environmental demands that cause stress.

A **stressor** is an environmental demand that causes people to feel stress. Stressors are common in organizational situations in which individuals are confronted

Cotham

"I suspect your problem is stress-related."
Wall Street Journal, *February 25, 1987. From the* Wall Street
Journal–*permission, Cartoon Features Syndicate.*

by circumstances in which their usual behaviors are inappropriate or insufficient and where negative consequences are associated with not properly dealing with the situation.[34] Organizational change is an obvious stressor. As Figure 11.9 on page 306 indicates, however, many other factors related to organizational policies, structure, physical conditions, and processes can also act as stressors.

In general, stress is not reduced significantly until the stressors causing it have been coped with satisfactorily or withdrawn from the environment. For example, if too much organizational change is causing undesirably high levels of stress, management may be able to reduce stress by improving organizational training that is aimed at preparing workers to deal with the job demands resulting from the change. Management might also deal with such stress by not making further organizational changes. Such action would be aimed at reducing the significance of organizational change as a stressor and thereby reducing stress levels.

Stressors are "keys" to managing stress.

In addition to working in a focused manner on organizational change and other organizational stressors after they are observed, management can adopt several strategies to help prevent the development of unwanted stressors in organizations. Three such strategies follow:[35]

The development of stressors can be prevented with three strategies:

1. *Create an organizational climate that is supportive of individuals* Organizations of today commonly seem to evolve into large bureaucracies with formal, inflexible, impersonal climates. This type of set-up can lead to considerable job stress. Making the organizational environment less formal and more supportive of employee needs will help prevent the development of unwanted organizational stressors.

1. A supportive organizational climate.

2. *Make jobs interesting* In general, routine jobs that do not allow employees some degree of freedom often result in undesirable employee stress. Manage-

2. Interesting jobs.

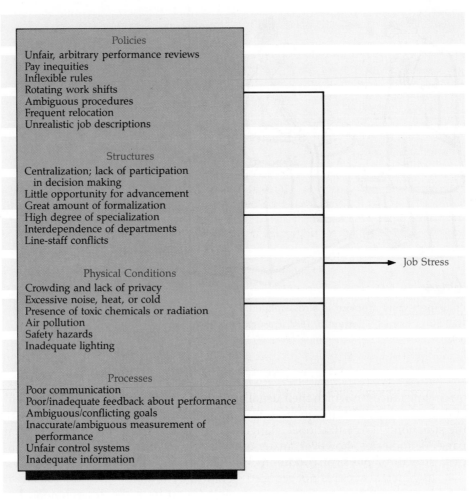

Policies
Unfair, arbitrary performance reviews
Pay inequities
Inflexible rules
Rotating work shifts
Ambiguous procedures
Frequent relocation
Unrealistic job descriptions

Structures
Centralization; lack of participation
   in decision making
Little opportunity for advancement
Great amount of formalization
High degree of specialization
Interdependence of departments
Line-staff conflicts

Physical Conditions
Crowding and lack of privacy
Excessive noise, heat, or cold
Presence of toxic chemicals or radiation
Air pollution
Safety hazards
Inadequate lighting

Processes
Poor communication
Poor/inadequate feedback about performance
Ambiguous/conflicting goals
Inaccurate/ambiguous measurement of
   performance
Unfair control systems
Inadequate information

Job Stress

FIGURE 11.9
Additional organizational stressors

ment's focus on making jobs as interesting as possible should help prevent the development of unwanted stressors related to routine, boring jobs.

3. *Design and operate career counseling programs* Considerable stress can be generated when employees do not know what their next career step might be or when they might take it. If management can show employees what the next step will probably be and when it realistically can be achieved, the development of unwanted organizational stressors in this area can be discouraged.

IBM is an example of a company that has focused on career planning for its employees.[36] IBM has a corporationwide program to encourage supervisors to conduct voluntary career planning sessions with employees on an annual basis. These sessions result in one-page career action plans. At the end of the sessions, the employees have a clear idea of where their careers are headed. The development of undesirable career related stressors at IBM has been discouraged as a result of this program.

3. Career counseling.

BACK TO THE CASE

Roger Smith should be careful not to create too much stress on other organization members as a result of his planned change. Such stress could be significant enough to eliminate any planned improvement at GM and could eventually result in such stress related effects on employees as physical symptoms and the inability to make sound decisions.

Although some additional stress on organization members as a result of Smith's planned change at GM could enhance productivity, too much stress could have a negative impact on production. Signs that Smith could look for include constant fatigue, increased aggression, temper outbursts, and chronic worrying.

If Smith determines that undesirably high levels of stress have resulted from his changes at GM, he should try to reduce the stress. He may be able to do so through training programs aimed at better equipping organization members to execute new job demands resulting from the change. Or he may want to simply slow the rate of his planned change.

It would probably be wise for Smith to take action that would prevent unwanted stressors from developing as a result of his planned change. In this regard, Smith could ensure that the organizational climate at GM is supportive of individual needs and that jobs resulting from the planned change are as interesting as possible.

Action Summary

Reread the learning objectives that follow. Each objective is followed by questions. Answering these questions accurately will help you retain the most important concepts discussed in this chapter. After answering each question, check your answer with the answer key at the end of this chapter. (*Hint:* If you have doubt regarding the correct response, consult the page whose number follows the answer.)

From studying this chapter, I will attempt to acquire: Circle:

1. **A working definition of** *changing an organization.*
   a. The purpose of organizational modifications is to increase the extent to   T, F
      which an organization accomplishes its objectives.
   b. Organizational modifications typically include changing: (a) overall goals   a, b, c, d, e
      and objectives; (b) established lines of organizational authority; (c) levels
      of responsibility held by various organization members; (d) b and c; (e) all
      of the above.

2. **An understanding of the relative importance of change and stability to an
   organization.**
   a. According to the Hellriegel and Slocum model, which of the following is   a, b, c, d, e
      the most likely outcome when both adaptation and stability are high:
      (a) high probability of slow death; (b) high survival probability; (c) high
      survival and growth probability; (d) certainty of quick death; (e) possibility
      of slow death.
   b. According to Hellriegel and Slocum, repeated changes in an organization   T, F
      without stability typically result in employees with a high degree of adaptability.

3. **Some ability to know what type of change should be made within an organization.**
   a. Although managers can choose to change an organization in many ways,   T, F
      most changes can be categorized as one of three types: (1) people change,
      (2) goal or objective change, and (3) technological change.

a, b, c, d, e

b. Decentralizing an organization is a structural change aimed at: (1) reducing the cost of coordination; (b) increasing the controllability of subunits; (c) increasing motivation; (d) all of the above; (e) a and b.

4. An appreciation for why individuals affected by a change should be considered when the change is being made.

a, b, c, d, e

a. Which of the following is not an example of personal loss that organization members fear as a result of change: (a) possibility of a reduction in personal prestige; (b) disturbance of established social relationships; (c) reduction in overall organizational productivity; (d) personal failure because of an inability to carry out new job responsibilities; (e) disturbance of established working relationships.

T, F

b. Support for a proposed change may be altered by focusing attention on possible individual gains that could materialize as a result of the change.

5. Some facility in evaluating change.

a, b, c, d, e

a. Symptoms indicating that further change is necessary are that organization members: (a) are oriented more to the future than to the past; (b) recognize the challenge of current problems more than the obligations of rituals; (c) owe allegiance more to overall company goals than to departmental goals; (d) none of the above; (e) a and b.

T, F

b. Change is an inevitable part of management and considered so important to organizational success that some managers encourage employees to suggest needed changes.

6. An understanding of how organizational change and stress are related.

T, F

a. Stress is simply the rate of wear and tear on the body.

T, F

b. From a managerial viewpoint, stress on employees can be either too high or too low.

T, F

c. Stressors are the factors within an organization that reduce employee stress.

INTRODUCTORY CASE WRAP-UP

"GM's Great Divide" (p. 286) and its related back-to-the-case sections were written to help you better understand the management concepts contained in this chapter. Answer the following discussion questions about this introductory case to further enrich your understanding of chapter content:

1. How complicated would it be for Roger Smith to actually implement his plan? Explain.
2. Assuming that Smith gets GM board approval to

make his proposed changes, do you think that certain employees will subtly resist the changes? Why or why not?
3. What reasons would Smith give to the GM board to explain why his changes must take so long (three years) to fully implement?
4. What elements of Smith's plan would cause organization members to experience stress, and what could Smith do to help alleviate this stress? Be specific.

Issues for Review and Discussion

1. What is meant in this chapter by phrase *changing an organization*?
2. Why do organizations typically undergo various changes?
3. Does an organization need both change and stability? Explain.
4. What major factors should a manager consider when changing an organization?

5. Define *change agent* and list the skills necessary to be a successful change agent.
6. Explain the term *organizational effectiveness* and describe the major factors that determine how effective an organization will be.
7. Describe the relationship between "determining what should be changed within an organization" and "choosing a type of change for the organization."
8. What is the difference between structural change and people change?
9. Is matrix organization an example of a structural change? Explain.
10. What is the difference between the overt and covert factors considered during organizational development?
11. Draw and explain the managerial grid.
12. Is grid OD an example of a technique used to make structural change? Explain.

13. What causes resistance to change?
14. List and explain the steps managers can take to minimize resistance to change.
15. Explain the significance of unfreezing, changing, and refreezing to changing the organization.
16. How and why should managers evaluate the changes they make?
17. Define *stress* and explain how it influences performance.
18. List three stressors that could exist within an organization. For each stressor, discuss a specific management action that could be aimed at eliminating the stressor.
19. What impact can career counseling have on employee stress? Explain.

Sources of Additional Information

Argyris, C. *Management and Organization Development.* New York: McGraw-Hill, 1972.

Barnes, Louis B. "Managing the Paradox of Organizational Trust." *Harvard Business Review* (March/April 1981): 107–16.

Chapman, Elwood N. *Your Attitude Is Showing: A Primer of Human Relations.* 5th ed. Chicago: Science Research Associates, 1987.

Dubinsky, Alan J. "Managing Work Stress." *Business* 35 (July/August/September 1985): 3–10.

Dyer, William G. *Contemporary Issues in Management and Organization Development.* Reading, Mass.: Addison-Wesley, 1983.

Goodman, Paul S. *Change in Organizations.* San Francisco: Jossey-Bass, 1982.

Harvey, Donald F., and Donald R. Brown. *An Experiential Approach to Organization Development.* Englewood Cliffs, N.J.: Prentice-Hall, 1982.

Janger, Allen J. *Matrix Organization of Complex Businesses.* New York: Conference Board, 1979.

Leavitt, Harold. "Applied Organization Change in Industry." In *Handbook on Organizations,* edited by James March. Chicago: Rand McNally, 1965.

Linder, Jane C. "Computers, Corporate Culture and Change." *Personnel Journal* 64 (September 1985): 48–55.

McLean, A. J., D. B. P. Sims, I. L. Mangham, and D. Tuffield. *Organization Development in Transition.* Chichester, England: Wiley, 1982.

Marchington, Mick. "Employee Participation—Consensus or Confusion?" *Personnel Management* 13 (April 1981): 38–41.

Pearson, Andrall E. "Muscle-Build the Organization." *Harvard Business Review* (July/August 1987): 49–55.

Umstot, Denis D. "Organization Development Technology and the Military: A Surprising Merger?" *Academy of Management Review* 5 (1980): 189–201.

Vancil, Richard F. "A Look at CEO Succession." *Harvard Business Review* (March/April 1987): 107–17.

Zierden, William E. "Managing Workplace Innovations: A Framework and a New Approach." *Management Review* 70 (June 1981): 57–61.

Notes

1. Ronald D. Daniel, "Reorganization for Results," *Harvard Business Review* (November/December 1966): 96–104.
2. Bridgford Hunt, "Managers of Change: Why They Are in Demand," *S.A.M. Advanced Management Journal* (Winter 1980): 40–44.
3. John S. Morgan, *Managing Change: The Strategies of Making Change Work for You* (New York: McGraw-Hill, 1972), 99.
4. Oliver L. Niehouse and Karen B. Massoni, "Stress—An Inevitable Part of Change," *S.A.M. Advanced Management Journal* (Spring 1979): 17–25.

5. Warren C. Bennis, K. D. Benne, and R. Chin, eds., *The Planning of Change: Readings in the Applied Behavioral Sciences* (New York: Holt, Rinehart & Winston, 1961), 69.

6. Alvin Toffler, *Future Shock* (New York: Bantam Books, 1971).

7. William C. Giegold and R. J. Craig, "Whatever Happened to OD?" *Industrial Management* (January/February 1976): 9–12.

8. W. F. Glueck, "Organization Change in Business and Government," *Academy of Management Journal* 12 (1969): 440–41.

9. C. J. Middleton, "How to Set Up a Project Organization," *Harvard Business Review* (March/April 1967): 73.

10. John F. Mee, "Matrix Organization," *Business Horizons* (Summer 1964).

11. Middleton, "How to Set Up a Project Organization," 74.

12. Harvey F. Kolodny, "Managing in a Matrix," *Business Horizons* 24 (March/April 1981): 17–24.

13. John C. Alpin and Duane E. Thompson, "Successful Organizational Change," *Business Horizons* (August 1974): 61–66.

14. This section is based primarily on R. Blake, J. Mouton, and L. Greiner, "Breakthrough in Organization Development," *Harvard Business Review* (November/December 1964): 133–55. For a discussion of other methods for implementing OD change, see William F. Glueck, *Organization Planning and Development* (New York: American Management Association, 1971).

15. Blake, Mouton, and Greiner, "Breakthrough in Organization Development."

16. L. G. Malouf, "Managerial Grid Evaluated," *Training Development Journal* 20 (1966): 6–15.

17. W. J. Heisler, "Patterns of OD in Practice," *Business Horizons* (February 1975): 77–84.

18. William E. Halal, "Organization Development in the Future," *California Management Review* 16 (Spring 1974): 35–41.

19. Martin G. Evans, "Failures in OD Programs—What Went Wrong," *Business Horizons* (April 1974): 18–22.

20. This strategy for minimizing the resistance to change is based on "How Companies Overcome Resistance to Change," *Management Review* (November 1972): 17–25.

21. John P. Kotter and Leonard A. Schlesinger, "Choosing Strategies for Change," *Harvard Business Review* (March/April 1979): 106–13.

22. "How Companies Overcome Resistance," 25.

23. Arnold S. Judson, *A Manager's Guide to Making Changes* (New York: Wiley, 1966), 118.

24. Kurt Lewin, "Frontiers in Group Dynamics: Concept, Method, and Reality of Social Sciences—Social Equilibria and Social Change," *Human Relations* 1 (June 1947): 5–14.

25. Edgar H. Schein, "Management Development as a Process of Influence," *Industrial Management Review* (May 1961): 59–76.

26. Newton Margulies and John Wallace, *Organizational Change: Techniques and Applications* (Chicago: Scott, Foresman, 1973), 14.

27. Larry E. Greiner, "Patterns of Organizational Change," *Harvard Business Review* (May/June 1967): 119–30.

28. Edgar C. Williams, "Changing Systems and Behavior: People's Perspectives on Prospective Changes," *Business Horizons* 12 (August 1969): 53.

29. Hans Selye, *The Stress of Life* (New York: McGraw-Hill, 1956).

30. James C. Quick and Jonathan D. Quick, *Organizational Stress and Preventive Management* (New York: McGraw-Hill, 1984).

31. Richard M. Steers, *Introduction to Organizational Behavior* (Glenview, Ill.: Scott, Foresman, 1981), 340–41.

32. For more discussion of this area, see Keith Davis and John W. Newstrom, *Human Behavior at Work: Organizational Behavior* (New York: McGraw-Hill, 1985), 469–70.

33. J. Clifton Williams, *Human Behavior in Organizations* (Cincinnati: South-Western, 1982), 212–13.

34. John M. Ivancevich and Michael T. Matteson, "Organizations and Coronary Heart Disease: The Stress Connection," *Management Review* 67 (October 1978): 14–19.

35. Fred Luthans, *Organizational Behavior* (New York: McGraw-Hill, 1985), 146–48.

36. Donald B. Miller, "Career Planning and Management in Organizations," *S.A.M. Advanced Management Journal* 43 (Spring 1978): 33–43.

Action Summary Answer Key

1. a. T, p. 287
   b. d, p. 287
2. a. c, p. 288
   b. F, p. 288

3. a. F, p. 291
   b. d, p. 293
4. a. c, p. 299
   b. T, p. 299

5. a. d, p. 302
   b. T, p. 287
6. a. T, pp. 302–303

b. T, p. 303
c. F, pp. 304–305

GE GAMBLES ON GROWTH

In 1955, a massive corporate decentralization program had left General Electric a loose confederation of companies under one commercial logo. Today, John F. Welch, Jr., presides over $37 billion GE. Although it is still a collection of businesses, it can no longer be considered "loose." Services and technology dominate, discipline is tight, and the manufacture of electric lamps no longer makes up much of the company. Services and advanced technology, not traditional manufacturing, are GE's strong suits for the 1980s. They currently account for about 70 percent of the annual earnings in GE's three basic business groupings. In contrast, basic manufacturing, which as recently as 1981 accounted for 50 percent of earnings, now produces 30 percent. And by 1991, manufacturing is expected to contribute only 20 percent.

GE today is definitely a "downsized" corporation from what it was just a few years ago. Although it has made 14 major acquisitions during the past six years, including the $6.4 billion purchase of RCA Corporation in 1986, it also has disposed of 10 major businesses and 222 smaller ones. The reorganization associated with all of these acquisitions and divestitures resulted in the jettisoning of an entire layer of senior management and the reducing of employee ranks by 132,000 people. GE employment now stands at 359,000. Even with the addition of 89,0000 RCA workers, that is 51,000 fewer employees than GE alone had in the early 1980s.

So frenetic has been the pace of change over the past six years that the fifty-one-year-old Welch, who is chairman and chief executive officer of GE, is now characterized by one associate as "an action junkie." And the days of fast-paced change at GE are far from over. "Change must be accepted as the rule rather than the exception," states the GE chairman. Not cautious change, big change. "Most bureaucracies—and ours is no exception—unfortunately still think in incremental terms, rather than in terms of fundamental change," complains Welch. "Nothing less than a reorientation of the culture of big institutions is needed—away from incrementalism. Quantum thinking must become a way of life." Quantum thinking at GE consists of being prepared to redeploy resources, purchase businesses, and sell strategic misfits. In GE's case, flexibility appears to be the only constant.

Welch is prepared to buy businesses that will sharpen GE's competitive edge. Less than a year after its RCA purchase, GE had $2.3 billion in cash and a comfortable 29 percent debt-to-equity ratio—the wherewithal to make another major acquisition. Although GE has phenomenal financial strength, Welch won't retain businesses, even profitable ones, that don't contribute to

GE diversified into plastics.

strategic strength. For example, because of a lack of strategic fit, GE sold its toasters, mixers, and other housewares businesses to Black & Decker Corporation for $300 million. Strategic misfit Utah International, a mining subsidiary, along with record, carpet, and life-insurance companies picked up in the RCA acquisitions, were also unloaded.

GE's primary strategic objective is to hold only businesses in GE's three basic operating circles ranked number 1 or number 2 in their respective markets. Businesses that do not meet that standard, or that run a high risk of being swamped by imports, are not likely to remain part of the GE organization for long. Currently GE's services circle includes its high-performing financial service units (GE Credit Corp.; Kidder, Peabody & Co.; and Employers Reinsurance Corp.), communication and services (including information services), and the National Broadcasting Company. Medical systems, aircraft engines, aerospace, plastics and other materials, and industrial electronics occupy the technology circle. In the manufacturing circle are lighting, major appliances, motors, locomotives, construction equipment, and power-generating systems.

Welch's second and third strategic objectives are to concentrate resources on critical businesses and to boost the percentage of technology and services in the corporate business mix. GE's technology businesses best illustrate how the company is carrying out these objectives. Between 1981 and 1986, GE's technology businesses garnered nearly half of the $11 billion in corporate funds budgeted for investment in buildings and machinery. Bricks, mortar, and machines accounted for a gigantic 87 percent of the $10 billion allocated for R&D.

Welch's final goal is to make GE more than a "GNP company." In other words, he wants GE's earnings to grow significantly faster than the rate at which the U.S. gross national product (GNP) is advancing. GE's recent performance must be encouraging to Welch. In a recent year, aircraft engines, major appliances, financial services, and aerospace businesses all posted 24 percent or better average annual earnings growth, nearly twice the advance in GNP in current dollars. Still, to stay in the good graces of Welch, GE businesses have to sustain the expected 10 to 15 percent annual net earnings gains.

There is no question that Welch has made fundamental changes in GE's traditionally conservative corporate culture. His style is confrontational and direct, whereas his predecessor, Reginald H. Jones, was courtly. An executive foolish enough to approach Welch with a dumb idea is likely to be told: "Get the hell out of here! We don't pay people for that kind of shoddy thinking." Welch expects every employee to give 150 percent every day, yet he is prepared to fire any GE manager who out-and-out brutalizes subordinates. There seems to be a good deal of truth to the observation of one GE executive that "as Reg Jones was the right chairman for the 1970s, Jack Welch is the right chairman for the rapidly changing '80s."

DISCUSSION ISSUES

1. What type of change is John Welch, Jr., chairman and CEO, implementing at General Electric? Explain.

2. Welch believes that today "nothing less than a reorientation of the culture of big institutions is needed— away from incrementalism. Quantum thinking must become a way of life." In GE's case, about the only constant is flexibility. Do any text concepts suggest some danger in the strategy that Welch is employing? Explain.

3. What "price" would you suspect is being paid by the organization and its members as a result of the extremely high volume and frequency of change occurring at GE? Explain.

THE CHICAGO CUBS—THE MAKING OF A CHAMPIONSHIP

Tuesday, March 27, 1984

Curses! Cubs lose again. If this is preparation for the regular season, are they already in mid-season form?

The Cubs have been edged, trounced, nipped, stomped, and dusted seventeen different ways between here and Yuma this spring. The remainder of the exhibition season, they'll be working on succumbing, falling, dropping, and basically bowing to opponents.

Just a week before their regular season opener in San Francisco, they're well on the way to earning the appellation "hapless" Chicago Cubs.

Monday, it was the Indians in Tucson—which is tantamount to saying the Cubbies lost another one. Bert Blyleven, who has won all three of his Cactus League games against the Cubs, improved his record to 3–1. Cleveland wants to move to the National League East.

The 5–4 score this windy afternoon sent the Chicago record plummeting to 3–17. That's ten losses in a row. But who's counting? It's only spring training, right? And the Cubs are simply getting ready, right? Manager Jim Frey keeps telling himself that. Maybe it will work for you, too.[1]

Tuesday, September 25, 1984

It's over. One of the longest dry spells in professional sports history ended when the Chicago Cubs clinched the National League East championship.

It ended with a flourish, a runaway by a team that was picked before the season to finish fifth or sixth.

It ended thirty-nine years of mediocrity and frustration.[2]

In less than six months, the Chicago Cubs National League Baseball Club went from a loser, stuck with a three and seventeen exhibition record, to National League Eastern Division champions. How this was accomplished provides an exciting lesson in organizational strategy.

The groundwork for this history-making about-face was laid shortly after Dallas Green took over as Cubs general manager in 1981. Soon after arriving in Chicago, Green initiated negotiations with the Phillies. That first season, he acquired, among others, Larry Bowa, Ryne Sandberg, and Keith Moreland. As a result of all of these trades with Philadelphia, the Cubs became known as "Philadelphia West."

However, the making of a championship team actually began in a manner that would go unnoticed to even the most astute baseball expert. On March 26, 1984, Green picked up reliever Tim Stoddard from Oakland for a pair of minor leaguers. According to Green, "That (trade) set everything up."[3]

During the final week of spring training, Green conjured up another deal with the Phillies. He traded relief pitcher Bill Campbell for outfielders Gary Matthews and Bob Dernier. According to manager Jim Frey, "Stoddard looked so good that we were able to trade Campbell to Philadelphia for Dernier and Matthews, and after that is was a domino effect. Everything began to fall into place."[4] Frey immediately put Matthews in left field and Dernier in center and moved Leon Durham in from the outfield to his natural position at first base. This decision was much to the chagrin of Bill Buckner, previously the Cubs' regular first baseman and the Cubs' leading hitter in the 1983 season.

Not only was Buckner unhappy, so was Moreland, who would now be platooning with Mel Hall in

---

[1] From Fred Mitchell, "Losing Cubs Land Big Reliever," *Chicago Tribune*, March 27, 1984.
[2] From "After 39 Years, Wait Is Over," *Daily Pantagraph* (Bloomington, Ill.), September 25, 1984.

[3] Ibid.
[4] Ibid.

right field. But it did give Frey a strong bench—and Green additional trading power.

A month later, Green pulled off the coup of the season: He traded Hall, outfielder Joe Carter, and pitcher Don Schulze to Cleveland for pitchers Rick Sutcliffe and George Frazier and catcher Ron Hassey. Sutcliffe won fifteen of his first sixteen decisions, including fourteen in a row, to quickly become Frey's "ace in the hole." Frazier also contributed by shoring up the bull pen. Finally, in May, Buckner was swapped to Boston for pitcher Dennis Eckersley.

These deals were sweet in many ways. With Hall gone, Moreland again became the regular right fielder. Furthermore, the pitching was finally set. With a lineup loaded with power, the Cubs could now be competitive against the best.

Frey rested key players, and the Cubs kept rolling. Late in July, the Cubs traveled to New York for a crucial series with the Mets, an equally surprising contender. While Chicago lost the first game to rookie sensation Dwight Gooden, they won the next three. Upon returning home, they won two of three from the Phillies and grabbed first place on August 1.

The Cubs then won three of four from Montreal and, against the visiting Mets, swept a four-game series to cement their hold on the lead in the National League East.

DISCUSSION ISSUES

1. Familiarize yourself with the Chicago Cubs' front office positions and personnel in Section Case Figure 3.1. Then complete parts *a* through *d*.
   a. From the position titles provided in the table, identify the type(s) of departmentalization used in the Cubs' front office.
   b. Does anything in the front office information suggest a violation of unity of command? Explain.
   c. In your examination of front office data, is there anything that suggests that both line and staff authority have been delegated?
   d. Draw the organization chart for the Cubs' front office as you believe it might appear.
2. From the information in the case, would you say that Dallas Green has hired appropriate human resources? Explain.
3. Is there an existing pool of employees already within the Cubs' organization that could have been promoted to meet the Cubs' pitching needs? Explain. If promotion from within improves morale, why weren't these individuals promoted? Explain.
4. Would it seem appropriate for the Cubs' organization to maintain some type of record-keeping forms for a human resource inventory? Explain.
5. Applying the adaptation/change model (Figure 11.1) to the Chicago Cubs' baseball organization, what sur-

CHICAGO CUBS DIRECTORY
CHICAGO NATIONAL LEAGUE BALL CLUB, INC.

BOARD OF DIRECTORS

Thomas G. Ayers   Dallas Green   Andrew J. McKenna
Stanton R. Cook   John W. Madigan

FRONT OFFICE

President and General Manager, Dallas Green
Executive Vice President, Business Operations, Donald C. Grenesko
Vice President, Planning and Special Projects, Mark McGuire
Vice President, E. R. Saltwell
Baseball Consultant to President and General Manager, Charlie Fox
Director of Minor Leagues and Scouting, Gordon Goldsberry
Director, Marketing, Jeff Odenwald
Assistant to General Manager and Traveling Secretary, John Cox
Director of Scouting, A. B. "Vedie" Himsl
Controller, Keith Bode
Assistant Controller, Joseph Kirchen
Secretary, Stanley J. Gardowski, Jr.
Director, Public Relations and Publications, Robert Ibach
Director, Ticket Sales, Frank Maloney
Director, Stadium Operations, Tom Cooper
Director, Ticket Services, Lamar Vernon
Director, Promotion and Sales, John McDonough
Assistant Director, Community Services, Connie Kowal
Assistant, Community Services, Steve Green
Associate Director, Minor Leagues, William Harford
Associate Director, Scouting, Scott Nelson
Assistant Director, Publications and Statistics, Ned Colletti
Associate Director, Public Relations and Publications, Sharon Pannozzo
Staff Accountant, Rick Grember
Assistant Director, Ticket Services, Larry Regan
Associate Director, Ticket Services, Frank Baltrusaitis
Assistant Director, Stadium Operations/Event Personnel, Paul Rathje
Assistant Director, Stadium Operations/Facilities, Lubie Veal
Assistant Group Sales, Edward Whalen
Team Physician, Jacob R. Suker, M.D.
Trainer, Tony Garofalo
Equipment Manager, Yosh Kawano

Administrative Assistants: Arlene Gill (President/General Manager); Doris Acosta (Administrative Assistant Public Relations); Trudy Kolak, Barbara Mueller (Administration); Elizabeth Riordan (Minor Leagues and Scouting); Susan Parkin (Marketing); Cherie Blake (Ticket Sales); Janet Peterson (Ticket Services); Mary Gutsell (Community Services). *Accounting:* Debbie Hodge, Deborah Wood. *Group Sales:* Tom Crepeau, Jim Bental, Steve Bornstein, Donna Mohr. *Mail Room:* Scott Nadolny. *Operations:* Anne Dikkers, Bill Galante, Tommy Hill. *Cinematographer:* Bob Searles. *Switchboard:* Desiree Brazelton, Rene Tobin. *Ticket Services:* Shareen Caithamer, Joe Geselter, Mike Ripoli, John Stroth.

SECTION CASE FIGURE 3.1
Front office Chicago Cubs directory, Chicago National League Ball Club, Inc.

vival and growth probability (number on the model) would you expect to find? Explain. What number do you believe probably represents the Cubs' organization during the past thirty-nine years?
6. Several special skills are necessary to be a successful change agent. How would you rate Dallas Green as a change agent? Explain.
7. How would you evaluate the Frey/Green approach to reducing resistance to change in the Cubs' organization? Explain.

INFLUENCING

Influencing is the third of the four major management functions that must be performed for organizations to have long-term success. The last two sections of the text focused on how managers plan and organize resources in order to reach organizational objectives. This section discusses important people oriented issues that managers must consider in influencing workers to become and remain productive. In general, the most important influencing tasks are communication, leadership, motivation, and managing groups.

The discussion of the fundamentals of influencing and communication defines *influencing* and presents it as a subsystem of the overall management system. The discussion also indicates that within this subsystem, communication is an important issue. It involves specific elements and processes, can be successful or unsuccessful, and can take various forms, such as verbal or nonverbal and formal or informal. The explanation of leadership will include the definition of *leadership*, specific leadership strategies that relate to decision making, the level of follower maturity, and the process of engineering situations to fit leadership styles.

This section will also include the definition of *motivation* and a discussion of three models that are used to describe it. It will describe three theories that focus on human needs as an integral part of motivation theory and several strategies that managers can use to motivate organization members.

Finally, the discussion on managing groups will stress that for managers to influence organization members, they must be able to manage groups of people. This discussion will define *groups*, distinguish between formal and informal groups, and suggest ways that managers can maximize group effectiveness.

Although the material in this section will be new and challenging, learning it is crucial to a comprehension of the new topics that will be presented later. As you study this material on influencing, remember what you have learned in the previous portions of the text so you can continue to build a comprehensive understanding of the management process.

STUDENT LEARNING OBJECTIVES

From studying this chapter, I will attempt to acquire:

1. An understanding of influencing.
2. An understanding of interpersonal communication.
3. A knowledge of how to use feedback.
4. An appreciation for the importance of nonverbal communication.
5. Insights on formal organizational communication.
6. An appreciation for the importance of the grapevine.
7. Some hints on how to encourage organizational communication.

FUNDAMENTALS OF INFLUENCING AND COMMUNICATION

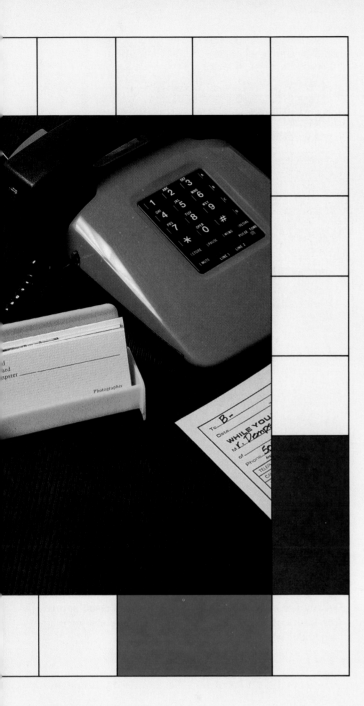

CHAPTER OUTLINE

TROUBLES AT MATTEL

In the beginning, the Barbie doll was Mattel, Inc. Now, after several unwieldy years of acquisitions and sometimes explosive growth, Barbie and the toy division she spawned may be all that survive.

Mattel has proclaimed itself a victim of the collapse of the video-game and low-cost-computer markets. Former Mattel officials, other industry executives, and even suppliers, however, say that Mattel's problems are much more severe than this market collapse. These individuals blame an isolated, lackluster management that got too greedy, moved too slowly, and never did understand some of Mattel's new ventures.

There are indeed several signs that Mattel's problems are complex and extensive. The company reported a loss of $176.5 million for only half of one operating year. Hundreds of employees, some hired in the very near past, were fired. The much-promoted Aquarius home computer system was abandoned, and a line of personal security products was sold to liquidators at a price much below cost. Profit margins were cut drastically on the Intellivision video game, and the entire Intellivision system itself faced an uncertain future. Even a longtime head of the toy division quit in frustration. Some people say that this crisis at Mattel was the company's worst in about twelve years.

Much of the crisis was blamed on Arthur S. Spear, Mattel's chief executive officer and past vice-president of operations. Even those who believe that Spear restored a vital level of confidence to the company admit that his management style is at least partly to blame for the problems. "Spear is something of a recluse," says a former top executive. Communicating with him is difficult.

To compound this communication problem with Spear, another former official at Mattel indicated, there are communication problems relating to divisional man-

agement. Division managers have always had a free rein in running their own units. Some believe that this freedom contributes to a lack of communication among divisions and between them and the corporate staff. According to a former executive, "There has always been this view at the division level to shut out the corporate staff and not let corporate know what was really happening."

Mattel officials have not been eager to respond to these comments. One corporate spokesperson, however, did say that former executives and outsiders certainly are neither knowledgeable nor unbiased sources of information regarding the appropriateness of management activities at Mattel.

What's Ahead

In the introductory case, Arthur S. Spear, Mattel's chief executive officer, has been accused of having a management style that is characterized by poor communication. The case raises two important questions: First, can poor communication be the major cause of Mattel's problems? Second, how can communication effectiveness be increased within an organization such as Mattel? The information in this chapter is designed to help managers such as Spear answer these questions. The chapter is divided into two main parts: fundamentals of influencing and communication.

⊞ FUNDAMENTALS OF INFLUENCING

The four basic managerial functions—planning, organizing, influencing, and controlling—were introduced in chapter 1. *Influencing* follows *planning* and *organizing*, to be the third of these basic functions covered in this text. A definition of *influencing* and a discussion of the influencing subsystem follow.

Defining "Influencing"

Influencing is the process of guiding the activities of organization members in appropriate directions. Appropriate directions, of course, are those that lead to the attainment of management system objectives. Influencing involves focusing on organization members as people and dealing with such issues as morale, arbitration of conflicts, and the development of good working relationships among individuals.

Influencing is guiding activities in appropriate directions.

The Influencing Subsystem

As with the planning and organizing functions, the influencing function can be viewed as a subsystem that is part of the overall management system process (see Figure 12.1, p. 322). The primary purpose of the influencing subsystem is to enhance the attainment of management system objectives by guiding the activities of organization members in appropriate directions.

Figure 12.2 on page 323 shows the specific ingredients of the influencing subsystem. The input of this subsystem is composed of a portion of the total resources of the overall management system, and the output is appropriate organization member behavior. The process of the influencing subsystem involves the performance of four primary management activities: (1) leading, (2) motivating, (3) considering groups, and (4) communicating. Managers transform a portion of organizational resources into appropriate organization member behavior mainly be performing these four activities.

As Figure 12.2 shows, leading, motivating, and considering groups are related influencing activities, each of which is accomplished, to some extent, by

Managers guide activities by leading, motivating, considering groups, and communicating.

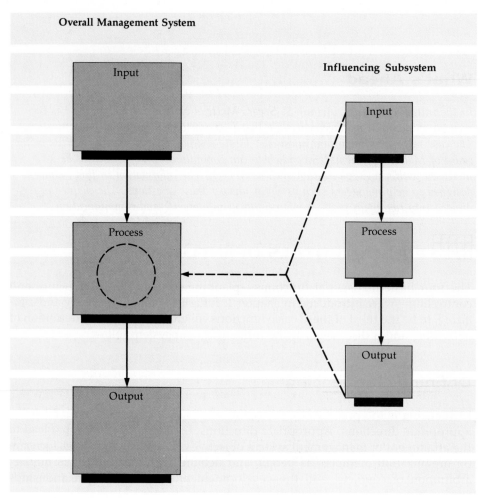

FIGURE 12.1
Relationship between overall management system and influencing subsystem

managers communicating with organization members. For example, managers decide what kind of leaders they should be only after they analyze the characteristics of various groups with which they will interact and determine how these groups can best be motivated. Then, regardless of the strategy they adopt, their leading, motivating, and working with groups will be accomplished, at least to some extent, by communication with other organization members.

Communication is the fundamental management skill.

In fact, as Figure 12.3 implies, all management activities are accomplished at least in part through communication or communication related endeavors.[1] Since communication is used repeatedly by managers, communication skills are often referred to as the fundamental management skill.

Supporting the notion that communication is the fundamental management skill are the results of a recent survey of chief executives. The results (which appear in Table 12.1, p. 324) show communication skill as the most important skill (along with interpersonal skills) to be taught to management students.

Communication is discussed further in the rest of this chapter. Leading, motivating, and considering groups are discussed in chapters 13, 14, and 15 respectively.

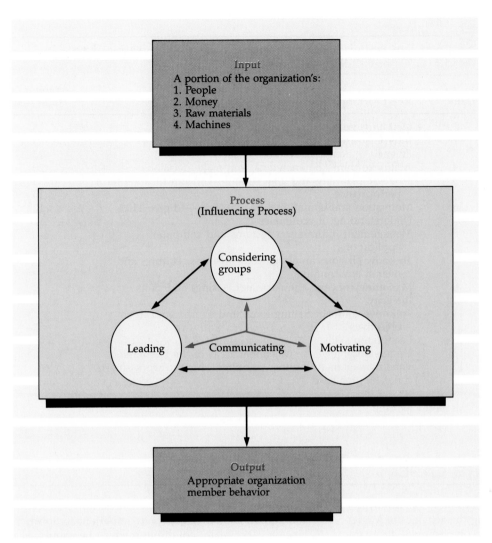

FIGURE 12.2
The influencing subsystem

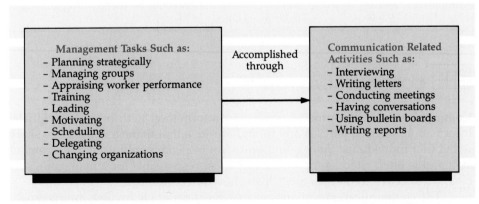

FIGURE 12.3
Management tasks and possible communication related behavior used to help accomplish those tasks

TABLE 12.1

Chief executives rank importance of skills to be taught to management students

Rank*	Key Learning Area	Frequency Indicated
1	Oral and written communication skills	25
1	Interpersonal skills	25
3	Financial/managerial account skills	22
4	Ability to think, be analytical, and make decisions	20
5	Strategic planning and goal setting—concern for long-term performance	13
6	Motivation and commitment to the firm—to give 110%	12
7	Understanding of economics	11
8	Management information systems and computer applications	9
8	To know all you can about your business, culture, and overall environment	9
8	Marketing concept (the customer is king) and skills	9
11	Integrity	7
11	To know yourself: Setting long- and short-term career objectives	7
13	Leadership skills	6
13	Understanding of the functional areas of the business	6
13	Time management: Setting priorities—how to work smart, not long or hard	1

* 1 is most important.

BACK TO THE CASE

One of the primary functions of Mattel's Arthur S. Spear is influencing—guiding the activities of Mattel employees to enhance the accomplishment of organizational objectives. Spear could perform this function by leading such individuals as the division managers or perhaps the corporate market research staff, by motivating them to do better jobs, by working well with various groups of Mattel employees, and by communicating successfully with Mattel employees.

Of all of these influencing activities, however, communication should be especially important to Spear, since it is the main tool through which he should, at least to some extent, accomplish his duties as chief executive officer. Although more facts would be needed before a final determination could be made, the introductory case suggests that Spear's lack of effective communication could be contributing substantially to problems at Mattel.

COMMUNICATION

Communication is sharing thoughts or ideas with others.

Communication is the process of sharing information with other individuals. Information, as used here, is any thought or idea that managers desire to share with other individuals. Since communication is a commonly used management skill and is often cited as the one ability most responsible for a manager's success, prospective managers must learn how to communicate.[2]

The communication activities of managers generally involve interpersonal communication—sharing information with other organization members. The following sections discuss both the general topic of interpersonal communication and the more specific topic of interpersonal communication in organizations.

Interpersonal Communication

To be a successful interpersonal communicator, a manager must understand (1) how interpersonal communication works, (2) the relationship between feedback and interpersonal communication, and (3) the importance of verbal versus nonverbal interpersonal communication.

How Interpersonal Communication Works

Interpersonal communication is the process of sharing information with other individuals.[3] To be complete, the process must have the following three basic elements:

Interpersonal communication has three elements:

1. *The source/encoder*   The **source/encoder** is the person in the interpersonal communication situation who originates and encodes information to be shared with another person. Encoding is the process of putting information in a form that can be received and understood by another individual. Putting thoughts into a letter is an example of encoding. Until information is encoded, it cannot be shared with others. (From here on, the source/encoder will be referred to simply as the source.)

1. The source/encoder of information.

2. *The signal*   Encoded information that the source intends to share constitutes a **message.** A message that has been transmitted from one person to another is called a **signal.**

2. The signal.

3. *The decoder/destination*   The **decoder/destination** is the person with whom the source is attempting to share information. This individual receives the signal and decodes, or interprets, the message to determine its meaning. Decoding is the process of converting messages back into information. In all interpersonal communication situations, message meaning is a result of decoding. (From here on, decoder/destination will be referred to as the destination.)

3. The decoder/destination.

The classic work of Wilbur Schramm helps us understand the role that each of the three elements of the interpersonal communication process plays. As implied in Figure 12.4, the source determines what information to share, encodes this information in the form of a message, and then transmits the message

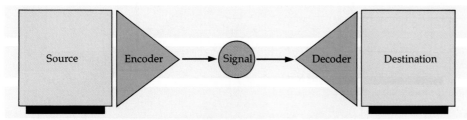

FIGURE 12.4
Role of the source, signal, and destination in the communication process

as a signal to the destination. The destination decodes the transmitted message to determine its meaning and then responds accordingly.

A manager who desires to assign the performance of a certain task to a subordinate would use the communication process in the following way: First, the manager would determine exactly what task she wanted the subordinate to perform. Then she would encode and transmit a message to the subordinate that would accurately reflect this assignment. The message transmission itself could be as simple as the manager telling the subordinate what the new responsibilities include. Next, the subordinate would decode the message transmitted by the manager to ascertain its meaning and then would respond to it appropriately.

Successful and Unsuccessful Interpersonal Communication

Successful communication is an interpersonal communication situation in which the information the source intends to share with the destination and the meaning the destination derives from the transmitted message are the same. Conversely, **unsuccessful communication** is an interpersonal communication situation in which the information the source intends to share and the meaning the destination derives from the transmitted message are different.

To increase the probability that communication will be successful, the message must be encoded to ensure that the source's experience with the way a signal should be decoded is equivalent to the destination's experience of the way it should be decoded. If this situation exists, the probability is high that the destination will interpret the signal as intended by the source. Figure 12.5 illustrates these overlapping fields of experience that ensure successful communication.

Barriers to Successful Interpersonal Communication

Factors that decrease the probability that communication will be successful commonly are called communication barriers. A clear understanding of these barri-

> If the message is decoded as the source intended, communication is successful.

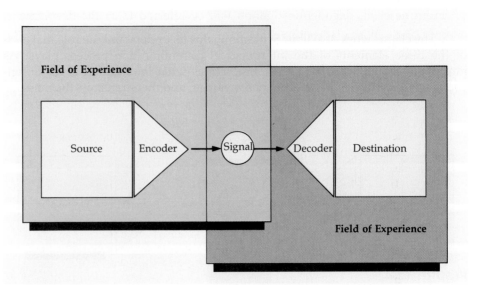

FIGURE 12.5
Overlapping fields of experience that ensure successful communication

ers is helpful to managers in their attempt to maximize communication success. The following sections discuss both communication macrobarriers and communication microbarriers.

Communication Macrobarriers. **Communication macrobarriers** are factors that hinder successful communication in a general communication situation.[4] These factors relate primarily to the communication environment and the larger world in which communication takes place. Among the macrobarriers are the following:[5]

To minimize communication macrobarriers, managers can:

1. *The increasing need for information* Because society is constantly and rapidly changing, individuals have a greater and greater need for information. This increased need tends to overload communication networks, thereby distorting communication. To minimize the effects of this barrier, managers should take steps to ensure that organization members are not overloaded with information. Only information critical to the performance of their jobs should be transmitted to them.

1. Limit the amount of communication transmitted to subordinates.

2. *The need for increasingly complex information* With today's rapid technological advances, most people are faced with complex communication situations in their everyday lives. If managers take steps to emphasize simplicity in communication, the effects of this barrier can be lessened. Also, furnishing organization members with adequate training to deal with more technical areas might be another strategy for overcoming this barrier.

2. Make messages to subordinates as simple as possible.

3. *The reality that individuals in the United States are increasingly coming in contact with individuals using languages other than English* As business becomes international in scope and as organization members travel more, the need to know other languages increases. The potential communication barrier of this multilanguage situation is obvious. Moreover, individuals who deal with foreigners need to be familiar not only with their languages but also with their cultures. Knowledge of a foreign language may be of little value if individuals don't know which words, phrases, and actions are culturally acceptable.

3. Encourage subordinates to learn and understand foreign languages and cultures.

Communication Microbarriers. **Communication microbarriers** are factors that hinder successful communication in a specific communication situation.[6] These factors relate directly to such variables as the communication message, the source, and the destination. Among the microbarriers are the following:[7]

To minimize communication microbarriers, managers can:

1. *The source's view of the destination* The source in any communication situation has a tendency to view the destination in a specific way and to influence the messages by this view. For example, individuals tend to speak differently to people they think are informed about a subject than to those they think are uninformed. The destination can sense the source's attitudes, which often block successful communication. Managers should keep an open mind about the people with whom they communicate and should be careful not to imply any negative attitudes through their communication behavior.

1. Be aware of their attitudes toward the destination.

2. *Message interference* Stimuli that compete with the communication message for the attention of the destination are called **message interference,** or noise.[8] An example of message interference is a manager talking to his secretary while the secretary is trying to correct a typing mistake. Correcting the mistake is message interference because it competes with the manager's communication message for the secretary's attention. Managers should attempt to communicate only when they have the total attention of the individuals with whom they wish to share information.

2. Try to monopolize their subordinates' attention.

3. Be aware of their attitudes toward the source.

3. *The destination's view of the source* The destination can have certain attitudes toward the source that also can hinder successful communication. If, for example, a destination believes that the source has little expertise in the area about which the source is communicating, the destination may filter out much of the source's message and only slightly consider the part of the message actually received. When communicating, managers should attempt to consider the worth of messages transmitted to them independent of their personal attitudes toward the source. They may lose many valuable ideas if personal feelings toward others influence which messages they listen to carefully.

4. Make messages specific.

4. *Perception* **Perception** is an individual's interpretation of a message. Different individuals can perceive the same message in very different ways. The two primary factors that influence the way in which a stimulus is perceived are the level of the destination's education and the destination's amount of experience. To minimize the negative effects of this perceptual factor on interpersonal communication, managers should try to send messages with precise meanings. Ambiguous words generally tend to magnify negative perceptions. The cartoon shows how a different interpretation of a message can result in unsuccessful communication.

5. Define their words in messages.

5. *Multimeaning words* Because many words in the English language have several different meanings, a destination may have difficulty deciding which meaning should be attached to the words of a message. A manager should not assume that a word means the same thing to all people who use it.

   A study by Lydia Strong substantiates this point. Strong concluded that for the 500 most common words in our language, there are 4,070 different dictionary definitions. On the average, each of these words has over 18 usages. The word *run* is an example:[9]

   Babe Ruth scored a *run*.
   Did you ever see Jesse Owens *run*?
   I have a *run* in my stocking.
   There is a fine *run* of salmon this year.
   Are you going to *run* this company or am I?
   You have the *run* of the place.
   What headline do you want to *run*?
   There was a *run* on the bank today.
   Did he *run* the ship aground?
   I have to *run* (drive the car) downtown.

Who will *run* for president this year?
Joe flies the New York-Chicago *run* twice a week.
You know the kind of people they *run* around with.
The apples *run* large this year.
Please *run* my bath water.

When encoding information, managers should be careful to define the terms they use whenever possible. They also should try to use words in the same way they see their destination use them.

BACK TO THE CASE

In discussing Arthur Spear's ability to communicate, we are actually discussing his ability to share ideas with other Mattel employees. For Spear to be a successful communicator, he must concentrate on the three essential elements of the communication process. The first element is the source—the individual who wishes to share information with another. In this case, the source is Spear. The second element is the signal—the message transmitted by Spear. The third element is the destination—the Mattel employee with whom Spear wishes to share information. Spear should communicate with Mattel employees by determining what information he wants to share, encoding the information, and then transmitting the message.

The subordinates would then interpret the message and respond accordingly. Spear's communication would be successful if subordinates interpreted messages as Spear intended.

If Spear is to be a successful communicator, he must minimize the impact of numerous communication barriers. These barriers include (1) Mattel employees' need to have more information and more complex information to do their jobs, (2) message interference, (3) Spear's view of the destination as well as the destination's view of Spear, (4) the perceptual process of the people involved in the communication attempt, and (5) multimeaning words.

Feedback and Interpersonal Communication

Feedback is the destination's reaction to a message. In general, feedback can be used by the source to ensure successful communication.[10] For example, if the destination's message reaction is inappropriate, the source can conclude that communication was not successful and that another message should be transmitted. If the destination's message reaction is appropriate, the source can conclude that communication was successful. This, of course, assumes that the appropriate reaction did not happen merely by chance. Because of the potentially high value of feedback, managers should encourage feedback whenever possible and evaluate it carefully.

Feedback can be either verbal or nonverbal.[11] To gather verbal feedback, the source could simply ask the destination pertinent message related questions. The destination's answers would probably indicate to the source whether the message was perceived as intended. To gather nonverbal feedback, the source may have to observe the destination's nonverbal response to a message. An example is a manager who has transmitted a message to a subordinate indicating new steps that must be taken in the normal performance of the subordinate's job. Assuming that no other problems exist, if the steps are not followed accurately, the manager has nonverbal feedback indicating the need for clarification of the initial message.

Robert S. Goyer has suggested other uses for feedback besides determining if a message is perceived as intended.[12] For example, over time a source can use

> Feedback is the destination's reaction to a message.

> Feedback can be either verbal or nonverbal.

> The communication effectiveness index evaluates personal communication effectiveness.

330 Section 4 Influencing

feedback to evaluate his personal communication effectiveness by determining the proportion of the destination's message reactions that he actually intended. A formula illustrating how this evaluation, the **communication effectiveness index,** can be calculated is shown in Figure 12.6. The higher this proportion, the greater the communication effectiveness of the source.

One communication problem may be a confusing vocabulary.

If managers discover that their communication effectiveness index is relatively low over an extended period of time, they should assess their situation to determine how to improve their communication skill. One problem they may discover is that they are repeatedly using a vocabulary confusing to the destination. For example, a study conducted by Group Attitudes Corporation found that if managers used certain words repeatedly in communicating with steelworkers, the steelworkers almost certainly would become confused.[13] Table 12.2 shows thirty words that Group Attitudes Corporation found to be misunderstood frequently by steelworkers. It also suggests phrases that managers should use instead.

The "ten commandments of good communication" are as follows:

Besides analyzing their vocabulary, managers should attempt to increase their communication effectiveness by following the "ten commandments of good communication" as closely as possible. These commandments are as follows:[14]

1. *Seek to clarify your ideas before communicating* The more systematically you analyze the problem or idea to be communicated, the clearer it becomes. This is the first step toward effective communication. Many communications fail because of inadequate planning. Good planning must consider the goals and attitudes of those who will receive the communication and those who will be affected by it.

2. Examine the purpose.

2. *Examine the true purpose of each communication* Before you communicate, ask yourself what you really want to accomplish with your message—obtain information, initiate action, change another person's attitude? Identify your most important goal and then adapt your language, tone, and total approach to serve that specific objective. Don't try to accomplish too much with each communication. The sharper the focus of your message, the greater its chances of success.

3. Consider the total setting.

3. *Consider the total physical and human setting whenever you communicate* Meaning and intent are conveyed by more than words alone. Many other factors influence the overall impact of a communication, and managers must be sensitive to the total setting in which they communicate. Consider, for example, your sense of timing, that is, the circumstances under which you make an announcement or render a decision; the physical setting—whether

$$\underset{\text{(Communication Effectiveness Index)}}{\text{CEI}} = \frac{\text{IMR (Intended Message Reaction)}}{\text{TM (Total Number of Messages Transmitted)}}$$

FIGURE 12.6
Calculation of communication effectiveness index

TABLE 12.2

Thirty words frequently misunderstood by steelworkers and suggested words or phrases to be used in their place

1. Accrue—*pile up; collect*
2. Compute—*figure*
3. Concession—*giving up (something)*
4. Contemplate—*think about; expect*
5. Delete—*cancel; take out; remove*
6. Designate—*name; appoint*
7. Deterioration—*breaking down; wearing away*
8. Detriment—*hurt; damage; harm*
9. Economic problem—*a cost problem*
10. Efficiency—*the way it should be (e.g., operating a machine the way it should be operated)*
11. Embody—*contain; include; hold*
12. Equitable—*fair; just*
13. Excerpt—*section; part*
14. Facilitate—*help along*
15. Fortuitously—*by chance; accidentally; luckily*
16. Generate—*create; build; produce*
17. Impediment—*barrier; roadblock*
18. Inadequate—*not enough*
19. Increment—*raise; increase*
20. Inevitably—*in the end; finally*
21. Initiate—*begin; start*
22. Injurious—*damaging; harmful*
23. Jeopardy—*danger*
24. Magnitude—*size*
25. Modify—*change; alter*
26. Objectivity—*fairness*
27. Pursuant—*in agreement with*
28. Perpetuate—*keep alive; continue*
29. Subsequently—*later*
30. Ultimate—*final; end*

you communicate in private or otherwise, for example; the social climate that pervades work relationships within the company or a department and sets the tone of its communications; custom and practice—the degree to which your communication conforms to, or departs from, the expectations of your audience. Be constantly aware of the total setting in which you communicate. Like all living things, communication must be capable of adapting to its environment.

4. *Consult with others, when appropriate, in planning communications* Frequently, it is desirable or necessary to seek the participation of others in planning a communication or in developing the facts on which to base the communication. Such consultation often lends additional insight and objectivity to your message. Moreover, those who have helped you plan your communication will give it their active support.

   4. Consult with others.

5. *Be mindful, while you communicate, of the overtones as well as the basic content of your message* Your tone of voice, your expression, your apparent receptiveness to the responses of others—all have tremendous impact on those you wish to reach. Frequently overlooked, these subtleties of communication often affect a listener's reaction to a message even more than its basic content. Similarly, your choice of language—particularly your awareness of the fine shades of meaning and emotion in the words you use—predetermine in large part the reactions of your listeners.

   5. Consider the overtones.

6. *Take the opportunity, when it arises, to convey something of help or value to the receiver* Consideration of the other person's interests and needs—trying to look at things from the other person's point of view—frequently points up opportunities to convey something of immediate benefit or long-range value to the other person. Subordinates are most responsive to managers whose messages take the subordinates' interests into account.

   6. Offer the receiver something of value.

7. *Follow up your communication* Your best efforts at communication may be wasted, and you may never know whether you have succeeded in express-

   7. Follow up the communication.

ing your true meaning and intent if you do not follow up to see how well you have put your message across. You can do this by asking questions, by encouraging the receiver to express his or her reactions, by follow-up contacts, and by subsequent review of performance. Make certain that every important communication has feedback so that complete understanding and appropriate action result.

8. Be aware of future needs.

8. *Communicate for tomorrow as well as today* While communications may be aimed primarily at meeting the demands of an immediate situation, they must be planned with the past in mind if they are to maintain consistency in the receiver's view. Most important, however, communications must be consistent with long-range interests and goals. For example, it is not easy to communicate frankly on such matters as poor performance or the shortcomings of a loyal subordinate, but postponing disagreeable communications makes these matters more difficult in the long run and is actually unfair to your subordinates and your company.

9. Have actions support communication.

9. *Be sure your actions support your communications* In the final analysis, the most persuasive kind of communication is not what you say, but what you do. When your actions or attitudes contradict your words, others tend to discount what you have said. For every manager, this means that good supervisory practices—such as clear assignment of responsibility and authority, fair rewards for effort, and sound policy enforcement—serve to communicate more than all the gifts of oratory.

10. Listen too.

10. *Last, but by no means least: Seek not only to be understood but to understand—be a good listener* When you start talking, you often cease to listen, at least in that larger sense of being attuned to the other person's unspoken reactions and attitudes. Even more serious is the occasional inattentiveness you may be guilty of when others are attempting to communicate with you. Listening is one of the most important, most difficult, and most neglected skills in communication. It demands that you concentrate not only on the explicit meanings another person is expressing, but also on the implicit meanings, unspoken words, and undertones that may be far more significant. Thus, you must learn to listen with the inner ear if you are to know the inner person.

Verbal and Nonverbal Interpersonal Communication

Interpersonal communication is generally divided into two types: verbal and nonverbal. Up to this point, the chapter has emphasized **verbal communication**—communication that uses either spoken or written words to share information with others.

Nonverbal communication is encoding without words.

Nonverbal communication may influence the impact of a message more than verbal communication.

Nonverbal communication is sharing information without using words to encode thoughts. Factors commonly used to encode thoughts in nonverbal communication are gestures, vocal tones, and facial expressions. In most interpersonal communication, verbal and nonverbal communications are not either-or occurrences. Instead, the destination's interpretation of a message generally is based not only on the words in the message but also on such factors as the source's gestures and facial expressions.

Managers must avoid contradictory verbal and nonverbal messages.

In an interpersonal communication situation in which both verbal and nonverbal factors are present, nonverbal factors may have more influence on the total impact of a message than verbal factors. Albert Mehrabian has developed a formula that shows the relative contributions of both verbal and nonverbal factors to the total impact of a message. This formula is as follows: Total message impact = .07 words + .38 vocal tones + .55 facial expressions.[15] Of course, both vocal tones and facial expressions are nonverbal factors. Besides vocal tones and facial expressions, gestures,[16] gender,[17] and dress[18] can influence the impact of a verbal message. Given the great potential influence of nonverbal factors on the impact of a message, managers should use nonverbal message ingredients to complement verbal message ingredients whenever possible.[19]

Nonverbal messages also can be used to add new content to verbal messages. To this end, a head might be nodded or a voice might be toned to show either agreement or disagreement.

Regardless of how managers decide to combine verbal and nonverbal factors, they must be sure that the two do not present contradictory messages. For instance, the words of a message might express approval while the nonverbal factors express disapproval. This type of situation creates message ambiguity and leaves the destination frustrated.

Organizational communication is interpersonal communication within organizations.

BACK TO THE CASE

The employees' reactions to Spear's messages can provide Spear with perhaps his most useful tool in making communication successful—feedback. When feedback does not seem appropriate, Spear should transmit another message to clarify the meaning of his first message. Spear must be alert to both verbal and nonverbal feedback. Over time, if feedback indicates that Spear is a relatively unsuccessful communicator, he should analyze his situation carefully to improve his communication effectiveness. Spear might find, for instance, that he is using a vocabulary that is generally inappropriate for certain employees or that

he is not following one or more of the ten commandments of good communication.

In addition, Spear must remember that he can communicate to others without using words. His facial expressions, gestures, and even the tone of his voice say things to people. Most of Spear's communication situations involve both verbal and nonverbal messages to Mattel employees. Since the impact of a message may be generated mostly by its nonverbal components, Spear must be certain that his nonverbal messages complement his verbal messages.

Interpersonal Communication in Organizations

To be effective communicators, managers must understand not only general interpersonal communication concepts but also the characteristics of interpersonal communication within organizations, called **organizational communication.** Organizational communication directly relates to the goals, functions, and structure of human organizations.[20] Organizational success, to a major extent, is determined by the effectiveness of organizational communication.[21]

Although organizational communication often was referred by early mangement writers, the topic began to receive systematic study and attention only after World War II.[22] From World War II to the 1950s, organizational communication as a discipline made significant advances in such areas as mathematical communication theory and behavioral communication theory.[23] In more recent times, emphasis on organizational communication has grown in colleges of business throughout the nation.[24] The following information focuses on three fundamental organizational communication topics: (1) formal organizational

Formal organizational communication follows the organization chart.

communication, (2) informal organizational communication, and (3) the encouragement of formal organizational communication.

Formal Organizational Communication

In general, organizational communication that follows the lines of the organization chart is called **formal organizational communication.**[25] As discussed in chapter 8, the organization chart depicts relationships of people and jobs and shows the formal channels of communication among them.

Types of Formal Organizational Communication
In general, there are three basic types of formal organizational communication: (1) downward, (2) upward, and (3) lateral.

Downward Organizational Communication. Communication that flows from any point on an organization chart downward to another point on the organization chart is called **downward organizational communication.** This type of formal organizational communication relates primarily to the direction and control of employees. Job related information that focuses on what activities are required, when the activities should be performed, and how the activities should be coordinated with other activities within the organization must be transmitted to employees. This downward communication typically includes a statement of organizational philosophy, management system objectives, position descriptions, and other written information relating to the importance, rationale, and interrelationships of various departments.[26]

Upward Organizational Communication. Communication that flows from any point on an organization chart upward to another point on the organization chart is called **upward organizational communication.** This type of organizational communication contains primarily the information managers need to evaluate the organizational area for which they are responsible and to determine if something is going wrong within the organization. For example, upward communication generally contains information about production reports, shipping reports, and customer complaints.[27] Organizational modifications based on this feedback enable the organization to be more successful in the future.

Lateral Organizational Communication. Communication that flows from any point on an organization chart horizontally to another point on the organization chart is called **lateral organizational communication.** Communication that flows across the organization usually focuses on coordinating the activities of various departments and developing new plans for future operating periods. Within the organization, all departments are related to all other departments. Only through lateral communication can these departmental relationships be coordinated well enough to enhance the attainment of management system objectives.

Patterns of Formal Organizational Communication
By nature, organizational communication creates patterns of communication among organization members. These patterns evolve from the repeated occur-

rence of various serial transmissions of information. According to Haney, a **serial transmission** involves passing information from one individual to another. It occurs when

> A communicates a message to B; B then communicates A's message (or rather his or her interpretation of A's message) to C; C then communicates his or her interpretation of B's interpretation of A's message to D; and so on. The originator and the ultimate recipient of the message are separated by middle people.[28]

Of course, one of the obvious weaknesses of a serial transmission is that messages tend to become distorted as the length of the serial transmission increases. Research has shown that message details may be omitted, altered, or added in a serial transmission.[29]

As presented in a classic article by Alex Bavelas and Dermot Barrett,[30] the potential inaccuracy of transmitted messages is not the only weakness of a serial transmission. Serial transmissions can also influence morale, the emergence of a leader, the degree to which individuals involved in the transmissions are organized, and their efficiency. Three basic organizational communication pattern studies and their corresponding effects on the variables just mentioned are shown in Figure 12.7.

Informal organizational communication ignores the organization chart.

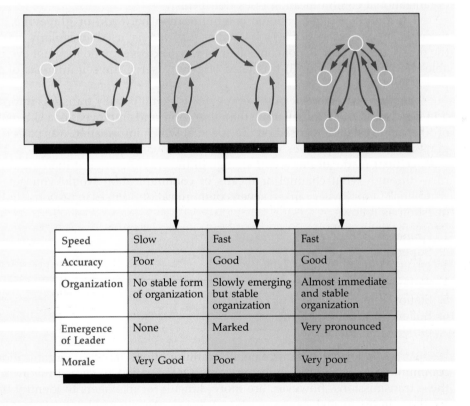

Speed	Slow	Fast	Fast
Accuracy	Poor	Good	Good
Organization	No stable form of organization	Slowly emerging but stable organization	Almost immediate and stable organization
Emergence of Leader	None	Marked	Very pronounced
Morale	Very Good	Poor	Very poor

FIGURE 12.7
Relationship between three patterns of organizational communication and group characteristics of speed, accuracy, organization, emergence of leader, and morale

BACK TO THE CASE

As chief executive officer at Mattel, Arthur Spear must strive to understand the intricacies of organizational communication—interpersonal communication as it takes place within the organization. The success of organizational communication at Mattel is an important factor in determining the company's level of success. Spear can communicate with his people in two basic ways: formally and informally.

In general, Spear's formal communication should follow the lines on the organization chart. Spear can communicate downward to, for example, divisional managers or upward to, for example, Mattel's board of directors. Spear's downward communication should focus on the activities subordinates should be performing. His upward communication should indicate how well the company is doing. Since Spear is chief executive officer and has no one at the same level within the organization, he would not communicate laterally. He should, however, take steps to ensure that lateral communication does occur at other organizational levels to enhance planning and coordination at Mattel.

The grapevine is the network of informal organizational communication.

Informal Organizational Communication. Organizational communication that does not follow the lines of the organization chart is called **informal organizational communication.** This type of communication typically follows the pattern of personal relationships among organization members. One friend communicates with another friend, regardless of their relative positions on the organization chart. Informal organizational communication networks generally exist because organization members have a desire for information that formal organizational communication does not furnish.

The grapevine usually follows one of four patterns.

The informal organizational communication network, or **grapevine,** has three main characteristics: (1) it springs up and is used irregularly within the organization; (2) it is not controlled by top executives, who may not even be able to influence it; and (3) it is used largely to serve the self-interests of the people within it.

Another characteristic of the grapevine is that it usually transmits information very quickly. A study of more than four thousand employees of a U.S. naval ordinance test station focused on the speed at which information was passed by grapevines. The employees were asked the following question: "Suppose that management made an important change in the way the organization would be run—through what channel or means of communication would you get the word first?" Employees ranked seven communication sources in response to this question as follows:[31]

1. Grapevine, 38 percent.
2. Supervisor, 27 percent.
3. Official memo, 17 percent.
4. Station newspaper, 7 percent.
5. Station directive system, 4 percent.
6. Bulletin boards, 4 percent.
7. Other, 3 percent.

Should grapevines be discouraged or encouraged?

As with formal organizational communication, informal organizational communication uses serial transmissions. Organization members involved in these transmissions, however, are more difficult for managers to identify than are those in the formal communication network. As Figure 12.8 illustrates, four patterns of grapevines tend to exist in organizations:[32]

1. *The single-strand grapevine* A tells B, who tells C, who tells D, and so on. This type of grapevine tends to distort messages more than any other.

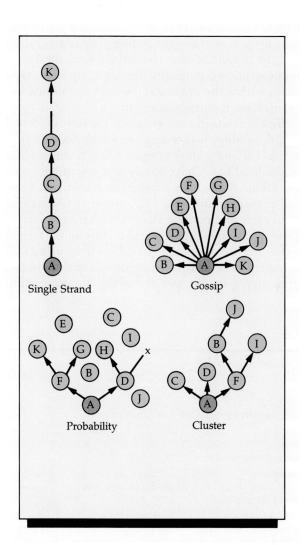

FIGURE 12.8
Four types of organizational grapevines

2. *The gossip grapevine* A informs everyone else on the grapevine.
3. *The probability grapevine* A communicates randomly, for example, to F and D. F and D then continue to inform other grapevine members in the same way.
4. *The cluster grapevine* A selects and tells C, D, and F. F selects and tells I and B, and B selects and tells J. Information in this grapevine travels only to selected individuals.

   Clearly, grapevines are a factor managers must deal with, since they can, and often do, generate rumors that can be detrimental to organizational success.[33] To minimize the development of such rumors, some managers advise distributing the maximum amount of information through formal communication channels.[34] Some writers argue, however, that managers should encourage the development of grapevines and strive to become grapevine members to gain feedback that could be very valuable in improving the organization.[35] Exactly how individual managers should deal with the grapevine, of course, depends on the specific organizational situation in which the managers find themselves.

Encouraging Formal Organizational Communication. Organizational communication often is called the nervous system of the organization. The organization acts only as its nervous system, or organizational communication, directs it. Since formal organizational communication is generally the more important type of communication that takes place within the organization, managers must encourage its free flow if the organization is to be successful.

Managers can use many different strategies to encourage the flow of formal organizational communication. One strategy is listening attentively to messages that come through formal channels. Listening shows organization members that managers are interested in what subordinates have to say and encourages employees to use formal communication channels in subsequent situations. General guidelines for listening are presented in Table 12.3. Another managerial strategy is to support the flow of clear and concise statements through formal communication channels. Receiving an ambiguous message through a formal organizational communication channel can discourage members from using that channel again. A third strategy managers can use is taking care to ensure that all organization members have free access to the use of formal communication

> Strategies for encouraging formal organizational communication include listening, sending clear messages, providing access to channels, and using staff personnel.

TABLE 12.3

Ten commandments for good listening

1. *Stop talking!*
   You cannot listen if you are talking.
   Polonius *(Hamlet):* "Give every man thine ear, but few thy voice."
2. *Put the talker at ease.*
   Help the talker feel free to talk.
   This is often called a permissive environment.
3. *Show the talker that you want to listen.*
   Look and act interested. Do not read your mail while he or she talks.
   Listen to understand rather than to oppose.
4. *Remove distractions.*
   Don't doodle, tap, or shuffle papers.
   Will it be quieter if you shut the door?
5. *Empathize with the talker.*
   Try to put yourself in the talker's place so that you can see his or her point
   of view.
6. *Be patient.*
   Allow plenty of time. Do not interrupt the talker.
   Don't start for the door or walk away.
7. *Hold your temper.*
   An angry person gets the wrong meaning from words.
8. *Go easy on argument and criticism.*
   This puts the talker on the defensive. He or she may "clam up" or get angry.
   Do not argue: even if you win, you *lose.*
9. *Ask questions.*
   This encourages the talker and shows you are listening.
   It helps to develop points further.
10. *Stop talking!*
    This is first and last, because all other commandments depend on it.
    You just can't do a good listening job while you are talking.
    Nature gave us two ears but only one tongue,
    which is a gentle hint that we should listen more than we talk.

COMMUNICATION WITH PEOPLE WORKING AT HOME

"Working at home" was perhaps initially looked upon by some as a euphemism for mowing the lawn—or even golfing. But managers of employees who now work away from the office say that they find these workers actually put in more hours, significantly improved their productivity—and are easier to manage.

"I was worried at the beginning [of becoming] a police officer," says Doug Murphy, manager of computer and telecommunications technology, Computer Systems Group, South Burlington, Vt., a division of Digital Equipment Corp. (DEC). In truth, he says, people tend to bring in projects much sooner when they work at home.

They may work more on off-hours, or even put in more hours. But probably the major benefit in managing people who work at home is avoidance of the considerable amount of office time spent on the telephone—often wasted time.

Originally it was called telecommuting, a word created by Dr. Jack Nilles, director of information technology, Center for Futures Research, University of Southern California, Los Angeles. It means working at home or at a satellite office and communicating with the home office or plant mainly by phone, usually with a terminal or computer.

This approach has been broadened of late; Electronic Services Unlimited (ESU), New York, has now coined the word "teleworking" for almost any kind of work done away from the office. Communications can be handled from a multitude of places—a client's phone via laptop computer or a mobile phone in a car—any phone, really. . . .

There's one downside: The system removes some of the face-to-face meetings that are needed to have a good daily contact balance.

Pacific Bell, a Pacific Telesis company, adopted a teleworking approach during the Los Angeles Summer Olympics in 1984 to allow employees to avoid the expected traffic hassles. After about three months it saw advantages in the system and decided to continue a pilot program, using one satellite office in southern California and one in northern California.

About 100 Pacific Bell managers from all functions were initially involved. By the time the pilot ended in December 1986, some 300 additional managers had volunteered for the program.

Pacific Bell has since closed the two satellite offices, plus another office, at a savings of 3,500 square feet, says Rick Higgins, the project manager who directed the southern California program. He regards teleworking as a boon for those employees who don't like to commute and as a savings for the company.

"We recommend that they stay at home not more than four days at a time, and come in one day to talk with the boss," he says. "That way, they don't feel isolated."

At present, only managers can participate in the Pacific Bell program, but Mr. Higgins foresees expanding the practice to hourly employees at some time in the future.

One Pacific Bell manager, Sandy Hale, manager of media relations, spends four days a week working at home, and has been doing so since her second baby was born recently. It seems the ideal answer for spending more time with her family while continuing her career. She places her two children with a babysitter next door and visits them twice a day. Doing that keeps her close to the children, yet saves her two hours a day in commuting. That conserves energy—for body and car, she says.

It's still important to get to the office one day a week, she says. "I need to meet specific people. That generates a lot of creativity. And I feel I'm not forgotten. I find I have to make an effort to remind people I'm working full-time."

Maintaining people-to-people communications seems to be a major point (and the potential trouble area) that managers and employees alike return to when discussing teleworking. Maintain that communications, most say, and the system can work to the advantage of both employers and employees.

channels within the organization. Obviously, organization members cannot communicate formally within the organization if they don't have access to the formal communication network. A fourth strategy is assigning specific communication responsibilities to staff personnel, who could be of enormous help to line personnel in spreading important information throughout the organization.

The "Management in Action" feature for this chapter focuses on a relatively new challenge that managers face in encouraging organizational communication—the challenge of employees working at home (sometimes called telecommuting or teleworking). Maintaining people-to-people communication seems to be a major potential trouble area that managers and employees alike return to in discussions of teleworking. Maintain that communication, most say, and teleworking can be an advantage for both employees and organizations.

BACK TO THE CASE

If the charge against Spear in the introductory case—that he is difficult to communicate with—is true, an extensive and often-used grapevine probably has developed at Mattel. Although the company grapevine must be dealt with, Spear may not be able to influence it significantly. Mattel employees, as well as employees for any company, typically are involved in grapevines for self-interest and because the formal organization has not furnished them with the information they believe they need.

By developing various social relationships, Spear could conceivably become part of the grapevine and obtain valuable feedback from it. Also, because grapevines generate rumors that could have a detrimental

effect on Mattel's success, Spear should try to ensure that Mattel personnel are given all the information they need to do their jobs well through formal organizational communication, thereby reducing the need for a grapevine.

Since formal organizational communication is vitally important to Mattel, Spear should try to encourage its flow as much as possible. He can do this by listening intently to messages that come to him over formal channels, supporting the flow of clear messages through formal channels, and making sure that all Mattel employees have access to formal communication channels.

Action Summary

Reread the learning objectives that follow. Each objective is followed by questions. Answering these questions accurately will help you retain the most important concepts discussed in this chapter. After answering each question, check your answer with the answer key at the end of this chapter. (*Hint:* If you have doubt regarding the correct response, consult the page whose number follows the answer.)

Circle:

From studying this chapter, I will attempt to acquire:

1. An understanding of influencing.

T, F   **a.** The influencing function can be viewed as forcing the activities of organization members in appropriate directions.

a, b, c, d, e   **b.** Which of the following activities is *not* a major component of the influencing process: (a) motivating; (b) leading; (c) communicating; (d) correcting; (e) considering groups.

2. An understanding of interpersonal communication.

a, b, c, d, e   **a.** Communication is best described as the process of: (a) sharing emotion; (b) sharing information; (c) sending messages; (d) feedback formulation; (e) forwarding information.

  b. The basic elements of interpersonal communication are: (a) source/encoder, signal, decoder/destination; (b) sender/message, encoder, receiver/decoder; (c) signal, source/sender, decoder/destination; (d) signal, source/decoder, encoder/destination; (e) source/sender, signal, receiver/destination.

      a, b, c, d, e

3. **A knowledge of how to use feedback.**
  a. Feedback is only verbal.
  b. Robert S. Goyer has suggested using feedback: (a) as a microbarrier; (b) as a way for sources to evaluate their communication effectiveness; (c) to ensure that instructions will be carried out; (d) evaluate the decoder; (e) all of the above.

4. **An appreciation for the importance of nonverbal communication.**
  a. In interpersonal communication, nonverbal factors may play a more influential role than verbal factors.

      T, F

  b. Nonverbal messages can contradict verbal messages, which can create frustration in the destination.

      T, F

5. **Insights on formal organizational communication.**
  a. Which of the following is not upward communication: (a) cost accounting reports; (b) purchase order summary; (c) production reports; (d) corporate policy statement; (e) sales reports.

      a, b, c, d, e

  b. The primary purpose served by lateral organizational communication is: (a) coordinating; (b) organizing; (c) direction; (d) evaluation; (e) control.

      a, b, c, d, e

6. **An appreciation for the importance of the grapevine.**
  a. Which of the following statements concerning the grapevine is *not* correct: (a) grapevines are irregularly used in organizations; (b) a grapevine can and often does generate harmful rumors; (c) the grapevine is used largely to serve the self-interests of the people within it; (d) some managers use grapevines to their advantage; (e) in time, and with proper pressure, the grapevine can be eliminated.

      a, b, c, d, e

  b. The grapevine is much slower than formal communication channels.

      T, F

7. **Some hints on how to encourage organizational communication.**
  a. To encourage formal organizational communication, managers should: (a) support the flow of clear and concise statements through formal channels; (b) ensure free access to formal channels for all organization members; (c) assign specific communication responsibilities to staff personnel; (d) a and b; (e) all of the above.

      a, b, c, d, e

  b. Since formal organizational communication is the most important type of communication within an organization, managers must restrict its flow if the organization is to be successful.

      T, F

■ INTRODUCTORY CASE WRAP-UP

"Troubles at Mattel" (p. 320) and its related back-to-the-case sections were written to help you better understand the management concepts contained in this chapter. Answer the following discussion questions about ths introductory case to further enrich your understanding of chapter content:

1. List three problems that could be caused at Mattel because of Spear's being a poor communicator.

2. Explain *how* the problems you listed in number 1 can be caused by Spear's being a poor communicator.

3. If Spear is a poor communicator, as charged, could he be contributing to communication problems relating to divisional management? Explain.

Issues for Review and Discussion

1. What is influencing?
2. Describe the relationship between the overall management system and the influencing subsystem.
3. What factors make up the input, process, and output of the influencing subsystem?
4. Explain the relationship between the factors that compose the process section of the influencing subsystem.
5. What is communication?
6. How important is communication to managers?
7. Draw the communication model presented in this chapter and explain how it works.
8. How does successful communication differ from unsuccessful communication?
9. Summarize the significance of field of experience to communication.
10. List and describe three communication macrobarriers and three communication microbarriers.
11. What is feedback, and how should managers use it when communicating?
12. How is the communication effectiveness index calculated, and what is its significance?
13. Name the ten commandments of good communication.
14. What is nonverbal communication? Explain its significance.
15. How should managers use nonverbal communication?
16. What is organizational communication?
17. How do formal and informal organizational communication differ?
18. Describe three types of formal organizational communication, and explain the general purpose of each type.
19. Can serial transmissions and other formal communication patterns influence communication effectiveness and the individuals using the patterns? If so, how?
20. Draw and describe the four main types of grapevines that exist in organizations.
21. How can managers encourage the flow of formal organizational communication?

Sources of Additional Information

Arnold, Hugh J., and Daniel C. Feldman. *Organizational Behavior.* New York: McGraw-Hill, 1986.

Barnlund, Dean. *Interpersonal Communication: Survey and Studies.* Boston: Houghton Mifflin, 1968.

Block, Peter. *The Empowered Manager: Positive Political Skills at Work.* San Francisco: Jossey-Bass, 1987.

Bosmajian, H. A., ed. *The Rhetoric of Nonverbal Communication.* Chicago: Scott, Foresman, 1971.

Costley, Dan L. *Human Relations in Organizations,* 3rd ed. New York: West Publishing Co., 1987.

Dunham, Randall B. *Organizational Behavior: People and Processes in Management.* Homewood, Ill.: Richard D. Irwin, 1984.

Ebenstein, Michael, and Leonard I. Krauss. "Strategic Planning for Information Resource Management." *Management Review* 70 (June 1981): 21–26.

Eisenberg, Abne M., and Ralph R. Smith. *Nonverbal Communication.* Indianapolis: Bobbs-Merrill, 1972.

French, Wendell L., Fremont E. Kast, and James E. Rosenzweig. *Understanding Human Behavior in Organizations.* New York: Harper & Row, 1985.

Friedman, Selma. "Where Employees Go for Information (Some Surprises!)." *Administrative Management* 42 (September 1981): 72–73.

Goldhaber, Gerald M. *Organizational Communication,* 4th ed. Dubuque, Iowa: Wm. C. Brown, 1983.

Gordon, William I., and John R. Miller. *Managing Your Communication.* Prospect Heights, Ill.: Waveland, 1983.

Gruneberg, Michael, and Toby Wall. *Social Psychology and Organizational Behavior.* New York: Wiley, 1984.

Lesikar, Raymond. *Business Communication.* Homewood, Ill.: Richard D. Irwin, 1972.

Micheli, Linda, Frank V. Cespedes, Donald Byker, and Thomas J. C. Raymond. *Managerial Communication.* Glenview, Ill.: Scott, Foresman, 1984.

Montgomery, Robert L. "Are You a Good Listener?" *Nation's Business* 69 (October 1981): 65–68.

Penrose, John. "Telecommunication, Teleconferencing, and Business Communication." *Journal of Business Communication* 21 (Winter 1984): 93–112.

Reinsch, N. L., and Phillip V. Lewis. "Communication Apprehension as a Determinant of Channel Preferences." *Journal of Business Communication* 21 (Summer 1984): 53–62.

Shatshat, H. M., and Bong-Gon P. Shin. "Organizational Communication—A Key to Successful Strategic Planning." *Managerial Planning* 30 (September/October 1981): 37–40.

Timm, Paul R. "Driving Out the Devils of Communication." *Management World* 13 (July 1984): 27–29.

Umstot, Denis D. *Understanding Organizational Behavior: Concepts and Applications*. New York: West Publishing, 1984.

Notes

1. See the following articles for insights into and examples of how communication is related to the performance of management activities: Larry Penley and Brian Hawkins, "Studying Interpersonal Communication in Organizations: A Leadership Application," *Academy of Management Journal* (June 1985): 309–26; Richard C. Huseman, Elmore R. Alexander III, and Russell W. Driver, "Planning for Organizational Change: The Role of Communication," *Managerial Planning* 28 (May/June 1980): 32–36; H. M. Shatshat and Bong-Gon P. Shin, "Organizational Communication—A Key to Successful Strategic Planning," *Managerial Planning* 30 (September/October 1981): 37–40.

2. James B. Strenski, "Two-Way Communication—A Management Necessity," *Personnel Journal* (January 1970): 29–35. See also Stephen C. Harper, "Business Education: A View from the Top," *Business Forum* (Summer 1987): 24–27.

3. This section is based on the following classic article on interpersonal communication: Wilbur Schramm, "How Communication Works," *The Process and Effects of Mass Communication*, ed. Wilbur Schramm (Urbana: University of Illinois Press, 1954), 3–10.

4. This section is based primarily on David S. Brown, "Barriers to Successful Communication: Part I, Macrobarriers," *Management Review* (December 1975): 24–29.

5. James K. Weekly and Raj Aggarwal, *International Business: Operating in the Global Economy* (New York: Dryden Press, 1987).

6. This section is based primarily on David S. Brown, "Barriers to Successful Communication: Part II, Microbarriers," *Management Review* (January 1976): 15–21.

7. Sally Bulkley Pancrazio and James J. Pancrazio, "Better Communication for Managers," *Supervisory Management* (June 1981): 31–37.

8. Gene E. Burton, "Barriers to Effective Communication," *Management World* (March 1977): 4–8.

9. Lydia Strong, "Do You Know How to Listen?" in *Effective Communications on the Job*, ed. M. Joseph Dooher and Vivienne Marquis (New York: American Management Association, 1956), 28.

10. Robert E. Callahan, C. Patrick Fleenor, and Harry R. Knudson, *Understanding Organizational Behavior: A Managerial Viewpoint* (Columbus, Ohio: Charles E. Merrill, 1986).

11. For more on nonverbal issues, see I.T. Sheppard, "Silent Signals," *Supervisory Management* (March 1986): 31–33; S. Strecker, "Opening Moves and Winning Plays: An Interview with Ken Delmar," *Executive Female* (January/February 1985): 24–48.

12. Robert S. Goyer, "Interpersonal Communication and Human Interaction: A Behavioral View," paper presented at the 138th annual meeting of the American Association for the Advancement of Science, 1971. For an article that complements this orientation toward feedback, see R. Abrams, "Do You Get What You Ask For?" *Supervisory Management* (April 1986): 32–34.

13. Verne Burnett, "Management's Tower of Babel," *Management Review* (June 1961): 4–11.

14. Reprinted, by permission of the publisher, from *Management Review* (October 1955). © 1955 American Management Association, Inc. All rights reserved.

15 Albert Mehrabian, "Communication without Words," *Psychology Today* (September 1968): 53–55.

16. For a practical article emphasizing the role of gestures in communication, see S.D. Gladis, "Notes Are Not Enough," *Training and Development Journal* (August 1985): 35–38.

17. Nicole Steckler and Robert Rosenthal, "Sex Differences in Nonverbal and Verbal Communication with Bosses, Peers, and Subordinates," *Journal of Applied Psychology* (February 1985): 157–63.

18. Andrew J. DuBrin, *Contemporary Applied Management* (Plano, Tex.: Business Publications, 1982), 127–34.

19. W. Alan Randolph, *Understanding and Managing Organizational Behavior* (Homewood, Ill.: Richard D. Irwin, 1985), 349–50.

20. Gerald M. Goldhaber, *Organizational Communication* (Dubuque, Iowa: Wm. C. Brown, 1983).

21. Don J. Baxter, "Employee Communication . . . A Matter of Organizational Survival," *Journal of Organizational Communication* 4, no. 1 (1974): 5–7.

22. Paul H. Pietri, "Organizational Communication: The Pioneers," *Journal of Business Communication* 11,

no. 4 (1974): 3–6.

23. Kenneth R. Van Voorhis, "Organizational Communication: Advances Made during the Period from World War II through the 1950s," *Journal of Business Communication* 11, no. 4 (1974): 11–18.

24. Phillip J. Lewis, "The Status of 'Organizational Communication,' in Colleges of Business," *Journal of Business Communication* 12, no. 4 (1975): 25–28.

25. This section is based primarily on Paul Preston, "The Critical 'Mix' in Managerial Communications," *Industrial Management* (March/April 1976): 5–9.

26. Arnold E. Schneider, William C. Donaghy, and Pamela J. Newman, "Communication Climate within an Organization," *Management Controls* (October/November 1976): 159–62.

27. Schneider, Donaghy, and Newman, "Communication Climate within an Organization."

28. William V. Haney, "Serial Communication of Information in Organizations," in *Concepts and Issues in Administrative Behavior*, ed. Sidney Mailick and Edward H. Van Ness (Englewood Cliffs, N.J.: Prentice-Hall, 1962), 150.

29. Haney, "Serial Communication," 150.

30. Alex Bavelas and Dermot Barrett, "An Experimental Approach to Organizational Communication," *Personnel* 27 (1951): 366–71.

31. Eugene Walton, "Communicating Down the Line: How They Really Get the Word," *Personnel* (July/August 1959): 78–82.

32. Keith Davis, "Management Communication and the Grapevine," *Harvard Business Review* (January/February 1953): 43–49.

33. Linda McCallister, "The Interpersonal Side of Internal Communications," *Public Relations Journal* (February 1981): 20–23.

34. Eugene Walton, "How Efficient Is the Grapevine?" *Personnel* (March/April 1961): 45–49.

35. For an article defending the value of grapevines, see W. Kiechel, "In Praise of Office Gossip," *Fortune*, August 19, 1985, 253–54.

Action Summary Answer Key

1. a. F, p. 321
   b. d, p. 321
2. a. b, p. 324
   b. a, p. 325

3. a. F, p. 329
   b. b, pp. 329–330
4. a. T, pp. 332–333
   b. T, p. 333

5. a. d, p. 334
   b. a, p. 334
6. a. e, pp. 336–337
   b. F, p. 336

7. a. e, p. 338
   b. F, pp. 338–340

PATIENT CARE AND EMPLOYEE SATISFACTION AT METHODIST MEDICAL

The communications department and the human resource department of Methodist Medical Center (MMC) in St. Joseph, Missouri, have planned, developed, and adopted an approach that addresses the complex issues of communication and motivation in health care environments. The approach can be summarized in just two words: "NO SURPRISES." Employees know what is going to happen before it occurs. Also, for the most part, they have some input into decision making or planning before anything becomes final.

The approach is probably best understood in the context of the medical center employees' overall understanding of, and support for, the organization and its objectives. The underlying principles of the approach are based on Maslow's perspective of higher-order needs. MMC administrators believe that when higher-order needs are met, employees become more supportive. The result is reduced absenteeism, increased voluntary service, and a positive attitude toward change.

Furthermore, the MMC administration believes that *understanding* is required for these supportive conditions to exist. That is, individuals must have a clear understanding of the organization's purpose and goals before they can be expected to be supportive.

The alternative to understanding is for the organization to demand support. In some cases, such as complying with patient care standards, this type of demand may be warranted. However, for the most part, MMC seeks voluntary cooperation or commitment instead of just compliance.

The key to MMC's beneficial two-way communication is its "Semi-Annual Report to Employees," a multimedia presentation designed to complement other communication tools. The semi-annual report is designed specifically to support the organization's corporate mission and philosophy: to provide the highest quality patient care at the most reasonable price while providing a work environment that is satisfying and rewarding to the staff. The format of the semi-annual report was developed to incorporate accomplishments and progress in the areas of patient care, employee relations, and administration. The report features MMC's plans and strategies for the next six months.

How the semi-annual report is presented is extremely important. Because patient care cannot be compromised, the presentations are made during all three shifts over an entire week. This amounts to thirty-eight one-hour meetings over a five-day period. Historically,

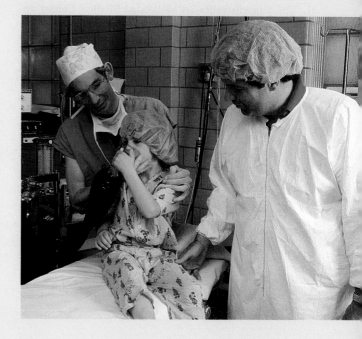

more than 90 percent of the sixteen hundred employees take part.

These semi-annual report meetings use three communication methods. The meetings begin with a slide show presentation outlining MMC's accomplishments during the past six months and describing what can be expected during the next six months. The slide presentation is narrated by the chief executive officer and the assistant administrator of human resources.

Next, the chief executive officer leads a discussion with MMC staff on ideas for future direction and growth of the medical center. This approach has proven to be a highly effective method of communication and has led to a continuing staff commitment to MMC. Finally, at the close of the meeting, each employee is handed a written copy of the "Semi-Annual Report to Employees."

Meeting times are set well in advance and announced through management meetings and employee publications. Notes, taken at all meetings, are reviewed by top management. Issues that can be quickly acted on are assigned to specific individuals. Issues with long-term implications are considered as part of MMC's annual strategic planning process.

Since most suggestions can be responded to quickly, management must be committed to providing immediate feedback. This feedback is reinforcing for staff members who worry about being heard. At MMC, the administration takes special care to complete this critical feedback loop.

1. The administration at Methodist Medical Center appears to be suggesting that good communication can play a significant role in reducing absenteeism, increasing voluntary service, and strengthening the positive attitude toward change. Does the material in the chapter support this perspective? Explain.

2. The second phase of the "Semi-Annual Report to Employees" involves the chief executive officer leading a discussion with MMC staff on ideas for future direction and growth of the medical center. What is this process called? What communication element must be added for this process to exist? Explain.

3. If the MMC administration came to you for advice on how to evaluate its communication effectiveness, what would you recommend? Explain.

4. Which of the basic "ten commandments of good communication" appear to be most important to the administration at MMC? Explain.

STUDENT LEARNING OBJECTIVES

From studying this chapter, I will attempt to acquire:

1. A working definition of leadership.
2. An understanding of the relationship between leading and managing.
3. An appreciation for the trait and situational approaches to leadership.
4. Insights on how to make decisions as a leader.
5. A strategy for using the life cycle theory of leadership.
6. An understanding of alternatives to leader flexibility.

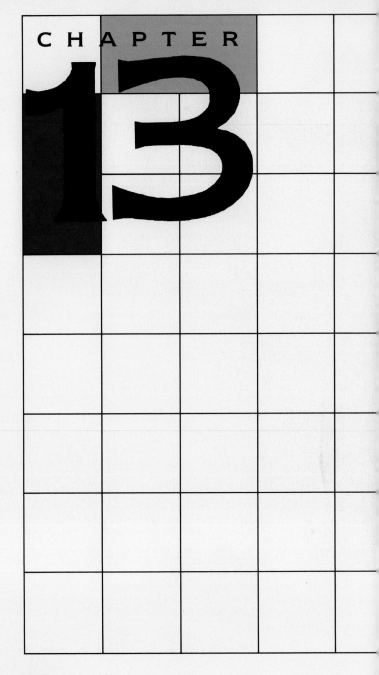

C H A P T E R

13

LEADERSHIP

CHAPTER OUTLINE

INTRODUCTORY CASE 13

BECOMING A SUCCESSFUL LEADER

John Rich is a dietitian and manager of the food services department in a large metropolitan hospital. One of Rich's strengths as a manager is that he continually reads management related articles to improve his managerial effectiveness. Last week he read an article that compared successful and unsuccessful organizational leaders. A summary of the main theme of this article is presented in Case Figure 13.1.

Rich was somewhat disturbed, because, as he attempted to evaluate himself in relation to the two profiles, he seemed to have more of the characteristics of the less successful leader than of the more successful leader. Rich developed a strategy, based on this article, for becoming a more successful leader. The strategy required that he change his interests and attitudes to be more consistent with the profile of the more successful leader. Rich reasoned that as his interests and attitudes came closer to those of more successful leaders, he would become a more successful leader himself.

CASE TABLE 13.1

A comparison of successful and unsuccessful organization leaders

Profile of More Successful Leaders	Profile of Less Successful Leaders
People who were usually in the upper 10 percent of their school class.	Less successful people tend to be from the middle or lower half of their school class.
Their favorite subject was probably one of the social sciences or English, even though they may have majored in engineering or business.	Their favorite subject was science or math.
They read the *New York Times*, are familiar with the Bible, and prefer French impressionist paintings and Tchaikovsky's music.	They read the *New York Times* less than their successful counterparts and the *Wall Street Journal* more.
Their TV habits tend toward news programs and sports, with occasional mixing of such programs as "All in the Family."	They prefer sports to news on TV and have limited interest in art and music.
Their most admired leader is Winston Churchill, although Richard M. Nixon rated high with them before Watergate. Dwight D. Eisenhower and John F. Kennedy are lesser choices, but in the top four.	They are politically more independent or neutral than successful people, and three times more often Republicans than Democrats.
Their average annual income is around $75,000, although their range might be as low as $25,000 or as high as $1,000,000. Their age range is the mid-fifties. More often than not they are Republicans rather than Independents or Democrats (3 to 2).	Their average income is $16,000, and their rate of salary growth over the past ten years is half that of the successful executives. Their choice of a leader is Nixon (pre-Watergate), almost three times over Churchill or Eisenhower.
Successful executives place a high priority on moral standards and integrity, on a sense of fairness to others, and a sense of personal worth. They are less interested in defeating communism or advancing capitalism than in being happy.	They place survival and return on investment on the same par as integrity. They are less interested in helping humanity than helping themselves. They no longer have their hearts set on making a fortune, but are more willing to settle for improving their financial security and their work situation.
In their scale of values, they place power and economics at the top of the list. However, they are significantly higher than less successful executives in their concern for people.	They place a great value on intelligence and place economics at the top of their list of values.

What's Ahead

John Rich, the dietitian-manager in the introductory case, is attempting to become a more successful leader by changing his interests and attitudes. The information in this chapter would be helpful to an individual such as Rich as the basis for developing a more useful leadership strategy. This chapter discusses (1) how to define leadership, (2) the difference between a leader and a manager, (3) the trait approach to leadership, and (4) the situational approach to leadership.

 DEFINING LEADERSHIP

Leadership is the process of directing the behavior of others toward the accomplishment of some objective. Directing, in this sense, means causing individuals to act in a certain way or to follow a particular course. Ideally, this course is perfectly consistent with such factors as established organizational policies, procedures, and job descriptions. The central theme of leadership is getting things accomplished through people. As indicated in chapter 12, leadership is one of the four main interdependent activities of the influencing subsystem and is accomplished, at least to some extent, by communicating with others. Leadership is of such great importance to organizational success that some management writers recommend that, when interviewing candidates to fill an open management position, the interviewer should try to find out each candidate's leadership style to see if it is appropriate for the needs of the organization.[1]

Leadership is guiding the behavior of others.

LEADER VERSUS MANAGER

Leading is not the same as managing.[2] Although some managers are leaders and some leaders are managers, leading and managing are not identical activities.[3] According to Theodore Levitt, management consists of

> the rational assessment of a situation and the systematic selection of goals and purposes (what is to be done); the systematic development of strategies to achieve these goals; the marshalling of the required resources; the rational design, organization, direction, and control of the activities required to attain the selected purposes; and, finally, the motivating and rewarding of people to do the work.[4]

Leadership, as one of the four primary activities of the influencing function, is a subset of management. Managing is much broader in scope than leading and focuses on behavioral as well as nonbehavioral issues. Leading emphasizes mainly behavioral issues. Figure 13.1 makes the point that although not all managers are necessarily leaders, the most effective managers, over the long term, are. Table 13.1 is a list of the primary activities that effective managers/leaders perform.

Leadership is part of management.

FIGURE 13.1
Most effective managers
over the long term are also
leaders

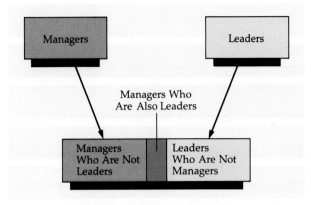

TABLE 13.1

Primary activities of the effective manager/leader

1. *In Terms of Attitudes toward Subordinates:*
   a. Has confidence in subordinates and conveys this confidence.
   b. Is approachable and friendly.
   c. Is eager to help subordinates to be more effective and works at removing obstacles to achievement.
   d. In dealing with subordinates, is emotionally supportive and is careful to avoid ego-threatening behavior.
   e. Tries to minimize stress in relationships with subordinates to avoid diminishing subordinates' use of intellectual capabilities.
   f. Permits subordinates to have latitude in the solution of work problems where the subordinates' ingenuity can result in gains and where standardization in method is not imperative.
   g. Is cognizant of the need for leadership styles to be somewhat different in different technological settings—for example, that it is easily possible to overstructure and be too directive in a laboratory setting and to understructure and be too participative in some factory settings.
   h. Encourages the participation of subordinates but only on the basis of a genuine interest in utilizing constructive suggestions and only where subordinates perceive participation as being legitimate.
2. *In Terms of Technology, Planning, and Selection:*
   a. Utilizes and encourages subordinates to utilize the appropriate technology in attaining these goals—e.g., work simplification, appropriate tools, proper layout, and so on.
   b. Is an effective planner in terms of both short-range and long-range goals and contingencies.
   c. Selects subordinates with appropriate qualifications.
3. *In Terms of Performance Standards and Appraisal:*
   a. Works with subordinates in establishing attainable but high performance standards and high goals—which are consistent with the goals of the enterprise.
   b. Appraises subordinates as nearly as possible on objective, measurable performance but makes compensation and promotion judgments on the basis of total performance.
4. *In Terms of the Linking Pin Function:*
   a. Is an effective link with higher management and other groups within the enterprise in facilitating task performances.
5. *In Terms of Rewards and Correction:*
   a. Gives recognition to good work.
   b. Uses subordinates' mistakes as an educational opportunity rather than an opportunity for punishment.

⊞ THE TRAIT APPROACH TO LEADERSHIP

The **trait approach to leadership** is based on early leadership research that seemed to assume that a good leader is born, not made. The mainstream of this research attempted to describe successful leaders as precisely as possible. The reasoning was that if a complete profile of the traits of a successful leader could be summarized, it would be fairly easy to pinpoint the individuals who should and should not be placed in leadership positions.

Many of the studies that attempted to summarize the traits of successful leaders have been documented.[5] One of these summaries concludes that successful leaders tend to possess the following characteristics:[6]

1. Intelligence, including judgment and verbal ability.
2. Past achievement in scholarship and athletics.
3. Emotional maturity and stability.
4. Dependability, persistence, and a drive for continuing achievement.
5. The skill to participate socially and adapt to various groups.
6. A desire for status and socioeconomic position.

An evaluation of a number of these trait studies, however, concludes that their findings tend to be inconsistent.[7] One researcher says that fifty years of study have failed to produce one personality trait or set of qualities that can be used consistently to discriminate leaders from nonleaders.[8] It follows, then, that no trait or combination of traits guarantees that a leader will be successful. Leadership is apparently a much more complex issue.

Traits cannot predict leadership success.

■ BACK TO THE CASE

From the preceding material, John Rich, the dietitian-manager in the introductory case, should be able to see that his leadership activities in the hospital involve directing the behavior of food services employees so that hospital goals are reached. Rich also should recognize that leading and managing are not the same thing. When managing, Rich is involved with planning, organizing, influencing, and controlling within the food services area. When leading, Rich is performing an activity that is part of the influencing function of management. To maximize his long-term success, Rich should strive to be both a manager and a leader.

The introductory case concludes with Rich attempting to increase his success as a leader by changing his interests and attitudes. Studies based on the trait approach to leadership should indicate to Rich that merely changing his characteristics will not guarantee his success as a leader.

⊞ THE SITUATIONAL APPROACH TO LEADERSHIP

The emphasis of leadership study has shifted from the trait approach to the situational approach. The more modern **situational approach to leadership** is based on the assumption that the instances of successful leadership are somewhat different and require a unique combination of leaders, followers, and leadership situations. This interaction commonly is expressed in formula form: SL = f (L,F,S). In this formula, SL is *successful leadership*, f stands for *function of*, and L,F, and S are, respectively, the *leader*, the *follower*, and the *situation*. A translation of this formula would be that successful leadership is a function of the

The situational approach to leadership in formula form is SL = f (L,F,S).

leader, the follower, and the situation. In other words, the leader, the follower, and the situation must be appropriate for one another if a leadership attempt is to be successful.

Leadership Situations and Decisions

Tannenbaum and Schmidt wrote one of the first and perhaps most well-known articles on the situational approach to leadership. The authors emphasize situations in which a leader makes decisions.[9] Since one of the most important tasks of a leader is making sound decisions, practical and legitimate leadership thinking should contain some emphasis on decision making. Figure 13.2 presents Tannenbaum and Schmidt's model of leadership behavior, which contains such a decision-making emphasis.

Leadership decision-making behavior can range from autocratic to democratic.

The model presented in the figure is actually a continuum, or range, of leadership behavior available to managers in making decisions. Each type of decision-making behavior in this model has both a corresponding degree of authority used by the manager and a related amount of freedom available to subordinates. Management behavior at the extreme left of the model characterizes the leader who makes decisions by maintaining high control and allowing little subordinate freedom. Behavior at the extreme right characterizes the leader who makes decisions by exercising little control and allowing much subordinate freedom and self-direction. Behavior between the extreme left and right reflects a gradual change from autocratic to democratic leadership, or vice versa. Managers displaying leadership behavior toward the right of the model are more democratic and are called subordinate-centered leaders. Managers displaying leadership behavior toward the left of the model are more autocratic and are called boss-centered leaders. Each type of leadership behavior in this model is explained in more detail in the following list:

1. *The manager makes the decision and announces it* This behavior is characterized by the manager (a) identifying a problem, (b) analyzing various alternatives

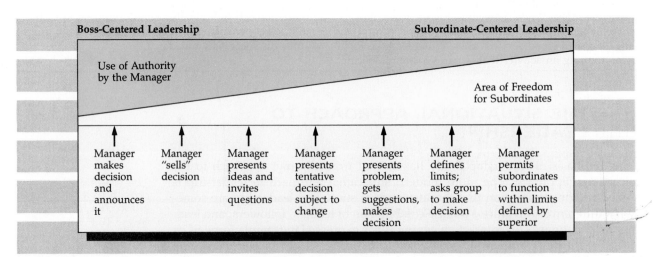

FIGURE 13.2
Continuum of leadership behavior that emphasizes decision making

available to solve the problem, (c) choosing the alternative that will be used to solve the problem, and (d) requiring followers to implement the chosen alternative. The manager may or may not use coercion, but the followers have no opportunity to participate directly in the decision-making process. (The cartoon depicts a manager who made a decision and announced it. As the Tannenbaum and Schmidt model implies, however, this is not *always* the best way to handle decision making.)

2. *The manager "sells" the decision* As before, the manager identifies the problem and independently arrives at a decision. Rather than announce the decision to subordinates for implementation, however, the manager tries to persuade subordinates to accept the decision.

3. *The manager presents ideas and invites questions* Here, the manager makes the decision and attempts to gain acceptance through persuasion. One additional step is taken, however, since subordinates are invited to ask questions about the decision.

4. *The manager presents a tentative decision subject to change* The manager allows subordinates to have some part in the decision-making process but retains the responsibility for identifying and diagnosing the problem. The manager then arrives at a tentative decision that is subject to change on the basis of subordinate input. The final decision is made by the manager.

5. *The manager presents the problem, gets suggestions, and then makes the decision* This is the first leadership activity described thus far that allows subordinates the opportunity to offer problem solutions before the manager does. The manager still identifies the problem in the first place, however.

6. *The manager defines the limits and requests the group to make a decision* This behavior is characterized by the manager first defining the problem and setting the boundaries within which a decision must be made. The manager then sets up a partnership with subordinates to arrive at an appropriate decision. However, if the group of subordinates does not perceive the manager as genuinely desiring a serious group decision-making effort, it will tend to arrive at conclusions that reflect what the group thinks the manager wants rather than what the group actually wants.

7. *The manager permits the group to make decisions within prescribed limits* Here the manager becomes an equal member of a problem-solving group. The entire

I DID IT MY WAY

Wall Street Journal, *February 5, 1987. From the Wall Street Journal–permission, Cartoon Features Syndicate.*

group identifies and assesses the problem, develops possible solutions, and chooses an alternative to be implemented. Everyone within the group understands that the group's decision will be implemented.

BACK TO THE CASE

The situational approach to leadership can give John Rich more insight on how to develop his leadership skill than can the trait approach. The situational approach would suggest that successful leadership within the hospital is determined by the appropriateness of a combination of three factors: (1) Rich as a leader, (2) the food services employees as followers, and (3) the situation within the food services department. Each of these factors plays a significant role in determining whether or not Rich is successful.

One of the most important activities Rich performs as a leader is making decisions. He can make decisions in any number of ways, ranging from authoritarian to democratic. For example, Rich could

make the decision to improve the hospital menu, announce to his employees how the menu will change, and require them to implement the change. Or Rich could define the changes that are needed on the menu, discuss them with the food services staff, and allow the staff to come up with an improved menu.

Of course, Rich could also be less extreme in his decision making, in that his leadership behavior could fall in the middle of the continuum. For example, he could suggest to his employees that a new menu is needed, ask them to develop ideas for improvement, and then make the decision on the basis of his own ideas and those of the staff.

Determining How to Make Decisions as a Leader

The true value of the model developed by Tannenbaum and Schmidt can be realized only if a leader can use it to make practical and desirable decisions. According to these authors, the three primary factors, or forces, that influence a manager's determination of which leadership behavior to use in making decisions are (1) forces in the manager, (2) forces in subordinates, and (3) forces in the leadership situation.

Forces in the manager include:

1. Values of the manager.

Forces in the Manager
Managers should be aware of four forces within themselves that influence their determination of how to make decisions as a leader. The first force is the manager's values, such as the relative importance to the manager of organizational efficiency, personal growth, the growth of subordinates, and company profits. For example, if subordinate growth is valued highly, the manager may want to give the group members the valuable experience of making a decision, even though he could have made the decision much more quickly and efficiently alone.

2. Confidence in subordinates.

The second influencing force within the manager is the level of confidence in subordinates. In general, the more confidence a manager has in subordinates, the more likely the style of decision making will be democratic, or subordinate-centered. The reverse is also true. The less confidence a manager has in subordinates, the more likely the style of decision making will be autocratic, or boss-centered.

3. Strengths of the leader.

The third influencing force within the manager is personal leadership strengths. Some managers are more effective in issuing orders than leading a group discussion, and vice versa. A manager must be able to recognize personal leadership strengths and to capitalize on them.

4. Tolerance for ambiguity.

The fourth influencing force within the manager is tolerance for ambiguity. The move from a boss-centered style to a subordinate-centered style means some loss of certainty about how problems should be solved. If this reduction of certainty is disturbing to a manager, it may be extremely difficult for the manager to be successful as a subordinate-centered leader.

Forces in Subordinates

A manager also should be aware of forces within subordinates that influence the manager's determination of how to make decisions as a leader.[10] To understand subordinates adequately, a manager should keep in mind that subordinates are both somewhat different and somewhat alike. Any cookbook approach for deciding how to lead all subordinates is therefore impossible. Generally speaking, however, a manager probably could increase success as a leader by allowing subordinates more freedom in making decisions if:[11]

1. The subordinates have a relatively high need for independence. (People differ greatly in the amount of direction they desire.)
2. They have a readiness to assume responsibility for decision making. (Some see additional responsibility as a tribute to their ability. Others see it as "passing the buck.")
3. They have a relatively high tolerance for ambiguity. (Some employees prefer to have clear-cut directives given to them. Others prefer a wider area of freedom.)
4. They are interested in the problem and believe it is important.
5. They understand and identify with goals of the organization.
6. They have the necessary knowledge and experience to deal with the problem.
7. They have learned to expect to share in decision making. (People who have come to expect strong leadership and who suddenly are confronted with the request to share more fully in decision making are often upset by this new experience. And people who have enjoyed a considerable amount of freedom resent the boss who begins to make all the decisions alone.)

If these characteristics of subordinates do not exist in a particular situation, a manager probably should move toward a more autocratic, or boss-centered, approach to making decisions.

> There are seven forces in subordinates that indicate the type of decision-making approach a manager should take.

Forces in the Situation

The last group of forces that influence a manager's determination of how to make decisions as a leader are forces in the leadership situation. The first such situational force involves the type of organization in which the leader works. Such organizational factors as the size of working groups and their geographical distribution become especially important in deciding how to make decisions as a leader. Extremely large work groups or a wide geographic separation of work groups, for example, could make a subordinate-centered leadership style impractical.

> Forces in the situation include:
> 1. The organization.

The second situational force is the effectiveness of group members working together. To this end, a manager should evaluate such issues as the experience of the group in working together and the degree of confidence group members have in their ability to solve problems as a group. As a general rule, a manager should assign decision-making responsibilities only to effective work groups.

> 2. The effectiveness of groups.

The third situational force is the problem to be solved. Before acting as a subordinate-centered leader, a manager should be sure that the group possesses the expertise necessary to make a decision about the existing problem. If it doesn't have the necessary expertise, the manager should move toward more boss-centered leadership.

> 3. The problem to be solved.

4. The time available to solve the problem.

The fourth situational force involves the time available to make a decision. As a general guideline, the less time available, the more impractical it becomes to have the decision made by a group. Typically, it takes a group more time than an individual to reach a decision.

Figure 13.3 summarizes the main forces that influence a manager's determination of how to make decisions as a leader and stresses that this determination is the result of the collective influence of all of these forces. As the situational approach to leadership implies, a manager will be successful as a decision maker only if the method used to make those decisions appropriately reflects the leader, the followers, and the situation.

Determining How to Make Decisions as a Leader: An Update

Forces within the manager, subordinates, and situation are increasingly interrelated and complex.

Tannenbaum and Schmidt's original article on leadership decision making was so widely accepted that the two authors were invited by *Harvard Business Review* to update their original work.[12] This update stresses that in modern organizations the relationship among forces within the manager, subordinates, and situation is becoming more complex and more interrelated than ever. As the relationship becomes increasingly complicated, it obviously becomes more difficult for the leader to determine how to lead.

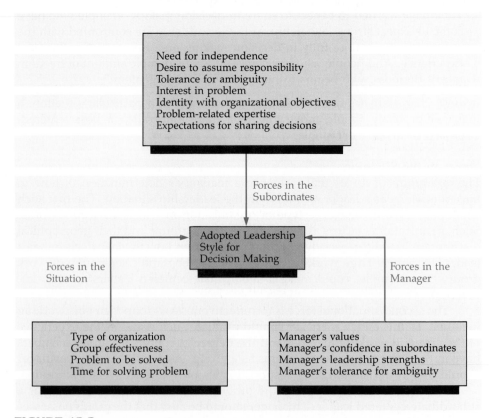

FIGURE 13.3
Collective influence of forces in the manager, the subordinates, and the situation on the leadership style adopted for decision making

The update also stresses both societal and organizational environments as more modern forces to consider in determining how to lead. Such societal and organizational values as affirmative action and pollution control should have some influence on the decision making of leaders.

The decision environments are also a force to be considered.

BACK TO THE CASE

In trying to decide exactly how to make his decisions as a leader, John Rich should consider forces in himself as manager, forces in his food services subordinates, and forces in the situation of the food services department. Forces within Rich include his own ideas about how to lead and his level of confidence in the food services staff. If Rich believes he is more knowledgeable about diet and food costs than his staff is, he will be likely to make boss-centered decisions about what items to put on the hospital's menu.

Forces within the food services subordinates, such as the need for independence, the readiness to assume responsibility, and the knowledge of and interest in the issues to be decided, also affect Rich's decisions as a leader. If Rich's staff is relatively independent and responsible and its members feel strongly that an improved menu is important to meet-

ing the hospital's objectives, then Rich will be inclined to allow his employees more freedom in deciding how to change the hospital menu.

Forces within the food services department include the number of people making decisions and the problem to be solved. For example, if Rich's staff is small, he will be more likely to use a democratic decision-making style, allowing his employees to become involved in such decisions as improving the hospital menu. He will also be likely to use a subordinate-centered leadership style if his staff is knowledgeable about the problem at hand, such as how to more efficiently serve hospital patients. In changing the hospital menu, however, Rich might use an autocratic style, since his employees may not be as knowledgeable as he is about dietary issues.

Leadership Situations in General

Decision-making behavior is a stream of leadership thought that focuses on leadership situations in more general terms. This stream of thought usually is said to have begun with a series of leadership studies whose researchers were affiliated with the Bureau of Business Research at Ohio State University. The studies are called the OSU studies.[13]

The OSU Studies

The OSU studies are a series of leadership investigations that concluded that leaders exhibit two main types of behavior. The first type, called **structure behavior,** is any leadership activity that delineates the relationship between the leader and the leader's followers or establishes well-defined procedures that followers should adhere to in performing their jobs. Over all, structure behavior limits the self-guidance of followers in the performance of their tasks. Although it would be correct to conclude that structure behavior can be, and sometimes is, relatively firm, it would be incorrect to assume that it is rude and malicious.[14]

Structure behavior restricts the self-guidance of subordinates.

Structure behavior can be useful to leaders as a means of minimizing follower activity that does not significantly contribute to organizational goal attainment. Leaders must be careful, however, that they do not discourage follower activity that will contribute to organizational goal attainment. The "Management in Action" feature for this chapter describes an unsuccessful attempt by IBM leadership to discourage certain activities by IBM research scientists. Fortunately for the company, the scientists disregarded the discouragement and continued with their work.[15]

ALMOST TOO MUCH STRUCTURE AT IBM

Rueschlikon, Switzerland—Four years ago, two scientists at International Business Machines Corp. began work on an idea so big that they were loath to share the details even with IBM.

The researchers, at IBM's Swiss laboratory here, wanted to solve one of the toughest problems in physics: finding a cheap, simple substance to conduct electricity without resistance. But they were searching where experts least expected this new "superconductor" to be found—in a ceramic that normally conducts electricity poorly.

Their idea made as little sense as making a picture window out of solid steel. "We were sure anybody would say, "These guys are crazy!"" recalls J. Georg Bednorz, one of the scientists. Indeed, when his partner, K. Alex Mueller, first mentioned the idea to an IBM official, he got a skeptical reaction. So the two scientists hunted quietly, telling a supervisor a half-truth and steering a curious visitor off the track.

Thus, it was quite a surprise when the scientists came up with one of the most significant electronics discoveries since the invention of the transistor in 1947. After 2½ years of lonely lab work conducted in spare moments, Messrs. Bednorz and Mueller discovered a new class of ceramic, superconducting materials. The announcement of the finding last fall triggered the current world-wide frenzy about superconductors. In time, the materials may affect industry as profoundly as the transistor did, making computers smaller, electric motors more efficient and electricity far cheaper.

The scientists' unlikely breakthrough was part painstaking work, part crazy thinking and part luck. Prof. Mueller, 60 years old, who also teaches physics at the University of Zurich, and Mr. Bednorz, 37, made a good team: a brainy, irascible Swiss physicist and his German protégé, a whiz at the lab bench. Their idea, based on a former colleague's theory, was "a farout notion," says Brown University Prof. Leon Cooper, a 1972 Nobel laureate in superconductivity. "It would never have occurred to me to look" where they did.

A superconducting ceramic

Indeed, other physicists initially scoffed at the discovery. But now scientists are squeezing, spraying, X-raying and re-formulating the IBM scientists' original, copper-based compound, trying to extend superconductor performance ever further. While other superconductor researchers had toyed with metal oxides a decade earlier without much luck, Prof. Cooper says that Messrs. Bednorz and Mueller were "the first ones to explore seriously this material and believe in it."

For IBM, the discovery has meant gloss for its scientific reputation and a head start on superconductor research. More than 50 company researchers now are exploring the materials. "We want to be the first to understand the implications of this new development for computers," says IBM's research director, John Armstrong.

The new superconductors may win their inventors a Nobel Prize, physicists speculate. At the least, the discovery has brought fame and an IBM cash bonus big enough "to eat a lot of restaurant dinners," Mr. Bednorz says.

The second main type of leadership behavior described by the OSU studies, **consideration behavior,** is leadership behavior that reflects friendship, mutual trust, respect, and warmth in the relationship between the leader and the followers. Consideration behavior generally is aimed at developing and maintaining a more human relationship between the leader and the followers.

Consideration behavior emphasizes a more human relationship.

The OSU studies resulted in a model that depicts four fundamental leadership styles (Figure 13.5). A **leadership style** is the behavior a leader exhibits while guiding organization members in appropriate directions. Each of the four leadership styles in Figure 13.4 is a different combination of structure behavior and consideration behavior. For example, the high structure/low consideration leadership style is that of a leader who emphasizes structure behavior and deemphasizes consideration behavior.

A leadership style is the behavior exhibited by the leader.

Effectiveness of Various Leadership Styles

An investigation of high school superintendents concluded that desirable leadership behavior seems to be associated with high leader emphasis on both structure and consideration and that undesirable leadership behavior tends to be associated with low leader emphasis on both dimensions.[16] Similarly, the managerial grid covered in chapter 11 implies that the most effective leadership style is characterized by high consideration and high structure.

One should be cautious, however, about concluding that any single leadership style is more effective than any other.[17] The leadership situation is so complex that pinpointing one leadership style as the most effective is an oversimplification. In fact, a successful leadership style for managers in one situation may be ineffective in another situation. Recognizing the need to link leadership styles to appropriate situations, A. K. Korman indicates that a worthwhile con-

Which leadership style is best depends on the situation.

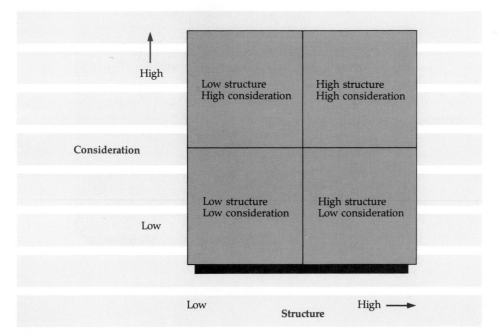

FIGURE 13.4
Four fundamental leadership styles based on structure behavior and consideration behavior

tribution to leadership literature would be a rationale for systematically linking appropriate styles with various situations so as to ensure effective leadership.[18] The life cycle theory of leadership, which is covered in the next section, provides such a rationale.

The Life Cycle Theory of Leadership

The life cycle theory is based on follower maturity, leader task behavior, and leader relationship behavior.

The **life cycle theory of leadership** is a rationale for linking leadership styles with various situations so as to ensure effective leadership. This theory uses essentially the same two types of leadership behavior as the OSU leadership studies, but it calls the dimensions "task" rather than "structure" and "relationships" rather than "consideration."

The life cycle theory of leadership links style and situations.

The life cycle theory is based primarily on the relationship of follower maturity, leader task behavior, and leader relationship behavior. In general terms, according to this theory, leadership style should reflect the maturity level of the followers. **Maturity** is defined as the ability of the followers to perform their job independently, their ability to assume additional responsibility, and their desire to achieve success. The more of each of these characteristics that followers possess, the more mature they are said to be. Maturity here is not necessarily linked to chronological age.

Figure 13.5 shows the life cycle theory of leadership model. The curved line in this model indicates the maturity level of the followers. As the maturity curve runs from right to left, the followers' maturity level increases. In more specific terms, the theory indicates that effective leadership behavior should shift from

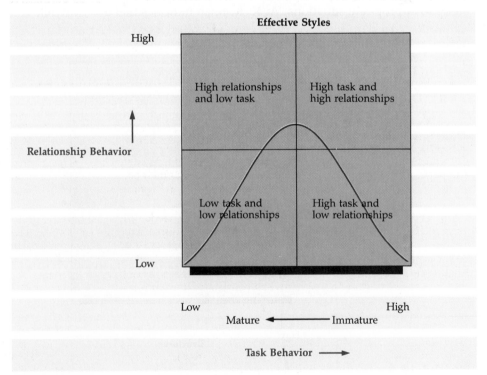

FIGURE 13.5
The life cycle theory of leadership model

"(1) high task/low relationships behavior to (2) high task/high relationships behavior to (3) high relationships/low task behavior to (4) low task/low relationships behavior, as one's followers progress from immaturity to maturity."[19]

The theory suggests, therefore, that a style of leadership will be effective only if it is appropriate for the maturity level of the followers. Table 13.2 describes how each of the four main leadership styles is perceived when it is both effective and ineffective, or appropriate and inappropriate, for followers' maturity levels.

There are some exceptions to the general philosophy of the life cycle theory. For example, if there is a short-term deadline to meet, a leader may find it necessary to accelerate production through a high task/low relationships style, rather than a low task/low relationships style, even if the followers are mature. A high task/low relationships leadership style carried out over the long term with such followers, however, typically results in a poor working relationship of the leader and followers.

There are exceptions to the life cycle theory.

Following is an example of how the life cycle theory applies to a leadership situation: A man has just been hired as a salesperson in a men's clothing store. At first, this individual is extremely immature—that is, unable to solve task related problems independently. According to the life cycle theory, the appropriate style for leading this salesperson at his level of maturity is high task/low relationships. The leader should tell the salesperson exactly what should be done and how it should be done. The salesperson should be shown how to make cash and charge sales and how to handle merchandise returns. The leader also should begin laying some of the groundwork for developing a personal relationship with the salesperson. Too much relationship behavior at this point, however, should be avoided, since it easily can be misinterpreted as permissiveness.

As time passes and the salesperson increases somewhat in job related maturity, the next appropriate style for leading him is high task/high relationships.

TABLE 13.2

How basic leadership styles are perceived by others as effective and ineffective

Basic Styles	Effective	Ineffective
High task and low relationships	Often seen as knowing what he or she wants and imposing personal methods for accomplishing this without creating resentment	Often seen as having no confidence in others, unpleasant, and interested only in short-term output
High task and high relationships	Often seen as satisfying the needs of the group for setting goals and organizing work, but also providing high levels of socioemotional support	Often seen as initiating more structure than is needed by the group and spending more time on socioemotional support than necessary
High relationships and low task	Often seen as having implicit trust in people and as being concerned primarily with developing their talents	Often seen as interested primarily in harmony and being seen as "a good person," and being unwilling to risk disruption of a relationship to accomplish a task
Low task and low relationships	Often seen as appropriately permitting subordinates to decide how the work should be done and playing only a minor part in their social interaction	Often seen as uninvolved and passive, as a "paper shuffler" who cares little about the task at hand or the people involved

Although the salesperson's maturity has increased somewhat, the leader needs to watch him closely, because he still needs some guidance and direction at various times. The main difference between this leadership style and the first leadership style is the amount of relationship behavior displayed by the leader. Building on the groundwork laid during the period of the first leadership style, the leader is now ready to start developing an atmosphere of mutual trust, respect, and friendliness between him and the salesperson.

As more time passes, the salesperson's maturity level increases still further. The next style appropriate for leading this individual is high relationships/low task. The leader can now deemphasize task behavior, because the salesperson is now of above-average maturity in his job and usually can solve job related problems independently. As with the previous leadership style, the leader still emphasizes the development of a human relationship with his follower.

As the salesperson's maturity level reaches its maximum, the appropriate style for leading him is low task/low relationships. Again, the leader can deemphasize task behavior, because the follower is thoroughly familiar with the job. The leader also can deemphasize relationship behavior, because he now has a good working relationship with the follower. Here, task behavior is seldom needed, and relationship behavior is used primarily to nurture the good working rapport that has developed between the leader and the follower. The salesperson, then, is left to do his job without close supervision, knowing that he has a positive working relationship with a leader who can be approached for additional guidance.

The life cycle theory of leadership has become widely accepted as a useful rationale on which to base leader behavior. The theory has served as the basis for leadership training in various organizations and has appeared in numerous management textbooks. Although at first glance it seems like a worthwhile leadership concept, some care probably should be exercised in its application because of the lack of scientific investigation verifying its worth.[20]

BACK TO THE CASE

The OSU leadership studies should furnish John Rich with insights on leadership behavior in general situations. According to these studies, Rich can exhibit two general types of leadership behavior: structure and consideration. Rich will be using structure behavior if he tells food services personnel what to do—for example, to work more quickly in serving meals to hospital patients. He will be using consideration behavior if he attempts to develop a more human rapport with his employees by discussing their concerns and developing friendships with them.

Of course, depending on how Rich emphasizes these two behaviors, his leadership style can reflect a combination of structure and consideration ranging from high structure/low consideration to low structure/high consideration. For example, if Rich stresses giving orders to employees and deemphasizes developing relationships, he will be exhibiting high structure/low consideration. If he emphasizes a good rapport with his staff and allows its members to function mostly independently of him, his leadership style will be termed low structure/high consideration.

Although no single leadership style is more effective than any other in all situations, the life cycle theory of leadership furnishes Rich with a strategy for using various styles in various situations. According to this theory, Rich should make his style consistent primarily with the maturity level of the food services personnel. As Rich's followers progress from immaturity to maturity, his leadership style should shift systematically from (1) high task/low relationships behavior to (2) high task/high relationships behavior to (3) high relationships/low task behavior to (4) low task/low relationships behavior.

Leader Flexibility

Situational theories of leadership, such as life cycle theory, are based on the concept of **leader flexibility**—that successful leaders must change their leadership style as they encounter different situations. Can leaders be so flexible as to span all major leadership styles? The only answer to this question is that some leaders can be flexible and some cannot. After all, a leadership style may be so ingrained in a leader that it takes years to even approach flexibility. Also, some leaders may have experienced such success in a basically static situation that they believe flexibility is unnecessary. Unfortunately, there are numerous obstacles to leader flexibility.

One strategy, proposed by Fred Fiedler, for overcoming these obstacles is changing the organizational situation to fit the leader's style, rather than changing the leader's style to fit the organizational situation.[21] Relating this thought to the life cycle theory of leadership, one finds that it may be easier to shift various leaders to situations appropriate for their leadership styles than to expect leaders to change styles as situations change. It probably would take three to five years to train managers to effectively use a concept such as life cycle theory.[22] Changing the situation a particular leader faces, however, can be done in the short term simply by exercising organizational authority.

According to Fiedler and his **contingency theory of leadership**, leader-member relations, task structure, and the position power of the leader are the three primary factors that should be used for moving leaders into situations appropriate for their leadership styles. *Leader-member relations* is the degree to which the leader feels accepted by the followers. *Task structure* is the degree to which the goals—the work to be done—and other situational factors are outlined clearly. *Position power* is determined by the extent to which the leader has control over the rewards and punishments the followers receive. How these three factors can be arranged in eight different combinations is presented in Table 13.3. Each of these eight combinations is called an octant.

Figure 13.6, p. 366, shows how effective leadership varies among the eight octants. From an organizational viewpoint, this figure implies that management should attempt to match permissive, passive, and considerate leaders with situations reflecting the middle of the continuum containing the octants. The figure also implies that management should try to match a controlling, active, and

Leader flexibility is adapting leadership style to the situation.

However, it may be easier to change the situation to fit the leader's style.

Possible actions to modify the leadership situation follow:

TABLE 13.3

Eight combinations, or octants, of three factors: leader-member relations, task structure, and leader position power

Octant	Leader-Member Relations	Task Structure	Leader Position Power
I	Good	High	Strong
II	Good	High	Weak
III	Good	Weak	Strong
IV	Good	Weak	Weak
V	Moderately poor	High	Strong
VI	Moderately poor	High	Weak
VII	Moderately poor	Weak	Strong
VIII	Moderately poor	Weak	Weak

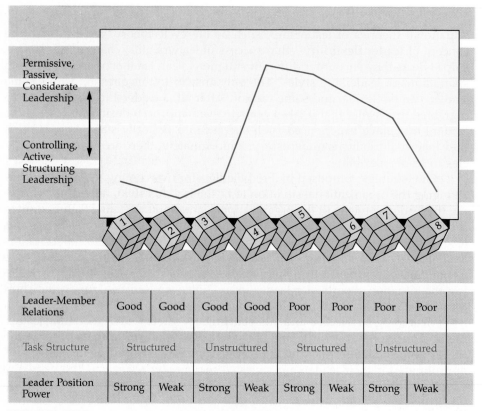

Leader-Member Relations	Good	Good	Good	Good	Poor	Poor	Poor	Poor
Task Structure	Structured		Unstructured		Structured		Unstructured	
Leader Position Power	Strong	Weak	Strong	Weak	Strong	Weak	Strong	Weak

FIGURE 13.6
How effective leadership style varies with Fiedler's eight octants

structuring leader with the extremes of this continuum. Possible actions that Fiedler suggests to modify the leadership situation are as follows:[23]

1. Task structure.

1. In some organizations, we can change the individual's task assignment. We may assign to one leader very structured tasks which have implicit or explicit instructions telling him what to do and how to do it, and we may assign to another the tasks that are nebulous and vague. The former are the typical production tasks; the latter are exemplified by committee work, by the development of policy, and by tasks which require creativity.

2. Position power.

2. We can change the leader's position power. We not only can give him a higher rank and corresponding recognition, we also can modify his position power by giving him subordinates who are equal to him in rank and prestige or subordinates who are two or three ranks below him. We can give him subordinates who are experts in their specialties or subordinates who depend upon the leader for guidance and instruction. We can give the leader the final say in all decisions affecting his group, or we can require that he make decisions in consultation with his subordinates, or even that he obtain their concurrence. We can channel all directives, communications, and information about organizational plans through the leader alone, giving him expert power, or we can provide these communications concurrently to all his subordinates.

3. Leader-member relations.

3. We can change the leader-member relations in this group. We can have the leader work with groups whose members are very similar to him in attitude, opinion, technical background, race, and cultural background. Or we can

assign him subordinates with whom he differs in any one or several of these important aspects. Finally, we can assign the leader to a group in which the members have a tradition of getting along well with their supervisors or to a group that has a history and tradition of conflict.

Over all, Fiedler's work helps destroy the myths that there is one best leadership style and that leaders are born, not made. Further, Fiedler's work supports the theory that almost every manager in an organization can be a successful leader if placed in a situation appropriate for the person's leadership style. This, of course, assumes that someone in the organization has the ability to assess the characteristics of the organization's leaders and of other important organizational variables and then to match the two accordingly.[24] Although criticism of Fiedler's work can be found,[25] his leadership research is probably the most rigorous to date, and his works are highly recommended to anyone seeking insights on the challenges and how-to's of leadership.

> Leaders can be successful in situations that suit their leadership styles.

■ BACK TO THE CASE

The life cycle theory suggests that John Rich should be flexible enough to behave as the situation requires. If Rich finds it extremely difficult to be flexible, however, he should attempt to structure his situation so as to make it appropriate for his style. As suggested by Fiedler, if Rich's leadership style is high task in nature, he generally will be a more successful leader in situations best described by octants 1, 2, 3, and 8 in Table 13.3 and Figure 13.6. If, however, Rich's leadership style is more relationship oriented, he will probably be a more successful leader in situations representative of octants 4, 5, 6, and 7. Over all, Fiedler's work provides Rich with insights on how to engineer situations in the food services department so they will be appropriate for his leadership style.

Action Summary

Reread the learning objectives that follow. Each objective is followed by questions. Answering these questions accurately will help you retain the most important concepts discussed in this chapter. After answering each question, check your answer with the answer key at the end of this chapter. (*Hint:* If you have doubt regarding the correct response, consult the page whose number follows the answer.)

From studying this chapter, I will attempt to acquire: **Circle:**

1. **A working definition of leadership.**
   a. The process of directing others toward the accomplishment of some objective is: (a) communication; (b) controlling; (c) leadership; (d) managing; (e) none of the above.   a, b, c, d, e
   b. Directing must be consistent with which of the following: (a) organizational policies; (b) procedures; (c) job descriptions; (d) none of the above; (e) all of the above.   a, b, c, d, e

2. **An understanding of the relationship between leading and managing.**
   a. Leading and managing are the same process.   T, F
   b. In the relationship between managers and leaders, one could say that: (a) all managers are leaders; (b) all leaders are managers; (c) some leaders are not managers; (d) managers cannot be leaders; (e) management is a subset of leadership.   a, b, c, d, e

3. An appreciation for the trait and situational approaches to leadership.

a, b, c, d, e   **a.** Which of the following is true about the conclusions drawn from the trait approach to leadership: (a) the trait approach identifies traits that consistently separate leaders from nonleaders; (b) there are certain traits that guarantee that a leader will be successful; (c) the trait approach is based on early research that assumes that a good leader is born, not made; (d) leadership is a simple issue of describing the traits of successful leaders; (e) none of the above.

a, b, c, d, e   **b.** The situational approach to leadership takes which of the following into account: (a) the leader; (b) the follower; (c) the situation; (d) a and b; (e) a, b, and c.

4. Insights on how to make a decision as a leader.

a, b, c, d, e   **a.** Forces in the manager that determine leadership behavior include: (a) the manager's values; (b) the manager's confidence in subordinates; (c) the manager's strengths; (d) the manager's tolerance for ambiguity; (e) all of the above.

a, b, c, d, e   **b.** Limiting the self-guidance of the follower and specifically defining procedures for the follower's task performance is called: (a) initiating behavior; (b) structure behavior; (c) maturity behavior; (d) consideration behavior; (e) relationship behavior.

5. A strategy for using the life cycle theory of leadership.

a, b, c, d, e   **a.** The ability of followers to perform their jobs independently and to assume additional responsibility in their desire to achieve success is called: (a) maturity; (b) authority; (c) aggressiveness; (d) assertiveness; (e) consideration.

a, b, c, d, e   **b.** Usually upon entrance into an organization, an individual is unable to solve task related problems independently. According to the life cycle theory, the appropriate style of leadership for this person is: (a) high task/low relationships; (b) high task/high relationships; (c) high relationships/low task; (d) low task/low relationships; (e) none of the above.

6. An understanding of alternatives to leader flexibility.

a, b, c, d, e   **a.** According to Fiedler, the three primary factors that should be used as a basis for moving leaders into more appropriate situations are: (a) task behavior, consideration behavior, maturity; (b) maturity, job knowledge, responsibility; (c) the worker, the leader, the situation; (d) leader-member relations, task structure, position power; (e) task structure, leadership style, maturity.

T, F   **b.** Fiedler's studies have proven true the myths that leaders are born, not made, and that there is one best leadership style.

INTRODUCTORY CASE WRAP-UP

"Becoming a Successful Leader" (p. 350) and its related back-to-the case sections were written to help you better understand the management concepts contained in this chapter. Answer the following discussion questions about this introductory case to further enrich your understanding of chapter content:

1. Evaluate John Rich's strategy.
2. How would you have reacted to the article summarized in Case Figure 13.1 if you had been Rich?

Issues for Review and Discussion

1. What is leadership?
2. How does leadership differ from management?
3. Explain the trait approach to leadership.
4. What relationship exists between successful leadership and leadership traits?
5. Explain the situational approach to leadership.
6. Draw and explain Tannenbaum and Schmidt's leadership model.
7. List the forces in the manager, the subordinates, and the situation that ultimately determine how a manager should make decisions as a leader.
8. What contribution did the OSU studies make to leadership theory?
9. Can any one of the major leadership styles resulting from the OSU studies be called more effective than the others? Explain.
10. What is meant by *maturity* as it is used in the life cycle theory of leadership?
11. Draw and explain the life cycle theory of leadership model.
12. What is meant by *leader flexibility*?
13. Describe some obstacles to leader flexibility.
14. In general, how might obstacles to leader flexibility be overcome?
15. In specific terms, how does Fiedler suggest that obstacles to leader flexibility be overcome?

Sources of Additional Information

Beggs, James M. "Leadership—The NASA Approach." *Long-Range Planning* 17 (April 1984): 12–24.

Culligan, Matthew J., Suzanne Deakins, and Arthur H. Young. *Back-to-Basics Management: The Lost Craft of Leadership.* New York: Facts on File, 1983.

Davis, Stanley M. *Managing Corporate Culture.* Cambridge, Mass.: Ballinger Publishing, 1984.

Derr, C. Brooklyn. "What Value Is Your Management Style?" *Personnel Journal* 66 (June 1987): 74–83.

Fiedler, Fred, and Martin Chemers. *Leadership and Effective Management.* Glenview, Ill.: Scott, Foresman, 1974.

Ford, Jeffrey D. "The Management of Organizational Crises." *Business Horizons* 24 (May/June 1981): 10–16.

Groocock, John M., and Richard A. Beaumont. "How Sound Employee Relations Contribute to Profitability." *AMA Forum* 71 (October 1982): 29–47.

Guest, David, and Robert Horwood. "Characteristics of the Successful Performance Manager." *Personnel Management* 13 (May 1981): 18–23.

Hayes, James L. *Memos for Management Leadership.* New York: Amacom, 1983.

Kirp, D. L., and D. S. Rice. "Fast Forward—Styles of California Management." *Harvard Business Review* 66 (January/February 1988): 74–83.

Kleiner, Brian H. "Tracing the Evolution of Leadership Styles." *Management World* (March 1981): 18–20.

Lattimer, Robert L., and Marvin L. Winitsky. "Unleashing Creativity." *Management World* 13 (April/May 1984): 22–24.

McGregor, Douglas. *Leadership and Motivation.* Cambridge, Mass.: M.I.T. Press, 1966.

May, Gregory D. "The Manager Within." *Personnel Journal* 67 (February 1988): 56–64.

Mintzberg, Henry. *The Nature of Managerial Work.* New York: Harper & Row, 1980.

Peters, Thomas J. "Leadership: Sad Facts and Silver Linings." *Harvard Business Review* (November/December 1979): 164–72.

Plachy, Roger J. "Leading vs. Managing: A Guide to Some Crucial Distinction." *Management Review* 70 (September 1981): 58–61.

Schein, Edgar H. *Organizational Culture and Leadership.* San Francisco, Calif.: Jossey-Bass Publishers, 1985.

Stogdill, R. M. *Handbook of Leadership.* New York: Free Press, 1974.

Vroom, Victor, and Philip Yetton. *Leadership and Decision Making.* Pittsburgh: University of Pittsburgh Press, 1973.

White, Donald D., and David A. Bednar. *Organizational Behavior: Understanding and Managing People at Work.* Boston: Allyn and Bacon, 1986.

Notes

1. Thomas J. Neff, "How to Interview Candidates for Top Management Positions," *Business Horizons* (October 1980): 47–52.

2. For more discussion on leader versus manager, see Joseph L. Massie and John Douglas, *Managing: A Contemporary Introduction* (Englewood Cliffs, N.J.: Prentice-Hall, 1977), 372–73.

3. Abraham Zaleznik, "Managers and Leaders: Are They Different?" *Harvard Business Review* (May/June 1977): 67–78.

4. Theodore Levitt, "Management and the Post-Industrial Society," *Public Interest* (Summer 1976): 73.

5. As an example, see R. D. Mann, "A Review of the Relationship between Personality and Performance in Small Groups," *Psychological Bulletin* 56, no.4 (1959): 241–70.

6. Ralph M. Stogdill, "Personal Factors Associated with Leadership: A Survey of the Literature," *Journal of Psychology* 25 (January 1948): 35–64.

7. Cecil A. Gibb, "Leadership," in *Handbook of Social Psychology*, ed. Gardner Lindzey (Reading, Mass.: Addison-Wesley, 1954).

8. Eugene E. Jennings, "The Anatomy of Leadership," *Management of Personnel Quarterly* 1 (Autumn 1961).

9. Robert Tannenbaum and Warren H. Schmidt, "How to Choose a Leadership Pattern," *Harvard Business Review* (March/April 1957): 95–101.

10. William E. Zierden, "Leading through the Follower's Point of View," *Organizational Dynamics* (Spring 1980): 27–46.

11. Tannenbaum and Schmidt, "How to Choose a Leadership Pattern."

12. Robert Tannenbaum and Warren H. Schmidt, "How to Choose a Leadership Pattern," *Harvard Business Review* (May/June 1973): 162–80.

13. Roger M. Stogdill and Alvin E. Coons, eds., *Leader Behavior: Its Description and Measurement*, Research Monograph no. 88 (Columbus: Ohio State University Bureau of Business Research, 1957).

14. "How Basic Management Principles Pay Off: Lessons in Leadership," *Nation's Business* (March 1977): 46–53.

15. For other discussion of how a leader's minimal amount of structure behavior can increase subordinate productivity, see David Clutterbuck, "Management by Anarchy," *International Management* (May 1980): 30–32.

16. Andrew W. Halpin, *The Leadership Behavior of School Superintendents* (Chicago: University of Chicago Midwest Administration Center, 1959).

17. W. J. Reddin, "The Tridimensional Grid," *Training and Development Journal* (July 1964).

18. A. K. Korman, "'Consideration,' 'Initiating Structure,' and Organizational Criteria—A Review," *Personnel Psychology* 19 (Winter 1966): 349–61.

19. P. Hersey and K. H. Blanchard, "Life Cycle Theory of Leadership," *Training and Development Journal* (May 1969): 26–34.

20. Claude L. Graeff, "The Situational Leadership Theory: A Critical View," *Academy of Management Review* 8, no. 2 (1983): 285–91.

21. Fred E. Fiedler, "Engineer the Job to Fit the Manager," *Harvard Business Review* 43 (September/October 1965): 115–22. See also Fred E. Fiedler, *A Theory of Leadership Effectiveness* (New York: McGraw-Hill, 1967).

22. Rensis Likert, *New Patterns of Management* (New York: McGraw-Hill, 1961).

23. From *A Theory of Leadership Effectiveness*, 255–256 by F. E. Fiedler. Copyright © 1967 by McGraw-Hill, Inc. Used with permission of McGraw-Hill Book Company.

24. Fred E. Fiedler, "How Do You Make Leaders More Effective: New Answers to an Old Puzzle," *Organizational Dynamics* (Autumn 1972): 3–18.

25. Timothy McMahon, "A Contingency Theory: Logic and Method Revisited," *Personnel Psychology* 25 (Winter 1972): 697–710.

Action Summary Answer Key

1. a. c, p. 351
   b. e, p. 351
2. a. F, p. 351
   b. c, p. 351
3. a. c, p. 353
   b. e, pp. 353–354
4. a, e, p. 356
   b. b, pp. 359–361
5. a. a, p. 362
   b. a, pp. 362–363
6. a. d, p. 365
   b. F, p. 367

JOHN EGAN—TOUGH LEADERSHIP RESTORES JAGUAR'S ROAR

In the 1970s and early 1980s, Jaguar had such a bad image it was often the topic of jokes at elite cocktail parties. Its poor reputation for durability led to a joke about selling the cars in pairs so the owner would have one to drive while the other was in the shop. The joke went on to suggest that the cars might also be used as a reliable winter thermometer, since they would start at 33 degrees but not at 32.

John Egan was named chief executive of Jaguar Company, a division of British Leyland, in 1980, and shortly thereafter things at Jaguar began to change. When Egan took the job, he was given a simple mandate—either make the company work or close it down: "We were given a certain amount of borrowing power, and when that was gone, we would have to go." Production had fallen from more than 32,000 cars in 1974 to 13,791 in 1980. The company was losing $1.5 million a week. Sales in the United States, Jaguar's principal overseas market, were down to just 3,000 cars, less than half of 1976 sales.

Egan recalls: "The company was in a terrible state. Morale was low and workmanship poor." He gave the company only a fifty-fifty chance of survival. The automaker's dismal productivity, strike-happy work force, and abysmal quality control were typical of the "British disease" that characterized general business conditions in Britain. "At the time," says Egan, "the country was not a good environment for making anything. The unions had become a completely destructive force, and management at most companies was ineffective. So poor quality and poor productivity were the rule. In addition, Jaguar itself had seen six or seven chief executives over the previous eight years. There was little leadership, and employees were demoralized."

Then Egan took charge and turned the company around in record time. He made it clear to management and workers at the factory that the company's future was on the line. To bring about change, he followed a three-step program, focusing on the poor quality control, then on lagging delivery schedules, and finally on poor productivity.

Correcting these problems was to require harsh measures. Typical of Egan's management style, he reduced labor costs by laying off nearly one-third of Jaguar's 10,000 employees and defying its union to do anything about it. To keep communication lines open with the employees who remained meant "bypassing" the union. "The day I arrived, the workers were all out on

strike. That got me into the job at a run," says Egan. Although workers were protesting a new set of conditions for all British Leyland employees, only Jaguar and one or two other divisions were striking. Egan lost no time making his position clear: "I told the strikers I'd been appointed to run Jaguar as an independent company, and that I thought there was a chance for success. Whereas, if they were all sacked [fired], that would be the end of it for them. It took about a week to resolve the strike, but in the end they decided to give me a try."

With limited time to make the turnaround, Egan first set his sights on quality control. Although customers liked the way the car looked and ran, there were just too many problems with maintenance. "Very simply, we put all our thought and engineering into making a better automobile." This meant sacking a lot of people who weren't doing their jobs right. Egan also initiated an ongoing customer service/market research program to learn about customers' experiences and complaints. In all, about 150 faults were discovered. A full 60 percent could be traced to components from outside suppliers. Egan told the manufacturers they would have to shape up. Those that didn't were dropped.

To control in-house efficiency, senior managers were dispatched to Japan to learn how to use Japanese-style quality control circles. Egan set up multidisciplinary task forces responsible for analyzing and fixing product flaws. Also introduced was a Jaguar innovation: Every car on the production line is rated for various features on a quality index. This allows immediate action to be taken on any faults.

The second step in Jaguar's turnaround was confronting the problem of late deliveries. "It was part of

371

the general British disease that nothing was done on time," says Egan. "If you're introducing a new model in the American market, it should be launched October 1. Our record was very bad; the cars would usually arrive the following March or April. They would, therefore, miss the best part of the selling season." Egan imposed a general crackdown on lateness. The better timing not only improved sales but also gave the company inventory control.

The third step in Egan's plan was to improve productivity. He explains: "First we sacked one-third of them [employees], then we made more cars with the remaining number of people. There were two or three people, it seemed, for every job. When we looked at the factories, we saw too many people standing around." With a work force cut by almost 30 percent, Egan invested heavily in advanced technology to update and streamline production. He also implemented productivity bonuses that would give employees shares of Jaguar's stock. "Everyone receives some kind of bonus,'" he says—hourly workers, staff, and top management.

Probably Egan's most impressive attribute is his style of labor relations. For instance, when management decided to cut an administrative division from three hundred to two hundred workers, the union threatened to call a strike the following Monday. Management identified the hundred workers who were to be cut, and put them outside the gates within two hours, and then explained that there was no use in striking because the workers were already gone. This was obviously a bold move, but it was effective. When the union called its strike, all the remaining two hundred workers stayed on the job.

Egan's tough leadership would not have been possible without the creation of new open communication channels with employees, the most effective being weekly employee briefings by foremen. "Every week the track [assembly line] stops for 20 to 30 minutes while the foreman briefs his troops," Egan says. The foreman's remarks are approved ahead of time, he adds. And if a foreman doesn't know the answer to a question, management tries to provide it within forty-eight hours.

These foreman contacts proved to be especially valuable during salary negotiations. The unions were demanding a 20 percent increase, which Jaguar was unable to give. When it became obvious that their differences were irreconcilable, Jaguar management began negotiating directly with the workers—through the foremen. "It was the most incredible negotiation, done with 10,000 people instead of a few dozen," says Egan. "The discussions going on between management and the unions were irrelevant. The *real* discussions were between the foremen and their troops. They would talk to the men, then come back and talk as a group to us. I met them all, to hear what the men thought of our offer." After these negotiations, the workers accepted a 7.5 percent increase, along with an altered profit-sharing package. The deal was reached over the objections of Jaguar's unions, which were still holding out for 20 percent.

For the first time in twenty years, people have begun boasting about working for Jaguar. Pride has returned, thanks to the leadership of John Egan.

DISCUSSION ISSUES

1. Where would you position John Egan along the Tannenbaum and Schmidt continuum of leadership? Explain.
2. Using the life cycle theory of leadership as your framework, describe the style of leadership Egan should be using at Jaguar.
3. Reflecting on your answer to question 1, and with Fiedler's contingency theory model in mind, would you characterize Egan's leadership style as more "controlling, active, structuring," or more "permissive, passive, considerate"? Explain.
4. Using Fiedler's three primary situational factors (leader-member relations, task structure, and leader position power), determine the situation facing Egan at Jaguar. Is Egan's leadership style (the style you identified in questions 1 and 3) appropriate for the situation? Explain.

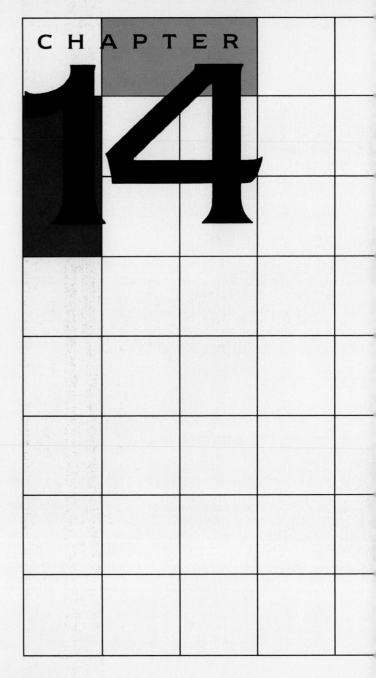
STUDENT LEARNING OBJECTIVES

From studying this chapter, I will attempt to acquire:

1. A basic understanding of human motivation.
2. Insights on various human needs.
3. An appreciation for the importance of motivating organization members.
4. An understanding of various motivation strategies.

MOTIVATION

CHAPTER OUTLINE

NORTH AMERICAN TOOL & DIE, INC.

Shortly after purchasing a small manufacturing company—North American Tool & Die, Inc., a San Leandro, California, manufacturer of computer components on a contract basis—Thomas H. Melohn and Garner Beckett realized that they had only a slightly profitable company and a relatively unenthusiastic work force. Even longtime employees were looking around for better jobs.

Since a concerned and involved work force is generally a prerequisite for a significant company turnaround, the new owners decided to concentrate on motivating the employees. In formulating their strategy, Melohn and Beckett probably asked themselves questions such as: (1) Why are we the only ones to initiate new ideas? (2) Why do our people avoid confronting tough situations facing our business? (3) Why do our middle managers seem to resist innovation? (4) Why are our employees cleaned up and ready to leave the plant fifteen minutes early?

Unfortunately, purchasers of operating companies often inherit problems created by prior owners and managers. Regardless of who created the problems at North American Tool & Die, however, disgruntled employees probably were asking themselves questions such as: (1) Why don't managers ever listen to my suggestions or ideas? (2) How is it that my job has become so boring? (3) For thirty years I have kept quiet and done my job, and for what?

Three years after Melohn and Beckett began their efforts to develop a motivated work force, a much different situation existed at North American Tool & Die. Company sales had tripled, and profits had grown six times. In addition, turnover of the company's seventy employees was almost nonexistent. A few employees told a visitor during a plant tour that they had never imagined that the company could become such a challenging and exciting place to work.

(Courtesy of North American Tool and Die)

Explaining why he and Beckett were so successful in turning their company around, Melohn indicated that when they took over the company, they had four objectives: expanding the company, increasing profits, sharing the wealth with employees, and having everyone experience satisfaction—and even fun—in performing the jobs. Furthermore, Melohn said, he and Beckett decided that the only way to attain these goals was to develop a feeling of trust between themselves and employees. According to Melohn, it was the successful creation of this trust that led to the turnaround in employee morale and, ultimately, to the financial turnaround at North American Tool & Die.

Melohn and Beckett, the new owners of North American Tool & Die in the introductory case, were faced with an unmotivated work force. In three years, they were able to transform dissatisfied, disillusioned workers into an involved, interested, motivated group of employees. The ability to motivate a work force is a skill that is extremely valuable to managers. The material in this chapter, by discussing the motivation process and the steps that can be taken to motivate organization members, explains how Melohn and Beckett could have accomplished the employee transformation.

 THE MOTIVATION PROCESS

To be successful in working with other people, managers first need a thorough understanding of the motivation process. To this end, a definition of *motivation*, various motivation models, and descriptions of people's needs are the main topics of discussion in this section of the chapter.

Defining Motivation

Motivation is the inner state that causes an individual to behave in a way that ensures the accomplishment of some goal.[1] In other words, motivation explains why people behave the way they do. The more managers understand organization members' behavior, the better able they should be to influence that behavior and make it more consistent with the accomplishment of organizational objectives. Since productivity is a result of the behavior of organization members, influencing this behavior is a manager's key to increasing productivity.

Motivation influences productivity.

Motivation Models

Three models that describe how motivation occurs are (1) the needs-goal model, (2) the Vroom expectancy model, and (3) the Porter-Lawler model. These models build on one another to furnish a description of the motivation process that begins at a relatively simple and easily understood level and culminates at a somewhat more intricate and realistic level.

The Needs-Goal Model of Motivation

The **needs-goal model** of motivation (see Figure 14.1) is the most fundamental of the three motivation models discussed in this chapter. As the figure indicates, motivation begins with an individual feeling a need. This need is then transformed into behavior directed at supporting, or allowing, the performance of goal behavior to reduce the felt need. Theoretically, goal-supportive behavior and goal behavior continue until the felt need has been reduced significantly.

For example, when an individual feels hunger (a need), this need typically is transformed first into behavior directed at supporting the performance of the goal behavior of eating. This supportive behavior could include such activities as buying, cooking, and serving the food to be eaten. The goal-supportive behaviors and the goal behavior itself—eating—typically continue until the individual's hunger substantially subsides. Once the individual experiences the hunger again, however, the entire cycle is repeated.

The Vroom Expectancy Model of Motivation

In reality, the motivation process is complex than is depicted by the needs-goal model. The **Vroom expectancy model** of motivation handles some of the additional complexities.[2] As with the needs-goal model, the Vroom expectancy model is based on the premise that felt needs cause human behavior. In addition, however, the Vroom model addresses the issue of **motivation strength**— an individual's degree of desire to perform a behavior. As this desire increases or decreases, motivation strength is said to fluctuate correspondingly.

Vroom's expectancy model is shown in equation form in Figure 14.2. According to this model, motivation strength is determined by the perceived value of the result of performing a behavior and the perceived probability that the behavior performed will cause the result to materialize. As both of these factors increase, the motivation strength, or the desire to perform the behavior, increases. In general, individuals tend to perform the behaviors that maximize personal rewards over the long term.

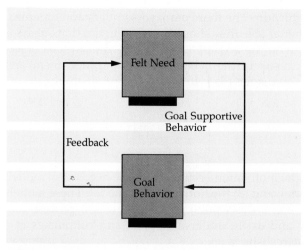

FIGURE 14.1
The needs-goal model of motivation

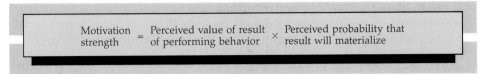

FIGURE 14.2
Vroom's expectancy model of motivation in equation form

An illustration of how Vroom's model applies to human behavior could be a college student who has been offered the summer job of painting three houses at the rate of two hundred dollars a house. Assuming that the student has a need for money, her motivation strength, or desire, to paint the houses is determined by two major factors: her perceived value of six hundred dollars and the perceived probability that she actually can paint the houses satisfactorily and, thus, receive the six hundred dollars. As the perceived value of the six hundred dollar reward and the probability that the houses can be painted satisfactorily increase, the student's motivation strength to paint the houses increases, and vice versa.

The Porter-Lawler Model of Motivation

Porter and Lawler developed a motivation model that presents a more complete description of the motivation process than either the needs-goal model or the Vroom expectancy model.[3] The **Porter-Lawler model** of motivation (see Figure 14.3) is consistent with the prior two models in that it accepts the premises that

The Porter-Lawler model is a more complete model because it stresses the following:

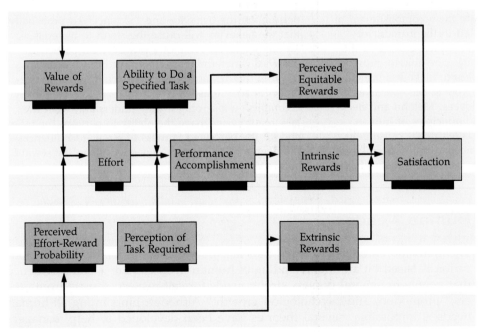

FIGURE 14.3
The Porter-Lawler model of motivation

felt needs cause human behavior and that effort expended to accomplish a task is determined by the perceived value of rewards that will result from the task and the probability that the rewards will materialize. In addition, however, the Porter-Lawler motivation model stresses three other characteristics of the motivation process:

1. Intrinsic and extrinsic rewards.

1. The perceived value of a reward is determined by both intrinsic and extrinsic rewards that result in need satisfaction when a task is accomplished. **Intrinsic rewards** come directly from performing a task, and **extrinsic rewards** are extraneous to the task. For example, when a manager counsels a subordinate about a personal problem, the manager may get some intrinsic reward in the form of personal satisfaction simply from helping another individual. In addition to this intrinsic reward, however, the manager also would receive an extrinsic reward in the form of the overall salary the manager is paid.[4]

2. Task requirements and ability.

2. The extent to which an individual effectively accomplishes a task is determined primarily by two variables: the individual's perception of what is required to perform the task and the individual's ability to perform the task. Naturally, the effectiveness at accomplishing a task increases as the perception of what is required to perform the task becomes more accurate and as the ability to perform the task increases.

3. The perceived fairness of rewards.

3. The perceived fairness of rewards influences the amount of satisfaction produced by those rewards. In general, the more equitable an individual perceives the rewards to be, the greater the satisfaction the individual will experience as a result of receiving them.

BACK TO THE CASE

Motivation is an inner state that causes individuals to act in certain ways that ensure the accomplishment of some goal. Melohn and Beckett in the introductory case obviously had an accurate understanding of the motivation process in that they were able to influence the behavior of their employees to make it more consistent with North American Tool & Die objectives.

To motivate their employees, Melohn and Beckett probably kept five specific principles of human motivation clearly in mind: (1) felt needs cause behavior aimed at reducing those needs, (2) the degree of desire to perform a particular behavior is determined by an individual's perceived value of the result of performing the behavior and the perceived probability that the behavior will cause the result to materialize, (3) the perceived value of a reward for a particular behavior is determined by both intrinsic and extrinsic rewards that result in need satisfaction when the behavior is accomplished, (4) individuals can effectively accomplish a task only if they understand what the task requires and have the ability to perform the task, and (5) the perceived fairness of a reward influences the degree of satisfaction generated when the reward is received.

Human Needs

Understanding motivation requires understanding human needs.

The motivation models discussed thus far imply that an understanding of motivation is based on an understanding of human needs. There is some evidence that people in general possess strong needs for self-respect, respect from others,[5] promotion, and psychological growth.[6] Although pinpointing all human needs is impossible, several theories have been developed to help managers better understand these needs: (1) Maslow's hierarchy of needs, (2) Argyris's maturity-immaturity continuum, and (3) McClelland's achievement motivation.

Maslow's Hierarchy of Needs

Perhaps the most widely accepted description of human needs is the hierarchy of needs concept developed by Abraham Maslow.[7] Maslow states that human beings possess five basic needs: (1) physiological needs, (2) security needs, (3) social needs, (4) esteem needs, and (5) self-actualization needs. He theorizes that these five basic needs can be arranged in a hierarchy of importance—the order in which individuals generally strive to satisfy them. The needs and their relative positions in the hierarchy of importance are shown in Figure 14.4.

Physiological needs relate to the normal functioning of the body. They include the needs for water, rest, sex, and air. Until these needs are met, a significant portion of an individual's behavior is aimed at satisfying them. Once the needs are satisfied, behavior is aimed at satisfying the security needs on the next level of Maslow's hierarchy.

Security, or safety, needs are the needs individuals feel to keep themselves free from harm, including both bodily and economic disaster. Management probably can best help employees satisfy their physiological and security needs through employee salaries, since it is with these salaries that employees can buy such things as food and housing.[8] As security needs are satisfied, behavior tends to be aimed at satisfying social needs.

Social needs include the desire for love, companionship, and friendship. Over all, these needs reflect a person's desire to be accepted by others. As the needs are satisfied, behavior shifts to satisfying esteem needs.

Esteem needs are the desire for respect. They generally are divided into two categories: self-respect and respect for others. Once esteem needs are satisfied, the individual emphasizes satisfying self-actualization needs.

Self-actualization needs are the desire to maximize whatever potential an individual possesses. For example, a high school principal who seeks to satisfy self-actualization needs would strive to become the best principal possible. Self-actualization needs are the highest level of Maslow's hierarchy.

Although many management theorists admit that Maslow's hierarchy can

> Maslow's hierarchy reflects a sequence of satisfaction of needs: physiological, security, social, esteem, and self-actualization.

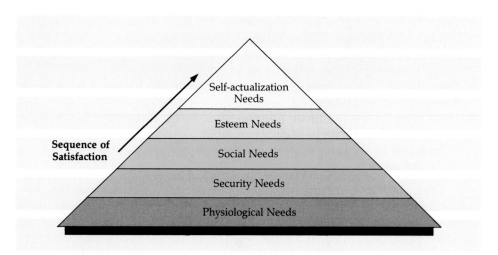

FIGURE 14.4
Maslow's hierarchy of needs

be useful in understanding human needs, they have also expressed concern about the hierarchy. Maslow himself has said:

Maslow's hierarchy should be used cautiously.

> I of all people should know just how shaky this foundation for the theory is as a final foundation. My work on motivation came from the clinic, from a study of neurotic people. The carryover of this theory to the industrial situation has some support from industrial studies, but certainly I would like to see a lot more studies of this kind before feeling finally convinced that this carryover from the study of neurosis to the study of labor in factories is legitimate. The same thing is true of my studies of self-actualizing people—there is only this one study of mine available. There were many things wrong with the sampling, so many in fact that it must be considered to be, in the classical sense anyway, a bad or poor or inadequate experiment. I am quite willing to concede this— because I'm a little worried about this stuff which I consider to be tentative being swallowed whole by all sorts of enthusiastic people who really should be a little more tentative in the way that I am.[9]

Among the concerns related to Maslow's hierarchy are an emphasis on its lack of a research base, [10] a questioning of whether Maslow has accurately pinpointed five basic human needs,[11] and some doubt as to whether human needs actually are arranged in a hierarchy.[12] Despite such concerns, Maslow's hierarchy is probably the most popular conceptualization of human needs to date. The concerns do, however, indicate that Maslow's hierarchy should be considered more a subjective statement than an objective description of human needs.

Argyris's Maturity-Immaturity Continuum

Argyris's maturity-immaturity continuum also furnishes insights on human needs.[13] According to Argyris, as people naturally progress from immaturity to maturity, they move:[14]

1. From a state of passivity as an infant to a state of increasing activity as an adult.
2. From a state of dependence on others as an infant to a state of relative independence as an adult.
3. From being capable of behaving only in a few ways as an infant to being capable of behaving in many different ways as an adult.
4. From having erratic, casual, shallow, and quickly dropped interests as an infant to having deeper interests as an adult.
5. From having a short time perspective as an infant to having a much longer time perspective as an adult.
6. From being in a subordinate position as an infant to aspiring to occupy an equal or superordinate position as an adult.
7. From a lack of awareness of self as an infant to awareness and control over self as an adult.

Argyris has proposed a natural maturation process.

Thus, according to Argyris's continuum, as individuals mature, they have increasing needs for more activity, a state of relative independence, behaving in many different ways, deeper interests, considering a relatively long time perspective, occupying an equal position with other mature individuals, and more awareness of themselves and control over their own destiny. Unlike Maslow's needs, Argyris's needs are not arranged in a hierarchy. Like Maslow's hierarchy, however, Argyris's continuum represents primarily a subjective position on the existence of human needs.

McClelland's Achievement Motivation

Another theory about human needs focuses on the need for achievement. This theory, popularized primarily by David C. McClelland, defines the **need for achievement (n Ach)** as the desire to do something better or more efficiently than it has ever been done before.[15] McClelland claims that in some business-people the need to achieve is so strong that it is more motivating than a quest for profits.[16] To maximize their satisfaction, individuals with high achievement needs tend to set goals for themselves that are challenging yet achievable.[17] Although these individuals do not avoid risk completely, they assess it very carefully. Individuals motivated by the need to achieve do not want to fail and will avoid tasks that involve too much risk. Individuals with a low need for achievement generally avoid challenges, responsibilities, and risk.

McClelland's need for achievement is the desire to do something better than before.

<table>
<tr><td>▮</td><td>BACK TO THE CASE</td></tr>
</table>

Even though Melohn and Beckett undoubtedly understood the basic motivation principle that felt needs cause behavior, they still had to be thoroughly familiar with the various human needs of their employees at North American Tool & Die before they could motivate them.

According to Maslow, people generally possess physiological needs, security needs, social needs, esteem needs, and self-actualization needs arranged in a hierarchy of importance. Argyris suggests that as people mature, they have increasing needs for activity, independence, flexibility, deeper interests, analyses of longer time perspectives, a position of equality with other mature individuals, and control over personal destiny. McClelland believes that the need for achievement—the desire to do something better or more efficiently than it has ever been done before—is a strong human need.

▦ MOTIVATING ORGANIZATION MEMBERS

People are motivated to perform behavior to satisfy personal needs. Therefore, from a managerial viewpoint, motivation is the process of furnishing organization members with the opportunity to satisfy their needs by performing productive behavior within the organization. As discussed in chapter 12, motivation is one of the four primary interrelated activities of the influencing function performed by managers to guide the behavior of organization members toward attainment of organizational objectives. The following sections discuss the importance of and strategies for motivating organization members.

Motivation of organization members requires satisfying human needs through work.

The Importance of Motivating Organization Members

Figure 14.5 on page 383 makes the point that unsatisfied needs of organization members can lead to either appropriate or inappropriate member behavior. Managers who are successful at motivating organization members minimize inappropriate behavior and maximize appropriate behavior. Correspondingly,

Motivation increases appropriate behavior, thereby increasing productivity.

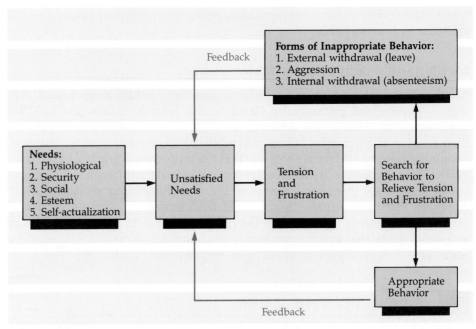

FIGURE 14.5
Unsatisfied needs of organization members resulting in either appropriate or inappropriate behavior

these managers raise the probability that productivity will increase and lower the probability that productivity will decrease.

The "Management in Action" feature for this chapter focuses on the outstanding success of Sam Walton in building the Wal-Mart chain of discount stores. Started just twenty-five years ago, Walton's chain is the fastest growing and perhaps the most influential force in the retailing industry today. Walton's success is attributed primarily to his ability to motivate employees and slash expenses. Certainly, Walton's experience underscores the importance of managers successfully motivating organization members.

Strategies for Motivating Organization Members

Managers have various strategies for motivating organization members. Each strategy is aimed at satisfying people's needs (consistent with those described by Maslow's hierarchy of needs, Argyris's maturity-immaturity continuum, and McClelland's achievement motive) through appropriate organizational behavior.[18] These managerial motivation strategies are (1) managerial communication, (2) Theory X–Theory Y, (3) job design, (4) behavior modification, and (5) Likert's management systems. The strategies are discussed in the sections that follow.

It is important to remember, however, that no single strategy will necessarily always be more effective for a manager than any other. In fact, a manager may find that some combination of these strategies is the most effective strategy in the organizational situation.

Theory Z is the effectiveness dimension.

Reddin proposes a **Theory Z**—an effectiveness dimension that implies that managers who use either Theory X or Theory Y assumptions when dealing with

MOTIVATION IS IMPORTANT TO SAM WALTON AT WAL-MART STORES

When a Wal-Mart discount store opens in your town—which could happen soon if it has not already—keep an eye out for a gray-haired 69-year-old wearing a flannel shirt and khaki pants. He may suddenly appear behind any Wal-Mart checkout counter to help the clerk approve a personal check. Or you may see the same grandfatherly figure driving his red-and-white 1984 Ford pickup through the parking lot, counting customers' cars as he goes. Or he may show up at the loading dock with a bag of doughnuts for a surprised crew of workers. Or, at a new-store opening, he may round up the employees for a pep rally at which he will serve as head cheerleader. "Give me a *W!* Give me an *A!*" he will yell, all the way to the last *T.* "Wal-Mart, we're No. 1!"

Who is this tireless senior citizen? He insists on being addressed as just Sam—or Mr. Sam, if you must—but people who have assessed his net worth call him America's richest man. He is Sam Walton, and the fortune he has amassed as founder and chairman of Wal-Mart Stores is estimated at $4.5 billion and growing. But Walton spends virtually no time counting his money, or even bothering to spend it. He is too busy as one of America's most restless and evangelical corporate leaders. Thanks to his uncanny ability to motivate employees and slash expenses, the chain of discount stores Walton started just 25 years ago has become the fastest-growing and most influential force in the retailing industry. "It's the best-managed company I've ever followed, and I've looked at hundreds," says Margaret Gilliam, a vice president at the First Boston investment firm. . . .

Right now Sam Walton's company is at a critical turning point as it expands beyond its regional, Sunbelt base to become a truly national presence. Can a folksy company with headquarters in the Ozark hill town of Bentonville, Ark. (pop. 9,900), cater to customers from California to New York? So far, shoppers say yes. The chain has opened stores in 23 states, having recently crossed into the Frost Belt states of Wisconsin, Minnesota and Indiana.

At the same time, Wal-Mart is expanding in other directions. It has opened 52 outlets of Sam's Wholesale Club, which are warehouse-style stores of 100,000 sq. ft., or about 2½ acres, that serve mainly as one-stop suppliers for small businesses. Next, taking a cue from Europe's successful hypermarkets, Walton plans to open

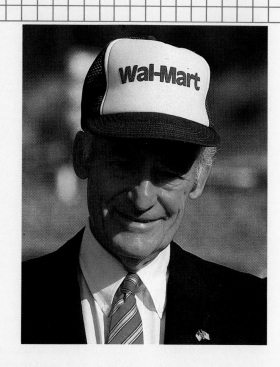

a chain of Wal-Mart Supercenters, which will offer consumers everything from groceries to hardware in one sprawling 220,000-sq.-ft. emporium. The first one, a test model, will debut this fall in a Dallas suburb. . . .

The fervor among Wal-Mart's 151,000 employees is inspired by a Walton philosophy in which ideas and profits are freely shared. All store employees, even the lowliest shelf stockers, are given the title "associate." Wal-Mart operates a liberal profit-sharing plan (1986 disbursements: $52 million) and offers bonuses for specific accomplishments like reducing pilferage. Workers are exhorted to make suggestions. "Most of the good ideas come from the bottom up," says Wal-Mart President David Glass. "We keep changing a thousand little things." . . .

Humility is Wal-Mart's watchword, which filters down from Mr. Sam. The billionaire, whose family owns 38% of the company's stock, lives in Bentonville with his wife Helen in a modest brick-and-wood ranch-style house. Their names are on the mailbox, and it was only a few years ago that they installed a security system. All their children, three sons and a daughter, are grown. Walton typically rises before dawn and eats breakfast at the Ramada Inn coffee shop on his way to work. Along the way he may stop at Barber John Mayhall's for his monthly haircut, for which he pays $5 (no tip). While Bentonville offers few diversions, a favorite Friday-night spot for the Waltons is Fred's Hickory Inn, known for its ribs and cheesecake.

FIGURE 14.6
Theory X, Theory Y, and the
effectiveness dimension Z

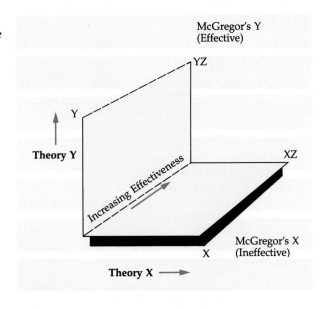

people can be successful, depending on their situation. Figure 14.6 shows Z as
an effectiveness dimension relating to Theory X and Theory Y.

Theory Y is more suc-
cessful in most cases.

The basic rationale for using Theory Y rather than Theory X in most situations is that managerial activities that reflect Theory Y assumptions generally
are more successful in satisfying the human needs of most organization members than are managerial activities that reflect Theory X assumptions. Therefore,
the activities based on Theory Y assumptions generally are more successful in
motivating organization members than are the activities based on Theory X
assumptions.

BACK TO THE CASE

Once Melohn and Beckett's managers understood that
felt needs cause behavior and were aware of people's
different types of needs, they were ready to apply
this information to motivating their work force at
North American Tool & Die. From Melohn and Beckett's viewpoint, motivating the employees meant furnishing them with the opportunity to satisfy their
human needs by performing their jobs. This was very
important to Melohn and Beckett because successful
motivation tends to increase employee productivity. If
Melohn and Beckett had not furnished their employees with an opportunity to satisfy their human needs
while working, low morale within the company probably would have continued. Few employees would
have continued to initiate new ideas, people would
have continued to avoid confronting tough situations,
and middle management would have continued to
resist innovation.

What could Melohn and Beckett actually do to

motivate North American Tool & Die workers? One
strategy they might have followed is merely taking
time to communicate with their employees. Manager-
employee communication can help satisfy employee
needs for recognition, belonging, and security. Another of Melohn and Beckett's strategies might have
been based on McGregor's Theory X–Theory Y concept. In following this concept when dealing with
employees, Melohn and Beckett would have assumed
that work was as natural as play; that employees
could be self-directed in goal accomplishment; that
the granting of rewards encouraged the achievement
of North American Tool & Die objectives; that employees sought and accepted responsibility; and that
most employees were creative, ingenious, and imaginative. The adoption of such assumptions by Melohn
and Beckettt could have led to the satisfaction of
many of the needs defined by Maslow, Argyris, and
McClelland.

Managerial Communication

Perhaps the most basic motivation strategy for managers is simply to communicate well with organization members. This manager-subordinate communication can satisfy such basic human needs as recognition, a sense of belonging, and security.[19] For example, such a simple action as a manager's attempting to become better acquainted with subordinates could contribute substantially to the satisfaction of each of these three needs. As another example, a message from a manager to a subordinate that praises the subordinate for a job well done can help satisfy the subordinate's recognition and security needs. As a general rule, managers should strive to communicate often with other organization members, not only because communication is the primary means of conducting organizational activities but also because it is a basic tool for satisfying the human needs of organization members.

Motivation through communication is one of the simplest strategies.

Theory X—Theory Y

Another motivation strategy involves managers' assumptions about the nature of people. Douglas McGregor identified two sets of assumptions: **Theory X** involves negative assumptions about people that McGregor believes managers often use as the basis for dealing with people. **Theory Y** represents positive assumptions that McGregor believes managers should strive to use.[20] Theory X and Theory Y assumptions are presented in Table 14.1.

McGregor implies that managers who use Theory X assumptions are "bad" and that those who use Theory Y assumptions are "good." Reddin, however, argues that production might be increased by using either Theory X or Theory Y assumptions, depending on the situation the manager faces: "Is there not a strong argument for the position that any theory may have desirable outcomes if

Theory X involves negative assumptions about people. Theory Y involves positive assumptions.

TABLE 14.1

McGregor's Theory X—Theory Y assumptions about the nature of people

Theory X Assumptions	Theory Y Assumptions
The average person has an inherent dislike for work and will avoid it if he or she can.	The expenditure of physical and mental effort in work is as natural as play or rest.
Because of this human characteristic of dislike of work, most people must be coerced, controlled, directed, and threatened with punishment to get them to put forth adequate effort toward the achievement of organizational objectives.	People will exercise self-direction and self-control in the service of objectives to which they are committed.
The average person prefers to be directed, wishes to avoid responsibility, has relatively little ambition, and wants security above all.	Commitment to objectives is a function of the rewards associated with achievement.
	The average person learns, under proper conditions, not only to accept but to seek responsibility.
	The capacity to exercise a relatively high degree of imagination, ingenuity, and creativity in the solution of organizational problems is widely, not narrowly, distributed in the population.

appropriately used? The difficulty is that McGregor had considered only the ineffective application of Theory X and the effective application of Theory Y."[21]

Job Design

A third strategy managers can use to motivate organization members involves the design of jobs that organization members perform. The following two sections discuss earlier and more recent job design strategies.

Earlier Job Design Strategies

Work simplification and specialization has produced job boredom.

A movement has existed in American business to make jobs simpler and more specialized so as to increase worker productivity. Theoretically, this movement is aimed at making workers more productive by enabling them to be more efficient. Perhaps the best example of this movement is the development of the automobile assembly line. A negative result of work simplification and specialization, however, is job boredom. As work becomes simpler and more specialized, it typically becomes more boring and less satisfying to the individuals performing the jobs. As a result, productivity suffers.

With job rotation, individuals move from job to job.

Perhaps the earliest major attempt to overcome job boredom was **job rotation**—moving individuals from job to job or not requiring individuals to perform only one simple and specialized job over the long term. For example, a gardener would do more than just mow lawns. He might also trim bushes, rake grass, and sweep sidewalks. Although job rotation programs have been known to increase organizational profitability, they typically are ineffective, because, over time, individuals become bored with all the jobs they are rotated into.[22] Job rotation programs, however, usually are more effective in achieving other objectives, such as training, by providing individuals with an overview of how the various units of the organization function.

Job enlargement increases the number of tasks an individual performs.

Job enlargement is another strategy developed to overcome the boredom of more simple and specialized jobs. **Job enlargement** means increasing the number of operations an individual performs and, in theory, thereby increasing the individual's satisfaction in work. According to the job enlargement concept, then, the gardener's job would become more satisfying as such activities as trimming bushes, raking grass, and sweeping sidewalks were added to the gardener's initial activity of mowing grass. Some research supports[23] the theory that job enlargement makes jobs more satisfying, and some does not.[24] Job enlargement programs, however, generally have been more successful in increasing job satisfaction than have job rotation programs.

More Recent Job Design Strategies

A number of other job design strategies have evolved since the development of job rotation and job enlargement programs. Two of these more recent strategies are job enrichment and flextime.

Hygiene factors influence job dissatisfaction. Motivating factors influence job satisfaction.

Job Enrichment. Frederick Herzberg has concluded from his research that the degrees of satisfaction and dissatisfaction that organization members feel as a result of performing a job are two different variables determined by two different set of items.[25] The items that influence the degree of job dissatisfaction are called **hygiene, or maintenance, factors.** The items that influence the degree of job satisfaction are called **motivating factors,** or motivators. Hygiene factors relate to the work environment, and motivating factors relate to the work itself. The items that make up Herzberg's hygiene and motivating factors are presented in Table 14.2.

Herzberg has indicated that if hygiene factors are undesirable in a particular job situation, organization members will become dissatisfied. Making these factors more desirable by, for example, increasing salary generally will not motivate people to do a better job, but it will keep them from becoming dissatisfied. In contrast, if motivating factors are high in a particular job situation, organization members generally are motivated to do a better job. In general, people tend to be more motivated and productive as more motivators are built into their job situation.

The process of incorporating motivators into a job situation is called **job enrichment.** Although such companies as Texas Instruments[26] and Volvo[27] have reported notable success in motivating organization members through job enrichment programs, experience indicates that for a job enrichment program to be successful, it must be carefully designed and administered.[28] An outline of a successful job enrichment program is presented in Table 14.3, p. 390.

> Job enrichment entails incorporating motivators into the job situation.

Herzberg's overall findings indicate that the most productive organization members are involved in work situations characterized by desirable hygiene factors and motivating factors. The needs on Maslow's hierarchy of needs that desirable hygiene factors and motivating factors generally satisfy are shown in Figure 14.7 on page 390. Esteem needs can be satisfied by both types of factors. An example of esteem needs satisfied by a hygiene factor could be a private parking space—a status symbol and a working condition evidencing the importance of the organization member. An example of esteem needs satisfied by a motivating factor could be an award received for outstanding performance—a display of importance through recognition of a job well done.

Flextime. Another more recent job design strategy for motivating organization members is based on a concept called flextime. Perhaps the most common traditional characteristic of work in the United States is that jobs are performed within a fixed eight-hour workday. Recently, however, this tradition has been challenged. Faced with motivation problems and absenteeism, many managers have turned to scheduling innovations as a possible solution.[29]

TABLE 14.2

Herzberg's hygiene factors and motivators

Dissatisfaction: Hygiene or Maintenance Factors	Satisfaction: Motivating Factors
1. Company policy and administration	1. Opportunity for achievement
2. Supervision	2. Opportunity for recognition
3. Relationship with supervisor	3. Work itself
4. Relationship with peers	4. Responsibility
5. Working conditions	5. Advancement
6. Salary	6. Personal growth
7. Relationship with subordinates	

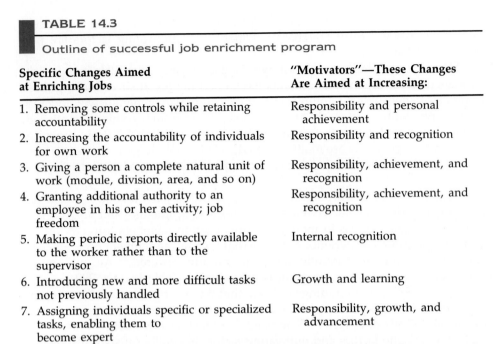

TABLE 14.3

Outline of successful job enrichment program

Specific Changes Aimed at Enriching Jobs	"Motivators"—These Changes Are Aimed at Increasing:
1. Removing some controls while retaining accountability	Responsibility and personal achievement
2. Increasing the accountability of individuals for own work	Responsibility and recognition
3. Giving a person a complete natural unit of work (module, division, area, and so on)	Responsibility, achievement, and recognition
4. Granting additional authority to an employee in his or her activity; job freedom	Responsibility, achievement, and recognition
5. Making periodic reports directly available to the worker rather than to the supervisor	Internal recognition
6. Introducing new and more difficult tasks not previously handled	Growth and learning
7. Assigning individuals specific or specialized tasks, enabling them to become expert	Responsibility, growth, and advancement

Flextime allows workers to arrange their own workweek hours.

The main purpose of these scheduling innovations is not to reduce the total number of work hours but to provide workers with greater flexibility in the exact hours during which they must perform their jobs. The main thrust of **flextime,** or flexible working hours programs, is that it allows workers to complete their

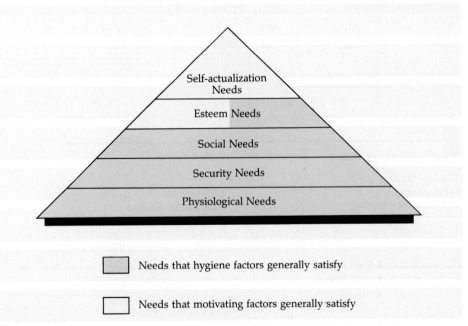

FIGURE 14.7
Needs on Maslow's hierarchy that desirable hygiene factors and motivating factors generally satisfy

TABLE 14.4

Advantages and disadvantages of using flextime programs

Advantages	Disadvantages
Improved employee attitude and morale	Lack of supervision during some hours of work
Accommodation of working parents	
Decreased tardiness	Key people unavailable at certain times
Fewer traffic problems—workers can avoid congested streets and highways	Understaffing at times
Accommodation of those who wish to arrive at work before interruptions begin	Problem of accommodating employees whose output is the input for other employees
Increased production	Employee abuse of flextime program
Facilitation of employee scheduling of medical, dental, and other types of appointments	Difficulty in planning work schedules
	Problem of keeping track of hours worked or accumulated
Accommodation of leisure-time activities of employees	Inability to schedule meetings at convenient times
Decreased absenteeism	Inability to coordinate projects
Decreased turnover	

jobs within a workweek (of a normal number of hours) that they arrange themselves.[30] The choices of starting and finishing times can be as flexible as the organizational situation allows. To ensure that flexibility does not become counterproductive within the organization, many flextime programs include a core period during which all employees must be on the job.

Various kinds of organizational studies have indicated that flextime programs have some positive organizational effects. Douglas Fleuter, for example, has reported that flextime contributes to greater job satisfaction, which typically results in greater productivity.[31] Other research concludes that flextime programs can result in higher motivation levels of workers.[32] (A listing of the advantages and disadvantages of flextime programs appears in Table 14.4.) Although many well-known companies, such as Scott Paper, Sun Oil, and Samsonite, have adopted flextime programs,[33] more research must be conducted to conclusively assess its true worth.

BACK TO THE CASE

Melohn and Beckett could have used two major job design strategies to motivate their employees at North American Tool & Die. With job enrichment, Melohn and Beckett could have incorporated into employee jobs such motivating factors as opportunities for achievement, recognition, and personal growth. However, for maximum success, hygiene factors at North American Tool & Die—company policy and administration, supervision, salary, and working conditions, for example—also would have had to be perceived as desirable by employees.

The second major job design strategy that Melohn and Beckett could have used to motivate their employees is flextime. With flextime, the employees would have some freedom in scheduling the beginning and ending of workdays. Of course, this freedom would have been somewhat limited by such organizational factors as seasonal demand or peak selling seasons.

Behavior Modification

A fourth strategy that managers can use in motivating organization members is based primarily on a concept known as behavior modification. As stated by B. F. Skinner, the Harvard psychologist considered by many to be the "father" of behavioral psychology, **behavior modification** focuses on encouraging appropriate behavior as a result of the consequences of that behavior.[34] According to the law of effect,[35] behavior that is rewarded tends to be repeated and behavior that is punished tends to be eliminated. Although behavior modification programs typically involve the administration of both rewards and punishments, rewards generally are emphasized, since they typically are more effective than punishments in influencing behavior. Obviously, the main theme of behavior modification is not new.[36]

Behavior modification theory asserts that if managers want to modify subordinates' behavior, they must ensure that appropriate consequences occur as a result of that behavior.[37] **Positive reinforcement** is a desirable consequence of a behavior, and **negative reinforcement** is the elimination of an undesirable consequence of a behavior. If a worker's arriving on time is positively reinforced, or rewarded, the probability increases that the worker will arrive on time more often. In addition, if the worker experiences some undesirable outcome on arriving late for work, such as a verbal reprimand, the worker is negatively reinforced when this outcome is eliminated by on-time arrival. According to behavior modification theory, positive reinforcement and negative reinforcement are both rewards that increase the likelihood that behavior will continue.

Punishment is the presentation of an undesirable behavioral consequence or the removal of a desirable behavioral consequence that decreases the likelihood of the behavior continuing.[38] Extending the earlier example, managers could punish employees for arriving late for work by exposing them to some undesirable consequence, such as a verbal reprimand, or by removing a desirable consequence, such as their wages for the amount of time they are late.[39] Although this punishment probably would quickly cause workers to come to work on time, it might be accompanied by undesirable side effects, such as high levels of absenteeism and turnover, if it were emphasized over the long term.

Behavior modification programs have been applied both successfully and unsuccessfully in a number of organizations.[40] The behavior modification efforts of Emery Air Freight Company, now called Emery Worldwide, resulted in the finding that the establishment and use of an effective feedback system is extremely important in making a behavior modification program successful.[41] This feedback should be aimed at keeping employees informed of the relationship between various behaviors and their consequences. Other ingredients that successful behavior modification programs include are (1) giving different levels of rewards to different workers depending on the quality of their performance, (2) telling workers what they are doing wrong, (3) punishing workers privately so as not to embarrass them in front of others, and (4) always giving rewards and punishments when earned to emphasize that management is serious about behavior modification efforts.[42]

Likert's Management Systems

Another strategy that managers can use for motivating organization members is based on the work of Rensis Likert.[43] As a result of studying several types and sizes of organizations, Likert has concluded that management styles in organizations can be categorized into the following systems:[44]

System 1 This style of management involves having no confidence or trust in subordinates. Subordinates do not feel free to discuss their jobs with superiors and are motivated by fear, threats, punishments, and occasional rewards. Information flow is directed primarily downward, and upward communication is viewed with great suspicion. The bulk of all decision making is at the top of the organization. (The cartoon shows how a manager with a system 1 management style might interact with a subordinate.)

System 1—treating people poorly.

System 2 This style of management involves condescending confidence and trust (such as master to servant) in subordinates. Subordinates do not feel very free to discuss their jobs with superiors and are motivated by rewards and some actual or potential punishment. Information flows mostly downward, and upward communication may or may not be viewed with suspicion. Although policies are made primarily at the top of the organization, decisions within a prescribed framework are made at lower levels.

System 2—treating people less poorly.

System 3 This style of management involves having substantial, but not complete, confidence in subordinates. Subordinates feel fairly free to discuss their jobs with superiors and are motivated by rewards, occasional punishment, and some involvement. Information flows both upward and downward. Upward communication is often accepted but at times may be viewed with suspicion. Although broad policies and general decisions are made at the top of the organization, more specific decisions are made at lower levels.

System 3—treating people fairly well.

System 4 This style of management involves having complete trust and confidence in subordinates. Subordinates feel completely free to discuss their jobs with superiors and are motivated by such factors as economic rewards based on a compensation system developed through participation and involvement in goal setting. Information flows upward, downward, and horizontally. Upward communication is generally accepted. However, if it is

System 4—treating people extremely well.

"I'm just a number here, like you, Caswell—but a higher number."
New Yorker, *May 4, 1987, p. 134. Drawing by Vietor; © 1987 The New Yorker Magazine, Inc.*

not, related questions are asked candidly. Decision making is spread widely throughout the organization and is well coordinated.

Likert has suggested that as the management style moves from system 1 to system 4, the human needs of individuals within the organization tend to be more effectively satisfied over the long term. Thus, as the organization moves toward system 4, it tends to become more productive over the long term.

Figure 14.8 illustrates the comparative long- and short-term effects of both system 1 and system 4 on organizational production. Managers may increase production in the short term by using a system 1 management style, since motivation by fear, threat, and punishment is generally effective in the short term. Over the long term, however, this style usually causes production to decrease, primarily because of the long-term nonsatisfaction of organization members' needs and the poor working relationships between managers and subordinates.

Conversely, managers who initiate a system 4 management style probably face some decline in production intially but an increase in production over the long term. The short-term decline occurs because managers must implement a new system to which organization members must adapt. The production increase over the long term materializes as a result of organization members' adjustment to the new management system, greater satisfaction of the human needs of organization members, and the good working relationships that tend to develop between managers and subordinates.

Likert has offered his **principle of supportive relationships** as the basis for management activity aimed at developing a system 4 management style. This principle states:

> The leadership and other processes of the organization must be such as to ensure a maximum probability that in all interactions and in all relationships within the organization, each member in light of his or her background, values,

FIGURE 14.8
Comparative long-term and short-term effects of system 1 and system 4 on organizational production

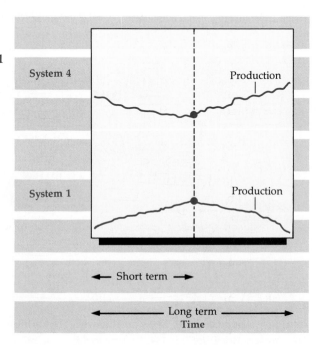

desires, and expectations will view the experience as supportive and one which builds and maintains his or her sense of personal worth and importance.[45]

■ BACK TO THE CASE

Melohn and Beckett could have applied behavior modification to their situation at North American Tool & Die by rewarding appropriate employee behavior and punishing inappropriate employee behavior. Punishment would have had to have been used very carefully, however. If used continually, the working relationship between Melohn and Beckett and their employees would have been destroyed. For the behavior modification program to have been successful, Melohn and Beckett would have had to furnish employees with feedback on which behaviors were appropriate and inappropriate, to have given workers different rewards depending on the quality of their performance, to have told workers what they were doing wrong, to have punished workers privately, and to have consistently given rewards and punishments when earned.

To have used Likert's system 4 management style to motivate employees over the long term, Melohn and Beckett would have had to demonstrate complete confidence in their workers and to encourage workers to feel completely free to discuss prob-

lems with them. In addition, communication at North American Tool & Die would have had to flow freely in all directions within the organization structure, with upward communication generally discussed candidly. Melohn and Beckett's decision-making process under system 4 would have had to involve many employees. Melohn and Beckett could have used the principle of supportive relationships as the basis for their system 4 management style. Melohn stated in the introductory case that he and Beckett believed that the development of a real feeling of trust between themselves and their employees was critical to the attainment of organizational goals. This statement definitely reflects a system 4 management style.

No single strategy mentioned in this chapter for motivating organization members would necessarily be more valuable to managers such as Melohn and Beckett than any other of the strategies. In reality, Melohn and Beckett could have easily found that some combination of all of these strategies was most useful in motivating the work force at North American Tool & Die.

Action Summary

Reread the learning objectives that follow. Each objective is followed by questions. Answering these questions accurately will help you retain the most important concepts discussed in this chapter. After answering each question, check your answer with the answer key at the end of this chapter. (*Hint:* If you have doubt regarding the correct response, consult the page whose number follows the answer.)

From studying this chapter, I will attempt to acquire:	**Circle:**

1. **A basic understanding of human motivation.**
   a. An individual's inner state that causes him or her to behave in such a way as to ensure accomplishment of a goal is: (a) ambition; (b) drive; (c) motivation; (d) need; (e) leadership. — a, b, c, d, e
   b. According to the needs-goal model, a fulfilled need is a motivator. — T, F
   c. Which of the following most comprehensively describes how motivation takes place: (a) the Vroom expectancy model; (b) the needs-goal model; (c) the Porter-Lawler model; (d) all of the above; (e) none of the above. — a, b, c, d, e

2. **Insights on various human needs.**
   a. Which of the following is a rank-ordered listing of Maslow's hierarchy of needs from lowest to highest: (a) self-actualization, social, security, physi- — a, b, c, d, e

ological, esteem; (b) social, security, physiological, self-actualization; (c) esteem, self-actualization, security, social, physiological; (d) physiological, security, social, esteem, self-actualization; (e) physiological, social, esteem, security, self-actualization.

a, b, c, d, e   b. According to Argyris, as individuals mature, they have an increasing need for: (a) greater dependence; (b) a shorter-term perspective; (c) more inactivity; (d) deeper interests; (e) youth.

a, b, c, d, e   c. The desire to do something better or more efficiently than it has ever been done before is known as the need for: (a) acceleration; (b) achievement; (c) acclamation; (d) actualization; (e) none of the above.

3. An appreciation for the importance of motivating organization members.

T, F   a. From a managerial veiwpoint, motivation is the process of furnishing organization members with the opportunity to satisfy their needs by performing productive behavior within the organization.

T, F   b. The concepts of motivation and appropriate behavior are closely related.

4. An understanding of various motivation strategies.

a, b, c, d, e   a. Which of the following is a Theory Y assumption: (a) the average person prefers to be directed; (b) most people must be threatened and coerced before they will put forth adequate effort; (c) commitment to objectives is a function of the rewards associated with achievement; (d) the average person seeks no responsibility; (e) all of the above.

a, b, c, d, e   b. The process of incorporating motivators into the job situation is called: (a) job enlargement; (b) flextime; (c) satisfying; (d) job enrichment; (e) Theory X.

a, b, c, d, e   c. Successful behavior modification programs can include: (a) giving rewards and punishments when earned; (b) giving rewards according to performance quality; (c) telling workers what they are doing wrong; (d) punishing workers privately; (e) all of the above.

INTRODUCTORY CASE WRAP-UP

"North American Tool & Die, Inc." (p. 376), and its related back-to-the-case sections were written to help you better understand the management concepts contained in this chapter. Answer the following discussion questions about this introductory case to further enrich your understanding of chapter content:

1. Do you think it is unusual for managers such as Melohn and Beckett to be faced with the challenge of motivating a work force? Explain.

2. What could the previous owners have done to alienate their employees to the extent indicated by the case?

3. It took three years for Melohn and Beckett to develop their motivated work force. Could they have realistically expected to accomplish this task sooner? Explain.

Issues for Review and Discussion

1. Define *motivation* and explain why managers should understand it.

2. Draw and explain the needs-goal model of motivation.

3. Summarize Vroom's expectancy model of motivation.

4. List and explain three characteristics of the motivation process contained in the Porter-

Lawler motivation model that are not contained in either the needs-goal model or Vroom's expectancy model.

5. What does Maslow's hierarchy of needs tell us about people's needs?
6. What concerns have been expressed about Maslow's hierarchy of needs?
7. Describe Argyris's maturity-immaturity continuum.
8. What is the need for achievement?
9. Summarize the characteristics of individuals who have high needs for achievement.
10. What does "motivating organization members" mean?
11. Is the process of motivating organization members important to managers? Explain.
12. How can managerial communication be used to motivate organization members?

13. What are Theory X, Theory Y, and Theory Z? What does each of these theories tell us about motivating organization members?
14. What is the difference between job enlargement and job rotation?
15. Describe the relationship of hygiene factors, motivating factors, and job enrichment.
16. Define *flextime.*
17. Define *behavior modification.*
18. What basic ingredients are necessary to make a behavior modification program successful?
19. In your own words, summarize Likert's four management systems.
20 What effect do Likert's systems 1 and 4 generally have on organizational production in both the short and long term? Why do these effects occur?

Sources of Additional Information

Argyris, C. *Integrating the Individual and the Organization.* New York: Wiley, 1964.

Arnold, Hugh J. "A Test of the Validity of the Multiplicative Hypothesis of Expectancy-Valence Theories of Work Motivation." *Academy of Management Journal* 24 (March 1981): 128–41.

Davis, Keith, and John W. Newstrom. *Human Behavior at Work: Organizational Behavior.* 7th ed. New York: McGraw-Hill, 1985.

Freedman, Sara M., and John R. Montanari. "An Integrative Model of Managerial Reward Allocation." *Academy of Management Review* 5, no. 3 (1900): 381–90.

Gardner, Jerry. "Creating Motivating Workplaces." *Personnel Journal* (May 1981): 406–408.

Glatthorn, Allan A., and Herbert R. Adama. *Listening Your Way to Management Success.* Glenview, Ill.: Scott, Foresman, 1983.

Hanna, John B. "Assessing Your People Potential." *Management World* 13 (April/May 1984): 30–31.

Kanter, Rosabeth Moss, and Barry A. Stein. "Ungluing the Stuck: Motivating Performance and Productivity through Expanding Opportunity." *Management Review* 70 (July 1981): 45–49.

Lawler, E. E. *Pay and Organizational Effectiveness.* New York: McGraw-Hill, 1971.

Locke, Edwin A. "The Nature and Causes of Job Satisfaction." In *Handbook of Industrial and Organizational Psychology,* edited by M. D. Dunnette. Chicago: Rand McNally, 1976.

Magnus, Margaret. "Employee Recognition: A Key to Motivation." *Personnel Journal* (February 1981): 103–107.

Miner, John B. *Organizational Behavior: Performance and Productivity.* New York: Random House, 1988.

Mischkind, Louis A. "Is Employee Morale Hidden behind Statistics?" *Personnel Journal* 65 (February 1986): 74–79.

Ryans, Adrian B., and Charles B. Weinberg. "Improving Productivity in the Sales Force—Learning from Our Own Experience: A Company-Focused Approach." *Business Quarterly* (Spring 1984): 67–69.

Seybolt, John W. "Dealing with Premature Employee Turnover." *California Management Review* 25 (Spring 1983): 107–17.

Skinner, B. F. *Beyond Freedom and Dignity.* New York: Knopf, 1971.

Steers, Richard M., and Lyman W. Porter, eds. *Motivation and Work Behavior,* 3rd ed. New York: McGraw-Hill, 1983.

Vroom, Victor H. *Work and Motivation.* New York: Wiley, 1982.

Notes

1. Bernard Berelson and Gary A. Steiner, *Human Behavior: An Inventory of Scientific Findings* (New York: Harcourt, Brace, and World, 1964), 239–40.
2. Victor H. Vroom, *Work and Motivation* (New York: Wiley, 1964).
3. L. W. Porter and E. E. Lawler, *Managerial Attitudes and Performance* (Homewood, Ill.: Richard D. Irwin, 1968).
4. For more information on intrinsic and extrinsic rewards, see H. J. Arnold, "Task Performance, Perceived Competence, and Attributed Causes of Performance as Determinants of Intrinsic Motivation," *Academy of Management Journal* 28 (December 1985): 876–88.
5. *Work in America: Report of the Special Task Force to the Secretary of Health, Education, and Welfare* (Cambridge, Mass.: M.I.T. Press, 1972).
6. H. Sheppard and N. Herrick, *Where Have All the Robots Gone?* (New York: Free Press, 1972).
7. Abraham Maslow, *Motivation and Personality*, 2d ed. (New York: Harper & Row, 1970).
8. Allen Flamion, "The Dollars and Sense of Motivation," *Personnel Journal* (January 1980): 51–53.
9. Abraham Maslow, *Eupsychian Management* (Homewood, Ill.: Richard D. Irwin, 1965).
10. Jack W. Duncan, *Essentials of Management* (Hinsdale, Ill.: Dryden Press, 1975), 105.
11. C. P. Adlerfer, "An Empirical Test of a New Theory of Human Needs," *Organizational Behavior and Human Performance* 4, no. 2 (1969): 142–75.
12. D. T. Hall and K. Nougaim, "An Examination of Maslow's Need Hierarchy in an Organizational Setting," *Organizational Behavior and Human Performance* 3, no. 1 (1968): 12–35.
13. Chris Argyris, *Personality and Organization* (New York: Harper & Bros., 1957).
14. Argyris, *Personality and Organization.*
15. David C. McClelland, "Power Is the Great Motivator," *Harvard Business Review* (March/April 1976): 100–10.
16. David C. McClelland and David G. Winter, *Motivating Economic Achievement* (New York: Free Press, 1969).
17. Burt K. Scanlan, "Creating a Climate for Achievement," *Business Horizons* 24 (March/April 1981): 5–9.
18. William H. Franklin, Jr., "Why You Can't Motivate Everyone," *Supervisory Management* (April 1980): 21–28.
19. Edwin Timbers, "Strengthening Motivation through Communication," *Advanced Management Journal* 31 (April 1966): 64–69.
20. Douglas McGregor, *The Human Side of Enterprise* (New York: McGraw-Hill, 1960).
21. W. J. Reddin, "The Tri-Dimensional Grid," *Training and Development Journal* (July 1964).
22. For more discussion on the implications of job rotation in organizations, see Alan W. Farrant, "Job Rotation Is Important," *Supervision* (August 1987): 14–16.
23. L. E. Davis and E. S. Valfer, "Intervening Responses to Changes in Supervisor Job Designs," *Occupational Psychology* (July 1965): 171–90.
24. M. D. Kilbridge, "Do Workers Prefer Larger Jobs?" *Personnel* (September/October 1960): 45–48.
25. This section is based on Frederick Herzberg, "One More Time: How Do You Motivate Employees?" *Harvard Business Review* (January/February 1968): 53–62.
26. Scott M. Meyers, "Who Are Your Motivated Workers?" *Harvard Business Review* (January/February 1964): 73–88.
27. John M. Roach, "Why Volvo Abolished the Assembly Line," *Management Review* (September 1977): 50.
28. Richard J. Hackman, "Is Job Enrichment Just a Fad?" *Harvard Business Review* (September/October 1975): 129–38.
29. E. G. Thomas, "Flexible Work Keeps Growing," *Management World* 15 (April/May 1986): 43–45.
30. D. A. Bratton, "Moving Away from Nine to Five," *Canadian Business Review* 13 (Spring 1986): 15–17.
31. Douglas L. Fleuter, "Flextime—A Social Phenomenon," *Personnel Journal* (June 1975): 318–19.
32. Lee A. Graf, "An Analysis of the Effect of Flexible Working Hours on the Management Functions of the First-Line Supervisor" (Ph.D. diss., Mississippi State University, 1976).
33. William Wong, "Rather Come in Late or Go Home Earlier? More Bosses Say OK," *Wall Street Journal*, July 12, 1973, 1.
34. B. F. Skinner, *Contingencies of Reinforcement* (New York: Appleton-Century-Crofts, 1969.
35. E. L. Thorndike, "The Original Nature of Man," *Educational Psychology* 1 (1903).
36. Keith E. Barenklaw, "Behavior Reinforcement," *Industrial Supervisor* (February 1976): 6–7.
37. Fred Luthans and Robert Kreitner, *Organizational Behavior Modification and Beyond* (Glenview, Ill.: Scott, Foresman, 1985).
38. Richard D. Arvey and John M. Ivancevich, "Punishment in Organizations: A Review, Proposal, and Research Suggestions," *Academy of Management Journal* (January 1980): 123–32; P. M. Padsokaff, "Rela-

tionships between Leader Reward and Punishment Behavior and Group Process and Productivity,'' *Journal of Management* 11 (Spring 1985): 55–73.

39. For another practical discussion on punishment, see Bruce R. McAfee and William Poffenberger, *Productivity Strategies: Enhancing Employee Job Performance* (Englewood Cliffs, N.J.: Prentice-Hall, Spectrum, 1982).

40. Ricky W. Griffin and Gregory Moorhead, *Organizational Behavior* (Boston: Houghton Mifflin, 1986), 183–89.

41. ''New Tool: Reinforcement for Good Work,'' *Psychology Today* (April 1972): 68–69.

42. W. Clay Hamner and Ellen P. Hamner, ''Behavior Modification on the Bottom Line,'' *Organizational Dynamics* 4 (Spring 1976): 6–8.

43. Rensis Likert, *New Patterns of Management* (New York: McGraw-Hill, 1961).

44. These descriptions are based on the table of organizational and performance characteristics of different management systems in Rensis Likert, *The Human Organization* (New York: McGraw-Hill, 1967), 4–10.

45. Likert, *New Patterns of Management*, 103.

Action Summary Answer Key

1. a. c, p. 377
   b. F, p. 378
   c. c, pp. 379–380
2. a. d, p. 381
   b. d, p. 382
   c. b, p. 383
3. a. T, p. 383
   b. T, p. 383
4. a. c, p. 387
   b. d, pp. 388–389
   c. e, p. 392

CLIMBING TO THE TOP— THE MOTIVATION BEHIND THE MAN

As if by fiendish design, the highest points on earth loom tantalizingly at the limits of mankind's physiological reach. Mountaineers and M.D.s agree that above 8,000 m (26,246 ft.), a physical curtain begins to fall. Higher than this, the air is so thin that ordinary people can live for only several hours—if at all. Trapped in the so-called death zone, says one climber who is familiar with these altitudes, "you can't shout for help anymore. You lose your sense of logic. And you die in euphoria, overestimating your own strength."

Only 14 summits, all of them in the crescent of mountains that runs from northern Pakistan southeast along the Himalayan chain to Sikkim, exceed this mysterious boundary between life and death. To climbers they are known as the eight-thousanders. And many of them, including Mount Everest, were conquered by mountaineers who fudged a little: they used bottled air. No one had ever conquered all 14—much less without oxygen—until [October 1986], when Reinhold Messner, 42, a brash, blond-bearded native of Italy's South Tirol, stood triumphantly atop Lhotse, the world's fourth highest mountain. Having conquered 13 other eight-thousanders in the past 16 years, all without oxygen, Messner had completed mountaineering's grand slam.

The sport's acknowledged master began knocking off the highest mountains in 1970, when he scaled Nanga Parbat (26,657 ft.) in the glacier-shrouded western bastion of the chain. Then he climbed Manaslu (26,781 ft.) in central Nepal and Pakistan's Gasherbrum I (26,470 ft.) with Peter Habeler, a longtime climbing partner. In 1978 Messner and Habeler, now 44, climbed oxygenless to the summit of Mount Everest (29,028 ft.), and the mountaineering world gasped. In 1979 Messner went back to the Pakistan-China border and conquered K2 (28,251 ft.), the world's second highest mountain, and, to top that, lumbered up Everest again in 1980, this time all by himself.

After climbing three more, Kangchenjunga (28,169 ft.), Gasherbrum II (26,361 ft.) and Broad Peak (26,401 ft.), it seemed that he had exhausted the possibilities. Or had he? "It was in 1982," he says, "after my hat trick, after the first time I was able to climb three mountains in one season, that I understood it was easy, or at least it was possible, for one human being to climb all the highest mountains in the world, all 14 eight-thousanders, in a lifetime."

It has not been easy. [In September] Messner made three separate attempts to conquer Makalu (27,765 ft.). On his last try, he [said] in a radio interview from base camp, "you could do 20 to 25 steps, and you had to stop for a while and breathe deeply ten to 20 times." [October's] triumph on Lhotse took only one attempt. Delayed an hour by adverse weather conditions, Messner and Partner Hans Kammerlander gained the summit with a moderating wind at their backs.

In Europe, especially in West Germany, Messner is a media darling, with an ebullient personality to match his outsize ambitions. He is the author (without any ghost) of numerous magazine stories chronicling his exploits, and he usually carries the photo credit as well. In addition, he has written 24 books, which have sold roughly 500,000 copies worldwide.

Messner has been called tactless and egocentric by his critics. After his solo ascent of Everest, for example, he told admiring fellow South Tyroleans, "I do this for myself because I am my own fatherland, and my handkerchief is my flag." On talk-show stints, he tends to shout down other guests. Indeed, a mountaineer who has known him for years thinks fame has been hard on a man who finds peace in solitude: "Everyone wants to shake his hand." He is divorced from West German Journalist Uschi Demeter, and lately, says one Messner watcher, "it seems there is a different woman in every base camp."

One secret of his mountaineering successes is that he travels light, as he might to climb an Alpine peak. The legendary pinnacles are, to him, small ascents stacked one on top of another. He scales the earth's greatest heights by what he calls "fair means," avoiding the rope networks, high-mountain camps and bottled air that were part of the historic eight-thousander sieges, which frequently involved ten or more climbers supported by dozens of Sherpas. The minimalist technique has attracted thousands of imitators. Says Swiss Mountain Guide Erhard Loretan, 27, who with his countryman Jean Troillet, 38, raced to the top of Everest last August and back down again to base camp in an astonishing 43 hours: "The reason we can now climb so quickly and easily is that Messner served as an example for us."

Indeed, his breakthroughs have led many to believe he has a mysterious physical edge over other mountaineers. Not so, says Oswald Oelz, a Swiss physician and one of Messner's former climbing partners, who conducted a series of tests on high-altitude climbers in a hypobaric chamber. Messner emerged with results similar to those of an above-average marathon runner. He and other mountaineers who had successfully penetrated the 8,000-m barrier proved to have what Oelz calls a "rather active respiratory center," meaning that as the air gets thinner, their rate of breathing involuntarily increases. "He's obviously got a superb high-altitude phy-sique," says Chris Bonington, who in 1975 led a successful British expedition to Mount Everest, "but what has given him the edge over everyone is creative innovation. There is a wall called 'impossible' that the great mass of people in any field face. Then one person who's got a kind of extra imaginative drive jumps that wall. That's Reinhold Messner."

DISCUSSION ISSUES

1. Using Maslow's hierarchy of needs as the framework, list the need categories that appear to underlie (be the motivating factors for) Messner's behavior. Give examples from the case to support the categories you identify.
2. Given Messner's emphasis on certain needs as established in question 1, use the basic determinants of the Porter-Lawler model to explain Messner's behavior in the satisfaction of these needs.
3. Messner's motivating forces appear to be derived intrinsically. Consider intrinsic and extrinsic factors to motivate employees. Which do you think would be the most effective motivators? Explain.
4. How can a manager use the needs-goal model to increase organizational effectiveness?

STUDENT LEARNING OBJECTIVES

From studying this chapter, I will attempt to acquire:

1. A definition of the term *group* as used within the context of management.
2. A thorough understanding of the difference between formal and informal groups.
3. Knowledge of the types of formal groups that exist in organizations.
4. An understanding of how managers can determine which groups exist in an organization.
5. An appreciation for how managers must evaluate formal and informal groups simultaneously to maximize work group effectiveness.

MANAGING GROUPS

CHAPTER OUTLINE

A MEETING ABOUT MANAGING GROUPS

All five vice-presidents of the Crutch Athletic Equipment Company were gathered for a special meeting. From the conversation taking place, it was easy to tell that none of the five knew what the meeting was about. Each had received a memo about the meeting from Jesse Flick, the president of the company, but the memo had given no hint as to the meeting's purpose.

Flick walked into the room, greeted everyone present, sat down, and then began the following speech:

> As you know, ladies and gentlemen, our company over the past two years has shown only moderate success. After considerable thought as to how we might excel over the next few years, I have determined that a sound strategy should include improving our use of groups within the company. Lately, I've noticed that though we are very structured in the sense that we have our design departments, marketing departments, production departments, and so on, these groups aren't working as well as they should. I don't think each group alone is as effective as it could be, and there's not enough communication among the different departments.

> I'd also like to see the development of some new groups. For example, I think there's a need to get a special group together to address the idea of manufacturing athletic clothes. Since this is a big step for us, I don't want to rely solely on our regular channels to handle it. I think we need to look at some new avenues for handling this type of situation.

> I'd also like to see some more informal interaction among the people in your respective departments. I don't think the attitudes of our employees are as good as they could be, and I think the overall work environment could benefit from more informal interactions. Of course, we need ways to get these groups going, and we all need to learn some management skills so the groups will be effective.

> What I'd like to do for the remainder of this meeting is to open the floor to all of you and hear some of your ideas about managing groups. Anyone want to start?

What's Ahead

Jesse Flick, the company president in the introductory case, is advising his vice-presidents on how to manage work groups. The material in this chapter develops a foundation for group management theory by (1) defining groups, (2) discussing the kinds of groups that exist in organizations, and (3) explaining what steps managers should take to manage groups appropriately.

The previous chapters in this section have dealt with three primary activities of the influencing function: (1) communication, (2) leadership, and (3) motivation. This chapter focuses on managing groups, the last major influencing activity to be discussed in this text. As with the other three activities, managing work groups requires guiding the behavior of organization members so as to increase the probability of reaching organizational objectives.

DEFINING GROUPS

To deal with groups appropriately, managers must have a thorough understanding of the nature of groups in organizations.[1] As used in management related discussions, a **group** is not simply a gathering of people. Rather it is "any number of people who (1) interact with one another, (2) are psychologically aware of one another, and (3) perceive themselves to be a group."[2] Groups are characterized by their members communicating with one another over time and being small enough that each member is able to communicate with all other members on a face-to-face basis.[3] As a result of this communication, each group member influences and is influenced by all other group members.[4]

> Group members interact, are aware of one another, and perceive themselves as a group.

The study of groups is important to managers, since the most common ingredient of all organizations is people and since the most common technique for accomplishing work through these people is dividing them into work groups. Cartwright and Lippitt list four additional reasons for studying groups:[5]

1. Groups exist in all kinds of organizations.
2. Groups inevitably form in all facets of organizational existence.
3. Groups can cause either desirable or undesirable consequences within the organization.
4. An understanding of groups can assist managers in increasing the probability that the groups with which they work will cause desirable consequences within the organization.

KINDS OF GROUPS IN ORGANIZATIONS

Groups that exist in organizations typically are divided into two basic types: formal and informal.

405

Formal Groups

A **formal group** is a group that exists within an organization, by virtue of management decree, to perform tasks that enhance the attainment of organizational objectives.[6] Figure 15.1 is an organization chart showing a formal group. The placement of organization members in such areas as marketing departments, personnel departments, or production departments involves establishing formal groups.

Organizations actually are made up of a number of formal groups that exist at various organizational levels. The coordination of and communication among these groups is the responsibility of managers, or supervisors, commonly called "linking pins." Figure 15.2 shows the various formal groups that can exist within an organization and the linking pins associated with those groups. The linking pins are organization members who belong to two formal groups.

Formal groups are clearly defined and structured. The following sections discuss (1) the basic kinds of formal groups, (2) examples of formal groups as they exist in organizations, and (3) the four stages of formal group development.

Kinds of Formal Groups

Formal groups commonly are divided into command groups and task groups.[7] **Command groups** are formal groups that are outlined on the chain of command on an organization chart. They typically handle the more routine organizational activities.

Task groups are formal groups of organization members who interact with one another to accomplish most of the organization's nonroutine tasks. Although task groups commonly are considered to be made up of members on the same organizational level, they can consist of people from different levels of the organizational hierarchy. For example, a manager could establish a task group to consider the feasibility of manufacturing some new product. Representatives

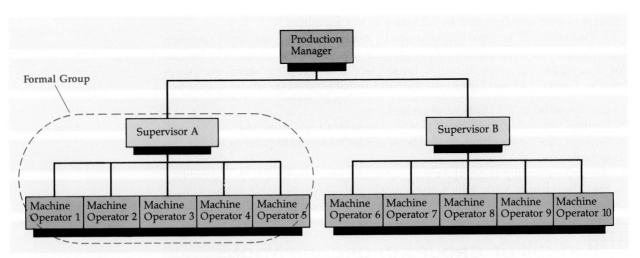

FIGURE 15.1
A formal group

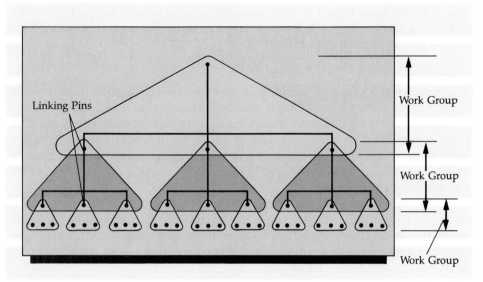

FIGURE 15.2
Formal groups and related linking pins

from various levels of such organizational areas as production, market research, and sales probably would be included as members.

BACK TO THE CASE

When Jesse Flick of Crutch Athletic Equipment in the introductory case, finished his introduction, there were a few minutes of silence while the vice-presidents considered what he had just said. Richard Simmons, the vice-president for design, was the first to respond:

> First of all, everyone, I think we need to define the term *group* and understand that there are several types of groups before we address how to handle these groups. To refresh your memories, a *group* is any number of people who interact, are psychologically aware of each other, and who perceive themselves as a group. Crutch Athletic is currently made up of formal groups—you know, the groups that appear on the company's organization charts, such as my design department, Susan Jamieson's marketing

department, and so on. Since we vice-presidents act as the ''linking pins'' among these departments, our ability to coordinate and communicate with these groups, as well as our success in dealing with our own departments, is certainly important to the success of the company as a whole.

Also, as Jesse mentioned, we can form new groups to handle some of our nonroutine challenges. I propose that we form a task group—that is, we should each choose two people from our own department and get them together on the athletic clothing concept. Then, of course, there are the informal groups Jesse mentioned, which we need to consider also. But I don't want to do all the talking. Perhaps we can get back to that subject later.

Examples of Formal Groups

Committees and work teams are two formal groups that can be established in organizations. Committees are a more traditional formal group. Work teams only recently have begun to gain popular acceptance and support. Since the organizing section of this text emphasized command groups, the examples in this section will emphasize task groups.

Committees

A **committee** is a group of individuals that has been charged with performing some type of activity. Therefore, it usually is classified as a task group. From a managerial viewpoint, the major reasons for establishing committees are (1) to allow organization members to exchange ideas, (2) to generate suggestions and recommendations that can be offered to other organizational units, (3) to develop new ideas for solving existing organizational problems, and (4) to assist in the development of organizational policies.[8]

Committees typically exist within all organizations and at all organizational levels. As Figure 15.3 suggests, the larger the organization, the greater the probability that committees will be used within that organization on a regular basis. The following two sections discuss why managers should use committees and what makes committees successful.

Why Managers Should Use Committees. Managers generally agree that committees have several uses in organizations. One is that committees can improve the quality of decision making.[9] As more people become involved in making a decision, the strengths and weaknesses of that decision tend to be discussed in more detail and the quality of the decision tends to increase.

Another reason for committees is that they encourage honest opinions. Committee members feel protected because the group output of a committee logically cannot be totally associated with any one member of that group.

Committees also tend to increase organization member participation in decision making and thereby enhance support of committee decisions. Also, as a result of this increased participation, committee work creates the opportunity for committee members to satisfy their social or esteem needs.

Finally, committees ensure the representation of important groups in the decision-making process. Managers must choose committee members wisely, however, to achieve this representation.

Executives vary somewhat in their opinions about using committees in organizations. A study reported by McLeod and Jones indicates that most execu-

Margin notes:

Committees are established for specific reasons.

Larger organizations use committees more regularly.

Committees tend to increase the quality of decision making.

They encourage honest opinions.

They enhance decision support and provide needs satisfaction.

They ensure group representation.

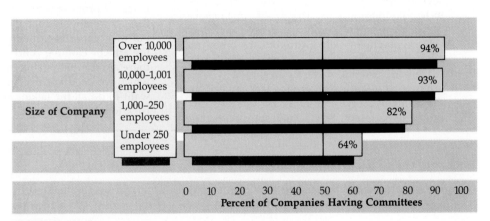

FIGURE 15.3
Percent of companies having committees by size of company

tives favor using committees in organizations.[10] According to this study executives claim to get significantly more information from organizational sources other than committees. However, they find that the information from committees is more valuable to them than the information from any other source (see Figure 15.4). However, some top executives show only qualified acceptance of committees as work groups, and others express negative feelings. Figure 15.5 on page 410 indicates that, in general, the executives who are negative about using committees are fewer in number than those who are positive about them or who display qualified acceptance of them.

Managers should take procedural steps to increase the probability of committee success.

What Makes Committees Successful. Although committees have become a commonly accepted management tool, managerial action taken to establish and run

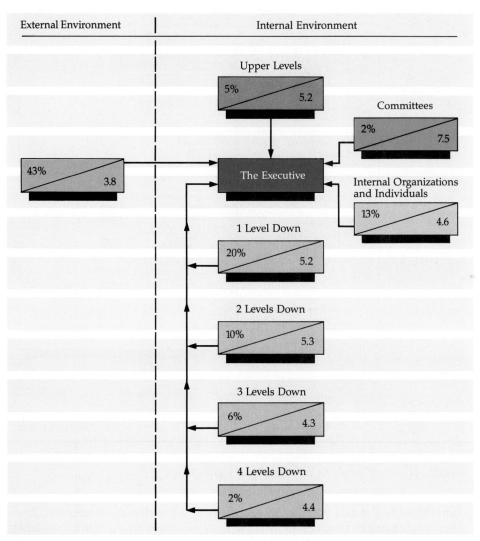

FIGURE 15.4
Comparing volume and value of information to executives from several organizational sources. *In each rectangle, the number* above *the diagonal is the percentage of overall volume for that source. The number* below *the diagonal is the average value, from 0 (no value) to 10 (maximum value), assigned the transaction. Figures may not total 100 percent because of rounding.*

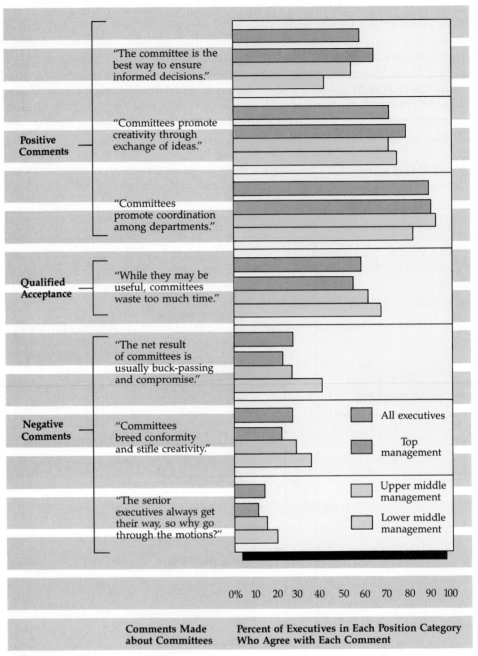

FIGURE 15.5
Feelings of executives about committees as work groups

committees is a major variable in determining their degree of success. Proce-dural steps that can be taken to increase the probability that a committee will be successful are the following:[11]

1. The committee's goals should be clearly defined, preferably in writing. This focuses the committee's activities and reduces the time devoted to discussing what the committee is supposed to do.

2. The committee's authority should be specified. Can the committee merely investigate, advise, and recommend, or is it authorized to implement decisions?

3. The optimum size of the committee should be determined. With fewer than five members, the advantages of group work may be diminished. With more than ten or fifteen members, the committee may become unwieldly. Although size varies with the circumstances, the ideal number of committee members for many tasks seems to range from five to ten.

4. A chairperson should be selected on the basis of the ability to run an efficient meeting—that is, the ability to keep the participation of all committee members from getting bogged down in irrelevancies and to see that the necessary paperwork gets done.

5. Appointing a permanent secretary to handle communications is often useful.

6. The agenda and all supporting material for the meeting should be distributed before the meeting. When members have a chance to study each item beforehand, they are likely to stick to the point and be ready with informed contributions.

7. Meetings should be started on time, and the time at which they will end should be announced at the outset.

In addition to these procedural steps, managers can follow a number of more people oriented guidelines to increase the probability of committee success. In this regard, a manager can increase the quality of discussion in committees by:[12]

Managers can also strive to improve the quality of committee discussion.

1. *Rephrasing ideas already expressed* This rephrasing makes sure that the manager as well as other individuals on the committee have a clear understanding of what has been said.

2. *Bringing a member into active participation* All committee members represent possible sources of information, and the manager should serve as a catalyst to spark individual participation whenever appropriate.

3. *Stimulating further thought by a member* The manager should encourage committee members to think ideas through carefully and thoroughly. Only this type of analysis generates high-quality committee output.

Managers should also help the committee avoid a phenomenon called "groupthink."[13] **Groupthink** is the mode of thinking that people engage in when seeking agreement becomes so dominant in a group that it tends to override the realistic appraisal of alternative problem solutions. Groups operate under groupthink when their members are so concerned with being too harsh in their judgments of other group members that objectivity in problem solving is lost. Such groups tend to adopt a softer line of criticism and to seek complete support on every issue, with little conflict generated to endanger the "we-feeling" atmosphere.

Groupthink involves a desire for unanimous agreement.

Work Teams

Work teams are another example of task groups used in organizations. A more recently developed management tool than committees, work teams generally are established to achieve greater organizational flexibility or to cope with rapid growth.

Consider the situation faced by William W. George, a corporate vice-president of Litton Industries. George created work teams within the Litton micro-

Work teams help organizations to be flexible and to cope with rapid growth.

wave cooking division to manage rapid growth.[14] One such team included members from the departments involved in new product development, manufacturing, marketing, cost reduction, facilities planning, and new business ventures. The team had a designated leader, representation from several functional departments, and involvement by top management on an as-required basis.

BACK TO THE CASE

When Richard Simmons had finished his explanation of formal groups, Susan Jamieson, the vice-president for marketing, expanded on his ideas about forming a task group:

> I agree with Richard. I think we should form a committee to develop the athletic clothing idea, the reason being that a committee would allow the departments to exchange ideas and generate suggestions. I feel that a committee would improve our decision making and encourage honest opinions in this new, unexplored area. We need to get some fresh ideas, and a committee would encourage member participation. Also, I think it is essential to represent all of the departments in this decision. When we introduce a new product, we must consider every angle, including design, production, marketing, sales, and so on.
>
> Then, when this new athletic line takes off, we can organize a different type of task group, a work team, to handle the company's tremendous growth. After all, we want to make sure we can produce these clothes as quickly as my department can market them!

Everyone smiled at Jamieson's enthusiasm. Then Henry Reed, the vice-president for production, interjected:

> Excuse me, Susan, but to get back to your committee idea, I think we need to consider what steps to take to make this committee successful. After all, while committees can be useful, a poorly run committee wastes a lot of time.
>
> First of all, we should clearly define this committee's goals and state its authority. Is the committee just going to come up with ideas and do some market research, or should it also take the initial steps toward manufacturing the clothes? And with two people from each department, as Richard suggested, we'd have a twenty-member committee. Perhaps one person from each department would be better. Of course, we need to address issues such as appointing a secretary to handle communications and appointing a chairperson who is good with people oriented issues. We need someone who can rephrase ideas clearly to ensure that everyone understands and who can get members to participate and think about the issues while avoiding "groupthink." We want original ideas to come out of this committee, not a unanimous opinion because everyone is avoiding conflict.
>
> But before we get that far, I think we must first understand how to develop the committee from scratch. Anyone have any thoughts on this?

Stages of Formal Group Development

Groups develop in four stages:

Another facet to managing formal groups is understanding the stages of formal group development. Bernard Bass has suggested that group development is a four-stage process influenced primarily by groups learning how to use their resources.[15] Although these stages may not occur sequentially, for the purpose of clarity the discussion that follows assumes that they do. The four stages can be labeled and defined as follows:

1. Acceptance.

1. *The acceptance stage* It is relatively common for members of a new group initially to mistrust each other somewhat. The acceptance stage occurs only after the initial mistrust within the group has been transformed into mutual trust and the general acceptance of group members by one another.

2. *The communication and decision-making stage* Once the acceptance stage has been passed, group members are better able to communicate frankly with one another. This frank communication provides the basis for effectively establishing and using some type of group decision-making mechanism.

3. *The group solidarity stage* Group solidarity comes naturally as the mutual acceptance of group members increases and communication and decision making continue within the group. This stage is characterized by members becoming more involved in group activities and cooperating, rather than competing, with one another. Group members find being a member of the group extremely satisfying and are committed to enhancing the group's overall success.

4. *The group control stage* A natural result of group solidarity is group control. This stage involves group members attempting to maximize group success by matching individual abilities with group activities and by assisting one another. Flexibility and informality tend to characterize this stage.

2. Communication and decision-making.

3. Group solidarity.

4. Group control.

In general terms, as a group passes through each of these four stages, it tends to become more mature and more effective—and therefore more productive. The group that reaches maximum maturity and effectiveness is characterized by:[16]

Mature groups are more productive.

1. *Members functioning as a unit* The group works as a team. Members do not disturb one another to the point of interfering with their collaboration.
2. *Members participating effectively in group effort* Members work hard when there is something to do. They usually do not loaf even if they get the opportunity to do so.
3. *Members being oriented toward a single goal* Group members work for common purposes and thereby do not waste group resources by moving in different directions.
4. *Members having the equipment, tools, and skills necessary to attain the group's goals* Group members are taught the various parts of their jobs by experts and strive to acquire whatever resources are needed to attain group objectives.
5. *Members asking and receiving suggestions, opinions, and information from one another* A member who is uncertain about something stops working and asks another member for information. Group members generally talk to one another openly and frequently.

▮ **BACK TO THE CASE**

In response to Henry Reed's question on how to develop a committee, Alan Green, vice-president for sales, spoke up about the stages of group development:

> We must understand that it's going to take some time for a new group to develop into a productive working unit. The different department members in any new committee must start by trusting and accepting one another and then begin communicating and exchanging ideas. Once this acceptance and communication increase, group solidarity and control come natu-

rally. In other words, the group members get involved, cooperate, and try to maximize the group's success.

So with this new committee we've been talking about, we must be patient and let the group mature before we can expect maximum effectiveness and productivity. Hopefully, if given time to grow, the group will function as a unit, members will participate willingly and effectively, and the group will reach some decisions about what we need to do to be productive and competitive in the athletic clothing market.

Informal Groups

Informal groups develop naturally as people interact.

Informal groups, the second major kind of group that can exist within an organization, are groups that develop naturally as people interact. As Figure 15.6 shows, informal group structures can deviate significantly from formal group structures. As in the case of Supervisor A in the figure, an organization member can belong to more than one informal group at the same time. In contrast to formal groups, informal groups typically are not highly structured in terms of procedure and are not formally recognized by management.

The following sections discuss (1) various kinds of informal groups that can exist in organizations, (2) the benefits usually reaped by membership in informal groups, and (3) encouraging the development of informal groups.

Kinds of Informal Groups

Interest groups have issues of common concern.

Informal groups generally are divided into two types: interest groups and friendship groups. **Interest groups** are informal groups that gain and maintain membership primarily because of a special concern each member possesses about a specific issue. An example is a group of workers pressing management for better pay or working conditions. Once the interest or concern that causes an informal group to form has been eliminated, the group tends to disband.

Friendship groups are basically social relationships.

As its name implies, **friendship groups** are informal groups that form in organizations because of the personal affiliation members have with one another. As with interest groups, the membership of friendship groups tends to change over time. Here, however, group membership changes as friendships dissolve or new friendships are made.

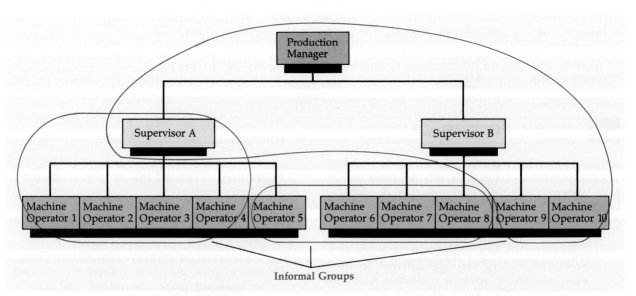

FIGURE 15.6
Three informal groups that deviate significantly from formal groups within the organization

Benefits of Informal Group Membership

Informal groups tend to develop in organizations because of various benefits that group members obtain. These benefits include (1) perpetuation of social and cultural values that group members consider important, (2) status and social satisfaction that might not be enjoyed without group membership, (3) increased ease of communication among group members, and (4) increased desirability of the overall work environment.[17] These benefits may be one reason that employees who are on fixed shifts or who continually work with the same groups are sometimes more satisfied with their work than employees whose shifts are continually changing.[18]

Informal group membership has many rewards.

Encouraging the Development of Informal Groups

Managers may be able to use quality circles to assist in the development of informal groups. **Quality circles** are simply small groups of factory workers who meet regularly with management to discuss quality related problems. During these meetings, management has opportunities to nurture relationships with various informal groups. In fact, quality circles may result in some managers and workers becoming members of the same informal groups. As the "Management in Action" feature, page 416, illustrates, some union leaders worry that management relations with workers may become too good as a result of quality circles.

Quality circles may help establish manager/worker informal groups.

BACK TO THE CASE

The vice-presidents of Crutch Athletic Equipment continued to share ideas about managing formal groups, until Jesse Flick again took control of the discussion:

> At this point, I would like to address the other issue I mentioned at the beginning of the meeting—working with informal groups in your departments. As you all know, employees group together at times because of certain issues. Remember last year, for example, when the nonsmokers in the company got together to pressure us into creating nonsmoking areas in their departments? And, of course, employees form friendship groups, which ease communication and provide feelings of satisfaction in the

company. In general, these informal groups can improve the work environment for everyone involved, and I strongly suggest that you encourage their development.

> Perhaps we could even try quality circles, where each manager in your department meets with subordinates on a regular basis. In fact, why don't each of you arrange for your managers to try a quality circle sometime in the next month? Have the managers report back to you about whether the effort was successful, and we can discuss the results at our next meeting. Now, let's get back to discussing how we can effectively manage our work groups.

▦ MANAGING WORK GROUPS

To manage work groups effectively, managers must simultaneously consider the impact of both formal and informal group factors on organizational productivity. This consideration requires three steps: (1) determining group existence, (2) understanding the evolution of informal groups, and (3) maximizing work group effectiveness.

QUALITY CIRCLES AT GM

Some labor officials are starting to worry that the growing use of "quality circles," or small groups of factory workers that meet regularly with management to discuss production problems, may turn out to be a potent anti-union tool.

Quality circles, often formed with labor's cooperation, are increasing rapidly. . . . The goal of such groups is to produce ideas that improve both productivity and conditions in the workplace. But some labor leaders are concerned that quality circles are being used by companies either to combat union organizing drives or to diminish a union's authority in a plant. They fear that quality circles will expand to include areas such as work rules and benefits that historically have been covered by collective bargaining.

"A number of well-meaning people believe that quality circles can lead to improvements in the work place," says William Roehl, the AFL-CIO's assistant director of organizing. "But what they don't know is that they can also be part of a company's union-busting strategy." Expressing organized labor's greatest fear, he worries that some companies "will give workers the impression that all their problems will be solved by quality circles, which implies that there's no need for unions."

UNIONS ADVISE COOPERATION

Nevertheless, the AFL-CIO's emerging strategy is to advise its unions to join the quality circles, rather than fight them. The federation [suggests that] labor should push for equal participation in the circles—and an equal share of the credit for any accomplishments.

Sometimes, companies beginning quality circles get off to a bad start by bypassing unions. . . . A consumer-electronics unit of North American Philips Corporation set up several quality circles at its Jefferson City, Tennessee, plant. Although 70 percent of the factory's 1,010 workers are represented by the International Union of Electrical Workers, the union wasn't consulted before the plan was started. Further, the company won't give the union a list of the workers in the quality circles, says Charles Wolfenbarger, local union president.

"My people are afraid that they'll wind up with some cost-saving ideas that will put them out on the street," says Wolfenbarger.

Bruce Handshu, the company's manager of quality training, concedes that "it's conceivable we made a mistake. In the future, we'll bring the union in from the beginning." He says that management met recently with union officials in an effort to get their support. The union says it's too early to judge the value of the company's circles.

ANTIUNION USES FEARED

Labor officials say that other companies see quality circles as a way to keep unions weak or to keep them out altogether. A copy of the minutes of a . . . meeting of Du Pont Company executives, in Nashville, Tennessee, says the motive "for entering into collaboration with the union" in worker committees "is more likely to be a recognition that the environment within the organization is rife with opportunity for the unions to make an issue of job pressure . . . if the company doesn't take the initiative itself. . . ." The company, which has local unions at some plants, is fighting a major organizing drive by the United Steelworkers union.

A Du Pont spokeswoman confirms that there were meetings . . . involving Du Pont's Old Hickory plant in Tennessee, but she can't vouch for the authenticity of the minutes. A spokesman adds that, to his knowledge, quality circles haven't been discussed as part of a strategy to keep out unions.

Despite labor's worries, some major unions support the quality-circle concept and are working closely with companies that have invited them to join as equal partners. These unions include the steelworkers, the autoworkers, and the communications workers. "We're not going to stand in the way of progress," says John Oshinski, the steelworkers' organizing director.

ENTHUSIASM AT GM

Even the electrical workers, while suspicious of North American Philips's efforts in Tennessee, are enthusiastic about a plan they participate in at a General Motors Corporation plant in Warren, Ohio. Edward Fire, the union's local president, says the quality circle discovered that high-paid workers were losing production time because of delays in getting them certain materials. The group suggested that four low-paid maintenance workers be hired to move material around the plant more efficiently. The suggestion was adopted by management.

However, some labor experts see quality circles moving from production problems into other areas. Kim Smith, former labor relations director for the National Association of Manufacturers and now a private consultant, predicts "companies using the concept will head slowly toward broader quality-of-worklife programs that include such issues as health and safety."

And, she concludes: "If I were in the unions' shoes, I'd be concerned. Quality circles are trying to achieve a lot of the things that are traditional union objectives."

Determining Group Existence

Perhaps the most important step that managers should take in managing work groups is determining what groups exist within the organization and who their members are. **Sociometry** is an analytical tool that managers can use to help determine such information. It can also provide information on the internal workings of an informal group, such as the group leader, the relative status level of various members within the group, and the group's communication networks.[19] This information on informal groups, along with an understanding of the established formal groups as shown on an organization chart, gives managers a complete picture of the group structure.

A sociometric analysis determines what groups exist and the membership of those groups.

The procedure involved in performing a sociometric analysis in an organization is quite basic.[20] Various organization members simply are asked, through either an interview or a questionnaire, to name several other organization members with whom they would like to spend some of their free time. A sociogram then is constructed to summarize the informal relationships among group members. **Sociograms** are diagrams that visually link individuals within the group according to the number of times they were chosen and whether the choice was reciprocal.

A sociogram is a graphic summary of the sociometric analysis.

Figure 15.7 (p. 418) shows two sample sociograms based on a study of two groups of boys in a summer camp—the Bulldogs and the Red Devils.[21] An analysis of these sociograms results in several interesting observations. For example, more boys within the Bulldogs than within the Red Devils were chosen as being desirable to spend time with. This probably implies that the Bulldogs are a closer-knit informal group than the Red Devils. Also, communication between L and most other Red Devils members is likely to occur directly, whereas communication between C and other Bulldogs is likely to pass through other group members. Lastly, the greater the number of times an individual is chosen, the more likely that individual will be the group leader. Thus individuals C and E would tend to be Bulldog leaders, and individuals L and S would tend to be Red Devil leaders.

Sociometric analysis can give managers many useful insights on the informal groups within an organization. Although managers may not want to perform a formal sociometric analysis, they can casually gather information that would indicate what form a sociogram might take in a particular situation. This information can be gathered through inferences made in normal conversations that managers have with other organization members and through observations of how various organization members relate to one another.

Understanding the Evolution of Informal Groups

Obviously, knowing what groups exist within an organization and what characterizes the membership of those groups is an important prerequisite for managing groups effectively. A second prerequisite is understanding how informal groups evolve, since this gives managers some insights on how to encourage informal groups to develop appropriately within an organization. Naturally, encouraging these groups to develop and maintaining good relationships with work group members can help ensure that organization members support management in the process of attaining organizational objectives.[22]

Perhaps the most widely accepted framework for explaining the evolution of informal groups was developed by George Homans.[23] Figure 15.8 on page 419

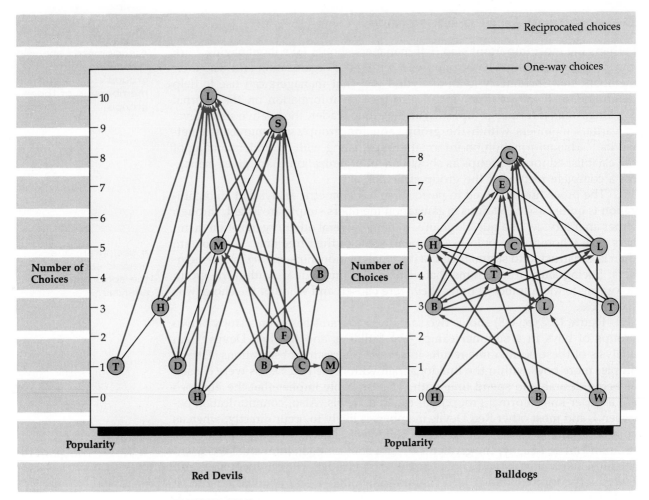

FIGURE 15.7
Sample sociograms

According to Homans, informal groups evolve from the sentiments, interactions, and activities of formal groups.

broadly summarizes his theory. According to Homans, the sentiments, interactions, and activities that emerge as part of an informal group result from the sentiments, interactions, and activities that exist within a formal group. In addition, the informal group exists to obtain the consequences of satisfaction and growth for its members. Feedback on whether the consequences are achieved can result in forces that attempt to modify the formal group so as to increase the probability that the informal group will achieve the consequences.

An example to illustrate Homans's concept involves twelve factory workers who are members of a formal work group that manufactures toasters. According to Homans, as these workers interact to assemble toasters, they might discover common personal interests that encourage the evolution of informal groups. In turn, these informal groups will tend to maximize the satisfaction and growth of their members. Once established, the informal groups will probably resist changes or established segments of formal groups that threaten the satisfaction and growth of the informal group's members.

FIGURE 15.8
Homans's ideas on how
informal groups develop

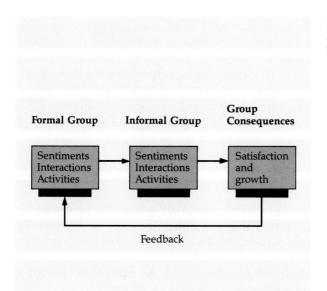

Formal Group	Informal Group	Group Consequences

Feedback

After Jesse Flick finished offering suggestions about informal groups, Henry Reed continued the discussion of managing groups:

> I think that, in order to be successful managers, we need to consider how both formal and informal groups affect our productivity. I think we need to determine what informal groups exist and who the group members are and then try to understand how these groups form. With this information, we can strive to make our groups more effective.

> One way we can get information about the groups in our departments is to use sociometry. We can design a questionnaire asking our employees whom they spend time with and then construct a sociogram to summarize this information. Of course, we can do a more casual analysis by just talking to our employees and observing how they interact with one another.

We should also try to understand how the informal groups evolve and should realize that our formal structure in the company influences the informal groups that develop. For example, in my department, I've got thirty men who work on baseball equipment. Needless to say, many of them love baseball, have become friends because of their common interest, and work well together as a result. If I needed to make some changes in the department, I would try to accommodate these friendship groups to keep everyone satisfied. I'd try not to do anything to threaten any one member, such as pull one guy off the baseball line and put him on something else. In other words, these informal groups are the result of the way we force people to interact. Therefore, the best way to influence these groups is to make appropriate changes within the formal dimensions of the company.

Maximizing Work Group Effectiveness

Once managers determine which groups exist within an organization and understand how informal groups evolve, they should strive to maximize work group effectiveness. As the following discussion emphasizes, maximizing work group effectiveness requires that managers continue to consider both formal and informal dimensions of the organization.[24]

Figure 15.9 indicates the four factors primarily responsible for collectively influencing work group effectiveness: (1) size of work group, (2) cohesiveness of work group, (3) work group norms, and (4) status of work group members. (The terms *work group* and *formal group* are used synonymously in the sections that follow.)

Size of Work Group

As work group size (the number of members in a work group) increases, forces usually are created within that group that can either increase or decrease its effectiveness.[25] The ideal number of members for a work group depends primarily on the group's purpose.[26] For example, the ideal size for a fact-finding work group usually is set at about fourteen members, and the maximum size for a problem-solving work group is approximately seven members.[27]

Work group size is a significant determinant of group effectiveness because it has considerable impact on three major components of a group: (1) leadership, (2) group members, and (3) group processes. A summary of how these factors can be influenced by group size is presented in Table 15.1.

Managers attempting to maximize group effectiveness by modifying formal group size also should consider informal group factors. For example, a manager may decide that a formal work group should be reduced in size to make it more effective. Before making this reduction, however, the manager should consider the existence of informal groups within the formal group. If the man-

FIGURE 15.9
Primary determinants of work group effectiveness

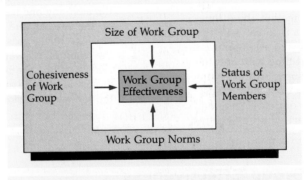

TABLE 15.1

Possible effects of group size on group leadership, group members, and group processes

| Dimensions | Group Size | | |
	2–7 Members	8–12 Members	13–16 Members
Leadership			
1. Demand on leader	Low	Moderate	High
2. Differences between leader and members	Low	Low to moderate	Moderate to high
3. Direction of leader	Low	Low to moderate	Moderate to high
Members			
4. Tolerance of direction from leader	Low to high	Moderate to high	High
5. Domination of group interaction by a few members	Low	Moderate to high	High
6. Inhibition in participation by ordinary members	Low	Moderate	High
Group processes			
7. Formalization of rules and procedures	Low	Low to moderate	Moderate to high
8. Time required for reaching decisions	Low to moderate	Moderate	Moderate to high
9. Tendency for subgroup to form	Low	Moderate to high	High

ager reduces the size of the formal group by transferring the informal group leader, the effectiveness of the work group could diminish considerably. The slight ineffectiveness of the overly large formal work group might be more advantageous than the greater ineffectiveness that could result from reducing the formal group size and possibly transferring the informal group leader.

Cohesiveness of Work Group

Another factor that can influence work group effectiveness is the degree of cohesiveness of the group. **Group cohesiveness** is the attraction group members feel for one another in terms of the desire to remain a member of the group and to resist leaving it.[28] The greater the desire, the greater the cohesiveness. In general, the cohesiveness of a work group is determined by the cohesiveness of the informal groups that exist within it. Therefore, to manage the degree of cohesiveness that exists within a work group, managers must manage the degree of cohesiveness that exists within the informal groups that constitute the work group.

Group cohesiveness is extremely important to managers, since the greater the cohesiveness, the greater the probability the group will accomplish its objectives. In addition, some evidence indicates that groups whose members have positive feelings toward one another tend to be more productive than groups whose members have negative feelings toward one another.[29]

Indicators of high group cohesiveness include the following:[30]

1. The members have a broad, general agreement on the goals and objectives of the informal group.

Group cohesiveness is based on a strong desire to remain a group member.

Cohesiveness tends to increase productivity.

2. A significant amount of communication and interaction is evident among participating members.
3. There is a satisfactory level of homogeneity in social status and social background among the members.
4. Members are allowed to participate fully and directly in the determination of group standards.
5. The size of the group is sufficient for interaction but is not so large as to stymie personal attention. Normally, the optimum size range of an informal group is from four to seven members.
6. The members have a high regard for their fellow members.
7. The members feel a strong need for the mutual benefits and protection the group appears to offer.
8. The group is experiencing success in the achievement of its goals and in the protection of important values.

Managers must consider the formal and informal dimensions of group cohesiveness.

Since the cohesiveness of informal groups is such an influential determinant of the cohesiveness of work groups and, as a result, of work group effectiveness, management should assist in the development of informal group cohesiveness whenever possible. (This, of course, assumes that the informal group is attempting to make a constructive contribution to organizational goal attainment.) To this end, managers should attempt to enhance the prestige of existing informal group members, design the overall organization to encourage informal group development, and eliminate organizational barriers to continuing informal group membership over an extended period of time.

If, however, managers determine that an informal group is attempting to attain objectives that are counterproductive to those of the organization, an appropriate strategy would be to attempt to reduce informal group cohesiveness. For example, managers could take action to limit the prestige of existing group members and design the overall organization to discourage further group cohesiveness. This type of action, however, could result in a major conflict between management and various informal groups that exist within the organization. Over all, managers must keep in mind that the greater the cohesiveness of informal groups with nonproductive objectives, the greater the probability that those nonproductive objectives will be attained.

Work Group Norms

Group norms are required behavior of group members.

Group norms are a third major determinant of work group effectiveness. In this chapter, **group norms** apply only to informal groups. These norms are appropriate or standard behavior that is required of informal group members. Therefore, they significantly influence the behavior of informal group members in their formal group. According to Hackman, group norms (1) are structured characteristics of groups that simplify the group-influence processes; (2) apply only to behavior, not to private thoughts and feelings of group members; (3) generally develop only in relation to the matters that most group members consider important; (4) usually develop slowly over time; and (5) sometimes apply only to certain group members.[31]

Systematic study of group norms has revealed that there is generally a close relationship between those norms and the profitability of the organization of which the group is a part.[32] Although it would be impossible to state all possible norms that might develop in a group, most group norms relate to one or more of the following: (1) organizational pride, (2) performance, (3) profitability, (4) teamwork, (5) planning, (6) supervision, (7) training, (8) innovation, (9) customer relations, and (10) honesty or security.

Norms usually are divided into two general types: negative and positive. **Negative norms** are required informal group behavior that limits organizational productivity. **Positive norms** are required informal group behavior that contributes to organizational productivity. Examples of both positive and negative norms are presented in Table 15.2. The cartoon on the next page illustrates a negative norm that allows informal group members to agree which nights they will leave work earlier so they can take turns looking good to the boss.

Some managers consider group norms to be of such great importance to the organization that they develop profiles of group norms to assess the norms' organizational impact. Figure 15.10 on page 425 shows a normative profile developed by one company manager. This particular profile is characterized by a number of norm differences. For example, a high level of organizational pride and good customer relations contrast with a lower concern for profitability. What actually happened in this company was that employees placed customer desires at such a high level that they were significantly decreasing organizational

Negative norms limit organizational productivity. Positive norms contribute to organizational productivity.

Normative profiles indicate norm variations.

TABLE 15.2

Examples of positive and negative group norms

	Negative Norms
Factory Workers	Keep your mouth shut when the boss is around.
Factory Workers	We stop working fifteen minutes before quitting time to wash up.
Utility Workers	We always take a nice long coffee break in the morning before climbing those poles.
Typing Pool	Don't rush the work—they'll just give you more to do.
Salesclerks	Don't hurry to wait on a customer—they'll keep.

	Positive Norms
Factory Workers	Do it right the first time.
Typing Pool	Make certain it looks nice—we want to be proud of our work.
Car Salespeople	We want to sell more cars than anyone else in the city.
Grocery Clerks	Go out of your way to satisfy customers—we want them to come back.
Factory Workers	Don't waste materials—they cost money.

"Come on Scott, be a buddy—look, if you leave the
office before me tonight, I'll leave before you any two
times you say."

*U.S. News & World Report, June 1, 1987. William Hamilton's
cartoon is reprinted by permission of Chronicle Features,
San Francisco.*

profitability to please customers. Once these norms were discovered, management took steps to make the situation more advantageous to the organization.

Characteristics of formal work groups can spawn negative norms in the informal group.

As the preceding information suggests, a key to managing behavior within a formal work group is managing the norms of the informal groups that exist within the formal group. More specifically, Homans's framework for analyzing group behavior indicates that informal group norms are mainly the result of the characteristics of the formal work group of which the informal group is a part. As a result, changing the existing norms within an informal group means changing the characteristics of the formal work group of which the informal group is a part.

For example, an informal group could have the negative norm: Don't rush the work—they'll just give you more to do. For a manager to change this norm, the factor in the formal work group from which the norm probably arose should be eliminated. The manager might find that this norm is a direct result of the fact that workers are formally recognized within the organization through pay and awards regardless of the amount of work performed. Changing the formal policy so the amount of work accomplished is considered in formal organizational recognition should help dissolve this negative norm. In some situations, norms may be difficult, if not impossible, to change.

Status of Work Group Members

Status is a group member's position within the group.

Status is the position of a group member in relation to other group members. Over all, an individual's status within a group is determined not only by the person's work or role within the group but by the nonwork qualities the individual brings to the group.[33] Work related determinants of status include titles,

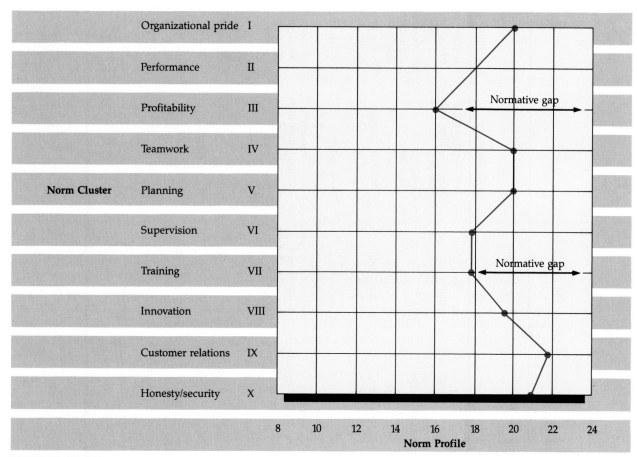

FIGURE 15.10
Sample normative profile

work schedules, and, perhaps most commonly, amounts of pay group members receive.[34] Nonwork related determinants of status include education level, race, age, and sex. Table 15.3 on page 426 is an entertaining but realistic treatment of how status symbols vary within the formal groups of an organizational hierarchy. These status symbols generally are used within formal work groups to reward individual productivity and to show the different levels of organizational importance.

To maximize the effectiveness of a work group, however, managers also should consider the status of members of the informal groups that exist within the formal group. For example, within a formal group, the formal group leaders have higher status than other group members. The informal groups that exist within the formal group also have informal leaders, who generally are different from the formal leader and of higher status than other informal group members. Management usually finds that, to increase productivity within a formal work group, the support of both the formal and the informal leaders must be gained. In fact, some evidence suggests that production is associated more with support from informal group leaders than with support from formal group leaders.[35]

TABLE 15.3

How status symbols vary with various levels of the organizational hierarchy

Visible Appurtenances	Top Dogs	VIPs	Brass	No. 2s	Eager Beavers	Hoi Polloi
Briefcases	None—they ask the questions	Use backs of envelopes	Someone goes along to carry theirs	Carry their own—empty	Daily—carry their own—filled with work	Too poor to own one
Desks, office	Custom-made (to order)	Executive style (to order)	Type A, "Director"	Type B, "Manager"	Castoffs from No. 2s	Yellow oak—or castoffs from eager beavers
Tables, office	Coffee tables	End tables or decorative wall tables	Matching tables, type A	Matching tables type B	Plain work table	None—lucky to have own desk
Carpeting	Nylon—one-inch pile	Nylon—one-inch pile	Wool-twist (with pad)	Wool-twist (without pad)	Used wool pieces—sewed	Asphalt tile
Plant stands	Several—kept filled with plants	Several—kept filled with strange, exotic plants	Two—repotted whenever they take a trip	One medium-sized—repotted annually during vacation	Small—repotted when plant dies	May have one in the department or bring their own from home
Vacuum water bottles	Silver	Silver	Chromium	Plain painted	Coke machine	Water fountains
Library	Private collection	Autographed or complimentary books and reports	Selected references	Impressive titles on covers	Books everywhere	Dictionary
Shoe-shine service	Every morning at 10:00	Every morning at 10:15	Every day at 9:00 or 11:00	Every other day	Once a week	Shine their own
Parking space	Private—in front of office	In plant garage	In company garage—if enough seniority	In company properties—somewhere	On the parking lot	Anywhere they can find a space—if they can afford a car

■■■ **BACK TO THE CASE**

After the vice-presidents had discussed ways to better understand group existence and evolution, Diane Lewis, the vice-president for customer relations, turned their attention to another component of managing work groups—maximizing group effectiveness:

Now that we understand more about our formal and informal groups, we should consider the four major factors that influence their effectiveness, so we can implement some changes. First of all, the size of the work group can be important to its productivity. As we noted earlier about the clothing committee, a twenty-person group for this type of committee could hamper the group's effectiveness. Also, we must consider informal groups before making changes in group size. As Henry alluded to earlier, he would not pull a few men, especially the more respected members, from his baseball group in order to reduce its size. The group could end up being less productive without its respected members than it would be if it were slightly too large.

This brings me to the second factor—group cohesiveness. Since a more cohesive group will tend to be more effective, we should try to increase the cohesiveness of our groups. Again, informal groups are very important here. We can increase the cohesiveness of our formal groups by doing such things as allowing members to take breaks together or rewarding informal group members for a job well done.

The group norms, or appropriate behaviors required within the informal group, are a third factor that affects the quality of formal group behavior. Since these norms affect our profitability, we must be aware of them and understand how to influence them within the formal group structure. For example, if the men in Henry's baseball group really care about the quality of the bats they produce and, as a result, are taking too much time to manufacture them, Henry could reward this positive norm by giving bonuses to group members who produce the best-quality bats in the shortest amount of time. This reward would increase the formal group productivity while encouraging a positive norm within the informal group.

Status within the informal groups comes into play here too. If Henry wants to increase his bat production, he should try to encourage the informal group's leaders, as well as the group's formal manager. Chances are that Henry's baseball group will be successful in producing more bats if its informal high-status members support that objective.

Over all, if we want to maximize group effectiveness, we must remember both the formal and informal dimensions of our groups while considering the four main factors that I've just mentioned.

At this point in this discussion, Jesse Flick interjected:

Thank you, Diane. I think we've covered enough material for today. This has been a very productive meeting, and you have all expressed important ideas about managing groups. Now, if there are no questions, I'd like you to think about and review what we've discussed here today. Any questions? Well then, this meeting is adjourned!

Action Summary

Reread the learning objectives that follow. Each objective is followed by questions. Answering these questions accurately will help you retain the most important concepts discussed in this chapter. After answering each question, check your answer with the answer key at the end of this chapter. (*Hint:* If you have doubt regarding the correct response, consult the page whose number follows the answer.)

Circle:

From studying this chapter, I will attempt to acquire:

1. **A definition of the term *group* as used within the context of management.**

T, F
   a. A group is made up of people who interact with one another, perceive themselves to be a group, and are primarily physically aware of one another.

a, b, c, d, e
   b. According to Cartwright and Lippitt, it is not true to say that: (a) groups exist in all kinds of organizations; (b) groups inevitably form in all facets of organizational existence; (c) groups cause undesirable consequences within the organization so their continued existence should be discouraged; (d) understanding groups can assist managers in increasing the probability that the groups with which they work will cause desirable consequences within the organization; (e) all of the above are true.

2. **A thorough understanding of the difference between formal and informal groups.**

T, F
   a. An informal group is a group that exists within an organization by virtue of management decree.

T, F
   b. A formal group is one that exists within an organization by virtue of interaction among organization members in proximity to one another.

3. **Knowledge of the types of formal groups that exist in organizations.**

a, b, c, d, e
   a. The type of group that generally handles more routine organizational activities is the: (a) informal task group; (b) informal command group; (c) formal task group; (d) formal command group; (e) none of the above.

a, b, c, d, e
   b. Managers should be encouraged to take which of the following steps to increase the success of a committee: (a) clearly define the goals of the committee; (b) rephrase ideas that have already been expressed; (c) select a chairperson on the basis of ability to run an efficient meeting; (d) a and b; (e) a, b, and c.

4. **An understanding of how managers can determine which groups exist in an organization.**

T, F
   a. The technique of sociometry involves asking people with whom they would like to manage.

a, b, c, d, e
   b. A sociogram is defined in the text as: (a) a letter encouraging group participation; (b) a diagram that visually illustrates the number of times that the individuals were chosen within the group and whether or not the choice was reciprocal; (c) a composite of demographic data useful in determining informal group choices; (d) a computer printout designed to profile psychological and sociological characteristics of the informal group; (e) none of the above.

5. **An appreciation for how managers must evaluate formal and informal groups simultaneously to maximize work group effectiveness.**

a, b, c, d, e
   a. Which of the following factors has the least influence on the effectiveness of a work group: (a) age of the work group; (b) size of the work group; (c) cohesiveness of the work group; (d) norms of the work group; (e) a and d.

T, F
   b. Knowing what informal groups exist within an organization and how informal groups evolve are prerequisites for managing groups effectively.

INTRODUCTORY CASE WRAP-UP

"A Meeting about Managing Groups" (p. 404) and its related back-to-the-case sections were written to help you better understand the management concepts contained in this chapter. Answer the following discussion questions about this introductory case to further enrich your understanding of chapter content:

1. Do you think that Flick chose an important topic on which to hold a meeting? Explain.
2. Do you think that the vice-presidents had good ideas for managing their groups? What additional suggestions could they have given?

Issues for Review and Discussion

1. How is the term *group* defined in this chapter?
2. Why is the study of groups important to managers?
3. What is a formal group?
4. Explain the significance of linking pins to formal groups in organizations.
5. List and define two types of formal groups that can exist in organizations.
6. Why should managers use committees in organizations?
7. What steps can managers take to ensure that a committee will be successful?
8. Explain how work teams can be valuable to an organization.
9. Describe the stages a group typically goes through as it becomes more mature.
10. What is an informal group?
11. List and define two types of informal groups in organizations.
12. What benefits generally accrue to members of informal groups?
13. What is the relationship between quality circles and informal groups?
14. Are formal groups more important to managers than informal groups? Explain.
15. Describe the sociometric procedure used to study informal group membership. What can the results of a sociometric analysis tell managers about members of an informal group?
16. Explain Homans's concept of how informal groups develop.
17. List and define the primary factors that influence work group effectiveness.
18. What is the relationship among formal groups, informal groups, and work group effectiveness?

Sources of Additional Information

Brightman, Harvey J., and Penny Verhoeven. "Why Managerial Problem-Solving Groups Fail." *Business* 36 (January/February/March 1986): 24–29.

Collins, B. E., and H. Guetzkow. *A Social Psychology of Group Processes for Decision Making.* New York: Wiley, 1964.

Delbecq, A., A. H. Van de Ven, and D. H. Gustafson. *Group Techniques for Program Planning.* Glenview, Ill.: Scott, Foresman, 1975.

Drucker, Peter F. "The Coming of the New Generation." *Harvard Business Review* 66 (January/February 1988): 45–53.

Earl, Michael J. *Perspectives on Management: A Multidisciplinary Analysis.* New York: Oxford University Press, 1983.

Ferraro, Vincent L., and Sheila A. Adams. "Interdepartmental Conflict: Practical Ways to Prevent and Reduce It." *Personnel* (July/August 1984): 12–23.

Franecki, Dennis J., Ralph F. Catalanello, and Curtiss K. Behrens. "Employee Committees: What Effect Are They Having?" *Personnel* (July/August 1984): 67–78.

Gordon, Judith R. *A Diagnostic Approach to Organizational Behavior,* 2d ed. Boston: Allyn and Bacon, 1987.

Halal, William E., and Bob S. Brown. ''Participative Management: Myth and Reality.'' *California Management Review* 23 (Summer 1981): 20–32.

Hare, A. P. *Handbook of Small Group Research.* New York: Free Press, 1962.

Homestead, Michael S. *The Small Group.* New York: Random House, 1981.

Levitt, Theodore. ''The Innovating Organization.'' *Harvard Business Review* 66 (January/February 1988): 7.

Luthans, Fred. *Organizational Behavior.* New York: McGraw-Hill, 1973.

Marsh, Arthur. ''Employee Relations—From Donovan to Today.'' *Personnel Management* 13 (June 1981): 34–36, 47.

Napier, R. W., and M. K. Gershenfeld. *Groups: Theory and Experience.* Boston: Houghton Mifflin, 1973.

Quible, Dr. Zane K. ''Quality Circles: A Well-Rounded Approach to Employee Involvement.'' *Management World* 10 (September 1981): 10–11, 38.

Scanlon, Burt, and Bernard Keys. *Management and Organizational Behavior,* 2nd ed. New York: Wiley, 1987.

Schweiger, David M., William R. Sandberg, and James W. Ragan. ''Group Approaches for Improving Strategic Decision Making: A Comparative Analysis of Dialectical Inquiry, Devil's Advocacy, and Consensus.'' *Academy of Management Journal* 29 (March 1986): 51–71.

Seashore, W. E. *Group Cohesiveness in the Industrial Work Group.* Ann Arbor, Mich.: Institute for Social Research, 1964.

Steele, Fred I. *Physical Settings and Organization Development.* Reading, Mass.: Addison-Wesley, 1973.

Wanous, John P., and Margaret A. Youtz. ''Solution Diversity and the Quality of Group Decisions.'' *Academy of Management Journal* 29 (March 1986): 149–58.

Notes

1. Robert L. Masson and Edward Jacobs, ''Group Leadership: Practical Points for Beginners,'' *Personnel and Guidance Journal* (September 1980): 52–55.
2. Edgar H. Schein, *Organizational Psychology* (Englewood Cliffs, N.J.: Prentice-Hall, 1965), 67.
3. George C. Homans, *The Human Group* (New York: Harcourt, Brace & World, 1950), 1.
4. Marvin E. Shaw, *Group Dynamics: The Psychology of Small Group Behavior* (New York: McGraw-Hill, 1971), 10.
5. Dorwin Cartwright and Ronald Lippitt, ''Group Dynamics and the Individual,'' *International Journal of Group Psychotherapy* 7 (January 1957): 86–102.
6. Edgar H. Schein, *Organizational Psychology,* 2d ed. (Englewood Cliffs, N.J.: Prentice-Hall, 1970), 82.
7. For more information on these groups, see Leonard R. Sayles, ''Research in Industrial Human Relations,'' in *Industrial Relations* (New York: Harper & Bros., 1957).
8. For a discussion of individual versus group decision making, see George P. Huber, *Managerial Decision Making* (Glenview, Ill.: Scott, Foresman, 1980), 140–48.
9. Ethel C. Glenn and Elliott Pood, ''Groups Can Make the Best Decisions, if You Lead the Way,'' *Supervisory Management* (December 1978): 2–6.
10. Raymond McLeod, Jr., and Jack W. Jones, ''Making Executive Information Systems More Effective,'' *Business Horizons* (September/October 1986): 29–37.
11. Cyril O'Donnell, ''Ground Rules for Using Committees,'' *Management Review* 50 (October 1961): 63–67. See also ''Making Committees Work,'' *Infosystems* (October 1985): 38–39.
12. These guidelines are taken from ''How Not to Influence People,'' *Management Record* (March 1958): 89–91. This article also can be consulted for additional guidelines.
13. Irving L. Janis, *Groupthink* (Boston: Houghton Mifflin, 1982).
14. For more information on the use of task teams in the Litton microwave cooking division, see William W. George, ''Task Teams for Rapid Growth,'' *Harvard Business Review* (March/April 1977): 71–80.
15. Bernard Bass, *Organizational Psychology* (Boston: Allyn and Bacon, 1965), 197–98.
16. Bass, *Organizational Psychology,* 199.
17. Keith Davis and John W. Newstrom, *Human Behavior at Work: Organizational Behavior* (New York: McGraw-Hill, 1985), 310–12.
18. Muhammad Jamal, ''Shift Work Related to Job Attitudes, Social Participation, and Withdrawal Behavior: A Study of Nurses and Industrial Workers,'' *Personnel Psychology* 34 (Autumn 1981): 535–47.
19. J. L. Moreno, ''Contributions of Sociometry to Research Methodology in Sociology,'' *American Psychological Review* 12 (June 1947): 287–92.
20. J. H. Jacobs, ''The Application of Sociometry to Industry,'' *Sociometry* 8 (Mary 1954): 181–98.

21. Muzafer Sherif, "A Preliminary Experimental Study of Intergroup Relations," in *Social Psychology at the Crossroads,* ed. John H. Rohrer and Muzafer Sherif (New York: Harper & Bros., 1951).

22. Edgar H. Schein, "SMR Forum: Improving Face-to-Face Relationships," *Sloan Management Review* 22 (Winter 1981): 43–52.

23. Homans, *The Human Group.*

24. For an interesting attempt to analyze characteristics of work groups in a small business, see James Curran and John Stanworth, "The Social Dynamics of the Small Manufacturing Enterprise," *Journal of Management Studies* 18 (April 1981): 141–58.

25. W. Alan Randolph, *Understanding and Managing Organizational Behavior* (Homewood, Ill.: Richard D. Irwin, 1985), 398–99.

26. Davis and Newstrom, *Human Behavior at Work,* 218.

27. Don Hellriegel and John W. Slocum, Jr., *Management* (Reading, Mass.: Addison-Wesley, 1986), 539–42.

28. Stanley E. Seashore, *Group Cohesiveness in the Industrial Work Group* (Ann Arbor: University of Michigan Press, 1954).

29. Raymond A. Van Zelst, "Sociometrically Selected Work Teams Increase Production," *Personnel Psychology* 4 (Autumn 1952): 175–85.

30. O. Jeff Harris, *Managing People at Work* (New York: Wiley, 1976), 122.

31. J. R. Hackman, "Group Influence on Individuals," in *Handbook for Industrial and Organizational Psychology,* ed. M. P. Dunnette (Chicago: Rand McNally, 1976).

32. This section is based primarily on P. C. André De la Porte, "Group Norms: Key to Building a Winning Team," *Personnel* (September/October 1974): 60–67.

33. A. Mazur, "A Cross-Species Comparison of Status in Small Established Groups," *American Sociological Review* 38, no. 5 (1973): 513–30.

34. Peter F. Drucker, "Is Executive Pay Excessive?" *Wall Street Journal,* May 23, 1977, 22.

35. T. N. Whitehead, "The Inevitability of the Informal Organization and Its Possible Value," in *Readings in Management,* ed. Ernest Dale (New York: McGraw-Hill, 1970).

Action Summary Answer Key

1. a. F, p. 405
   b. c, p. 405
2. a. F, pp. 406–414
   b. F, pp. 406–414
3. a. d, p. 406
   b. e, p. 408
4. a. F, p. 417
   b. b, p. 417
5. a. a, p. 420
   b. T, p. 417

WORK TEAMS AT GOODYEAR AND FRITO-LAY

Many early managers of U.S. business organizations were retired military officers. As in their military days, they issued orders and expected followers to obey them. However, with the rise of unions and more militant workers, the autocratic style has fallen by the wayside. In fact, some plants have no line management at all. What has replaced the manager is teams of workers who manage their own jobs. This "open system" setup is being used in selected plants by such companies as Control Data, Shell Oil, Exxon, and PepsiCo. Most of these plants are nonunion, and most of the jobs in them are routine. Two of the latest companies to try this "open" approach are Goodyear Tire & Rubber Company and Frito-Lay.

For several years, Goodyear concealed from the outside world just what was going on at its new Lawton, Oklahoma, facility. As it turns out, the place was an incubator for a bold experiment that put workers in total charge of what they do. The Lawton plant is a combination of advanced technology equipment and a unique employee involvement process. But according to Stanley J. Mihelick, an executive vice-president at Goodyear, "Without the people-involvement concept, this would merely be a good high-technology plant."

Goodyear believes so strongly in the Lawton success that it is instilling the same culture at other facilities. Although the concrete numbers that prove Lawton's superiority remain a corporate secret, chairman Robert E. Mercer appears convinced: "The Lawton-delivered tire cost will beat the cost of comparable tires from the lowest-cost foreign producers, meaning the Koreans, who think the Japanese are lazy." Commenting on his own presence at a Lawton flag-raising ceremony to designate the Oklahoma plant as the company's first "World-Class Competitor," Mercer indicated how much is riding on what Goodyear has discovered there: "This is the most significant trip I've made since I've been chairman. This plant proves that working smarter beats foreign producers and low labor costs any time, that the worker-as-his-own-manager works."

According to plant manager E. J. Rodia, all Lawton workers view themselves as "business centers": "They work for a business, but they still have the freedom to do their own thing. They are not afraid to fail, only of not trying." Vice-president Mihelick goes a bit further: "I can't give you figures. But in tires per employee per year, a usual measurement, Lawton blows those numbers out of the water. We don't even talk about that mea-

surement anymore. Lawton has 35% fewer managers than a traditional plant and is going to 50%. . . . We're producing 50,000 tires a day where at a comparable-sized plant they do 25,000. Already at our Gadsden, Ala., plant, where the Lawton approach is being put in, we've saved $30 million."

"What did you do perfect today?" and "Set a world record today?" are serious questions workers ask each other. The goal at Lawton is for every tire to be perfect. The plant has 164 worker teams, or natural work groups, with 5 to 27 people per group. The groups meet regularly to discuss goals, problems, and ways to make improvements. Their thinking is then funneled into 4 larger plant teams. "Forcing strategies" are used to create dissatisfaction with the status quo. For example, Lawton's repair department for imperfect tires was abolished, forcing workers to find ways of producing "perfect" tires. Imperfect tires are not fixed; they are scrapped. An even more recent refinement is the concept of each work group as a "business center" responsible for its own goals, productivity, costs, waste, and all other performance measurements.

Attendance is 99.1 percent. And when employees have their ten-minute break, they don't go to the smoking room. They "pick up a can and paint," according to Mihelick. Lawton has no distinguishing clothing or badges for managers, no designated parking, and no time clocks. Potential new hires are carefully screened, with participation by the team they'll join. Goodyear now is indoctrinating employees at other plants in the Lawton way.

Similar changes have been made at Frito-Lay's 300 employee plant in Kern County, California, near Bakersfield, and at its plant in Casa Grande, Arizona. According to a Frito-Lay spokesman, the Kern County plant reached full production one week after start-up, compared with the usual six to thirteen week initiation period.

At both plants, teams of workers run their own operations with virtually no supervision. Usually made up of eight workers, a team sets its own goals and inspects its own output. Management's job is to give feedback on costs, quality, and output and to provide technical assistance when asked. Each worker learns at least two and sometimes three jobs. Thus a delivery-truck driver can choose to load the truck or pack boxes if a temporary job switch between workers can be arranged. Each employee has the power to shut down the production line if he or she sees poor quality. Three members elected by the group approve the hiring of new team members. Although Frito-Lay has offered them the power to fire members, they don't want it. Teams meet regularly in conference rooms adjoining their work areas to discuss operations. As one worker put it, "We attack problems, not people. . . . We decide what's right, not who's right."

The Frito-Lay project is noteworthy if only because of the size of the company and the fact that elements of the "open" system are being used in about six of Frito-Lay's forty plants. Yet, according to James O'Neal, senior vice-president of operations in Dallas, "The open system, which we call 'the high-performance system,' has an influence beyond the plants in which it is used. People in all the plants know about it, of course, and since we continually circulate cost and quality reports among the plants, they try to beat the high-performance plants just to show that their way works, too."

DISCUSSION ISSUES

1. Are the work teams at Goodyear and Frito-Lay command groups or task groups? Explain.
2. At what stage of formal group development are Goodyear's work teams? Frito-Lay's work teams? Explain.
3. Would you categorize work teams at either Goodyear or Frito-Lay as mature? Explain.
4. Work teams at Frito-Lay are characterized as problem-solving groups ("we attack problems, not people). Is the work team size of eight appropriate for this type of group? Is the work team size of between five and twenty-seven appropriate for Goodyear's work groups? Explain.

TRAVEL INCENTIVES PAY OFF FOR PANASONIC AND APPLE®

When Panasonic's office systems division entered the U.S. copier market, it discovered quickly that the standard industry sales incentive was travel—the more exotic and luxurious, the better. Panasonic's 35-member sales staff sells office copiers through 275 dealerships. Only 30 percent of these dealerships deal exclusively in Panasonic equipment, which means that most dealers can win trips or receive other incentives from several manufacturers. Competition to come up with the best trip or incentive is therefore keen.

Panasonic's solution was the "Panasonic Grand Prix." In keeping with the theme of a "grand prix," each of Panasonic's four sales regions is assigned a racing car to serve as the team's symbol and each copier model is assigned a specific number of points. The sales force receives "Grand Prix" points for selling copiers. The dealers receive points for buying them. Every month, individual and team results are tabulated and reported in a newsletter appropriately titled *The Racer's Edge*. The newsletter includes quotes from the major "drivers"

Apple is a registered trademark of Apple Computer, Inc., Cupertino, CA 95014.

(salespeople) and data on team standings. Although individuals, not teams, qualify for the trip on the basis of their own performance, Jack Kelleher, assistant general manager of the division and national sales manager for the copier group, believes that the team idea builds cohesiveness and encourages competition.

When the five-month competition for 1984 ended, all but 1 of 28 eligible salespeople had qualified, as had 50 percent of the dealerships. Because trips were awarded to dealerships on the basis of every thousand points accumulated, several won more than one trip. These trips could be used by dealers to reward their employees.

The trip itself lasted nine days and followed a pattern Kelleher hopes to continue: four days in a major European city for culture and local color and the remainder of the trip in a beach resort with a more relaxed atmosphere. Formal business was covered in about a half-day. The remainder of the trip was devoted to social activities, including cocktail parties and banquets, tours, day-long cruises, and evenings at local night spots. The schedule also provided for considerable free time for sightseeing and shopping.

According to Kelleher, the only problem relates to the size of the group. With a group of approximately 320 salespeople, dealers, and spouses, and with five-star hotel accommodations required, the choice of location is somewhat limited. As a result, Panasonic is considering restructuring the qualifying rules to create two separate trips for different levels of achievement. The two-tier framework will permit small dealers to compete. In the past, they had little chance of qualifying.

Although he is unable to put a dollar figure on it, Kelleher feels strongly that incentive travel is a motivator. In fact, the trip has become so important symbolically that a dealer will buy extra inventory just to qualify and a salesperson will sell harder in order not to get left behind.

Apple Computer is also convinced that incentive travel is a motivator for its sales force. Incentive travel results in maximum team effort, explains Dave Bowman, director of U.S. sales. Apple's growth historically has been somewhere between 50 and 100 percent each year, so the trips are used to get everybody to pitch in.

The team incentive approach is especially evident in the Apple sales managers' annual trip—an all-or-nothing proposition. If all go over 100 percent of plan, everyone goes; if there is anyone less than 100 percent, nobody goes. One year, the group spent a week in Hong Kong. Another year included Monte Carlo and Paris. The qualifying period is Apple's fiscal year, which runs from October 1 to September 30.

The sales staff has the same qualifying period for its trip, but the destination and rules are different. Members of the sales staff can qualify for a week-long cruise by going 25 percent over their annual goal. One year, winners cruised from Miami to Nassau, San Juan, and St. Thomas. Another year, winners cruised to Grand Cayman Island, Montego Bay, and Cozumel. Salespeople who hit 150 percent of quota get an additional reward: their spouses are handed a tidy little $1,000 check for spending money on the trip.

It is Bowman's belief that travel incentives work best when spouses are involved. Each month, he sends home information, photos, and small souvenirs to inform spouses about what is happening and how close the salesperson is to the goal. According to Bowman, the response has been outstanding. He states, "Any time you have help from home, it keeps everybody on their toes."

The prospect of the trip, according to Bowman, is a motivator all year long. Furthermore, the trip itself fosters camaraderie and gives salespeople a chance to compare business concerns in an informal setting. Bowman believes that a trip is much more effective than money as an incentive: "If we gave them the equivalent in cash, say, $8,000 to $10,000 per couple, they'd probably spend it on the house or pay some bills. The trip gives them something to remember—and associate with Apple—for the rest of their lives."

DISCUSSION ISSUES

1. Will Panasonic's travel incentive necessarily motivate all salespeople and dealers? Explain from the Vroom expectancy theory perspective and from the Porter-Lawler perspective.
2. Do the Panasonic and Apple travel incentive approaches reflect a Theory X or Theory Y philosophy? Explain.
3. Are travel incentives motivator or hygiene factors? Explain.
4. Chapter 14 suggests that the most basic motivation strategy for managers is simply to communicate with organization members. In Panasonic's situation, is there any evidence that supports the communication → motivation → performance relationship? Explain.
5. From the life cycle theory of leadership perspective, what style of leadership appears to be called for to guide Panasonic and Apple salespeople? Explain.
6. Chapter 15 identifies numerous types of groups found in formal organizations. How would you classify the Apple sales manager group involved in the all-or-nothing annual trip contest?
7. If only individual points count in the contest, what was Panasonic hoping to gain by specifying team symbols (racing cars) and tabulating and reporting team standings as well as individual points in the newsletter?
8. Do you see any evidence of a status system and status symbols at Panasonic and Apple? Explain.

CONTROLLING

The purpose of this section is to introduce controlling, the fourth and last major management function. The previous three sections showed that managers must be able to plan, organize, and influence organizational variables. This section will explain that managers must also control these variables in order for their organizations to achieve long-term success. In general, the section will discuss the principles of controlling, the fundamentals of production management and control, and how information relates to the control function.

The discussion of the principles of controlling will open with a definition of *control function*. It will then present the three main steps in controlling and discuss the three main types of control. In addition, it will address the job of a controller and the elements necessary for managers to successfully perform the control function.

Production is an area that requires careful control. Therefore the discussion of the fundamentals of production management and control will emphasize operations management, productivity, and control tools that relate directly to production control. These tools include management by exception, breakeven analysis, materials requirements planning, and quality control.

Lastly, the section will explain how information relates to the control function, what factors influence the value of information, and how managers can use computers for generating and analyzing information. It will also discuss two information-related systems: the management information system (MIS) and the management decision support system (MDSS).

As you study the new material presented in this section, think about how the other functions of management relate to the process of controlling. Once you understand this last major function, you should have a thorough knowledge of how controlling must interact with planning, organizing, and influencing if organizations are to achieve long-term success.

STUDENT LEARNING OBJECTIVES

From studying this chapter, I will attempt to acquire:

1. A definition of *control.*
2. A thorough understanding of the controlling subsystem.
3. An appreciation for various kinds of control and for how each kind can be used advantageously by managers.
4. Insights on the relationship between power and control.
5. Knowledge of the various potential barriers that must be overcome for successful control.
6. An understanding of steps that can be taken to increase the quality of a controlling subsystem.

PRINCIPLES OF CONTROLLING

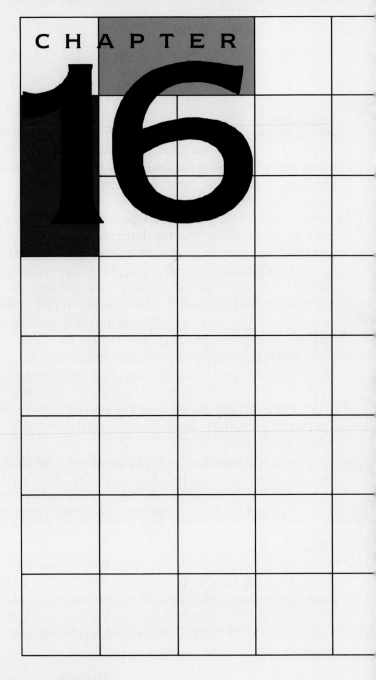

CHAPTER OUTLINE

HOSPITAL SERVICES, INC.

In the 1960s, considerable interest was generated in hospital care. The aged and the poor were heavily subsidized by government programs aimed, among other things, at helping those in need to get adequate hospital care. During the same time, the cost of hospital services doubled, and still there were not enough beds for patients. Federal and state governments saw the need to distinguish between the types of care that were most suitable. It was clear that not everyone needed the full-service care of general hospitals. The law contemplated that, once patients were discharged from such a facility, they would be sent for a limited time to a convalescent hospital, where the service level and costs were much lower. And, theoretically, having completed the allowed time, or as much of it as was needed, in this institution, patients would be returned to their homes, where they could receive needed services.

Jules McDonald was among several people who had the idea of building or buying a chain of convalescent hospitals to serve the growing need for beds. He thought that a chain probably could achieve some economies of operation that a single hospital would not find possible. He intended to broaden his business by purchasing land, securing a mortgage to take care of the hospitals, and selling the whole package to investors. He would place his own optical stores and drugstores within each hospital, have his own wholesalers in drugs and hospital equipment, and create his own construction companies.

McDonald needed money to do these things. He knew that the stocks of convalescent hospital chains were being traded in multiples from 60 to 200 times earnings, and so he determined to tap the investment market for capital. He got together a few scattered assets, packaged them attractively, and took his business public. It could not be said that he could show any earnings, but he stressed his prospective earnings per share. Amazingly, the idea sold, and he raised about $15 million.

With cash in the bank and an attractive vision in his head, McDonald was ready to go with his Hospital Services, Inc. Plush offices came first. Then a group of lawyers and tax accountants was added. A salesman sold him a computer. Convalescent hospitals were pur-

chased at high prices. Land was bought across the country, and construction was begun. Acquisitions were eagerly sought. McDonald did not do this all by himself. He was specially gifted in his public relations, government relations, and negotiations skills and tended to specialize in them. Managers were hired to take care of construction, hospital management, and finance.

As the months passed, the cash raised from the public issue was fast used. On paper, the cash flow from operations should have been adequate, but it did not actually materialize. No one, it seemed, was able to get a reading on hospital finances. In some cases, there were no profits; in other cases, the individual institution kept its own cash balance; and in others, there was a heavy drain of funds to cover expenses. The government did not help either. Its agencies were new at this activity; interpretations were being made in the law so frequently that no one knew what practice to follow.

Throughout this period of operation, there was no slowdown in activity. McDonald was in his element, but his controller failed to warn him of imminent bankruptcy. There did come a day when he ran out of money. This occurred at a time when bankers were tightening up credit and the stock market was falling fast.

As he looked over his wreck, he inquired, "What control system should I have had?"

What's Ahead

Perhaps the most significant managerial weakness of Jules McDonald in the introductory case was his failure to design and implement an effective control system for Hospital Services, Inc. The material in this chapter would help a manager such as McDonald overcome this weakness. The chapter emphasizes four main topics: (1) fundamentals of controlling, (2) the controller and control, (3) power and control, and (4) performing the control function.

⊞ FUNDAMENTALS OF CONTROLLING

Prospective managers need a working knowledge of the essentials of the controlling function.[1] To this end, the following sections provide a definition of control, a definition of controlling, and a discussion of the various types of control that can be used in organizations.

Defining Control

Stated simply, **control** is making something happen the way it was planned to happen.[2] As implied in this definition, planning and control are virtually inseparable.[3] In fact, the two have been called the Siamese twins of management.[4] According to Robert L. Dewelt:

> The importance of the planning process is quite obvious. Unless we have a soundly charted course of action, we will never quite know what actions are necessary to meet our objectives. We need a map to identify the timing and scope of all intended actions. This map is provided through the planning process.
>
> But simply making a map is not enough. If we don't follow it or if we make a wrong turn along the way, chances are we will never achieve the desired results. A plan is only as good as our ability to make it happen. We must develop methods of measurement and control to signal when deviations from the plan are occurring so that corrective action can be taken.[5]

Figure 16.1 on page 442 is a newsletter sent to General Tire employees by the corporate personnel office of the General Tire Company. Although the newsletter is essentially a lighthearted discussion of Murphy's Law, it does make the serious point that managers should continually control, checking to make sure that organizational activities and processes are going as planned.

Control is making things happen as planned.

441

MANAGEMENT IN GENERAL

A Newsletter for Management from Corporate Personnel-Akron

MALICE IN BLUNDERLAND

Thomas L. Martin wrote a book published in 1973 called
<u>Malice</u> in <u>Blunderland</u>. If you haven't read it, you might
want to obtain it from your local library or the Corporate
Research Library. The following are some excerpts:

"MURPHY'S LAWS"

First Law:	If something can go wrong, it will.
Second Law:	When left to themselves, things always go from bad to worse.
Third Law:	Nature always sides with the hidden flaw.

"REVISION OF MURPHY'S FIRST LAW"

If anything can go wrong (with a mechanical system),
it will, and generally at the moment the system becomes
indispensable.

"COROLLARIES TO MURPHY'S FIRST LAW"

It is impossible to make anything foolproof because fools
are so ingenious.

Any wire or tube cut to length will be too short.

Interchangeable parts won't.

Identical units tested under identical conditions will not
perform identically in the field.

After any machine or unit has been completely assembled,
extra components will be found on the bench.

Components that must not and cannot be assembled improperly,
will be.

All constants are variables.

In any given computation, the figure that is most obviously
correct will be the source of the error.

The book goes on and on with other laws as well. The thought hit us that
you might have your own contributions. So, if you have corollaries to
"Murphy's First Law," send them to us and we will publish them in a later
issue of Management in General.

FIGURE 16.1
Newsletter emphasizing the importance of managerial control

Defining Controlling

Controlling is the process managers go through to control. According to Robert Mockler, controlling is

> a systematic effort by business management to compare performance to predetermined standards, plans, or objectives to determine whether performance is in line with these standards and presumably to take any remedial action required to see that human and other corporate resources are being used in the most effective and efficient way possible in achieving corporate objectives.[6]

For example, production workers generally have production goals they must achieve per day and week. At the end of each working day, the number of units produced by each worker is recorded so weekly production levels can be determined. If the weekly totals are significantly below the weekly goals, the supervisor must take action to ensure that actual production levels are equivalent to planned production levels. If production goals are met, the supervisor probably should allow work to continue as it has in the past.

The following sections discuss the controlling subsystem and provide more details about the control process itself.

■ BACK TO THE CASE

Jules McDonald in the introductory case should have had a clearer understanding of control. Control within McDonald's organization would have entailed making things happen at Hospital Services, Inc., the way they were planned to happen. In essence, McDonald's control would have had to be closely related to his planning activities.

Going one step further, controlling at Hospital

Services would have been the steps or process that McDonald would have had to go through to control. Ideally, this process would have included a determination of plans, standards, and objectives at Hospital Services so action could be taken to eliminate organizational characteristics that caused deviation from these factors.

The Controlling Subsystem

As with the planning, organizing, and influencing functions described in earlier chapters, controlling can be viewed as a subsystem that is part of the overall management system (see Figure 16.2, p. 444). The purpose of the controlling subsystem is to help managers enhance the success of the overall management system through effective controlling. Figure 16.3 on page 445 shows the specific ingredients of the controlling subsystem.

The Controlling Process

As the process segment of Figure 16.3 implies, the three main steps of the controlling process are (1) measuring performance, (2) comparing measured performance to standards, and (3) taking corrective action.

Measuring Performance
Before managers can determine what must be done to make an organization more effective and efficient, they must measure current organizational performance. And before such a measurement can be taken, some unit of measure that

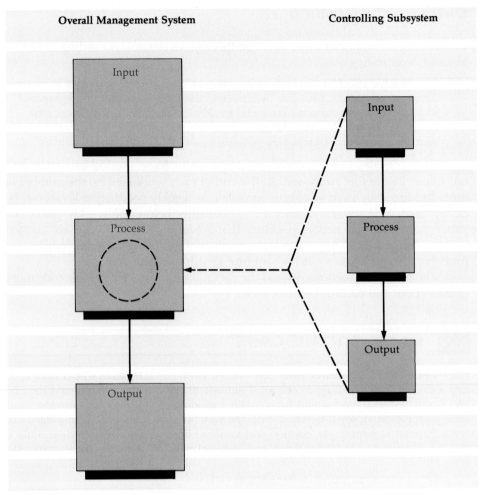

FIGURE 16.2
Relationship between overall management system and controlling subsystem

gauges performance must be established, and the quantity of this unit generated by the item whose performance is being measured must be observed.

For example, a manager who wants to measure the performance of five janitors first has to establish units of measure that represent janitorial performance, such as the number of floors swept, the number of windows washed, or the number of light bulbs changed. After designating these units of measures for janitorial performance, the manager then has to determine the number of each of these units associated with each janitor. This process of determining the units of measure and the number of units per janitor furnishes the manager with a measure of janitorial performance.

Managers also must keep in mind that a wide range of organizational activities can be measured as part of the control process. For example, the amounts and types of inventory kept on hand are commonly measured to control inventory, and the quality of goods and services being produced is commonly measured to control product quality. Performance measurements also can relate to various effects of production, such as the degree to which a particular manufacturing process pollutes the atmosphere.

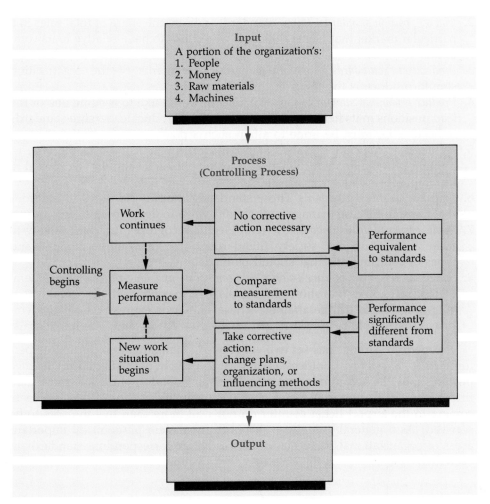

FIGURE 16.3
The controlling subsystem

As one might suspect, the degree of difficulty in measuring various types of organizational performance is determined primarily by the activity being measured. For example, the degree of difficulty in measuring the performance of a ditch-digger would differ greatly from the degree of difficulty in measuring the performance of a student enrolled in a college-level management course.[7]

The difficulty of measuring performance varies greatly.

Comparing Measured Performance to Standards

Once managers have taken a measure of organizational performance, their next step in controlling is to compare this measure against some standard. A **standard** is the level of activity established to serve as a model for evaluating organizational performance. In essence, standards are the yardsticks that determine if organizational performance is adequate or inadequate.[8] General Electric set performance standards for itself in each of the following general areas:[9]

Standards are yardsticks of performance.

1. *Profitability standards* In general, these standards indicate how much money General Electric would like to make as profit over a given time period—that is, its return on investment.

2. *Market position standards* These standards indicate the share of total sales in a particular market that General Electric would like to have relative to its competitors.
3. *Productivity standards* How much various segments of the organization should produce is the focus of these standards.
4. *Product leadership standards* General Electric would like to assume one of the lead positions in its field in product innovation. Product leadership standards indicate what must be done to attain such a position.
5. *Personnel development standards* Standards in this area indicate the type of training programs to which General Electric personnel should be exposed to develop appropriately.
6. *Employee attitudes standards* These standards indicate the types of attitudes that General Electric management should strive to develop in its employees.
7. *Public responsibility standards* General Electric recognizes its responsibility to make a contribution to society. Standards in this area outline the level and types of contributions that should be made.
8. *Standards reflecting relative balance between short- and long-range goals* General Electric recognizes that short-range goals exist to enhance the probability that long-range goals will be attained. These standards express the relative emphasis that should be placed on attaining various short- and long-range goals.

Standards should be established in all important areas of organizational performance.

American Airlines has set two very specific standards for appropriate performance of airport ticket offices: (1) at least 95 percent of the flight arrival times posted should be accurate in that actual arrival times do not deviate more than fifteen minutes from posted times, and (2) at least 85 percent of the customers coming to the airport ticket counter do not wait more than five minutes to be serviced. As a general guideline, successful managers pinpoint all important areas of organizational performance and establish corresponding standards in each area.

BACK TO THE CASE

McDonald should have viewed his controlling activities at Hospital Services, Inc., as a subsystem of the organization's overall management system. For him to have achieved organizational control, his controlling subsystem would have required a portion of the people, money, raw materials, and machines available at Hospital Services.

The process portion of the controlling subsystem at Hospital Services should have involved McDonald's taking three steps: (1) measuring the performance levels of various productive units, (2) comparing these performance levels to predetermined performance standards for these units, and (3) taking any corrective action necessary to make the planned performance levels at Hospital Services consistent with actual performance levels.

Areas in which McDonald probably should have developed standards at Hospital Services include the desired profitability of various hospitals, the performance levels needed to achieve this profit level, and the training necessary to equip employees to reach the desired performance levels.

Taking Corrective Action
Once managers have measured actual performance and compared this performance with established performance standards, they should take corrective action if necessary. **Corrective action** is managerial activity aimed at bringing organizational performance up to the level of performance standards. In other

words, corrective action focuses on correcting the mistakes in the organization that are hindering organizational performance. Before taking any corrective action, however, managers should make sure that the standards being used were properly established and that the measurements of organizational performance are valid and reliable. The "Management in Action" feature for this chapter gives some examples of corrective action that Jack Nicklaus took to gain control of his company Golden Bear International Inc.

At first glance, it seems fairly simple to state that managers should take corrective action to eliminate **problems**—factors within organizations that are barriers to organizational goal attainment. In practice, however, it may be difficult to pinpoint the problem causing some undesirable organizational effect. For example, a performance measurement may indicate that a certain worker is not adequately passing on critical information to fellow workers. If the manager is satisfied that the communication standards are appropriate and that the performance measurement information is valid and reliable, corrective action should be taken to eliminate the problem causing this substandard performance.

However, what exactly is the problem causing substandard communication? Is it that the individual is not communicating because she doesn't want to communicate? Or is she not communicating because the job makes communication difficult? Does she have the training needed to enable her to communicate in an appropriate manner? The manager must determine whether the individual's lack of communication is a problem in itself of a **symptom**—a sign that a problem exists. For example, the individual's lack of communication could be a symptom of inappropriate job design or a cumbersome organizational structure.

Once an organizational problem has been identified, necessary corrective action can focus on one or more of the three primary management functions of planning, organizing, and influencing. Correspondingly, corrective action can include such activities as modifying past plans to make them more suitable for future organizational endeavors, making an existing organizational structure more suitable for existing plans and objectives, or restructuring an incentive program to make sure that high producers are rewarded more than low producers. In addition, since planning, organizing, and influencing are closely related,

> Corrective action is action to bring performance up to standard.

> Symptoms are signs that problems exist.

> Corrective action should focus on planning, organizing, and influencing.

TABLE 16.1

Corrective action programs commonly used by managers and frequency of use

Corrective Action Program	Frequency of Program Use
Cost reduction	2.3
Employee participation	3.1
Productivity incentives	3.3
Goal setting with productivity focus	3.5
Increased automation	3.8
Quality improvement	3.9
Increased employee training	4.7
Better labor-management relations	4.9
Increased research and development	5.3

Note: The lower the frequency, the higher the relative use of the program.

JACK NICKLAUS IN CONTROL AT GOLDEN BEAR INTERNATIONAL

North Palm Beach, Fla.—In November 1985, Jack Nicklaus visited Chemical Bank in New York. Chemical had loaned his company $35 million for a golf community in Westchester County, N.Y., but the golfer told a group of stunned bankers the project was far behind schedule and he wasn't sure he could finish it.

"We recognize that we have a problem," Mr. Nicklaus said. In short, one of America's richest and most popular athletes faced a financial crisis.

The project was his most serious—but far from his only—business misadventure. It was also a turning point in his long and often painful education as a businessman. After relying on a series of appointed managers, Mr. Nicklaus had decided shortly before the Chemical meeting to take charge himself of his wholly owned Golden Bear International Inc.

"If you let someone else run the business, they'll follow their own philosophy," he says now. His last manager at Golden Bear "was looking for a home run. I am looking to run a good business."

GOOD AND THE BAD

Mr. Nicklaus's endorsements and golf course designs certainly are good business. But over the years, he has been guided by various managers into a Pontiac dealership, a radio station, a travel agency, a home-security company, an oil and gas general partnership, a golf-club management concern and real-estate development. None has turned out well.

"You shouldn't be involved with things you really don't know about," the 47-year-old, still-blond golfer says. "It's taken me 25 years of being on the periphery of my business to learn that."

Tales of sports figures with financial problems are common in the age of the athlete millionaire. Because of their wealth and fame, athletes attract myriad business offers; because most are relatively young and know little about handling money, they often plunge into ventures and investments that fizzle. Jack Nicklaus's problems reflect the hazards many athletes face as they try to turn their sports careers into financial security.

The entrance to Golden Bear's headquarters in North Palm Beach is distinctive, adorned with golf clubs and bags, photos of Mr. Nicklaus in action, his signature clothing lines and the golfer's books (in English, French and Japanese). Inside Mr. Nicklaus's office, however, there are no trophies, no putting machine—no trappings of his unrivaled career.

And Mr. Nicklaus isn't a figurehead. Since taking over, he has slashed debt by half, shrunk a high-priced corporate staff, cut overhead by 30% to 40% and narrowed the scope of his once-sprawling companies.

Most importantly, he worked out of trouble with Chemical. He offered to promote the luxury condominium project, called St. Andrews, and to take a $3 million loss; in return, Chemical forgave the rest of the loan, took over the property and hired a new developer. Chemical bankers decline to comment on the subject.

DESIGNING COURSES

Now, Mr. Nicklaus is concentrating on businesses he knows: golf course design, at which he is regarded as perhaps the best; MacGregor Golf Co., which makes golf gear; and a growing stream of endorsements, including Nabisco, Hartmarx and Manville. Business occupies at least part of his time almost every day; he plans to reduce his tournament schedule by more than a third this year.

And Golden Bear is doing well. Revenue [in 1987] was over $100 million, double that of 1984; profit surged to over $10 million, more than double 1984 earnings as well as the $5 million Mr. Nicklaus has earned in prize money during a lifetime of golf.

As a pudgy athlete who left Ohio State University without a diploma, Jack Nicklaus wasn't interested in business. If he hadn't become a golfer, he says, he probably would have been a pharmacist, like his father in Columbus, Ohio.

"He was smart, but he had no more business smarts than any college student," says Mark McCormack, Mr. Nicklaus's agent when he turned pro in 1961. Mr. McCormack, head of International Management Group, a sports-management firm in Cleveland, created and ran Golden Bear (after the golfer's nickname) as a vehicle for Mr. Nicklaus's businesses. Aside from endorsements, Mr. Nicklaus stuck to his sport.

there is a good chance that corrective action taken in one area will necessitate some corresponding change in one or both of the other two areas.

A study by Y. K. Shetty surveyed 171 managers from *Fortune's* list of the thirteen hundred largest U.S. industrial and nonindustrial companies.[10] One purpose of the study was to investigate the types of corrective action programs managers use and the frequency with which they are used. Table 16.1 on page 447 presents the results of this study. The corrective action programs listed in the table are only a sample of such programs, not an exhaustive list.

■ BACK TO THE CASE

If McDonald had determined that corrective action was necessary at Hospital Services, Inc., he would have had to be certain that the action was aimed at organizational problems rather than at symptoms of problems. Once Hospital Services' problems had been solved through corrective action, related symptoms eventually would have disappeared.

McDonald's corrective action at Hospital Services inevitably would have had to focus on past planning, organizing, or influencing efforts. In addition, as McDonald made changes in one of these areas, he probably would have found that some corresponding changes in another area were needed.

Types of Control

There are three types of management control: (1) precontrol, (2) concurrent control, and (3) feedback control. The type is determined primarily by the time period in which the control is emphasized in relation to the work being performed.

Precontrol

Control that takes place before work is performed is called **precontrol,** or feedforward control.[11] In this regard, management creates policies, procedures, and rules aimed at eliminating behavior that will cause undesirable work results. For example, the manager of a small record shop may find that a major factor in developing return customers is having salespeople discuss various records with customers. This manager might use precontrol by establishing a rule that salespeople cannot talk to one another while a customer is in the store. This rule is a precontrol because it is aimed at eliminating anticipated problems with salespeople before the salespeople are faced with a customer. Precontrol focuses on eliminating predicted problems.

Precontrol— controlling before people work.

Concurrent Control

Control that takes place as work is being performed is called **concurrent control.** It relates not only to human performance but also to such areas as equipment performance and department appearance. For example, most supermarkets have rigid rules about the amount of stock that should be placed on the selling floor. In general, these stores want to display generous amounts of all products on the shelves, with no empty spaces. A concurrent control aimed at ensuring that shelves are stocked as planned could be a stock manager's making periodic

Concurrent control— controlling while people work.

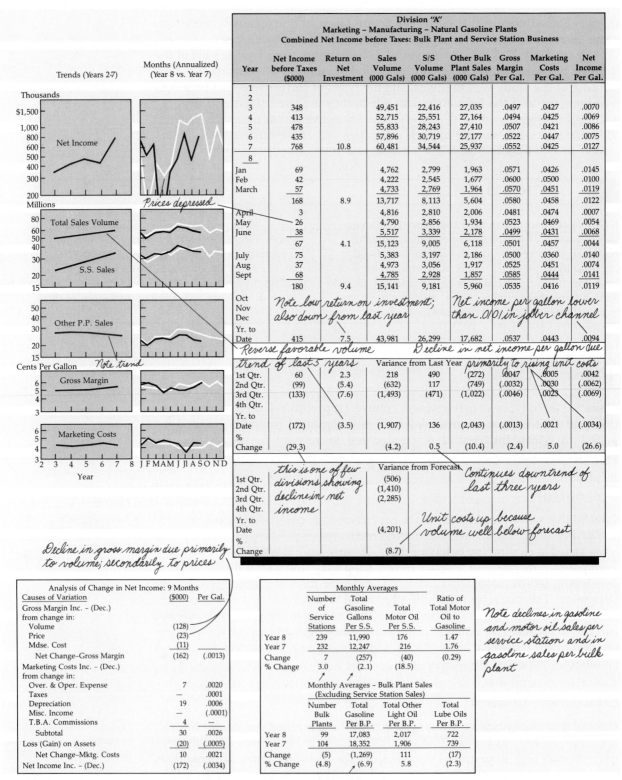

FIGURE 16.4
Example of a report that can serve as the basis for feedback control

450

visual checks throughout a work period to evaluate the status of the sales shelves and, correspondingly, the performance of the stock crew.

Feedback Control

Control that concentrates on past organizational performance is called **feedback control.** Managers exercising this type of control are attempting to take corrective action within the organization by looking at organizational history over a specified time period. This history may concentrate on only one factor, such as inventory levels, or on the relationships among many factors, such as net income before taxes, sales volume, and marketing costs.

Feedback control—controlling after people work.

Figure 16.4 is an example of a report, developed for an oil company, that can serve as the basis for feedback control. This particular report contains graphs that show various trends over a number of years as well as handwritten notes that highlight major trends. Management would use this report to compare actual organizational performance with planned organizational performance and then to take whatever corrective action is necessary to bring together actual and planned performance. Of course, the structure of such reports varies from organization to organization, depending on the various types and forms of information needed to present an overview of specific organizational activities.

BACK TO THE CASE

In controlling Hospital Services, Inc., McDonald probably would have found good use for some combination of precontrol, concurrent control, and feedback control. Precontrol would have emphasized the elimination of the factors at Hospital Services that could cause poor productivity before the work itself actually began. Through concurrent control, McDonald would have been able to assess work performance at Hospital Services while the work was being performed.

Lastly, McDonald's feedback control would have improved future performance by analyzing the history of Hospital Services. Some use of each of these types of control would have increased the probability of eliminating production problems before those problems caused too much damage. Perhaps McDonald's main mistake was that he emphasized feedback control to the exclusion of concurrent control and precontrol.

THE CONTROLLER AND CONTROL

Organization charts developed for medium- and large-sized companies typically contain a position called controller. The sections that follow explain more about controllers and their relationship to the control function by discussing the job of the controller and how much control is needed within an organization.

The Job of the Controller

The **controller** (also sometimes called the comptroller) is usually a staff person who gathers information that helps managers control. From the preceding discussion, it is clear that managers have the responsibility of comparing planned and actual performance and of taking corrective action when necessary. In smaller organizations, managers may be completely responsible for gathering information about various aspects of the organization and developing necessary reports based on this information. In medium- or large-sized companies, however, the controller handles much of this work. The controller's basic responsibility is assisting line managers with the controlling function by gathering appropriate information and generating reports that reflect this information.[12] The controller usually works with information about the following financial dimensions of the organization: (1) profits, (2) revenues, (3) costs, (4) investments, and (5) discretionary expenses.[13]

The sample job description of a controller in Table 16.2 shows that the controller is responsible for generating information on which a manager can base the exercising of control. Since the controller generally is not directly responsible for taking corrective action within the organization but instead advises a manager of what corrective action should be taken, the controller position is primarily a staff position.

TABLE 16.2

Sample job description for a controller in a large company

Objectives
The Controller (or Comptroller) is responsible for all accounting activities within the organization.

Functions
1. *General accounting* Maintain the company's accounting books, accounting records, and forms. This includes:
   a. Preparing balance sheets, income statements, and other statements and reports.
   b. Giving the president interim reports on operations for the recent quarter and fiscal year to date.
   c. Supervising the preparation and filing of reports to the SEC.
2. *Budgeting* Prepare a budget outlining the company's future operations and cash requirements.
3. *Cost accounting* Determine the cost to manufacture a product and prepare internal reports to management of the processing divisions. This includes:
   a. Developing standard costs.
   b. Accumulating actual cost data.
   c. Preparing reports that compare standard costs to actual costs and highlight unfavorable differences.
4. *Performance reporting* Identify individuals in the organization who control activities and prepare reports to show how well or how poorly they perform.
5. *Data processing* Assist in the analysis and design of a computer-based information system. Frequently, the data processing department is under the controller, and the controller is involved in management of that department as well as other communications equipment.
6. *Other duties* Other duties may be assigned to the controller by the president or by corporate bylaws. Some of these include:
   a. Tax planning and reporting.
   b. Service departments such as mailing, telephone, janitors, and filing.
   c. Forecasting.
   d. Corporate social relations and obligations.

Relationships
The Controller reports to the Vice-president for Finance.

How Much Control Is Needed?

As with all organizational endeavors, control activities should be pursued if the expected benefits of performing such activities are greater than the costs of performing them.[14] The process of comparing the cost of any organizational activity with the expected benefit of performing the activity is called **cost-benefit analysis.** In general, managers and controllers should collaborate to determine exactly how much controlling is justified in a given situation.

Figure 16.5 shows controlling activity over an extended period of time. According to this figure, controlling costs increase steadily as more and more controlling activities are performed. In addition, since the controlling function requires start-up costs, controlling costs at first usually are greater than the income generated from increased controlling. As controlling starts to correct major organizational errors, however, the income from increased controlling eventually equals controlling costs (point X_1 on the graph) and ultimately surpasses them by a large margin.

As more and more controlling activity is added beyond X_1, however, controlling costs and the income from increased controlling eventually become equal again (point X_2 on the graph). As more controlling activity is added beyond X_2, controlling costs again surpass the income from increased controlling. The main reason this last development takes place is that major organizational

Managers should perform a cost-benefit analysis to determine how much controlling activity is justified.

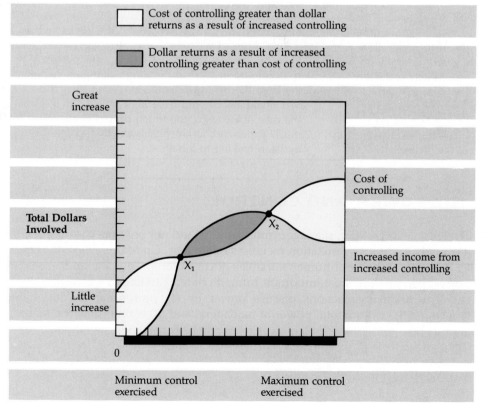

FIGURE 16.5
Value of additional controlling

problems probably have been detected much earlier, and corrective measures taken now are aimed primarily at smaller and more insignificant problems.

The following information about Franklin M. Jarman, a past chief executive of Genesco, Inc., makes the point that a manager can exercise too much control.[15] In 1973, Jarman fought his father, W. Maxey, for control of Genesco, a $1 billion retailing and apparel conglomerate. Jarman won. One of his first moves was to initiate a system of financial controls. These controls saved the company from ruin in 1973, when it lost $52 million. However, they ultimately may have been responsible for Jarman's downfall four years later.

According to people within Genesco, Jarman became obsessed with controls. Red tape and paperwork caused many delays and paralyzed operations. Management was centralized to the point of frustrating company executives. In its 1975 annual report, Genesco announced that in 1976 it would spend $8 million to open 63 stores and renovate 124 others. According to insiders, Jarman required so much analysis for these projects that decisions were postponed. Six months into fiscal year 1976, little of the projected work had been completed.

Because most of Genesco's business is in the fast-moving areas of apparel and retailing, delays and indecision can be very damaging. As a result, in January 1977 two dozen Genesco executives participated in a "palace revolt" that relieved Jarman of his responsibilities.

BACK TO THE CASE

The introductory case ends with the statement that McDonald's controller "failed to warn him of imminent bankruptcy." The basic job of the controller at Hospital Services, Inc., was to gather information for reports that McDonald could use to take corrective action. The controller was not to take any corrective action at Hospital Services but simply should have advised McDonald as to what corrective action should be taken. The root of the problem, however, was with McDonald. He failed to control the controller.

To have operated properly, McDonald should have determined, with or without the advice of his controller, exactly how much control was necessary at Hospital Services. In general, McDonald should have continued to increase controlling as long as the benefits from the control activities exceeded their cost. McDonald also should have kept in mind that, as in the case of Genesco, too much control could cause too much paperwork at Hospital Services and could bring decision making to a halt.

POWER AND CONTROL

The human related aspect of controlling is power.

To control successfully, managers must understand not only the control process itself but also how organization members relate to it. Up to this point, the chapter has emphasized nonhuman variables of controlling. This section focuses on power, perhaps the most important human related variable in the control process. The following sections discuss power by (1) presenting its definition, (2) elaborating on the total power of managers, and (3) listing the steps managers can take to increase their power over other organization members.

A Definition of Power

Power is the ability to influence others.

Perhaps the two most often confused terms in management are *power* and *authority*. Authority was defined in chapter 9 as the right to command or give orders. The extent to which an individual is able to influence others so they respond to orders is called **power.** The greater this ability, the more power an individual is said to have.

Obviously, power and control are closely related. To illustrate, after a manager compares actual performance with planned performance and determines that corrective action is necessary, orders usually are given to implement this action. Although the orders are issued through the manager's organizational authority, they may or may not be followed precisely, depending on how much power the manager has over the individuals to whom the orders are addressed.

Total Power of a Manager

The **total power** a manager possesses is made up of two different kinds of power: position power and personal power.[16] **Position power** is power derived from the organizational position a manager holds. In general, moves from lower-level management to upper-level management accrue more position power for a manager. **Personal power** is power derived from a manager's human relationships with others.

Total power = position power + personal power.

Steps for Increasing Total Power

Managers can increase their total power by increasing their position power or their personal power. Position power generally can be increased by a move to a higher organizational position, but managers usually have little personal control over moving upward in an organization. Managers do, however, have substantial control over the amount of personal power they hold over other organization members. John P. Kotter stresses the importance of developing personal power:

Managers can increase total power by increasing position power or personal power.

> To be able to plan, organize, budget, staff, control, and evaluate, managers need some control over the many people on whom they are dependent. Trying to control others solely by directing them and on the basis of the power associated with one's position simply will not work—first, because managers are always dependent on some people over whom they have no formal authority, and second, because virtually no one in modern organizations will passively accept and completely obey a constant stream of orders from someone just because he or she is the ''boss.''[17]

To increase personal power, a manager can attempt to develop:[18]

1. *A sense of obligation in other organization members that is directed toward the manager* If a manager is successful in developing this sense of obligation, other organization members think they should rightly allow the manager to influence them within certain limits. The basic strategy generally suggested to create this sense of obligation is to do personal favors for people.

2. *A belief in other organization members that the manager possesses a high level of expertise within the organization* In general, a manager's personal power increases as organization members perceive that the manager's level of expertise is increasing. To increase the perceived level of expertise, the manager must quietly make significant achievement visible to others and rely heavily on a successful track record and respected professional reputation.

3. *A sense of identification that other organization members have with the manager* The manager can strive to develop this identification by behaving in ways that other organization members respect and by espousing goals, values, and

A manager can increase personal power by:

1. Making people feel obligated.

2. Being seen as an expert in an area.

3. Having others identify with them.

ideals commonly held by them. The following description illustrates how a certain sales manager took steps to increase the degree to which his subordinates identified with him:

> One vice-president of sales in a moderate-sized manufacturing company was reputed to be so much in control of his sales force that he could get them to respond to new and different marketing programs in a third of the time taken by the company's best competitors. His power over his employees was based primarily on their strong identification with him and what he stood for. Emigrating to the United States at age seventeen, this person worked his way up "from nothing." When made a sales manager in 1965, he began recruiting other young immigrants and sons of immigrants from his former country. When made vice-president of sales in 1970, he continued to do so. In 1975, 85 percent of his sales force was made up of people whom he hired directly or who were hired by others he brought in.[19]

4. Holding the purse strings.

4. *The perception in other organization members that they are dependent on the manager* Perhaps the main strategy the manager should adopt in this regard is a clear demonstration of the amount of authority the manager possesses over organizational resources. Action taken in this regard should emphasize not only influence over resources necessary for organization members to do their jobs but also influence over resources organization members personally receive in such forms as salaries and bonuses. This strategy is aptly reflected in the managerial version of the Golden Rule: "He who has the gold makes the rules."

BACK TO THE CASE

For McDonald to have been successful in controlling at Hospital Services, Inc., he would have had to have been aware of not only the intricacies of the control process itself but also of how to deal with people as they relate to the control process. With regard to people and control, McDonald would certainly have had to consider the amount of power he held over organization members—that is, his ability to encourage them to follow orders. Most of these orders would have related to implementing corrective action that McDonald had deemed advisable for Hospital Services.

The total amount of power that McDonald possessed came from the position he held and from his personal relationships with other organization members. Since McDonald was head of Hospital Services, he already possessed more position power than anyone else in the organization. Therefore, to increase his total power, McDonald would have had to develop his personal power. He could have attempted to do this by developing (1) a sense of obligation in other organization members toward himself, (2) the belief in other organization members that he had a high level of task related expertise, (3) a sense of identification that other organization members had with him, and (4) the perception in organization members that they were dependent on him as a manager.

PERFORMING THE CONTROL FUNCTION

Controlling can be a detailed and intricate process, especially as the size of the organization increases. The two sections that follow furnish valuable guidelines for successfully executing this potentially complicated controlling function. These sections discuss potential barriers to successful controlling and making controlling successful.

Potential Barriers to Successful Controlling

Managers should take steps to avoid the following potential barriers to successful controlling:[20]

1. *Control activities can create an undesirable overemphasis on short-term production as opposed to long-term production* As an example, in striving to meet planned weekly production quotas, a manager might "push" machines in a particular area and not allow these machines to be serviced properly. This kind of management behavior would ensure that planned performance and actual performance are equivalent in the short term but may cause the machines to deteriorate to the point that long-term production quotas are impossible to meet.

2. *Control activities can increase employee frustration with their jobs and thereby reduce morale* This reaction tends to occur primarily when management exerts too much control. Employees get frustrated because they perceive management as being too rigid in its thinking and not allowing the freedom necessary to do a good job.[21] Another feeling that employees may have from overcontrol is that control activities are merely a tactic to pressure workers to higher production.

3. *Control activities can encourage the falsification of reports* The following excerpt makes this point:

> Not long ago, the Boy Scouts of America revealed that the membership figures coming from the field had been falsified. In response to the pressures of a national membership drive, people within the organization had vastly overstated the number of new Boy Scouts. To their chagrin, the leaders found something that other managers have also discovered: organizational control systems often produce unintended consequences. The drive to increase membership had motivated people to increase the number of new members reported, but it had not motivated them to increase the number of Boy Scouts actually enrolled.[22]

Employees may perceive management as basing corrective action solely on department records with no regard to extenuating circumstances. (The cartoon on the next page implies that people would sometimes prefer to have management consider extenuating circumstances when controlling.) If this is the case, employees may feel pressured to falsify reports so corrective action regarding their organizational unit will not be too drastic. For example, actual production may be overstated so it will look good to management or it may be understated to create the impression that planned production is too high, thereby tricking management into thinking that a lighter work load is justified.

4. *Control activities can cause the perspective of organization members to be too narrow for the good of the organization* Although controls can be designed to focus on relatively narrow aspects of an organization, managers must keep in mind that any corrective action should be considered not only in relation to the specific activity being controlled but also in relation to all other organizational units.

For example, a manager may determine that actual and planned production are not equivalent in a specific organizational unit because of various periods when a low inventory of needed parts causes some production workers to pursue other work activities instead of producing a product. Although the corrective action to be taken in this situation would seem to be simply

"I guess no man's a hero to his controller—right, Higgins?"

New Yorker, *January 19, 1987, p. 36. Drawing by D. Reilly;*
© *1987 The New Yorker Magazine, Inc.*

raising the level of inventory, this probably would be a very narrow perspective of the problem. The manager should seek to answer questions such as the following before any corrective action is taken: Is there enough money on hand to raise current inventory levels? Are there sufficient personnel presently in the purchasing department to effect a necessary increase? Who will do the work the production workers presently are doing when they run out of parts?

5. *Remember that controlling is a means, not an end.*

5. *Control activities can be perceived as the goals of the control process rather than the means by which corrective action is taken* Managers must keep in mind that information should be gathered and reports should be designed to facilitate the taking of corrective action within the organization. In fact, these activities can be justified only if they yield some organizational benefit that extends beyond the cost of performing them.

Making Controlling Successful

To make the control process more effective, managers should:

In addition to avoiding the potential barriers to successful controlling mentioned in the previous section, managers can perform certain activities to make the control process more effective. In this regard, managers should make sure that:

1. *Verify that controlling suits the situation.*

1. *Various facets of the control process are appropriate for the specific organizational activity being focused on*[23] As an example, standards and measurements concerning a line worker's productivity are much different from standards and measurements concerning a vice-president's productivity. Controlling ingredients related to the productivity of these individuals, therefore, must be different if the control process is to be applied successfully.

2. *Use control to achieve many ends.*

2. *Control activities are used to achieve many different kinds of goals* According to Jerome, control can be used for such purposes as standardizing performance,

protecting organizational assets from theft and waste, and standardizing product quality.[24] Managers should keep in mind that the control process can be applied to many different facets of organizational life and that, for the organization to receive maximum benefit from controlling, each of these facets should be emphasized.

3. *Information used as the basis for taking corrective action is timely*[25] Some time necessarily elapses as managers gather control related information, develop necessary reports based on this information, decide what corrective action should be taken, and actually take the corrective action. However, information should be gathered and acted on as promptly as possible to ensure that the situation, as depicted by this information, has not changed and that the organizational advantage of corrective action will, in fact, materialize.

3. Act on information quickly.

4. *The mechanics of the control process are understandable to all individuals who are in any way involved with implementing the process*[26] Managers should take steps to ensure that people know exactly what information is necessary for a particular control process, how that information is to be gathered and used to compile various reports, what the purposes of various reports actually are, and what corrective actions are appropriate given various possible types of reports. The lesson here is simple: For control to be successful, all individuals involved in controlling must have a working knowledge of how the control process operates.

4. Make controlling understood.

■ BACK TO THE CASE

In addition to understanding the intricacies of control and how people fit into the control process, McDonald should have been aware of the potential barriers to successful controlling and the action he could have taken to increase the probability that his controlling activities would be successful.

To overcome the potential control related barriers at Hospital Services, Inc., McDonald should have balanced his emphasis on short-term versus long-term objectives, minimized the negative influence controlling might have had on the morale of Hospital Services organization members, eliminated forces that might have led to the falsification of control related reports, implemented a control perspective that would have appropriately combined narrow and broad organizational focuses, and stressed controlling as a means rather than an end.

With regard to the action that could have been taken to increase the probability of effective controlling activities, McDonald should have made sure that various facets of his controlling subsystem were appropriate for Hospital Services activities, that components of the controlling subsystem were flexible and suited to many purposes, that corrective action was based on timely information, and that the controlling subsystem was understood by all organization members involved in its operation.

Action Summary

Reread the learning objectives that follow. Each objective is followed by questions. Answering these questions accurately will help you retain the most important concepts discussed in this chapter. After answering each question, check your answer with the answer key at the end of this chapter. (*Hint:* If you have doubt regarding the correct response, consult the page whose number follows the answer.)

Circle:

From studying this chapter, I will attempt to acquire:

1. A definition of *control*.

a, b, c, d, e
    a. Managers must develop methods of measurement to signal when deviations from standards are occurring so that: (a) the plan can be abandoned; (b) quality control personnel can be notified; (c) the measurement standards can be checked; (d) corrective action can be taken; (e) none of the above.

T, F
    b. Control is making something happen the way it was planned to happen.

2. A thorough understanding of the controlling subsystem.

a, b, c, d, e
    a. The main steps of the controlling process include all of the following *except:* (a) taking corrective action; (b) establishing planned activities; (c) comparing performance to standards; (d) measuring performance; (e) all of the above are steps in controlling.

T, F
    b. Standards should be established in all important areas of organizational performance.

3. An appreciation for various kinds of control and for how each kind can be used advantageously by managers.

a, b, c, d, e
    a. Which of the following is not one of the basic types of management control: (a) feedback control; (b) precontrol; (c) concurrent control; (d) exception control; (e) all are basic types of control.

a, b, c, d, e
    b. An example of precontrol established by management would be: (a) rules; (b) procedures; (c) policies; (d) budgets; (e) all of the above are examples.

4. Insights on the relationship between power and control.

T, F
    a. According to Kotter, controlling others solely on the basis of position power will not work.

a, b, c, d, e
    b. The extent to which an individual is able to influence others to respond to orders is: (a) power; (b) sensitivity; (c) authority; (d) communication skills; (e) experience.

5. Knowledge of the various potential barriers that must be overcome for successful control.

a, b, c, d, e
    a. Potential barriers to successful controlling can result in: (a) an overemphasis on short-term production as opposed to long-term production; (b) employees' frustration with their jobs and thereby reduced morale; (c) the falsification of reports; (d) causing the perception of organization members to be too narrow for the good of the organization; (e) all of the above.

T, F
    b. Control activities should be seen as the means by which corrective action is taken.

6. An understanding of steps that can be taken to increase the quality of a controlling subsystem.

a, b, c, d, e
    a. All of the following are suggestions for making controlling successful *except:* (a) managers should make sure the mechanics of the control process are understood by organization members involved with controlling; (b) managers should use control activities to achieve many different kinds of goals; (c) managers should ensure that control activities are supported by most organization members; (d) managers should make sure that information used as the basis for taking corrective action is timely; (e) all of the above are suggestions.

b. The standards and measurements concerning a line worker's productivity are much the same as the standards and measurements concerning a vice-president's productivity.

T, F

INTRODUCTORY CASE WRAP-UP

"Hospital Services, Inc." (p. 440) and its related back-to-the-case sections were written to help you better understand the management concepts contained in this chapter. Answer the following discussion questions about this introductory case to further enrich your understanding of chapter content:

1. At the end of the introductory case, McDonald asked, "What control system should I have had?"

What do you think McDonald meant by *control system?*

2. Do you think that McDonald could have controlled Hospital Services by himself? Explain.

3. List several areas of Hospital Services that McDonald's controlling activities should have emphasized.

Issues for Review and Discussion

1. What is control?
2. Explain the relationship between planning and control.
3. What is controlling?
4. What is the relationship between the controlling subsystem and the overall management system?
5. Draw and explain the controlling subsystem.
6. List and discuss the three main steps of the controlling process.
7. Define the term *standards*.
8. What is the difference between a symptom and a problem? Why is it important to differentiate between a symptom and a problem in controlling?
9. What types of corrective action can managers take?
10. List and define the three basic types of control that can be used in organizations.
11. What is the relationship between controlling and the controller?
12. What basis do managers use to determine how much control is needed in an organization?
13. What is the difference between power and authority? Describe the role of power within the control process.
14. What determines how much power a manager possesses?
15. How can a manager's personal power be increased?
16. Describe several potential barriers to successful controlling.
17. What steps can managers take to ensure that control activities are successful?

Sources of Additional Information

Bartolomé, Fernando, and André Laurent. "The Manager: Master and Servant of Power." *Harvard Business Review* (November/December 1986): 77–81.

Bruns, William J., Jr., and F. Warren McFarlan. "Information Technology Puts Power in Control Systems." *Harvard Business Review* (September/October 1987): 89–94.

Drake, Rodman L., and Lee M. Caudill. "Management of the Large Multinational: Trends and Future Challenges." *Business Horizons* 24 (May/June 1981): 83–91.

Hecht, Maurice R. *What Happens in Management: Principles and Practices.* New York: Amacom, 1980.

Hogan, Peter. "Using the Behavioural Sciences to Measure Management Performance." *Personnel Management* 13 (February 1981): 36–39.

"How TRW Tracks Multiple Programs." *Management Review* (March 1983): 44–45.

Hutchins, David. *Quality Circles Handbook*. New York: Nichols Publishing, 1985.

Kaplan, R. S. "One Cost System Isn't Enough." *Harvard Business Review* 66 (January/February 1988):61–66.

Kotter, John P. *Power and Influence*. New York: Free Press, 1985.

Lawler, Edward E., III, and John Grant Rhode. *Information and Control in Organizations*. Santa Monica, Calif.: Goodyear, 1976.

Ludwig, Richard. "A Team Approach to Cost Cutting." *Management World* 15 (July/August 1986): 18–19.

McTague, Michael. "Signposts on the Road to Excellence." *Business* 36 (April/May/June 1986): 3–12.

Moravec, Milan. "Performance Appraisal: A Human Resource Management System with Productivity Payoffs." *Management Review* 70 (June 1981): 51–54.

Rhodes, David, and Mike Wright. "Management Control for Effective Corporate Planning." *Long-Range Planning* 17 (August 1984): 115–21.

Rubin, Leonard R. "Planning Trees: A CEO's Guide through the Corporate Planning Maze." *Business Horizons* 27 (September/October 1984): 66–70.

Shanklin, William L. "Strategic Business Planning: Yesterday, Today, and Tomorrow." *Business Horizons* 22 (October 1979): 7–14.

Tannenbaum, A. *Control in Organizations*. New York: McGraw-Hill, 1968.

Notes

1. L. R. Bittle and J. E. Ramsey (eds.), *Handbook for Professional Managers* (New York: McGraw-Hill, 1985).

2. K. A. Merchant, "The Control Function of Management," *Sloan Management Review* 23 (Summer 1982): 43–55.

3. For an example of how a control system can be used with a formal planning model, see A. M. Jaeger and B. R. Baliga, "Control Systems and Strategic Adaptations: Lessons from the Japanese Experience," *Strategic Management Journal* 6 (April/June 1985): 115–34.

4. Donald C. Mosley and Paul H. Pietri, *Management: The Art of Working with and through People* (Encino, Calif.: Dickenson, 1975), 29–43.

5. Robert L. Dewelt, "Control: Key to Making Financial Strategy Work," *Management Review* (March 1977): 18.

6. Robert J. Mockler, ed., *Readings in Management Control* (New York: Appleton-Century-Crofts, 1970), 14.

7. Insights concerning how such measurements can influence employee performance can be found in Mark K. Hirst, "Accounting Information and the Evaluation of Subordinate Performance: A Situational Approach," *Accounting Review* 56 (October 1981): 771–84.

8. For a discussion of how standards are set, see James B. Dilworth, *Production and Operations Management: Manufacturing and Nonmanufacturing* (New York: Random House, 1986), 637–50.

9. Robert W. Lewis, "Measuring, Reporting, and Appraising Results of Operations with References to Goals, Plans, and Budgets," in *Planning, Managing, and Measuring the Business: A Case Study of Management Planning and Control at General Electric Company* (New York: Controllership Foundation, 1955).

10. Y. K. Shetty, "Product Quality and Competitive Strategy," *Business Horizons* (May/June 1987): 46–52.

11. Harold Koontz, Cyril O'Donnell, and Heinz Weihrich, *Essentials of Management* (New York: McGraw-Hill, 1986), 454–59.

12. Vijay Sathe, *Controller Involvement in Management* (Englewood Cliffs, N.J.: Prentice-Hall, 1982).

13. James D. Wilson, *Controllership: The Work of the Managerial Accountant* (New York: Wiley, 1981).

14. For other ways in which cost-benefit analysis can be used by managers, see G. S. Smith and M. S. Tseng, "Benefit-Cost Analysis as a Performance Indicator," *Management Accounting* (June 1986): 44–49; "The IS (Information System) Payoff," *Infosystems* (April 1987): 18–20.

15. Adapted from "What Undid Jarman: Paperwork Paralysis," *Business Week*, January 24, 1977, 67.

16. Amitai Etzioni, *A Comparative Analysis of Complex Organizations* (New York: Free Press, 1961), 4–6.

17. John P. Kotter, "Power, Dependence, and Effective Management," *Harvard Business Review* (July/August 1977): 128.

18. Kotter, "Power, Dependence, and Effective Management," 135–36.

19. Kotter, "Power, Dependence, and Effective Management," 131.

20. For further discussion of overcoming the potential negative effects of control, see Ramon J. Aldag and Timothy M. Stearns, *Management* (Cincinnati, Ohio: South-Western Publishing, 1987), 653–54.

21. Arnold F. Emch, "Control Means Action," *Harvard Business Review* (July/August 1954): 92–98. See also K. Hall and L. K. Savery, "Tight Rein, More Stress," *Harvard Business Review* (January/February 1986): 160–64.

22. Cortlandt Cammann and David A. Nadler, "Fit Control Systems to Your Managerial Style," *Harvard Business Review* (January/February 1976): 65.

23. Peter F. Drucker, *Management: Tasks, Responsibilities, Practices* (New York: Harper & Row, 1974).

24. W. Jerome III, *Executive Control: The Catalyst* (New York: Wiley, 1961), 31–34.

25. William Bruns, Jr., and E. Warren McFarlan, "Information Technology Puts Power in Control Systems," *Harvard Business Review* (September/October 1987): 89–94.

26. C. Jackson Grayson, Jr., "Management Science and Business Practice," *Harvard Business Review* (July/August 1973): 41–48.

Action Summary Answer Key

1. a. d, p. 443
   b. T, p. 441
2. a. b, p. 443
   b. T, pp. 446–447

3. a. d, p. 449
   b. e, p. 449
4. a. T, p. 455
   b. a, pp. 454–455

5. a. e, p. 457
   b. T, p. 457
6. a. c, pp. 458–459
   b. F, p. 458

THE FINAL MISSION OF THE SPACE SHUTTLE CHALLENGER

On the morning of January 28, 1986, mission 51-L of the space shuttle *Challenger* began on an ice-encrusted pad at the Kennedy Space Center at Cape Canaveral. It ended 73 seconds after blastoff, killing all seven members of its crew. The evidence suggests that the cause of the accident was the failure of two rubber O rings on the shuttle's solid-fuel booster rockets.

The O rings are a pair of synthetic rubber washers similar to those used in a faucet. They keep the superhot gases from squirting through tiny gaps in the joint between sections of the solid-fuel rocket. When the O rings failed, the escaping gases cut into the shuttle's liquid-fuel booster and triggered a massive explosion. It is thought that the low temperatures the morning of the flight reduced the resiliency and hardness of the rings, preventing them from sealing.

Time magazine, in its March 10, 1986, issue, described the events leading up to the tragedy:

> As early as Dec. 17, 1982, . . . NASA [the National Aeronautics and Space Administration] had been concerned enough about the possibility that the O rings might fail during lift-off to designate them as "criticality 1" items, components whose failures would doom the mission. . . .
>
> In July 1985 NASA Budget Analyst Richard Cook had warned in an internal memo that unless the O rings were improved, a "catastrophic" failure might follow. . . . Engineer Roger Boisjoly, Thiokol's top expert on the rings, [said] that he had sent a similar memo to his superiors only days after Cook sent his. . . . One month later, yet another Thiokol engineer, Arnold Thompson, urged his company to ask NASA to suspend all flights until the seal problem was fixed. Thiokol management apparently did not convey these warnings to NASA.
>
> . . . After hearing forecasts that the Florida temperature might fall to as low as 18°F [the] night [of January 27], Robert Ebeling, a Thiokol engineer at the company's plant in Brigham City, Utah, telephoned [Allan] McDonald [Thiokol's director of the solid-fuel rocket project and the company's senior official at Cape Canaveral] at the Cape about 4 P.M. He said that he and other engineers at the plant were worried about the seals. McDonald then got the latest prediction, about 22°, and, finding this "very serious," called Robert Lund, the vice president for engineering at Thiokol, to urge a full-scale analysis to determine if the seals could perform safely at that temperature. It should be "an engineering decision," McDonald told Lund, "not a program-management decision."

As a result of McDonald's statement, a teleconference was set up among the engineers in Utah; officials at Marshall Space Flight Center in Huntsville, Alabama; and managers at Cape Canaveral. Among the teleconferees were Lawrence Mulloy, the chief of the booster program at Marshall; Judson Lovingood, deputy manager of the shuttle projects office at Marshall; Stanley Reinartz, Lovingood's boss; George Hardy, an engineering official at Marshall; Joe Kilminster, vice president for booster programs at Thiokol; Jerald Mason, senior vice president; Calvin Wiggins, vice president for space projects; Boisjoly; Lund; and a dozen Thiokol engineers.

The March 10 issue of *Time* continued:

> Boisjoly presented six charts that had been transmitted to the others and argued that "lower temperature was a factor" in O-ring performance. Lund, the highest engineering officer, said flatly that unless the temperature reached at least 53°, "I don't want to fly."
>
> Mulloy and Hardy led the NASA challenge to this conclusion. Hardy said that he was "appalled" by the reasoning behind the no-fly stance of Thiokol, while Mulloy insisted that there was no demonstrable link between temperature and O-ring erosion. He contended that despite NASA's placing the booster seals on the criticality-1 list because of a lack of redundancy, the backup ring would certainly seat in the critical early-ignition phase of the launch and provide a seal even if gases got by the first ring. Since NASA had not established a minimum launch temperature for the boosters, he and Hardy both complained that Thiokol was trying to change the flight criteria on the night before a scheduled mission. Said Mulloy: "You can't do

that." In his testimony [later on], he did not deny having said, "My God, Thiokol, when do you want me to launch, next April?" But he argued that his listeners had taken his highly publicized remark out of context.

After some two hours of debate, Kilminster, who had supported Thiokol's no-go position, asked for a five-minute recess to consider NASA's objections. The break stretched on for half an hour. Caucusing in Utah, the engineers remained unanimous against the launch. Nonetheless, Mason declared that "we have to make a management decision," then turned to Lund and asked him to "take off his engineering hat and put on his management hat." In front of the surprised engineers, Mason polled only the management officials, getting Lund, Wiggins and Kilminster to join him in giving NASA a recommendation from Thiokol to launch.

When the teleconference resumed and Kilminster announced the startling turnabout, Marshall's shuttle manager Reinartz asked if anyone on the network had any comment on the decision. There was no response. Thiokol was now on record as no longer opposing the launch, and the telephone hookup was ended. Kilminster telefaxed a memo to the Cape and Huntsville formalizing the change.

Following the disaster, a presidential commission headed by former Secretary of State William Rogers and a House Science and Technology Committee were established to investigate the *Challenger* catastrophe. The reports of these two groups suggest that shuttle workers were motivated to make unsound decisions in large part because of pressure to achieve a planned flight rate of twenty-four missions a year. It was clear to both groups that the shuttle launch system was not functioning well and had become increasingly unsafe as the flight rate was increased.

In addition, as *Aviation Week & Space Technology* noted: "The Rogers Commission concluded that safety representatives had lost their independence because they reported to the programs they were overseeing rather than to an independent safety organization." The Reagan administration, Congress, and the House committee agreed that the blame for the accident was both Thiokol's and NASA's. They concluded that NASA must never again set unreasonable goals that stress the system beyond its safe functioning.

Today NASA is rebuilding its safety and quality assurance program by increasing its staff levels, expanding its scope, and strengthening the independence of safety personnel. George Rodney, who was appointed Associate Administrator for Safety, Reliability, and Quality Assurance, said that his first objective was to reestablish the presence of Safety, Reliability and Quality Assurance management in individual NASA programs. In the future, these people will be present at all significant flight readiness events.

One of Rodney's top priorities was to redesign NASA's internal communication system. He planned to create a problem-reporting system to manage the flow routinely. Included would be some type of "channel" through which middle- and lower-level managers and workers could voice safety concerns to senior management. Another step to improve safety would be to establish a number of independent watchdog groups. One of these groups was to be a small full-time team within Rodney's safety office to independently assess potential problems. This team would have the right to look into safety matters through all the program phases.

A second operational safety group was to be headed by astronaut Frederick Gregory. In addition, two advisory groups—the Aerospace Safety Advisory Panel and an internal safety panel focusing on manned flight safety issues and headed by astronaut Bryan O'Connor—would provide direction and guidance to the safety office.

Even with all these changes, Rodney has argued, there will always be some risks involved in a high-technology business such as NASA. Although risk can never be totally eliminated, he believes it can be reasonably managed. As Rodney has said: "It is our job to manage that risk, recognize where we have risk, and minimize and control it."

DISCUSSION ISSUES

1. Explain how the control activity of an imposed rate of twenty-four shuttle flights per year created a barrier to successful controlling.
2. How was the launch/no-launch decision flawed by NASA's original power structure?
3. Considering the launching violations that were documented in the case, which type of control (by timing) was the most ineffective? How was feedback control exercised?
4. In NASA's new system, a "hotline" to be used as a channel for middle- and lower-level managers and workers to voice safety concerns to senior management was decided against. Potential barriers to successful controlling point to employee frustration as a factor. How might this factor relate to the decision against a hotline?
5. Which control activities for making controlling successful appear to have been overlooked or at least given very little emphasis in the final few hours leading up to the infamous last mission of the space shuttle *Challenger*?

STUDENT LEARNING OBJECTIVES

From studying this chapter, I will attempt to acquire:

1. Definitions of both *production* and *production control*.
2. An understanding of how productivity and layout patterns relate to the production process.
3. An appreciation for the significance of operations management.
4. Insights on how management by exception and breakeven analysis can be used to control production.
5. An understanding of how quality control and materials requirements planning and control can contribute to production control.
6. Knowledge of how budgets and ratio analysis can be used to achieve overall or broader organizational control.

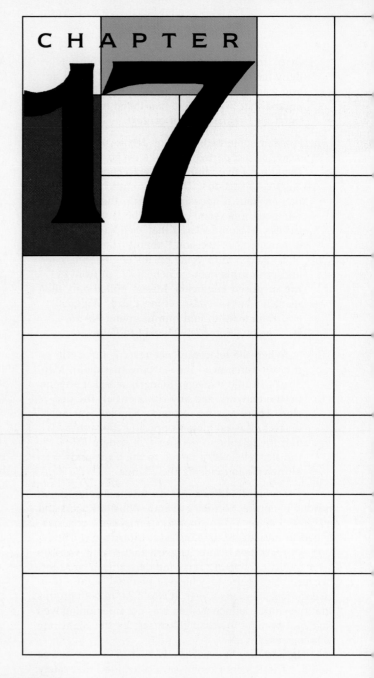

PRODUCTION MANAGEMENT AND CONTROL

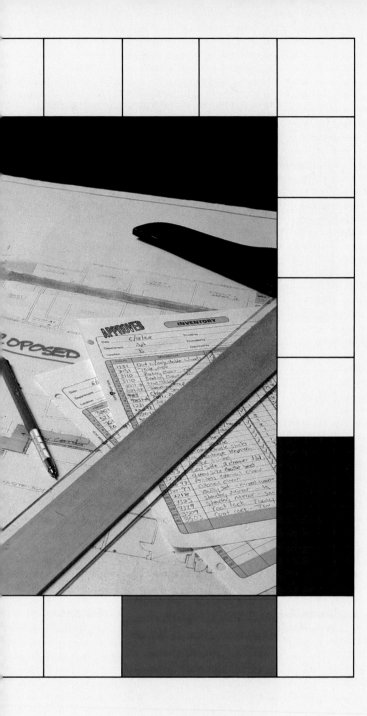

CHAPTER OUTLINE

PRODUCTION SNAGS AT COMMODORE

When Commodore International Limited, a home computer maker, began selling its Commodore 64 to mass merchandisers, only 5 to 7 percent of the machines were returned for defects. Only a few months later, however, the rate had risen sharply. The president of CSI Distributors, Inc., in Spring Valley, New York, said that when CSI began selling the Commodore 64, the defect rate started off at 30 percent and then went down to 15 percent. A year later, the defect rate was back up again.

Many of Commodore's problems centered around the Commodore 64 disk drive, the part of the computer that uses a floppy disk. To begin with, Commodore had opted to have the disk drives made in the Far East because of a potential savings of about $15 million annually. This decision proved troublesome for several reasons. First, the Far East manufacturer shipped the disk drives by sea, which significantly slowed deliveries. Then, an entire shipment of 170,000 Commodore disk drives was discovered to be defective. The situation apparently worsened shortly thereafter, when Commodore's disk drive maker abruptly halted production temporarily. The resulting shortage left many distributors without disk drive shipments for an average of about three months.

In an attempt to make disk drives available to its distributors, Commodore sent a rush order to its manufacturer for more than 100,000 of the drives to be sent air freight. Industry officials said, however, that Commodore's disk drive maker had a production capacity of only 50,000 units per month—far below the 8,000 to 10,000 a day capacity at Commodore's assembly plants.

In addition to the disk drive shortages and defects, Commodore had still other production problems. For

example, one shipment of video screen monitors didn't fit the Commodore 64 properly. Another of Commodore's production problems involved its highest-priced letter quality printer. The printer was pulled off the market because it "froze" on the print command.

Commodore's top executives, while refusing to provide any details, generally dismissed the reports of production problems as overblown. They set the defect rate of the Commodore 64 at 7 percent. Don Richard, acting vice-president at Commodore's U.S. unit, said: "Our manufacturing problems are our internal affairs. We just don't want to discuss some of this."

Despite these production problems at Commodore, the company has made significant progress.* Think how much more progress management might have made, however, if the problems had never existed.

* Lewis, Geoff. "Commodore Is Anything But Dead" *Business Week*, March 9, 1987, pp. 96–97.

What's Ahead

The introductory case describes the reported high defect rates of various goods produced at Commodore International Limited. This chapter is designed to help managers, such as those at Commodore, who are confronted with high defect rates as well as other production related problems.

This chapter emphasizes the fundamentals of **production control**—ensuring that an organization produces goods and services as planned. The three primary discussion areas in the chapter are (1) production, (2) operations management, and (3) production and control.

 PRODUCTION

To reach organizational goals, all managers must plan, organize, influence, and control to produce some type of goods or services. Naturally, these goods and services vary significantly from organization to organization. This section of the chapter defines *production* and discusses productivity and the production facility.

Defining Production

Production is the transformation of organizational resources into products.[1] In this definition, *organizational resources* are all assets available to a manager to generate products, *transformation* is the set of steps necessary to change these resources into products, and *products* are various goods or services aimed at meeting human needs. Figure 17.1 on page 470 contains examples of organizational resources (inputs), transformation processes, and goods and services produced (outputs) for each of three different types or organizations.

> Production is the transformation of organizational resources into products.

Productivity

Productivity is an important consideration in designing, evaluating, and improving modern production systems. The two sections that follow define *productivity* and discuss robotics, a means of increasing productivity.

Defining Productivity

Productivity is the relationship between the total amount of goods or services being produced (output) and the organizational resources needed (input) to produce them. This relationship is usually expressed by the following equation:[2]

> Productivity is the ratio of outputs to inputs.

$$\text{Productivity} = \frac{\text{Outputs}}{\text{Inputs}}$$

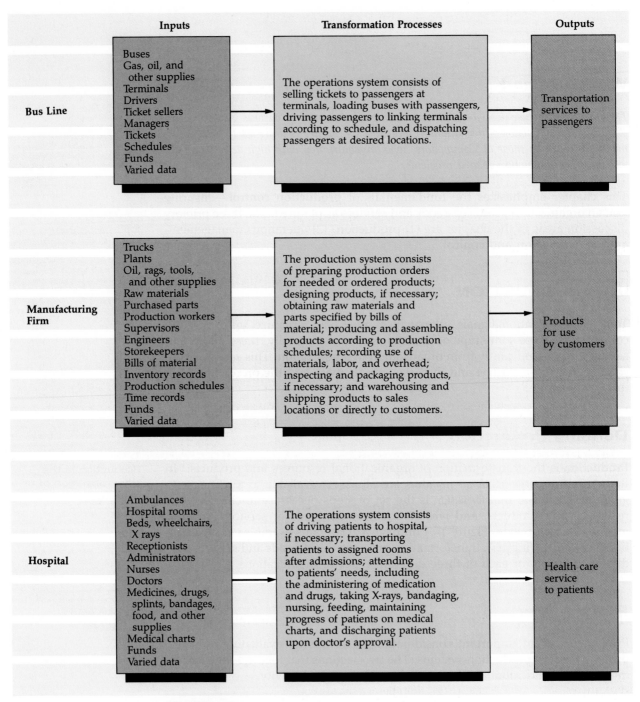

FIGURE 17.1
Inputs, transformation processes, and outputs for three different types of organizations

The higher the value of the ratio of outputs to inputs, the higher the productivity of the operation.

Although managers should continually strive to make their production processes as productive as possible, it is no secret that over the last twenty years

Five traditional strategies can increase productivity.

productivity growth related to production management and innovation in manufacturing within the United States has lagged significantly behind that of countries such as Japan, West Germany, and France.[3] Some of the more traditional strategies for increasing productivity include (1) improving the effectiveness of the organizational work force through training, (2) improving the production process through automation, (3) improving product design to make products easier to assemble, (4) improving the production facility by purchasing more modern equipment, and (5) improving the quality of workers hired to fill open positions.

Robotics: A Means of Increasing Productivity

The preceding section presented a number of traditional means of increasing productivity within organizations. Robotics shows promising signs of increasing productivity in a more revolutionary way.

Robotics is the area of study dealing with the development and use of robots. A **robot** is a machine in the form of a human being that performs the mechanical functions of a human being but lacks sensitivity. Three of today's most commonly used applications of robots during production are presented in Table 17.1. The role of the robot of the future, however, will become far more complex in industrial applications, as robot manufacturers master higher levels of robot design. The use of robots as standalone pieces of manufacturing equipment will diminish in importance. Linking robots to many forms of production in order to achieve full factory automation will be stressed.[4]

The use of robots is a growing trend.

Naturally, there are potential advantages and disadvantages to using robots to perform work functions. One advantage, of course, is that robots can take over boring factory jobs and allow people to perform more interesting and more motivating jobs. One disadvantage is that since workers are generally threatened by job loss, the use of robots can strain relations between management and labor.[5]

Robotics has its advantages and disadvantages.

TABLE 17.1

Three common applications of robots during production

Robot Operations	Description of Operations
Assembly operations	Activities involved in constructing products. Various types of welding, parts insertion, wiring, and soldering are stressed. The automobile industry and the electronics industry commonly use robots for assembly operations.
Materials handling operations	Activities that involve moving materials from one point to another during the manufacturing process—including point-to-point transfers, machine loading, and loading and unloading palletized goods. Materials handling is one area where growth in robotics is anticipated for smaller manufacturing firms.
Spraying operations	Activities that involve applying necessary liquids during various stages of the production process. The application of paint, stain, lacquer, sealants, and rustproofing is common. Automobile and major appliance manufacturers are among the largest users of robots for spraying operations.

The Production Facility: Layout Patterns

A layout pattern is an arrangement of a number of variables to maximize productivity.

In addition to understanding the production process and how productivity relates to it, managers also should be aware of various layout patterns that can be used within a production facility. A **layout pattern** is the overall arrangement of machines, equipment, materials handling areas, aisles, service areas, storage areas, and work stations within a production facility. The primary objective of a layout is to optimize the arrangement of these variables so their total contribution to the production process is maximized.[6] There are three basic layout patterns:

1. **Process layout** is a layout pattern based primarily on the grouping of similar types of equipment. Hospitals, automobile repair shops, and department stores would use process layout.
2. **Product layout** is a layout pattern based on the progressive steps by which a product is made. The automobile assembly line and furniture manufacturing are areas where product layout could be used.
3. **Fixed position layout** is a layout pattern that, because of the weight or bulk of the product being manufactured, has workers, tools, and materials rotating around a stationary product. Ships and airplanes usually are manufactured with the fixed position layout.

Figure 17.2 illustrates each of the three basic layout patterns.

In practice, what constitutes the best, or most appropriate, layout pattern differs from organization to organization. There are, however, several criteria for judging the effectiveness and efficiency of a layout pattern, regardless of the organization in which it exists. Several of these criteria are listed in Table 17.2.[7]

OPERATIONS MANAGEMENT

Operations management deals with managing production in organizations. The sections that follow define *operations management* and discuss the steps involved in its use.

Defining Operations Management

Operations management is managing production systems.

According to Chase and Aquilano, **operations management** is the performance of the managerial activities entailed in selecting, designing, operating, controlling, and updating production systems.[8] Figure 17.3, p. 474, describes each of these activities and categorizes them as being either periodic or continual. The distinction between periodic and continual activities is based on the relative frequency of their performance: Periodic activities are performed from time to time, and continual activities are performed essentially without interruption.

Steps in Operations Management

Successful operations management requires that managers determine:

There are four major steps to managing production successfully. Normally, these steps should be performed in the following order:

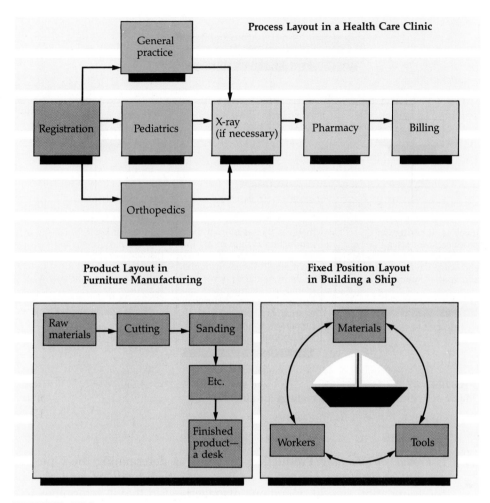

FIGURE 17.2
Three basic layout patterns

TABLE 17.2

Criteria for effective and efficient plant layout

Effective and efficient plant layout has:

1. Straight aisles to minimize worker and materials movement
2. Minimum handling of materials between manufacturing or assembly operations
3. Short distances over which materials must be moved
4. Beginning production steps occurring as close as possible to place where resources are received from suppliers
5. Ending production steps occurring as close as possible to place where finished goods are shipped to customers
6. Adequate storage for tools and equipment
7. The ability to be changed easily as circumstances change
8. Maximum use of all production facilities
9. Desirable levels of control for production nuisances, such as noise, dust, and heat
10. An effective and efficient system for scrap removal

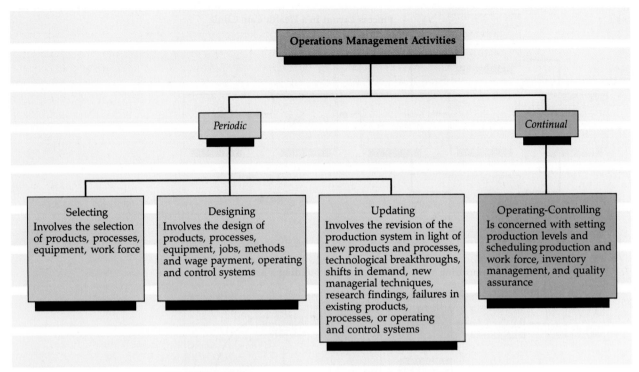

FIGURE 17.3
Major activities performed to manage production

1. The type and amount of resources needed.

Step 1: Production planning **Production planning** is determining the type and amount of resources needed to produce specified goods or services. It is the foundation step in operations management in that it determines to a large degree the effectiveness of the operations management steps that follow. Other issues involved in production planning are (1) how much to produce, (2) what level inventory should be kept at, and (3) what materials should be ordered and from which suppliers.

2. The sequencing of work.

Step 2: Routing **Routing** is determining the sequence in which work must be completed to produce specified goods or services. In essence, routing determines the path through a plant that materials acquired during production planning must take to become finished products. For example, wood acquired to produce furniture must be cut, sanded, glued, painted, and so on.

3. How to get the work done.

Step 3: Scheduling **Scheduling** is the process of (1) formulating detailed listings of activities that must be performed to accomplish a task, (2) allocating resources necessary to complete the task, and (3) setting up and following timetables for completing the task. Gantt charts and PERT networks are two useful scheduling tools.[9]

4. How to put the other steps into operation.

Step 4: Dispatching **Dispatching** is issuing orders to the individuals involved in producing goods or services. It takes the results of production planning, routing, and scheduling and puts them into operation within the organization.

BACK TO THE CASE

The high defect rate of manufactured goods at Commodore International Limited, as presented in the introductory case, may be a result of the way in which resources such as people, equipment, and materials at Commodore are transformed into products—for example, the Commodore 64 and video screen monitors.

Although the level of productivity at Commodore is not specifically mentioned in the case, company managers must strive to increase it to obtain the maximum number of products manufactured for the level of resources invested in the production process. In striving to increase productivity at Commodore, managers can take such actions as implementing more effecting training programs for employees and being more selective in hiring people. In addition, Commodore managers should evaluate the possibility of using robots to produce products. Besides increasing productivity, robots probably would make fewer production errors than humans.

Product layout probably would be the most ad-

visable layout pattern for Commodore. Most high-tech manufacturers have found that efficient and effective production requires using progressive steps, a type of assembly-line situation. Indeed, rotating workers, materials, and tools around a single Commodore 64 (fixed position layout) probably would be inefficient. Commodore might also want to consider if there would be any advantages to using process layout instead of product layout.

As the introductory case implies, managers at Commodore must spend much time managing production, or performing operations management activities. In essence, these managers are involved in selecting, designing, operating, controlling, and updating the Commodore production process. To carry out their operations management responsibilities, Commodore managers perform the sequential steps of production planning, routing, scheduling, and dispatching.

PRODUCTION AND CONTROL

A **control tool** is a specific procedure or technique that presents pertinent organizational information in a way that helps managers develop and implement appropriate control strategy. That is, it helps managers pinpoint the organizational strengths and weaknesses on which a useful control strategy must focus. This section discusses specific control tools for production as well as tools for broader organizational control.

Control tools provide information for implementing control strategy.

Control Tools for Production

Some of the best-known and most commonly used control tools are (1) management by exception, (2) breakeven analysis, (3) materials requirements planning and control, and (4) quality control. The specific purpose of these tools is to control the production of organizational goods and services.

Management by Exception

Management by exception is a control technique that allows only significant deviations between planned and actual performance to be brought to a manager's attention.[10] Actually, management by exception is based on the exception principle, a management principle that appears in early management literature.[11] The exception principle recommends that subordinates handle all routine

Management by exception ensures that managers handle only exceptional issues.

organizational matters, leaving managers to handle only nonroutine, or exceptional, organizational issues.

Although exceptional issues might be uncovered when managers themselves detect significant deviation between standards and performance, some managers establish special rules that allow exceptional issues to surface as a matter of normal operating procedure. Two examples of such rules are the following:[12]

1. A department manager must immediately inform the plant manager if actual weekly labor costs exceed estimated weekly labor costs by more than 15 percent.
2. A department manager must immediately inform the plant manager if actual dollars spent plus estimated dollars to be spent on a special project exceed the funds approved for the project by more than 10 percent.

These two rules focus on production related expenditures. However, such rules can be established in virtually any organizational area.

If appropriately administered, management by exception yields the added advantage of ensuring the best use of a manager's time. Since it brings only significant issues to the manager's attention, the possibility that the manager will spend valuable time working on relatively insignificant issues is automatically eliminated.

Of course, the significant issues brought to the manager's attention could be organizational strengths as well as organizational weaknesses. The manager should try to eliminate the weaknesses and reinforce the strengths.

Breakeven Analysis

Breakeven analysis summarizes levels of profit or loss associated with levels of production.

Another production related control tool commonly used by managers is breakeven analysis. **Breakeven analysis** is the process of generating information that summarizes various levels of profit or loss associated with various levels of production. The following sections discuss (1) the basic ingredients of breakeven analysis, (2) the types of breakeven analysis available to managers, and (3) the relationship between breakeven analysis and controlling.

Basic Ingredients of Breakeven Analysis

Breakeven analysis typically includes reflection, discussion, reasoning, and decision making relative to the following seven major ingredients:

1. *Fixed costs* **Fixed costs** are expenses incurred by the organization regardless of the number of products produced. Some examples are real estate taxes, upkeep to the exterior of a business building, and interest expenses on money borrowed to finance the purchase of equipment.
2. *Variable costs* Expenses that fluctuate with the number of products produced are called **variable costs.** Some examples are costs of packaging a product, costs of materials needed to make the product, and costs associated with packing products to prepare them for shipping.

Total costs = fixed costs + variable costs.

3. *Total costs* **Total costs** are simply the sum of fixed costs and variable costs associated with production.
4. *Total revenue* **Total revenue** is all sales dollars accumulated from selling manufactured products. Naturally, total revenue increases as more products are sold.

5. *Profits* **Profits** are defined as the amount of total revenue that exceeds the total costs of producing the products sold.

Profits = total revenue − total costs.

6. *Loss* **Loss** is the amount of the total costs of producing a product that exceeds the total revenue gained from selling the product.

7. *Breakeven point* The **breakeven point** is the situation wherein the total revenue of an organization equals its total costs—that is, the point at which the organization is generating only enough revenue to cover its costs. The company is neither gaining a profit nor incurring a loss.

Types of Breakeven Analysis

There are two somewhat different procedures for determining the same breakeven point for an organization: algebraic breakeven analysis and graphic breakeven analysis.[13]

Algebraic Breakeven Analysis. The following simple formula is commonly used to determine the level of production at which an organization breaks even:

The algebraic break-even analysis formula is

$$BE = \frac{FC}{P - VC}$$

$$BE = \frac{FC}{P - VC}$$

where—

BE = the level of production at which the firm breaks even
FC = total fixed costs of production
 P = price at which each individual unit is sold to customers
VC = variable costs associated with each product manufactured and sold

Two sequential steps must be followed in using this formula to calculate a breakeven point. First, the variable costs associated with producing each unit must be subtracted from the price at which each unit will sell. The purpose of this calculation is to determine how much of the selling price of each unit sold can go toward covering total fixed costs incurred from producing all products. The second step is to divide the remainder calculated in the first step into total fixed costs. The purpose of this calculation is to determine how many units must be produced and sold to cover fixed costs. This number of units is the breakeven point for the organization.

For example, a textbook publisher could face the fixed costs and variable costs per textbook presented in Table 17.3, p. 478. If the publisher wants to sell each textbook for $12, the breakeven point could be calculated as follows:

$$BE = \frac{\$88,800}{\$12 - \$6}$$

$$BE = \frac{\$88,800}{\$6}$$

$$BE = 14,800 \text{ copies}$$

This calculation indicates that if expenses and selling price remain stable, the textbook publisher will incur a loss if book sales are fewer than 14,800 copies, will break even if book sales equal 14,800 copies, and will make a profit if book sales exceed 14,800 copies.

TABLE 17.3

Fixed costs and variable costs for a textbook publisher

Fixed Costs (Yearly Basis)		Variable Costs per Textbook Sold	
1. Real estate taxes on property	$ 1,000	1. Printing	$2.00
2. Interest on loan to purchase equipment	5,000	2. Artwork	1.00
3. Building maintenance	2,000	3. Sales commission	.50
4. Insurance	800	4. Author royalties	1.50
5. Salaried labor	80,000	5. Binding	1.00
Total fixed costs	$88,800	Total variable costs per textbook	$6.00

Graphic Breakeven Analysis. Graphic breakeven analysis entails the construction of a graph that shows all the critical elements in a breakeven analysis. Figure 17.4 is a breakeven graph for the textbook publisher.

Using the Algebraic and Graphic Breakeven Methods. Both the algebraic and the graphic methods of breakeven analysis for the textbook publisher result in the same breakeven point–14,800 books produced and sold. However, the processes used to arrive at the point are quite different.

The situation managers face usually determines which breakeven method they should use. For example, if managers simply desire a quick yet accurate determination of a breakeven point, the algebraic method generally suffices. If

> The algebraic method is quick, but the graphic method gives a more complete picture.

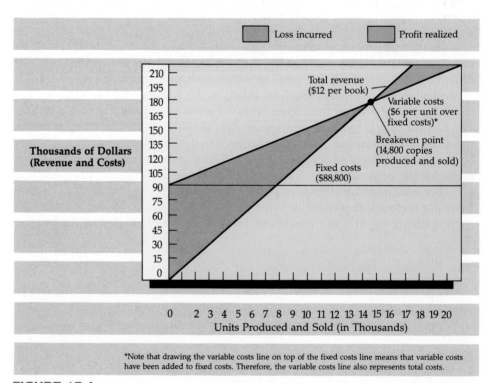

FIGURE 17.4
Breakeven analysis for a textbook publisher

they prefer a more complete picture of the cumulative relationships between the breakeven point, fixed costs, and escalating variable costs, the graphic breakeven method probably is more useful. The textbook publisher could quickly and easily see from Figure 17.4 the cumulative relationships of fixed costs, escalating variable costs, and potential profit and loss associated with various levels of production.

Control and Breakeven Analysis

Breakeven analysis is a useful control tool because it helps managers understand the relationships between fixed costs, variable costs, total costs, and profit and loss within an organization. Once these relationships are understood, managers can take steps to modify one or more of the variables to reduce significant deviation between planned and actual profit levels.[14] Increasing costs or decreasing selling prices have the overall effect of increasing the number of units an organization must produce and sell to break even. Conversely, the managerial strategy for decreasing the number of products an organization must produce and sell to break even entails lowering or stabilizing fixed and variable costs or increasing the selling price of each unit. The exact breakeven control strategy a particular manager should develop and implement is dictated primarily by the manager's unique organizational situation.

Breakeven analysis helps managers control profit levels.

BACK TO THE CASE

There are useful production control tools that Commodore management could use to ensure that the Commodore 64 and other products are produced as planned. Management by exception is one of these tools. The implementation of management by exception would allow Commodore workers to handle all routine production and to bring only exceptional matters to management's attention. The successful use of management by exception at Commodore probably would be characterized by a number of carefully designed rules. One such rule might be that when 10 percent or more of materials purchased to be used in the production of the Commodore 64 are defective, a production worker must bring this fact to the attention of the production supervisor and the purchasing manager. The production supervisor could then inspect products more carefully to ensure that a significant number are not manufactured with defective parts, and the purchasing manager could contact the supplier for an upgrading of future delivered materials and an allowance for defective materials already delivered.

In addition to management by exception, Commodore management could use breakeven analysis as a control tool. Breakeven analysis would furnish management with information about various levels of profit or loss associated with various levels of production. To use breakeven analysis, Commodore manage-

ment would have to determine the total fixed costs necessary to operate a production facility, the price at which each unit is to be offered, and the variable costs associated with producing each of those units.

For example, if Commodore management wanted to determine how many Commodore 64s had to be sold before the company would break even on that product alone, management could arrive at the breakeven point algebraically by following three steps. First, management would have to total all fixed costs attributable to the Commodore 64—for example, lighting expenses and real estate taxes. Second, Commodore management would have to total all variable costs associated with selling each Commodore 64 and subtract this total from the price at which each unit is to be sold. Variable costs would include such expenses as the costs of materials and labor needed to produce the Commodore 64. Finally, Commodore management would have to divide the answer calculated in step 2 into the answer derived in step 1. This figure would tell management how many 64s had to be sold to break even.

Commodore management also could arrive at this breakeven point by constructing a graph that showed fixed costs, variable costs, and selling price. The graph probably would provide management with a more useful picture for formulating profit oriented production plans.

Materials Requirements Planning and Control

Materials require-
ments planning plots
the flow of materials.

Materials requirements planning is the third control tool that can increase the effectiveness and efficiency of the production process. **Materials requirements planning** is the process of creating schedules that identify specific parts and materials required to produce an item, the exact quantities of each needed to enhance the organizational production process, and the dates when orders for these quantities should be released to suppliers and be received for best timing within the production cycle.[15]

Figure 17.5 shows the main elements of a materials requirements planning system. As can be seen from this figure, the computer can be an important part of the materials requirements planning process. Input data for the computer come from three main sources: (1) a master production schedule based on orders from consumers, sales forecasts or product demand, and plant capacity; (2) a bill of material file that considers product design changes in determining the types and quantities of materials needed within the production process; and (3) an inventory file that shows the types and quantities of materials presently on hand. The computer then generates output reports that indicate what materials should be ordered or canceled as well as what materials should be expedited or de-expedited.

A Japanese management technique sometimes considered a component of materials requirements planning is just-in-time (JIT) inventory control. The discussion of that technique, which appears in Chapter 20, will provide a richer

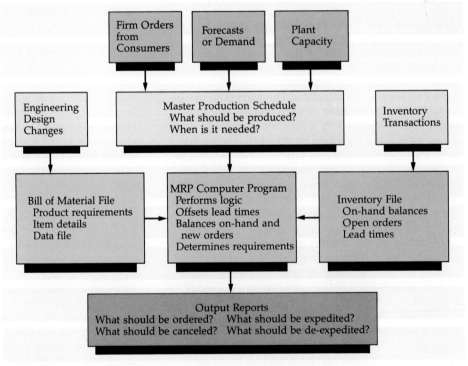

FIGURE 17.5
Basic elements of a materials requirements planning system

understanding of the potential value of materials requirements planning to the organization.

Naturally, materials requirements planning is closely related to materials requirements control. **Materials requirements control** is simply the process of making things happen the way they were planned to happen in materials requirements planning.

Quality Control

Quality control is the process of making the quality of finished goods and services what it was planned to be. Managers compare product quality to organizational quality standards and take steps to increase, decrease, or maintain the level of product quality as dictated by the situation.[16] Products too high in quality can be too expensive to produce, while products too low in quality can alienate customers.

Product inspection may be limited to finished products or be extended to such areas as materials purchased for inventory, materials available from various suppliers, and progress inspections at different stages of production. As the cartoon illustrates, customers of today are becoming intolerant of low-quality and defective merchandise.

Managers must determine not only what products or product components to inspect but also how many units or components to inspect. One method of addressing this question is called statistical quality control.[17] **Statistical quality control** is a process used to determine how many units of a product should be inspected to calculate a probability that the total number of units meets organizational quality standards. Although managers limit inspection expenses by not examining all units, they must be careful to ensure that the number of units inspected gives an accurate measurement of the quality of the products being produced.

Quality control measures planned versus actual product quality.

Statistical quality control determines how many units to inspect.

"Unless I'm misinterpreting the signs, gentlemen, we are approaching the end of the golden age of shoddy merchandise."

New Yorker, *December 19, 1983, p. 45. Drawing by Weber;*
© 1983 The New Yorker Magazine, Inc.

BACK TO THE CASE

Two additional production control tools that probably would be useful to Commodore management are materials requirements planning and control and quality control. Materials requirements planning for the Commodore 64 would involve creating work schedules that identify the specific parts and materials necessary to produce the units, determining the quantities of each needed to get maximum use of the Commodore production system, and pinpointing dates when orders for these items should be released and materials actually received from suppliers. Commodore management undoubtedly would find that the Commodore 64 itself would be invaluable in administering the complex materials requirements planning process.

Materials requirements control at Commodore would involve Commodore management following up to make sure that events occur as planned during the process of materials requirements planning. If shipments of materials are not arriving as planned, for example, Commodore management must contact suppliers to expedite deliveries.

Since the most serious issue at Commodore, as depicted in the introductory case, is that of poor-quality products, quality control should be an important concern. Commodore management must plan for some desirable level of quality—neither too high nor too low—and then take steps to ensure that planned levels of quality are indeed present in the finished computers. An important part of this quality control process would involve inspection. Commodore management first must determine *what* should be inspected—materials purchased for inventory, materials available from various suppliers, units at different stages of Commodore 64 production, or finished Commodore 64s. Then management must decide *how many* should be inspected—every Commodore 64 unit in production, all materials purchased from all suppliers, or only some proportion of each. Statistical quality control is a tool Commodore management can use to minimize inspection expenses without sacrificing the measurement accuracy for product quality.

As implied in the introductory case, Commodore in the past somewhat limited its alternatives concerning when to inspect by subcontracting the manufacturing of certain product components. Commodore inspected subcontracted components only after they were completed, and that was too late, since the components were already defective on delivery.

Tools for Broader Organizational Control

Organizational control requires an understanding of production.

The control tools already discussed are commonly applied directly to the production process. The following sections discuss control tools that do not relate as directly to the production process: budgets and ratio analysis. Since the production process has an impact on virtually all phases of organizational existence, however, a thorough understanding of the production process is a prerequisite for the successful use of even these control tools.

Budgets

A budget is a planning tool *and* a control tool.

As described in chapter 7, a budget is a single-use financial plan that covers a specified length of time. The **budget** of an organization is the financial plan outlining how funds in a given period will be obtained and spent.

In addition to being a financial plan, however, a budget is also a control tool.[18] As managers gather information on actual receipts and expenditures within an operating period, significant deviations from budgeted amounts may be uncovered. In such a case, managers can develop and implement a control strategy aimed at making actual performance more consistent with planned performance. This, of course, assumes that the plan contained in the budget is appropriate for the organization.

An illustration of how a budget can be used as an organizational plan as well as an organizational control tool is the following fictitious situation concerning a Father Walter James, rector and manager of St. Matthew's Church. In response to organizational objectives, Father James developed a simple budget for St. Matthew's (see Table 17.4). The budget is actually Father James's financial plan of how money will be spent to achieve organizational objectives.

In addition, however, Father James can use this budget as a control tool. For example, as actual office supplies and expenses approach their maximum budgeted allowance of $2,250 during an operating period, Father James conceivably can take steps to minimize further expenditures in this area. Or, after analyzing the entire situation carefully, Father James may decide to increase the budgeted amount for office supplies and expenses. Since the total amount of

TABLE 17.4

Operating budget for St. Matthew's Church

St. Matthew's Operating Budget
Year 1989

Disbursements		*Receipts*		
Diocesan assessment	$ 17,220.00	For general purposes:		
Clergy salary	16,368.00	Plate offerings	$ 501.47	
Secretary salary	7,200.00	Pledge payments	74,761.11	
Sexton	6,463.00	Parish organizations:		
Organist/St. Matthew's		Treasure House	1,320.00	
choirmaster salary	4,576.00	St. Thomas's Guild	2,019.32	
Social security	2,000.00	From diocese	325.00	
Housing allowance	3,000.00	Other miscellaneous sources	828.59	
Auto lease	3,072.00	Investment income	16,645.00	$ 96,400.49
Auto gas allowance	1,100.00			
Pastoral care	350.00	For special parish use:		
Pension premium	3,500.00	Communion alms	1,240.19	
Utilities	7,920.00	Building fund (steeple repair)	1,050.00	
Housekeeping	2,400.00	Designated gifts and memorials	1,239.25	
Repairs to property		Miscellaneous sources	485.00	$ 4,014.44
(bldg. fund)	5,000.00	For work outside parish	$ 152.55	
Telephone	1,760.00	Nonincome receipts:		
Office supplies & expenses	2,250.00	From endowment trust		
Postage	700.00	transfers		$ 13,552.75
Bulletins & printing	1,500.00	Day school		16,918.28
Kitchen supplies & expense	3,000.00	Total receipts		$131,038.51
Organ maintenance	200.00			
T. H. Greater Fed. of Churches	2600.00			
Church school				
Worship commission				
Planning commission				
Social concerns commission				
Youth commission				
Rector's funds (music, adult				
education, special programs)	4,500.00			
Other expenses	3,200.00			
Convention delegate expense	800.00			
Insurance	5,500.00			
Sexton's insurance	500.00			
Clergy assistance	1,000.00			
Altar supplies	2,000.00			
Garden maintenance	500.00			
Total Disbursements	$110,179.00			

resources for this church or any other organization probably is fixed, an increase in the budgeted amount for one expense typically requires an equal decrease in the budgeted amount for another expense. For example, increasing the budgeted allowance for office supplies and expenses from $2,250 to $3,250 typically would require a $1,000 reduction in the budgeted amounts for other organizational expenses.

The following sections discuss potential pitfalls of budgets and people considerations in using budgets.

Potential Pitfalls of Budgets

In using budgets, managers should:

To maximize the benefits of using budgets, managers must be able to avoid several potential pitfalls. These pitfalls include:

1. Emphasize significant expenses.

1. *Placing too much emphasis on relatively insignificant organizational expenses* In preparing and implementing a budget, managers should allocate more time for dealing with significant organizational expenses and less time for relatively insignificant organizational expenses. For example, the amount of time managers spend on developing and implementing a budget for labor costs typically should be much more than the amount of time managers spend on developing and implementing a budget for office supplies.

2. Justify expenses each year.

2. *Increasing budgeted expenses year after year without adequate information* It does not necessarily follow that items contained in last year's budget should be increased this year. Perhaps the best-known method developed to overcome this potential pitfall is zero-base budgeting.[19] **Zero-base budgeting** is the planning and budgeting process that requires managers to justify their entire budget request in detail rather than simply to refer to budget amounts established in previous years.[20]

The Department of Agriculture's Office of Budget and Finance used the following instructions to implement its zero-base budgeting program:

> A new concept has been adopted for [this year's] agency estimates; namely, that of zero-base budgeting. This means that all programs will be reviewed from the ground up and not merely in terms of changes proposed for the budget year. . . . The total work program of each agency must be subjected to an intensive review and evaluation. . . . Consideration must be given to the basic need for the work contemplated, the level at which the work should be carried out, the benefits to be received, and the costs to be incurred.
>
> The fact that certain activities have been carried out for a number of years will not, per se, adequately justify their continuation. Nor will the fact that programs are prescribed by statutory law necessarily be a controlling consideration. Program goals based on statutes enacted to meet problems or needs that are today of lesser priority must be reevaluated in terms of present conditions.
>
> It is implied in the zero-base budget approach that the need for programs and their recommended magnitude in [this] fiscal year . . . be clearly and specifically demonstrated. . . . The justification should be prepared on the assumption that all information needed for making budget decisions should be included.[21]

3. Change budgets periodically.

3. *Ignoring the fact that budgets must be changed periodically* Managers should recognize that such factors as costs of materials, newly developed technology, and product demand constantly are changing and that budgets should be reviewed and modified periodically in response to these changes. A special type of budget called a variable budget is sometimes used to determine automatically such needed changes in budgets. **Variable budgets** outline various

levels of resources to be allocated for each organizational activity, depending on the level of production within the organization. It follows, then, that a variable budget automatically indicates increases or decreases in the amount of resources allocated for various organizational activities, depending on whether production levels increase or decrease. Variable budgets also have been called flexible budgets.

People Considerations in Using Budgets

Many managers believe that although budgets are valuable planning and control tools, they can result in major human relations problems in an organization. For example, in a classic article by Chris Argyris, budgets are shown to build pressures that unite workers against management, cause harmful conflict between management and factory workers, and create tensions that result in worker inefficiency and worker aggression against management.[22] Depending on the severity of such problems, budgets may result in more harm to the organization than good.

Several strategies have been suggested to minimize the human relations problems caused by budgets. The most often recommended strategy is to design and implement appropriate human relations training programs for finance personnel, accounting personnel, production supervisors, and all other key people involved in the formulation and use of budgets. These training programs should be designed to emphasize both the advantages and disadvantages of applying pressure on people through budgets and the possible results of using budgets to imply organization member success or failure.[23]

Budgets can cause people problems.

Training can help minimize the problems.

BACK TO THE CASE

Budgets and ratio analysis are control tools available to Commodore management for broader organizational control. The prerequisite for gaining maximum benefit from the use of these tools is a thorough understanding of Commodore's production process.

A budget would be Commodore's financial plan indicating how much money should be spent on such items as salaries, materials, and equipment. The budget, once prepared, would be a source of information to Commodore management regarding what steps for control, if any, should be taken. For example, if 60 percent of the annual allowance for production workers is already used up and 70 percent of the year still remains, Commodore management must assess the situation carefully to determine what, if anything, must be done. Management could decide to cut

wages, lay off certain workers, or increase the salary allowance in the budget and decrease the monetary commitment to some other budget item, such as advertising.

To use budgets successfully, Commodore management must focus on significant expenses rather than minor ones, attempt to rejustify budgeted expenses at Commodore each time a budget is revised, and change the amounts allocated to various budgeted expenses as conditions change. Commodore management also must keep in mind that budgets can cause human relations problems and that training that focuses on how to minimize such problems should be provided for all people involved in formulating and using Commodore budgets.

Ratio Analysis

The second tool for broader organizational control is ratio analysis.[24] A *ratio* is a relationship between two numbers that is calculated by dividing one number into the other. **Ratio analysis** is the process of generating information that summarizes the financial position of an organization through the calculation of ratios based on various financial measures that appear on the organization's balance

Ratios are relationships.

sheet and income statements.[25] The ratios available to managers for controlling organizations typically are divided into four categories: (1) liquidity ratios, (2) leverage ratios, (3) activity ratios, (4) profitability ratios.

Liquidity Ratios

Liquidity ratios indicate the ability to meet financial obligations:

Ratios that indicate an organization's ability to meet upcoming financial obligations are called **liquidity ratios.** The better an organization is at meeting these obligations, the more liquid it is said to be. As a general rule, organizations should be liquid enough to meet their obligations, yet not so liquid that too many financial resources are sitting idle in anticipation of meeting upcoming debts. The two main types of liquidity ratios are the current ratio and the quick ratio.

1. Can the organization meet current debts?

The **current ratio** is calculated by dividing the dollar value of the organization's current assets by the dollar value of its current liabilities:

$$\text{Current ratio} = \frac{\text{Current assets}}{\text{Current liabilities}}$$

Current assets typically include cash, accounts receivable, and inventory. Current liabilities generally include accounts payable, short-term notes payable, and any other accrued expenses. The current ratio indicates to managers the organization's ability to meet its financial obligations in the short term.

2. Can the organization meet current debts without inventory?

The **quick ratio,** sometimes called the acid-test ratio, is computed by subtracting inventory from current assets and then dividing the difference by current liabilities:

$$\text{Quick ratio} = \frac{\text{Current assets} - \text{Inventory}}{\text{Current liabilities}}$$

The quick ratio is the same as the current ratio except that it does not include inventory in current assets. Since inventory can be difficult to convert into money or securities, the quick ratio gives managers information on the organization's ability to meet its financial obligations with no reliance on inventory.

Leverage Ratios

Leverage ratios deal with using borrowed funds:

Leverage ratios indicate the relationships between organizational funds supplied by the owners of an organization and organizational funds supplied by various creditors. The more organizational funds furnished by creditors, the more leverage an organization is said to be employing. As a general guideline, an organization should use leverage to the extent that borrowed funds can be used to generate additional profit without a significant amount of organizational ownership being established by creditors. Perhaps the two most commonly used leverage ratios are the debt ratio and the times interest earned ratio.

1. Who provides organizational funding?

The **debt ratio** is calculated by dividing total organizational debt by total organizational assets:

$$\text{Debt ratio} = \frac{\text{Total debts}}{\text{Total assets}}$$

In essence, this ratio gives the percentage of all organizational assets provided by organizational creditors. Whereas some managers strongly caution against using too much debt to finance an organization, Barclay Morely, the chairman and chief executive of Stauffer's, supports the theory that experiencing some debt is a critical ingredient of building a successful organization.[26]

The **times interest earned ratio** is calculated by dividing gross income, or earnings before interest and taxes, by the total amount of organizational interest charges incurred from borrowing needed resources:

2. Can the organization pay interest expenses?

$$\text{Times interest earned ratio} = \frac{\text{Gross income}}{\text{Interest charges}}$$

This ratio indicates the organization's ability to pay interest expenses directly from gross income.

Activity Ratios

Activity ratios indicate how well an organization is selling its products in relation to its available resources. Obviously, management's goal is to maximize the amount of sales per dollar invested in organizational resources. Three main activity ratios are (1) inventory turnover, (2) fixed assets turnover, and (3) total assets turnover.

Activity ratios evaluate organizational performance:

Inventory turnover is calculated by dividing organizational sales by inventory:

1. Is too much invested in inventory?

$$\text{Inventory turnover} = \frac{\text{Sales}}{\text{Inventory}}$$

This ratio indicates whether an organization is maintaining an appropriate level of inventory in relation to its sales volume. In general, as sales volume increases or decreases, an organization's inventory level should fluctuate correspondingly.

Fixed assets turnover is calculated by dividing fixed assets, or plant and equipment, into total sales:

2. Is too much invested in fixed assets?

$$\text{Fixed assets turnover} = \frac{\text{Sales}}{\text{Fixed assets}}$$

This ratio indicates the appropriateness of the amount of funds invested in plant and equipment relative to the level of sales.

Total assets turnover is calculated by dividing sales by total assets:

3. Is too much invested in total assets?

$$\text{Total assets turnover} = \frac{\text{Sales}}{\text{Total assets}}$$

The focus of this ratio is on the appropriateness of the level of funds the organization has tied up in all assets relative to its rate of sales.

Profitability Ratios

Profitability ratios focus on assessing overall organizational profitability and improving it wherever possible. Major profitability ratios include the profit to sales ratio and the profit to total assets ratio.

Profitability ratios focus on making a profit:

The **profit to sales ratio** is calculated by dividing the net profit of an organization by its total sales:

1. Is the organization making enough profit per sales dollar?

$$\text{Profit to sales ratio} = \frac{\text{Net profit}}{\text{Sales}}$$

This ratio indicates whether the organization is making an adequate net profit in relation to the total dollars coming into the organization.

The **profit to total assets ratio** is calculated by dividing the net profit of an organization by its total assets:

2. Is the organization making enough profit per dollar invested in total assets?

$$\text{Profit to total assets ratio} = \frac{\text{Net profit}}{\text{Total assets}}$$

This ratio indicates whether the organization is realizing enough net profit in relation to the total dollars invested in assets.

Using Ratios to Control Organizations

Managers can use ratio analysis in three ways to control an organization.[27] First, managers should evaluate all ratios simultaneously. This strategy ensures that managers will develop and implement a control strategy appropriate for the organization as a whole rather than one that suits only one phase or segment of the organization.

Second, managers should compare computed values for ratios in a specific organization with the values of industry averages for those ratios. (The values of industry averages for the ratios can be obtained from Dun & Bradstreet; Robert Morris Associates, a national association of bank loan officers; the Federal Trade Commission; and the Securities and Exchange Commission.) Managers can increase the probability of formulating and implementing appropriate control strategies by comparing their financial situation to that of competitors.

Third, managers' use of ratios to control an organization also should involve trend analysis. Managers must remember that any set of ratio values is actually only a determination of relationships that exist in a specified time period, perhaps a year. To use ratio analysis to its maximum advantage, values for ratios should be accumulated for a number of successive time periods to uncover specific organizational trends. Once these trends are uncovered, managers can formulate and implement appropriate strategies for dealing with them.

The "Management in Action" feature for this chapter is an account of how Allen Murray, chairman of Mobil Corporation, used ratio analysis to control his organization. Sensing that the total debt of the company was too high relative to total assets and that net profit was too low relative to sales, Murray took steps to both retire debt and reduce the unnecessary operating costs that were holding down net profits.

Managers should review all ratios at once.

Managers should compare organizational values to industry averages.

Managers should use ratios to determine financial trends.

■ BACK TO THE CASE

Ratio analysis is another tool available to Commodore managers for broader organizational control. Ratio analysis would indicate the financial position of Commodore by determining relationships between various financial factors on Commodore's income statement and balance sheet. More specifically, Commodore management could use liquidity ratios to indicate Commodore's ability to pay its debts, leverage ratios to indicate the appropriateness of the amount of debt used to run Commodore, activity ratios to indicate the level of activity at Commodore relative to its resources, and profitability ratios to indicate the appropriateness of Commodore's profit level.

As with all control tools, Commodore management must use these ratios as a basis for a more subjective development and implementation of appropriate control strategies. Commodore management should evaluate all ratio information simultaneously, compare Commodore ratio values to the values of industry averages for the same ratios, and analyze ratio values for several successive time periods to identify and control any financial trends that might exist at Commodore.

USING RATIO ANALYSIS TO CONTROL MOBIL CORPORATION

One sultry morning, Allen Murray, then four months into his job as chairman of Mobil Corp., strode into a headquarters conference room. Discarding his jacket and lighting a cigar, he waded into an hour's verbal fencing with a visiting banker. The subject: an offer to take Mobil's disappointing Container Corp. subsidiary off the oil giant's hands.

Once satisfied with the numbers, Mr. Murray set a deadline for a contract and ended the meeting. "He said he didn't want to make a career" out of the sale of the subsidiary, recalls the banker, Morgan Stanley & Co.'s managing director, Donald Brennan. "He wanted it settled one way or the other by July 25."

Since Mr. Murray became chairman, he has projected an image of rapid-fire decision making. With the oil industry reeling under falling prices, he has shed an estimated $1.5 billion to $2 billion in Mobil assets, applying most of the proceeds to reduce the company's debt. He quietly lopped more than 10,000 jobs from Mobil's worldwide work force, nearly equaling on a percentage basis the highly publicized cuts at Exxon Corp. He has raised the company's profile on Wall Street and begun a drive to bring Mobil's headquarters closer to line operations.

WIELDING THE AX

So far, Mr. Murray's most prominent symbol of authority has been the ax. Through attrition, early retirements and layoffs, he pared 6% of Mobil's work force in one year. "I was told by Mobil that it had reduced its head count by 10,000, to 154,000, between January and the end of June," says Michael Mayer, an analyst with Wertheim & Co. and once a Mobil executive. The company won't comment on the figures—or on anything else in this story.

The same year, Mobil announced the sale of Container Corp. to Morgan Stanley and Jefferson Smurfit Corp. in the deal negotiated with Mr. Brennan. This reduced Mobil's payroll by an additional 18,000.

Mobil employees also say they received a letter at their homes warning of more cuts on the way. "Murray told us we need to do more," one Mobil executive said. "'Root out every savings you can find,' he told us."

Overseas operations have been shaved and some managers repatriated. But the sharpest cuts have come in the U.S. Tape recorders take messages at corporate headquarters for some executives who must now share

secretaries. One executive tells of a colleague who came to work in the morning, was offered early retirement before his coffee had cooled, and told to be gone that afternoon.

OTHER CUTBACKS

Some 10% to 12% of the exploration and production staff has been eliminated. Regional marketing offices have disappeared, and the overall marketing and refining staff was cut 3%, according to one executive.

At least 6,000 employees have left Montgomery Ward, Mobil's retail subsidiary, helping spark what Wertheim's Mr. Mayer calls a dramatic turnaround there. Ward's net earnings soared an estimated 152% from the previous year's, to an estimated $106 million. If Ward's strategy to focus on specialty retailing is successful, adds Mr. Mayer, profits should continue upward, ending the unit's financial dependence on Mobil. Mobil has done well to pay down over $1 billion in debt "during the worst crisis in oil history," says Paul Mlotok, analyst for Salomon Brothers. Operating earnings, excluding one-time items, were up only slightly, although net after reflecting the heavy special charges was up 35%.

"Compared to many U.S. major internationals, Mobil has been a bright star," says Philip Dodge, an analyst for Donaldson, Lufkin & Jenrette Inc.

But Mr. Murray has his work cut out for him. Mobil still carries one of the most burdensome debt loads in the industry, with the borrowings representing 39% of Mobil's capitalization. It receives little cash flow from its Superior Oil acquisition. At least one-third of Superior's North American natural-gas capacity is idled because of lagging demand.

Action Summary

Reread the learning objectives that follow. Each objective is followed by questions. Answering these questions accurately will help you retain the most important concepts discussed in this chapter. After answering each question, check your answer with the answer key at the end of this chapter. (*Hint:* If you have doubt regarding the correct response, consult the page whose number follows the answer.)

Circle:

From studying this chapter, I will attempt to acquire:

1. Definitions of both *production* and *production control*.

a, b, c, d, e
    a. *Production* is defined simply as the transformation of organizational resources into: (a) profits; (b) plans; (c) forecasts; (d) processes; (e) products.

T, F
    b. *Production control* is ensuring that an organization produces goods and services as planned.

2. An understanding of how productivity and layout patterns relate to the production process.

a, b, c, d, e
    a. The ratio that defines productivity is: (a) inputs/outputs; (b) outputs/profit; (c) outputs/inputs; (d) profits/inputs; (e) none of the above.

a, b, c, d, e
    b. Which of the following layout patterns is usually used to manufacture airplanes: (a) process layout; (b) product layout; (c) fixed position layout; (d) customer layout; (e) assembly-line layout.

3. An appreciation for the significance of operations management.

a, b, c, d, e
    a. Which of the following is *not* one of the operations management activities: (a) selecting; (b) designing; (c) updating; (d) operating-controlling; (e) all of the above are operations management activities.

T, F
    b. Scheduling is the first step to be taken in operations management.

4. Insights concerning how management by exception and breakeven analysis can be used to control production.

T, F
    a. Management by exception is a control technique that allows only significant deviations between planned and actual performance to be brought to the manager's attention.

a, b, c, d, e
    b. The overall effect on the breakeven point of increasing costs or decreasing selling prices is that: (a) the number of products an organization must sell to break even increases; (b) the amount of profit a firm will receive at a fixed number of units sold increases; (d) the number of products an organization must sell to break even decreases; (d) a and b; (e) there is no effect on the breakeven point.

5. An understanding of how quality control and materials requirements planning and control can contribute to production control.

a, b, c, d, e
    a. A process used to determine how many units of a product from a larger number should be inspected to calculate a probability that the total number of units meets organizational quality standards is: (a) quality control; (b) materials requirements planning; (c) materials requirements control; (d) statistical quality control; (e) all of the above.

a, b, c, d, e
    b. Input data for the computer in a materials requirements planning system come from all of the following sources except: (a) an accounts receivable file; (b) a master production schedule; (c) a bill of material file; (d) an inventory file; (e) all of the above are sources.

6. Knowledge of how budgets and ratio analysis can be used to achieve overall or broader organizational control.

    a. Potential pitfalls of using budgets as control tools include: (a) too much emphasis placed on relatively insignificant organizational expenses; (b) changing budgets periodically; (c) increasing budgeted expenses year after year without adequate information; (d) a and c; (e) a and b.   a, b, c, d, e

    b. Which of the following is an activity ratio: (a) inventory turnover ratio; (b) current ratio; (c) debt ratio; (d) quick ratio; (e) times interest earned ratio.   a, b, c, d, e

INTRODUCTORY CASE WRAP-UP

"Production Snags at Commodore" (p. 468) and its related back-to-the-case sections were written to help you better understand the management concepts contained in this chapter. Answer the following discussion questions about this introductory case to further enrich your understanding of chapter content:

1. What problems could be causing a high defect rate at Commodore? List as many problems as possible.

2. What would you do to solve the problems identified in question 1?
3. Does a high defect rate represent a serious situation for Commodore? Explain fully.

Issues for Review and Discussion

1. Define both *production* and *production control*.
2. Thoroughly explain the equation used to define productivity.
3. Discuss several traditional strategies that managers can use to increase organizational productivity.
4. Discuss the importance of robots in building productive organizations in the future.
5. What is a layout pattern, and what is its relationship to productivity?
6. Name the three basic types of layout patterns and give an example of each.
7. List five criteria for efficient and effective plant layout and explain how each can contribute to increasing productivity.
8. Explain the term *operations management* as well as the major managerial activities involved in operations management.
9. What steps usually are recommended to manage production successfully? Be sure to discuss each step as well as the relationships among the steps.
10. What is a control tool?
11. Define *management by exception* and describe how it can help managers control production.
12. List and define seven major ingredients of breakeven analysis.
13. How can managers use breakeven analysis as an aid in controlling production?
14. What is materials requirements planning, and how can it aid in production control?
15. Define *statistical quality control* and describe its role in production control.
16. Define *budget*. How can managers use a budget to control an organization?
17. List three potential pitfalls of budgets.
18. What is ratio analysis?
19. List and define the four basic types of ratios.
20. What can the profit to sales ratio and the profit to total assets ratio tell managers about organizational profitability?
21. What guidelines would you recommend to managers using ratio analysis to control an organization?

Sources of Additional Information

Ackoff, Russell L., Jamshid Gharajedaghi, and Elsa Vergara Finnel. *A Guide to Controlling Your Corporation's Future.* New York: Wiley, 1984.

Frankson, Fred M. "A Simplified Approach to Financial Planning," *Journal of Small Business Management* (January 1981): 7–15.

Hayes, Robert H., and Kim B. Clark. "Why Some Factories Are More Productive than Others." *Harvard Business Review* (September/October 1986): 66–73.

Haywood-Farmer, John, Anthony Alleyne, Balteano Duffus, and Mark Downing. "Controlling Service Quality." *Business Quarterly* 50 (Winter 1985–86): 62.

Higgins, James M. *Human Relations: Behavior at Work,* 2d ed. New York: Random House, 1988.

Kauffman, Mort. "An Administrator's Guide to Expense Account Management." *Administrative Management* 42 (July 1981): 30–32, 39.

Mace, Edward E., and Russell Valentine. "Profit Improvement: Hope Springs Internal." *Management Focus* 31 (January/February 1984): 26–29.

McDonald, Alonzo L. "Of Floating Factories and Mating Dinosaurs." *Harvard Business Review* (November/December 1986): 82–86.

McNamee, Patrick B. "The V-Matrix—A New Tool for Plotting Earnings." *Long-Range Planning* 17 (February 1984): 19, 22

Mockler, R. J. *The Management Control Process.* New York: Appleton-Century-Crofts, 1972.

Quelch, John A., Paul W. Farris, and James M. Olver. "The Product Management Audit." *Harvard Business Review* (March/April 1987): 30–37.

Radhakrishnan, K. S., and L. A. Soenen. "Why Computerized Financial Reporting and Consolidation Systems?" *Managerial Planning* 33 (July/August 1984): 32–36.

Raiborn, Mitchell H., and William C. Scurry, Jr. "Equity to Debt Conversion—Promoting Investments in Small Business Firms." *Financial Executive* (September 1980): 42–46, 48, 50.

Richman, Eugene, and Denis Coleman. "Monte Carlo Simulation for Management." *California Management Review* 23 (Spring 1981): 92–96

Sadhwani, Arjan T., and Mostafa H. Sarhan. "Putting JIT Manufacturing Systems to Work." *Business* 37 (April/May/June 1987): 30.

Schwan, Edward S. "Understanding Financial Statements." *Business* 34 (April/May/June 1984): 37–40.

Thornton, Billy M., and Paul Preston. *Introduction to Management Science: Quantitative Approaches to Managerial Decisions.* Columbus, Ohio: Charles E. Merrill, 1977.

Williamson, Nicholas C. "Japanese Productivity: Advances in Production and Marketing." *Business* 34 (April/May/June 1984): 16–22.

Wilson, Richard M.S. *Cost Control Handbook.* New York: Wiley, 1975.

Notes

1. James B. Dilworth, *Production and Operations Management: Manufacturing and Non-Manufacturing* (New York: Random House, 1986), 3.

2. John W. Kendrick, *Understanding Productivity: An Introduction to the Dynamics of Productivity Change* (Baltimore: Johns Hopkins University Press, 1977), 14.

3. Lester C. Thurow, "Other Countries Are as Smart as We Are," *New York Times,* April 5, 1981.

4. John A. Mearman, *U.S. Industrial Outlook, 1987* (Washington D.C.: U.S. Department of Commerce), p. 21-6.

5. Joann S. Lubin, "As Robot Age Arrives, Labor Seeks Protection against Work Loss," *Wall Street Journal,* October 26, 1981.

6. Jack R. Meredith, *The Management of Operations* (New York: Wiley, 1987), 243–44.

7. For more information on plant layout, see Joseph G. Monks, *Operations Management: Theory and Problems* (New York: McGraw-Hill, 1987), 122–35.

8. Richard B. Chase and Nicholas J. Aquilano, *Production and Operations Management: A Life Cycle Approach* (Homewood, Ill.: Richard D. Irwin, 1981), 4.

9. At this point, it probably would be worthwhile to review the general topic of scheduling and the more specific topics of the Gantt chart and PERT networks (pp. 179–181).

10. Lester R. Bittle, *Management by Exception* (New York: McGraw-Hill, 1964).

11. Frederick W. Taylor, *Shop Management* (New York: Harper & Bros., 1911), 126–27.

12. These two rules are adapted from *Boardroom Reports* 5 (May 15, 1976): 4.

13. For a clear discussion of more of the intricacies of breakeven analysis, see Lee J. Krajewski and Larry P. Ritzman, *Operations Management: Strategy and Analysis* (Reading, Mass.: Addison-Wesley, 1987), 41–43.

14. Robert J. Lambrix and Surendra S. Singhvi, "How to Set Volume-Sensitive ROI Targets," *Harvard Business Review* (March/April 1981): 174.

15. Chase and Aquilano, *Production and Operations Management*, 516.

16. Elwood S. Buffa, *Modern Production/Operations Management* (New York: Wiley, 1983), 501.

17. Roger G. Schroeder, *Operations Management: Decision Making in the Operations Function* (New York: McGraw-Hill, 1985), 597–98.

18. Robert L. Dewelt, "Control: Key to Making Financial Strategy Work," *Management Review* (March 1977): 20.

19. George S. Minmier, "Zero-Base Budgeting: A New Budgeting Technique for Discretionary Costs," *Mid-South Quarterly Business Review* 14 (October 1976): 2–8.

20. Peter A. Phyrr, "Zero-Base Budgeting," *Harvard Business Review* (November/December 1970): 111–21. See also E. A. Kurbis, "The Case for Zero-Base Budgeting," *CA Magazine* (April 1986): 104–105.

21. Aaron Wildausky and Arthur Hammann, "Comprehensive versus Incremental Budgeting in the Department of Agriculture," in *Planning Programming Budgeting: A Systems Approach to Management*, ed. Fremont J. Lyden and Ernest G. Miller (Chicago: Markham Publishing, 1968), 143–44.

22. Chris Argyris, "Human Problems with Budgets," *Harvard Business Review* (January/ February 1953): 108.

23. Argyris, "Human Problems with Budgets," 109.

24. This section is based primarily on J. Fred Weston and Eugene F. Brigham, *Essentials of Managerial Finance*, 7th ed. (Hinsdale, Ill.: Dryden Press, 1985).

25. F. L. Patrone and Donald duBois, "Financial Ratio Analysis for the Small Business," *Journal of Small Business Management* (January 1981): 35.

26. "How Stauffer Outperforms the Industry," *Business Week*, November 22, 1976, 129–30.

27. For an excellent discussion of ratio analysis in a small business, see Patrone and duBois, "Financial Ratio Analysis," 35–40.

Action Summary Answer Key

1. a. e, p. 469
   b. T, p. 469
2. a. c, pp. 469–471
   b. c, p. 472

3. a. e, p. 472
   b. F, pp. 472–474
4. a. T, pp. 475–476
   b. a, p. 479

5. a. d, p. 481
   b. a, p. 480
6. a. d, pp. 484–485
   b. a, p. 487

WEAK PRODUCTION CONTROLS AT GENERAL MOTORS

In mid-October 1984, General Motors Corporation agreed to an Environmental Protection Agency request to recall another 750,000 cars because of suspected design defects in the catalytic converter. This latest EPA move brought recalls to about 3.5 million cars since December 1982, when the first 131,000 1979 GM four-cylinder cars were recalled for exhaust emission violations.

Since the initial recall in late 1982, either the EPA or GM has instituted seven other major pollution related callbacks. In February 1983, 174,000 eight-cylinder Buicks and Pontiacs of 1980 vintage were called back for similar exhaust emission violations. In March 1983, this number mushroomed to 527,000 1978 Chevrolet, Pontiac, Oldsmobile, and Buick models. EPA officials claimed that these cars exceeded federal emission standards for nitrogen oxide by an average of more than 20 percent. Furthermore, the EPA indicated that the problem stemmed primarily from the way the engines were assembled.

April 1983 brought yet another sizable recall— 861,000 1978 and 1979 six-cylinder GM cars were suspected of being polluters. This recall was followed by 800,000 1981 and 1982 Chevrolet six- and eight-cylinder autos in July 1983. This recall was attributed to faulty catalytic converters that reduced the car's acceleration. A GM spokesperson intimated that catalyst beads in the converters of recalled cars could fragment and fall into the lower chambers of the converters, blocking engine exhaust and noticeably reducing engine performance. GM's solution to the problem was the installation of a converter shell with a new type of basket to hold the catalyst beads.

Next, the EPA ordered GM to recall 112,000 of its 1979 Chevrolet Chevettes for violating federal clean air standards. This October 1983 directive indicated that Chevettes with four-cylinder engines and automatic transmissions exceeded the government's maximum standard for carbon monoxide emissions by an average of more than 20 percent. According to the EPA, GM had previously offered to voluntarily recall this model but would not provide free repair on cars driven more than fifty thousand miles. Under the EPA-ordered recall, GM had to pay for all repairs, regardless of the mileage on the vehicle.

EPA-initiated pollution related recalls continued into 1984. In March, the government ordered GM to recall about 186,000 of its 1980 Buick and Oldsmobile cars equipped with large V–8 engines. The EPA stated that

the cars, all having 5 or 5.7 liter engines, exceeded standards for hydrocarbon emissions by an average of more than 20 percent. Hydrocarbons contribute to the formation of ozone pollution, which can cause respiratory problems. Following standard operating procedures, the agency indicated that GM had forty-five days to submit a plan to fix the cars free of charge or to appeal the recall order.

As mentioned earlier, the most recent recall occurred in October 1984. The 750,000 cars recalled were suspected to have design defects in the catalytic converter. Catalytic converters, mufflerlike devices attached to exhaust pipes to bring exhaust emission into conformance with federal standards, became standard equipment on many cars in 1975. GM indicated that this last recall could cost more than $150 million.

DISCUSSION ISSUES

1. Do you believe GM has an operations management problem? Explain.
2. Which initially overlooked production control tools created the existing catalytic converter problem? Explain.
3. What major production management activities (see Figure 17.3) should be performed to correct the catalytic converter problem at GM? Explain.
4. Which production control tools would be especially relevant in correcting the catalytic converter problem? Explain.

STUDENT LEARNING OBJECTIVES

From studying this chapter, I will attempt to acquire:

1. An understanding of the relationship between data and information.
2. Insights on the main factors that influence the value of information.
3. Knowledge of some potential steps for evaluating information.
4. An appreciation for the role of computers in handling information.
5. An understanding of the importance of a management information system (MIS) to an organization.
6. A feasible strategy for establishing an MIS.
7. Information about what a management decision support system is and how it operates.

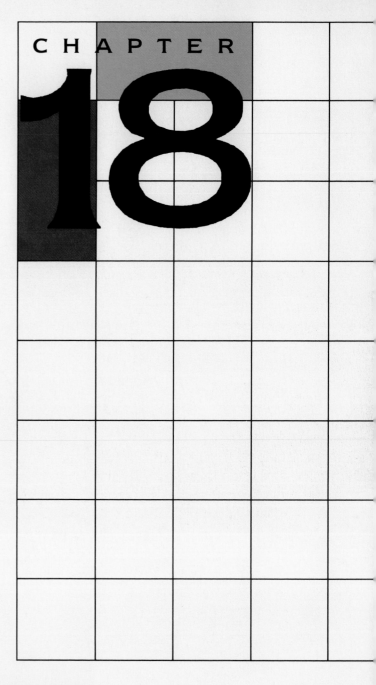

CHAPTER

18

INFORMATION

CHAPTER OUTLINE

A QUESTION OF MEASUREMENT

"Out of control? That's nonsense. Our organization has one of the most thorough control systems in the industry. I simply can't accept that statement." As Jack Wilkenson, president of Mega-Systems, Inc., made these comments, several members of the executive committee nodded in agreement. A smaller number showed no expression, while Natalie Greenberg, a new member of the executive committee, appeared unconvinced. Greenberg, a recently hired division manager, had drawn the heated remarks from the president by pointing out cost overruns on several recent projects. She had suggested that these overruns pointed to a lack of effective controls in key parts of the organization.

"We're all aware of the overruns, Natalie," said Warren Turner, the controller, "But I don't think we should blame our reporting system. It's probably the most thorough series of checks and measurements we could devise at the present time. For example, our production supervisors alone receive at least fourteen monthly measures of their department's productivity. Everything from output per hour to equipment utilization reports is made available to them. Have you seen the stack of computer printouts they receive every month? They've got everything they need to control their operations if they will only study those reports carefully."

"And we enlarged and improved our overall reporting system two years ago," added Ed Simpson, director of information systems. "We brought in a man-

agement consulting group that worked with our system design staff to create a thorough and sophisticated management information system. Then we conducted a massive campaign to 'sell' the control tools to the managers who would be using them. We've literally left no stone unturned to develop a first-class control system. I'm very satisfied with its thoroughness."

"Without trying to appear cynical," said Greenberg, "I wonder if the system is too thorough."

"Natalie, I think you'd better explain your comment," said the president, looking quizzically at the new division manager.

What's Ahead

The introductory case concludes with Natalie Greenberg, a recently hired division manager, implying that Mega-Systems, Inc., is not being controlled effectively because of the inadequacy of the control related information that managers presently are receiving. This chapter presents material that Jack Wilkenson, president of Mega-Systems, should use in assessing the validity of Greenberg's implications and in evaluating the overall status of information within his organization.

Controlling is the process of making things happen as planned. Of course, managers cannot make things happen as planned if they lack information on the manner in which various events in the organization occur. This chapter discusses the fundamental principles of handling information in an organization by first presenting the essentials of information and then examining both the management information system (MIS) and the management decision support system (MDSS).

⊞ ESSENTIALS OF INFORMATION

The process of developing information begins with the gathering of some type of facts or statistics, called **data.** Once gathered, data typically are analyzed in some manner. In general terms, **information** is the conclusions derived from data analysis. In management terms, information is the conclusions derived from the analysis of data that relate to the operation of an organization.

> Data are facts. Information is derived from data analysis.

The information that managers receive heavily influences managerial decision making, which in turn determines the activities that will be performed within the organization, which in turn dictate the eventual success or failure of the organization.[1] Some management writers consider information to be of such fundamental importance to the management process that they define *management* as the process of converting information into action through decision making.[2] The following sections discuss (1) factors that influence the value of information, (2) how to evaluate information, and (3) computer assistance in using information.

> The benefit derived from using information defines the information's value.

Factors Influencing the Value of Information

Some information is more valuable than other information.[3] The value of information is defined in terms of the benefit that can accrue to the organization through the use of the information. The greater this benefit, the more valuable the information.

Four primary factors determine the value of information: (1) information appropriateness, (2) information quality, (3) information timeliness, and (4) information quantity. In general, management should encourage the generation, distribution, and use of organizational information that is appropriate, of high quality, timely, and of sufficient quantity. Following this guideline will not necessarily guarantee sound decisions, but it will ensure that important resources necessary to make such decisions are available.[4] Each of the factors that determine information value is discussed in more detail in the paragraphs that follow.

Information Appropriateness

Appropriate informa-tion is information rel-evant to the decision.

Information appropriateness is defined in terms of how relevant the information is to the decision-making situation faced by the manager. If the information is quite relevant, then it is said to be appropriate. Generally, as the appropriateness of information increases, the value of that information increases.

Figure 18.1 shows the characteristics of information appropriate for the following common decision-making situations: (1) operational control, (2) management control, and (3) strategic planning.[5]

Operational control decisions relate to assuring that specific organizational tasks are carried out effectively and efficiently. Management control decisions relate to obtaining and effectively and efficiently using the organizational resources necessary to reach organizational objectives. Strategic planning decisions relate to determining organizational objectives and designating the corresponding action necessary to reach them.

As Figure 18.1 shows, the characteristics of appropriate information change as managers shift from making operational control decisions to making management control decisions to making strategic planning decisions. Strategic

Characteristics of Information	Operational Control	Management Control	Strategic Planning
Source	Largely internal	⟶	External
Scope	Well defined, narrow	⟶	Very wide
Level of aggregation	Detailed	⟶	Aggregate
Time horizon	Historical	⟶	Future
Currency	Highly current	⟶	Quite old
Required accuracy	High	⟶	Low
Frequency of use	Very frequent	⟶	Infrequent

FIGURE 18.1
Characteristics of information appropriate for decisions related to operational control, management control, and strategic planning

planning decision makers need information that focuses on the relationship of the organization to its external environment, emphasizes the future, is wide in scope, and presents a broad view. Appropriate information for this type of decision is usually old and not completely accurate.

Information appropriate for making operational control decisions has dramatically different characteristics than information appropriate for making strategic planning decisions. Operational control decision makers need information that focuses for the most part on the internal organizational environment, emphasizes the performance history of the organization, and is well defined, narrow in scope, and detailed. In addition, appropriate information for this type of decision is both highly current and highly accurate.

Information appropriate for making management control decisions generally has characteristics that fall somewhere between the extreme characteristics of appropriate operational control information and appropriate strategic planning information.

Information Quality

The second primary factor that determines the value of information is **information quality**—the degree to which information represents reality. The more closely information represents reality, the higher the quality and the greater the value of the information. In general, the higher the quality of information available to managers, the better equipped the managers are to make appropriate decisions and the greater the probability that the organization will be successful over the long term.

High-quality information is information that represents reality.

Information Timeliness

Information timeliness, the third primary factor that determines the value of information, is the extent to which the receipt of information allows decisions to be made and action to be taken so the organization can gain some benefit from possessing the information. Information received by managers at a point when it can be used to the advantage of the organization is said to be timely.

Timely information is information received in time to benefit the organization.

For example, a product may be selling poorly because its established market price is significantly higher than that of competitive products. If this information is received by management after the product has been discontinued, the information will be untimely. If, however, it is received soon enough to adjust the selling price of the product and thereby significantly increase sales, it will be timely.

Information Quantity

The fourth and final determinant of the value of information is **information quantity**—the amount of decision related information managers possess. Before making a decision, managers should assess the quantity of information they possess that relates to the decision being made. If this quantity is judged to be insufficient, more information should be gathered before the decision is made. If the amount of information is judged to be as complete as necessary, managers can feel justified in making the decision.

Sufficient information quantity is necessary for making justifiable decisions.

BACK TO THE CASE

Information at the introductory case's Mega-Systems, Inc., is the conclusions derived from the analysis of data relating to the way in which Mega-Systems operates. Natalie Greenberg has implied that managers currently are unable to make sound control decisions at Mega-Systems primarily because of the type of decision related information they are receiving.

If Jack Wilkenson, the president of Mega-Systems, finds that the control related information Mega-Systems managers currently are receiving is relatively valueless, he cannot fault his managers for making poor control decisions. Instead, he should strive to provide them with more valuable control related information. Wilkenson might be able to increase the value of the information his managers presently are receiving by forcing it to more closely represent activities as they actually occur at Mega-Systems, by making sure that the information is received by managers in sufficient quantity and in time to make controlling decisions, and by ensuring that the information is relevant to the control decisions of the managers receiving the information.

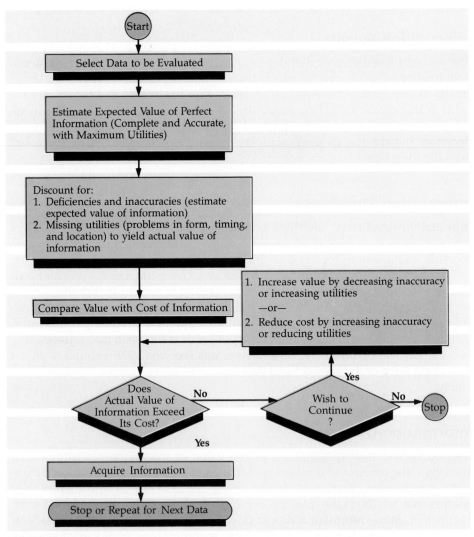

FIGURE 18.2
Flowchart of main activities in evaluating information

Evaluating Information

Evaluating information is the process of determining whether the acquisition of specified information is justified. As with all evaluations of this type, the primary concern of management is to weigh the dollar value of benefit gained from using some quantity of information against the cost of generating that information.

According to the flowchart in Figure 18.2, the first major step in evaluating organizational information is determining the value of that information by pinpointing the data to be analyzed and then determining the expected value or return to be received from obtaining perfect information based on these data. Next, this expected value should be reduced by the amount of benefit that will not be realized because of deficiencies and inaccuracies expected to appear in the information.

Then the expected value of organizational information should be compared with the expected cost of obtaining that information. If the expected cost does not exceed the expected value, the information should be gathered. If it does exceed the expected value, managers either must increase the information's expected value or decrease its expected cost before the information gathering can be justified. If neither of these objectives is possible, management cannot justify gathering the information.

One generally accepted strategy for increasing the expected value of information is to eliminate the characteristics of the information that tend to limit its usefulness. Table 18.1 lists some of these characteristics and the possible actions management can take to eliminate them.

Evaluating information involves determining whether the expected value of the information exceeds the expected cost.

TABLE 18.1

Characteristics that tend to limit the usefulness of information and how to eliminate them

Characteristics That Tend to Limit the Usefulness of Information	Possible Actions to Eliminate These Characteristics*
Language or format not understood	Translate, revise, or change format
Volume excessive: Time required to examine information exceeds the intuitive estimate of the value of the contents	Condense
Received before need perceived	Store for possible future need
Received after needed	Ensure against future occurrence
Inaccessible	Create access
Time or cost of access excessive	Relocate data, change access
No right of use, or closed communication channels because of conflicting subunit goals, authority relationships, and so forth	Relocate information; alter or open transmission channels; change relationships

* The organization will incur some additional cost by taking one or more of these actions.

BACK TO THE CASE

Jack Wilkenson's analysis of the status of organizational information at Mega-Systems should include a determination of whether all of the information furnished to Mega-Systems managers can be justified. To make this determination, Wilkenson should compare the value of the information with its cost. If its value is greater than its cost, the information received by managers can be justified. If its cost is greater than its value, however, the process of furnishing information should be modified—and Greenberg's inference that managers are receiving too much control related information would be valid. Wilkenson also should consider the possibility of increasing the value of organizational information by increasing its usefulness.

Computer Assistance in Using Information

Managers have an overwhelming amount of data to gather, analyze, and transform into information before making numerous decisions. Materials distributed by the Xerox corporation indicate that American businesses currently have more than 324 billion documents to generate annually, and this number is increasing by 72 billion each year.[6] A computer is a tool managers can use to assist in the complicated and time-consuming task of generating this information. A **computer** is an electronic tool capable of accepting data, interpreting data, performing ordered operations on data, and reporting on the outcome of these operations.

Computers are extremely helpful in generating information from raw data.

In general terms, Joseph D. Wessekamper, a director of the Haskins and Sells computer services department, indicates that computers give managers the ability to store vast amounts of financial, inventory, and other data so the data will be readily accessible for making day-to-day decisions.[7] Table 18.2 lists several specific computer operations for handling information.

Of course, the mere possession of a computer does not guarantee that management will receive a desirable level of data-processing support. Managers must strive to acquire appropriate computers for their organization and take steps to ensure that the computers are performing the necessary data-processing functions. The "Management in Action" feature for this chapter illustrates this point. John McBride, the deputy executive director of CARE, found on his arrival that the organization possessed a computer that was giving management virtually no data-processing support. To remedy this situation, CARE purchased and installed a new computer system.

The sections that follow discuss the main functions of computers and possible pitfalls in using computers.

Main Functions of Computers

The five functions of a computer involve:

A computer function is a computer activity that must be performed to generate organizational information. Computers perform five main functions: (1) input, (2) storage, (3) control, (4) processing, and (5) output. The relationships among these functions are shown in Figure 18.3 on page 508.

1. Getting material into the computer.

The **input function** consists of computer activities through which the computer enters the data to be analyzed and the instructions to be followed to analyze the data appropriately. As Figure 18.3 implies, the purpose of the input function is to provide data and instructions to be used in the performance of the storage, processing, control, and output functions.

TABLE 18.2

Computer operations that assist management in handling information

Operation	How a Computer Can Aid Managers
Billing	Control of buying, inventory, selling; rapid paying cycle; improved cash position; data about customers, products, items, costs, prices, sales representatives, sales statistics
Accounts receivable	Shorten average collections of accounts receivables; highlight past due statements, improve cash flow, invoice summary
Sales analysis	Review sales volume on the basis of profit contributions as well as gross profit contribution; compute sales representatives' commission plans; pinpoint sales improvement for customers and sales representatives
Inventory	Provide control of inventory, generation of distribution-by-value report—i.e., quantity sold annual sales are accumulated and printed as percentage of total number of items and total annual sales; pinpoint marginal items; segment inventory; establish order quantities and order points; cycle reviewing of vendor lines
Payroll	Construct payroll accounting system; produce reports to management, employees, government agencies; reduce peak workloads, strengthen managerial control over human resources
Materials planning	Determine components requirements; plan inventory per item by time period; determine how change in order quantity or delivery will affect production schedule; consolidate requirements of multiple-use items; reduce materials planning costs
Purchasing	Provide performance figures by item, supplier, and buyer in terms of cost, quality, and delivery; achieve tangible savings by meeting discount dates through faster processing of invoices; simplify analysis of historical data, expedite purchase orders based on production shortages and late deliveries
Dispatching and shop floor control	Reduce expediting costs because job status records are current; give early notification of exceptions requiring corrective action plus daily revisions of order priority by machine group
Capacity planning and operation scheduling	Make available labor requirements by time period in time to take corrective action; provide immediate information about effect of changes on work orders, simplified planning on availability of tools, realistic order release dates

The **storage function** consists of computer activities involved with retaining the material entered into the computer during the performance of the input function. The storage unit, or memory, of a computer is similar to the human memory in that various facts can be stored until they are needed for processing. In addition, facts can be stored, used in processing, and then restored as many times as necessary. As Figure 18.3 implies, the storage, processing, and control activities are dependent on one another and ultimately yield computer output.

2. Retaining material that has been input.

CHANGING COMPUTERS AT CARE

In 1946, the first CARE package arrived at Le Havre, France. By 1980, it looked as if the organization itself needed help.

CARE Inc., the American arm of the international aid organization, was reeling from a financial crisis that had forced cutbacks in some programs. Employee morale was low. Then, to cap it off, scandal struck: A senior CARE official was convicted of embezzling funds.

The troubles convinced CARE's directors of something they had long suspected: With annual revenue then at $200 million (now at $400 million) and projects in 37 countries, CARE had grown too big for its management systems. "CARE . . . was running on love, compassion and doing the right thing," says Philip Johnston, executive director, who joined CARE in 1963.

The solution: new management, new computers, a new head office, some new professional staff and the development of financial systems like those used by for-profit companies. After five years of top-to-bottom management shake-ups, "it's unquestionably a stronger and better organization," says Edwin J. Wesley, a lawyer who in 1980 was chairman of CARE and now is president, both volunteer positions. . . .

CARE was born after World War II as Americans banded together to find ways to send packages of food and clothing to Europe. It was originally very personal, with people designating specific friends and relatives to receive aid.

But CARE gradually expanded, through government grants and private and corporate donations. It started school-lunch and maternal-health programs, and did disaster relief. It pushed into forestation programs, agribusiness development and job training as its focus broadened to include the underdeveloped countries of Asia, Latin America and Africa. The phrase behind the acronym—originally Cooperative for American Remittances to Europe—was changed to Cooperative for American Relief Everywhere.

CARE's management and management systems grew as the organization did, without changing fundamentally. But in 1979, donations from corporations, foundations and individuals fell about $5 million short of the projected $24 million. The shortfall caused a crisis. It also drove CARE's directors to conclude that they needed new people and methods.

Mr. Johnston, who was promoted in 1980 from director of CARE Europe to executive director of the U.S. organization, was encouraged by the board to hire

outside managers. They found their work cut out for them. "There were management problems throughout," says John McBride, who was vice president of finance and administration at Barnard College before becoming CARE's deputy executive director. "There were horrible facilities, the wrong people in the wrong jobs, a computer that didn't do any good, no cohesive salary structure, no employment manual and no salary grades."

Some financial changes yielded quick results. About $1.7 million was moved from a checking account into interest-bearing accounts. Short-term investments were swapped for long-term ones. Such moves increased interest income to over $1 million a year . . . from an annual range of $200,000 to $500,000 in the several years before the change. . . .

CARE bought a new computer system. J. Hampson Sinker, who became CARE's budget director this year after taking early retirement from Westinghouse Electric Corp., says CARE's current computerized accounting system is as good as Westinghouse's.

Although CARE was doing larger and more complex projects, the systems to evaluate them hadn't be-

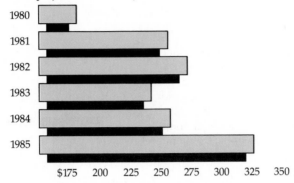

International Aid
CARE's spending for food aid, disaster relief and other projects (*In millions of dollars*)

1980	
1981	
1982	
1983	
1984	
1985	

$175 200 225 250 275 300 325 350

come more sophisticated. Beryl Levinger, an assistant executive director who joined CARE in 1984, says a water system was funded in the Sudan three or four years ago, without any program for maintaining it. A program to give good aid to mothers and children in Guatemala, Haiti and the Philippines didn't monitor weight gains.

In the past two years, CARE has tried to plan projects in relation to each other, rather than separately, to get better feedback from the field, and to give projects better technical help. For example, the water project in the Sudan now includes a program for maintaining the system and training people in managing it, and a health-education program.

FIGURE 18.3
Relationships among the five
main functions of a computer

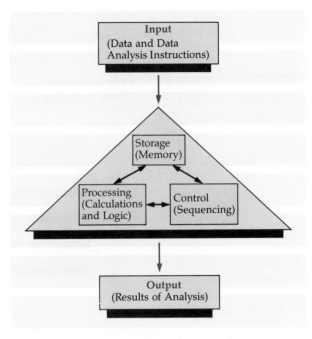

3. Analyzing data.

The **processing function** consists of the computer activities involved with performing both logic and calculation steps necessary to analyze data appropriately. Calculation activities include virtually any numerical analysis. Logic activities include such analysis as comparing one number to another to determine which is larger. Data, as well as directions for processing the data, are furnished by input and storage activities.

4. Ordering computer activities.

Computer activities that dictate the order in which other computer functions are performed compose the **control function.** Control activities indicate (1) when data should be retrieved after storage, (2) when and how the data should be analyzed, (3) if and when the data should be restored after analysis, (4) if and when additional data should be retrieved, and (5) when output activities (described in the next paragraph) should begin and end.

5. Communicating computer analysis results.

The **output function** comprises the activities that take the results of the input, storage, processing, and control functions and transmit them outside the computer. These results can appear in such diverse forms as data on magnetic tape or characters typed on paper. Obviously, the form in which output appears is determined primarily by how the output is to be used. Output that appears on magnetic tape, for example, can be used as input for another computer analysis but is of little value for analysis by human beings.

Possible Pitfalls in Using Computers

Managers should keep in mind that:

The computer is a sophisticated management tool with the potential of making a significant contribution to organizational success. For this potential to materialize, however, the following possible pitfalls should be avoided:

1. Computers are not self-directed.

1. *Thinking that a computer is capable of independently performing creative activities* A computer is capable only of following precise and detailed instructions provided by the computer user. The individual using the computer must tell the

computer exactly what to do, how to do it, and when to do it. One computer expert describes his working with a computer as follows:

> It's like talking to a moron. You have to tell it every little detail. . . . When I was working my way through college, I used to work in a laundry. One of the boys . . . there had very low intelligence. I could say, "Jimmy, go over to the bench and pick up that empty bucket and bring it to me." Jimmy would do it. But, if he found that the bucket was full of water instead of empty, he would become very confused. So I would have to tell him to take it to the sink and pour the water out. The trouble was that I had left out a step in his instructions, and he didn't have the ability to think what to do. It's the same with machines.[8]

This section points out that computers are simply pieces of equipment that must be directed very precisely by computer users to perform some function. The cartoon makes much the same point by implying that people and computers are equals.

2. *Spending too much money on computer assistance*[9] In general, computers can be of great assistance to managers. The initial cost of purchasing a computer as well as updating it when necessary, however, can be very high.[10] Managers need to keep comparing the benefit obtained from computer assistance with the cost of obtaining this assistance. A. R. Zipf makes the point that this comparison can help managers eliminate the seeming desire of many organization members to purchase computers simply to "play with a new toy."[11]

   2. Using computers is expensive.

3. *Overestimating the value of computer output* Some managers fall into the trap of assuming that they have "the answer" once they have received information generated by computer analysis. Managers must recognize that computer output is only as good as the quality of data and directions for analyzing that data that human beings have put into the computer. Inaccurate data or inap-

   3. People determine the worth of computer output.

Reprinted by permission of the cartoonist, Douglas Blackwell.

propriate computer instructions yield useless computer output. A commonly used phrase to describe such an occurrence is "garbage in, garbage out."

BACK TO THE CASE

Part of Wilkenson's investigation of the status of information at Mega-Systems should include an analysis of the company's present computer assistance in handling information. Not only should the computer be storing and processing data related to performing the control function at Mega-Systems, but it also should be handling additional operations related to such areas as payroll, sales analysis, billing, and purchasing. To encourage wise use of Mega-Systems' computer, Wilkenson should tell organization members using the computer to keep in mind that a computer is not capable of performing creatively, that the benefits of using a computer should be greater than the costs of using it, and that computer output should be scrutinized carefully and not used as "the answer."

THE MANAGEMENT INFORMATION SYSTEM (MIS)

An MIS gets information to where it is needed.

In simple terms, a **management information system (MIS)** is a network established within an organization to provide managers with information that will assist them in decision making. The following, more complete definition of an MIS was developed by the Management Information System Committee of the Financial Executives Institute:

> An MIS is a system designed to provide selected decision-oriented information needed by management to plan, control, and evaluate the activities of the corporation. It is designed within a framework that emphasizes profit planning, performance planning, and control at all levels. It contemplates the ultimate integration of required business information subsystems, both financial and non-financial, within the company.[12]

The title of the specific organization member responsible for developing and maintaining an MIS varies from organization to organization. In smaller organizations, a president or vice-president may possess this responsibility. In larger organizations, an individual with a title such as "director of information systems" may be solely responsible for appropriately managing an entire MIS department. The term *MIS manager* is used in the sections that follow to indicate the person within the organization who has the primary responsibility for managing the MIS. The term *MIS personnel* is used to designate the nonmanagement individuals within the organization who possess the primary responsibility of actually operating the MIS. Examples of nonmanagement individuals are computer operators and computer programmers. The sections that follow describe an MIS more fully and outline the steps managers take to establish an MIS.

Describing the MIS

The MIS is perhaps best described by a summary of the steps necessary to properly operate an MIS and by a discussion of the different kinds of information various managers need to make job related decisions.

Operating the MIS

MIS personnel generally perform six sequential steps to properly operate an MIS.[13] (Figure 18.4 summarizes the steps and indicates the order in which they are performed.) The first step is to determine what information is needed within the organization, when it will be needed, and in what form it will be needed. Since the basic purpose of the MIS is to assist management in making decisions, one way to begin determining management information needs is to analyze (1) decision areas in which management makes decisions, (2) specific decisions within these decision areas that management actually must make, and (3) alternatives that must be evaluated to make these specific decisions. Table 18.3 on page 512 presents such an analysis for a manager making decisions related to production and operations management.

The second major step in operating the MIS is pinpointing and collecting the data that will yield needed organizational information. This step is just as important as determining the information needs of the organization. If collected

The six-step process of operating an MIS involves:

1. Determining what information is needed.

2. Gathering data to fill information needs.

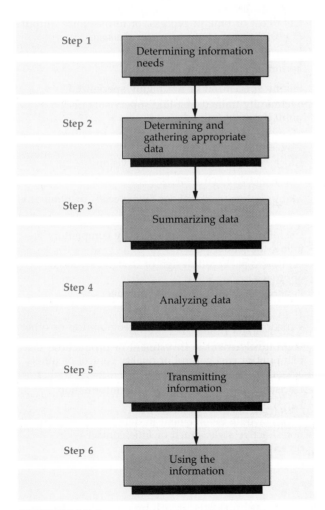

FIGURE 18.4
The six steps necessary to operate an MIS properly in order of their performance

TABLE 18.3

Decision areas, decisions, and alternatives related to production and operations management

Decision Areas	Decisions	Alternatives
Plant and equipment	Span of process	Make or buy
	Plant size	One big plant or several smaller ones
	Plant location	Locate near markets or locate near materials
	Investment decisions	Invest mainly in buildings or equipment or inventories or research
	Choice of equipment	General-purpose or special-purpose equipment
	Kind of tooling	Temporary, minimum tooling or "production tooling"
Production planning and control	Frequency of inventory taking	Few or many breaks in production for buffer stocks
	Inventory size	High inventory or a lower inventory
	Degree of inventory control	Control in great detail or in lesser detail
	What to control	Controls designed to minimize machine downtime or labor cost or time in process, or to maximize output of particular products or material usage
	Quality control	High reliability and quality or low costs
	Use of standards	Formal or informal or none at all
Labor and staffing	Job specialization	Highly specialized or not highly specialized
	Supervision	Technically trained first-line supervisors or nontechnically trained supervisors
	Wage system	Many job grades or few job grades; incentive wages or hourly wages
	Supervision	Close supervision or loose supervision
	Industrial engineers	Many or few such men
Product design/ engineering	Size of product line	Many customer specials or few specials or none at all
	Design stability	Frozen design or many engineering change orders
	Technological risk	Use of new processes unproved by competitors or follow-the-leader policy
	Engineering	Complete packaged design or design-as-you-go approach
	Use of manufacturing engineering	Few or many manufacturing engineers
Organization and management	Kind of organization	Functional or product focus or geographical or other
	Executive use of time	High involvement in investment or production planning or cost control or quality control or other activities
	Degree of risk assumed	Decisions based on much or little information
	Use of staff	Large or small staff group
	Executive style	Much or little involvement in detail; authoritarian or nondirective style; much or little contact with organization

data do not relate properly to information needs, it will be impossible to generate needed information.

3. Summarizing the data.

After the information needs of the organization have been determined and appropriate data have been pinpointed and gathered, summarizing the data and analyzing the data are, respectively, the third and fourth steps MIS personnel generally should take to properly operate an MIS. It is in the performance of these steps that MIS personnel find computer assistance of great benefit.

The fifth and sixth steps are transmitting the information generated by data analysis to appropriate managers and having the managers actually use the information. The performance of these last two steps results in managerial decision making. Although each of the six steps is necessary if an MIS is to run properly, the time spent on performing each step naturally will vary from organization to organization.

4. Analyzing the data.

5. Transmitting the information.

6. Using the information.

Different Managers Need Different Kinds of Information

For maximum benefit, an MIS must collect relevant data, transform that data into appropriate information, and transmit that information to the appropriate managers. Appropriate information for one manager within an organization, however, may not be appropriate information for another. Robert G. Murdick suggests that the degree of appropriateness of MIS information for a manager

MIS information should be appropriate for the manager receiving it.

Organizational level	Type of Management	Manager's Organizational Objectives	Appropriate Information from MIS	How MIS Information is Used
1. Top management	CEO, president, vice-president	Survival of the firm, profit growth, accumulation and efficient use of resources	Environmental data and trends, summary reports of operations, "exception reports" of problems, forecasts	Corporate objectives, policies, constraints, decisions on strategic plans, decisions on control of the total company
2. Middle management	Middle managers such as marketing, production, and financial	Allocation of resources to assigned tasks, establishment of plans to meet operating objectives, control of operations	Summaries and exception reports of operating results, corporate objectives, policies, contraints, decisions on strategic plans, relevant actions and decisions of other middle managers	Operating plans and policies, exception reports, operating summaries, control procedures, decisions on resource allocations, actions and decisions related to other middle managers
3. First-line management	First-line managers whose work is closely related	Production of goods to meet marketing needs, supplying budgets, estimates of resource requirements, movement and storage of materials	Summary reports of transactions, detailed reports of problems, operating plans and policies, control procedures, actions and decisions of related first-line managers	Exception reports, progress reports, resource requests, dispatch orders, cross-functional reports

FIGURE 18.5
Appropriate MIS information under various sets of organizational circumstances

depends on the activities for which the manager will use the information, the organizational objectives assigned to the manager, and the level of management at which the manager functions.[14] All of these factors, of course, are closely related.

Murdick's thoughts on this matter are best summarized in Figure 18.5 on page 513. As can be seen from this figure, since the overall job situations of top managers, middle managers, and first-line managers are significantly different, the types of information these managers need to satisfactorily perform their jobs also are significantly different.

BACK TO THE CASE

Wilkenson's analysis of the status of information at Mega-Systems should include an assessment of the MIS within the organization. The MIS at Mega-Systems is the organizational network established to provide managers with information that helps them make job related decisions. In assessing the MIS, Wilkenson should check to see that activities performed by MIS personnel include determining information needs at Mega-Systems, determining and collecting appropriate Mega-Systems data, summarizing and analyzing these data, transmitting analyzed data to appropriate Mega-Systems managers, and having managers actually use received MIS information. Wilkenson also should check to see if information sent to managers through the MIS is appropriate for their respective levels within the organization.

Establishing an MIS

The process of establishing an MIS involves four stages: (1) planning for the MIS, (2) designing the MIS, (3) implementing the MIS, and (4) improving the MIS.

Planning for the MIS

Planning for an MIS is critical for MIS success.

The planning stage is perhaps the most important stage of establishing an MIS. Commonly cited factors that make planning for the establishment of an MIS an absolute necessity are the typically long periods of time needed to acquire MIS related data-processing equipment and to integrate it within the operation of the organization, the difficulty of hiring competent operators of the equipment, and the major amounts of financial and managerial resources typically needed to operate an MIS.[15]

The specific types of plans for an MIS vary from organization to organization. However, a checklist of topics that should be addressed in all such plans is presented in Table 18.4. In general, the more topics on this checklist that an MIS plan thoroughly addresses, the greater the probability the plan will be successful.

A sample plan for the establishment of an MIS at General Electric is shown in Figure 18.6 on page 516. This particular plan, of course, is abbreviated. Much more detailed outlines of each of the areas in this plan would be needed before it could be implemented. It is interesting to note that this plan includes a point (about a third of the way down the figure) at which management must decide if there is enough potential benefit to be gained from the existence of the MIS to continue the process of establishing it. This particular plan specifies that if man-

TABLE 18.4

Checklist for the contents of an MIS plan

1. *Introduction*
   a. Summary of major goals, a statement of their consistency with corporate goals, and current state of planning vis-à-vis these goals
   b. Summary of aggregate cost and savings projections
   c. Summary of human resource requirements
   d. Major challenges and problems
   e. Criteria for assigning project priorities
2. *Project Identification*
   a. Maintenance projects, all projects proposed, and development projects
   b. Estimated completion times
   c. Human resource requirements, by time period and job category
   d. Computer capacity needed for system testing and implementation
   e. Economic justification by project—development costs, implementation costs, running costs, out-of-pocket savings, intangible savings
   f. Project control tools
   g. Tie-ins with other systems and master plans
3. *Hardware Projections (Derived from Projects)*
   a. Current applications—work loads and compilation and testing requirements
   b. New applications—work loads and reruns
   c. Survey of new hardware, with emphasis on design flexibility, which will allow the company to take full advantage of new developments in hardware and software
   d. Acquisition strategy, with timing contingencies
   e. Facilities requirements and growth in hardware, tape storage, offices, and supplies
4. *Human Resource Projections (Derived from Projects)*
   a. Human resources needed by month for each category
      1. General—management, administrative, training, and planning personnel
      2. Developmental—application analysts, system designers, methods and procedures personnel, operating system programmers, and other programmers
      3. Operational—machine operators and input/output control clerks
   b. Salary levels, training needs, and estimated turnover
5. *Financial Projections by Time Period*
   a. Hardware rental, depreciation, maintenance, floor space, air conditioning, and electricity
   b. Human resources—training and fringe benefits
   c. Miscellaneous—building rental, outside service, telecommunications, and the like

agement decides there is not sufficient potential benefit to be gained by establishing the MIS, given its total costs, the project should be terminated.

Designing the MIS

Although data-processing equipment is normally an important ingredient of management information systems, the designing of an MIS should not begin with a comparative analysis of the types of such equipment available. Many MIS managers mistakenly think that data-processing equipment and an MIS are synonymous.

Stoller and Van Horn indicate that, since the purpose of an MIS is to provide information that will assist managers in making better decisions, the designing of an MIS should begin with an analysis of the types of decisions the

The design of an MIS should stress decision making.

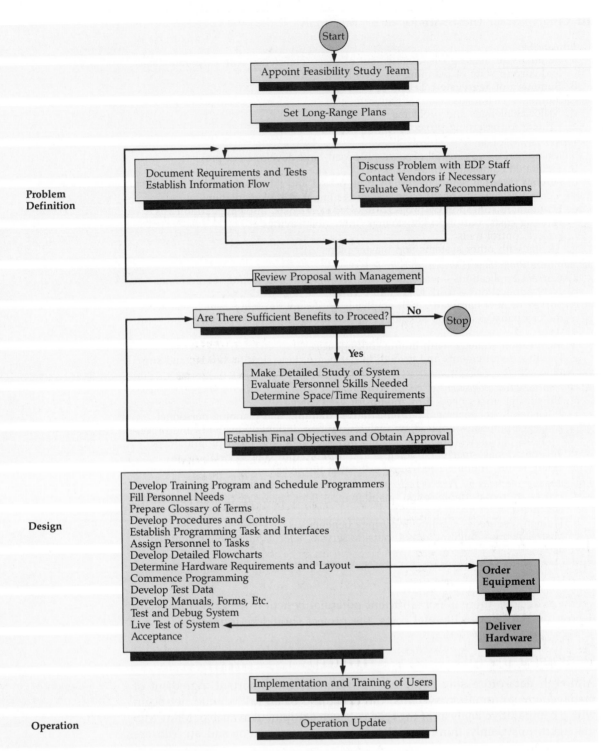

FIGURE 18.6
Plan for establishing an MIS at General Electric

managers actually make in a particular organization.[16] These authors suggest that designing an MIS should consist of four steps: (1) defining various decisions that must be made to run an organization, (2) determining the types of existing management policies that may influence the ways in which these decisions should be made, (3) pinpointing the types of data needed to make these decisions, and (4) establishing a mechanism for gathering and appropriately processing the data to obtain needed information.[17]

Implementing the MIS

The third stage in the process of establishing an MIS within an organization is implementation—that is, putting the planned for and designed MIS into operation. In this stage, the equipment is acquired and integrated into the organization. Designated data are gathered, analyzed as planned, and distributed to appropriate managers within the organization. And line managers make decisions based on the information they receive from the MIS.

Implementation is putting the MIS into action.

Improving the MIS

Once the MIS is operating, MIS managers should continually strive to maximize its value. The two sections that follow provide insights on how MIS improvements might be made.

Symptoms of Inadequate MIS

To improve an MIS, MIS managers must first find symptoms or signs that the existing MIS is inadequate. A list of such symptoms, developed by Bertram A. Colbert, a principal of Price Waterhouse & Company, is presented in Table 18.5, p. 518.[18]

Managers must evaluate the symptoms of an inadequate MIS to determine MIS weaknesses.

Colbert divides the symptoms into three types: (1) operational, (2) psychological, and (3) report content. Operational symptoms and psychological symptoms relate, respectively, to the operation of the organization and the functioning of organization members. Report content symptoms relate to the actual makeup of the information generated by the MIS.

Although the symptoms in the table are clues that an MIS is inadequate, the symptoms themselves may not actually pinpoint MIS weaknesses. Therefore, after such symptoms are detected, MIS managers usually must gather additional information to determine what MIS weaknesses exist. Answering questions such as the following would be of some help to MIS managers in determining these weaknesses:[19]

1. Where and how do managers get information?
2. Can managers make better use of their contacts to get information?
3. In what areas is managers' knowledge weakest, and how can managers be given information to minimize these weaknesses?
4. Do managers tend to act before receiving information?
5. Do managers wait so long for information that opportunities pass them by and the organization becomes bottlenecked?

Typical Improvements to an MIS

MIS inadequacies vary from situation to situation, depending on such factors as the quality of an MIS plan, the appropriateness of an MIS design, and the type of

To improve an MIS, managers should:

TABLE 18.5

Symptoms of an inadequate MIS

Operational	Psychological	Report Content
Large physical inventory adjustments	Surprise at financial results	Excessive use of tabulations of figures
Capital expenditure overruns	Poor attitude of executives about usefulness of information	Multiple preparation and distribution of identical data
Inability of executives to explain changes from year to year in operating results	Lack of understanding of financial information on part of nonfinancial executives	Disagreeing information from different sources
Uncertain direction of company growth	Lack of concern for environmental changes	Lack of periodic comparative information and trends
Cost variances unexplainable	Executive homework reviewing reports considered excessive	Lateness of information
No order backlog awareness		Too little or excess detail
No internal discussion of reported data		Inaccurate information
Insufficient knowledge about competition		Lack of standards for comparison
Purchasing parts from outside vendors when internal capability and capacity to make is available		Failure to identify variances by cause and responsibility
Record of some "sour" investments in facilities, or in programs such as R&D and advertising		Inadequate externally generated information

individuals operating an MIS. However, several activities have the potential of improving the MIS of most organizations:

1. Build cooperation.

1. *Building cooperation among MIS personnel and line managers*[20] Cooperation of this sort encourages line managers to give MIS personnel honest opinions of the quality of information being received. Through this type of interaction, MIS designers and operators should be able to improve the effectiveness of an MIS.

2. Stress decision making.

2. *Constantly stressing that MIS personnel should strive to accomplish the purpose of the MIS—providing managers with decision related information* In this regard, it probably would be of great benefit to hold line managers responsible for continually educating MIS personnel on the types of decisions organization managers make and the corresponding steps taken to make these decisions. The better MIS personnel understand the decision situations that face operating managers, the higher the probability that MIS information will be appropriate for decisions these managers must make.

3. Use cost-benefit analysis.

3. *Holding, wherever possible, both line managers and MIS personnel accountable for MIS activities on a cost-benefit basis*[21] This accountability reminds line managers and MIS personnel that the benefits the organization receives from MIS functions must exceed the costs. In effect, this accountability emphasis helps increase the cost consciousness of both line managers and MIS personnel.

4. Consider people.

4. *Operating an MIS in a "people conscious" manner* An MIS, like the formal pyramidal organization, is based on the assumption that organizational affairs can and should be handled in a completely logical manner.[22] Logic, of course, is important to the design and implementation of an MIS. In addition, however, MIS activities also should include people considerations.[23] After all, even if

TABLE 18.6

Causes for four different working groups' resistance to an MIS

	Operating (Nonclerical)	Operating (Clerical)	Operating Management	Top Management
Threats to economic security		X	X	
Threats to status or power		X	X*	
Increased job complexity	X		X	X
Uncertainty or unfamiliarity	X	X	X	X
Changed interpersonal relations or work patterns		X*	X	
Changed superior-subordinate relationships		X*	X	
Increased rigidity or time pressure	X	X	X	
Role ambiguity		X	X*	X
Feelings of insecurity		X	X*	X*

X = The reason is possibly the cause of resistance to MIS development.
X* = The reason has a strong possibility of being the cause of resistance.

MIS activities are well thought out and completely logical, an MIS can be ineffective simply because people do not use it as intended.

According to Dickson and Simmons, several factors can cause people to resist using an MIS.[24] A summary of these factors according to working groups is presented in Table 18.6. This table implies that for managers to improve MIS effectiveness, they may have to take steps to reduce such factors as threats to power and status that might be discouraging MIS use.

BACK TO THE CASE

Mega-Systems presently has an MIS. Wilkenson, however, may be able to gain valuable insights on the status of information at Mega-Systems by evaluating the way in which the existing MIS was established. For example, Wilkenson should ask the following questions about the planning stage of Mega-Systems' MIS: Was appropriate data-processing equipment acquired and integrated? Have appropriate personnel been acquired to operate the equipment?

About the design and implementation stages of Mega-Systems' MIS, Wilkenson should seek answers to such questions as: Did the design of the present MIS begin with an analysis of managerial decision making? Does the present MIS exist as designed and implemented?

Wilkenson also should try to determine whether MIS managers, other MIS personnel, and line managers are continually trying to improve the MIS. All such organization members should be aware of the symptoms of an inadequate MIS and should be attempting to pinpoint and eliminate corresponding MIS weaknesses.

Finally, Wilkenson should consider the possibilities of improving his MIS by (1) building additional cooperation between MIS managers, MIS personnel, and line managers; (2) stressing that the purpose of the MIS is to provide managers with decision related information; (3) using cost-benefit analysis to evaluate MIS activities; and (4) ensuring that the MIS operates in a people-conscious manner.

THE MANAGEMENT DECISION SUPPORT SYSTEM (MDSS)

Traditionally, the MIS that uses electronic assistance in gathering data and providing related information to managers has been invaluable. This MIS assistance has been especially useful in areas where programmed decisions (see chapter 5)

Electronic assistance is invaluable to an MIS.

are necessary, since the computer continually generates the information that helps managers make these decisions. An example is using the computer to track cumulative labor costs by department. The computer can be used to automatically gather and update the cumulative labor costs per department, compare the costs to corresponding annual budgets, and calculate the percentage of the budget that each department has reached to date. Such information would normally be useful in controlling departmental labor costs.

Closely related to the MIS is the **management decision support system (MDSS)**—an interdependent set of decision aids that help managers make nonprogrammed decisions (see chapter 5).[25] Figure 18.7 illustrates possible components of the MDSS and describes what they do. The MDSS is typically characterized by the following:[26]

Management decision support systems are characterized by:

1. Corporate databases.

1. *One or more corporate databases* A **database** is a reservoir of corporate facts consistently organized to fit the information needs of a variety of organization members. These databases (also termed corporate databases) tend to contain facts about all important facets of company operations, including financial as well as nonfinancial information. These facts are used to explore issues important to the corporation. For example, a manager might find it helpful to use facts from the corporate database to forecast profits for each of the next three years.

2. User databases.

2. *One or more user database* In addition to the corporate database, an MDSS tends to contain several additional user databases. A **user database** is a database developed by an individual manager or other user. These databases may be derived from but are not necessarily limited to the corporate database. They tend to address specific issues peculiar to the individual users. For example, a production manager might be interested in exploring the specific issue of lowering production costs. To do so, the manager might build a

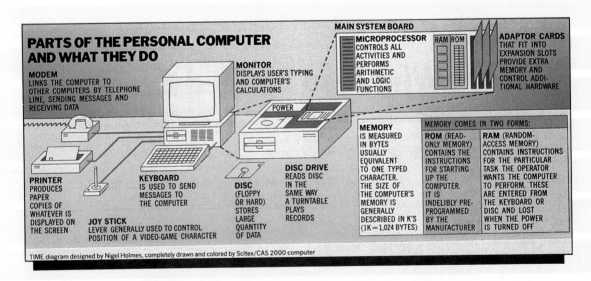

FIGURE 18.7
Possible components of a management decision support system (MDSS) and what they do

simple user database that includes departmental facts about reject rates of materials purchased from various suppliers. The manager might be able to lower production costs by eliminating the materials from the suppliers with the highest reject rates.

3. *A set of quantitative tools stored in a model base* A **model base** is a collection of quantitative computer programs that can assist MDSS users in analyzing data in databases. For example, the production manager discussed in item 2 might use a correlation analysis program stored in a model base to accurately determine any relationships that might exist between reject rates and the materials from various suppliers.

    One desirable feature of a model base is its ability to allow the user to perform **"what if" analysis**—the simulation of a business situation over and over again using somewhat different data for selected decision areas. For example, a manager might first determine the profitability of a company under present conditions. The manager might then ask *what* would happen *if* materials costs increased by 5 percent. Or *if* products were sold at a different price. Popular programs such as Lotus 1–2–3 and the Interactive Financial Planning System (IFPS)[27] allow managers to ask as many "what if's" as they want to and to save their answers without changing their original data.

4. *A dialogue capability* The ability of an MDSS user to interact with an MDSS is **dialogue capability.** Such interaction typically involves extracting data from a

3. Model databases.

4. Dialogue capability.

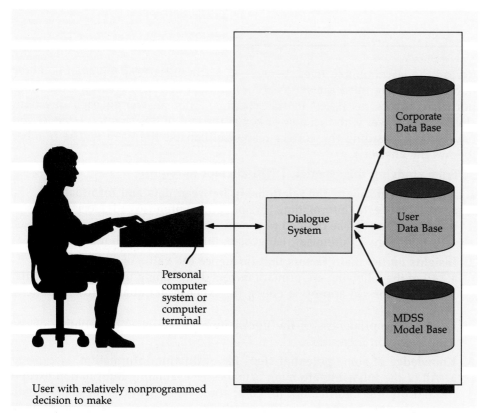

FIGURE 18.8
How dialogue capability interacts with other MDSS ingredients

database, calling various models stored in the model base, and storing analysis results in a file. How this dialogue capability interacts with other MDSS ingredients is depicted in Figure 18.8 on page 521.

The continued technological developments related to microcomputers have made the use of the MDSS concept feasible and its application available to virtually all managers. In addition, the continued development of extensive software to support information analysis related to more subjective decision making is contributing to the popularity of MDSS.

BACK TO THE CASE

The information about MDSS should be particularly interesting to Wilkenson in evaluating Greenberg's comments. Perhaps information is not being appropriately used at Mega-Systems simply because managers are not familiar with the use of the MDSS. Wilkenson should make sure that managers are balancing MIS reports for programmed decisions with MDSS reports for nonprogrammed decisions.

In exploring this issue, Wilkenson must answer several questions: Do managers have adequate equipment to operate an MDSS? Do they have adequate access to a corporate database? Are managers properly employing user databases? Is there an appropriate model base available to managers? Is there adequate dialogue capability within the existing MDSS? If the answers to these and other related questions are yes, then the probability is high that the Mega-Systems MDSS is being properly used. If the answers are no, then Wilkenson would probably be able to improve operations within his company by encouraging his managers to appropriately use an MDSS.

Action Summary

Reread the learning objectives that follow. Each objective is followed by questions. Answering these questions accurately will help you retain the most important concepts discussed in this chapter. After answering each question, check your answer with the answer key at the end of this chapter. (*Hint:* If you have doubt regarding the correct response, consult the page whose number follows the answer.)

Circle:

From studying this chapter, I will attempt to acquire:

1. **An understanding of the relationship between data and information.**

a, b, c, d, e   **a.** Data can be: (a) information; (b) opinion; (c) premises; (d) facts; (e) gossip.

a, b, c, d, e   **b.** Information can be defined as conclusions derived from: (a) data analysis; (b) opinion; (c) premises; (d) gossip; (e) none of the above.

2. **Insights on the main factors that influence the value of information.**

a, b, c, d, e   **a.** All of the following are primary factors determining the value of information except: (a) appropriateness; (b) expense; (c) quality; (d) timeliness; (e) quantity.

T, F   **b.** The appropriateness of the information increases as the volume of the information increases.

3. **Knowledge of some potential steps for evaluating information.**

a, b, c, d, e   **a.** All of the following are main activities in evaluating information except: (a) acquiring information; (b) comparing value with cost of information; (c) selecting data to be evaluated; (d) using information in decision making; (e) discounting expected value for deficiencies and inaccuracies.

b. The primary concern of management in evaluating information is the dol-   T, F
lar value of the benefits gained compared to the cost of generating the
information.

4. **An appreciation for the role of computers in handling information.**
   a. All of the following are main computer functions except: (a) input; (b) stor-   a, b, c, d, e
   age; (c) control; (d) heuristic; (e) output.
   b. All of the following are possible pitfalls in using the computer except: a, b, c, d, e
   (a) thinking that a computer is independently capable of creative activities;
   (b) failing to realize that a computer is capable only of following precise
   and detailed instructions; (c) training and retraining all computer operating personnel; (d) spending too much money on computer assistance;
   (e) overestimating the value of computer output.

5. **An understanding of the importance of a management information system
   (MIS) to an organization.**
   a. A management information system is a network established within an   T, F
   organization to provide managers with information that will assist them in
   decision making.
   b. "Determining information needs" is which of the steps necessary to oper-   a, b, c, d, e
   ate an MIS: (a) first; (b) second; (c) third; (d) fourth; (e) none of the above.

6. **A feasible strategy for establishing an MIS.**
   a. All of the following are stages in the process of establishing an MIS except: a, b, c, d, e
   (a) planning; (b) designing; (c) improving; (d) implementing; (e) all of the
   above are stages.
   b. Which of the following activities has the potential of improving an MIS: a, b, c, d, e
   (a) stressing that MIS personnel should strive to accomplish the purpose
   of an MIS; (b) operating an MIS in a "people conscious" manner; (c) encouraging line managers to continually request additional information
   through the MIS; (d) a and b; (e) all of the above.

7. **Information about what a management decision support system is and how
   it operates.**
   a. A management decision support system is a set of decision aids aimed at   T, F
   helping managers make nonprogrammed decisions.
   b. There is basically no difference between a corporate database and a user   T, F
   database.
   c. Dialogue capability allows the MDSS user to interact with an MIS.   T, F

▮ INTRODUCTORY CASE WRAP-UP

"A Question of Measurement" (p. 498) and its related
back-to-the-case sections were written to help you better understand the management concepts contained in
this chapter. Answer the following discussion questions about this introductory case to further enrich
your understanding of chapter content:

1. How does the series of "checks and measurements" mentioned by Turner fit into the control
   process of Mega-Systems, Inc.?

2. What do you think Greenberg meant by, "I wonder if the system is too thorough"?
3. How do managers determine if too many checks
   and measurements are being taken during the controlling process?

Issues for Review and Discussion

1. What is the difference between data and information?
2. List and define four major factors that influence the value of information.
3. What are operational control decisions and strategic planning decisions? What characterizes information appropriate for making each of these decisions?
4. Discuss the major activities involved in evaluating information.
5. What factors tend to limit the usefulness of information, and how can these factors be overcome?
6. Is a computer a flexible management tool? Explain.
7. How do the main functions of a computer relate to one another?
8. Summarize the major pitfalls managers must avoid when using a computer.
9. Define *MIS* and discuss its importance to management.
10. What steps must be performed to operate an MIS properly?
11. What major steps are involved in establishing an MIS?
12. Why is planning for an MIS such an important part of establishing an MIS?
13. Why does the designing of an MIS begin with analyzing managerial decision making?
14. How should managers use the symptoms of an inadequate MIS as listed in Table 18.5?
15. How could building cooperation between MIS personnel and line managers improve an MIS?
16. How can management use cost-benefit analysis to improve an MIS?
17. Describe five possible causes of resistance to using an MIS. What can managers do to ensure that these causes do not affect their organization's MIS?
18. How does an MDSS differ from an MIS? Define *"what if" analysis* and give an illustration of how a manager might use it.

Sources of Additional Information

Ahituv, Niv, and Seev Neumann. *Principles of Information Systems for Management.* Dubuque, Iowa: Wm. C. Brown, 1982.

Attaran, Mohsen, and Hossein Bidgoli. "Developing an Effective Manufacturing Decision Support System." *Business* 36 (October/November/December 1986): 9–16.

Berg, Norman A. *General Management: An Analytical Approach.* Homewood, Ill.: Richard D. Irwin, 1984.

Brabb, George J. *Computers and Information Systems in Business.* Boston: Houghton Mifflin, 1980.

Chen, Dr. Richard. "Hospital Information System Design." *Journal of Systems Management* (May 1984): 24–28.

Ehrlemark, Ulla. "Design Your Own Management Information Systems." *Long-Range Planning* 17 (April 1984): 85–95.

Gillenson, Mark L., and Robert Goldberg. *Strategic Planning, Systems Analysis, and Database Design.* New York: Wiley, 1984.

Henderson, Marjorie, Marti J. Rhea, and Joe L. Welch.

"How to Manage the Information Resource—The Xerox Case." *Business* 37 (April/May/June 1987): 3–10.

Middaugh, J. Kendall, III. "Data Transmission: Guarding the System." *Business* 35 (January/February/March 1985): 3–10.

Murray, John P. "How an Information Center Improved Productivity." *Management Accounting* (March 1984): 38–44.

Orlicky, Joseph A. *The Successful Computer System.* New York: McGraw-Hill, 1969.

Panko, Raymond R. "A Different Perspective on Office Systems." *Administrative Management* 42 (August 1981): 30–32ff.

"The Spreading Danger of Computer Crime." *Business Week,* April 20, 1981, 86–92.

Wagner, G. R. "Decision Support Systems: Computerized Mind Support for Executive Problems." *Managerial Planning* 30 (September/October 1981): 3–8, 16.

Notes

1. Henry Mintzberg, "The Myths of MIS," *California Management Review* (Fall 1972): 92–97.
2. Jay W. Forrester, "Managerial Decision Making," in *Management and the Computer of the Future*, ed. Martin Greenberger (Cambridge, Mass., and New York: MIT Press and Wiley, 1962), 37.
3. The following discussion is based largely on Robert H. Gregory and Richard L. Van Horn, "Value and Cost of Information," in *Systems Analysis Techniques*, ed. J. Daniel Conger and Robert W. Knapp (New York: Wiley, 1974), 473–89.
4. John T. Small and William B. Lee, "In Search of MIS," *MSU Business Topics* (Autumn 1975): 47–55.
5. G. Anthony Gorry and Michael S. Scott Morton,"A Framework for Management Information Systems," *Sloan Management Review* 13 (Fall 1971): 55–70.
6. "A Wealth of Information Can Be Worthless," *Newsweek*, August 7, 1978, 28.
7. *H & S Reports: For the People of Haskins and Sells* 14 (Autumn 1977): 28.
8. Robert Sanford, "Some Loose Talk about and with Computers," *Beehive* (United Aircraft Corporation), Fall 1960.
9. John Dearden and Richard L. Nolan, "How to Control the Computer Resource," *Harvard Business Review* (November/December 1973): 68–78.
10. Martin D. J. Buss, "Penny-wise Approach to Data Processing," *Harvard Business Review* (July/August 1981): 111.
11. A. R. Zipf, "Retaining Mastery of the Computer," *Harvard Business Review* (September/October 1968): 70.
12. Robert W. Holmes, "Twelve Areas to Investigate for Better MIS," *Financial Executive* (July 1970): 24.
13. This section is based on Richard A. Johnson, R. Joseph Monsen, Henry P. Knowles, and Borge O. Saxberg, *Management, Systems, and Society: An Introduction* (Santa Monica, Calif.: Goodyear, 1976), 113–20.
14. Robert G. Murdick, "MIS for MBO," *Journal of Systems Management* (March 1977): 34–40.
15. F. Warren McFarlan, "Problems in Planning the Information System," *Harvard Business Review* (March/April 1971): 75.
16. David S. Stoller and Richard L. Van Horn, *Design of a Management Information System* (Santa Monica, Calif.: Rand Corporation, 1958).
17. More detail on the design of an MIS can be found in Robert G. Murdick, "MIS Development Procedures," *Journal of Systems Management* 21 (December 1970): 22–26.
18. Bertram A. Colbert, "The Management Information System," *Management Services* 4 (September/October 1967): 15–24.
19. Adapted from Henry Mintzberg, "The Manager's Job: Folklore and Fact," *Harvard Business Review* (July/August 1975): 58.
20. William R. King and David I. Cleland, "Manager-Analysts Teamwork in MIS," *Business Horizons* 14 (April 1971): 59–68.
21. Regina Herzlinger, "Why Data Systems in Nonprofit Organizations Fail," *Harvard Business Review* (January/February 1977): 81–86.
22. Chris Argyris, "Management Information Systems: The Challenge of Rationality and Emotionality," *Management Science* (February 1971): 275–92.
23. Robert W. Holmes, "Developing Better Management Information Systems," *Financial Executive* 38 (July 1970): 24–31.
24. G. W. Dickson and John K. Simmons, "The Behavioral Side of MIS," *Business Horizons* (August 1970): 59, 71.
25. Steven L. Mandell, *Computers and Data Processing: Concepts and Applications with BASIC* (St. Paul, Minn.: West Publishing, 1982), 370–91.
26. Mark G. Simkin, *Computer Information Systems for Business* (Dubuque, Iowa: Wm. C. Brown, 1987), 299–301.
27. For additional information on these software packages, see *Lotus 1–2–3 Reference Manual* (Cambridge, Mass.: Lotus Development Corporation, 1985); *IFPS User's Manual* (Austin, Tex.: Execucom Systems Corporation, 1984).

Action Summary Answer Key

1. a. d, p. 499
   b. a, p. 499
2. a. b, pp. 499–500
   b. F, pp. 500–501
3. a. d, p. 503
   b. T, p. 503
4. a. d, pp. 504–508
   b. c, pp. 508–511
5. a. T, p. 510
   b. a, pp. 511–513
6. a. e, p. 514
   b. d, pp. 517–518
7. a. T, p. 520
   b. F, p. 520
   c. F, pp. 521–522

CHERNOBYL—AN INFORMATION MELTDOWN

At 9 A.M. on Monday, April 28, 1986, workers at the Forsmark Nuclear Power Plant in Sweden began receiving distressing signals on their computer screens. As *Time* magazine reported in its May 12, 1986, issue:

> Those signals revealed abnormally high levels of radiation, a sure sign of serious trouble. At first suspecting difficulties in their own reactors, the engineers searched frantically for a leak. When they found nothing, they lined up some 600 workers at the plant and tested them with a Geiger counter. This time the signals were even more alarming: the workers' clothing gave off radiation far above contamination levels. Outside, monitors took Geiger counter readings of the soil and greenery surrounding the plant. The result showed four to five times the normal amount of radioactive emissions. . . .

> Somewhere, some mysterious source was spewing dangerous radiation into the atmosphere. . . . The Swedes quickly confirmed that the source was not in their country. They immediately turned their suspicions southward, to their powerful neighbor, the Soviet Union.

> A glance at prevailing wind patterns confirmed their fear. For several days currents of air had been whipping up from the Black Sea, across the Ukraine, over the Baltic and into Scandinavia. But when the Swedes and their neighbors demanded an explanation from Moscow, they were met by denials and stony silence. For six hours, as officials throughout Scandinavia insisted that something was dangerously amiss, the Soviets steadfastly maintained that nothing untoward had happened.

> Finally, at 9 P.M. on Monday, an expressionless newscaster on Moscow television read a four-sentence statement from the Council of Ministers . . . : "An accident has taken place at the Chernobyl power station, and one of the reactors was damaged. Measures are being taken to eliminate the consequences of the accident. Those affected by it are being given assistance. A government commission has been set up." . . .

> Soviet officials were reluctant to seek much outside assistance while still trying to pretend that not much had happened. Tuesday morning at 8:10, a scientific liaison officer from the Soviet embassy in Bonn appeared . . . at the office of [a West German nuclear power agency]. He asked . . . if the Germans knew anyone who could advise his country on how to put out a graphite fire. A similar request went out the same day to the Swedish nuclear authority. . . .

> In the first few hours of the Chernobyl disaster, lethal forms of iodine and cesium were released into the atmosphere. . . . By week's end an ominous pall of radiation had spread across Eastern Europe and toward the shores of the Mediterranean. . . .

> In the absence of detailed information, Europeans and their governments took frantic steps. Polish authorities banned the sale of milk from cows fed on fresh grass and said children from birth to age 16 would receive iodine solutions to keep their bodies from absorbing the element in radioactive form. . . .

> The Austrian state of Carinthia asked that pregnant women and children under six remain indoors. . . . The British embassy in Moscow organized an airlift of more than 100 British students from the Soviet Union, and cautioned 30 who had been in Minsk when the nuclear cloud passed overhead to shower and wash their hair every two hours. . . .

> Because the Soviets kept details secret, Moscow and the Western press contradicted each other with pronouncements that left the world

mystified about the actual developments at Chernobyl. . . .

One Soviet official made an unprecedented appearance before a House committee Thursday [May 1] to give Moscow's view of events. In a deft and tough-minded performance, Vitali Churkin, 34, second secretary of the Washington embassy, offered little new information but acknowledged that the crisis was not yet over. "Definitely there has been an accident which has not been liquidated yet and theoretically poses a threat to people outside the Soviet Union," Churkin said. "We are still trying to manage the situation." He added that the Soviets initially withheld news of the disaster because they wanted to know the extent of the damage before making an announcement.

Finally, four months after the accident, the Soviets reported to the International Atomic Energy Agency that operators at the Chernobyl plant were responsible for the accident. As *Time* recounted in its September 1, 1986, issue:

Said Andronik M. Petrosyants, chairman of the Soviet Committee for the Peaceful Uses of Atomic Energy: "The accident took place as a result of a whole series of gross violations of operating regulations by the workers." . . .

The Chernobyl calamity occurred, ironically, in the course of a safety test. According to the report, workers were trying to determine how long the reactor's turbine generators would continue to operate as a result of inertia in the event of an unforeseen reactor shutdown. To prevent the automatic safety systems from interfering with the experiment, the technicians disconnected them, opening the way for a chain of fatal mishaps.

The report indicated that the technicians made six serious mistakes:

1. They turned off the emergency cooling system to conduct the test.
2. They lowered the reactor power output too much, making it difficult to control.
3. They turned on all the water circulation pumps, exceeding the recommended flow rates.
4. They blocked the automatic signal that shuts down the reactor if the turbines stop.
5. They turned off the safety devices that shut down the reactor if steam pressure or water levels become abnormal.
6. They pulled almost all the control rods out of the core.

As *Time* also noted in its September 1, 1986, issue:

So far, 31 people who were in or near the plant at the time of the accident have died, and that number only begins to state the extent of the health damage. . . . American experts conclude that a total of more than 5,000 people are likely to die prematurely from radiation-induced cancer.

Swedish energy minister Birgitta Dahl stated, "We shall reiterate our demand that the whole Soviet civilian nuclear program be subject to international control." This demand was echoed at a meeting of about eighty nations to approve a new accord for sharing information about future nuclear accidents.

DISCUSSION ISSUES

1. The first real admission that a nuclear accident had occurred came at the 9 P.M. news broadcast on Monday, April 28, at least forty-eight hours after the accident had actually occurred. Evaluate the value of the information provided by this announcement to the people in the neighboring countries of the Soviet Union.
2. The Swedish energy minister's comment that the "whole Soviet civilian nuclear power program [should] be subject to international control" may reflect a need for a global "nuclear information system (NIS)." Using the framework and concepts from the section of the text entitled "Establishing an MIS," describe the key issues that must be considered in establishing the "NIS."
3. Does the information in Table 18.1 give any hint about the specific characteristics that limited the usefulness of the information related to the Chernobyl accident? The possible actions that could be taken to eliminate these characteristics? Explain.
4. Extremely costly computer enhanced satellite photography permitted U.S. officials to determine the occurrence of the Chernobyl accident and to assess its magnitude. Do you believe the United States is justified in expending such a large sum of money on computer enhanced surveillance techniques? Explain.

THE COMPUTER PIRATES: THEY'RE NOT STEALING MACHINES

For the American businessperson, the computer has become an indispensable tool and, more recently, a constant source of apprehension. Wherever they turn, executives are warned how vulnerable their computer systems are to trade secret theft or embezzlement. In a not-too-dated episode of the television series "Simon and Simon," a fourteen-year-old boy connected his home computer to a telephone line, tapped into the computer of a neighborhood bank, and transferred money to his personal account. In scripts and on the screen, computer criminals are fast becoming the Butch Cassidys of the electronic age.

However, these fictional tales of "computer piracy" are far from being futuristic fantasies. They were inspired by numerous real life cases. For example, in 1981 the Wells Fargo Bank discovered that an employee had used a computer to embezzle $21.3 million, the largest U.S. electronic bank fraud on record. In another case, seven employees at a state welfare office in Miami were convicted of stealing at least $300,000 worth of food stamps by falsifying data fed into the agency's computer. In yet another example, a clerk at People's Savings Bank in Bridgeport, Connecticut, was arrested for electronically lifting $37,487. She allegedly used the bank's computer to credit the money to three of her own accounts.

What most concerns businesspeople is that the prevalence of computer crime is unknown and probably unknowable. And even when culprits are caught, victimized companies often try to "hush up" the scandal and absorb the losses rather than admit to poor computer security. According to banking sources, a Washington, D.C. bank has yet to report a huge fraud that occurred there. It seems that one Washington bank teller electronically transferred $1.5 million to a Swiss bank account.

With the bad press that computers have been getting, computer manufacturers are moving to defend their machines. As they argue, computers do not commit crimes, people do. An IBM advertisement depicts a computer terminal in a police lineup of suspects. The headline reads: "The Computer Didn't Do It." The ad emphasizes that, with proper precautions against human misuse, the computer is a safe place to store information.

With the increasing frequency of computer piracy, a whole new industry has sprung up to help companies protect stored information. Literally hundreds of companies sell advice on security, market various watchdog gadgets, and rent out detectives to track down evidence of wrongdoing. An estimated $200 million was spent by industry on safeguards in 1982, and yearly market growth is estimated at $100 million. The Security Pacific National Bank in Los Angeles, which suffered a $10 million electronic fraud in 1978, used some sixty people and spent $1.5 million to protect its computers in 1982. Diamond Shamrock Corporations, a Dallas-based oil, mineral, and chemical producer, invested almost $500,000 to upgrade its computer security plan.

Perhaps the most common protective devices are special programs (software) used to restrict computer access. In most systems, the computer user must type in the password before the machine will answer commands. But some passwords are changed so infrequently that they become known to most employees, many of whom are not authorized to access the computer. Another concern is that a single password sometimes allows an employee to probe into any part of the computer's memory, even into files that may be confidential, such as personnel records.

Several new programs have been developed to fill these gaps in the computer's defenses. One best-seller is mysteriously titled the ACF2. Introduced in 1978 by SKK, a small firm outside Chicago, the ACF2 allows the computer to restrict each employee to only those parts of the system for which he or she has authorization. In addition, employees with proper clearance can choose their own password and change that password as frequently as they want.

However, such programs are no deterrent when the pirate is a trusted employee with authorization to roam through the computer system. In that situation, a

company can hope to catch the criminal only after the misdeed. Several companies have developed programs that enable auditors to check computer transactions for irregularities. One such program is designed to uncover unusually large or frequent transfers of money. Cullinane Database System of Westwood, Massachusetts, a leading producer of these audit programs, experienced a 66 percent sales growth in one year. Computer audit program are selling so well that leading accounting firms such as Peat, Marwick, Mitchell & Company are now marketing their own programs.

Though computers are most vulnerable to piracy by company employees, security specialists are increasingly concerned about the threat from outsiders. Because banks and other corporations use complex systems in which computers communicate with other computers over telephone lines between cities, it is possible for interlopers armed with home computers to call telephones hooked up with business computers and to give the machines orders, for example, to transfer money into personal bank accounts. The best defense against this type of wiretapping piracy is the use of encryption devices, machines that turn electronic messages into gibberish. The armed forces have long used such equipment to protect national secrets. A few aggressive small firms, for example, Datotek in Dallas, have adapted the encryption idea for business uses.

Some of Datotek's best customers are oil firms that fear that competitors will pirate the results of oil-field tests and reveal promising drilling sites. Computer security specialists predict that the demand for scrambling devices will soon explode. Encryption is expected to become the control of the future.

DISCUSSION ISSUES

1. Are the facts and figures that individuals are pirating from computers data or information? Explain.
2. With the volume of data stored in computers, it would appear that all pirated data would not be of the same value to the pirate. What factors influence the value of pirated data? Explain.
3. If a person was contemplating becoming a "computer pirate," how would he or she determine whether the acquisition of specific information was justified? Explain.
4. Is the theft of computer data a control problem? Explain.
5. Do you find any evidence in the case that precontrol measures are being established to diminish the pirating of data? Concurrent control measures? Feedback control measures? Explain.
6. What do you see as the relationship between loss of confidential data or information through pirating and productivity? Explain

TOPICS FOR
SPECIAL EMPHASIS

The first five sections of this text introduced the subject of management and presented detailed discussions of the four major management functions. The purpose of this section is to emphasize some carefully selected topics that present special challenges for modern managers. This last portion of the text covers social responsibility and ethics, international management, and management skills for the future.

The social responsibility material focuses on managerial obligation to take action that protects and improves the welfare of society, to spend a significant amount of time dealing with social issues, and to utilize the four management functions effectively and efficiently in pursuing social responsibility activities. The role of ethics as it relates to the issue of social responsibility is also examined. The discussion of international management defines *international management* and *multinational corporations*, explains the complexities and risks involved in managing internationally, and examines, through a study of Japanese management techniques, how the four management functions and the process of comparative management relate to the field of international management.

The last topic for discussion is the skills that managers will need to be successful in the future. Future managers will have to apply systems and functional theory to unique organizational situations. In general, these situations will involve larger, more complex management systems, an older work force, and energy that is in short supply. The discussion also emphasizes that training programs aimed at preparing managers for the future must help managers see themselves as future oriented professionals with ever-changing attitudes about what constitutes sound management.

Once you have studied the final section of this text, you should understand the most important principles of modern management. The purpose of this text was to introduce you to these principles and to prepare you for becoming a manager in the future. Keep this text in your professional library as a reference book that can help you meet the many challenges you will face throughout your management career.

STUDENT LEARNING OBJECTIVES

From studying this chapter, I will attempt to acquire:

1. An understanding of the term *social responsibility*.
2. An appreciation for the arguments both for and against business assuming social responsibilities.
3. Useful strategies for increasing the social responsiveness of an organization.
4. Insights on the planning, organizing, influencing, and controlling of social responsibility activities.
5. A practical plan for how society can help business meet its social obligations.
6. An understanding of the relationship between social responsibility and ethics.

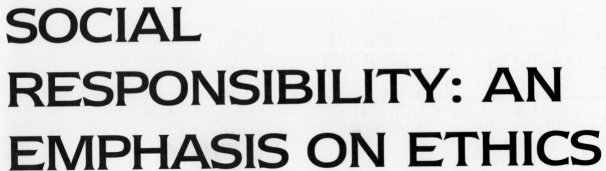

SOCIAL RESPONSIBILITY: AN EMPHASIS ON ETHICS

CHAPTER OUTLINE

ASSISTING THE HANDICAPPED

Nick Vicaro is president of Stylistics, a chain of thirty-six beauty shops spread out over Denver, Minneapolis, St. Louis, and New Orleans. Vicaro presently resides in Denver, where company headquarters are located. By almost any criteria, Stylistics shops have been extremely successful over the past several years. In fact, Vicaro has completed plans for opening seven new Stylistics shops in Baltimore.

It was Tuesday morning, and Vicaro had just arrived at his office. His secretary handed him a special delivery envelope that had been delivered only twenty minutes earlier. Vicaro opened the envelope and began to read the following letter from a woman in St. Louis:

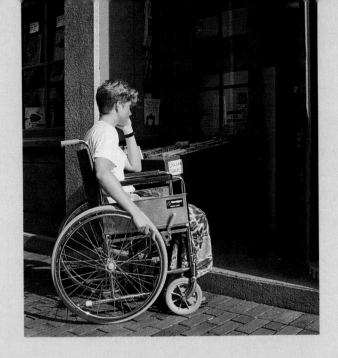

```
Mr. Nick Vicaro, President
Stylistics
1322 Manford Avenue
Denver, CO 80212

Dear Mr. Vicaro:
     I have a special problem that I
hope you can help me to solve.  I live
in the St. Louis area and hear nothing
but fantastic comments about the
beauticians you have in your shops in
our city.  I also hear very good
things about how clean and well kept
the shops themselves actually are.
     My problem is that I am handi-
capped and am confined to a wheel-
chair.  I can arrange transportation
to and from any of your shops but
cannot climb the several steps in
front of each of them.  From what I
hear, it also would be difficult for
me to have my hair washed in one of
your basins, even if I could get into
one of your shops.  Friends also tell
me that your shops are somewhat
cramped and that there may be some
areas where I would find it difficult
to maneuver.
     To solve my problem, I thought
you might be able to install a ramp on
the outside of your shops so that
wheelchair customers like myself could
enter your place of business.  I also
wonder if you can alter your equipment
and facility somewhat so that indi-
viduals like myself can get hair
washed and maneuver wheelchairs once
within one of your establishments.
     Thank you for your attention to
this matter, and I hope you can make
it easier for the handicapped to be
your customers.

Sincerely yours,

Tiffany Ware

Tiffany Ware
```

When Vicaro had finished the letter, he was quite perplexed. All of Tiffany Ware's information about his beauty salons was accurate. He wondered, however, if he could or really should do anything about Tiffany Ware's problem.

What's Ahead

The introductory case ends with Nick Vicaro, the president of Stylistics, reflecting on a customer request to modify his beauty shops so they will be more easily accessible to the handicapped. This chapter presents material that a manager such as Vicaro needs to assess his social responsibility in this situation. Specifically, the chapter discusses (1) fundamentals of social responsibility, (2) social responsiveness, (3) social responsibility activities and management functions, (4) how society can help business meet social obligations, and (5) ethics and social responsibility.

⊞ FUNDAMENTALS OF SOCIAL RESPONSIBILITY

The term *social responsibility* means different things to different people.[1] For purposes of this chapter, however, **social responsibility** is the managerial obligation to take action that protects and improves the welfare of society as a whole and organizational interests as well.[2] The manager in the cartoon is not being socially responsible, because he is stressing societal goals and deemphasizing organizational goals. According to the concept of social responsibility, a manager must strive to achieve both organizational and societal goals.

The amount of attention given to the area of social responsibility by both management and society has increased in recent years and probably will con-

> Social responsibility is the managerial obligation to protect the interests of society and the organization.

"You know what I think, folks? Improving technology isn't important. Increased profits aren't important. What's important is to be warm, decent human beings."
New Yorker, June 1, 1987, p. 39. Drawing by Handelsman; © 1987 The New Yorker Magazine, Inc.

tinue to increase in the future.[3] The following sections present the fundamentals of social responsibility of businesses by discussing (1) the Davis model of social responsibility, (2) areas of social responsibility activity, and (3) varying opinions on social responsibility.

The Davis Model of Social Responsibility

A generally accepted model of social responsibility was developed by Keith Davis.[4] Stated simply, Davis's model is a list of five propositions that describe why and how business should adhere to the obligation to take action that protects and improves the welfare of society and the organization:

Davis has proposed the following:

1. Social responsibility comes from social power.

Proposition 1: Social responsibility arises from social power This proposition is built on the premise that business has a significant amount of influence on, or power over, such critical social issues as minority employment and environmental pollution. In essence, the collective action of all businesses in the country determines to a major degree the proportion of minorities employed and the prevailing condition of the environment in which all citizens must live.

Building on this premise, Davis reasons that since business has this power over society, society can and must hold business responsible for social conditions that result from exercising this power.[5] Davis explains that society's legal system does not expect more of business than it does of each individual citizen exercising personal power.

2. Society and business must be partners.

Proposition 2: Business shall operate as a two-way open system, with open receipt of inputs from society and open disclosure of its operation to the public According to this proposition, business must be willing to listen to society's representatives in regard to what must be done to sustain or improve societal welfare. In turn, society must be willing to listen to the reports of business on what it is doing to meet its social responsibilities. Davis suggests that ongoing honest and open communications between business and society's representatives must exist if the overall welfare of society is to be maintained or improved.

3. Business must consider how proposed activities will affect society.

Proposition 3: The social costs and benefits of an activity, product, or service shall be thoroughly calculated and considered in deciding whether to proceed with it This proposition stresses that technical feasibility and economic profitability are not the only factors that should influence business decision making. Business also should consider both the long- and short-term societal consequences of all business activities before such activities are undertaken.

4. Society must ultimately pay for business's social costs.

Proposition 4: Social costs related to each activity, product, or service shall be passed on to the consumer This proposition states that business cannot be expected to finance completely activities that may be socially advantageous but economically disadvantageous. The cost of maintaining socially desirable activities within business should be passed on to consumers through higher prices for the goods or services related to the socially desirable activities.

5. Business must be willing to help others to help society.

Proposition 5: Business institutions, as citizens, have the responsibility to become involved in certain social problems that are outside their normal areas of operation This last proposition makes the point that if a business possesses the expertise to solve a social problem with which it may not be directly associated, it should be held responsible for helping society solve that problem. Davis reasons that since business eventually will share increased profit from a generally improved society, business should share in the responsibility of all citizenry to generally improve society.

■ BACK TO THE CASE

Social responsibility is the obligation of a business manager to take action that protects and improves the welfare of society along with the interests of the organization. Nick Vicaro, the president of Stylistics in the introductory case presently is considering his social responsibility to the handicapped.

Following the logic of Davis's social responsibility model, Vicaro should attempt to service Tiffany Ware because such an activity generally would help improve society and thereby would profit Vicaro as well as others. For example, with a new hair style from Stylistics, Ware might be able to get a job that would help her make some additional contribution to society. Vicaro probably would profit from Ware's job as well, because Ware would be able to return to the salon more often and might even recommend Stylistics to the people with whom she works.

The information presented thus far in this chap-

ter also implies that Vicaro should decide what to do about Ware's situation by considering not only the technical feasibility and economic profitability of various actions but also the possible effects of those actions on society as a whole. Of course, depending on what Vicaro actually does about this situation, the costs he would incur as a result of taking action would be passed on to his patrons. Obviously, he should not do so much that his prices are no longer competitive.

As a result of handling Ware's problem, Vicaro could acquire some expertise in the general area of assisting the handicapped. This expertise could benefit society if Vicaro shared it with businesspeople in other areas. For example, Vicaro might be able to help the president of another company make barbershops more accessible to handicapped customers.

Areas of Social Responsibility Activity

The areas in which business can become involved to protect and improve the welfare of society are numerous and diverse (see Table 19.1 on page 538). Perhaps the most publicized of these areas are urban affairs, consumer affairs, and environmental affairs.[6]

Varying Opinions on Social Responsibility

Although numerous businesses are involved in and will continue to be involved in social responsibility activities, much controversy persists about whether such involvement is necessary or appropriate. The two sections that follow present some of the arguments for and against businesses performing social responsibility activities.[7]

Arguments FOR Business Performing Social Responsibility Activities

The best-known argument supporting the performance of social responsibility activities by business was alluded to earlier in this chapter. This argument be-

Proponents of social responsibility argue that all members of society must maintain society.

TABLE 19.1

Major social responsibility areas in which business can become involved

Categories of Social Responsibility Issues

Product Line

Internal standards for product
- Quality, e.g., does it last?
- Safety, e.g., can it harm users or children finding it?
- Disposal, e.g., is it biodegradable?
- Design, e.g., will its use or even "easy" misuse cause pain, injury, or death?

Average product life comparisons versus
- Competition
- Substitute products
- Internal standards or state-of-the-art regular built-in obsolescence

Product performance
- Efficacy, e.g., does it do what it is supposed to do?
- Guarantees/warranties, e.g., are guarantees sufficient, reasonable?
- Service policy
- Service availability
- Service pricing
- Utility

Packaging
- Environmental impact (degree of disposability; recyclability)
- Comparisons with competition (type and extent of packaging)

Marketing Practices

Sales practices
- Legal standards
- "Undue" pressure (a qualitative judgment)

Credit practices against legal standards

Accuracy of advertising claims—specific government complaints

Consumer complaints about marketing practices.
- Clear explanation of credit terms
- Clear explanation of purchase price
- Complaint answering policy
  - Answered at all
  - Investigated carefully
  - Grievances redressed (and cost)

—Remedial action to prevent future occurrences

Adequate consumer information on
- Product use, e.g., dosage, duration of use, etc.
- Product misuse

Fair pricing
- Between countries
- Between states
- Between locations

Packaging

Employee Education and Training

Policy on leaves of absence for
- Full-time schooling
- Courses given during working hours

Dollars spent on training
- Formal vocational training
- Training for disadvantaged worker
- OJT (very difficult to isolate)
- Tuition (job-related versus non-job-related)
- Special upgrading and career development programs
- Compare versus competition

Special training program results (systematic evaluations)
- Number trained in each program per year
- Cost per trainee (less subsidy)
- Number or percent workers still with company

Plans for future programs

Career training and counseling

Failure rates

Extend personnel understanding
- Jobs
- Skills required later
- Incentive system now available
- Specific actions for promotion

Corporate Philanthropy

Contribution performance
- By category, for example:
  - Art
  - Education
  - Poverty

—Health
—Community development
—Public service advertising
- Dollars (plus materials and work hours, if available)
  - As a percent of pretax earnings
  - Compared to competition

Selection criteria for contributions

Procedures for performance tracking of recipient institutions or groups

Programs for permitting and encouraging employee involvement in social projects
- On company time
- After hours only
- Use of company facilities and equipment
- Reimbursement of operating units for replaceable "lost" time
- Human resource support
  - Number of people
  - Work hours

Extent of employee involvement in philanthropy decision making

Environmental Control

Measurable pollution resulting from
- Acquisition of raw materials
- Production processes
- Products
- Transportation of intermediate and finished products

Violations of government (federal, state, and local) standards

Cost estimates to correct current deficiencies

Extent to which various plants exceed current legal standards, e.g., particulate matter discharged

Resources devoted to pollution control
- Capital expenditures (absolute and percent)
- R & D investments
- Personnel involved full time, part time
- Organizational "strength" of personnel involved

TABLE 19.1

(continued)

Environmental Control (*Continued*)

Competitive company performance, e.g., capital expenditures

Effort to monitor new standards as proposed

Programs to keep employees alert to spills and other pollution-related accidents

Procedures for evaluating environmental impact of new packages or products

External Relations

Community Development

Support of minority and community enterprises through
- Purchasing
- Subcontracting

Investment practices
- Ensuring equal opportunity before locating new facilities
- Identifying opportunities to serve community needs through business expansion (e.g., housing rehabilitation or teaching machines)
- Funds in minority banks

Government Relations

Specific input to public policy through research and analysis

Participation and development of business/government programs

Political contributions

Disclosure of Information/ Communications

Extent of public disclosure of performance by activity category

Measure of employee understanding of programs such as:
- Pay and benefits
- Equal opportunity policies and programs
- Position on major economic or political issues (as appropriate)

Relations/communications with constituencies such as stockholders, fund managers, major customers, and so on

International

Comparisons of policy and performance between countries and versus local standards

Employee Relations, Benefits, and Satisfaction with Work

Comparisons with competition (and/or national averages)
- Salary and wage levels
- Retirement plans
- Turnover and retention by level
- Profit sharing
- Day care and maternity
- Transportation
- Insurance, health programs, and other fringes
- Participation in ownership of business through stock purchases

Comparisons of operating units on promotions, terminations, hires against breakdowns by
- Age
- Sex
- Race
- Education level

Performance review system and procedures for communication with employees whose performance is below average

Promotion policy—equitable and understood

Transfer policy

Termination policy (i.e., how early is "notice" given)

General working environment and conditions
- Physical surroundings
  —Heat
  —Ventilation
  —Space/person
  —Lighting
  —Air conditioning
  —Noise
- Leisure, recreation, cultural opportunities

Fringe benefits as a percent of salary for various salary levels

Evaluation of employee benefit preferences (questions can be posed as choices)

Evaluation of employee understanding of current fringe benefits

Union/industrial relations
- Grievances
- Strikes

Confidentiality and security of personnel data

Minority and Women Employment and Advancement

Current hiring policies in relation to the requirements of all affirmative action programs

Specific program of accountability for performance

Company versus local, industry, and national performance
- Number and percent minority and women employees hired in various job classifications over last five years
- Number and percent of new minority and women employees in last two or three years by job classification
- Minority and women and nonminority turnover
- Indictments for discriminatory hiring practices

Percent minority and women employment in major facilities relative to minority labor force available locally

Number of minority group and women members in positions of high responsibility

Promotion performance of minority groups and women

Specific hiring and job upgrading goals established for minority groups and women
- Basic personnel strategy
- Nature and cost of special recruiting efforts
- Risks taken in hiring minority groups and women

Programs to ease integration of minority groups and women into company operations, e.g., awareness efforts

Specialized minority and women career counseling

Special recruiting efforts for minority groups and women

Opportunities for the physically handicapped
- Specific programs
- Numbers employed

TABLE 19.1

(continued)

Employee Safety and Health

Work environment measures
- OSHA requirements (and extent of compliance)
- Other measures of working conditions

Safety performance
- Accident severity—work hours lost per million worked
- Accident frequency (number of lost time accidents per million hours)

- Disabling injuries
- Fatalities

Services provided (and cost of programs and human resources) for
- Addictive treatment (alcohol, narcotics)
- Mental health

Spending for safety equipment
- Required by law/regulation
- Not required

Special safety programs (including safety instruction)

Comparisons of health and safety performance with competition and industry in general

Developments/innovations in health and safety

Employee health measures, e.g., sick days, examinations

Food facilities
- Cost/serving to employee, to company
- Nutritional evaluation

gins with the premise that business as a whole is a subset of society and exerts a significant impact on the way in which society exists. The argument continues that since business is such an influential member of society, it has the responsibility to help maintain and improve the overall welfare of society. After all, since society asks no more and no less of any of its members, why should business be exempt from such responsibility?

In addition, some make the argument that business should perform social responsibility activities because profitability and growth go hand in hand with responsible treatment of employees, customers, and the community. In essence, this argument implies that performing social responsibility activities is a means of earning greater organizational profit.[8]

The "Management in Action" feature for this chapter focuses on recent environmental protection efforts at the Florida Power & Light Company. Ross Wilcox, the company's chief ecologist, describes organizational efforts focusing on environmental assistance for crocodiles, manatees, and other wildlife. Ross argues that environmental protection makes good business sense. At the very least, it can help enlist the understanding and cooperation of consumer groups and government agencies, thereby reducing the risk of expensive fines and costly litigation.

Arguments AGAINST Business Performing Social Responsibility Activities

Friedman argues that business exists mainly to make profits.

The best-known argument against business performing social responsibility activities is advanced by Milton Friedman, one of America's most distinguished economists. Friedman argues that to make business managers simultaneously responsible to business owners for reaching profit objectives and to society for enhancing societal welfare represents a conflict of interest that has the potential to cause the demise of business as it is known today.[9] According to Friedman, this demise almost certainly will occur if business continually is forced to perform socially responsible behavior that is in direct conflict with private organizational objectives.[10]

Friedman also argues that to require business managers to pursue socially

ENVIRONMENTAL PROTECTION MAKES GOOD BUSINESS SENSE AT FLORIDA POWER & LIGHT

As a great blue heron glides off from the bank ahead, two Florida Power & Light Co. airboats rip down a cooling canal near the company's nuclear plant here and ease to a stop on a muddy bank. Ross Wilcox climbs out of the first of the boats, walks up the bank and pauses to examine a small indentation in the mud.

It is a crocodile nest.

Before FPL built its plant here in the early 1970s, crocodiles didn't nest at Turkey Point, a finger of land on the southeast edge of the Florida peninsula. But as a condition for approving the plant, regulations required FPL to dig a huge grid of cooling canals to prevent the plant's warm-water discharges from harming the marine life in adjacent Biscayne Bay. The canals soon began attracting crocodiles. Today, there seems to be a population of 25 or 30 adults, making the nuclear plant one of only three places in the U.S. known to have breeding populations of the endangered species. The others are Everglades National Park, nearby to the west of here, and a national wildlife refuge on North Key Largo, to the south.

EXTRA EFFORT

Mr. Wilcox, as FPL's chief ecologist, is the utility's point man for the big reptiles. This morning, he is lobbying plant managers, who have joined him on the inspection tour, to create buffer zones around any crocodile nests they find. By afternoon, the managers agree.

"What we're trying to show is that with a little extra effort on our part or understanding of the species, our activities can be compatible with the needs of wildlife. They can go about their business and we can go about ours," says Mr. Wilcox, who has a doctorate in oceanography.

In addition to his crocodile responsibilities, Mr. Wilcox is also the point man for manatees, sea turtles, wood storks, bald eagles, indigo snakes and the many other endangered or threatened species that live on FPL property. His job is a sign of how the environmental movement of the 1970s continues to affect business in the 1980s, as environmental management becomes an increasingly mainstream corporate specialty. It is also part of an effort that has made FPL, Florida's largest electric utility and a unit of FPL Group Inc., a company that even environmentalists praise for its efforts to fit in with the natural world.

More than most companies, FPL can't avoid dealing with environmental issues. Its service area, covering roughly half of Florida, spans one of the most ecologically fragile and diverse parts of the country. More than 50 federally protected plants and animals are found in the state, and Florida itself lists more than 500 species of concern. In producing and transmitting electricity, FPL—like most utilities, a major landholder—encounters many of them.

Whenever the weather turns cold, for instance, manatees seek out the waters near power plants, because they are warmed by the plants' effluents. FPL has counted as many as 866 of the endangered animals, also known as sea cows, at five of its plants—or more than two-thirds of the 1,200 manatees that are officially estimated to live in Florida waters.

UNUSUAL STEPS

The company often takes unusual steps to accommodate the manatees, which, in addition to being protected by law, are extremely popular with the public. In January 1985, under pressure from the Florida governor's office, FPL kept one unit at its Fort Myers plant running for 11 days—when economics justified closing it down—solely to keep the water warm for the roughly 100 manatees gathered there. Management agreed only on condition it not be asked to do so again; subsequently, FPL drilled three underground wells, at a cost of nearly $500,000, to tap warmer ground water.

"We're involved with a lot of endangered species just because we are where we are," says Samuel Tucker, director of the environmental-affairs department. "There is no way we can avoid it. We can't put our plants somewhere else." He says FPL, because of its service area, may well deal with more endangered species than any other utility in the country, "if not any other company in the country."

FPL formed its environmental-affairs department in 1972, after it was burned badly in a battle over construction of the Turkey Point plant. The company originally planned to discharge the plant's cooling water directly into Biscayne Bay; but environmentalists and others persuaded regulators to require FPL to dig some 168 miles of cooling canals (the same ones that later attracted crocodiles). The changes in plans, as well as delays, pushed the project millions of dollars over budget.

Like many companies in those days, FPL was caught completely off guard by the ferocity of the environmental attack. "They had no concept that warmwater pollution might be a problem," says Audubon's Mr. Lee. But, he adds: "They got smart and realized that if they brought some good environmental scientists on board, they would be in a much better position to watch their own operations."

responsible objectives may in fact be unethical, since it requires managers to spend money that really belongs to other individuals:

> In a free enterprise, private property system, a corporate executive is an employee of the owners of the business. He has direct responsibility to his employers. That responsibility is to conduct the business in accordance with their desires, which generally will be to make as much money as possible while conforming to the basic rules of society, both those embodied in law and those embodied in ethical custom. . . . Insofar as his actions reduce returns to stockholders, he is spending their money. Insofar as his actions raise the price to customers, he is spending the customers' money.[11]

Many more arguments for and against business performing social responsibility activities are presented in Table 19.2.

TABLE 19.2

Major arguments for and against business performing social responsibility activities

Major Arguments for Social Responsibility

1. It is in the best interest of the business to promote and improve the communities where it does business.
2. Social actions can be profitable.
3. It is the ethical thing to do.
4. It improves the public image of the firm.
5. It increases the viability of the business system. Business exists because it gives society benefits. Society can amend or take away its charter. This is the "iron law of responsibility".
6. It is necessary to avoid government regulation.
7. Sociocultural norms require it.
8. Laws cannot be passed for all circumstances. Thus, business must assume responsibility to maintain an orderly, legal society.
9. It is in the stockholders' best interest. It will improve the price of stock in the long run because the stock market will view the company as less risky and open to public attack and therefore award it a higher price-earnings ratio.
10. Society should give business a chance to solve social problems that government has failed to solve.
11. Business, by some groups, is considered to be the institution with the financial and human resources to solve social problems.
12. Prevention of problems is better than cures—so let business solve problems before they become too great.

Major Arguments against Social Responsibility

1. It might be illegal.
2. Business plus government equals monolith.
3. Social actions cannot be measured.
4. It violates profit maximization.
5. Cost of social responsibility is too great and would increase prices too much.
6. Business lacks social skills to solve societal problems.
7. It would dilute business's primary purposes.
8. It would weaken U.S. balance of payments because price of goods will have to go up to pay for social programs.
9. Business already has too much power. Such involvement would make business too powerful.
10. Business lacks accountability to the public. Thus, the public would have no control over its social involvement.
11. Such business involvement lacks broad public support.

BACK TO THE CASE

Table 19.1 indicates that there probably are many social responsibility areas in which Stylistics could become involved. Ware's situation, however, can be categorized under the heading of marketing practices, since Ware is suggesting that Stylistics' present method of marketing its services makes it extremely difficult for the handicapped to be consumers of those services.

Whatever Vicaro would do to ease Ware's problem probably would cost him money and, as a result, would raise the cost of his services to his customers. Although this action would cost him profits and perhaps seem unbusinesslike, performing such social responsibility activities could improve the public image of Stylistics and therefore seem very businesslike. Vicaro must decide to what degree (if at all) he will try to solve Ware's problem.

Conclusions about Business Performing Social Responsibility Activities

The preceding two sections presented several major arguments for and against businesses performing social responsibility activities. Regardless of which argument or combination of arguments particular managers might support, they generally should make a concerted effort to (1) perform all legally required social responsibility activities, (2) consider voluntarily performing social responsibility activities beyond those legally required, and (3) inform all relevant individuals of the extent to which their organization will become involved in performing social responsibility activities.

Performing Required Social Responsibility Activities

Laws require certain social responsibility activities.

Federal legislation requires that businesses perform certain social responsibility activities. In fact, several government agencies have been established and are maintained to develop such business related legislation and to make sure the laws are followed (see Table 19.3). The Environmental Protection Agency does indeed have the authority to require businesses to adhere to certain socially responsible environmental standards. Examples of specific legislation that require the performance of social responsibility activities are (1) the Equal Pay Act of 1963, (2) the Federal Water Pollution Control Act Amendments of 1972, (3) the Clear Air Act Amendments of 1977, (4) the Quiet Communications Act of 1978, and (5) the Highway Safety Act of 1978.

Voluntarily Performing Social Responsibility Activities

Adherence to legislated social responsibilities represents the minimum standard of social responsibility performance that business managers must achieve. Managers must ask themselves, however, how far beyond the minimum they should attempt to go.

Managers must determine how much social responsibility is enough.

The process of determining how far to go is simple to describe yet difficult and complicated to implement. It entails assessing the positive and negative outcomes of performing social responsibility activities over both the short and long term and then performing only the social responsibility activities that maximize management system success while making some desirable contribution to maintaining or improving the welfare of society.

TABLE 19.3

Primary functions of several federal agencies involved with social responsibility legislation

Federal Agency	Primary Agency Activities
Equal Employment Opportunity Commission	Investigates and conciliates employment discrimination complaints that are based on race, sex, or creed
Office of Federal Contract Compliance Programs	Ensures that employers holding federal contracts grant equal employment opportunity to people regardless of race or sex
Environmental Protection Agency	Formulates and enforces environmental standards in such areas as water, air, and noise pollution
Consumer Product Safety Commission	Strives to reduce consumer inquiries related to product design, labeling, etc. by promoting clarity of these messages.
Occupational Safety and Health Administration	Regulates safety and health conditions in nongovernment workplaces
National Highway Traffic Safety Administration	Attempts to reduce traffic accidents through the regulation of transportation-related manufacturers and products
Mining Enforcement and Safety Administration	Attempts to improve safety conditions for mine workers by enforcing all mine safety and equipment standards

Sandra Holmes asked top executives in 560 of the major firms in such areas as commercial banking, life insurance, transportation, and utilities to indicate the possible negative and positive outcomes their firms could expect to experience from performing social responsibility activities.[12] Table 19.4, p. 546, lists the outcomes and indicates the percentage of executives questioned who expected to experience them. Although this information furnishes managers with general insights on how involved their organizations should become in social responsibility activities, it does not and cannot furnish them with a clear-cut statement about what to do. Managers can determine the appropriate level of social responsibility involvement for a specific organization only by examining and reacting to specific factors related to that organization.

Communicating the Degree of Social Responsibility Involvement

Determining the extent to which a business should perform social responsibility activities beyond legal requirements is a subjective process. Despite this subjectivity, however, managers should have a well-defined position in this vital management area, should establish a personal code of ethics that relates to this position and should inform all organization members of the position.[13] Taking these steps will ensure that managers and organization members behave consistently to support the position and that societal expectations of what a particular organization will achieve in this area will be realistic.

An organization's position on social responsibility should be known.

TABLE 19.4

Outcomes of social responsibility involvement expected by executives and the percent who expected them

	Percent Expecting
Positive Outcomes	
Enhance corporate reputation and goodwill	97.4
Strengthening of the social system in which the corporation functions	89.0
Strengthening of the economic system in which the corporation functions	74.3
Greater job satisfaction among all employees	72.3
Avoidance of government regulation	63.7
Greater job satisfaction among executives	62.8
Increased chances for survival of the firm	60.7
Ability to attract better managerial talent	55.5
Increased long-term profitability	52.9
Strengthening of the pluralistic nature of American society	40.3
Maintaining or gaining customers	38.2
Investor preference for socially responsible firms	36.6
Increased short-term profitability	15.2
Negative Outcomes	
Decreased short-term profitability	59.7
Conflict of economic or financial and social goals	53.9
Increased prices for consumers	41.4
Conflict in criteria for assessing managerial performance	27.2
Disaffection of stockholders	24.1
Decreased productivity	18.8
Decreased long-term profitability	13.1
Increased government regulation	11.0
Weakening of the economic system in which the corporation functions	7.9
Weakening of the social system in which the corporation functions	3.7

BACK TO THE CASE

Some social responsibility activities are legislated and therefore must be performed by business. Most of the legislated activities, however, are aimed at larger companies. There probably is no existing legislation that would require Vicaro to make Stylistics beauty shops more accessible to the handicapped.

Since Vicaro probably is not required by law to modify his shops for the benefit of the handicapped, whatever modifications he might decide to make would be strictly voluntary. In making his decision, Vicaro should assess the positive and negative outcomes of modifying his shops over both the long and short term and then make whatever modifications would maximize the success of Stylistics as well as offer some desirable contribution to the welfare of the handicapped. Vicaro should let all organization members, as well as Tiffany Ware, know what he decides and, perhaps, his reasons for that decision.

⊞ SOCIAL RESPONSIVENESS

The previous section discussed social responsibility as the business obligation to take action that protects and improves the welfare of society along with business's own interests. This section defines and discusses **social responsiveness** as the degree of effectiveness and efficiency an organization displays in pursuing its social responsibilities.[14] The greater the degree of effectiveness and efficiency, the more socially responsive the organization is said to be.[15] The two sections that follow discuss (1) social responsiveness and decision making and (2) approaches to meeting social responsibilities.

Social responsiveness is the degree of effectiveness and efficiency in pursuing social responsibilities.

Social Responsiveness and Decision Making

The socially responsive organization that is both effective and efficient meets its social responsibilities and does not waste organizational resources in the process. Deciding exactly which social responsibilities an organization should pursue and then deciding how to pursue them are perhaps the two most critical decision-making aspects of maintaining a high level of social responsiveness within an organization.

Figure 19.1 on page 548 is a flowchart that managers can use as a general guideline for making social responsibility decisions that enhance the social responsiveness of their organization. This figure implies that for managers to achieve and maintain a high level of social responsiveness within an organization, they must pursue only the social responsibilities that their organization actually possesses and has a right to undertake. Furthermore, once managers decide to meet a specific social responsibility, they must decide the best way to undertake activities related to meeting this obligation. That is, managers must decide if their organizations should undertake the activities on its own or acquire the help of outsiders with more expertise in the area.

Socially responsive organizations must decide which social responsibilities to pursue and how best to pursue them.

Approaches to Meeting Social Responsibilities

In addition to decision making, various managerial approaches to meeting social obligations are another determinant of an organization's level of social responsiveness. According to Lipson, a desirable and socially responsive approach to meeting social obligations (1) incorporates social goals into the annual planning process; (2) seeks comparative industry norms for social programs; (3) presents reports to organization members, the board of directors, and stockholders on social responsibility progress; (4) experiments with different approaches for measuring social performance; and (5) attempts to measure the cost of social programs as well as the return on social program investments.[16]

S. Prakash Sethi presents three management approaches to meeting social obligations: (1) the social obligation approach, (2) the social responsibility approach, and (3) the social responsiveness approach.[17] Each of these approaches and the types of behavior typical of them on several dimensions are presented in Table 19.5 on page 549.

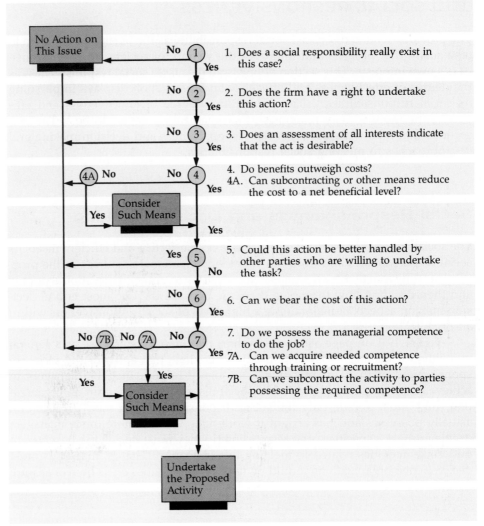

FIGURE 19.1
Flowchart of social responsibility decision making that will generally enhance the social responsiveness of an organization

Sethi's approaches reflect three different business dispositions toward social responsibility.

As the table indicates, each of Sethi's three approaches contains behavior that reflects a somewhat different attitude with regard to business performing social responsibility activities. The **social obligation approach,** for example, considers business as having primarily economic purposes and confines social responsibility activity mainly to conformance to existing legislation. The **social responsibility approach** sees business as having both economic and societal goals. The **social responsiveness approach** considers business as having both societal and economic goals as well as the obligation to anticipate upcoming social problems and to work actively toward preventing their appearance.

Organizations characterized by attitudes and behaviors consistent with the social responsiveness approach generally are more socially responsive than organizations characterized by attitudes and behaviors consistent with either the social responsibility approach or the social obligation approach. Also, organizations characterized by the social responsibility approach generally achieve

TABLE 19.5

Three approaches to social responsibility and the types of behavior associated with each

Dimensions of Behavior	Approach 1: Social Obligation Prescriptive	Approach 2: Social Responsibility Prescriptive	Approach 3: Social Responsiveness Anticipatory and Preventive
Search for legitimacy	Confines legitimacy to legal and economic criteria only; does not violate laws; equates profitable operations with fulfilling social expectations	Accepts the reality of limited relevance of legal and market criteria of legitimacy in actual practice; willing to consider and accept broader extralegal and extramarket criteria for measuring corporate performance and social role	Accepts its role as defined by the social system and therefore subject to change; recognizes importance of profitable operations but includes other criteria
Ethical norms	Considers business value-neutral; managers expected to behave according to their own ethical standards	Defines norms in community-related terms, i.e., good corporate citizen; avoids taking moral stand on issues that may harm its economic interests or go against prevailing social norms (majority views)	Takes definite stand on issues of public concern; advocates institutional ethical norms even though they may be detrimental to its immediate economic interest or prevailing social norms
Social accountability for corporate actions	Construes narrowly as limited to stockholders; jealously guards its prerogatives against outsiders	Construes narrowly for legal purposes, but broadened to include groups affected by its actions; management more outward looking	Willing to account for its actions to other groups, even those not directly affected by its actions
Operating strategy	Exploitative and defensive adaptation; maximum externalization of costs	Reactive adaptation; where identifiable, internalizes previously external costs; maintains current standards of physical and social environment; compensates victims of pollution and other corporate related activities even in the absence of clearly established legal grounds; develops industry-wide standards	Proactive adaptation; takes lead in developing and adapting new technology for environmental protectors; evaluates side effects of corporate actions and eliminates them prior to the action's being taken; anticipates future social changes and develops internal structures to cope with them
Response to social pressures	Maintains low public profile, but if attacked, uses PR methods to upgrade its public image; denies any deficiencies; blames public dissatisfaction on ignorance or failure to understand corporate functions; discloses information only where legally required	Accepts responsibility for solving current problems; will admit deficiencies in former practices and attempt to persuade public that its current practices meet social norms; attitude toward critics conciliatory; freer information disclosures than in approach 1	Willingly discusses activities with outside groups; makes information freely available to public; accepts formal and informal inputs from outside groups in decision making; is willing to be publicly evaluated for its various activities
Activities pertaining to government actions	Strongly resists any regulation of its activities except when it needs help to protect its market position; avoids contact; resists any demands for information beyond that legally required	Preserves management discretion in corporate decisions, but cooperates with government in research to improve industrywide standards; participates in political processes and encourages employees to do likewise	Openly communicates with government; assists in enforcing existing laws and developing evaluations of business practices; objects publicly to government activities that it feels are detrimental to the public's good **(continued)**

TABLE 19.5

(continued)

Dimensions of Behavior	Approach 1: Social Obligation Prescriptive	Approach 2: Social Responsibility Prescriptive	Approach 3: Social Responsiveness Anticipatory and Preventive
Legislative and political activities	Seeks to maintain status quo; actively opposes laws that would internalize any previously externalized costs; seeks to keep lobbying activities secret	Willing to work with outside groups for good environmental laws; concedes need for change in some status quo laws; less secrecy in lobbying than in approach 1	Avoids meddling in politics and does not pursue special-interest laws; assists legislative bodies in developing better laws where relevant; promotes honesty and openness in government and in its own lobbying activities
Philanthropy	Contributes only when direct benefit to it clearly shown; otherwise, views contributions as responsibility of individual employees	Contributes to noncontroversial and established causes; matches employee contributions	Activities of approach 2 *plus* support and contributions to new, controversial groups whose needs it sees as unfulfilled and increasingly important

higher levels of social responsiveness than organizations characterized by the social obligation approach.

BACK TO THE CASE

Vicaro should strive to maintain a relatively high level of social responsiveness in pursuing issues such as those brought up by Tiffany Ware. To do this, he should make decisions appropriate to his social responsibility area and should approach the meeting of those social responsibilities in an appropriate way.

In terms of decision making in the Tiffany Ware situation, Vicaro must first decide if Stylistics has a social responsibility to service customers such as Ware. Assuming that Vicaro decides that Stylistics has such a responsibility, he must then determine exactly how to accomplish the activities necessary to meet the responsibility. For example, can the people presently employed by Stylistics install ramps in front of the beauty shops, or should Vicaro hire independent contractors to make the installations? Making appropriate decisions will help Stylistics meet social obligations effectively and efficiently.

In terms of an approach to meeting social responsibilities that probably will increase Stylistics' social responsiveness, Vicaro should try to view his organization as having both societal and economic goals. In addition, he should attempt to anticipate the arrival of social problems, such as the one depicted by Ware's situation, and actively work to prevent their appearance.

SOCIAL RESPONSIBILITY ACTIVITIES AND MANAGEMENT FUNCTIONS

This section discusses social responsibility as a major organizational activity. As such, it should be subjected to the same management techniques used for other major organizational activities, such as production, personnel, finance, and marketing activities. Managers have known for some time that to achieve desirable results in these areas, managers must be effective in planning, organizing, influencing, and controlling. Achieving social responsibility results is not any different.[18] The following sections discuss planning, organizing, influencing, and controlling social responsibility activities.

Planning Social Responsibility Activities

Planning was defined in chapter 4 as the process of determining how the organization will achieve its objectives, or get where it wants to go. Planning social responsibility activities therefore involves determining how the organization will achieve its social responsibility objectives, or get where it wants to go in the area of social responsibility. The following sections discuss how the planning of social responsibility activities is related to the overall planning process of the organization and how the social responsibility policy of the organization can be converted into action.

The Overall Planning Process

The model shown in Figure 19.2 below depicts how social responsibility activities can be handled as part of the overall planning process of the organization. According to this figure, social trends forecasts should be performed within the organizational environment along with the more typically performed economic, political, and technological trends forecasts. Examples of social trends are prevailing and future societal attitudes toward water pollution and safe working conditions. Each of the forecasts would influence the development of the strategic and tactical plans of the organization as well as the activities undertaken.

Social responsibility activities can be integrated into the overall planning effort.

Converting Organizational Policies on Social Responsibility into Action

A *policy* is a standing plan that furnishes broad guidelines for channeling management thinking in specific directions. Managers should establish organizational policies in the social responsibility area just as they do in some of the more generally accepted areas, such as hiring, promotion, and absenteeism.

   To be effective, however, social responsibility policies must be converted

Social responsibility policies are converted into action by:

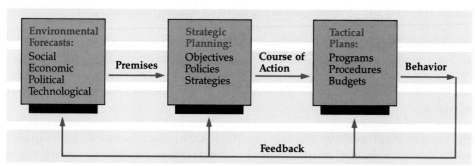

FIGURE 19.2
Integration of social responsibility activities and planning activities

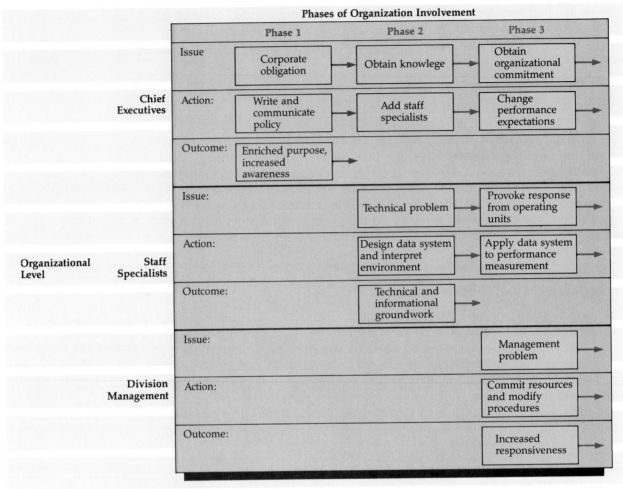

FIGURE 19.3
Conversion of social responsibility policy into action

into appropriate action. According to Figure 19.3, this conversion involves three distinct and generally sequential phases.

1. Top management.

Phase 1 consists of top management recognizing that its organization possesses some social obligation. Top management then must formulate and communicate some policy about the acceptance of this obligation to all organization members.

2. Staff personnel.

Phase 2 involves staff personnel as well as top management. In this phase, top management gathers information related to meeting the social obligation accepted in phase 1. Staff personnel generally are involved at this point to give advice on technical matters related to meeting the accepted social obligation.

3. Division management.

Phase 3 involves division management in addition to organization personnel already involved from the first two phases. During this phase, top management strives to obtain the commitment of organization members to live up to the accepted social obligation and attempts to create realistic expectations about the effects of such a commitment on organizational productivity. Staff specialists encourage the responses within the organization that are necessary to meet the accepted social obligation properly. And division management commits resources and modifies existing procedures so appropriate socially oriented activities can and will be performed within the organization.

BACK TO THE CASE

Vicaro should know that pursuing social responsibility objectives probably will be a major management activity at Stylistics. Therefore, Vicaro must plan, organize, influence, and control Stylistics' social responsibility activities if the company is to be successful in reaching social responsibility objectives.

In terms of planning social responsibility activities, Vicaro should determine how Stylistics will achieve its social responsibility objectives. He can do this by incorporating social responsibility planning into his overall planning process. That is, Vicaro can make social trends forecasts along with his economic, political, and technological trends forecasts. In turn, these forecasts would influence the development of strategic plans, tactical plans, and, ultimately, the action taken by Stylistics in the area of social responsibility.

Vicaro also must be able to turn Stylistics' social responsibility policy into action. For example, Vicaro may want to make Stylistics beauty shops more accessible to handicapped customers. To convert this policy into action, he should first communicate the policy to all organization members. Next, he should obtain additional knowledge of exactly how to make his shops more accessible and retain staff personnel who can help him with technical problems in this area. Finally, Vicaro should make sure all people at Stylistics are committed to meeting this social responsibility objective and that lower-level managers are allocating funds and establishing appropriate opportunities for organization members to fulfill this commitment.

Organizing Social Responsibility Activities

Organizing was defined in chapter 8 as the process of establishing orderly uses for all resources within the organization. These uses, of course, emphasize the attainment of management system objectives and flow naturally from management system plans. Correspondingly, organizing for social responsibility activities entails establishing for all organizational resources logical uses that emphasize the attainment of the organization's social objectives and that are consistent with the organization's social responsibility plans.

Figure 19.4, p. 554, shows how Standard Oil Company of Indiana decided to organize for the performance of its social responsibility activities. The vice-president for law and public affairs holds the primary responsibility in the area of societal affairs within this company and is responsible for overseeing the related activities of numerous individuals. This figure, of course, is intended only as an illustration of how a company might include its social responsibility area on its organization chart. The specific organizing in this area always should be tailored to the unique needs of each company.

> Organizational resources should be organized to attain the organization's social responsibility objectives.

Influencing Individuals Performing Social Responsibility Activities

Influencing was defined in chapter 12 as the management process of guiding the activities of organization members in directions that enhance the attainment of

> Activities of organization members should be guided toward reaching social responsibility objectives.

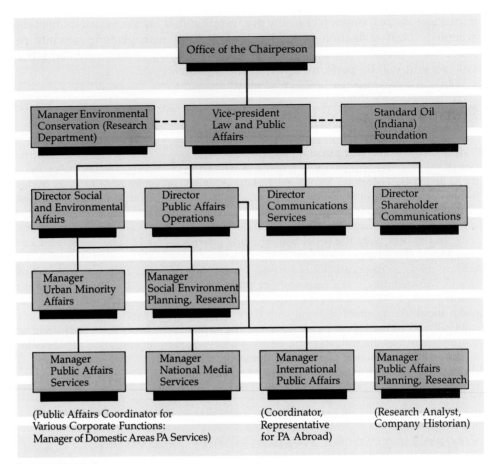

FIGURE 19.4
How Standard Oil Company of Indiana includes social responsibility in its organization chart

organizational objectives. As applied to the social responsibility area, influencing is simply the process of guiding the activities of organization members in directions that will enhance the attainment of the organization's social responsibility objectives. More specifically, to influence appropriately in this area, managers must lead, communicate, motivate, and work with groups in ways that result in the attainment of existing social responsibility objectives.

Controlling Social Responsibility Activities

Controlling involves determining whether social responsibility activity is going as planned.

Controlling, as defined in chapter 16, is making things happen as they were planned to happen. To control, managers assess or measure what is occurring in the organization and, if necessary, change these occurrences in some way to make them conform to plans. Controlling in the area of social responsibility entails the same two major tasks. The following sections discuss various areas in which social responsibility measurement takes place and examine the social audit, a tool for determining and reporting progress in the attainment of social responsibility objectives.

Areas of Measurement

To be consistent, measurements to gauge organizational progress in reaching social responsibility objectives could be taken in any of the areas listed in Table 19.1. The specific areas in which individual companies actually take such measurements vary, of course, depending on the specific social responsibility objectives of the companies. All companies, however, probably should take such social responsibility measurements in at least the following four major areas.[19]

1. *The economic function area* A measurement should be made of whether the organization is performing such activities as producing goods and services that people need, creating jobs for society, paying fair wages, and ensuring worker safety. This measurement gives some indication of the economic contribution the organization is making to society.
2. *The quality of life area* The measurement of quality of life should focus on whether the organization is improving or degrading the general quality of life in society. Producing high-quality goods, dealing fairly with employees and customers, and making an effort to preserve the natural environment are all indicators that the organization is upholding or improving the general quality of life in society. As an example of not upholding the quality of life, some people believe that cigarette companies, because they produce goods that actually can harm the health of society over all, are socially irresponsible.[20]
3. *The social investment area* The measurement of social investment deals with the degree to which the organization is investing both money and human resources to solve community social problems. Here, the organization could be involved in assisting community organizations involved in education, charities, and the arts.
4. *The problem-solving area* The measurement of problem solving should focus on the degree to which the organization deals with social problems. Such activities as participating in long-range community planning and conducting studies to pinpoint social problems generally could be considered dealing with social problems.

Social responsibility measurements should be taken in at least four areas.

The Social Audit: A Progress Report

A **social audit** is the process of taking measurements of social responsibility to assess organizational performance in the social responsibility area. The basic steps in conducting a social audit are monitoring, measuring, and appraising all aspects of an organization's social responsibility performance. The audit can be performed by organization personnel or by an outside consultant.[21]

Table 19.6 on page 556 is an example of a social audit that would be prepared by a bank. This table does not illustrate any type of standard format used for writing up the results of a social audit. In fact, probably no two organizations conduct and present the results of a social audit in exactly the same way.[22]

A social audit monitors, measures, and appraises social responsibility performance.

TABLE 19.6

Portion of sample social audit report

Social Performance Report
Part 1—Mainstream Issues

Priority—Consumer Issues

Issue—Discrimination in Credit—Minorities

Potential	New legislation pending in Congress, which should be enacted within two years. Growing public awareness due to increased press coverage. Class actions a possibility.
Progress	New guidelines instituted for small loans (under $5,000), credit cards. Race no longer part of the application, emphasis on employment and credit history. No automatic restrictions.
Problems	No progress in increasing applications from minorities.
Position	Keeping pace with the competition. Better advertising of new policies would help generate new business.

Issue—Complaints and Errors

Potential	Most stated reason for customer choosing another bank is errors. Three percent reduction in closed accounts would be the equivalent of increased profits of $320,000. This could be dramatically increased if complaints were handled more quickly.
Progress	Instituted toll-free line to handle complaints. Feedback has been positive. Cost: $50,000. New manager hired in checking. Instituted a system whereby all checks are double-processed. Errors down 18%. Cost: $80,000.
Problems	No progress in ridding checking and savings account statements of errors.
Position	Perception in the marketplace regarding our service is improved. Substantial reduction in closed accounts (7%).

Priority—Employee Development

Issue—Affirmative Action

Potential	Continued close monitoring by government. Potential liability by class actions now $1 million to $10 million. Program to upgrade underutilized talent in bank (especially women) could significantly increase productivity, as well as decrease recruitment costs. Growing number of qualified minorities in area increase pool of qualified candidates.
Progress	Strong minority program instituted during the year with goals, timetables, and mechanisms for enforcement. The recent record is good: 1985, 18.3 percent of employees minority; 1986, 19.9 percent; 1987, 23.7 percent; 1988 goal is parity. Plans to institute a similar program are underway for 1990.
Problems	Minorities and women still concentrated in the lower ranks:

Percent of Bank Officers Who Are:	1985	1986	1987	1990 Goal
Minority	4.3%	5.8%	7.1%	10.8%
Women	16.9%	19.7%	22.0%	30.0%

	To reach 1990 goals, we must concentrate on developing programs to identify and train potential candidates for promotion.
Position	The above effort is largely required. It will offer no competitive advantage or disadvantage, since it is mandated industry-wide.

■ BACK TO THE CASE

In addition to planning social responsibility activities at Stylistics, Vicaro also must organize, influence, and control them. To organize social responsibility activities, Vicaro must establish orderly use of all resources at Stylistics to carry out the company's social responsibility plans. Despite the relatively small size of his company, developing an organization chart that shows the social responsibility area at Stylistics along with corresponding job descriptions, responsibilities, and specifications for the positions on this chart might be an appropriate step for Vicaro to take.

To influence social responsibility activities, Vicaro must guide the activities of organization members in directions that will enhance the attainment of Stylistics' social responsibility objectives. He must lead, communicate, motivate, and work with groups in ways appropriate for meeting these objectives.

To control, Vicaro must make sure that social responsibility activities at Stylistics are happening as planned. If they are not, he should make changes to ensure that they will be handled properly in the near future. One tool Vicaro can use to check Stylistics' progress in meeting social responsibilities is the social audit. With the audit, he can check and assess management system performance in such areas as economic function, quality of life, social investment, and problem solving.

▦ HOW SOCIETY CAN HELP BUSINESS MEET SOCIAL OBLIGATIONS

Although the point has been made that there must be an open and honest involvement of both business and society for business to meet desirable social obligations, the bulk of this chapter has focused on what business should do in the area of social responsibility. This section emphasizes action that society should take to help business accomplish its social responsibility objectives.

Jerry McAfee, chairman of the board and chief executive officer of Gulf Oil Corporation, indicates that, although business has some responsibilities to society, society also has the following responsibilities to business:[23]

Society has responsibilities to business:

1. *Set rules that are clear and consistent* This is one of the fundamental things that society, through government, ought to do. Although it may come as a surprise to some, I believe that industry actually needs an appropriate measure of regulation. By this I mean that the people of the nation, through their government, should set the bonds within which they want industry to operate.

    But the rules have got to be clear. Society must spell out clearly what it is it wants the corporations to do. The rules can't be vague and imprecise. Making the rules straight and understandable is really what government is all about. One of my colleagues described his confusion when he read a section of a regulation that a federal regulatory representative had cited as the reason for a certain decision that had been made. "You're right," the official responded, "that's what the regulation says, but that's not what it means."

    1. Clear and consistent rules.

2. *Keep the rules technically feasible* Business cannot be expected to do the impossible. Yet the plain truth is that many of today's regulations are unworkable. Environmental standards have on occasion exceeded those of Mother Nature. For example, the Rio Blanco shale-oil development in Colorado was delayed by the fact that the air-quality standards, as originally proposed, required a higher quality of air than existed in the natural setting.

    2. Technically feasible rules.

3. *Make sure the rules are economically feasible* Society cannot impose a rule that

    3. Economically feasible rules.

society is not prepared to pay for because, ultimately, it is the people who must pay, either through higher prices or higher taxes, or both. Furthermore, the costs involved include not only those funds constructively spent to solve problems, but also the increasingly substantial expenditures needed just to comply with the red-tape requirements. Although the total cost of government regulation of business is difficult to compute, it is enormous. To cite an example, the Commission on Federal Paperwork estimated the energy industry's annual cost of complying with federal energy-reporting requirements at possibly $335 million per year.

4. Rules with a future orientation.

4. *Make the rules prospective, not retroactive* Nowadays, there is an alarming, distressing trend toward retroactivity, toward trying to force retribution for the past. Certain patterns of taxation and some of the regulations and applications of the law are indications of this trend.

A case in point is the "Notices of Proposed Disallowance" issued by the Federal Energy Administration (now the Department of Energy) in 1977 against Gulf Oil for alleged overcharges on imported crude oil during the 1973–74 oil embargo. The fact is that during those difficult months we were struggling to supply the nation's energy needs, and increasing imports with the government's support.

We were doing our level best to follow the existing regulations on pricing imports. The charges against us, as well as many other issues raised by the DOE, were the result of retroactive applications of vague, poorly written and confusing regulations.

It is counterproductive to make today's rules apply retroactively to yesterday's ball game.

5. An emphasis on ends—not means.

5. *Make the rules goal-setting, not procedure-prescribing* The proper way for the people of the nation, through their government, to tell their industries how to operate is to set the goals, set the fences, set the criteria, set the atmosphere, but don't tell us how to do it. Tell us what you want made, but don't tell us how to make it. Tell us the destination we're seeking, but don't tell us how to get there. Leave it to the ingenuity of American industry to devise the best, the most economical, the most efficient way to get there, for industry's track record in this regard has been pretty good.

⊞ ETHICS AND SOCIAL RESPONSIBILITY

Ethics is a catalyst for socially responsible actions.

The study of ethics can be approached from many different viewpoints. Perhaps the most practical approach is to view ethics as a catalyst, causing managers to take socially responsible actions. According to Dr. Albert Schweitzer, a famous humanitarian, **ethics** is "our concern for good behavior. We feel an obligation to consider not only our own personal well-being, but also that of other human beings." Over all, ethics is similar to following the golden rule: Do unto others as you would have them do unto you. In general, the more ethical its manager, the more socially responsible the organization.

Some important criteria for determining if actions are ethical:

General Dynamics, McDonnell Douglas, Chemical Bank, and American Can Company are examples of corporations that conduct training programs aimed at encouraging ethical practices within their organizations.[24] Such programs do not attempt to teach managers what is moral or ethical but rather give managers criteria they can use to help determine how ethical a certain action might be. Managers can feel confident that a potential action will be considered ethical by the general public if it is consistent with one or more of the following standards:[25]

1. *The golden rule* Act in a way you would expect others to act toward you.
2. *The utilitarian principle* Act in a way that results in the greatest good for the greatest number.
3. *Kant's categorical imperative* Act in such a way that the action taken under the circumstances could be a universal law, or rule, of behavior.
4. *The professional ethic* Take actions that would be viewed as proper by a disinterested panel of professional peers.
5. *The TV test* Managers should always ask, "Would I feel comfortable explaining to a national TV audience why I took this action?"

1. Golden rule.
2. Utilitarian principle.

3. Kant's categorical imperative.
4. Professional ethic.

5. TV test.

Encouraging ethical practices is good business.

Top management in many organizations commonly strives to encourage ethical practices not only to be morally correct but to gain whatever business advantage there may be in having potential consumers as well as employees view their companies as being ethical. In addition to preserving their corporate image, such companies are concerned about future ethical dilemmas that could prove costly. Unethical practices commonly result in expensive consequences, such as fines, loss of company reputation, and legal fees.

Instances of companies pursuing ethical issues are plentiful. For example, Martin Marietta, a major supplier of missile systems and aircraft components, has established a corporate ethics office. Table 19.7 explains what this office is and how it functions. And Johnson & Johnson, a leading manufacturer of health care products, included in its annual report the code of ethics it developed to guide company practices (see Table 19.8, p. 560.).

TABLE 19.7

Martin Marietta's corporate ethics office

To ensure continuing attention to matters of ethics and standards on the part of all Martin Marietta employees, the Corporation has established the Corporate Ethics Office. The Director of Corporate Ethics is charged with responsibility for monitoring performance under this Code of Ethics and for resolving concerns presented to the Ethics Office.

Martin Marietta calls on every employee to report any violation or apparent violation of the Code. The Corporation strongly encourages employees to work with their supervisors in making such reports and, in addition, provides to employees the right to report violations directly to the Corporate Ethics Office. Prompt reporting of violations is considered to be in the best interest of all.

Employee reports will be handled in absolute confidence. No employee will suffer indignity or retaliation because of a report he or she makes to the Ethics Office. . . .

The Chairman of the Corporate Ethics Committee will be the President of the Corporation. The Committee will consist of five other employees of the Corporation including representatives of the Corporation's operating elements, each of whom will be appointed by the Chairman of the Committee subject to the approval of the Audit and Ethics Committee of the Corporation's Board of Directors.

The Chairman of the Corporate Ethics Committee reports to the Audit and Ethics Committee of the Martin Marietta Corporation Board of Directors.

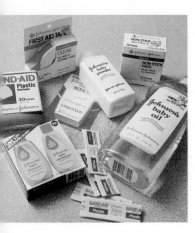

TABLE 19.8

The Johnson & Johnson code of ethics

We believe our first responsibility is to the doctors, nurses and patients, to mothers and all others who use our products and services.
In meeting their needs everything we do must be of high quality.
We must constantly strive to reduce our costs in order to maintain reasonable prices.
Customers' orders must be serviced promptly and accurately.
Our suppliers and distributors must have an opportunity to make a fair profit.

We are responsible to our employees, the men and women who work with us throughout the world.
Everyone must be considered as an individual.
We must respect their dignity and recognize their merit.
They must have a sense of security in their jobs.
Compensation must be fair and adequate, and working conditions clean, orderly and safe.
Employees must feel free to make suggestions and complaints.
There must be equal opportunity for employment, development and advancement for those qualified.
We must provide competent management, and their actions must be just and ethical.

We are responsible to the communities in which we live and work and to the world community as well.
We must be good citizens—support good works and charities and bear our fair share of taxes.
We must encourage civic improvements and better health and education.
We must maintain in good order the property we are privileged to use, protecting the environment and natural resources.

Our final responsibility is to our stockholders.
Business must make a sound profit.
We must experiment with new ideas.
Research must be carried on, innovative programs developed and mistakes paid for.
New equipment must be purchased, new facilities provided and new products launched.
Reserves must be created to provide for adverse times.
When we operate according to these principles, the stockholders should realize a fair return.

BACK TO THE CASE

As indicated earlier, there probably is no legislation that would require Vicaro to modify his beauty shops to make them more accessible to handicapped customers. If such legislation were being developed, however, there are certain steps legislators could take to help Vicaro meet social responsibilities in this area. For example, laws should be clear, consistent, and technically feasible. This would ensure that Vicaro would know what action was expected of him and that technology existed to help him take this action.

Laws should also be economically feasible, emphasize the future, and allow flexibility. Vicaro should be able to follow them without going bankrupt and should not be penalized for what has happened in the past. Vicaro also should be given the flexibility to follow these laws to the best advantage of Stylistics. In other words, he should not be told to conform to laws by following specific steps.

Assuming that Vicaro is an ethical manager, he would be inclined to consider the well-being of other people. As a result, he would be likely to seriously consider reasonable action to aid handicapped customers such as Tiffany Ware. If Vicaro assisted handicapped customers to an extent that significantly limited the success of his company, however, he could probably be accused of being unethical in regard to his employees or anyone else who had a genuine interest in organizational success.

Action Summary

Reread the learning objectives that follow. Each objective is followed by questions. Answering these questions accurately will help you retain the most important concepts discussed in this chapter. After answering each question, check your answer with the answer key at the end of this chapter (*Hint:* If you have doubt regarding the correct response, consult the page whose number follows the answer.)

	Circle:
From studying this chapter, I will attempt to acquire:	

1. **An understanding of the term** *social responsibility.*
   - **a.** According to Davis, since business has certain power over society, society can and must hold business responsible for social conditions that result from the exercise of this power. — T, F
   - **b.** Major social responsibility areas in which business can become involved include all of the following except: (a) urban affairs; (b) consumer affairs; (c) pollution control; (d) natural resource conservation; (e) all of the above are areas of potential involvement. — a, b, c, d, e

2. **An appreciation for the arguments both for and against business assuming social responsibilities.**
   - **a.** Some argue that performing social responsibility activities is a means for a business to gain greater profit. — T, F
   - **b.** Milton Friedman argues that business cannot be held responsible for performing social responsibility activities. He does not argue that: (a) doing so has the potential to cause the demise of American business as we know it today; (b) doing so is in direct conflict with the organizational objectives of business firms; (c) doing so would cause the nation to creep toward socialism, which is inconsistent with American business philosophy; (d) doing so is unethical because it requires business managers to spend money that rightfully belongs to the firm's investors; (e) doing so ultimately would either reduce returns to the firm's investors or raise prices charged to consumers. — a, b, c, d, e

3. **Useful strategies for increasing the social responsiveness of an organization.**
   - **a.** When using the flowchart approach in social responsibility decision making, which of the following questions is out of appropriate sequential order: (a) can we afford this action? (b) does a social responsibility actually exist? (c) does the firm have a right to undertake this action? (d) does an assessment of all interests indicate that the act is desirable? (e) do benefits outweigh costs? — a, b, c, d, e
   - **b.** The social obligation approach to performing social responsibility activities is concerned primarily with complying with existing legislation on the topic. — T, F

4. **Insights on the planning, organizing, influencing, and controlling of social responsibility activities.**
   - **a.** Organizational policies should be established for social responsibility matters in the same manner as, for example, for personnel relations problems. — T, F
   - **b.** Companies should take social responsibility measurements in all of the following areas except: (a) economic utility area; (b) economic function area; (c) quality of life area; (d) social investment area; (e) problem-solving area. — a, b, c, d, e

5. **A practical plan for how society can help business meet its social obligations.**

T, F
    a. Ultimately, the citizens in a society must pay for the social responsibility activities of business by paying higher prices or higher taxes or both.

a, b, c, d, e
    b. Which of the following is *not* one of the responsibilities that society has to business, as listed by Jerry McAfee: (a) setting rules that are clear and concise; (b) making rules prospective, not retroactive; (c) making rules goal-setting, not procedure-prescribing; (d) making rules that are subjective, not objective; (e) making sure the rules are economically feasible.

6. **An understanding of the relationship between social responsibility and ethics.**

T, F
    a. The utilitarian principle suggests that managers should act in such a way that the action taken under the circumstances could be a universal law, or rule, of behavior.

a, b, c, d, e
    b. Management might strive to encourage ethical behavior in organizations in order to: (a) be morally correct; (b) gain a business advantage by having employees perceive their company as ethical; (c) gain a business advantage by having customers perceive the company as ethical; (d) avoid possible costly legal fees; (e) all of the above.

INTRODUCTORY CASE WRAP-UP

"Assisting the Handicapped" (p. 534) and its related back-to-the-case sections were written to help you better understand the management concepts contained in this chapter. Answer the following discussion questions about this introductory case to further enrich your understanding of chapter content:

1. Do you think that Vicaro has a responsibility to make it possible for customers such as Ware to enter his beauty salons? Explain.

2. Assuming that Vicaro has such a responsibility, when would it be relatively easy for him to be committed to living up to it?
3. Assuming that Vicaro has such a responsibility, when would it be relatively difficult for him to be committed to living up to it?

Issues for Review and Discussion

1. Define *social responsibility*.
2. Explain three of the major propositions in the Davis model of social responsibility.
3. Summarize three arguments that support business pursuing social responsibility objectives.
4. Summarize Milton Friedman's arguments against business pursuing social responsibility objectives.
5. What is meant by the phrase *performing required social responsibility activities*?
6. What is meant by the phrase *voluntarily performing social responsibility activities*?

7. List five positive and five negative outcomes a business could experience as a result of performing social responsibility activities.
8. What is the difference between social responsibility and social responsiveness?
9. Discuss the decision-making process that can help managers increase the social responsiveness of a business.
10. In your own words, explain the main differences among Sethi's three approaches to meeting social responsibilities.
11. Which of Sethi's approaches has the most po-

tential for increasing the social responsiveness of a management system? Explain.

12. What is the overall relationship between the four main management functions and performing social responsibility activities?

13. What suggestions does this chapter make about planning social responsibility activities?

14. Describe the process of turning social responsibility policy into action.

15. How do organizing and influencing social responsibility activities relate to planning social responsibility activities?

16. List and define four main areas in which any management system can take measurements to control for social responsibility activities.

17. What is a social audit? How should the results of a social audit be used by management?

18. How can society help business meet its social responsibilities?

19. What is the relationship between ethics and social responsibility?

20. Explain how managers can try to judge if a particular action is ethical.

Sources of Additional Information

Anshen, Melvin, ed. *Managing the Socially Responsible Corporation.* New York: Macmillan, 1974.

Christopher, William F. *Management for the 1980s.* New York: Amacom, 1980.

Cowan, William M. "Office Accidents: Painful, Profitless—and Preventable." *Administrative Management* 42 (September 1981): 68–70, 78.

Cressey, Donald R., and Charles A. Moore. "Managerial Values and Corporate Codes of Ethics." *California Management Review* 25 (Summer 1983): 53–77.

Davis, Keith, and Robert L. Blomstrom. *Business and Society: Environment and Responsibility,* 3d ed. New York: McGraw-Hill, 1975.

Diebold, John. *The Role of Business in Society.* New York: Amacom, 1982.

Donaldson, Thomas. *Corporations and Morality.* Englewood Cliffs, N.J.: Prentice-Hall, 1982.

Harding, Charles F. "Why Administrative Offices Are Moving to Smaller Cities." *Administrative Management* 42 (September 1981): 40–42, 66.

Hay, Robert D., and Edmund R. Gray. *Business and Society: Cases and Text.* Cincinnati, Ohio: South-Western, 1981.

Hosmer, LaRue Tone. *The Ethics of Management.* Homewood, Ill.: Richard D. Irwin, 1987.

"Johnson & Johnson Suspends Shipments of Some Tylenol." *Wall Street Journal,* September 1983, 21.

Kapp, K. William. *The Social Costs of Private Enterprise.* New York: Schocken, 1971.

Kinicki, Angelo, Jeffrey Bracker, Robert Kreitner, Chris Lockwood, and David Lemak. "Socially Responsible Plant Closings." *Personnel Administrator* 32 (June 1987): 116–36.

McGuire, Joseph F. *Business and Society.* New York: McGraw-Hill, 1963.

Rose, Robert L. "Ethics Policies Gain Favor but Leave Major Questions." *Wall Street Journal,* November 24, 1986, 35.

Ruth, Stephen R., and Linda Samuels. "Perspectives on Computer Ethics and Crime." *Business* 36 (January/February/March 1986): 30–36.

Scott, William G., and Terrence R. Mitchell. "The Moral Failure of Management Education." *Chronicle of Higher Education,* December 11, 1985, 35.

Soothill, Keith. "The Extent of Risk in Employing Ex-Prisoners." *Personnel Management* 13 (April 1981): 35–37, 43.

Steiner, George A., and John F. Steiner. *Business, Government, and Society: A Managerial Perspective,* 5th ed. New York: Random House, 1988.

Stone, Christopher D. *Where the Law Ends: The Social Control of Corporate Behavior.* New York: Harper & Row, 1975.

Sutton, Robert I., and Anat Rafaeli. "Characteristics of Work Stations as Potential Occupational Stressors." *Academy of Management Journal* 30 (June 1987): 260–76.

Thomas, Dr. Edward (C.A.M.). "Conserving Energy—What's Being Done." *Management World* 10 (March 1981): 14–17.

Walton, Clarence C. *Corporate Social Responsibilities.* Belmont, Calif.: Wadsworth, 1967.

Watson, John H., III. *20 Company-Sponsored Foundations: Programs and Policies.* New York: Conference Board, 1970.

Weidenbaum, Murray L. "The True Obligation of the Business Firm to Society." *Management Review* 70 (September 1981): 21–22.

Notes

1. D. Votaw and S. P. Sethi, *The Corporate Dilemma: Traditional Values versus Contemporary Problems* (Englewood Cliffs, N.J.: Prentice-Hall, 1973), 9–46, 167–91.
2. Keith Davis and Robert L. Blomstrom, *Business and Society: Environment and Responsibility*, 3d. ed. (New York: McGraw-Hill, 1975), 6.
3. Peter L. Berger, "New Attack on the Legitimacy of Business," *Harvard Business Review* (September/October 1981): 82–89.
4. Keith Davis, "Five Propositions for Social Responsibility," *Business Horizons* (June 1975): 19–24.
5. Stahrl W. Edmunds, "Unifying Concepts in Social Responsibility," *Academy of Management Review* (January 1977): 38–45.
6. For a worthwhile study on these social responsibility areas, see Vernon M. Buehler and Y. K. Shetty, "Managerial Response to Social Responsibility Challenge," *Academy of Management Journal* (March 1976): 66–78.
7. For a more detailed summary of the arguments for and against businesses pursuing social responsibility activities, see Keith Davis, "The Case for and against Business Assumptions of Social Responsibilities," *Academy of Management Journal* (June 1973): 312–22.
8. Elizabeth Gatewood and Archie B. Carroll, "The Anatomy of Corporate Social Response: The Rely, Firestone 500, and Pinto Cases," *Business Horizons* 24 (September/October 1981): 9–16.
9. Milton Friedman, "The Social Responsibility of Business Is to Increase Profits," *New York Times Magazine*, September 13, 1970, 33, 122–26.
10. Neil M. Brown and Paul F. Haas, "Social Responsibility: The Uncertain Hypothesis," *MSU Business Topics* (Summer 1974): 48.
11. Milton Friedman, "Does Business Have Social Responsibility?" *Bank Administration* (April 1971): 13–14.
12. Sandra L. Holmes, "Executive Perceptions of Corporate Social Responsibility," *Business Horizons* (June 1976): 34–40.
13. William C. Gergold, "Corporate Responsibility and the Industrial Professional," *Industrial Management* (November/December 1976): 5–8.
14. Frederick D. Sturdivant, *Business and Society: A Managerial Approach* (Homewood, Ill.: Richard D. Irwin, 1977), 109–25.
15. For an interesting discussion of the comparative social responsiveness of Ford, Firestone, and Procter & Gamble, see Gatewood and Carroll, "The Anatomy of Corporate Social Response."
16. Harry A. Lipson, "Do Corporate Executives Plan for Social Responsibility?" *Business and Society Review* (Winter 1974–75): 80–81.
17. S. Prakash Sethi, "Dimensions of Corporate Social Performance: An Analytical Framework," *California Management Review* (Spring 1975): 58–64.
18. Donald S. McNaughton, "Managing Social Responsiveness," *Business Horizons* (December 1976): 19–24.
19. Frank H. Cassell, "The Social Cost of Doing Business," *MSU Business Topics* (Autumn 1974): 19–26.
20. Donald W. Garner, "The Cigarette Industry's Escape from Liability," *Business and Society Review*, no. 33 (Spring 1980): 22.
21. Archie B. Carroll and George W. Beiler, "Landmarks in the Evolution of the Social Audit," *Academy of Management Journal* (September 1975): 589–99.
22. Raymond A. Bauer and Dan H. Fenn, Jr., "What Is a Corporate Social Audit?" *Harvard Business Review* (January/February 1973): 37–48.
23. Condensed from Jerry McAfee, "How Society Can Help Business," *Newsweek*, July 3, 1978, 15. Copyright 1978 by Newsweek, Inc. All rights reserved. Reprinted by permission.
24. Alan L. Otten, "Ethics on the Job: Companies Alert Employees to Potential Dilemmas," *Wall Street Journal*, July 14, 1986, 25.
25. Gene R. Laczniak, "Framework for Analyzing Marketing Ethics," *Journal of Macromarketing* (Spring 1983): 7–18.

Action Summary Answer Key

1. a. T, p. 535
   b. e, p. 537
2. a. T, p. 540
   b. c, pp. 540–543

3. a. a, pp. 547–548
   b. T, pp. 547–549
4. a. T, pp. 550–551
   b. a, p. 555

5. a. T, pp. 557–558
   b. d, pp. 557–558
6. a. F, p. 559
   b. e, p. 559

ETHICAL ISSUES AT PRESBYTERIAN-UNIVERSITY HOSPITAL

At age seventy-six, Iola Miller came to Pittsburgh's Presbyterian-University Hospital to see Dr. Thomas Starzl, renowned transplant surgeon. When Dr. Starzl met Miss Miller in her hospital room, he saw signs of her worsening disease. Her jaundiced condition had deepened, her abdomen and legs were swollen with fluid, and a few of her vertebrae had collapsed. But her blue eyes were clear, and her manner was determined. For two years, the liver disease, called primary biliary cirrhosis, had barely slowed her activities. She helped her senior citizens' group raise money, went to card parties, and bowled. Then, things went amiss and she was given as little as six months to live.

Miss Miller told Dr. Starzl that she wanted a transplant but, suddenly subdued, added that she did not know how she would be able to pay for the operation. Dr. Starzl indicated that the money didn't really matter, that he'd just have to have a fight with the governor of Pennsylvania, her home state, to obtain the needed funding. Before leaving the room, he warned of the fight that she herself would face, at her age, to get through the operation. "You may be too old to fight," he tested. She looked him in the eye and shook her head no.

Thus began another case at Presbyterian, the nation's busiest organ transplant hospital, where every twelve hours, on the average, another patient gets a new liver, heart, or kidney. This case, however, was somewhat different. It would match an aging woman willing to make a prayerful gamble with a workaholic surgeon eager to test the limits of his skills. It was also one more case illuminating the ethical and financial issues associated with the growing field of transplant surgery.

How should a tight supply of donor organs be allocated? Who should pay the bill, typically running at least $100,000? How old must a person be before being judged too old for transplant surgery? Iola Miller would have been turned away at many of the three dozen other U.S. hospitals that do liver transplants, including the Mayo Clinic. Ruud Krom, head of the Mayo Clinic transplant program, defends age tests partly because of the scarcity of donor organs. Dr. Starzl, in contrast, is trying to prove that fixed age limits are unrealistic. Although he has set his own current age of sixty as a tentative limit, he believes that each case should be examined on its own merits and is now recommending exceptions. As Dr. Starzl indicates, Miss Miller's case shows the need for expanding the liver transplant program. By the time Miss Miller entered Presbyterian, Dr. Starzl had already

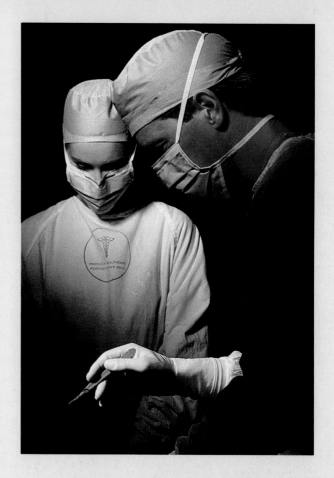

accepted twenty candidates in their sixties. As recently as 1982, the cutoff had been fifty.

Whether to favor the young over the aged is a troublesome problem, because a great many people in the United States (over four hundred on any given day) are awaiting liver transplants. The shortage of donor livers is also a variable problem. It tends to be worse for small children. Furthermore, the competition for transplants can be muddled by shifting circumstances, such as the availability of surgeons when organs suddenly become available. Mayo Clinic's Dr. Krom argues that if transplants are less successful in the elderly, scarce resources are being wasted. He wonders whether younger candidates shouldn't get preference because they may have more years ahead of them and may carry heavier responsibilities, such as supporting a family. In Miss Miller's case, Presbyterian's ethics committee, an advisory panel of doctors and hospital officials, held that age alone should not bar her operation.

Yet, for Iola Miller, one additional issue remained: Who would pay for the operation? Presbyterian requires $127,000 up front for a liver transplant for patients lacking insurance. Hospital officials argue that they simply cannot write off the huge bills, which have run as high as $500,000. Miss Miller had only Medicare, the federal health insurance program for the elderly and disabled. But it doesn't pay for liver transplants (except for a sharply restricted provision for children). Since Miss Miller had no insurance, Presbyterian had to look for someone to pay her hospital expenses. In this case, the hospital was successful. It lined up coverage through a state medical aid agency that has become a payer of last resort for transplants.

Age does not appear to be the only battleground over who gets transplants. The *Pittsburgh Press* last year reported that the Starzl team had given kidney transplants to wealthy Saudi Arabians. The paper linked alleged favoritism to what it called financial "bonuses." For example, King Fahd and other Saudis donated $650,000 to the University of Pittsburgh for transplant research. Of course, the word *university* in the hospital's name denotes the affiliation between the hospital and the university. Dr. Starzl denies that favorites were played. Yet today Presbyterian limits foreign patients to no more than 5 percent of all kidney transplants, and the question of how transplants were allocated is now before a grand jury.

DISCUSSION ISSUES

1. Would Presbyterian-University Hospital be acting in a socially responsible manner if it performed liver transplants for wealthy Saudis while denying the treatment to less wealthy U.S. citizens? To senior citizens while denying the treatment to younger citizens? Explain.

2. Is there a link between ethics and social responsibility? Explain.

3. Do you believe that the decision reached by the ethics committee of Presbyterian-University Hospital to provide transplants to Saudis and to more elderly citizens was ethical? Do any of the ethics standards described in the chapter (the golden rule, the utilitarian principle, Kant's categorical imperative, the professional ethic, or the TV test) appear to have been violated by the actions taken by the hospital? Explain.

4. Is it proper to deny medical treatment to certain segments of society? What about individuals who have been incarcerated for serious crimes? What criteria should be used for determining who should receive life saving medical treatment such as liver, kidney, and heart transplants? Should the main criterion be age, academic achievement, professional or social contribution, ability to pay, or anything else? Explain.

STUDENT LEARNING OBJECTIVES

From studying this chapter, I will attempt to acquire:

1. An understanding of international management and its importance to modern managers.
2. An understanding of what constitutes a multi-national corporation.
3. Insights concerning the risk involved in investing in international operations.
4. Knowledge about planning and organizing in multinational corporations.
5. Knowledge about influencing and controlling in multinational corporations.
6. Insights about what comparative management is and how it might help managers do their jobs better.
7. Ideas on how to be a better manager through the study of Japanese management techniques.

INTERNATIONAL

MANAGEMENT

CHAPTER OUTLINE

NABISCO BRANDS IN THE INTERNATIONAL ARENA

In 1985, Nabisco merged with R. J. Reynolds to form a new company called RJR Nabisco. Nabisco Brands, a subsidiary of RJR Nabisco, is the leading U.S. producer of cookies and crackers. The Nabisco Brands North American product line includes such recognizable brands as Oreos, Chips Ahoy!, Fig Newtons, Ritz, and Saltines. Nabisco Brands also produces nuts and snack products, candy products, dog food products, margarine products, and cereal products for North American markets. Popular product names in these areas include Planters, Baby Ruth, Life Savers, Milk Bone, Blue Bonnet, and Shredded Wheat.

Although many North Americans are very familiar with the Nabisco Brands products mentioned in the previous paragraph, they probably are less familiar with Nabisco Brands product penetration in other parts of the world. In some years, product sales to "other parts of the world" have contributed over 40 percent of total company annual sales at Nabisco Brands. The following excerpts from the 1987 Nabisco Brands annual report indicate how involved this company is in the international arena:

> In the United Kingdom, International Nabisco's largest single market, good volume growth came from Walkers and Smiths crisps and snacks, as well as Nabisco cereals. Successful product introductions included Smiths Jackets crisps, a chip made using unpeeled potatoes, and Team Flakes cereal.
>
> In France, volume and market share increases for the Belin line of cookies extended the company's position as one of the country's top biscuit producers. The acquisition of ULA Bahlsen, a French frozen pastry business, made Nabisco the leading marketer of this popular French dessert.
>
> Other major European markets also showed good progress. In Italy, Nabisco continued to register market share gains for the Saiwa line of cookies. In Spain, the company's biscuit business achieved sharply higher volume and market share improvements. To enhance its distribution channels there, the company entered into a partnership with Tabacalera, S.A., Spain's government-owned tobacco and foods company.

> International Nabisco expanded its operations in a number of other countries as well. Britannia Industries, Nabisco's 38 percent–owned business in India, began operating a new soya processing plant and maintained its leadership position in the biscuit category. In New Zealand, the company added to its number one position in biscuit products by acquiring the country's leading snack producer, Abels Industries, Ltd.
>
> Nabisco Brands' joint venture in the People's Republic of China completed construction and began start-up of a new bakery in late 1987. The Beijing bakery will begin producing crackers for sale in China and other Far East countries during 1988. In addition, a joint-venture business in Thailand began operating a new bakery during 1987.

Nabisco Brands does business in several countries in addition to those just mentioned. Although there is great potential reward for such an international focus, the task of managing an organization such as Nabisco Brands is generally much more involved than that of managing most organizations of similar size that focus on doing business in only one country.

What's Ahead

The introductory case gives examples of Nabisco Brands operations in the United Kingdom, France, Italy, and Latin America. The material in this chapter provides insights on how to manage in diverse multinational circumstances such as those at Nabisco Brands. Major topics covered are fundamentals of international management, the multinational corporation, management functions and multinational corporations, and comparative management.

FUNDAMENTALS OF INTERNATIONAL MANAGEMENT

International management is simply the performance of management activities across national borders. In essence, international management entails reaching organizational objectives by extending management activities to include an emphasis on organizations in foreign countries.

In practice, this emphasis may take any of several different forms and can vary from simply analyzing and fighting foreign competition to establishing a formal partnership with a foreign company. An example of analyzing the competition is the U.S. automobile industry. Some researchers believe that Japanese car manufacturers can deliver a compact automobile to California for 23 percent less than it can be produced in the United States.[1] Certainly, U.S. car manufacturers must consider such information in managing their own organizations. An example of a formal partnership is National Steel, a U.S. company that has formed an equal partnership with Nippon Kokan, a Japanese steel company, in an effort to gain a competitive advantage over other world steel producers.[2]

Outstanding progress in areas such as transportation, communication, and technology makes access to foreign countries more feasible and attractive as time passes. As a result, many modern managers face numerous international issues that can have a direct and significant impact on organizational success. For example, the following situation was facing managers at Xerox a few years ago:

> Xerox corporation is racing to meet deadlines at once. It must slim its copier business fast enough to beat the Japanese. Japanese competition in small copiers, a nagging worry since the mid-1970s, has shrunk Xerox's market share in America to roughly half of total copier revenue. In Europe, its other big market, Xerox has only a quarter of the revenues. Xerox has had to accept slimmer profit margins to stop the rot.[3]

The notable trend that already exists in the United States and other countries toward developing business relationships in and with foreign countries is expected to accelerate even more in the future.[4] As Figures 20.1 and 20.2 indi-

International management is management activities that cross national borders.

Business with foreign countries is growing.

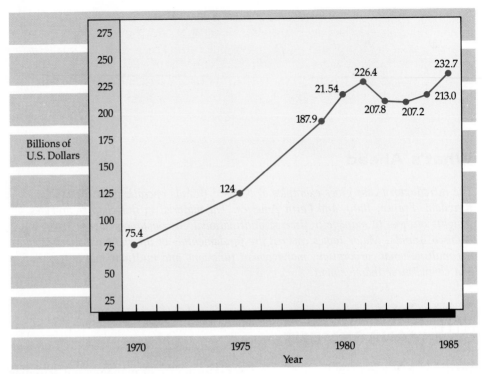

FIGURE 20.1
Growth in U.S. investment abroad

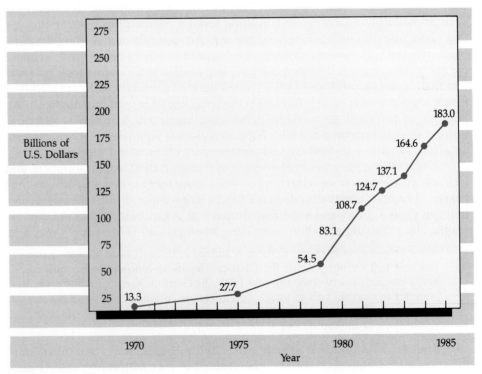

FIGURE 20.2
Growth in foreign investment in the United States

cate, U.S. investment in foreign countries and investment by foreign countries in the United States has been growing since 1970 and is expected to continue growing. Information of this nature has caused many management educators as well as practicing managers to voice the opinion that an understanding of international management is necessary for a thorough and contemporary understanding of the fundamentals of management.[5]

BACK TO THE CASE

As the introductory case shows, Nabisco Brands is an organization involved in international management. Managers within Nabisco perform management activities across national borders of such countries as Italy and France. Given the international trend toward greater foreign investment, Nabisco is likely to continue to emphasize worldwide expansion. In addition, this trend will likely be characterized by foreign companies attempting to compete with Nabisco in the United States.

THE MULTINATIONAL CORPORATION

This section presents more specifics about managing organizations in the international arena by defining *multinational corporation* and discussing the complexities and risks of managing the multinational corporation.

Defining the Multinational Corporation

The term *multinational corporation* first appeared in the dictionary sometime in the 1970s and has been defined in several ways in conversation and textbooks alike.[6] For the purposes of this text, a **multinational corporation** is a company that has significant operations in more than one country. In essence, a multinational corporation is an organization that is involved in doing business at the international level. It carries out its activities on an international scale that disregards national boundaries and on the basis of a common strategy from a corporation center.[7]

A multinational corporation has significant operations in more than one country.

A list of multinational corporations in this country would include such companies as Ford, General Motors, Mobil Oil, Firestone Tire, and Massey-Ferguson. A Massey-Ferguson executive has described his company's international involvement as combining French-made transmissions, British-made engines, Mexican-made axles, and U.S.-made sheet metal parts to produce in Detroit a tractor for sale in Canada.[8] Examples of foreign multinational corporations that have various levels of ownership in certain companies located in the United States are presented in Table 20.1 on page 574. As the table implies, foreign revenue, related profit, and foreign assets owned can be significant for multinational corporations.

Neil H. Jacoby implies that companies go through six stages to reach the highest degree of multinationalization (see Table 20.2, p. 574).[9] As the table indicates, companies can range from slightly multinationalized organizations that simply export products to a foreign country to highly multinationalized organizations that have some of their owners in other countries.

There are six stages of multinationalization.

TABLE 20.1

The impact of foreign operations on several multinational organizations

Company	Foreign Revenue as Percent of Total	Foreign Profit as Percent of Total Profits	Foreign Assets as Percent of Total Profits
Citicorp	49.8	51.2	53.7
Coca-Cola	38.0	55.6	25.3
Colgate Palmolive	52.3	48.1	38.4
Dow Chemical	53.6	55.3	45.9
Exxon	69.4	55.4	43.0
Gilette	51.8	54.0	45.5
IBM	40.4	39.4	36.1
Texaco	50.1	46.1	30.1

In general, the larger the organization, the greater the likelihood that it participates in international operations of some sort. Companies such as General Electric, Lockheed, and du Pont, which have annually accumulated over $1 billion from export sales, support this generalization. Exceptions, however, also exist. BRK Electronics, for example, a small firm in Aurora, Illinois, has won a substantial share of world sales by smoke detectors. By setting up local distributors in Italy, France, and England, BRK caused its export sales to climb from $124,000 in one year to $4 million five years later.[10] In the future, an increasing number of smaller organizations almost certainly will become involved in international operations.

Complexities of Managing the Multinational Corporation

International management is more complex than domestic management.

The definition of *international management* and the discussion of what constitutes a multinational corporation clearly indicate that international management and domestic management are quite different. International management differs from domestic management because it involves operating:[11]

TABLE 20.2

Six stages of multinationalization

Stage 1	Stage 2	Stage 3	Stage 4	Stage 5	Stage 6
Exports its products to foreign countries	Establishes sales organizations abroad	Licenses use of its patents and know-how to foreign firms that make and sell its products	Establishes foreign manufacturing facilities	Multinationalizes management from top to bottom	Multinationalizes ownership of corporate stock

1. Within different national sovereignties.
2. Under widely disparate economic conditions.
3. With people living within different value systems and institutions.
4. In places experiencing the industrial revolution at different times.
5. Often over greater geographical distance.
6. In national markets varying greatly in population and area.

Figure 20.3 on page 576 shows some of the more important management implications of the six variables and some of the relationships among them. For example, according to the "different national sovereignties" variable, different national sovereignties generate different legal, monetary, and political systems. In turn, each legal system implies a unique set of rights and obligations involving property, taxation, antitrust (control of monopoly) law, corporate law, and contract law. These, in turn, require the firm to acquire new skills to assess the international legal considerations. The skills are new in the sense of being different from those required in a purely domestic setting. The cartoon emphasizes the point that the management process generally becomes more complicated when an organization functions in the international business arena.

"Problems with your conference call—Los Angeles is out to breakfast, New York's out to lunch and London's out to dinner."

Wall Street Journal, *February 24, 1987. From the Wall Street Journal—permission, Cartoon Features Syndicate.*

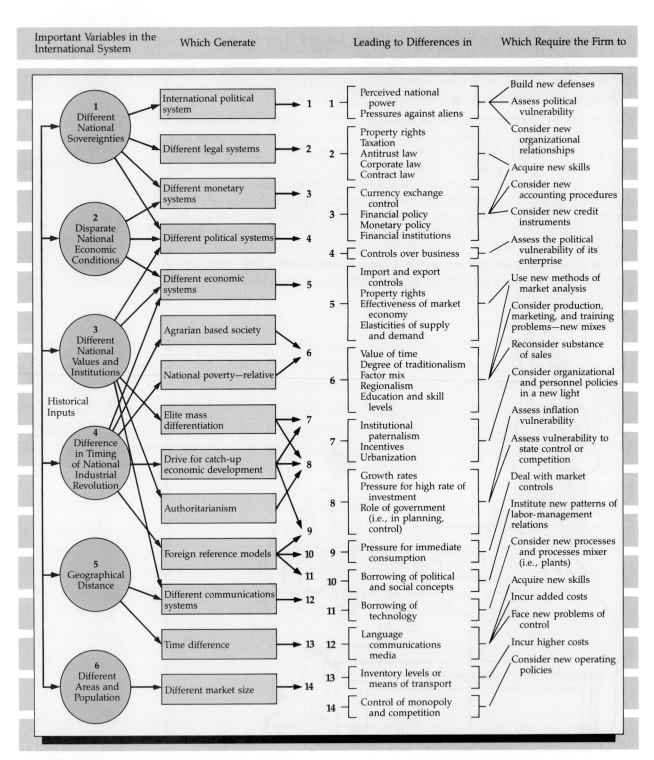

FIGURE 20.3
Management implications based on six variables in international systems and relationships among them

Risk and the Multinational Corporation

Naturally, developing a multinational corporation requires a substantial investment in foreign operations. Normally, managers who make foreign investments
believe that such investments (1) reduce or eliminate high transportation costs;
(2) allow participation in the rapid expansion of a market abroad; (3) provide
foreign technical, design, and marketing skills; and (4) earn higher profits.[12]

*Foreign investments
bring several benefits.*

There is, however, some risk associated with the decision to invest in foreign operations. For example, political complications involving the **parent company** (the company investing in the international operations) and various factions within the **host country** (the country in which the investment is made)
could keep the outcomes in the preceding paragraph from materializing. Table
20.3 lists various possible sources of political risk, several groups within the host
country that might generate the risk, and possible effects of the risk on the
investing organization.

*Foreign investments
also involve several
kinds of risk.*

The likelihood of desirable outcomes related to foreign investments probably always will be somewhat uncertain and will vary from country to country.
Nevertheless, managers faced with making a foreign investment must assess
this likelihood as accurately as possible. Obviously, a poor decision to invest in
another country can cause serious financial problems for the organization. Table
20.4 on page 578 explains how some managers subscribe to services that weigh
political, economic, and social factors to assess various risk levels associated
with investing in different foreign countries.

TABLE 20.3

Political risk in investing in a foreign country

Sources of Political Risk	Groups through Which Political Risk Can Be Generated	Political Risk Effects: Types of Influence on Business Operations
Competing political philosophies (nationalism, socialism, communism)	Government in power and its operating agencies	Confiscation: Loss of assets without compensation
Social unrest and disorder	Nonparliamentary opposition groups (e.g., anarchist or guerilla movement working from within or outside of country)	Expropriation with compensation: Loss of freedom to operate
Vested interests of local business groups		Operational restrictions: Market shares, product characteristics, employment policies, locally shared ownership, and so forth
Recent and impending political independence	Nonorganized common interest groups: students, workers, peasants, minorities, and so forth	
Armed conflicts and internal rebellions for political power	Foreign governments or inter-government agencies such as the European Economic Community	Loss of transfer freedom: Financial (e.g., dividends, interest payments), goods, personnel, or ownership rights
New international alliances	Foreign governments willing to enter into armed conflict or to support internal rebellion	Breaches or unilateral revisions in contracts and agreements
		Discrimination, such as taxes, compulsory subcontracting
		Damage to property or personnel from riots, insurrections, revolutions, and wars

TABLE 20.4

How some managers assess the risk of doing business abroad

Can a Computer Tell the Ratio of Risk?

To help them cope with the uncertainties of doing business abroad, many companies subscribe to services that publish country risk indexes, somewhat like Moody's bond or Value Line stock ratings. Though there is some debate about the usefulness of numerically rating countries for risk, the client lists of the three organizations read like the Fortune 500.

A company considering expanding into Indonesia, for example, might well consult all three of that country's ratings. It could look at the BERI (for Business Environment Risk Index) rating, which ranks countries on a scale of 1 to 100. Indonesia scores a 45.5, a low enough rating to be marked a "high risk." A similar index put out by Business International (BI), an advisory service for multinations, gives Indonesia a slightly more respectable 58. Finally, the World Political Risk Forecasts (WPRF) service of Frost & Sullivan, a business research organization, expresses its own rather dim view of Indonesia in its January, 1980 forecast: a company doing business there stands a 31 percent chance of a major business loss owing to political developments in the next eighteen months and a 45 percent chance of loss within five years. A better bet for investment would be nearby Singapore—BERI score 74.9, BI rating 79, WRPF loss probability of only 19 percent in the next five years.

Executives appreciate these rating services because they are relatively cheap ($500 a year for BERI, $1,500 for WPRF), and they boil down the complex forecast to simple numbers. Says Frederick Haner, the University of Delaware business professor who compiles the BERI rating, "Executives treat these numbers as though they came from God directly." In fact, they are derived from weighting and averaging the evaluations of economic, political, and social factors in foreign countries made by panels of "experts." BI's information comes from its employees around the world; WPRF and BERI don't identify their panelists beyond describing them as experts from business, government, and academia.

The most frequent criticism of this indexing is that, although it is based on largely subjective evaluations, the figures imply a mathematical precision that really isn't there. One risk analyst for a major U.S. corporation calls indexing "a substitute for thought." But the purveyors of risk ratings—and many of their clients—claim indexing is a useful tool, though obviously not the only one, for assessing risk. In any case, the troubled world of international business has made risk rating a growth industry.

BACK TO THE CASE

It is apparent from the introductory case that Nabisco Brands is a multinational corporation—an organization with significant operations in more than one country. In addition, Nabisco can be classified as being in the sixth stage of multinationalization—multinational ownership of corporate stock.

Managing at Nabisco under such international circumstances is a complex matter. This complexity is caused mostly by Nabisco managers managing within different foreign countries that are separated by significant distances and that are characterized by different economic conditions, people, levels of technology, and market sizes. A comparison of Nabisco's Latin American and United Kingdom markets on each of these variables, for example, illustrates how complex management at Nabisco can be.

Naturally, management has attempted to minimize risk in making foreign investments. In the past few years, the political situations in France, Italy, and the United Kingdom have seemed mostly stable. Of course, political situations can change quickly and should be constantly monitored by multinational corporations. On such additional dimensions as economy and social factors, Nabisco management obviously has decided that investments in these countries represent a tolerable amount of risk when weighed against the prospect of increased return from foreign operations.

▦ MANAGEMENT FUNCTIONS AND MULTINATIONAL CORPORATIONS

The sections that follow discuss the four major management functions—planning, organizing, influencing, and controlling—as they occur at multinational corporations.

Planning for Multinational Corporations

Planning was defined in chapter 4 as determining how the management system will achieve its objectives. This definition is applicable to the management of both domestic and multinational organizations. In general, such management tools as policies, procedures, rules, budgets, forecasting, Gantt charts, and the program evaluation and review technique (PERT) are equally valuable in planning for either domestic or multinational organizations.

Perhaps the primary difference between planning in multinational versus domestic organizations involves strategic planning. Organizational strategy for the multinational organization must include provisions that focus on the international arena, whereas such strategy for the domestic organization does not. Increased environmental uncertainties along with a growing sense of international competition are causing more and more managers to evaluate internationalization as an organizational strategy.

> Multinational corporations must have an international strategy.

To develop appropriate international strategies, managers explore issues such as (1) establishing a new sales force in a foreign country, (2) developing new manufacturing plants in other countries through purchase or construction, (3) financing international expansion, and (4) determining which countries represent the most suitable candidates for international expansion. Although international strategies vary, most include some emphasis on one or more of the following areas: imports/exports, license agreements, direct investing, and joint ventures.

> International strategies usually involve imports and exports, license agreements, direct investing, and joint ventures.

Imports/Exports

Strategy in imports/exports emphasizes reaching organizational objectives by **importing** (buying goods or services from another country) or **exporting** (selling goods or services to another country).

Organizations of all sizes are importing and exporting. On the one hand, there are very small organizations, such as People's Car Company, which is made up basically of two people who import cars from Mexico to be sold to American dealers for resale.[13] On the other hand, there are extremely large and complex organizations, such as Eastman Kodak, which exports photographic products to a number of foreign countries.[14]

License Agreements

A **license agreement** is a right granted by one company to another to use its brand name, technology, product specifications, and so on in the manufacture or sale of goods and services. Naturally, the company to which the license is extended pays some fee for the privilege. International strategy in this area involves reaching organizational objectives through either the purchase or sale of licenses at the international level.

For example, Ohio Mattress Company, a relatively small mattress manufacturer, has generated outstanding profits by making and selling Sealy bedding in Ohio, Texas, and Puerto Rico. A license purchased by Ohio Mattress from Sealy gives Ohio Mattress the right to manufacture and sell Sealy's well-known products.[15]

Direct Investing

Direct investing is using the assets of one company to purchase the operating assets (for example, factories) of another company. International strategy in this area emphasizes reaching organizational objectives through the purchase of operating assets of a company in another country.

For example, Robinson Nugent, Inc., of New Albany, Indiana, manufactures sophisticated electronic parts that are used in other products assembled by high-tech manufacturers throughout the world. The company opened a manufacturing facility in Delemont, Switzerland, in an effort to maintain its share of the European market. Over all, the company believes that this Swiss plant has had a good effect on European sales and has even increased demand for exports from the United States to Europe by 40 percent.[16]

Joint Ventures

A **joint venture** is a partnership formed by a company in one country with a company in another country for the purpose of pursuing some mutually desirable business undertaking. International strategy that includes joint ventures emphasizes the attainment of organizational objectives through partnerships with foreign companies.

Joint ventures between car manufacturers in Europe are becoming more and more common as companies strive for greater economies of scale and higher standards in product quality and delivery. Renault, for example, formulated a network of deals for diesel engines from Fiat, gasoline engines from Volvo, forgings and castings from Peugeot, and gearboxes from Volkswagen.[17]

Organizing Multinational Corporations

Organizing was defined in chapter 8 as the process of establishing orderly uses for all resources within the organization. This definition applies equally to the management of either domestic or multinational organizations. Two organizing topics regarding multinational corporations, however, bear further discussion. These topics are organization structure and the selection of managers.

Organization Structure

Five factors usually determine the organization structure of multinational corporations: function, product, territory, customer, and manufacturing process.

Organization structure was defined in chapter 8 as established relationships among resources within the management system, and the *organization chart* is the graphic illustration of organization structure. Chapter 8 also noted that departments shown on organization charts are most commonly established according to function, product, territory, customers, or manufacturing process. Internationally oriented organizations also normally establish structure based on these five areas (see Figure 20.4).

As with domestic organizations, there is no best way to organize all multinational corporations. Instead, managers of these organizations must analyze the multinational circumstances that confront them and develop an organization structure that best suits the circumstances.

Selection of Managers

For multinational organizations to thrive, they must of course have competent managers. One important characteristic that is believed to be a primary determinant of how competently managers can guide multinational organizations is their attitude toward how such organizations should operate.

Over the years, management theorists have identified three basic managerial attitudes toward the operations of multinational corporations: ethnocentric, polycentric, and geocentric.[18] The **ethnocentric attitude** reflects a belief that multinational corporations should regard home country management practices as

Managerial attitudes toward the operations of a multinational corporation can range from ethnocentric to polycentric to geocentric.

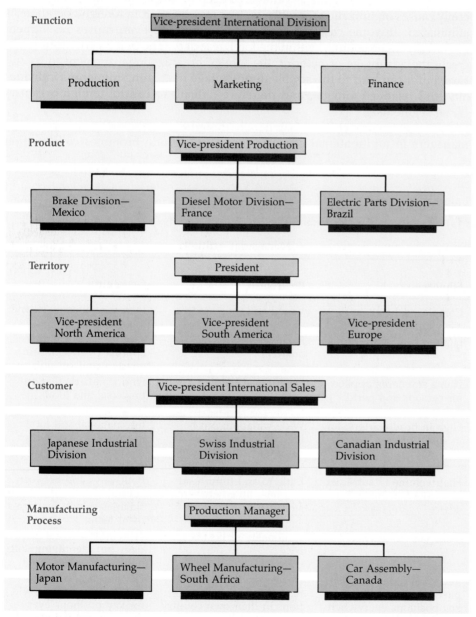

FIGURE 20.4
Partial multinational organization charts based on function, product, territory, customers, and manufacturing process

superior to foreign country management practices. The **polycentric attitude** reflects a belief that since foreign managers are closer to foreign organizational units, they probably understand them better, and therefore foreign management practices should generally be viewed as more insightful than home country management practices. Managers with a **geocentric attitude** believe that the overall quality of management recommendations, rather than the location of managers, should determine the acceptability of management practices used to guide multinational corporations.

Understanding the potential worth of these three attitudes within multinational corporations is extremely important. The ethnocentric attitude, although perhaps having the advantage of keeping the organization simple, generally causes organizational problems, since feedback from foreign operations is eliminated. In some cases, the ethnocentric attitude even causes resentment toward the home country within the foreign society. The polycentric attitude can create the advantage of tailoring the foreign organizational segment to its culture, but it can lead to the sizable disadvantage of creating numerous individually run, relatively unique, and therefore difficult to control foreign organizational segments.

The geocentric attitude is generally thought to be the most appropriate for managers in multinational corporations. This attitude promotes collaboration

The geocentric attitude generally is considered most appropriate for long-term organizational success.

TABLE 20.5

Different organizational characteristics typical of ethnocentric, polycentric, and geocentric

Organizational Characteristics	Managerial Attitudes		
	Ethnocentric	Polycentric	Geocentric
Complexity of organization	Complex in home country, simple in subsidiaries	Varied and independent	Increasingly complex and interdependent
Authority, decision making	High in headquarters	Relatively low in headquarters	Aim for a collaborative approach between headquarters and subsidiaries
Evaluation and control	Home standards applied for persons and performance	Determined locally	Find standards that are universal and local
Rewards and punishments, incentives	High in headquarters, low in subsidiaries	Wide variation; can be high or low for subsidiary performance	International and local executives rewarded for reaching local and worldwide objectives
Communicating, information flow	High volume to subsidiaries: orders, commands, advice	Little to and from headquarters, little between subsidiaries	Both ways and between subsidiaries: heads of subsidiaries part of management team
Identification	Nationality of owner	Nationality of host country	Truly international company but identifying with national interests
Perpetuation (recruiting, staffing, development)	Recruit and develop people of home country for key positions everywhere in the world	Develop people of local nationality for key positions in their own country	Develop best people everywhere in the world for key positions everywhere in the world

between foreign and home country management and encourages the development of managerial skill regardless of the organizational segment or country in which managers operate. An organization characterized by the geocentric attitude generally incurs high travel and training expenses, and many decisions are made by consensus. Although risks such as the wide distribution of power in such an organization are real, payoffs such as better-quality products, worldwide utilization of the best human resources, increased managerial commitment to worldwide organizational objectives, and increased profit generally outweigh potential harm. Over all, managers with a geocentric attitude create organizations that contribute more to the long-term success of the multinational corporation. Table 20.5 compares in more detail the types of organizations generally created by managers who possess ethnocentric, polycentric, and geocentric attitudes.

BACK TO THE CASE

Planning tools such as policies and procedures are equally valuable at Nabisco Brands in managing either domestic or foreign operations. Being a multinational corporation, Nabisco has strategies that focus on the international sector, whereas a totally domestic organization would not. Such strategies could include Nabisco buying products (importing) from foreign companies or selling products (exporting) to foreign companies, selling the rights (license agreements) to a foreign company to manufacture and sell such products as Oreos, purchasing facilities (direct investing) in foreign countries, or entering a partnership (joint venture) with a foreign company to pursue some mutually desirable opportunity.

Regarding organizing a multinational corporation such as Nabisco, organization structure generally should be based on one or more of the important variables of function, product, territory, customers, or manufacturing process. Nabisco managers must consider all of the variables within the situations that confront them and then design the organization structure that is most appropriate for those situations.

Over the long term, management at Nabisco should try to select for multinational positions the managers who possess geocentric attitudes, as opposed to polycentric or ethnocentric attitudes. Such managers would tend to build operating units in, say, France and the United Kingdom that would use the best human resources available and be highly committed to the attainment of organizational objectives.

Influencing People in Multinational Corporations

Influencing was defined in chapter 12 as guiding the activities of organization members in appropriate directions through such activities as communicating, leading, motivating, and managing groups. Influencing people in a multinational corporation, however, is more complex and challenging than in a domestic organization.

The factor that probably contributes most to this increased complexity and challenge is culture. **Culture** is the total characteristics of a given group of people and their environment. Factors generally designated as important components of a culture include customs, beliefs, attitudes, habits, skills, state of technology, level of education, and religion. As a manager moves from a domestic corporation involving basically one culture to a multinational corporation involving several, the task of influencing usually becomes progressively more difficult.

To successfully influence people, managers in multinational corporations should:

Influencing within multinational corporations is more complex because of culture.

Multinational managers should:

1. Understand the languages.

2. Understand the attitudes.

3. Understand the personal needs.

1. *Acquire a working knowledge of the languages used in countries that house foreign operations* Multinational managers attempting to operate without such knowledge are prone to making costly mistakes. For example, one American company was shaken when it discovered that the Spanish brand name of the well-known cooking oil it had just introduced in Latin America translated as "jackass oil."[19] Naturally, such a mistake could have been avoided if the management of this organization had had a working knowledge of the Spanish language.

2. *Understand the attitudes of people in countries that house foreign operations* An understanding of these attitudes can help managers design business practices that are suitable for unique foreign situations. For example, Americans generally accept competition as a tool to encourage people to work harder. As a result, U.S. business practices that include some competitive aspects seldom create significant disruption within organizations. Such practices, however, could cause disruption if introduced in either Japan or the typical European country. Table 20.6 compares the American, European, and Japanese attitudes toward competition in more detail.

3. *Understand the needs that motivate people in countries housing foreign operations* For managers in multinational corporations to be successful in motivating people in different countries, they must present these individuals with the opportunity to satisfy personal needs while being productive within the organization. In designing motivation strategies, multinational managers must understand that people in different countries often have different personal needs. For example, people in Switzerland, Austria, Japan, and Argentina tend to have high security needs, whereas people in Denmark, Sweden, and Norway tend to have high social needs. People in Great Britain, the United States, Canada, New Zealand, and Australia tend to have high self-actualization needs.[20] Thus, to be successful at influencing, multinational managers must understand their employees' needs and mold such organizational components as incentive systems, job design, and leadership style to correspond to these needs.

Controlling Multinational Corporations

Controlling was defined in chapter 16 as making something happen the way it was planned to happen. As with domestic corporations, control in multinational corporations requires that standards be set, performance be measured and compared to standards, and corrective action be taken if necessary. In addition, control in such areas as labor costs, product quality, and inventory is important to organizational success regardless of whether the organization is domestic or international.

Controlling in multinational corporations is complicated by different currencies.

It is also complicated by geographical separation.

Control of a multinational corporation, however, has additional complexities. First, there is the problem of difficult currencies. Management must decide how to compare profit generated by organizational units located in different countries and therefore expressed in terms of different currencies.

Another complication is that organizational units in multinational corporations are generally more geographically separated. This increased distance normally makes it difficult for multinational managers to keep a close watch on operations in foreign countries. For example, physical distance certainly contributed to the adverse publicity PepsiCo received when an employee in Pepsi's overseas bottling branch blew the whistle on an elaborate scam that had puffed

TABLE 20.6

Comparison of American, European, and Japanese viewpoints on competition

Competition	Typical American Viewpoints	Typical European Viewpoints	Typical Japanese Viewpoints
Nature of competition	Competition is a strong moral force; it contributes to character building.	Competition is neither good nor bad.	There is conflict inherent in nature. To overcome conflicts, individuals must compete; but our final goal is harmony with nature and other human beings.
Business competition compared	Business competition is like a big sport game.	Business competition affects the livelihood of people and quickly develops into warfare.	The company is like a family. Competition has no place in a family. Aggressive action against competitors in the marketplace is for the survival and growth of the company.
Motivation	One cannot rely on an employee's motivation unless extra monetary inducements for hard work are offered in addition to a base salary or wage.	A key employee is motivated by the fact that he or she has been hired by the company.	Same as the European viewpoint.
Reward system	Money talks. A person is evaluated on the basis of his or her image (contribution) to the company. High tipping in best hotels, restaurants, etc., is expected.	An adequate salary, fringe benefits, opportunities for promotion, but no extra incentives—except in sales. Very little tipping (service charge is included in added-value tax).	Same as the European viewpoint.
Excessive competition	Competition must be tough for the sake of the general welfare of society. No upper limit on the intensity and amount of competition is desirable.	Too much competition is destructive and is in conflict with brotherly love and the Christian ethic.	Excessive competition is destructive and can create hatred. Only restrained competition leads to harmony and benefits society.
Hiring policy	Aggressive individuals who enjoy competition are ideal employees. Individuals who avoid competition are unfit for life and company work.	Diversity of opinion. How competitiveness or aggressive behavior of an individual is viewed varies with national ideology and the type of work. In England, it is not a recommendation to describe a job applicant as being aggressive.	Individuals are hired usually not for specific jobs but on the basis of their personality traits and their ability to become honorable company members. Team play and group consensus are stressed.

up unit profits for several previous years. Using stacks of false documents, finance staffers in the Philippines and Mexico had overstated assets and profits and deferred expenses. As a result, PepsiCo's financial position was overstated by $224 million.[21]

BACK TO THE CASE

Influencing people at Nabisco Brands must be a complicated process. The cultures of people in Italy, France, the United Kingdom, and Latin America, as well as the United States, must be thoroughly understood. Nabisco managers of foreign operations must have a working knowledge of the languages spoken in the country and an understanding of the attitudes and personal needs that motivate individuals within the foreign work force. If motivation strategy is to be successful for Nabisco as a whole, rewards used to motivate Latin American workers may need to be much different from rewards used to motivate United Kingdom workers.

The control process at Nabisco should involve standards, measurements, and needed corrective action just as it should within a domestic company. The different currencies used in France, Italy, the United States, the United Kingdom, and Latin America, however, tend to make control more complicated for Nabisco than for a domestic organization. The significant distance of all of the other countries from the United States also tends to complicate control at Nabisco.

COMPARATIVE MANAGEMENT: AN EMPHASIS ON JAPANESE MANAGEMENT

Perhaps the most popular international management topic today is comparative management. The sections that follow define *comparative management* and provide insights on Japanese management practices that can be of value to U.S. managers.

Defining Comparative Management

Comparative management is studying management in other countries.

Comparative management is the study of the management process in different countries to examine the potential of management action under different environmental conditions. Whereas international management focuses on management activities across national borders,[22] comparative management analyzes management practices in one country for their possible application in another country.[23]

The sections that follow discuss motivation and management practice insights that were formulated by analysis of Japanese management methods. These insights currently are being applied by many U.S. managers.

Insights from Japanese Motivation Strategies

The one country that is being studied the most from a comparative management viewpoint is Japan, and knowledge of the overall success of today's Japanese managers is widespread.[24] Perhaps the most analyzed area of this success deals with how Japanese managers effectively motivate organization members. So successful are the Japanese in this area that Americans are traveling to Japan to try to gain insights on Japanese motivation strategies.[25]

Japanese managers motivate by:

Japanese managers seem to be able to motivate their organization members by:

1. *Hiring employees for life rather than for some shorter period of time* A close relationship between workers and the organization is built through this lifetime employment. Since workers know that they have a guaranteed job and that their future is therefore heavily influenced by the future of the organization, they are willing to be flexible and cooperative.[26]

1. Hiring for life.

2. *Elevating employees to a level of organizational status equal to that of management* In Japanese factories, employees at all levels wear the same work clothes, eat in the same cafeteria, and use the same restrooms.[27]

2. Treating everyone equally.

3. *Making employees feel that they are highly valued by management and that the organization will provide for their material needs.*[28] New workers and their relatives attend a ceremony at which the company president welcomes them to the firm. The newcomers often live in company-built housing for several years until they can afford to buy their own housing. Also, much employee life outside work is spent in company social clubs, with weddings and receptions often being held in company facilities. Some Japanese companies even help pay for wedding expenses.

3. Making employees feel valued and secure.

Japanese managers obviously go to great lengths to build positive working relationships with their employees. In addition, there is some evidence that similar actions have been applied successfully by Japanese managers in motivating American employees at the Sony plant in San Diego.[29] Since the general Japanese culture has been shown to be a significant factor influencing the success of Japanese management,[30] however, managers of other countries should imitate Japanese actions with extreme caution.[31] After all, what Japanese workers find desirable or need-satisfying may not be the same as what workers from other countries find desirable or need-satisfying.[32]

Imitating Japanese management in other countries could backfire.

The "Management in Action" feature for this chapter highlights the training that Americans are undergoing in Hofu, Japan, as employees of Mazda, the third largest Japanese automaker. Mazda trainers seem very aware that their culture is an important factor influencing the success of Japanese management methods. As a result, they spend time attempting to change certain ingrained American attitudes in order to make them more consistent with Japanese culture and more instrumental in ensuring the success of Japanese management methods.

Insights from Japanese Management Practices: Theory Z

Given the success of organizations such as Nissan and Sanyo, many U.S. management writers have been carefully analyzing Japanese organizations and comparing them to American organizations. The purpose is to make recommendations about how Japanese management practices can be used to improve the operation of American organizations.

One such recommendation, called Theory Z, was introduced by William Ouchi in 1981.[33] **Theory Z** suggests that significant management practices in the United States and Japan be combined into one middle-ground, improved framework. Ouchi studied the following management practices in American and Japanese organizations: (1) the length of time workers were employed, (2) the way decisions were made, (3) where responsibility existed, (4) the rate at which employees were evaluated and promoted, (5) the type of control tools used, (6) the

Ouchi proposed Theory Z, which integrates U.S. and Japanese management practices.

TRAINING AT MAZDA FOCUSES ON AMERICAN CULTURE

After a hard day at the auto plant last week, Mark Daniel and his co-workers played a couple of games of softball, then went out for pizza and a few beers. But the scene was not Detroit or any other American factory town. Instead, the unlikely site of Daniel's work and play was Hofu (pop. 120,000), a city 56 miles southwest of Hiroshima in Japan. Daniel, along with 47 other Americans who work for the U.S. subsidiary of Mazda, the third largest Japanese automaker, was finishing up a four-week stint at the firm's Hofu assembly plant. Their goal: to learn how to build cars the Japanese way. Said Daniel, a Michigan native whose father and grandfather worked for General Motors: "I'm the first member of my family to go foreign."

Mazda will be bringing hundreds of American workers, most of them supervisors, to Hofu in preparation for [the 1987] opening of its first U.S. factory, an assembly plant in Flat Rock, Mich. Much like the fictional Assan Motors in the . . . Michael Keaton movie *Gung Ho,* Mazda bought a closed-down factory from Ford, which owns 25% of the Japanese company, and is building a new $450 million facility on the site. It is Mazda's largest single investment ever, and the Japanese are sparing no effort to ensure the factory's success.

Labor-management relations will be especially delicate. As Mazda fills the 3,500 jobs at the new facility, the company has been giving preference to laid-off Ford workers, most of whom are members of the United Auto Workers. The U.A.W., which has saluted Mazda's Hofu training program as part of an "enlightened approach" to operating in the U.S., intends to organize the entire Flat Rock work force. That would create the closest partnership yet between a Japanese car company and an American union. Although Toyota's joint car-building venture with General Motors in Fremont, Calif., employes U.A.W. members, the union does not deal directly with the Japanese firm. Both Honda and Nissan use nonunion labor in their American plants.

In Japan last week, Mazda's new American employees were learning things they never heard much about at the union hall. In particular, they were lectured about the Japanese tradition of *kaizen,* meaning a worker's commitment to finding ways to do his job better and more efficiently. On the Hofu assembly line, a group of Americans clutching stopwatches and clipboards hovered around Kazuyuki Toda, a Japanese worker, as he demonstrated how to do a job poorly, with too much *muda,* or wasted motion. The Americans were then asked to suggest ways of doing the job faster. Their ideas ranged from simple improvements, like grabbing a handful of bolts at once instead of stepping back to the bolt tray after using each one, to the installation of a moving parts tray, which would save even more time. The object of Mazda's training program, said its supervisor, Keishi Motoyama, is to erase the "traditional American separation between the planner and the person responsible for doing a job."

Mazda officials praised their American students for being hardworking and eager to learn but noted that some ingrained attitudes needed changing. Said Motoyama: "The Americans don't seem to be very good at deciding things in groups. Each individual has a very strong opinion of his own. They have to learn to step back and accept other ideas."

After a month of training in Mazda's factory methods, whipping their new Japanese buddies at softball and sampling local wateringholes, the Americans were fired up. "It's the cleanest assembly plant I've ever seen," marveled Douglas Goodman, who worked for Chrysler for 22 years before moving to Mazda as Flat Rock's maintenance manager. Goodman even faintly praised the Japanese practice of holding group calisthenics at the start of each working day: "I didn't think I'd like doing exercises every morning, but I kind of like it."

"I'm really impressed with how hard people work and how genuinely concerned the company seems about human beings," said Daniel. Nonetheless, he added, "taking what we're learning here into America won't be easy. As supervisors we're going to have to ask workers to grab their lunch pails and come spend part of their lunch hour sitting around a table talking about quality." Still, employees might be willing to do that for supervisors like Brad Stiving, a former GM production supervisor and Hertz manager. Displaying a couple of nasty blisters acquired while helping to install weather stripping around Mazda trucks at Hofu, Stiving boasted, "You won't find managers getting blisters on their fingers in the States."

degree to which employees had specialized career paths, and (7) the type of concern organizations showed for employees. Figure 20.5 summarizes Ouchi's findings about how management practices differ in American and Japanese organizations.

In addition, the figure contains Ouchi's suggestions for how to integrate American and Japanese management practices to develop a new, more successful American organization, called a Type Z organization. According to Ouchi, the Type Z organization is characterized by the "individual responsibility" of American organizations as well as the "collective decision making, slow evaluation and promotion, and holistic concern for employees" of Japanese organizations. The length of employment, control, and career path characteristics of the Type Z organization are essentially compromises between American and Japanese organizations.

In a very short time, Ouchi's Theory Z concept gained popularity not only among management theoreticians but also among practicing managers. Anecdotes abound about how the application of Theory Z principles has aided managers in such organizations as Chrysler and Mead Merchants.[34] However, some question has arisen regarding the quality of Ouchi's research methods,[35] and the validity of his Theory Z conclusions has been questioned. Much more investigation is needed before Ouchi's Theory Z can be conclusively evaluated.

The Type Z organization combines American and Japanese management practices.

Theory Z is popular, but Ouchi's research methods are being questioned.

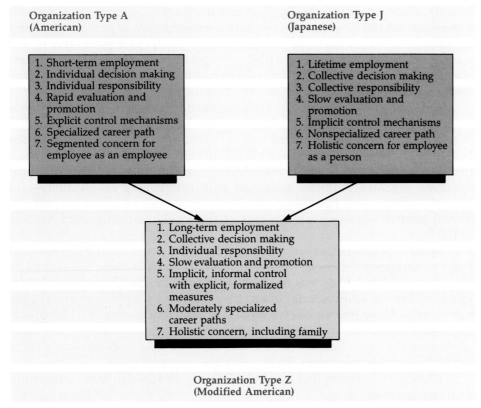

Organization Type A
(American)

1. Short-term employment
2. Individual decision making
3. Individual responsibility
4. Rapid evaluation and promotion
5. Explicit control mechanisms
6. Specialized career path
7. Segmented concern for employee as an employee

Organization Type J
(Japanese)

1. Lifetime employment
2. Collective decision making
3. Collective responsibility
4. Slow evaluation and promotion
5. Implicit control mechanisms
6. Nonspecialized career path
7. Holistic concern for employee as a person

1. Long-term employment
2. Collective decision making
3. Individual responsibility
4. Slow evaluation and promotion
5. Implicit, informal control with explicit, formalized measures
6. Moderately specialized career paths
7. Holistic concern, including family

Organization Type Z
(Modified American)

FIGURE 20.5
Combining significant American and Japanese management practices to form the Type Z organization

Insights from Japanese Manufacturing: Just-in-Time Inventory Control

JIT reduces inventory to a minimum.

The previous two sections focused on improving U.S. companies through the use of Japanese motivation strategies and management practices. This section focuses on improving U.S. companies through the use of **just-in-time (JIT) inventory control,** the inventory control technique that reduces inventories to a minimum by arranging for them to be delivered to the production facility "just in time" to be used. The concept, developed primarily by the Toyota Motor Company of Japan,[36] is also called "zero inventory" and "kanban"—the latter a Japanese term referring to purchasing raw materials by using a special card ordering form.

JIT is based on the management philosophy that products should be manufactured when customers need them and in the quantities customers need them in order to minimize levels of raw materials and finished goods inventories kept on hand.[37] It is sometimes considered a component of materials requirements planning (MRP). The discussion of MRP, which appears in chapter 17, will provide a more complete understanding of JIT and its potential role in organizations. Over all, JIT emphasizes maintaining operations within a company by using only the resources that are absolutely necessary to meet customer demand.

JIT is most suitable for companies with standardized products and consistent demand for them.

JIT works best in companies that manufacture relatively standardized products and that have consistent product demand. Such companies can comfortably order materials from suppliers and assemble products in several small, continuous batches. The result is a smooth, consistent flow of purchased materials and assembled products and little inventory buildup. Companies that manufacture nonstandardized products that have sporadic or seasonal demand generally must face more irregular purchases of raw materials from suppliers, more uneven production cycles, and greater accumulations of inventory.

JIT can enhance organizational performance.

If implemented successfully, JIT can enhance organizational performance in several important ways. First, it can reduce unnecessary labor expenses generated by products manufactured but not sold. Second, it can minimize the tying up of monetary resources needed to purchase production related materials that do not result in sales on a timely basis.[38] Third, it can help management minimize expenses normally associated with maintaining an inventory—for example, storage and handling costs. Better inventory management and improved control of labor costs are two of the most commonly cited benefits of JIT.[39]

Many U.S. businesses are adopting JIT as a means of improving organizational performance.[40] General Motors has used JIT since 1980 and has slashed its annual inventory related costs from $8 billion to $2 billion. One American Motors plant has cut its inventories to less than one day's supply, compared to the more usual six-day reserve. Recent reports indicate that the use of JIT is spreading from the automotive industry to other industries—for example, the small appliances industry. General Electric and RCA are two small appliance firms seriously experimenting with JIT.[41]

Four common characteristics of JIT programs are:

Experience indicates that successful JIT programs tend to have certain common characteristics:[42]

1. Short distances.

1. *Closeness of suppliers* Manufacturers using JIT find it beneficial to have suppliers of raw materials within short distances of them. As companies begin to order smaller quantities of raw materials, suppliers sometimes must be asked

to make one or more deliveries per day. Short distances make multiple deliveries per day feasible.

2. *High quality of materials purchased from suppliers* Manufacturers using JIT find it difficult to overcome problems caused by defective materials purchased from suppliers. Since the materials inventory is kept small, defective materials may mean that the manufacturer must wait until the next delivery from the supplier before the production process can continue. Such production slowdowns can be disadvantageous, causing late delivery to customers or lost sales because finished products are unavailable.

2. Avoidance of defective materials.

3. *Well-organized receiving and handling of materials purchased from suppliers* Companies using JIT must be able to receive and handle raw materials effectively and efficiently. Such materials must be available for the production process where and when they are needed. Naturally, if the materials are not available, extra costs are built into the production process.

3. Well-organized receiving and handling of materials.

4. *Strong management commitment* Management must be strongly committed to the concept of JIT. The system takes time and effort to plan, install, and improve—and is therefore expensive to implement. Management must be willing to commit funds to initiate the JIT system and to support it once it is functioning.

4. Management commitment.

BACK TO THE CASE

Managers at Nabisco Brands undoubtedly are involved with comparative management. In this regard, they study the management practices in foreign operations for the purpose of applying them to improve operations at Nabisco. Company managers probably take a number of trips annually to see firsthand how foreign operations are run.

One comparative management insight that Nabisco managers might want to consider applying within their company involves Japanese motivation strategies. Japanese managers seem to be very successful in motivating their workers by implementing such strategies as elevating the workers to the same status as managers and making workers believe that the organization will provide for their material needs. Since the Japanese culture is much different than the French, Italian, United Kingdom, Latin American, and U.S. cultures with which Nabisco deals, however, Nabisco managers should be careful in applying Japanese methods to workers in other countries.

Another comparative management insight that could be valuable to Nabisco managers is Theory Z, which suggests a blend of American and Japanese management practices. With Theory Z, Nabisco managers could make their company more successful by implementing such strategies as hiring employees for the long term and having only moderately specialized career paths for workers. If Theory Z is to be implemented in a non-Japanese company, however, the worth and impact of the concept should be carefully monitored. More research is needed to test Theory Z's true worth.

JIT, another Japanese concept, could prove to be a valuable inventory control method for Nabisco. Keeping inventory to a minimum by ordering materials from suppliers only as they are needed for production could significantly enhance organizational performance. Minimizing storage and handling costs related to inventories and engaging only the organizational resources needed to meet customer needs are advantages that Nabisco could gain by using JIT.

Action Summary

Reread the learning objectives that follow. Each objective is followed by questions. Answering these questions accurately will help you retain the most important concepts discussed in this chapter. After answering each question, check your answer with the answer key at the end of this chapter. (*Hint:* If you have doubt regarding the correct response, consult the page whose number follows the answer.)

Circle:

From studying this chapter, I will attempt to acquire:

1. **An understanding of international management and its importance to modern managers.**

T, F,
   a. To reach organizational objectives, management may extend its activities to include an emphasis on organizations in foreign countries.

a, b, c, d, e
   b. It has been estimated that by 1995 the investments in foreign countries made by U.S. companies will be: (a) $275 billion; (b) $213 billion; (c) $124 billion; (d) $75 billion; (e) none of the above.

2. **An understanding of what constitutes a multinational corporation.**

a, b, c, d, e
   a. According to Jacoby, which of the following is the first stage in a corporation's multinationalization: (a) multinationalizes ownership of corporate stock; (b) multinationalizes management from top to bottom; (c) establishes foreign manufacturing facilities; (d) establishes sales organizations abroad; (e) exports its products.

T, F
   b. In general, the smaller the organization, the greater the likelihood that it participates in international operations of some sort.

3. **Insights concerning the risk involved in investing in international operations.**

a, b, c, d, e
   a. Which of the following factors affect the risk of an organization doing business in a foreign country: (a) economic factors; (b) political factors; (c) social factors; (d) a and b; (e) a, b, and c.

T, F
   b. Before a company does business in a foreign country, some managers think it should check the country's BERI rating, its BI rating, and its WPRF rating.

4. **Knowledge about planning and organizing in multinational corporations.**

T, F
   a. The primary difference between planning in multinational versus domestic organizations probably involves operational planning.

a, b, c, d, e
   b. The feeling that multinational corporations should regard home country management practices as superior to foreign country practices is known as which of the following attitudes: (a) egocentric attitude; (b) ethnocentric attitude; (c) polycentric attitude; (d) geocentric attitude; (e) isocentric attitude.

5. **Knowledge about influencing and controlling in multinational corporations.**

a, b, c, d, e
   a. The factor that probably contributes most to the increased complexity and challenge of influencing in multinational organizations is: (a) language; (b) attitudes; (c) personal needs; (d) culture; (e) none of the above.

T, F
   b. Different currencies and distance are the two major contributors to the difficulty of controlling in multinational corporations.

6. **Insights about what comparative management is and how it might help managers do their jobs better.**

T, F
   a. Comparative management emphasizes analyzing management practices in one country to determine how to best counteract the effectiveness of a foreign competitor.

a, b, c, d, e
   b. A group of American autoworkers visiting a Toyota plant in Japan to gather ideas that can be applied in their plant back home is an example of: (a) industrial sabotage; (b) comparative management; (c) kibutshi; (d) foreign intervention; (e) none of the above.

7. **Ideas on how to be a better manager through the study of Japanese management techniques.**

   a. Since the Japanese have been so successful and there is little relationship between their culture and their success, American management would be wise to immediately implement the Japanese techniques.   T, F

   b. Which of the following is *not* one of the significant management practices that Ouchi studied in American and Japanese organizations: (a) the length of time workers were employed; (b) the way in which decisions were made; (c) the type of incentive plan used; (d) where responsibility existed within the organization; (e) the rate at which employees were evaluated and promoted.   a, b, c, d, e

   c. JIT emphasizes the improvement of organizational performance primarily through more accurate sales forecasts.   T, F

▮ INTRODUCTORY CASE WRAP-UP

"Nabisco Brands in the International Arena" (p. 570) and its related back-to-the case sections were written to help you better understand the management concepts contained in this chapter. Answer the following discussion questions about this introductory case to further enrich your understanding of chapter content:

1. Do you think that at some point in your career you will become involved in international management? Explain.

2. Assuming that you become involved in international management, what challenges do you think will be the most difficult for you to meet? Why?

3. Evaluate the following statement: We can learn to manage our organizations better by studying how successful managers in other countries run their organizations.

Issues for Review and Discussion

1. Define *international management.*
2. How significant is the topic of international management to the modern manager? Explain fully.
3. What is meant by the term *multinational corporation?*
4. List and explain four factors that contribute to the complexity of managing multinational corporations.
5. Should managers be careful in making investments in foreign operations? Explain.
6. List and define four areas in which managers can develop internationally oriented strategies.
7. What is the difference between direct investing and joint ventures at the international level?
8. Draw segments of organization charts that organize a multinational corporation on the basis of product, function, and customers.
9. Is there one best way to organize all multinational corporations? Explain fully.
10. What are the differences between ethnocentric, polycentric, and geocentric attitudes? Describe advantages and disadvantages of each.
11. How does culture affect the international management process?
12. Discuss three suggestions that would be helpful to a manager attempting to influence organization members in different countries.
13. How does geographic distance relate to controlling multinational corporations?
14. How can comparative management help managers of today?
15. What insights can be learned from Japanese

managers about ways to motivate people? Should caution be exercised by a Canadian manager in applying these insights? Explain.

16. Discuss what is meant by Theory Z. How much value should a manager place on the Theory Z concept? Explain.

17. What is JIT, and how can it improve organizational performance?

Sources of Additional Information

Berenbeim, Ronald. *Managing the International Company: Build a Global Perspective.* New York: Conference Board, 1982.

Bylinsky, Gene. "America's Best-Managed Factories." *Fortune,* May 1984, 16–24.

Frame, J. Davidson. *International Business and Global Technology.* Lexington, Mass.: D. C. Heath, 1983.

Garvin, David A. "Quality Problems, Policies, and Attitudes in the United States and Japan: An Exploratory Study." *Academy of Management Journal* 29 (December 1986): 653–73.

Goehle, Donna A. *Decision Making in Multinational Corporations.* Ann Arbor: University of Michigan Research Press, 1980.

Gregory, Gene. "The Japanese Enterprise: Sources of Competitive Strength." *Business and Society* 24 (Spring 1985): 13–21.

Herbert, Theodore T. "Strategy and Multinational Organization Structure: An Interorganizational Perspective." *Academy of Management Review* 9, no. 2 (1984): 259–71.

Keys, J. Bernard, and Thomas R. Miller. "The Japanese Management Theory Jungle." *Academy of Management Review* 9, no. 2 (1984): 342–53.

Marr, Norman E. "Impact of Customer Service in International Markets." *International Journal of Physical Distribution and Materials Management* 14, no. 1 (1984): 33–40.

Negandhi, Anant R. *International Management.* Boston: Allyn and Bacon, 1987.

Scott, Bruce R. "National Strategies for Stronger U.S. Competitiveness." *Harvard Business Review* (March/April 1984): 77–91.

Sloan, Michael P. "Strategic Planning by Multiple Political Futures Techniques." *Management International Review* 24, no. 1 (1984): 4–17.

Tung, Rosalie L. "Selection and Training Procedures of U.S., European, and Japanese Multinationals." *California Management Review* 25 (Fall 1982): 57–71.

Tyson, Laura, and John Zysman. *American Industry and International Competition: Government Policies and Corporate Strategies.* Ithaca, N.Y.: Cornell University Press, 1983.

Vlachoutsicos, Charalambos A. "Where the Ruble Stops in Soviet Trade." *Harvard Business Review* (September/October 1986): 82–86.

Notes

1. W. J. Abernathy, K. B. Clark, and A. M. Kantrow, "The New Industrial Competition," *Harvard Business Review* (September/October 1981): 68–81.

2. Lee Smith, "Japan Hustles for Foreign Investment," *Fortune,* May 28, 1984, 163.

3. "Trying to Copy Past Success," *Economist,* February 6, 1982, 70.

4. Ben J. Wattenberg, "Their Deepest Concerns," *Business Month* (January 1988): 27–33.

5. American Assembly of Collegiate Schools of Business, *Accreditation Council Policies, Procedures, and Standards, 1980–1981.* St. Louis, Mo.; Sylvia Nasar, "America's Competitive Revival," *Fortune,* January 4, 1988, 44–52.

6. J. Behrman, *Some Patterns in the Rise of the Multinational Enterprise* (Chapel Hill: University of North Carolina Press, 1969).

7. U.S. Department of Commerce, *The Multinational Corporation: Studies on U.S. Foreign Investment,* vol. 1 (Washington, D.C.: Government Printing Office).

8. Robert W. Stevens, "Scanning the Multinational Firm," *Business Horizons* 14 (June 1971): 53.

9. Neil H. Jacoby, "The Multinational Corporation," *Center Magazine* 3 (May 1970): 37–55.

10. Grover Starling, *The Changing Environment of Business* (Boston: Kent, 1980), 140.

11. This section is based primarily on Richard D. Robinson, *International Management* (New York: Holt, Rinehart & Winston, 1967), 3–5.

12. 1971 Survey of National Foreign Trade Council, cited in Frederick D. Sturdivant, *Business and Society: A Managerial Approach* (Homewood, Ill.: Richard D. Irwin, 1977), 425.

13. "The Bug Comes Back," *Newsweek,* April 4, 1983, 60.

14. Karen Paul, "Fading Images at Eastman Kodak," *Business and Society Review* 48 (Winter 1984): 56.

15. "The Mattress Maker That Woke Up Wall Street," *Fortune,* August 20, 1984, 37.

16. Joan Servaas Marie, "Robinson Nugent, Inc.: Working Smarter, Not Harder," *Indiana Business* (June 1983): 4–7.

17. Peter J. Mullins, "Survival through Joint Ventures," *Automotive Industries* (May 1983): 17–18.

18. Howard V. Perlmutter, "The Tortuous Evolution of the Multinational Corporation," *Columbia Journal of World Business* (January/February 1969): 9–18.

19. John S. Hill and Richard R. Still, "Adapting Products to LDC Tastes," *Harvard Business Review* (March/April 1984): 92.

20. Geert Hofstede, "Motivation, Leadership, and Organization: Do American Theories Apply Abroad?" *Organizational Dynamics* 9 (Summer 1980): 42–63.

21. Anne B. Fisher, "Peering Past Pepsico's Bad News," *Fortune,* November 14, 1983, 124.

22. R. N. Farmer, "International Management," in *Contemporary Management Issues and Viewpoints,* ed. J. W. McGuire (Englewood Cliffs, N.J.: Prentice-Hall, 1974), 302.

23. Frank Ching, "China's Managers Get U.S. Lessons," *Wall Street Journal,* January 23, 1981, 27.

24. Peter F. Drucker, "Behind Japan's Success," *Harvard Business Review* (January/February 1981): 83–90.

25. "How Japan Does It," *Time,* March 30, 1981, 55.

26. Charles McMillan, "Is Japanese Management Really So Different?" *Business Quarterly* (Autumn 1980): 26–31.

27. Masaru Ibuka, "Management Opinion," *Administrative Management* (May 5, 1980): 86.

28. "How Japan Does It."

29. "Consensus in San Diego," *Time,* March 30, 1981, 58.

30. Lane Kelly and Reginald Worthley, "The Role of Culture in Comparative Management," *Academy of Management Journal* 24, no. 1 (1981): 164–73.

31. Linda S. Dillon, "Adopting Japanese Management: Some Cultural Stumbling Blocks," *Personnel* (July/August 1983): 73–77.

32. Isaac Shapiro, "Second Thoughts about Japan," *Wall Street Journal,* June 5, 1981.

33. William Ouchi, *Theory Z* (Reading, Mass.: Addison-Wesley, 1981).

34. Charles W. Joiner, "One Manager's Story of How He Made the Theory Z Concept Work," *Management Review* (May 1983): 48–53.

35. William Bowen, "Lessons from behind the Kimono," *Fortune,* June 15, 1981, 247–50.

36. Lee J. Krajewski and Larry P. Ritzman, *Operations Management: Strategy and Analysis* (Reading, Mass.: Addison-Wesley, 1987), 573.

37. Krajewski and Ritzman, *Operations Management,* 572–84.

38. A. Ansari and Modarress Batoul, "Just-in-Time Purchasing: Problems and Solutions," *Journal of Purchasing and Materials Management* (August 1986): 11–15.

39. Albert F. Celley, William H. Clegg, Arthur W. Smith, and Mark A. Vonderembse, "Implementation of JIT in the United States," *Journal of Purchasing and Materials Management* (Winter 1987): 9–15.

40. Jack R. Meredith, *The Management of Operations,* 3d ed. (New York: Wiley, 1987), 391–92.

41. Information about companies that have adopted JIT methods appears in Sumer C. Aggarwal, "MRP, JIT, OPT, FMS?" *Harvard Business Review* (September/October 1985): 8–16.

42. John D. Baxter, "Kanban Works Wonders, but Will It Work in U.S. Industry?" *Iron Age,* June 7, 1982, 44–48.

Action Summary Answer Key

1. a. T, p. 571
   b. a, p. 572
2. a. e, pp. 573–574
   b. F, p. 574

3. a. e, p. 577
   b. T, pp. 577–578
4. a. F, p. 579
   b. b, pp. 581–582

5. a. d, p. 583
   b. T, pp. 584–585
6. a. F, p. 586
   b. b, p. 586

7. a. F, p. 587
   b. c, pp. 587–589
   c. F, p. 590

TENNESSEE WORKERS ADOPT JAPANESE WAYS AT NEW NISSAN PLANT

At Nissan's new light truck plant in Smyrna, Tennessee, all the employees are on a first-name basis. They can't really help but be, since all have their names embroidered on their uniform shirts and hats. Even Marvin Runyon has "Marvin" boldly stitched over the pocket of his white dress shirt. Who is this Marvin? Oh, just the company president. Nissan officials and now Runyon believe strongly that the first-name basis helps create a familial atmosphere and a level of politeness conducive to high performance.

In the sprawling complex, with sixty-nine acres under one roof, work team decisions are made by consensus, cursing is seldom heard, supervisors cheerfully substitute for ill employees, and line workers consult with vice-presidents on suggestions.

"I've never had a harsh word voiced to me from anyone here," states thirty-year-old Bobby Sims, a Nashville commuter who works in the production training program. "I can ask something here, and I can get an answer," comments Alan Jakes, twenty-seven, a Nissan production technician. "That really helps. That way you think someone cares." The production technician position at Nissan is the same as the assembly-line worker position in Detroit plants.

The bosses at the plant, from former Ford executive Marvin Runyon down through the plant's five management levels, are determined to preserve the positive climate that exists by applying participatory management, by encouraging employee initiative, by using new production techniques that give the dirty and most monotonous work to robots, and by screening job applicants (there were eighty thousand) for their ability to work in a team. Applicants then audition for jobs by putting themselves through unpaid training programs held on evenings and weekends.

Runyon has indicated that the Nissan approach is a "better way of doing business." Nissan sent 383 production employees and supervisors to Japan for firsthand observations of teamwork, management techniques, and production processes. Management hoped to make each person feel a part of the "Nissan family." The production employees and supervisors visiting Japan were told to judge which Japanese techniques would work best at the Smyrna plant. One of their decisions was to wear the blue Nissan uniforms (provided free to workers). They also decided to adopt the Japanese idea of minimizing differences among executive, administrative, and production workers by having only

one cafeteria for all employees, including executives. But Japanese-style plant dormitories, a pay scale based on age and responsibility for aging parents and in-laws, a promotional system that requires employees to work twelve to fourteen years before being considered for managerial positions, and a lump-sum retirement payment instead of a pension were voted down.

The group also decided against a guarantee of a lifetime job for assembly-line workers. Nissan, however, continues to give strong signals that even though there is no guarantee, employees are working toward creating jobs for a lifetime. Nissan plans to preserve this assurance by avoiding large expansions or contractions and by contracting out as much in-plant work as possible. If jobs such as security and food service are contracted out, then when hard times come, subcontractors can be laid off and those jobs can be given to production employees. Although this is not a "set-in-concrete" guarantee, it is definitely an assurance that is unmatched in most manufacturing plants. "I may be a gate guard if times get bad enough," states Bob Creekbaum, forty, an electronics technician who is now training others. "That's a pretty nice little factor you can count on it you've got a mortgage to meet."

Line workers are trained in many skills so both they and management have more flexibility. Runyon believes that a multiskilled employee is happier than the specialist in Detroit. And Nissan is willing to pay more for the person who masters more skills.

Runyon also has adopted the Japanese approach to inspection. Except for the final inspection, or at one or two quality assurance stations between stamping, welding, and painting, the employees who do the work are their own inspectors. They also do their own tool and equipment maintenance. As Creekbaum testifies, "I love it, but it sure puts the monkey on your back. Now if a piece of work passes your station, it better be right."

Each day begins with team discussions. Suggestions for improvements are agreed upon by consensus and either implemented at the work station or routed to the appropriate supervisor. Staff meetings also are held, and questions for Runyon are submitted on three-by-five-inch cards.

One of the biggest, if not *the* biggest, difference between the Nissan plant and old-line Detroit plants is the absence of abusive language and humiliation. Chewing out the line workers for making a mistake is the way Dan Demara, operations manager of the stamping division, was brought up. "But I believe there's a better way," he states. Most at Nissan agree, however, that when one gets caught up in a system that works, the person can't get out and it becomes contagious.

"Here, they don't tell you, 'Hey, you screwed up!' They tell you, 'Hey, maybe the tool's not right,' or 'How about some more training?' " states Creekbaum. It's hard to find a Nissan worker on or off the plant grounds who does not express job satisfaction. And management would like to keep it that way.

DISCUSSION ISSUES

1. Should Nissan be categorized as a multinational corporation? Explain. Which stage of multinationalization? Explain.
2. Which attitude (ethnocentric, polycentric, or geocentric) does it appear that Nissan has adopted? Explain.
3. What action has Nissan taken to bring the Japanese corporate culture to Smyrna, Tennessee? Explain. What has Nissan done to incorporate American perspectives into the management of the Smyrna plant? Explain.
4. How closely does Nissan's approach to employee motivation match the Japanese motivation approaches mentioned in the chapter? Explain.

STUDENT LEARNING OBJECTIVES

From studying this chapter, I will attempt to acquire:

1. An understanding of how systems skill relates to management in the future.
2. Insights about how functional skill relates to management in the future.
3. An understanding of how situational analysis skill relates to management in the future.
4. A better understanding of the labor force of the future.
5. An appreciation for the impact of such factors as system size, energy, and technology on management in the future.
6. A practical strategy for training managers for the future.

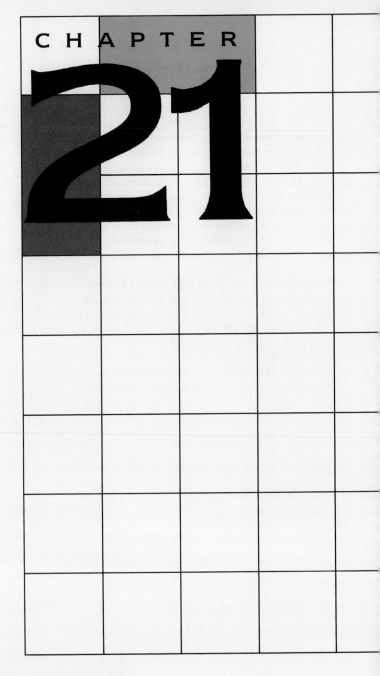

MANAGEMENT SKILLS FOR THE FUTURE

CHAPTER OUTLINE

WHAT ABOUT TOMORROW?

Max Barton was feeling a real sense of accomplishment. He had worked at the Pleasant Ridge Candy Company managing the molded chocolate candy department for twelve months and was just receiving a well-deserved compliment from his supervisor, Judy Shull.

Shull was telling Barton that his people had been very productive as a unit, having increased their output of molded candy by 12 percent over the past six months. She also mentioned that the department's efficiency was above average and that Barton's people seemed to identify with the company's goal of becoming the largest producer of chocolate candy on the West Coast during the next five years. Barton could only surmise from Shull's statements that, over all, he was doing an excellent job as department manager.

Shull's concluding statements, however, left Barton somewhat perplexed. Shull indicated that Barton certainly would have a good future with the Pleasant Ridge Candy Company if he decided to remain. This, of course, pleased Barton. What puzzled him was that, as Shull left, she turned around and advised him to prepare himself carefully for managing in the future.

Barton had never really thought about consciously and systematically trying to prepare himself for a management position later on. He was managing well today, but what about tomorrow? How would the company's

growth affect his department? How could technological advances change the production of molded candy? Would he be able to continue the efficiency and productivity of his department in the face of rising costs and greater company demands? After giving some thought to these issues, Barton concluded that Shull was right. He did need to plan carefully for the future as manager of the molded chocolate candy department. The question was: How?

What's Ahead

The introductory case ends with Max Barton, a relatively new department manager at the Pleasant Ridge Candy Company, thinking about conscientiously and systematically preparing himself to be a good manager in the future. This chapter gives managers such as Barton insights on what such preparation involves. More specifically, the chapter discusses various skills that managers of the future should possess and how a management system can train its present managers for the challenges they inevitably will face in the future.

⊞ ESSENTIAL SKILLS FOR FUTURE MANAGERS

Up to this point, the text has recommended that, to manage successfully, managers should apply both knowledge of systems theory and the four basic management functions to the unique management situations they face. However, will this recommendation change sometime in the future? The sections that follow attempt to answer this question by discussing (1) systems skill in the future, (2) functional skill in the future, and (3) situational analysis skill in the future.

Systems Skill in the Future

Systems skill is the ability to view and manage a business or some other concern as a number of components that work together and function as a whole to achieve some objective. In essence, the systems approach to management is a way of analyzing and solving managerial problems.[1] Managers analyze problems and implement solutions only after examining the system parts related to the problems and evaluating the effect of each solution on the functioning of all other system parts.[2]

> Systems skill involves seeing parts as a whole.

Frank T. Curtin, vice-president of machine tools at Cincinnati Milacron, has seen the value of applying the systems approach to management problems in the past and indicates that the systems approach will be an extremely valuable tool for managers of the future.[3] According to Curtin, only after managers understand the "big picture," or see all parts of a company as a whole, will they be able to solve managerial problems appropriately. For the systems approach to management to become more useful to businesses in the future, however, Curtin suggests that more individuals be formally educated in the value of this approach and shown the steps that can be taken to implement it.

Functional Skill in the Future

Functional skill is the ability to apply appropriately the concepts of planning, organizing, influencing, and controlling to the operation of a management system. The application of these four basic functions is of such vital concern to management that this text presents them as subsystems of the overall management system (Figure 21.1).

> Functional skill involves applying managerial functions to the operation of the management system.

601

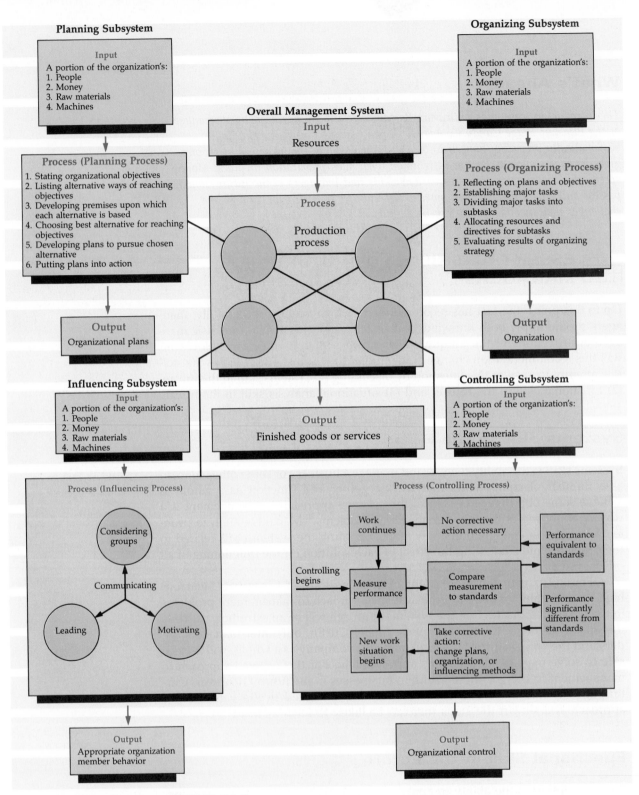

FIGURE 21.1
Relationships among the four major functional subsystems and the overall management system

The application of these four functions to managerial problems has long been suggested as sound management practice. In fact, the evolution of theory related to each of these functions has evolved over many decades as a result of insights contributed and accumulated by both management practitioners and management researchers. The probability is quite high, therefore, that functional skill will continue to be extremely valuable to managers of the future.

BACK TO THE CASE

Max Barton, in the introductory case, probably has achieved his present level of managerial success primarily by applying systems skill and functional skill to the fundamental aspects of his job at Pleasant Ridge. Systems skill enables Barton to see and manage all parts of his department as a group of components that function as a whole with other departments to help his company achieve its objectives. For example, Barton is able to understand how his department's increased productivity will affect the chocolate making and the packaging departments and how changes in these other departments will affect the company as a whole.

Functional skill enables Barton to successfully plan, organize, influence, and control the various components in his department. He is able to plan to produce more chocolate candy, and he can then implement his plan by organizing his work force, encouraging his people to produce, and controlling each part of his department to ensure that the department as a whole will be coordinated with other departments to obtain the company's goal of increased production.

Because these skills are so entrenched in management theory, a sound strategy for Barton in preparing himself for a future management position would be to continue developing his systems and functional skills.

Situational Analysis Skill in the Future

Situational analysis skill is the ability to apply both systems theory and functional theory to the particular situations managers face. This skill emphasizes that managers must thoroughly understand their own unique management situations before they can use systems and functional skills to their best advantage. Obviously, the importance of situational analysis skill is supported by the thoughts and ideas of the contingency approach to management.

Situational analysis skill probably will be extremely important to managers of the future. However, these managers almost certainly will face much different situational factors than either past or present managers[4]—for example, (1) the size of future management systems, (2) the characteristics of future management system members, (3) the amount of energy available to future management systems, and (4) the technology available to future management systems. The following sections discuss each of these future situational factors in more detail and offer strategies for dealing with them.

Situational analysis skill involves managers understanding their unique management situations.

Size of Management Systems of the Future

Generally speaking, a tendency exists in American society for successful businesses and other types of concerns to grow larger over time. As this trend continues into the future, managers of the future, as a group, probably will be faced with managing larger systems than have any other generations of managers.[5] Also, since growing management systems tend to become more difficult to man-

Situational factors of the future will be different.

age, managers of the future, as a group, probably also will be challenged by the most difficult to manage set of management systems that has ever existed. Specific characteristics of large management systems that tend to make the systems more difficult to manage include:

Large management systems are hard to manage because:

1. Comprehension of the overall system is difficult.

1. *A diminishing ability of individuals within the system to comprehend the overall system* As a system increases in size, fewer and fewer individuals within it are able to understand all system parts and the complicated relationships among those parts. Generating and disseminating information that adequately defines system parts and their relationships becomes a formidable but important task for managers of large management systems. One of the trends emerging to counter the problems created by size is stated by John Naisbitt in *Megatrends:* "We will restructure our business into smaller and smaller units, more entrepreneurial units, more participatory units."[6]

2. Fewer people participate in decision making.

2. *A diminishing level of participation in decision making* Over all, as management systems grow larger, managers tend to believe that large-group involvement in decision making becomes less and less feasible, and thus some system members are excluded from decision making. As a general guideline, even as management systems grow larger, managers should continue to try to raise the quality of their decisions by allowing other system members to participate in the making of decisions.[7]

3. Communication between top management and system members diminishes.

3. *A declining access of organization members to top decision makers within the system* As the number of system members increases, the proportion of those members who can communicate directly with upper management becomes smaller and smaller. If not overcome in some way—perhaps through special meetings of various kinds with system members—this characteristic of a large management system can put top management completely out of touch with its people.

4. Experts offer hard-to-understand advice.

4. *A growing involvement of experts in decision making within the system* As systems grow, they necessarily become more and more complex. As problem complexity related to those systems increases, managers tend to ask various kinds of experts for help in solving the problems. These experts can be of help, however, only if they can discuss specialized information in a way that managers can understand and apply. This can be, and often is, very challenging for experts. Managers, however, must do everything possible to ensure that experts meet this challenge.

5. The costs of running the system are high.

5. *Increasing costs of coordination and control* As management systems grow larger, more and more authority must be delegated to various system levels and segments. To maintain coordination and control, however, managers must establish adequate communication among the various levels and segments and establish effective plans to guide the segments. The cost of coordinating and controlling system segments never should exceed the contribution those segments can make to the system as a whole.

6. The system becomes less flexible.

6. *Increasing system rigidity* As systems grow in size, rules and regulations must be established so new system segments will operate in a predetermined and predictable fashion. Managers must recognize, however, that too many rules and regulations create a rigid and inflexible system. Large systems should have enough regulations to ensure order but not so many that flexibility and creativity in solving unique management system problems become nonexistent.

7. The system's weaknesses go undetected.

7. *A growing deterioration of the overall system* The point was made earlier that as management systems grow larger, fewer and fewer system members are able

to understand them fully. As a result of this lack of understanding, the deterioration of various segments of the systems will likely go unnoticed and therefore will remain uncorrected. Managers of growing management systems must take steps to ensure that such deterioration is noticed and eliminated as soon as possible.

BACK TO THE CASE

Since Max Barton is presently successful, he probably possesses situational analysis skill in addition to the systems and functional skills discussed earlier. In other words, Barton is able to look at and analyze the unique issues in his own department before he uses his systems and functional skills to solve problems.

Barton should consider that his department will grow and be more difficult to manage as the Pleasant Ridge Candy Company becomes more successful. Barton will need to analyze his department's growth and instill in its members, as well as in himself, an understanding of the department's components and how they relate to one another and to the rest of the company. He must also recognize that it is important to continue to involve department members in decision making, despite the fact that group involvement will become more difficult as the department gets larger.

Other issues, such as Barton's accessibility to his subordinates and the amount of control he exerts over them, will also come into play as the molded candy department grows. Currently, Barton is available to listen to employee suggestions and complaints. He spends time walking through the production line, talking to and encouraging his workers. He is also relaxed about his employees' hours and vacation time. As Pleasant Ridge grows, however, Barton will probably have less time for his employees and will also have to establish new rules to keep his growing department under control. If he uses his situational analysis skill effectively, he will find ways to make himself accessible to his workers and provide some flexibility in the new regulations, despite the department's increased size.

It seems, then, that Barton's situational analysis skill is very valuable to him as manager of the molded chocolate candy department. He should continue to develop this skill as he prepares for management in the future.

Characteristics of Future Management System Members

The characteristics of future management system members is another significant situational factor that will face managers of the future. The sections that follow discuss union membership of professional workers in the future and characteristics of the work force of the future.

Union Membership of Professional Workers in the Future

A significant number of management theorists predict that in the future an increasing number of professional workers, such as engineers, professors, and doctors, will join unions and that the traditional image of the union member as a factory employee fighting for better wages will change. This probably will be especially true for professionals employed by government agencies.[8] It appears that the needs of professionals in management systems simply are not being met by management.[9] Unless this trend is reversed, managers of the future probably can look forward to dealing with professional workers primarily through union representatives.

Future professional workers will turn to unions.

Characteristics of the Work Force of the Future

Characteristics of the future human resources of management systems can be obtained by studying the general makeup of the work force from which those resources will come. The next sections discuss the following characteristics of this work force of the future: (1) average age of the work force, (2) size of the work force, (3) number of professional workers in the work force, (4) jobs performed by the work force, (5) employment of the work force according to industry, (6) interest of the work force in the quality of work life, and (7) number of women in management.

The work force of the future will consist of older workers.

Average Age of Work Force. Over all, the work force of the future will have a higher average age than the work force of today. In addition, older workers will not be forced to retire because of age and generally will be sought by managers much more intensely than their counterparts today.[10] As a result, managers of the future probably will have to deal with generally older workers who may have been employed for much longer periods of time.[11] As shown in Figure 21.2, the increase in the average age of the work force is projected to occur mainly as a result of a significant increase in the number of twenty-five to fifty-four year old workers.

There will be fewer workers than once expected.

Size of Work Force. The work force of the future probably will be smaller than was at one time anticipated. (As Figure 21.3 indicates, labor force growth has been slowing down for several years.) As a result, managers of the future probably will have to face higher labor costs and more intense competition in hiring good employees than was predicted earlier. The decreasing national population rate generally is cited as the basis for this prediction of a smaller work force:

> So now it appears that the average American woman will bear only 2.1 children in her lifetime, instead of 3.1. If the trend continues, the United States population in the year 2000 will reach only 262 million instead of 340 million projected earlier. The increase is still large: the population today is only 214 million. But the lowered birthrate already means that more than 12 million Americans who

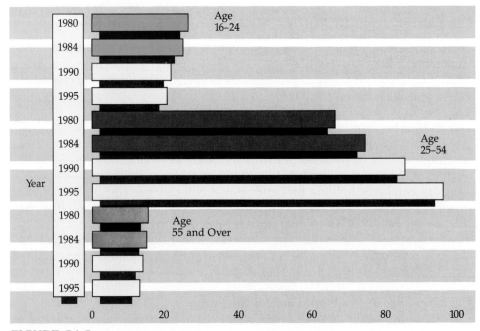

FIGURE 21.2
Growth in the number of workers between 25 and 54 years of age through the mid-1990s

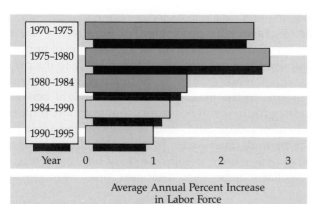

FIGURE 21.3
Labor force growth rate through the mid-1990s

had been expected to exist will not exist; the forecast ten years ago projected 226 million people in 1976.

The number of Americans in the year 2000 could, in fact, be even lower than now foreseen. The smallest of three estimates recently made by the Commerce Department is only 245 million, and many economists and other analysts think this figure may turn out to be the most accurate.[12]

Number of Professional Workers in Work Force. Another characteristic of the work force of the future probably will be that the number of white-collar, or professionally and technically trained, workers will increase relative to the number of blue-collar, or nonprofessional, workers. This growth of professional and technical workers implies that managers of the future probably will have to modify their strategies to suit generally more sophisticated workers.[13] In addition, the competition for managerial positions will become more intense. Naisbitt's *Megatrends* suggests that in the near future, the number of workers competing for such positions will double.[14]

There will be more professionals than once expected.

Jobs Performed by Work Force. A fourth characteristic of the work force of the future is that it will be performing somewhat different jobs than the work force of today. In addition, its members will want to be responsible and efficient if they perceive their work as serving some meaningful purpose.[15] There probably will be three main types of jobs that people will perform in management systems:

There will be a few "workers"—probably a smaller part of the total labor force than today—who will be part of the in-line production, primarily doing tasks requiring relatively flexible eye-brain-hand coordination.

The work force of the future will work less in production areas and more in maintenance and professional areas.

There will be a substantial number of people whose task is to keep the system operating by preventative and remedial maintenance. Machines will play an increasing role, of course, in maintenance functions, but machine power will not likely develop as rapidly in this area as in-line activities. Moreover, the total amount of maintenance work—to be shared by people and machines—will increase. In the near future at least, this group can be expected to make up an increasing fraction of the total work force.

There will be a substantial number of people at professional levels responsible for the design of product, for the design of the productive process, and for general management.[16]

If these three types of jobs materialize as predicted, managers of the future will be faced with a number of challenging problems. For example, if fewer employees work in production areas, differences in the perceived level of importance of production work groups in the management system relative to the perceived level of importance of other work groups in the management system could develop. Other work groups in the management system might believe that since they are larger than the production work group, they are more important. Naturally, this type of situation easily could result in jealousy and a lack of cooperation between production and other work groups. Another problem managers of the future will have to face is the determination of how to use their blue-collar employees as blue-collar jobs begin to disappear.[17]

In the future, more people will work for service industries.

Employment of Work Force According to Industry. As Figure 21.4 below indicates, a greater percentage of the work force of the future will be employed in service industries, such as retailing, banking, insurance, and education. Service industries do not directly produce goods—as do manufacturing, farming, and construction industries. Although Figure 21.4 projects only to 1995, many management theorists believe that this trend will continue well beyond that year.[18] Since service jobs probably will become more prevalent as society continues to grow, managers' ability to apply management concepts to this particular job situation will become increasingly important.

The work force of the future will be interested in making decisions about work situations.

Interest of Work Force in Quality of Work Life. Generally, the work force of the future probably will be more seriously interested in the overall quality of work life than any other work force preceding it. **Quality of work life** is the opportu-

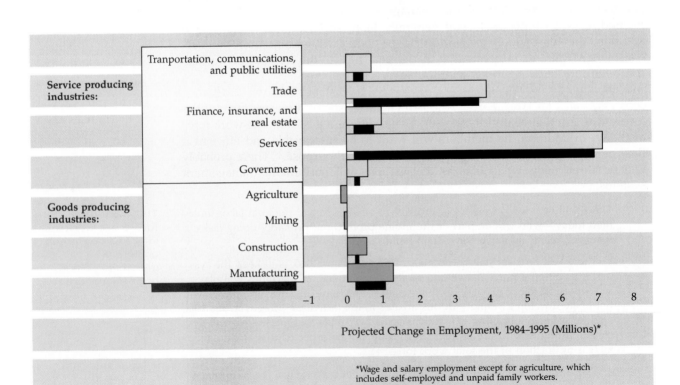

Projected Change in Employment, 1984–1995 (Millions)*

*Wage and salary employment except for agriculture, which includes self-employed and unpaid family workers.

FIGURE 21.4
Employment growth by industry through 1995

nity of workers to make decisions that influence their work situation. The greater the opportunity of workers to make such decisions, the higher the quality of work life is said to be. Over all, the work force of the future probably will strive to make decisions that tend to create:[19]

1. Jobs that are interesting, challenging, and responsible.
2. Worker rewards through fair wages and recognition for worker contributions.
3. Workplaces that are clean, safe, quiet, and bright.
4. Minimal but available supervision.
5. Secure jobs that promote the development of friendly relationships with other system members.
6. Organizations that provide for personal welfare and medical attention.

Managers of the future, as managers of both the present and the past, will have to emphasize the attainment of management system objectives. Unlike managers of the past, however, future managers may find that providing workers with a high-quality work life is an extremely important prerequisite for attaining these objectives.[20]

Women in Management. As Figure 21.5 indicates, women are expected to account for over three-fifths of labor force growth from 1990 to 1995. And, as in the recent past, the future should contain a number of legal, educational, and social developments that will move a greater percentage of women into the mainstream of corporate management (a point touched on by the cartoon).[21] As an indication of this trend, not only is the percentage of women attending four-year colleges increasing faster than that of men, but a significant number of business schools are now offering courses aimed specifically at preparing women for management positions.[22] Naisbitt's *Megatrends* indicates that "by 1990, the number of women earning business B.A.'s will be eight times that of the 1960s.[23]

Although, at first glance, "more women in management" may seem to be a simple variable with which managers of the future must deal, in reality it is extremely complex. For example, Baron and Witte have determined that several factors seem to increase the difficulty of men and women working together productively.[24] Table 21.1 on page 610 shows these factors divided into four categories: (1) organizational problems and inequities, (2) personal characteristics of men and women, (3) men's perception of women, and (4) women's perception of men. The "Management in Action" feature, which reports on a survey of over seven hundred female executives, furnishes insights on the factors

Women will fill more managerial positions in the future.

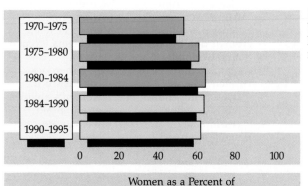

FIGURE 21.5
Women as major factor in labor force growth through the mid-1990s

© *Lee Lorenz 1987. Reprinted with permission from the* Harvard Business Review *(July/August 1987).*

contributing to the strained male/female working relationships, which are likely to continue for some time into the future.

Naturally, managers of the future must strive to minimize the effects of these factors if organizations are to maximize gains through men and women working together. Perhaps special training programs can help men and women better understand one another and, as a result, work more productively as a team.

TABLE 21.1

Factors that seem to make it difficult for men and women to work together productively

Organizational Problems and Inequities	Characteristics of Men and Women	Men's Perception of Women	Women's Perception of Men
Many women feel they are left out of the informal communication network.	Men seem to have difficulty understanding the subtle ways in which they discriminate against or treat women.	Women are obsessed with terminology (a "he" rather than a "he/she," etc.).	Men treat women differently than men.
Women are seen by men as making advances because of government regulations and not ability.	Women compete and discriminate more against each other than do men.	Women use the idea of discrimination as a "crutch."	Men exhibit niceties, not acceptance.
Customers may have difficulty dealing with women.	Women appear to give their marriages and family roles greater importance relative to their jobs than men.	Women don't make a real commitment.	Men don't help women grow.
Women feel they are discriminated against for promotions.	Women behave with more emotion than men.	Women misconstrue being courteous as being patronizing.	Men don't relate to problems women have.
Women are seen as having more problems than men in relocating in another community.	Women are required to be more competent than men in comparable positions.	Women overreact.	Men either lack confidence in women's abilities or are afraid women are capable.
Men are seen by other men as having more long-term career goals than women.			

GALLUP PROFILES FEMALE EXECUTIVES

These women are the pioneers.

They have impressive titles. They earn comfortable salaries. Through persistence, adaptability, and hard work, they have climbed to positions of influence in a corporate world dominated by men. And they like their jobs.

Yet they share a sense of frustration—and in some cases, anger—toward the people and attitudes that have made their professional lives anything but easy. "You have to prove that you are not just a pretty face or a pushy broad," says a fifty-year-old bank vice-president. "The male attitude has made it very difficult. You live in a fishbowl when you're the only woman. You have to be more credible than a man would—every day." Adds a thirty-five-year-old record company vice-president, "I think being a woman has held me back. You have to work ten times as hard to prove yourself."

The *Wall Street Journal* and the Gallup Organization surveyed 722 female executives to find out what their lives are like—how their careers have taken shape and how they feel about the business world and the rewards and sacrifices it involves.

All of the women surveyed have the title of vice-president or higher in listed companies with annual sales of $100 million or more. Fifty-eight percent are under forty-five, younger than the typical male executive. The younger ones have educational backgrounds similar to their male counterparts. They also have higher incomes than female executives over the age of forty-five, who rarely had the same educational opportunities.

EXHILARATION

The women hold positions in a wide range of areas, including formerly male domains like operations and finance. At least half were the first women to reach management level in their companies, and they're exhilarated by their success. "You're just trying, and then, oh my God, all of a sudden you're there," says a sixty-year-old bank vice-president.

All know what it's like to be part of a small minority in a male corporate world. "At a conference, if there are three hundred men and six women, people know what you've said," says a thirty-seven-year-old vice-president in manufacturing. "You're always on display." At times, that minority status can be an advantage. "Everything I do stands out," says a forty-three-year-old insurance company vice-president. "If I do a good job, everyone knows."

At the same time, these women are painfully

aware of how unaccustomed most men are to dealing with women at their own professional level. Sixty-one percent say they've been mistaken for a secretary at a business meeting.

Many of the women have conflicting views toward men. On one hand, they depend on men for career advancement. Most are grateful to a particular man: 82 percent say the most helpful person in their career has been a man. And among those who have a preference, many more would rather work for a man (29 percent) than for a woman (4 percent).

DISADVANTAGES

Still, more than four out of five of the women interviewed say there are disadvantages to being female in the business world. More than 25 percent say they have been thwarted on their way up the ladder by male attitudes toward women. Men, they say, don't take them seriously—they patronize them and undervalue their experience. The younger women in positions of authority complain that men resent them and resist taking orders from them. And a sizable majority—70 percent—feel they are paid less than men of equal ability.

The women frequently describe the business world as a "male club" from which they are excluded. Almost half of them say men treat them differently than they treat other male executives; most say this treatment is negative. One woman in five, for example, complains of being shut out from male executives' social activities. "You're not invited to many functions," says one, "not to the golf course or for the drink after work, where a lot of business gets transacted." A forty-year-old manufacturing company treasurer says, "I'm not one of the boys. I can't hook into the informal chain of communications." As a result, she says, "it's easy to be ignored."

As women slowly move up in the business world, their lives seem to become more like men's—up to a point. They work hard, from fifty to sixty hours a week; 63 percent admit to losing sleep over work problems. And, like men, they feel that they have made personal and family sacrifices for their careers.

Successful male executives have, of course, traditionally put their jobs before their personal lives. Female executives do that too—but it's often more difficult for them. A forty-one-year-old bank vice-president says, "More time is required of me in my job because of a need to prove that a woman can do equal or better work. This translates into time away from my family."

COOKING DINNER

The woman executive returning late from a business trip may find herself cooking dinner for her husband. A thirty-six-year-old senior vice-president in a bank points out that her male colleagues don't have to walk such a tightrope between jobs and family. "They have a spouse at home," she says.

Given the difficulty of the situation, it's not surprising that many female executives are unmarried and that the married ones tend to have helpful husbands. A top executive with three children says she sees herself as having two full-time jobs. "But my husband helps with the children," she says, "and he's thrown in a load of laundry now and then."

Women executives are more likely to be single (26 percent) and divorced or separated (16 percent) than the national norms for women. The most senior women are the least likely to be married, and the divorce rate is highest among the age group with the highest status: one-fourth of the women aged forty to forty-four are now divorced or separated. Less than half (48 percent) of female corporate executives have had children, and fewer than three in ten now have a child at home.

These executives take feminist political positions. Seventy-two percent favor passage of the Equal Rights Amendment, compared with 61 percent of American women sampled earlier by Gallup. On the issue of abortion, executives are much more likely than other American women to feel it should be legal under all circumstances (59 percent, compared with 22 percent of the women surveyed in another Gallup Poll).

GENDER GAP

The survey also reflects that some of the senior women think that things are getting easier for young women, who have been able to take advantage of affirmative action legislation and changing attitudes. A bank vice-president with thirty-two years of experience says that even a few years ago, as an assistant vice-president, she found herself at meetings with forty men and only one or two women. Now, she says, she sees younger men and women lunching together and think that for the first time women are being accepted.

The younger women tend to agree. But as they compete with men for prestige and power, they find themselves making large sacrifices. "I have compromised spontaneity in my personal life," laments a vice-president in a service industry. Another vice-president in an electric company says, "My job has definitely stood in the way of marriage." This woman has a serious relationship with a man, but, she says, "I feel that if I were to marry him, there'd be a new set of expectations, and I would be unable to fulfill them at the same time as doing my job."

BACK TO THE CASE

One reason the management situation Barton will face in the future will probably be different is that the nature of the work force in his department and in the company as a whole will be different. Barton will probably find that the professionals in his department will be represented by unions, making it necessary for him to abide by union rules regarding wages, hours, and working conditions.

Barton will also have to consider that the number of blue-collar workers and the types of jobs they perform will probably decrease. This will result in fewer assembly-line workers making the chocolate candy and more employees at the professional level planning and designing the candy-making process.

In addition, Barton may find that the average age of his employees is rising and that more of his fellow managers are women, making it necessary for

him to adapt his working conditions and relationships. Over all, Barton will need to recognize that his employees (and all the other employees at Pleasant Ridge Company) will be more concerned with the quality of their work life, making it necessary for him to provide more challenging positions, a clean, comfortable workplace, and appropriate compensation for jobs well done.

Of course, Barton should not view any of these people oriented issues as unmanageable. Instead, he should strive to apply systems and functional theory to help him plan for managing in the future. He can begin by considering such issues as how to accommodate more professionals in his department, how to alter regulations to abide by union rules, and how to make assembly-line jobs more interesting.

Energy in the Future

The previous two sections discussed management system size and characteristics of system members as two major situational variables for managers of the future. Energy is a third such variable.

In the past, managers seem to have operated under the assumption that an unlimited supply of energy could be obtained for such worthwhile and important purposes as powering equipment and providing adequate working light. Energy sources as known in the past, however, probably will become more and more scarce in the future. Although this scarcity is not expected to be crippling, the cost of energy in the future probably will be very high. This prediction is based primarily on the premise that the world's oil supply is expected to begin vanishing in about 1990.[25]

As new ways of using coal, solar, and nuclear energy are discovered in years to come, energy may again become readily available. Managers of the more immediate future, however, probably will need to involve themselves in such activities as investing in reserve supplies of energy, finding or developing alternative sources of energy, and quickly cutting back production activities because of unexpected depletion of energy supplies.

Future energy shortages probably will force managers to modify somewhat the way in which they operate their management systems. The most significant modifications typically will be forced on managers who are directly responsible for management systems that exist primarily to supply energy products to consumers.

In the future, there will be less energy at higher cost.

Technology in the Future

Technology is the fourth major situational factor that will face managers of the future. The future undoubtedly will contain numerous technological improvements that managers will have to evaluate for use in the management system.[26]

Future technological improvements will have to be evaluated on a cost-benefit basis.

This evaluation, of course, necessarily must weigh the cost of using such technological improvements against the contribution they can make toward the attainment of management system objectives. In essence, managers of the future will be faced with the hard fact that sophisticated equipment is expensive to use and therefore must make a substantial contribution to the attainment of management system objectives.

Specific technological improvements available to managers of the future undoubtedly will be many and varied. The further sophistication of computers and calculators for use in the area of information handling is likely. Indeed, Naisbitt's *Megatrends* identifies the "new information economy" as the "most important megatrend." Naisbitt devotes his first chapter to the proposition that "we have shifted from an industrial society to one based on the creation and distribution of information."[27] New and different means of distributing products to customers, as well as faster and safer means of human transportation, are expected. In addition, further developments in the area of communication will make it easier for people to share information more effectively and efficiently.[28]

BACK TO THE CASE

In the future, Barton may find that the energy supply to his company is diminished, making it necessary for him to consider such conservation measures as cutting down the hours of the night shift, utilizing fewer machines for production, and purchasing more energy-efficient equipment. However, Barton will not need to be as concerned about energy shortages as will managers who supply energy products to consumers.

Barton could also be greatly affected by improved technology. Faster, more efficient machines could lead to an increase in the amount of molded candy Barton's department can produce but could also result in a decrease in the need for assembly-line workers. Of course, Barton will have to evaluate technological improvements to decide if the increase in production will be more valuable than the cost of the improved machinery.

▦ TRAINING MANAGERS FOR THE FUTURE

Organizations can prepare their managers for the future.

Managers of tomorrow, if they are competent, certainly will be in high demand and of critical importance to the success of management systems. One strategy a company can adopt to ensure an adequate supply of future managers is to train its managers of today so they will be ready to cope with tomorrow's challenges. The sections that follow discuss three main issues related to this training of managers for the future: (1) objectives in training managers for the future, (2) developing future oriented managers, and (3) emphasizing professionalism and change.

Objectives in Training Managers for the Future

Objective for training managers for the future should consider skills, decisions, and practices.

To develop and maintain an effective and efficient program for training managers for the future, an appropriate set of objectives for such a program must be developed and pursued. These objectives should consider skills that managers will need in the future, decisions future managers will have to make, and practices that managers of the future will follow.

An earlier section of this chapter discussed three skills that inevitably will be helpful to managers of the future: systems skill, functional skill, and situa-

TABLE 21.2

Skillful managers of the past and future

Past Manager	Future Manager
Familiar problem solver	Novel problem solver
Intuitive problem solver	Analytic problem solver
Conservative risk taker	Entrepreneurial risk taker
Convergent diagnostician	Divergent diagnostician
Lag controller	Lead controller

tional analysis skill. In addition, Table 21.2 indicates that managers of the future probably will need somewhat different skills than their predecessors. Thus objectives for training managers for the future should focus on developing managers who are imaginative problem solvers, analytical problem solvers, risk takers, divergent diagnosticians, and lead controllers.

Objectives for training managers for the future also should take into consideration the decisions that these managers will have to make. Table 21.3 compares the content of decisions, the decision process, and decision information as used in the company of today versus the company of the future. Since these two decision-making situations are dramatically different, objectives for training

TABLE 21.3

Decision making in the firm of today and the firm of the future

Firm of Today	Firm of the Future
Content of Decisions	
Operating issues, corporate policies	Strategy formulation, design of systems for strategy implementation
Exploitation of firm's current position	Innovation in patterns of form's products, markets, and technology
Economic, technological, national, intraindustry perspective	Economic, sociopolitical, technological, multinmational, multi-industry perspective
Decision Process	
Emphasis on historical experience, judgment, past programs for solving similar problems	Emphasis on anticipation, rational analysis, pervasive use of specialist experts, techniques for coping with novel decision situations
Personnel intensive process	Technology intensive process
Information for Decisions	
Formal information systems for internal performance history	Formal systems for anticipatory, external environment information
One-way, top down, flow of information	Interactive two-way communication channels linking managers and other professionals with knowledgeable workers
Computer systems emphasizing volume and fast response information for general management	Computer systems emphasizing richness, flexibility, and accessibility of information for general management
Emphasis on periodic operation plans, capital, and operating expenditure budgets	Emphasis on continuous planning, covering operations, projects, system resource development; control based on cost-benefit forecasts

managers for the future should reflect these differences. For example, the objectives should emphasize the relationship between managerial decision making and such factors as strategy formulation, the use of expert specialists, and the use of computer systems to increase management system flexibility. Table 21.3 indicates that objectives for training managers of today that relate to these same areas typically emphasize the relationship between managerial decision making and existing corporate policies, the use of personal judgment and operating history, and the use of computer systems to analyze large amounts of information quickly.

Objectives for training managers for the future also should consider the management practices that managers will be following. Naturally, such objectives should be aimed at training managers to carry out these future practices both effectively and efficiently. Table 21.4 compares past and future management practices. According to this table, training objectives for developing managers for the future should emphasize such factors as carrying out long-range comprehensive planning as opposed to short-term intuitive planning, meeting social responsibilities as opposed to meeting only profit responsibilities, and establishing a decentralized decision process in the management system as opposed to a primarily centralized decision process.

Developing Future Oriented Managers

Future oriented managers participate in creating their own future.

In addition to developing and pursuing appropriate objectives, the process of training managers for the future should involve encouraging today's managers

TABLE 21.4

Past and future management practices

Past Practices	Future Practices
Assumption that a business manager's sole responsibility is to optimize stockholder wealth	Profit still dominant but modified by the assumption that a business manager has social responsibilities
Business performance measured only by economic standards	Application of both economic and social measures of performance
Emphasis on quantity of production	Emphasis on quantity and quality
Authoritarian management	Permissive/democratic management
Short-term intuitive planning	Long-range comprehensive structured planning
Entrepreneurship	Renaissance managing
Control	Creativity
People subordinate to machines	People dominant over machines
Financial accounting	Human resource accounting
Caveat emptor ("let the buyer beware")	Ombudsmen
Centralized decision making	Decentralized and small-group decision making
Concentration on internal functioning	Concentration on external ingredients for company success
Dominance of economic forecasts in decision making	Major use of social, technical, and political forecasts as well as economic forecasts
Business viewed as single system	Business viewed as system within larger social system
Business ideology calling for aloofness from government	Business-government cooperation and convergence of planning
Business having little concern for social costs of production	Increasing concern for internalizing social costs of production

to be future oriented.[29] According to Nanus, **future oriented managers** attempt to create their own future whenever possible and adapt to this future, when necessary, through a continuous process of research about the future, long-range planning, and the setting of objectives. Such managers make no important decisions without a systematic and thorough analysis of the future consequences of such decisions. Future oriented managers see the future not as an uncontrollable development but as a factor that can be influenced significantly by present managerial behavior. Here, Nanus is suggesting that managers are best prepared for the future when they are shown how to participate in creating that future to the best advantage of the management system.

Emphasizing Professionalism and Change

Besides emphasizing an appropriate set of objectives and a future orientation, the process of training managers for the future should emphasize both professionalism and change. The extremely complex nature of the future manager's job indicates that this job can best be learned by those who approach its study as the learning of a profession. A **profession** is a vocation whose practice is based on an understanding of a specific body of knowledge and the corresponding abilities necessary to apply this understanding to vital human problems. Additionally, professionalism stresses that knowledge related to a profession should be seen as constantly evolving and being modified as a result of insights derived from individuals practicing the profession.[30]

> Management is a profession.

Professionalism necessarily involves changes. Managers trained for the future, therefore, should be warned of the inevitable changes that will occur over time. This warning should help them overcome "future shock," or an inability to adapt to changes.[31] Although some management theorists argue that such changes probably will be insignificant,[32] others believe strongly that the changes will be both extensive and significant.[33]

BACK TO THE CASE

Even though the discussion has focused primarily on the process a company can implement to prepare its managers for future challenges, there are many things Max Barton can do as an individual to prepare himself for his own management position. For example, Barton should realize that, in addition to using his excellent systems, functional, and situational analysis skills, he will need to be an imaginative problem solver and risk taker. In other words, he must look at new and innovative ways to accomplish his department's objectives rather than simply relying on what has worked well in the past.

In addition, Barton must recognize that the decision making process in the future will be quite different from the way it is now. As he prepares himself for the future, Barton should consider how he can use computers and expert specialists to aid him in future decision-making situations.

Barton must also become future oriented and learn to anticipate the inevitable changes that will occur as the company grows. As he makes decisions such as increasing the number of employees in his department or purchasing improved machinery, he should look ahead and analyze how such changes will lead to other developments. In other words, Barton must see his present managerial decisions as factors that will help shape the developments to come.

Over all, Barton must recognize that his role as manager is a professional one, requiring him not only to understand the workings of his department but to modify this understanding as the department evolves. By developing his professionalism, learning to be future oriented, and improving his decision-making and other managerial skills, Max Barton should be well prepared for his future management position at Pleasant Ridge Candy Company.

Action Summary

Reread the learning objectives that follow. Each objective is followed by questions. Answering these questions accurately will help you retain the most important concepts discussed in this chapter. After answering each question, check your answer with the answer key at the end of this chapter. (*Hint:* If you have doubt regarding the correct response, consult the page whose number follows the answer.)

Circle:

From studying this chapter, I will attempt to acquire:

1. **An understanding of how systems skill relates to management in the future.**

   T, F
   a. In solving organizational problems, managers of the future must understand the "big picture," seeing all parts of the company as a whole.

   T, F
   b. Systems skill is intuitive to most managers; and according to Curtin, successful managers don't require any type of formal education to develop systems skill.

2. **Insights about how functional skill relates to management in the future.**

   a, b, c, d, e
   a. The functional skill of a manager requires the application of activities associated with: (a) the influencing subsystem; (b) the implementing subsystem; (c) the organizing subsystem; (d) a and b; (e) a and c.

   T, F
   b. To manage successfully, a manager need only apply knowledge of the four basic management functions to the unique management situation faced.

3. **An understanding of how situational analysis skill relates to management in the future.**

   a, b, c, d, e
   a. Which of the following is *not* a major situational factor that managers of the future will face: (a) the characteristics of future management system members; (b) the technology available for future management systems; (c) the amount of energy available for future management systems; (d) the size of future management systems; (e) all of the above are major factors.

   a, b, c, d, e
   b. All of the following are characteristics of a large management system that tend to make this system harder to manage except: (a) a decrease in the overall number of component units that compose the total system; (b) increasing costs of coordinating and controlling the system; (c) a diminishing level of participation in decision making; (d) a declining access of organization members to top decision makers in the system; (e) an increase in system rigidity.

4. **A better understanding of the labor force of the future.**

   T, F
   a. Projections for future employment opportunities indicate that there will be more blue-collar than white-collar workers in the labor force in the future.

   a, b, c, d, e
   b. Which of the following is *not* an organizational problem that causes inequities between men and women workers: (a) women tend to overreact; (b) customers may have difficulty in dealing with women employees; (c) women tend to feel they are omitted from the organization's informal communication network; (d) men are perceived by other men as having more long-term career goals than women; (e) women are perceived as having more difficulty than men in relocating to another community.

5. **An appreciation for the impact of such factors as system size, energy, and technology on management in the future.**

a. Technological improvement in equipment can be expected in the future in all of the following areas except: (a) communication; (b) legislation; (c) information processing; (d) product distribution; (e) human transportation.   a, b, c, d, e

b. In the future, managers will need to recognize that sophisticated equipment will have to contribute significantly to meeting organizational objectives to be justified.   T, F

6. A practical strategy for training managers for the future.

a. In the future, a manager will need to be everything except: (a) a lag controller; (b) a divergent diagnostician; (c) an analytical problem solver; (d) an entrepreneurial risk taker; (e) a solver of novel problems.   a, b, c, d, e

b. The process of training future oriented managers should stress a need for professionalism and change.   T, F

INTRODUCTORY CASE WRAP-UP

"What about Tomorrow?" (p. 600) and its related back-to-the-case sections were written to help you better understand the management concepts contained in this chapter. Answer the following discussion questions about this introductory case to further enrich your understanding of chapter content:

1. What skills does Barton probably possess now that should still be valuable to him five or ten years from now?

2. Do you agree that Barton should be preparing himself for managing in the future? Explain.

3. If you were Barton, what would you do to prepare yourself for managing in the future at the Pleasant Ridge Candy Company?

Issues for Review and Discussion

1. Define *systems skill* and describe its probable value to managers of the future.
2. What is functional skill? How valuable will this skill probably be to managers of the future?
3. What is the relationship between situational analysis skill, systems skill, and functional skill?
4. List and discuss four factors that can make large management systems difficult to manage.
5. If the predicted trend of more professional workers of the future joining unions actually materializes, how do you think it will affect management practices in the future?
6. State three probable characteristics of the work force of the future. Explain how each of these characteristics could affect the practice of management in the future.
7. What is meant by the phrase *quality of work life?*

8. Describe the types of decisions that employees of the future will attempt to make to increase the quality of their work life.
9. How will the predicted energy shortage, if it materializes, probably affect the practice of management in the future?
10. What is the major criterion that managers of the future should use to decide if a particular technological improvement will be employed in their management system?
11. Describe a strategy that a company can adopt to ensure that its managers will be able to face management challenges of the future.
12. Considering the decision-making situation future managers will face, how should managers be trained for the future?
13. What is a future oriented manager?
14. Fully explain the implications of the following statement: Management is a profession.

Sources of Additional Information

Amara, Roy, and Andrew J. Lipinski. *Business Planning for an Uncertain Future: Scenarios and Strategies.* New York: Pergamon, 1983.

Bowonder, B. "The Energy Manager and His Corporate Role." *Long-Range Planning* 17 (August 1984): 74–78.

Flamholtz, Eric G., Yvonne Randle, and Sonja Sackmann. "Personnel Management: The Tone of Tomorrow." *Personnel Journal* 66 (July 1987): 42–65.

Guth, William D. *Handbook of Business Strategy 1986/1987 Yearbook.* New York: Warren, Gorham & Lamont, 1986.

Harris, Philip R. *New World, New Ways, New Management.* New York: Amacom, 1983.

Hickok, Richard S. "Looking to the Future: A Key to Success." *Journal of Accountancy* (March 1984): 77–82.

"High Technology—Wave of the Future or a Market Flash in the Pan?" *Business Week,* November 10, 1980, 86–98.

Leavitt, Harold J. *Corporate Pathfinds: Building Vision and Values into Organizations.* Homewood, Ill.: Richard D. Irwin, 1986.

Lehrer, Robert N. *Participative Productivity and Quality of Work Life.* Englewood Cliffs, N.J.: Prentice-Hall, 1982.

Mills, D. Quinn. *The New Competitors: A Report on American Managers from D. Quinn Mills of the Harvard Business School.* New York: Wiley, 1985.

Naisbitt, John. *Megatrends.* New York: Warner Books, 1984.

Nykodym, Nick, Jack L. Simonetti, Joseph C. Christen, and Judith A. Kasper. "Stress and the Working Woman." *Business* 37 (January/February/March 1987): 8–12.

Pascarella, Perry. "Futurists Sound a More Positive Note." *Industry Week* (August 1982): 79–86.

Quinn, James Brian, and Christopher E. Gagnon. "Will Services Follow Manufacturing into Decline?" *Harvard Business Review* (November/December 1986): 95–105.

Sample, Robert L. "Coping with the 'Work-at-Home' Trend." *Administrative Management* 42 (August 1981): 24–27.

Suojanen, Waino W., Tricia Working, Jane S. Goldner, Kelley Ort, and Sherrie Cribbs. "The Emergence of the Type E Woman." *Business* 37 (January/February/March 1987): 3–7.

Talpaert, Roger. "Looking into the Future: Management in the Twenty-first Century." *Management Review* (March 1981): 21–25.

"What's Ahead for In-House Training." *Administrative Management* 42 (July 1981): 41–47.

Whitsett, David A., and Lyle Yorks. "Looking Back at Topeka: General Foods and the Quality-of-Work-Life Experiment." *California Management Review* 25 (Summer 1983): 93–109.

Zoffer, H. J. "Restructuring Management Education." *Management Review* 70 (April 1981): 37–41.

Notes

1. J. Buckley, "Goal-Process-System Interaction in Management: Correcting an Imbalance," *Business Horizons* 14 (December 1971): 81–92.
2. Paul Adler, Jr., "Toward a System of General Management Theory," *Southern Journal of Business* (July 1969).
3. "Stressing the System Approach," *Manufacturing Engineering* (August 1969): 75.
4. Richard Allen Stull, "A View of Management to 1980," *Business Horizons* (June 1974): 5–12.
5. Duane S. Elgin and Robert A. Bushnell, "The Limits to Complexity: Are Bureaucracies Becoming Unmanageable?" *Futurist* (December 1977): 493–99.
6. John Naisbitt, *Megatrends* (New York: Warner Books, 1984), 229.
7. Kenneth A. Kovach, Ben F. Sands, Jr., and William W. Brooks, "Management by Whom?—Trends in Participative Management," *S.A.M. Advanced Management Journal* (Winter 1981): 4–14.
8. Thomas A. DeScisciolo, "Labor Relations—Friends and Future," Third National Capitol Conference, International Personnel Management Association, Washington, D.C., May 28, 1975.
9. Dennis Chamot, "Professional Employees Turn to Unions," *Harvard Business Review* (May/June 1976): 119–28.
10. Patricia Skalka, "Farewell to the Youth Culture," *Ambassador* (April 1978): 43–48.
11. Susan R. Rhodes, Michael Schuster, and Mildred Doering, "The Implications of an Aging Work Force," *Personnel Administrator* (October 1981): 19–22.

12. Alfred L. Malabre, Jr., "The Future Revised—U.S. Unlikely to Be as Big—or as Rich—as Analysts Thought," *Wall Street Journal*, March 15, 1976, 1.

13. Peter F. Drucker, "Management's New Role," *Harvard Business Review* (November/December 1969): 49–54.

14. Naisbitt, *Megatrends*, 223.

15. Frederick Herzberg, "Herzberg on Motivation for the '80s," *Industry Week* (October 1979): 58–61.

16. Herbert A. Simon, "The Corporation: Will It Be Managed by Machines?" in *Management and Corporations—1985*, ed. Anshen and Bach (New York: McGraw-Hill, 1960), 17–55.

17. Robert Schrank, "Horse-Collar, Blue-Collar Blues," *Harvard Business Review* (May/June 1981): 133.

18. Keith Davis, "Some Basic Trends Affecting Management in the 1980s," *Arizona Business* (November 1976): 18–22.

19. Tom Lupton, "Efficiency and the Quality of Work Life," *Organizational Dynamics* (Autumn 1975): 68.

20. John F. Mee, "The Manager of the Future," *Business Horizons* (June 1973): 5–14.

21. Linda Keller Brown, "Women and Business Management," *Signs: Journal of Women in Culture and Society* 5, no. 2 (1979): 266–88.

22. Rose K. Reha, "Preparing Women for Management Roles," *Business Horizons* (April 1979): 68–71.

23. Naisbitt, *Megatrends*, 264.

24. Alma S. Baron and Robert L. Witte, "The New Work Dynamic: Men and Women in the Work Force," *Business Horizons* (August 1980): 56–60.

25. "The Future Revised: No Crippling Shortage of Energy Expected, but Cost Will Be High," *Wall Street Journal*, March 29, 1976, 1.

26. Henry B. Schacht, "The Impact of Changes in the Seventies," *Business Horizons* (August 1970): 29–34.

27. Naisbitt, *Megatrends*, xxii.

28. Douglas P. Brush, "Internal Communications and the New Technology," *Public Relations Journal* (February 1981): 10–13.

29. Burt Nanus, "The Future-Oriented Corporation," *Business Horizons* (February 1975): 5–12.

30. For more information on professionalism, see Kenneth R. Andrews, "Toward Professionalism in Business Management," *Harvard Business Review* (March/April 1969): 49–60.

31. Alvin Toffler, *Future Shock* (New York: Random House, 1970), 4.

32. Charles Perrow, "Is Business Really Changing?" *Organization Dynamics* 3 (Summer 1974): 30–62.

33. Gordon H. Coperthwaite, "Management: Its Changing Patterns," *Management Controls* (December 1972): 281–86.

Action Summary Answer Key

1. a. T, p. 601
   b. F, p. 601
2. a. e, pp. 601–602
   b. F, p. 603

3. a. e, p. 603
   b. a, p. 604
4. a. F, pp. 605–606
   b. a, pp. 609–610

5. a. b, p. 614
   b. T, pp. 613–614
6. a. a, p. 615
   b. T, pp. 616–617

GM, APPLE, GE, AND PHILIP MORRIS TAP WOMEN FOR TOP SPOTS

In the plant manager's office at the huge General Motors factory in Bay City, Michigan, all expected artifacts appear to be in place. A model of a carburetor rests on a nearby credenza, a GM pen set graces the desk. Only the plant manager's Styrofoam coffee cup hints that there is something out of the ordinary in this office: The cup is rimmed with lipstick. "I'm a woman," states Patricia M. Carrigan, acknowledging the lipstick. "I don't become something else when I come to work."

Ms. Carrigan, fifty-seven years old, is also a pioneer in one segment of today's work force—plant management—which has provided some of the stiffest resistance for women. In 1982, she became GM's first woman plant manager in the United States, and by many accounts remains one of its most outstanding. Her career also does much to explode the usual explanation as to why there are so few women at her level. The job requires an engineering background, and only recently have women begun graduating from engineering school in large numbers.

What background was required for a woman to capture this first GM plant manager job? Maybe not what one would expect. Ms. Carrigan has a doctorate in clinical psychology, worked for several years in the Ann Arbor, Michigan, school system, and served a stint as corporate director of human resources at Bendix Corporation before initiating her tour of duty with GM. Then, she crammed into five years—with only two of those years actually managing a production shift—enough plant experience to capture the top job. How was she able to leap the technology barrier? Constant questioning and much hard work, according to Ms. Carrigan. In addition, she has a strong belief that to succeed, one must learn from one's people.

Not many women are even getting the chance to ply their skills, at least not yet. Although women have made significant headway into middle management in such professions as marketing and finance, plant management remains a distinctly male business. For example, Chrysler Corporation and Ford Motor Company operate 109 U.S. plants but do not have a single woman plant manager. Hewlett Packard Company's 54 U.S. manufacturing managers are all men. The same is true for du Pont Company and Goodyear Tire & Rubber Company. R. J. Reynolds Industries Incorporated has only two women among its 71 plant managers.

However, a few women have begun to break the barrier to plant management. Debi Coleman and Claire

Deborah Coleman

Heiss are two of those elite few. Ms. Coleman is vice-president of manufacturing at Apple Computer. She is recognized as possibly the only female plant manager in Silicon Valley. Ms. Heiss, thirty-nine, a plant manager for General Electric in Daytona Beach, Florida, has what some human resource experts consider the perfect credentials for the job: an undergraduate degree in engineering and an MBA.

Ms. Heiss—and others in her field—has risen through the ranks without the benefit of female role models or mentors. In charting her own path, she has discovered that the plant floor is more open and less encumbered by politics than most white-collar offices. According to Ms. Heiss, blue-collar workers "are very straightforward with their thoughts," which has made sexism easier to deal with. Ms. Heiss, whose plant manufactures computerized training simulators, found the biggest obstacle to be establishing credibility. Male contractors, who "always wanted to talk to the boss," "were surprised to find out that I was the boss." In fact, one who was bidding to construct a new GE building balked at dealing with a woman and lost the contract.

Today GE has a special program to train its future manufacturing managers. About 20 percent of the employees in the program are women. But all of the employees in the program must hold an engineering degree. As one might suspect, manufacturing is becoming increasing complex as new technology supplants the labor-intensive jobs of the past. GE is counting on people who can master the technology in a plant and later move up to jobs with broad responsibilities.

Like Ms. Carrigan at GM, there are other women who have bucked convention. Audrey Dixon, thirty-eight, for example, manages a plant for Philip Morris Incorporated in Richmond, Virginia, where about three hundred employees process tobacco for export. Although she now spends her day surrounded by feeders, dryers, and big conveyors, her formal education provided little direction for this type of job. Ms. Dixon studied economics in college and later earned an MBA with a concentration in finance. Although she finds it important to have a good understanding of the technological aspects of a plant, she doesn't believe one has to be an engineer to succeed in plant management. In fact, she says, engineers sometime lack critical skills in such areas as employee relations and long-range planning.

Ms. Dixon joined Philip Morris in 1978 after gaining business experience at E. F. Hutton Group Inc. and Celanese Corporation in New York. Over about a five-year stint at the tobacco company, she moved up from a position as coordinator between operations and marketing to that of assistant vice-president for plant operations. However, she spent only about three months of the five years as an assistant plant manager before becoming head of one of the company's fifteen U.S. plants. When asked to compare her New York business experiences with those in Richmond, she says: "I don't miss the New York corporate offices at all. . . . There's just more action in a plant. You're responsible for costs, getting the product out on time, the people there. There's more of a sense of urgency." Her most satisfying moments on the job, she says, have been "managing catastrophes," such as the time a boiler exploded and the time the plant was flooded.

GM's Pat Carrigan has a background markedly different from that of Audrey Dixon. Ms. Carrigan's first job was in personnel. However, when her boss, Charles Katko, now with GM's Truck and Bus Group, recognized her ability to manage people, he asked her to consider manufacturing. Ms. Carrigan does not mind climbing around the oil slick, nor is she fearful of getting dirty.

GM first sent her to manage its aging Atlanta assembly plant. Labor and management had been at each other's throats for years, the plant's truck operations already had been closed, and lagging sales had forced car production to shut down three months after Ms. Carrigan's arrival. Not a very auspicious beginning. Yet Ms. Carrigan was able to win over union leaders by encouraging more cooperation. By 1984, the plant was again building cars. When Ms. Carrigan left the Atlanta plant to take a new job with GM, workers and union leaders honored her as "one of us" with a plaque labeled "Ms. Boss."

DISCUSSION ISSUES

1. The text identifies three essential skills that managers of the future must possess if they wish to be successful. Is there any evidence in the case that female plant managers may possess and, in some instances, may already be applying one or more of these skills? Explain.

2. What difficulties relative to men and women being unable to work together productively (see Table 21.1) have Pat Carrigan and the other women in the case encountered on their way to plant manager status? Which would you suspect they have been able to overcome? Explain.

3. It has been predicted that managers of the future will have to make decisions that are somewhat different from those that managers are making in today's firms (see Table 21.3). What in the case suggests that these predictions may already be coming to pass? Explain.

4. What future management practices (see Table 21.4) do female plant managers already appear to be displaying? Explain.

ARCO NOW HIRING A NEW TYPE OF MANAGER

In February of 1981, many business executives, still gleeful over Ronald Reagan's inauguration, were looking forward to four years of a probusiness, conservative government. However, the outlook was not quite as optimistic at Atlantic Richfield company (Arco) headquarters in Los Angeles. A new group of Arco executives called "issues managers" were predicting that Reagan's budget-cutting election promises would diminish federal money flowing to state governments and, as a result, would increase state tax rates for businesses. If their speculations were correct, Arco, a profitable oil and natural resources company operating in twenty-eight states, would be a prime target for such rate increases.

An issues-management task force at Arco was assigned this tax related issue. By the summer, the task force had developed a report on likely state tax proposals and had prepared lobbyists and top executives. As predicted, a deluge of state tax bills were introduced, but well-prepared Arco representatives were able to respond quickly. Although four states did raise corporate taxes, bills in several states aimed specifically at oil companies were defeated.

To Arco, this episode proved the usefulness of the new issues manager concept. Arco's issues managers now alert decision centers to emerging political, social, and economic trends and controversies. The company can then mobilize company resources to deal with them.

An issues manager is not a futurist who tries to tell management what will happen ten or twenty years down the road. Rather, he or she considers the immediate future—the next one to five years. The issues manager is charged not only with identifying issues but also with specifying ways to deal with them.

The impetus for issues management at Arco began in the late 1970s. Corporate executives were tired of unpleasant surprises. In response to feelings of uncertainty, Arco set up special trend spotting departments, assigning them tasks previously performed in somewhat haphazard fashion by top executives, planners, government relations people, and public relations staffs.

Arco established its current issues management system partly because it believed its planning was too numbers oriented. "Single-line numbers forecasting typically done by economic planners didn't predict the Arab oil embargo or the environmental revolution," explains Breck Arrington, who heads Arco's twenty-eight-member governmental issues team. "We needed a wider, more qualitative approach to supplement the other work."

Today Arco has a large staff of full-time issues managers. They include people trained as petroleum, chemical, and aeronautical engineers, lawyers, marketing managers, congressional consultants, legislative analysts, a former journalist, and a former English professor. Issues managers at Arco emphasize legislative and governmental issues. However, Arco also uses issues managers to spot emerging concerns for their communities and philanthropic programs. Arco's system is organized around five clusters of issues: resources, environment, corporate and planning (including tax, antitrust, and labor matters), manufacturing processes, and participation in its many trade associations.

The Arco issues management group presently monitors hundreds of publications, opinion polls, and think-tank projects. It provides five hundred Arco middle managers and executives with a daily publication called *Scan*, which summarizes governmental actions—federal, state, and local legislation, regulations and rules, court and agency decisions, and hearing notices and investigations. The group is presently tracking 140 issues.

Many in the emerging issues management field believe issues tend to follow an eight-year curve. For the first five years or so, emerging issues begin to take shape in local newspapers, are enumerated by public interest groups, and can be detected through public opinion polls. At this stage, issues are plastic and moldable. If the issue affects their interests, companies can intervene to prevent the issue from reaching the action stage. In the fifth or sixth year of the eight-year cycle, the national media become interested. Governmental action typically results in the seventh or eighth year. If a company gets caught up in an issue in the seventh or eighth year, it can only react. A proactive stance necessitates getting involved in the third to fifth year.

Issues management is more complicated than just identifying the issues. The team must also determine the position the company ought to take. For instance, under natural gas decontrol, the higher process would aid Arco's gas and oil operations but would harm its refining and chemicals operations. The issues managers' responsibility is to build a consensus among operating units before the issue gets to corporate management. This type of analysis and compromise eventually moves the company to action.

For example, a House bill on Alaska lands proposed a ban on evaluation of oil and gas potential at the William O. Douglas Arctic Wildlife Refuge. Arco's issues managers marshaled a bevy of experts to head this bill off in the Senate. They sent maps, data, and survey information to Arco's Washington lobbying office. Furthermore, they sent letters to all members of Congress and flew in oil and environmental experts from Alaska and Los Angeles to point up the high oil and gas potential of the wildlife range. Finally, experts were called to assure senators of the harmless effects of seismic testing on caribou herds in the refuge.

The Alaska lands bill that was eventually passed allowed oil companies to test for hydrocarbons in the wildlife refuge. Arco executives are convinced that testing in the whole area would have been restricted for years had it not been for the efforts of their issues managers.

DISCUSSION ISSUES

1. What are the organizational responsibilities of an issues manager?
2. Which, if any, of the essential skills for future managers identified in chapter 21 will be important to the issues manager of the future? Explain.
3. Of what value to management is having an awareness of the eight-year emerging issues curve? Explain.
4. Is there any evidence in the case that issues managers assist Arco in meeting its social responsibilities? Explain.
5. Where, if at all, does international management fit into Arco's issues management framework or system? Explain.
6. What are some of the current international management issues that might merit inclusion in an international issues management examination?

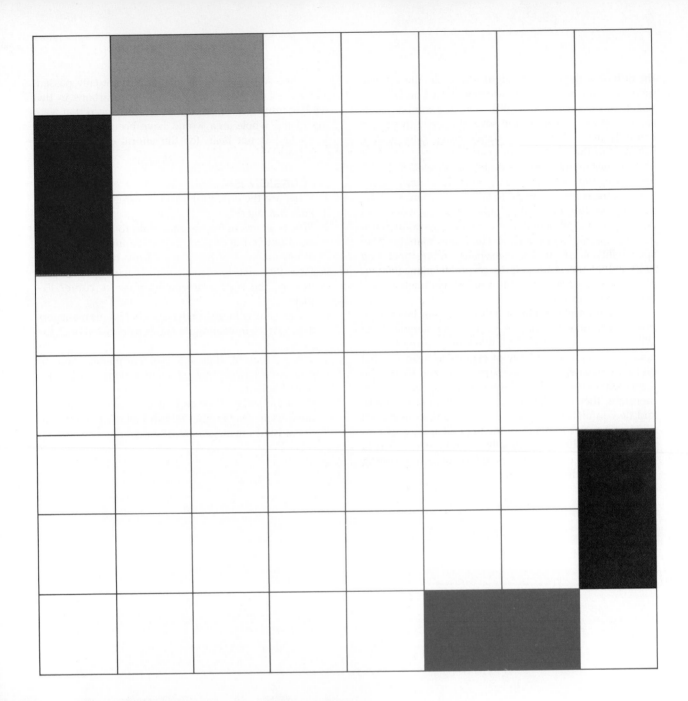

APPENDIX
Video Cases

This is a unique appendix designed to give you another means of applying the management theory you are learning. Four video-assisted cases appear on the following pages:

Fired: A Focus on Management Careers.
Battle of the Blimps: A Focus on Strategic Planning.
The Parable of the Sadhu: A Focus on Ethics.
The Colonel Comes to Japan: A Focus on International Management.
    Your instructor will inform you when to use this material.

VIDEO CASE 1

FIRED: A FOCUS ON MANAGEMENT CAREERS

(An extension of materials in Chapter 1—Introducing Management and Management Careers)

SYNOPSIS: Tens of thousands of executives lose their jobs each year. "Fired" is the true story of one of those executives. 44-year-old Douglas "Biff" Wilson.

Before he was dismissed, Biff Wilson was Vice-President of Marketing for Universal Foods (fictional name), a multi-divisional packaged-goods firm. After 15 years, Wilson's career at Universal was terminated by a man who had reached the presidency after vying with Biff for the position. The new president wanted to aim toward a new era for Universal, and Biff was part of the old era. Clearly, the new president and Biff had contrasting personalities and styles, so Biff was out. One Monday morning, in less than an hour, Biff Wilson had gone from a vice-president of a large company to unemployment.

Douglas Wilson was shaken. For $10,000, Universal hired an executive outplacement firm to help Biff find a job elsewhere. Eric Barton, Biff's counselor and a former sales representative, met his client at Universal minutes after the firing. His challenge: To help piece together Biff Wilson's shattered professional life.

The first step was a visit to the outplacement center, which, like a hospital, has its patients. Only these patients are some 100 fired executives seeking a new job in mid-life. As in a hospital, counselors prescribed a protocol for each patient, or client. Wilson's protocol included self-exploration exercises, fitness training, new clothing, new hairstyle, and most importantly, a new confidence in this exciting new product—himself.

After mock interviewing and evaluation, Biff's counselors determined that he was out of his league in attempting another career with a large packaged-goods firm. They felt he should set his sights lower; Wilson did not agree. He answered newspaper advertisements, called on friends, and contacted executive search firms. From his search, one job possibility emerged. After interviewing, Biff did not get the job; he claimed age was the deciding factor.

Finally, Wilson lowered his expectations and followed Eric Barton's advice: "Use people like never before and don't be ashamed to do it." After talking with several people in the food industry, Wilson homed in on a medium-sized organization, run by its owner, Ray Morris. Before seeing Morris, Biff chatted with suppliers, buyers and employees, and eventually landed the all-important interview with Ray Morris. Biff Wilson was lucky, he was offered the job with Morris—replacing a man that Ray Morris was about to fire.

INTRODUCTION: Now that you have had the opportunity to read and reflect on the chapter 1 materials and concepts pertaining to management and management careers, you are ready to view the video case entitled "Fired." This case vividly portrays the true story of forty-four-year-old Douglas "Biff" Wilson, one of the tens of thousands of managers who lose their jobs each year. The major difference in the video case situation and the background reading you have done in chapter 1 is that this type of career change is not within the control of the individual . . . or is it? After you view the case and discuss its implications, your perspective on management careers will be broadened. Management is one of the most challenging and rewarding of all careers. It is also one of the most demanding and, in some instances, one of the least secure career choices.

PART 1: In preparation for viewing the video, familiarize yourself with the following questions. When the video is shown, make notes on the case issues that appear especially relevant:

a. Is there anything in the text that provides a hint that Biff Wilson's career could be approaching a period of transition?

b. Which management skills did Wilson appear to be lacking to cause the new president to view him as he did? Jot down specific examples and statements from the video to support your contentions. Was there any evidence at the end of the video that Wilson had made adjustments and upgraded his skills? Explain.

c. When Wilson finally realized that he was going to have to lower his sights and get serious about the search process if he was to find a job, how did he approach the job search process? Would the steps he took be helpful for anyone else looking for a job? Explain.

d. One of the recommendations made to Wilson by outplacement executive Eric Barton was to "use people" to make the contacts necessary to get the job he wanted. Is this type of behavior appropriate job search behavior? If it is, should college students begin developing links to individuals in business organizations who can assist them in making career moves? If so, how?

e. What specific strategy did Wilson follow to land the job at Morris Corporation? Would it be beneficial to you to tuck away this strategy for your own future reference? Explain.

f. Was Wilson in a position to do anything about being fired after the decision was made? Could he have taken action earlier to keep this from occurring? Explain.

PART 2: After you view the case and document the issues you find especially pertinent, meet with three or four of your classmates to discuss and develop a group reaction to each question. Groups may be asked to share their views (or case analysis) with the rest of the class. The presenting group's comments will provide the basis for a class discussion of the issue at hand.

PART 3: Now that you have viewed the video case and have answered and discussed the questions, what specific points do you want to remember to assist you in your management career? ■

VIDEO CASE 2

BATTLE OF THE BLIMPS: A FOCUS ON STRATEGIC PLANNING

(An extension of materials in Chapter 6—Types of Planning: Strategic and Tactical)

SYNOPSIS: Founded in 1979 by Roger Munk, the small British company Airship Industries has built eight airships with seven more in the works. Using Porsche engines and sporting $4 million price tags, Airship Industries' products are presently the best in the field, making Airship the undisputed leader in modern airship technology. Yet being a technological leader is of little advantage when the market for your product is practically nonexistent. In late 1984, $14 million in debt, Airship Industries was sold to Australian tycoon Alan Bond.

The only other major producer of blimps, Goodyear Aerospace (a wholly-owned subsidiary of Goodyear Tire and Rubber), did not even compete for Airship Industries' few customers. Goodyear's heyday for blimps lasted from World War I until the early 1960s, when it built almost 300 airships for the U.S. Navy. Now Goodyear has only four blimps, which it uses for its own promotional purposes.

Unlike balloons, blimps or airships have a propulsion system and a steering mechanism. Although the first successful airship was built in 1852, the age of commercial use really began in 1900 when Count Ferdinand von Zeppelin of Germany designed a "rigid airship." Dubbed "Zeppelins," these aircraft had aluminum frames and gas-filled cells inside.

Zeppelins were used for military purposes during World Wars I and II, and for long-distance passenger travel until 1937, when the hydrogen-filled *Hindenberg* exploded in Lakehurst, New Jersey. Today's blimps are far smaller than the zeppelins of the 1930s; they do not have internal frames, and are filled with helium, a stable gas that will not explode.

The market for airships reawakened in the early 1980s when the U.S. Coast Guard announced its intention to use blimps in surveillance and search-and-rescue operations. Both Goodyear and Airship Industries showed early interest in participating in the Coast Guard's six-month feasibility trials.

Airship Industries spent the summer of 1985 pursuing a contract for the Coast Guard trials, a move they hoped would put $4 million into their cash-poor coffers. Goodyear, realizing that extensive modifications to its 30-year-old blimp designs would be necessary just to participate in the trials, decided to withdraw from the competition. In the end, this conservative action turned out to be the right course: as of September, 1985, the Coast Guard indefinitely postponed its airship program. Airship Industries' summer of negotiations had gained them nothing.

In the meantime, the U.S. Navy decided to re-enter the airship market. For the first time since 1963, the Navy was making plans to use airships for surveillance. Airships are large enough to carry the 100-foot radar antennae necessary to track smaller, faster targets. The Navy contract would be worth an estimated $3 to $5 billion. To date, three groups have submitted proposals for the Navy contract:

- Airship Industries, teamed with the American company Westinghouse
- Goodyear, in conjunction with Sperry and Litton
- A consortium led by aircraft manufacturer Boeing

All three groups have been lobbying intensively for the contract, particularly at the Navy League's annual Sea and Air Exposition. Each competitor's position is unique:

630

- *Airship Industries* represents the latest in airship technology, with its vectored-thrust propellers and greater lifting capacity. The company's small size and lack of a history in the market, however, could be detrimental.
- *Goodyear's* airships are of an older design, but it has a longstanding relationship with the Navy and a name that has been closely associated with blimps.
- *Boeing*, the dark horse in the competition, has drawn on its experience in aircraft technology to create a design radically different from either Airship Industries' or Goodyear's. Boeing's airship has a rigid internal structure, like the zeppelins of the 1930s, for greater stability and safety.

At the time this program was filmed, the Navy's final decision was not known. The company that wins the Navy contract could become the dominant force in a market few people even know exists. Whether there is room for competitors in that market remains to be seen.

INTRODUCTION: Now that you have read and reflected on the Chapter 6 materials and concepts pertaining to strategic and tactical planning, you are ready to analyze the decisions and actions of a small British company called Airship Industries. This video case, entitled "Battle of the Blimps," provides a unique behind-the-scenes opportunity to evaluate the strategy and tactics of the organizations involved in an apparent revival of the lighter-than-air airship industry.

PART 1: Part of this video case analysis will be carried out in work teams. Your instructor will assign specific questions to various teams. It will be the responsibility of each team to extract the requested information from the video as the case is played out. If more than one team is assigned the same question, teams may be asked to pool their findings in preparation for presenting them to the rest of the class.

a. An organization can be successful only if it is appropriately matched to its environment. With information provided in the video, your group is to perform an environmental analysis of the situation facing Airship Industries. Use Figure 6.2 in the text as the framework for your analysis.

b. An organization's strategy can be systematically developed through the use of one of a number of specially formulated techniques. The responsibility of your group is to conduct a SWOT analysis of Airship Industries' situation, using the points appearing in Table 6.5, in an attempt to judge the appropriateness of the company's existing strategy.

c. What is Airship Industries' organizational strategy? Would you categorize it as a growth, stability, retrenchment, or divestiture strategy? Explain.

d. What specific tactics were implemented to support the established strategy?

e. One of the companies competing for the Navy's contract has resurrected technology that may make its design the most competitive of all. What is this design feature and what is its special advantage?

f. Which company do you think will secure the Navy's contract? Why? Justify your answer with the information that your group assimilated in the team assignment in either a or b above.

PART 2: After fulfilling your team's assignment, answer questions c through f. Be prepared to present your views to your classmates if called upon to do so.

PART 3: Now that you have viewed the video case and have answered and discussed the questions, what specific points do you want to note so you will be able to effectively handle strategic and tactical planning in a similar situation? ■

VIDEO CASE 3

THE PARABLE OF THE SADHU: A FOCUS ON ETHICS

(An extension of materials in Chapter 19—Social Responsibility: An Emphasis on Ethics)

INTRODUCTION: Now that you have had the opportunity to read and reflect on the chapter 19 materials and concepts pertaining to social responsibility and the closely related subject of ethics, you are ready to view the video case entitled "The Parable of the Sadhu." This case portrays the real-life ethical dilemma of Bowen H. "Buzz" McCoy, a managing director of Morgan Stanley & Co., after encountering a dying pilgrim in an 18,000-foot-high pass in the Himalayas. The pilgrim, an Indian holy man, or sadhu, had apparently taken the wrong trail and had been overcome by the low temperature and the altitude. The story provides many valuable lessons related to individual and corporate ethics. After viewing the case and discussing its implications, you should have not only a much expanded understanding of the ethical dilemmas you may be faced with as a member of corporate America but also a much better understanding of how to manage them.

PART 1: In preparation for viewing the video, familiarize yourself with the following questions. When the video is shown, make notes on the case issues that appear especially relevant. Your instructor may stop the film from time to time to conduct a brief discussion of some of the case related issues.

a. Do you think that there was a breakdown in ethical responsibility in the mountain climbing experience that you just saw? Use the five criteria specified on p. 559 in your text to make this judgment.
b. Where is the limit of an individual's responsibility in a situation such as this?
c. How do the following excerpts from the case[1] relate to the ethical decisions sometimes faced at work in corporate America? Explain.

> Just after daybreak, while we rested at 15,500 feet, one of the New Zealanders, who had gone ahead, came staggering down toward us with a body slung across his shoulders. He dumped the almost naked, barefoot body of an Indian holy man—a sadhu—at my feet. . . . He said, "Look, I've done what I can. You have porters and Sherpa guides. You care for him. We're

1. Excerpts from Bowen H. McCoy, "The Parable of the Sadhu," *Harvard Business Review* (September/October 1983), 103–108. Reprinted by permission of the *Harvard Business Review*. Copyright © 1983 by the President and Fellows of Harvard College; all rights reserved.

going on!" He turned and went back up the mountain to join his friends.

I took a carotid pulse and found that the sadhu was still alive. . . . Stephen and the four Swiss began stripping off outer clothing and opening their packs. The sadhu was soon clothed from head to foot. He was not able to walk, but he was very much alive. I looked down the mountain and spotted below the Japanese climbers marching up with a horse.

Without a great deal of thought, I told Stephen and Pasang [our Sherpa leader] that I was concerned about withstanding the heights to come and wanted to get over the pass. I took off after several of our porters who had gone ahead.

. . . I stopped for a breather, allowing the Swiss to catch up with me. I inquired about the sadhu and Stephen. They said that the sadhu was fine and that Stephen was just behind. I set off again for the summit. . . .

After I had gone, and the Swiss had departed not long after, Stephen had remained with the sadhu. When the Japanese had arrived, Stephen had asked to use their horse to transport the sadhu down to the hut. They had refused. . . .

The Sherpas had carried the sadhu down to a rock in the sun at about 15,000 feet and had pointed out the hut another 500 feet below. The Japanese had given him food and drink. . . .

We do not know if the sadhu lived or died.

d. Are there collective or institutional ethics beyond the ethics of the individual?
e. Do you believe that a code of ethics such as Johnson & Johnson's (see Table 19.8) provides assistance for managers facing ethical dilemmas?
f. In the context of corporate America today, what is the great lesson of "The Parable of the Sadhu?"

PART 2: Your instructor may have chosen to stop the video and discuss some of the above-mentioned issues. Now meet with three or four of your classmates to discuss and prepare a group reaction to the remaining questions. Groups will probably be called upon to share with the rest of the class their views about one of the issues yet to be discussed.

PART 3: Now that you have viewed the video case and have answered and discussed the questions, what specific points do you want to remember to assist you as you face ethical dilemmas in your life? ■

VIDEO CASE 4

THE COLONEL COMES TO JAPAN: A FOCUS ON INTERNATIONAL MANAGEMENT

(an extension of materials in chapter 20—International Management)

SYNOPSIS: Japan is the restaurant capital of the world. The country has one eating establishment for every 81 people. Competition, understandably, is fierce.

One outfit that has been able to penetrate the market is Kentucky Fried Chicken. KFC was actually asked by the enormous Japanese conglomerate Mitsubishi to participate in a joint fast-food venture. The gesture was not simply hands-across-the water generosity. Mitsubishi just happens to be the largest chicken grower in Japan. KFC would have had trouble finding enough chicken to fry elsewhere in the country, and imported birds develop skin disease. The partnership has turned out to be mutually rewarding, with Mitsubishi leading the Colonel through the maze of the Japanese bureaucracy, and KFC netting a solid profit.

The program follows the opening of one restaurant in a relatively traditional Tokyo neighborhood. While the product itself is the same as in the United States, just about everything else is not. KFC is positioned differently in the market, appealing to a higher-paying customer. The familiar restaurant design is altered to fit a limited space. Outside, the restaurant displays little plastic models of the food available inside, as is customary in Japan. In one scene, the Japanese store manager and workers go door-to-door to drum up new business.

KFC seems to be catching on. The Japanese have obviously developed a fondness for the Colonel and his chicken. And the total operation is bringing in $200 million a year.

INTRODUCTION: Now that you have become thoroughly familiar with the chapter 20 materials and concepts pertaining to international management, you are ready to view the video case entitled "The Colonel Comes to Japan." This case should provide you with a great deal of insight into what is required to successfully set up and run a business in a foreign country.

PART 1: In preparation for viewing the video, familiarize yourself with the following questions.[1] When the video is shown, make notes on the case issues that appear especially pertinent.

a. What examples of planning, organizing, influencing, and controlling did you see in the video case? Does there appear to be any difference in the way these management functions are carried out in an international setting?
b. At what stage of multinationalization is Kentucky Fried Chicken? Explain.
c. Think of some American-made goods that, following the example of Kentucky Fried Chicken, might be successfully exported to Japan. What cultural, linguistic, or technological barriers would have to be overcome before the enterprises would flourish?
d. If you were an American entrepreneur trying to start up a chain of Kentucky Fried Chicken restaurants in Tokyo, what typical Japanese policies should you implement toward your employees?
e. What characteristics should a manager possess if the manager is to be transferred to a foreign location?

PART 2: After you view the case and document the issues you find especially pertinent, meet with three or four of your classmates to discuss and develop a group reaction to each question. Groups may be asked to share their views (or case analysis) with the rest of the class. The comments of the presenting group will provide the basis for a class discussion of the issues.

PART 3: Now that you have viewed the video case and have answered and discussed the questions, what generalizations can you make about managing in a foreign setting? ◾

1. Some of the questions are adapted from *A Guide to Enterprise: The Colonel Comes to Japan*, Learning Corporation of America, distributed by Coronet/MTI Film & Video, 108 Wilmot Road, Deerfield, IL 60015.

GLOSSARY

This glossary contains important management terms and their definitions as used in this text. Since it is sometimes difficult to understand a term fully simply by reading its definition, page numbers after each definition indicate where a more complete discussion of the term can be found.

Accountability Management philosophy that individuals are held liable, or accountable, for how well they use their authority and live up to their responsibility of performing predetermined activities. (page 236)

Activities In the PERT network, specified sets of behavior within a project. (page 180)

Activity ratios In ratio analysis, ratios that indicate how well an organization is selling its products in relation to its available resources. (page 487)

Affirmative action programs In the area of equal employment opportunity, programs whose basic purpose is to eliminate barriers against and increase opportunities for underutilized or disadvantaged individuals. (page 261)

Appropriate human resources The individuals in the organization who make a valuable contribution to management system goal attainment. (page 253)

Assessment centers Programs in which participants engage in and are evaluated on a number of individual and group exercises constructed to simulate important activities at the organizational levels to which these participants aspire. (page 265)

Authority The right to perform or command. (page 229)

Behavioral approach to management Management approach that emphasizes increasing organizational success by focusing on human variables within the organization. (page 40)

Behavior modification Program that focuses on managing human activity by controlling the consequences of performing that activity. (page 392)

Breakeven analysis Control tool based on the process of generating information that summarizes various levels of profit or loss associated with various levels of production. (page 476)

Breakeven point The situation wherein the total revenue of an organization equals its total costs. (page 477)

Budget Control tool that outlines how funds in a given period will be spent, as well as how they will be obtained. (pages 169, 482)

Bureaucracy Management system with detailed procedures and rules, a clearly outlined organizational hierarchy, and, mainly, impersonal relationships among organization members. (page 201)

Business portfolio analysis The development of business related strategy that is based primarily on the market share of businesses and the growth of markets in which businesses exist. (page 143)

Career An individual's perceived sequence of attitudes and behaviors associated with the performance of work related experiences and activities over the span of the person's working life. (page 17)

Centralization The situation in which a minimal number of job activities and a minimal amount of authority are delegated to subordinates. (page 239)

Change agent Anyone inside or outside the organization who tries to modify an existing organizational situation. (page 289)

Changing The second of Kurt Lewin's three related conditions, or states, that result in behavioral change—the state in which individuals begin to experiment with performing new behaviors. (page 300)

Changing an organization The process of modifying an existing organization to increase organizational effectiveness. (page 287)

Classical approach to management Management approach that emphasizes organizational efficiency to increase organizational success. (page 31)

Classical organizing theory The cumulative insights of early management writers on how organizational resources can best be used to enhance goal attainment. (page 201)

Closed system System that is not influenced by and does not interact with its environment. (page 44)

Command groups Formal groups that are outlined in the chain of command on an organization chart. (page 406)

Commitment principle Management guideline that advises managers to commit funds for planning

Commitment principle (continued)
only if they can anticipate, in the foreseeable future, a return on planning expenses as a result of the long-range planning analysis. (page 133)

Committee   Task group that is charged with performing some type of specific activity. (page 408)

Communication   The process of sharing information with other individuals. (page 324)

Communication effectiveness index   Intended message reactions divided by the total number of transmitted messages. (page 330)

Communication macrobarriers   The factors that hinder successful communication and that relate primarily to the communication environment and the larger world in which communication takes place. (page 327)

Communication microbarriers   The factors that hinder successful communication and that relate primarily to such variables as the communication message, the source, and the destination. (page 327)

Comparative management   The study of the management process in different countries to examine the potential of management action under different environmental conditions. (page 586)

Complete certainty condition   The decision-making situation in which the decision maker knows exactly what the results of an implemented alternative will be. (page 119)

Complete uncertainty condition   The decision-making situation in which the decision maker has absolutely no idea what the results of an implemented alternative will be. (page 120)

Computer   Electronic tool capable of accepting data, interpreting data, performing ordered operations on data, and reporting on the outcome of these operations. (page 504)

Conceptual skills   Skills that involve the ability to see the organization as a whole. (page 15)

Concurrent control   Control that takes place as some unit of work is being performed. (page 449)

Consensus   Agreement on a decision by all individuals involved in making the decision. (page 113)

Consideration behavior   Leadership behavior that reflects friendship, mutual trust, respect, and warmth in the relationship between the leader and the followers. (page 361)

Contingency approach to management   Management approach that emphasizes that what managers do in practice depends on a given set of circumstances—a situation. (page 44)

Contingency theory of leadership   Leadership concept that hypothesizes that, in any given leadership situation, success is determined primarily by (1) the degree to which the task being performed by the followers is structured, (2) the degree of position

power possessed by the leader, and (3) the type of relationship that exists between the leader and the followers. (page 365)

Control   Making something happen the way it was planned to happen. (page 441)

Control function   Computer activities that dictate the order in which other computer functions are performed. (page 508)

Controller   Staff individual whose basic responsibility is assisting line managers with the controlling function by gathering appropriate information and generating necessary reports that reflect this information. (page 451)

Controlling   The process the manager goes through to control. (page 443)

Control tool   Specific procedure or technique that presents pertinent organizational information in such a way that a manager is aided in developing and implementing appropriate control strategy. (page 475)

Coordination   The orderly arrangement of group effort to provide unity of action in the pursuit of a common purpose. (page 208)

Corporate database   *See* Database.

Corrective action   Managerial activity aimed at bringing organizational performance up to the level of performance standards. (page 446)

Cost-benefit analysis   The process of comparing the cost of some activity to the benefit or revenue that results from the activity to determine the total worth of the activity to the organization. (page 453)

Critical path   The sequence of events and activities within a program evaluation and review technique (PERT) network that requires the longest period of time to complete. (page 181)

Critical question analysis   Strategy development tool composed mainly of four questions: What are the purposes and objectives of the organization? Where is the organization presently going? In what kind of environment does the organization presently exist? What can be done to better achieve organizational objectives in the future? (page 143)

Culture   The total characteristics of a given group of people and their environment. (page 583)

Current ratio   The liquidity ratio that indicates the organization's ability to meet its financial obligations in the short run. (page 486)

$$\text{Current ratio} = \frac{\text{Current assets}}{\text{Current liabilities}}$$

Data   Facts or statistics. (page 499)

Database   A reservoir of corporate facts consistently

organized to fit the information needs of a variety of organization members. Also termed corporate database. (page 520)

Debt ratio The leverage ratio that indicates the percentage of all organizational assets provided by organizational creditors. (page 486)

$$\text{Debt ratio} = \frac{\text{Total debts}}{\text{Total assets}}$$

Decentralization The situation in which a significant number of job activities and a maximum amount of authority are delegated to subordinates. (page 239)

Decision Choice made between two or more available alternatives. (page 109)

Decision-making process The steps a decision maker takes to make a decision. (page 116)

Decision tree Graphic decision-making tool typically used to evaluate decisions containing a series of steps. (page 122)

Decline stage The fourth and last stage in career evolution, which occurs near retirement and during which individuals about sixty-five years of age or older show declining productivity. (page 19)

Decoder/destination The person or people in the interpersonal communication situation with whom the source/encoder attempts to share information. (page 325)

Delegation The process of assigning job activities and related authority to specific individuals in the organization. (page 237)

Demographics The statistical characteristics of a population. (page 137)

Department Unique group of resources established by management to perform some organizational task. (page 202)

Departmentalization The process of establishing departments in the management system. (page 202)

Dialogue capability The ability of a management decision support system (MDSS) user to interact with a management decision support system. (page 521)

Direct investing Using the assets of one company to purchase the operating assets of another company. (page 580)

Dispatching Issuing orders to the individuals involved in producing goods or services. (page 474)

Divestiture Strategy generally adopted to eliminate a strategic business unit that is not generating a satisfactory amount of business and has little hope of doing so in the future. (page 146)

Division of labor The assignment of various portions of a particular task among a number of organization members. (page 208)

Downward organizational communication Communication that flows from any point on an organiza-tion chart downward to another point on the organization chart. (page 334)

Economics Science that focuses on understanding how people of a particular community or nation produce, distribute, and use various goods and services. (page 137)

Environmental analysis Study of the organizational environment to pinpoint environmental factors that can significantly influence organizational operations. (page 136)

Equal Employment Opportunity Commission (EEOC) Agency established to enforce the laws that regulate recruiting and other managerial practices. (page 261)

Establishment stage The second stage in career evolution, during which individuals of about twenty-five to forty-five years of age typically start to become more productive or higher performers. (page 18)

Esteem needs Maslow's fourth set of human needs—including the desire for self-respect and respect from others. (page 381)

Ethics Our concern for good behavior; our obligation to consider not only our own personal well-being but also that of other human beings. (page 558)

Ethnocentric attitude Attitude that reflects a belief that multinational corporations should regard home country management practices as superior to foreign country management practices. (page 581)

Events In the PERT network, the completions of major product tasks. (page 180)

Expected value Measurement of the anticipated value of some event; determined by multiplying the income an event would produce by its probability of making that income. (page 121)

Exploration stage The first stage in career evolution, which occurs at the beginning of a career and is characterized by self-analysis and the exploration of different types of available jobs by individuals of about fifteen to twenty-five years of age. (page 18)

Exporting Selling goods or services to another country. (page 579)

Extrinsic rewards Rewards that are extraneous to the task accomplished. (page 380)

Feedback In the interpersonal communication situation, the decoder/destination's reaction to a message. (page 329)

Feedback control Control that takes place after some unit of work has been performed. (page 451)

Financial objectives Organizational targets relating to monetary issues. (66)

Fixed assets turnover The activity ratio that indicates the appropriateness of the amount of funds invested in plant and equipment relative to the level of sales. (page 487)

$$\text{Fixed asset turnover} = \frac{\text{Sales}}{\text{Fixed assets}}$$

Fixed costs Expenses incurred by an organization regardless of the number of products produced. (page 476)

Fixed position layout Layout pattern that, because of the weight or bulk of the product being manufactured, has workers, tools, and materials rotating around a stationary product. (page 472)

Flat organization chart Organization chart that is characterized by few levels and relatively large spans of management. (page 211)

Flextime Program that allows workers to complete their jobs within a workweek of a normal number of hours that they schedule themselves. (page 390)

Forecasting Planning tool used to predict future environmental happenings that will influence the operation of the organization. (page 173)

Formal group Group that exists in an organization by virtue of management decree to perform tasks that enhance the attainment of organizational objectives. (page 406)

Formal organizational communication Organizational communication that follows the lines of the organization chart. (page 334)

Formal structure Relationships among organizational resources as outlined by management. (page 201)

Friendship groups Informal groups that form in organizations because of the personal affiliation members have with one another. (page 414)

Functional authority The right to give orders within a segment of the management system in which the right is normally nonexistent. (page 234)

Functional objectives Targets relating to key organizational functions. (page 67)

Functional similarity method Method for dividing job activities in the organization. (page 224)

Functional skill Skill involving the ability to apply appropriately the concepts of planning, organizing, influencing, and controlling to the operation of a management system. (page 601)

Future oriented managers Managers who attempt to create their own future, whenever possible, and adapt to this future, when necessary, through a continuous process of research about the future, long-term planning, and setting objectives. (page 617)

Gangplank Communication channel extending from one organizational division to another but not shown in the lines of communication outlined on an organization chart. (page 213)

Gantt chart Scheduling tool composed essentially of a bar chart with time on the horizontal axis and the resource to be scheduled on the vertical axis. (page 179)

General environment The level of an organization's external environment that contains components normally having broad long-term implications for managing the organization. (page 137)

Geocentric attitude Attitude that reflects a belief that the overall quality of management recommendations, rather than the location of managers, should determine the acceptability of management practices used to guide multinational corporations. (page 582)

Geographic contiguity The degree to which subordinates are physically separated. (page 210)

Goal integration Compatibility between individual and organizational objectives. (page 61)

Graicunas's formula Formula that makes the span of management point that as the number of a manager's subordinates increases arithmetically, the number of possible relationships between the manager and the subordinates increases geometrically. (page 210)

Grapevine Network for informal organizational communication. (page 336)

Grid organization development (grid OD) Commonly used organization development technique based on a theoretical model called the managerial grid. (page 296)

Group Any number of people who (1) interact with one another, (2) are psychologically aware of one another, and (3) perceive themselves to be a group. (page 405)

Group cohesiveness The attraction group members feel for one another in terms of the desire to remain a member of the group and to resist leaving it. (page 421)

Group norms Appropriate or standard behavior that is required of informal group members. (page 422)

Groupthink The mode of thinking that people engage in when seeking agreement becomes so dominant in a group that it tends to override the realistic appraisal of alternate problem solutions. (page 411)

Growth Strategy adopted by management to increase the amount of business that a strategic business unit is currently generating. (page 146)

Hierarchy of objectives The overall organizational objective(s) and the subobjectives assigned to the various people or units of the organization. (page 67)

Host country The country in which an investment is made by a foreign company. (page 577)

Human resource inventory Accumulation of information concerning the characteristics of organization members; this information focuses on the past performance of organization members as well as on how they might be trained and best used in the future. (page 258)

Human resource planning Input planning that involves obtaining the human resources necessary for the organization to achieve its objectives. (page 173)

Human resources *See* Appropriate human resources.

Human skills Skills involving the ability to build cooperation within the team being led. (page 15)

Hygiene, or maintenance, factors Items that influence the degree of job dissatisfaction. (page 388)

Importing Buying goods or services from another country. (page 579)

Individual objectives Personal goals that each organization member would like to reach as a result of personal activity in the organization. (page 61)

Influencing The process of guiding the activities of organization members in appropriate directions, involving the performance of four primary management activities: (1) leading, (2) motivating, (3) considering groups, and (4) communicating. (page 321)

Informal groups Groups that develop naturally in organizations as people interact. (page 414)

Informal organizational communication Organizational communication that does not follow the lines of the organization chart. (page 336)

Informal structure Patterns of relationships that develop because of the informal activities of organization members. (page 202)

Information Conclusions derived from data analysis. (page 499)

Information appropriateness The degree to which information is relevant to the decision-making situation that faces the manager. (page 500)

Information quality The degree to which information represents reality. (page 501)

Information quantity The amount of decision related information a manager possesses. (page 501)

Information timeliness The extent to which the receipt of information allows decisions to be made and action to be taken so the organization can gain some benefit from possessing the information. (page 501)

Input function Computer activities through which the computer enters the data to be analyzed and the instructions to be followed to analyze the data appropriately. (page 504)

Input planning Development of proposed action that will furnish sufficient and appropriate organizational resources for reaching established organizational objectives. (page 170)

Interest groups Informal groups that gain and maintain membership primarily because of a special concern each member possesses about a specific issue. (page 414)

Intermediate-term objectives Targets to be achieved within one to five years. (page 64)

Internal environment The level of an organization's environment that exists inside the organization and normally has immediate and specific implications for managing the organization. (page 141)

International management Performing management activities across national borders. (page 571)

Intrinsic rewards Rewards that come directly from performing a task. (page 380)

Inventory turnover The activity ratio that indicates whether an organization is maintaining an appropriate level of inventory in relation to its sales volume. (page 487)

$$\text{Inventory turnover} = \frac{\text{Sales}}{\text{Inventory}}$$

Job analysis Technique commonly used to gain an understanding of what a task entails and the type of individual who should be hired to perform the task. (page 254)

Job description Specific activities that must be performed to accomplish some task or job. (pages 223, 254)

Job enlargement The process of increasing the number of operations an individual performs in a job. (page 388)

Job enrichment The process of incorporating motivators into a job situation. (page 389)

Job rotation The process of moving individuals from one job to another and not requiring individuals to perform only one job over the long term. (page 388)

Job specifications Characteristics of the individual who should be hired to perform a specific task or job. (page 254)

Joint venture Partnership formed by a company in one country with a company in another country for the purpose of pursuing some mutually desirable business undertaking. (page 580)

Jury of executive opinion method Method of predicting future sales levels primarily by asking appropriate managers to give their opinions on what will happen to sales in the future. (page 175)

Just-in-time (JIT) inventory control An inventory control technique that reduces inventories to a mini-

Just-in-time (JIT) inventory control (continued)
mum by arranging for them to be delivered to the production facility just in time to be used. (page 590)

Lateral organizational communication   Communication that flows from any point on an organization chart horizontally to another point on the organization chart. (page 334)

Layout patterns   The overall arrangement of machines, equipment, materials handling, aisles, service areas, storage areas, and work stations within a production facility. (page 472)

Leader flexibility   The ability of leaders to change their leadership styles. (page 365)

Leadership   The process of directing the behavior of others toward the accomplishment of objectives. (page 351)

Leadership style   Behavioral pattern a leader establishes while guiding organization members in appropriate directions. (page 361)

Lecture   Primarily one-way communication situation in which an instructor trains by orally presenting information to an individual or group. (page 268)

Level dimension (of plans)   The level of the organization at which plans are aimed. (page 164)

Leverage ratios   In ratio analysis, the ratios that indicate the relationship between organizational funds supplied by the owners of an organization and organizational funds supplied by creditors. (page 486)

License agreement   Right granted by one company to another to use its brand name, technology, product specifications, and so on in the manufacture or sale of goods and services. (page 579)

Life cycle theory of leadership   Leadership concept that hypothesizes that leadership styles should reflect primarily the maturity level of the followers. (page 362)

Line authority   The right to make decisions and to give orders concerning the production, sales, or finance related behavior of subordinates. (page 230)

Liquidity ratios   In ratio analysis, the ratios that indicate an organization's ability to meet upcoming financial obligations. (page 486)

Long-term objectives   Targets to be achieved within five to seven years. (page 64)

Loss   The amount of the total costs of producing a product that exceeds the total revenue gained from selling the product. (page 477)

Maintenance stage   The third stage in career evolution, during which individuals of about forty-five to sixty-five years of age become more productive, stabilize, or become less productive. (page 18)

Management   The process of reaching organizational goals by working with and through people and other organizational resources. (page 8)

Management by exception   Control tool that allows only significant deviations between planned and actual performance to be brought to the manager's attention. (page 475)

Management by objectives (MBO)   Management approach that uses organizational objectives as the primary means by which to manage organizations. (page 71)

Management decision support system (MDSS)   An interdependent set of computer-oriented decision aids that help managers make nonprogrammed decisions. (page 520)

Management functions   Activities that make up the management process, including planning, organizing, influencing, and controlling. (page 8)

Management information system (MIS)   Network established in an organization to provide managers with information that will assist them in decision making. (page 510)

Management inventory card   Form used in compiling a human resource inventory—containing an organizational history of an individual and an explanation of how the individual might be used in the future. (page 258)

Management manpower replacement chart   Form used in compiling a human resource inventory—people-oriented and presenting a total composite view of the individuals whom management considers significant to human resource planning. (page 259)

Management responsibility guide   Tool that can be used to clarify the responsibilities of various managers in the organization. (page 226)

Management science approach   Management approach that emphasizes the use of the scientific method and quantitative techniques to increase organizational success. (page 42)

Management system   Open system whose major parts are organizational input, organizational process, and organizational output. (page 45)

Managerial effectiveness   The degree to which management attains organizational objectives. (page 12)

Managerial efficiency   The degree to which organizational resources contribute to productivity. (page 13)

Managerial grid   Theoretical model based on the premise that concern for people and concern for production are the two primary attitudes that influence management style. (page 296)

Materials requirements control   The process of making things happen the way they were planned to happen in materials requirements planning. (page 481)

Materials requirements planning (MRP)   Creating schedules that identify the specific parts and materials required to produce an item, the exact quantities of each needed to enhance the production process, and the dates when orders for these quantities should be released to suppliers and be received for best timing in the production cycle. (page 480)

Matrix organization   Traditional organizational structure that is modified primarily for the purpose of completing some type of special project. (page 293)

Maturity   As used in the life cycle theory of leadership, an individual's ability to independently perform the job, to assume additional responsibility, and to desire success. (page 362)

Means-ends analysis   The process of outlining the means by which various objectives, or ends, in the organization can be achieved. (page 70)

Message   Encoded information that the source/encoder intends to share with others. (page 325)

Message interference   Stimuli that compete with the communication message for the attention of the decoder/destination. (page 327)

Model base   A collection of quantitative computer programs that can assist management decision support system (MDSS) users in analyzing data within databases. (page 521)

Motion study   Finding the one best way to accomplish a task by analyzing the movements necessary to perform the task. (page 35)

Motivating factors   Items that influence the degree of job satisfaction. (page 388)

Motivation   The inner state that causes an individual to behave in a way that ensures the accomplishment of some goal. (page 377)

Motivation strength   Individual's degree of desire to perform a behavior. (page 378)

Multinational corporation (MNC)   Company that has significant operations in more than one country. (page 573)

Need for achievement (n Ach)   The desire to do something better or more efficiently than it has ever been done before. (page 383)

Needs-goal model   Motivation model that hypothesizes that felt needs cause human behavior. (page 378)

Negative norms   Informal group standards that limit organizational productivity. (page 423)

Negative reinforcement   Reward that is the elimination of an undesirable consequence of behavior. (page 392)

Nonprogrammed decisions   Decisions that typically are one-shot occurrences and usually are less structured than programmed decisions. (page 110)

Nonverbal communication   The sharing of ideas without the use of words. (page 332)

On-the-job training   Training technique that blends job related knowledge with experience in using that knowledge in the job. (page 268)

Open system   System that is influenced by and is constantly interacting with its environment. (page 44)

Operating environment   Level of the organization's external environment that contains components normally having relatively specific and immediate implications for managing the organization. (page 139)

Operational objectives   Objectives that are stated in observable or measurable terms. (page 69)

Operations management   The process of managing production in organizations. (page 472)

Organizational communication   Interpersonal communication in organizations. (page 333)

Organizational objectives   Targets toward which the open management system is directed. (page 57)

Organizational purpose   What the organization exists to do, given a particular group of customers and customer needs. (page 58)

Organizational resources   Assets available for activation during normal operations, among which are human resources, monetary resources, raw materials resources, and capital resources. (page 11)

Organization chart   Graphic representation of organizational structure. (page 201)

Organization development   Process that emphasizes changing an organization by changing organization members and that bases these changes on an overview of structure, technology, and all other organizational ingredients. (page 296)

Organizing   The process of establishing orderly uses for all resources in the organization. (page 197)

Output function   Computer activities that take the results of input, storage, processing, and control functions and transmit them outside the computer. (page 508)

Overlapping responsibility   Situation in which more than one individual is responsible for the same activity. (page 224)

Parent company   The company investing in international operations. (page 577)

People change   Changing certain aspects of organization members to increase organizational effectiveness. (page 295)

People factors   Attitudes, leadership skills, communication skills, and all other characteristics of the organization's employees. (page 290)

Perception   Interpretation of a message as observed by an individual. (page 328)

Performance appraisal   The process of reviewing past productive activity to evaluate the contribution individuals have made toward attaining management system objectives. (page 271)

Personal power   Power derived from the relationship that one person has with another. (page 455)

PERT   *See* Program evaluation and review technique (PERT). (page 180)

Physiological needs   Maslow's first set of human needs—for the normal functioning of the body—including the desire for water, food, rest, sex, and air. (page 381)

Plan   Specific action proposed to help the organization achieve its objectives. (page 161)

Plan for planning   Listing of all steps that must be taken to plan for an organization. (page 93)

Planning   The process of determining how the management system will achieve its objectives. (page 85)

Planning tools   Techniques managers can use to help develop plans. (page 173)

Plant facilities planning   Input planning that involves developing the type of work facility an organization will need to reach its objectives. (page 170)

Policy   Standing plan that furnishes broad guidelines for channeling management thinking in specified directions. (page 167)

Polycentric attitude   Attitude that reflects a belief that since foreign managers are closer to foreign organizational units, they probably understand them better—and therefore that foreign management practices generally should be viewed as more insightful than home country management practices. (page 582)

Porter-Lawler model   Motivation model that hypothesizes that felt needs cause human behavior and that motivation strength is determined primarily by the perceived value of the result of performing the behavior and the perceived probability that the behavior performed will cause the result to materialize. (page 379)

Position power   Power derived from the organizational position that one holds. (page 455)

Position replacement form   Form used in compiling a human resources inventory—summarizing information about organization members who could fill a position should it open. (page 258)

Positive norms   Informal group standards that contribute to organizational productivity. (page 423)

Positive reinforcement   Reward that is a desirable consequence of behavior. (page 392)

Power   The extent to which an individual is able to influence others so they respond to orders. (page 455)

Precontrol   Control that takes place before some unit of work is actually performed. (page 449)

Premises   Assumptions on which alternate ways of accomplishing objectives are based. (page 88)

Principle of supportive relationships   Management guideline that indicates that all human interaction with an organization should build and maintain the sense of personal worth and the importance of those involved in the interaction. (page 394)

Principle of the objective   Management guideline that recommends that before managers initiate any action, organizational objectives should be clearly determined, understood, and stated. (page 65)

Probability theory   Decision-making tool used in risk situations—situations in which the decision maker is not completely sure of the outcome of an implemented alternative. (page 121)

Problems   Factors within organizations that are barriers to organizational goal attainment. (page 447)

Procedure   Standing plan that outlines a series of related actions that must be taken to accomplish a particular task. (page 167)

Processing function   Computer activities involved with performing the logic and calculation steps necessary to analyze data appropriately. (page 508)

Process layout   Layout pattern based primarily on grouping together similar types of equipment. (page 472)

Production   The transformation of organizational resources into products. (page 469)

Production control   Ensuring that an organization produces goods and services as planned. (page 469)

Production planning   Determining the type and amount of resources needed to produce specified goods or services. (page 474)

Productivity   The relationship between the total amount of goods or services being produced (output) and the organizational resources needed (input) to produce the goods or services. (page 469)

Product layout   Layout pattern based mostly on the progressive steps by which the product is made. (page 472)

Product life cycle   Five stages through which most new products and services pass—introduction, growth, maturity, saturation, and decline. (page 175)

Product-market mix objectives   Objectives that outline

which products and the relative number or mix of these products the organization will attempt to sell. (page 66)

Profession Vocation whose practice is based on an understanding of a specific body of knowledge and the corresponding abilities necessary to apply this understanding to vital human problems. (page 617)

Profitability ratios In ratio analysis, the ratios that indicate the ability of an organization to generate profits. (page 487)

Profits The amount of total revenue that exceeds total costs. (page 477)

Profit to sales ratio The profitability ratio that indicates whether the organization is making an adequate net profit in relation to the total dollars coming into the organization. (page 487)

$$\text{Profit to sales ratio} = \frac{\text{Net profit}}{\text{Sales}}$$

Profit to total assets ratio The profitability ratio that indicates whether the organization is realizing enough net profit in relation to the total dollars invested in assets. (page 487)

$$\frac{\text{Profit to}}{\text{total assets ratio}} = \frac{\text{Total assets}}{\text{Net profit}}$$

Program Single-use plan designed to carry out a special project in an organization. (page 169)

Program evaluation and review technique (PERT) Scheduling tool that is essentially a network of project activities showing estimates of time necessary to complete each activity and the sequential relationship of activities that must be followed to complete the project. (page 180)

Programmed decisions Decisions that are routine and repetitive and that typically require specific handling methods. (page 109)

Programmed learning Technique for instructing without the presence of a human instructor—small pieces of information requiring responses are presented to individual trainees. (page 268)

Punishment The presentation of an undesirable behavioral consequence or the removal of a desirable one that decreases the likelihood of the behavior continuing. (page 392)

Quality circles Small groups of workers that meet regularly with management to discuss quality related problems. (page 415)

Quality control The process of making the quality of finished goods and services what it was planned to be. (page 481)

Quality of work life Opportunity of workers to make decisions that influence their work situation. (page 608)

Quick ratio The liquidity ratio that indicates an organization's ability to meet its financial obligations with no reliance on inventory. (page 486)

$$\frac{\text{Quick}}{\text{ratio}} = \frac{\text{Current assets} - \text{Inventory}}{\text{Current liabilities}}$$

Ratio analysis Control tool based on the process of generating information that summarizes the financial position of an organization by calculating ratios based on various financial measures appearing on balance sheets and income statements. (page 485)

Recruitment The initial screening of the total supply of prospective human resources available to fill a position. (page 254)

Refreezing The third of Kurt Lewin's three related conditions, or states, that result in behavioral change—the state in which an individual's experimentally performed behaviors become part of the person. (page 300)

Relevant alternatives Alternatives that are considered feasible for implementation and for solving an existing problem. (page 116)

Repetitiveness dimension (of plans) The extent to which plans are used again and again. (page 161)

Responsibility The obligation to perform assigned activities. (page 223)

Responsibility gap Situation in which certain organizational tasks are not included in the responsibility area of any individual organization member. (page 224)

Retrenchment Strategy adopted by management to strengthen or protect the amount of business a strategic business unit is currently generating. (page 146)

Risk condition The decision-making situation in which the decision maker has only enough information to estimate how probable the outcome of implemented alternatives will be. (page 120)

Robot Machine in the form of a human being that performs the mechanical functions of a human being but lacks sensitivity. (page 471)

Robotics The area of study dealing with the development and use of robots. (page 471)

Routing Determining the sequence in which work must be completed to produce specified goods or services. (page 474)

Rule Standing plan that designates specific required action. (page 168)

Sales force estimation method Method of predicting future sales levels primarily by asking appropriate

Sales force estimation method (continued) salespeople for their opinions of what will happen to sales in the future. (page 175)

Scalar relationships   The chain of command positioning of individuals on an organization chart. (page 212)

Scheduling   The process of formulating detailed listings of activities that must be performed to accomplish a task, allocating resources necessary to complete the task, and setting up and following timetables for completing the task. (pages 178, 474)

Scientific management   Management approach that emphasizes the one best way to perform a task. (page 34)

Scientific method   Problem-solving method that entails the following sequential steps: (1) observing a system, (2) constructing a framework that is consistent with the observations and from which the consequences of changing the system can be predicted, (3) predicting how various changes would influence the system, and (4) testing to see if these changes influence the system as intended. (page 42)

Scope dimension (of plans)   The portion of the total management system at which the plans are aimed. (page 164)

Scope of the decision   The proportion of the total management system that a particular decision will affect. (page 112)

Security, or safety, needs   Maslow's second set of human needs—reflecting the human desire to keep free from physical harm. (page 381)

Selection   Choosing an individual to hire from all of those who have been recruited. (page 262)

Self-actualization needs   Maslow's fifth set of human needs—reflecting the human desire to maximize potential. (page 381)

Serial transmission   The passing of information from one individual through a series of individuals. (page 335)

Short-term objectives   Targets to be achieved in one year or less. (page 64)

Signal   A message that has been transmitted from one person to another. (page 325)

Single-use plans   Plans that are used only once or several times because they focus on organizational situations that do not occur repeatedly. (page 165)

Site selection   Determining where a plant facility should be located. (page 170)

Situational analysis skill   Skill involving the ability to apply both systems theory and functional theory to the unique conditions of a particular organizational situation. (page 603)

Situational approach to leadership   Relatively modern view of leadership that suggests that successful leadership requires a unique combination of leaders, followers, and leadership situations. (page 353)

Social audit   The process of measuring the social responsibility activities of an organization. (page 555)

Social needs   Maslow's third set of human needs—reflecting the human desire to belong, including the desire for friendship, companionship, and love. (page 381)

Social obligation approach   Approach to meeting social obligations that reflects an attitude that considers business to have primarily economic purposes and confines social responsibility activity mainly to conformance to existing legislation. (page 548)

Social responsibility   The managerial obligation to take action that protects and improves the welfare of society as a whole and organizational interests as well. (page 535)

Social responsibility approach   Approach to meeting social obligations that is characterized by an attitude that considers business as having both societal and economic goals. (page 548)

Social responsiveness   The degree of effectiveness and efficiency an organization displays in pursuing its social responsibilities. (page 547)

Social responsiveness approach   Approach to meeting social obligations that reflects an attitude that considers business to have societal and economic goals as well as the obligation to anticipate upcoming social problems and to work actively toward preventing their appearance. (page 548)

Social values   The relative degrees of worth society places on the manner in which it exists and functions. (page 138)

Sociogram   Sociometric diagram that summarizes the personal feelings of organization members about the people in the organization with whom they would like to spend free time. (page 417)

Sociometry   Analytical tool that can be used to determine what informal groups exist in an organization and who the members of those groups are. (page 417)

Source/encoder   The person in the interpersonal communication situation who originates and encodes information that the person wants to share with others. (page 325)

Span of management   The number of individuals a manager supervises. (page 209)

Stability   Strategy adopted by management to maintain or slightly improve the amount of business a strategic business unit is generating. (page 146)

Staff authority   The right to advise or assist those who possess line authority. (page 231)

Standard   The level of activity established to serve as a model for evaluating organizational performance. (page 445)

Standing plans   Plans that are used over and over because they focus on organizational situations that occur repeatedly. (page 165)

Statistical quality control   Process used to determine how many products from a larger number should be inspected to calculate a probability that the total number of products meets organizational quality standards. (page 481)

Status   The positioning of importance of a group member in relation to other group members. (page 424)

Storage function   Computer activities involved with retaining the material entered into the computer during the performance of the input function. (page 505)

Strategic business unit (SBU)   In business portfolio analysis, a significant organizational segment that is analyzed to develop organizational strategy aimed at generating future business or revenue. (page 144)

Strategic planning   Long-term planning that focuses on the organization as a whole. (page 133)

Strategy   Broad and general plan developed to reach long-term organizational objectives. (page 133)

Strategy management   The process of ensuring that an organization possesses and benefits from the use of an appropriate organization strategy. (page 134)

Stress   The bodily strain that an individual experiences as a result of coping with some environmental factor. (page 302)

Stressor   Environmental demand that causes people to feel stress. (page 304)

Structural change   Type of organizational change that emphasizes modifying an existing organizational structure. (page 293)

Structural factors   Organizational controls, such as policies and procedures. (page 290)

Structure   Designated relationships among resources of the management system. (page 201)

Structure behavior   Leadership activity that (1) delineates the relationship between the leader and the leader's followers or (2) establishes well-defined procedures that the followers should adhere to in performing their jobs. (page 359)

Suboptimization   Condition wherein organizational subobjectives are conflicting or not directly aimed at accomplishing overall organizational objectives. (page 67)

Subsystem   System created as part of the process of the overall management system. (page 90)

Successful communication   Interpersonal communica-

tion situation in which the information the source/encoder intends to share with the decoder/destination and the meaning the decoder/destination derives from the transmitted message are the same. (page 326)

Suppliers   Individuals or agencies that provide organizations with resources needed to produce organizational goods or services. (page 141)

SWOT analysis   Strategy development tool that matches internal organizational strengths and weaknesses with external opportunities and threats. (page 143)

Symptom   Sign that a problem exists. (page 447)

System   Number of interdependent parts functioning as a whole for some purpose. (page 44)

System approach to management   Management approach based on general system theory—the theory that to understand fully the operation of an entity, the entity must be viewed as a system. (page 44)

Systems skill   The ability to view and manage a business or some other concern as a number of components that work together and function as a whole to achieve some objective. (page 601)

Tactical planning   Short-range planning that emphasizes current operations of various parts of the organization. (page 147)

Tall organization chart   Organization chart that is characterized by many levels and relatively small spans of management. (page 211)

Task groups   Formal groups of organization members who interact with one another to accomplish mostly nonroutine organizational tasks (members of any one task group can and often do come from various levels and segments of an organization). (page 406)

Technical skills   The ability to apply specialized knowledge and expertise to work related techniques and procedures. (page 15)

Technological change   Type of organizational change that emphasizes modifying the level of technology in the management system. (page 291)

Technological factors   Any types of equipment or processes that assist organization members in the performance of their jobs. (page 290)

Testing   Examining human resources for qualities relevant to performing available jobs. (page 263)

Theory X   Set of essentially negative assumptions about the nature of people. (page 387)

Theory Y   Set of essentially positive assumptions about the nature of people. (page 387)

Theory Z   Effectiveness dimension that implies that managers who use either Theory X or Theory Y assumptions when dealing with people can be

Theory Z (continued)
successful, depending on their situation. (pages 384, 587)

Time dimension (of plans)   The length of time plans cover. (page 164)

Time series analysis method   Method of predicting future sales levels by analyzing the historical relationship in an organization between sales and time. (page 175)

Times interest earned ratio   The leverage ratio that indicates an organization's ability to pay interest expenses directly from gross income. (page 487)

$$\frac{\text{Times interest}}{\text{earned ratio}} = \frac{\text{Gross income}}{\text{Interest charges}}$$

Total assets turnover   The activity ratio that indicates the appropriateness of the level of funds an organization has tied up in all assets relative to its rate of sales. (page 487)

$$\frac{\text{Total assets}}{\text{turnover}} = \frac{\text{Sales}}{\text{Total assets}}$$

Total costs   The sum of fixed costs and variable costs associated with production. (page 476)

Total power   The entire amount of power an individual in an organization possesses, mainly the amount of position power and the amount of personal power possessed by the individual. (page 455)

Total revenue   All sales dollars accumulated from selling goods or services that are produced. (page 476)

Training   The process of developing qualities in human resources that ultimately will enable them to be more productive and thus to contribute more to organizational goal attainment. (page 265)

Training need   Information or skill area of an individual or group that requires further development to increase the organizational productivity of the individual or group. (page 266)

Trait approach to leadership   Outdated view of leadership that sees the personal characteristics of an individual as the main determinants of how successful the individual could be as a leader. (page 353)

Triangular management   Management approach that emphasizes using information from the classical, behavioral, and management science schools of thought to manage the open management system. (page 46)

Unfreezing   The first of Kurt Lewin's three related conditions, or states, that result in behavioral change—the state in which individuals experience a need to learn new behaviors. (page 300)

Unity of command   Management principle that recommends that an individual have only one boss. (page 213)

Universality of management skills   The idea that the principles of management are universal, or applicable to all types of organizations and organizational levels. (page 16)

Unsuccessful communication   Interpersonal communication situation in which the information the source/encoder intends to share with the decoder/destination and the meaning the decoder/destination derives from the transmitted message are different. (page 326)

Upward organizational communication   Communication that flows from any point on an organization chart upward to another point on the organization chart. (page 334)

User database   Database developed by an individual manager or other user. (page 520)

Variable budgets   Budgets that outline various levels of resources to be allocated for each organizational activity, depending on the level of production within the organization. Also called flexible budgets. (page 484)

Variable costs   Organizational expenses that fluctuate with the number of products produced. (page 476)

Verbal communication   The sharing of ideas through words. (page 332)

Vroom expectancy model   Motivation model that hypothesizes that felt needs cause human behavior and that motivation strength depends on an individual's degree of desire to perform a behavior. (page 378)

"What if" analysis   The simulation of a business situation over and over again using somewhat different data for selected decision areas. (page 521)

Work team   Task group used in organizations to achieve greater organizational flexibility or to cope with rapid growth. (page 411)

Zero-base budgeting   The planning and budgeting process that requires managers to justify their entire budget request in detail rather than simply to refer to budget amounts established in previous years. (page 484)

INDEXES

COMPANY NAME INDEX

NAME INDEX

SUBJECT INDEX

CREDITS

Chapter 1 **Introductory case:** Based on Kenneth Labich, "A Steel Town's Bid to Save Itself," *Fortune*, April 18, 1983. **Figure 1.2:** Used by permission of Sibson & Company, Inc. **Table 1.1:** From Joseph L. Massie and John Douglas, *Managing: A Contemporary Introduction* (Englewood Cliffs, N.J.: Prentice-Hall, 1973), p. 24; Robert Kreitner, *Management*, 2d ed. (Boston: Houghton Mifflin, 1983); Henry L. Sisk, *Management and Organization*, 2d ed. (Cincinnati: South-Western, 1974), p. 13; Harold Koontz and Cyril O'Donnell, *Principles of Management: An Analysis of Managerial Functions*, 5th ed. (New York: McGraw-Hill, 1972), p. 42; James H. Donnelly, Jr., James L. Gibson, and John M. Ivancevich, *Fundamentals of Management: Functions, Behavior, Models* (Homewood, Ill.: Business Publications, 1975), p. 4. **Management in Action:** From Robert McGough, "A Passion for Fine-Tuning." Reprinted by permission of *Forbes* magazine, May 4, 1987, p. 44. © Forbes Inc., 1987. **Table 1.2:** "The Eight Attributes" from pp. 13–16 of *In Search of Excellence* by Thomas J. Peters and Robert H. Waterman, Jr. Copyright © 1982 by Thomas J. Peters and Robert H. Waterman, Jr. Reprinted by permission of Harper & Row, Publishers, Inc. **Figure 1.6:** From Paul Hersey/Kenneth Blanchard, *Management of Organizational Behavior: Utilizing Human Resources*, 5e, © 1988, p. 8. Reprinted by permission of Prentice-Hall, Inc., Englewood Cliffs, N.J. **Figure 1.7:** From *Careers in Organizations* by Douglas T. Hall, © 1976 Scott, Foresman and Company. Reprinted by permission. **Table 1.3:** From Lynn Slavenski, "Career Development: A Systems Approach," *Training and Development Journal* (February 1987): 58. Copyright 1987, *Training and Development Journal*, American Society for Training and Development. Reprinted with permission. **Table 1.4:** Reprinted by permission from Paul H. Thompson, Robin Zenger Baker, and Norman Smallwood, "Improving Professional Development by Applying the Four-Stage Career Model," *Organizational Dynamics* (Autumn 1986): 59. © 1986 American Management Association, Inc. All rights reserved. **Table 1.5:** © 1976 by the Regents of the University of California. Reprinted from Ross A. Webber, "Career Problems of Young Managers," *California Management Review*, Vol. 18, No. 4 (Summer 1976): 29, by permission of the Regents. **Concluding case:** Adapted from Toni Mack, "It's Time to Take Risks." Adapted by permission of *Forbes* magazine, October 6, 1986, pp. 125–133. © Forbes Inc., 1986.

Chapter 2 **Introductory case:** Based on "Recipe for Success in the Fast-Food Game," *U.S. News & World Report*, November 21, 1983. **Management in Action:** Excerpted from John S. DeMott, "In Old Milwaukee: Tomorrow's Factory, Today," *Time*, June 16, 1986, pp. 66–67. Copyright 1986 Time Inc. All rights reserved. Reprinted by permission from *Time*. **Table 2.2:** From William R. Spriegel and Clark E. Myers, *The Writings of the Gilbreths* (Easton, Pa.: Richard D. Irwin, 1953), p. 56. By permission of Hive Publishing Company. **Concluding case (including illustration):** Adapted from Gary Forger, "How Frito-Lay Justifies New Handling Equipment," *Modern Materials Handling* (May 1987): 78–80. Copyright 1987 by Cahners Publishing, Div. of Reed Publishing USA.

Chapter 3 **Introductory case:** Based on Virginia Inman, "Flow General Tries to Settle on Future Path," *Wall Street Journal*, July 11, 1983. **Table 3.2:** © 1979 by the Regents of the University of California. Reprinted from Y. K. Shetty, "New Look at Corporate Goals," *California Management Review*, Vol. 22, No. 2, p. 73, by permission of the Regents. **Management in Action:** From Seth H. Lubove, "In the Computer Age Certain Workers Are Still Vital to Success," *Wall Street Journal*, August 3, 1987, pp. 1, 13. Reprinted by permission of the *Wall Street Journal*, © Dow Jones & Company, Inc., 1987. All rights reserved. **Figure 3.2:** From Jon H. Barrett, *Individual Goals and Organizational Objectives: A Study of Integration Mechanisms*, p. 5. Copyright © 1970 by the Institute for Social Research, The University of Michigan. Reprinted with permission. **Figure 3.4:** From Joseph L. Massie and John Douglas, *Managing*, © 1985, p. 244. Reprinted by permission of Prentice-Hall, Inc. Englewood Cliffs, New Jersey. **Table 3.3:** From *Management Concepts and Situations* by Howard M. Carlisle. © 1976, Science Research Associates, Inc. Adapted and reprinted by permission of the publisher. **Table 3.4:** Reprinted by permission from A. N. Geller, *Executive Information Needs in Hotel Companies* (New York: Peat Marwick Mitchell, 1984), p. 17. © Peat Marwick Main & Co., 1984. **Concluding case:** Based on "Alcan's Integration of Management Techniques Raises Their Effectiveness," *AMA Forum* (April 1984). **Section 1 integrative case:** Based on "Playboy Makes the Boss's Daughter Boss," *Fortune*, August 23, 1982; James E. Ellis, with Geraldine Fabrikant and Elizabeth Ames, "Now Even Playboy Is Bracing for a Midlife Crisis," *Business Week*, April 15, 1985, pp. 66–68 (quotation from p. 68); "Playboy Enterprises," *Advertising Age*, June 30, 1986, pp. 556–557; "Playboy: Buddy Down the Line," *Economist*, April 11, 1987, p. 69; Stephen Kindel, "A Rabbit's Tale," *Financial World*, May 5, 1987, p. 6; "Playboy's Progress," *Fortune*, October 12, 1987, p. 9.

Chapter 4 **Introductory case:** Based on Leslie Schultz, "A Compression of Old and New," *Inc.* (February 1983). **Management in Action:** Excerpted by permission from *Wendy's International Inc. Annual Report, 1986*, pp. 2–4. **Figure 4.5:** From William R. King and David I. Cleland, "A New Method for Strategic Systems Planning," *Business Horizons* (August 1975): 56. Copyright, 1975, by the Foundation for the School of Business at Indiana University. Reprinted by permission. **Concluding case:** Adapted from Bruce G. Posner, "Real Entrepreneurs Don't Plan." Reprinted with permission, *Inc.* magazine (November 1985): 129–135. Copyright © 1985 by *Inc.* Publishing Company, 38 Commercial Wharf, Boston, MA 02110.

Chapter 5 **Introductory case:** Based on Jill Andresky, "Another Mile to Go," *Forbes*, April 25, 1983. **Table 5.1:** From Herbert A. Simon, *The Shape of Automation* (New York: Harper & Row, 1965), p. 62. Used with permission of the author. **Management in Action:** Excerpted from Stephen Koepp, "A Hard Decision to Swallow," *Time*, March 3, 1986, p. 59. Copyright 1986 Time Inc. All rights reserved. Reprinted by permission from *Time*. **Figure 5.3:** Republished with permission of E. I. du Pont de Nemours & Company. **Table 5.2:** Reprinted from "Characteristics of Organizational Environments and Perceived Environmental Uncertainty" by Robert B. Duncan. Published by *Administrative Science Quarterly*, Vol. 17, No. 3 (September 1972). By permission of *Administrative Science Quarterly*. **Figure 5.8:** Reprinted by permission of the *Harvard Business Review*. An exhibit from "Decision Trees for Decision Making" by John F. Magee (July/August 1964): 130. Copyright © 1964 by the President and Fellows of Harvard College; all rights reserved. **Concluding case:** Excerpt from Myron Magnet, "How Top Managers Make a Company's Toughest Decision," *Fortune*, March 18, 1985, pp. 52–57. © 1985 Time Inc. All rights reserved.

Chapter 6 **Introductory case:** Based on "Prescription for Profits," *Time*, July 4, 1983. **Table 6.1:** (a) and (b) based on E. Meadows, "How Three Companies Increased Their Productivity," *Fortune*, March 10, 1980, pp. 92–101. (c) based on William B. Johnson, "The Transformation of a Railroad," *Long-Range Planning* 9 (December 1976): 18–23. **Figure 6.1:** From Arthur A. Thompson, Jr., and A. J. Strickland III, *Strategy and Policy: Concepts and Cases*, rev. ed., p. 24. Copyright © 1981 Business Publications, Inc. Reprinted by permission. **Table 6.2:** From William F. Glueck and Lawrence R. Jauch, *Business Policy and Strategic Management*. © 1984 McGraw-Hill Book Company, New York. Reprinted by permission. **Management in Action:** Reprinted by permission from Nancy J. Perry, "Letting the Sun Shine In," *Fortune*, August 3, 1987, p. 29. © 1987 Time Inc. All rights reserved. **Table 6.3:** Adapted from Arvind V. Phatak, *International Dimensions of Management* (Boston: Kent Publishing, 1983), p. 6. © by Wadsworth, Inc. Reprinted by permission of PWS-Kent Publishing Co., a division of Wadsworth, Inc. **Table 6.5:** From Arthur A. Thompson, Jr., and A. J. Strickland III, *Strategy Formulation and Implementation*, 3d ed. Copyright © 1986 Business Publications, Inc. Reprinted by permission. **Figure 6.3:** © 1970 The Boston Consulting Group, Inc. All rights reserved. Published by permission. **Figure 6.5:** Reprinted with the special permission of *Dun's Review* from R. M. Besse, "Company Planning Must Be Planned," April 1957, p. 48. Copyright 1957, Dun & Bradstreet Publications Corporation. **Concluding case:** Based on Howard Rudnitsky, "Making Money at the Low End of the Market," *Forbes*, December 17, 1984.

Chapter 7 **Introductory case 7:** First two paragraphs from Earl F. Lundgren, *Organizational Management Systems and Process*, pp. 153–154. © 1974 Harper & Row, Publishers, Inc. Reprinted by permission of the author. **Management in Action:** Excerpted from Cathy Trost, "Child-Care Center at Virginia Firm Boosts Worker Morale and Loyalty," *Wall Street Journal*, February 12, 1987, p. 27. Reprinted by permission of the *Wall Street Journal*, © Dow Jones & Company, Inc., 1987. All rights reserved. **Table 7.1:** Copyright © 1969 by the Trustees of Columbia University in the City of New York. **Table 7.2:** Reprinted by permission from *Indiana State University Handbook* 1969. Revised in 1970 and in 1972, Terre Haute, Indiana. **Tables 7.3, 7.4:** Adapted from E. S. Groo, "Choosing Foreign Locations: One Company's Experience," *Columbia Journal of World Business* (September/October 1977): 77. Used with permission. **Figure 7.4:** From Bruce Coleman, "An Integrated System for Manpower Planning," *Business Horizons* (October 1970): 89–95. Copyright, 1970, by the Foundation for the School of Business at Indiana University. Reprinted by permission. **Table 7.5:** Adapted, with permission, from W. C. House, "Environmental Analysis: Key to More Effective Dynamic Planning," *Managerial Planning* (January/February 1977): 27, published by the Planning Executive Institute, Oxford, Ohio 45046. **Figure 7.6:** From Philip Kotler, *Marketing Management Analysis, Planning and Control,* © 1967, p. 291. Adapted by permission of Prentice-Hall, Inc., Englewood Cliffs, N.J. **Table 7.6:** Material in table adapted from *Sales Forecasting* (New York: The Conference Board, Inc., 1978), pp. 11–12, 31–44, 47–80. **Figure 7.8:** Reprinted by permission of the Sperry Rand Corporation. **Concluding case:** Adapted by permission from Robert C. Baldwin, "Streamlining Operations at the Aro Corporation," *Plant Engineering,* April 9, 1987, pp. 42–47. **Section 2 integrative case:** Based on "More Effective Strategic Planning for Organizations," *CPA Journal* (May 1984): 18–23. **Unnumbered table in case:** Reprinted with permission of *The CPA Journal* (May 1984): 18–23. Copyright 1984, New York State Society of Certified Public Accountants.

Chapter 8   Figure 8.11: © 1972 by the Regents of the University of California. Reprinted from Y. K. Shetty and H. M. Carlisle, "A Contingency Model of Organizational Behavior," *California Management Review,* Vol. 15, No. 1, p. 44, by permission of the Regents. **Management in Action:** Excerpted from George J. Church, "Behind the Help-Wanted Signs," *Time,* July 20, 1987, p. 55. Copyright 1987 Time Inc. All rights reserved. Reprinted by permission from *Time.* **Table 8.2:** From *Principles of Management,* p. 253, by Harold Koontz and Cyril O'Donnell. Copyright © 1972 by McGraw-Hill, Inc. Used with permission of McGraw-Hill Book Co. **Figure 8.14:** From H. Fayol, *General and Industrial Management,* trans. Constance Storrs (London: Sir Isaac Pitman & Sons, Ltd., 1963), p. 34. Used with permission. **Concluding case:** Based on Kenneth Labich, "How Long Can Quilting-Bee Management Work?" *Fortune,* November 25, 1985, p. 132; Bill Powell, "Donald Burr: A Fallen Hero," *Newsweek,* July 7, 1986, pp. 36–37; William M. Carley, "Bumpy Flights: Many Travelers Gripe about People Express, Citing Overbooking," *Wall Street Journal,* May 19, 1986, pp. 1, 12; William M. Carley, "New Flight Plan: Struggling to Survive, People Express Alters Operations and Image," *Wall Street Journal,* July 31, 1986, pp. 1, 17; Amanda Bennett, "Airline's Ills Point Out Weaknesses of Unorthodox Management Style," *Wall Street Journal,* August 11, 1986, p. 15; Teri Agins, "People Express Holders Approve Firm's Acquisition," *Wall Street Journal,* December 30, 1986, p. 2; Paulette Thomas, "Again, Burr and Lorenzo Part Company as People's Founder Leaves Texas Air," *Wall Street Journal,* April 13, 1987, p. 6.

Chapter 9   **Table 9.1:** Reprinted, by permission of the publisher, from "Roles and Relationships Clarifying the Manager's Job," by Robert D. Melcher, *Personnel* (May/June 1967): 35, 38–39. © 1967 American Management Association, New York. All rights reserved. **Management in Action:** Excerpted from Robert E. Kelley, "Poorly Served Employees Serve Customers Just as Poorly," *Wall Street Journal,* October 12, 1987, p. 21. Reprinted by permission of the *Wall Street Journal,* © Dow Jones & Company, Inc., 1987. All rights reserved. **Figure 9.2:** Reprinted by permission of the publisher, from "Roles and Relationships Clarifying the Manager's Job," by Robert D. Melcher, *Personnel* (May/June 1967): 35, 38–39. © 1967 American Management Association, New York. All rights reserved. **Table 9.3:** From Louis A. Allen, "Developing Sound Line and Staff Relationships," from *Studies in Personnel Policy* No. 153. National Industrial Conference Board, 1956. Used with permission. **Table 9.4:** Adapted from ASPA-BNA Survey No. 47, "Personnel Activities, Budgets, and Staffs: 1983–1984," *Bulletin to Management* No. 1785—Part II, June 21, 1984. Reprinted by permission. **Table 9.5:** Reprinted with permission of Macmillan Publishing Company from *The New Management* by Robert M. Fulmer. Copyright © 1974 by Robert M. Fulmer. **Figure 9.4:** From David B. Starkweather, "The Rationale for Decentralization in Large Hospitals," *Hospital Administration* 15 (Spring 1970): 139. Courtesy of Dr. P. N. Ghei, Secretary General, Indian Hospital Association, New Delhi. **Concluding case:** Reprinted by permission of the author from Peter F. Drucker, "Management Lessons of Irangate," *Wall Street Journal,* March 24, 1987.

Chapter 10   **Introductory case:** Based on Joel Dreyfuss, "Handing Down the Old Hands' Wisdom," *Fortune,* June 13, 1983. **Figure 10.2:** Reprinted with permission of Macmillan Publishing Company from *Personnel: The Management of People at Work* by Dale S. Beach. Copyright © 1970 by Dale S. Beach. **Table 10.1:** From U.S. Civil Service Commission. **Figures 10.3, 10.4, 10.5:** From Walter S. Wikstrom, "Developing Manage-

rial Competence: Concepts, Emerging Practices," *Studies in Personnel Policy* No. 189, pp. 14, 9. Used with permission. **Table 10.2:** From Gene E. Burton, Dev S. Pathak, David B. Burton, "Equal Employment Opportunity: Law and Labyrinth," *Management World,* published by Administrative Management Society, September 1976, pp. 29, 30. **Figure 10.6:** Reprinted by permission from L. C. Megginson, *Providing Management Talent for Small Business* (Baton Rouge, La. Division of Research, College of Business Administration, Louisiana State University, 1961), p. 108. **Table 10.3:** Reprinted from John B. Miner, *Personnel Psychology* (New York: Macmillan, 1969). Courtesy John B. Miner. **Table 10.4:** From Dale Feuer, "Where the Dollars Go," reprinted from the October 1985 issue of *Training,* The Magazine of Human Resources Development, p. 53. Copyright 1985, Lakewood Publications Inc., Minneapolis, MN (612)333–0471. All rights reserved. **Figure 10.8:** From George R. Terry and Leslie W. Rue, *Personal Learning Aid for Principles of Management,* p. 138. Copyright © 1982 Dow Jones–Irwin. Reprinted by permission. **Table 10.5:** Compiled from *Personnel Administration and Human Resource Management* by Andrew F. Sikula (New York: John Wiley & Sons, 1976), pp. 208–211. **Management in Action:** Reprinted from *Iacocca: An Autobiography* by Lee Iacocca with William Novak. Copyright © 1984 by Lee Iacocca. By permission of Bantam Books, Inc. All rights reserved. **Concluding case:** Adapted from Tom Richman, "Mississippi Motivators." Reprinted with permission, *Inc.* magazine (October 1986): 83–88. Copyright © 1986 by *Inc.* Publishing Company, 38 Commercial Wharf, Boston, MA 02110.

Chapter 11   Introductory case: Based on "GM Plans a Great Divide," *Newsweek,* January 9, 1984. **Figure 11.1:** From Don Hellriegel and John W. Slocum, Jr., "Integrating Systems Concepts and Organizational Strategy," *Business Horizons* 15 (April 1972): 73. Copyright, 1972, by the Foundation for the School of Business at Indiana University. Reprinted by permission. **Management in Action:** From Katherine M. Hafner, "Apple Is Getting a Few Gray Hairs." Reprinted from the January 19, 1987, issue of *Business Week,* p. 88, by special permission, copyright © 1987 by McGraw-Hill, Inc. Lyrics from Bob Dylan song "Forever Young," copyright 1973, 1974 by Ram's Horn Music. All rights reserved. International copyright secured. Reprinted by permission. **Figures 11.4, 11.5:** From John F. Mee, "Matrix Organization," *Business Horizons* (Summer 1964): 71. Copyright, 1964, by the Foundation for the School of Business at Indiana University. Reprinted by permission. **Figure 11.6:** From Richard J. Selfridge and Stanley I. Sokolik, "A Comprehensive View of Organization Development," p. 47, *MSU Business Topics* (Winter 1975). Reprinted by permission of the publishers, Division of Research, Graduate School of Business Administration, Michigan State University. **Figure 11.7:** Reprinted by permission of *Harvard Business Review,* from "Breakthrough in Organization Development," by Robert R. Blake, Jane S. Mouton, Louis Barnes, and Larry Greiner (November/December 1964): 136. Copyright © 1964 by the President and Fellows of Harvard College; all rights reserved. **Figure 11.9:** Reprinted by permission of the authors from Arthur P. Brief, Randall S. Schuler, and Mary Van Sell, *Managing Job Stress* (Boston: Little, Brown, 1981), p. 66. **Concluding case:** Adapted from John S. McClenahen, "The Welch Years: GE Gambles on Growth." Reprinted with permission from *Industry Week,* April 20, 1987, pp. 30–32. Copyright, Penton Publishing, Inc., Cleveland, Ohio. **Section 3 integrative case figure:** Courtesy Chicago National League Ball Club, Inc.

Chapter 12   Introductory case: Based on Stephen J. Sansweet, "Troubles at Mattel Seen Extending beyond Fallout in Electronics Line," *Wall Street Journal,* May 6, 1983. **Table 12.1:** Reprinted by permission from Stephen C. Harper, "Business Education: A View from the Top," *Business Forum* (Summer 1987): 25. **Figures 12.4, 12.5:** From Wilbur Schramm, *The Process and Effects of Mass Communication.* © 1954 University of Illinois Press, Champaign, IL. Reprinted by permission. **Table 12.2:** Reprinted, by permission of the publisher, from "Management's Tower of Babel," by Verne Burnett, *Management Review* (June 1961): 7. © 1961 American Management Association, Inc. All rights reserved. **Figure 12.7:** Reprinted, by permission of the publisher, from "An Experimental Approach to Organizational Communication," by Alex Bavelas and Dermot Barrett, *Personnel* (March 1951): 370. © 1951 American Management Association, Inc. All rights reserved. **Figure 12.8:** Reprinted by permission of the *Harvard Business Review.* An exhibit from "Management Communication and the Grapevine" by Keith Davis (September/October 1953): 45. Copyright © 1953 by the President and Fellows of Harvard College; all rights reserved. **Table 12.3:** From *Human Behavior at Work,* p. 396, by Keith Davis. Copyright © 1972 by McGraw-Hill, Inc. Used with permission of McGraw-Hill Book Company. **Management in Action:** Excerpted from Lad Kuzela, "Sandy's Working at Home Today." Reprinted with permission from *Industry Week,* June 1, 1987, pp. 34–35. Copyright, Penton Publishing, Inc., Cleveland, Ohio. **Concluding case:** Based on Donald L. Currier, "Improved Employee Involvement in a Health Care Facility," *Training and Development Journal* (July 1983).

Chapter 13 **Introductory case table:** From Henry A. Singer, "Human Values and Leadership," *Business Horizons* (August 1975): 85–88. Copyright, 1975, by the Foundation for the School of Business at Indiana University. Reprinted by permission. **Table 13.1:** From Wendell L. French, *Personnel Management Process*, 5th ed. © 1982 Houghton Mifflin Company, Boston, MA. Reprinted by permission. **Figure 13.2:** Reprinted by permission of the *Harvard Business Review*, from "How to Choose a Leadership Pattern," by Robert Tannenbaum and Warren H. Schmidt (May/June 1973). Copyright © 1973 by the President and Fellows of Harvard College; all rights reserved. **Management in Action:** Richard L. Hudson, "How Two IBM Physicists Triggered the Frenzy over Superconductors," *Wall Street Journal*, August 19, 1987, pp. 1, 6. Reprinted by permission of the *Wall Street Journal*, © Dow Jones & Company, Inc., 1987. All rights reserved. **Figure 13.5:** From Paul Hersey, Kenneth H. Blanchard, *Management of Organizational Behavior: Utilizing Human Resources*, 3d ed., © 1977, p. 103. Reprinted by permission of Prentice-Hall, Inc., Englewood Cliffs, New Jersey. **Table 13.2:** From Paul Hersey, Kenneth H. Blanchard, *Management of Organizational Behavior: Utilizing Human Resources*, 3d ed., © 1977 by Prentice-Hall, Inc., Englewood Cliffs, New Jersey. Used with permission of Dr. W. J. Reddin, University of New Brunswick. **Table 13.3:** From *A Theory of Leadership Effectiveness* by F. E. Fiedler, p. 34. Copyright © 1967 by McGraw-Hill, Inc. Used by permission of McGraw-Hill Book Company. **Figure 13.6:** Reprinted by permission of the *Harvard Business Review*, from "Engineer the Job to Fit the Manager," by Fred E. Fiedler (September/October 1965). Copyright © 1965 by the President and Fellows of Harvard College; all rights reserved. **Concluding case:** Adapted from Minda Zetlin, "John Egan: Tough Leadership Turns Jaguar Around," *Management Review* (May 1986): 20–22. © 1986 American Management Association. All rights reserved. Supplementary information from David Fairlamb, "Comeback of a Class Car," *Dun's Business Month* (November 1985): 64–66; and Michael H. Dale, "How We Rebuilt Jaguar in the U.S.," *Fortune*, April 28, 1986, pp. 110–120.

Chapter 14 **Introductory case:** Based on Thomas H. Melohn, "How to Build Employee Trust and Productivity," *Harvard Business Review* (January/February 1983). **Figure 14.3:** From Lyman Porter and Edward Lawler III, *Managerial Attitudes and Performance*. Copyright © 1968 Richard D. Irwin, Inc. Reprinted by permission. **Figure 14.5:** Adapted from B. Kolasa, *Introduction to Behavioral Science in Business* (New York: Wiley, 1969), p. 256. Used with permission. **Management in Action:** Excerpted from Stephen Koepp, "Make That Sale, Mr. Sam," *Time*, May 18, 1987, pp. 54–55. Copyright 1987 Time Inc. All rights reserved. Reprinted by permission from *Time*. **Table 14.1:** From *The Human Side of Enterprise* by Douglas McGregor. Copyright © 1960 by McGraw-Hill, Inc. Used with permission of McGraw-Hill Book Company. **Figure 14.6:** From W. J. Reddin, "The Tri-Dimensional Grid." Reproduced by special permission from the July 1964 *Training and Development Journal*. Copyright 1964 by the American Society for Training and Development Inc. **Tables 14.2, 14.3:** Reprinted by permission of the *Harvard Business Review*, from "One More Time: How Do You Motivate Employees?" by Frederick Herzberg (January/February 1968). Copyright © 1968 by the President and Fellows of Harvard College; all rights reserved. **Table 14.4:** Reprinted by permission from Edward G. Thomas, "Workers Who Set Their Own Time Clocks," *Business and Society Review* (Spring 1987): 50. **Concluding case:** Reprinted from Jamie Murphy, "Hail to the Mountain King!" *Time*, October 27, 1986, p. 106. Copyright 1986 Time Inc. All rights reserved. Reprinted by permission from *Time*.

Chapter 15 **Figure 15.2:** From *New Patterns of Management* by Rensis Likert, p. 104. Copyright © 1961 by McGraw-Hill, Inc. Used with permission of McGraw-Hill Book Company. **Figure 15.3:** Reprinted by permission of the *Harvard Business Review* from "Committees on Trial" (Problems in Review) by Rollie Tillman, Jr. (May/June 1960): 163. Copyright © 1960 by the President and Fellows of Harvard College; all rights reserved. **Figure 15.4:** Adapted from Raymond McLeod, Jr., and Jack W. Jones, "Making Executive Information Systems More Effective," *Business Horizons* (September/October 1986): 32. Copyright, 1986, by the Foundation for the School of Business at Indiana University. Reprinted by permission. **Figure 15.5:** Reprinted by permission of the *Harvard Business Review* from "Committees on Trial" (Problems in Review) by Rollie Tillman, Jr. (May/June 1960). Copyright © 1960 by the President and Fellows of Harvard College; all rights reserved. **Management in Action:** From Robert S. Greenberger, "Quality Circles Grow, Stirring Union Worries," *Wall Street Journal*, September 22, 1981, p. 33. Reprinted by permission of the *Wall Street Journal*, © Dow Jones & Company, Inc. 1981. All rights reserved. **Figure 15.7:** Figure 11.5 from p. 238 of *Social Psychology* by Muzafer Sherif and Carolyn W. Sherif. Copyright © 1969 by Muzafer Sherif and Carolyn W. Sherif. Reprinted by permission of Harper & Row, Publishers, Inc. **Table 15.1:** Reprinted with permission from Don Hellriegel and John W. Slocum, Jr.'s "Organizational Behavior Contingency Views," p. 166. Copyright © 1976 by West Publishing Co. **Table 15.2:** From T. W. Johnson & J. E. Stinson, *Managing Today and Tomorrow*. © 1978, Addison-Wesley Publishing Co., Inc., Reading, Massachusetts. Figure on page 69. Reprinted with permission. **Figure 15.10:** Reprinted, by permission of the publisher, from "Group Norms Key to Building a Winning Team," by P. C. Andre dela Porte, *Personnel* (September/October 1974): 64. © 1974 American Management Association, New York. All rights reserved. **Table 15.3:** Reprinted, by permission of the publisher, from "What Raises a Man's Morale," by Morris S. Viteles, *Personnel* (January 1954): 305. © 1954 American Management Association, Inc. All rights reserved. **Concluding case:** Adapted from Donald B. Thompson, "Everybody's a Boss: Goodyear Bets Its Future on Plant's Success." Reprinted with permission from *Industry Week*, February 23, 1987, pp. 16–17. Also adapted from Thomas M. Rohan, "Bosses—Who Needs 'Em? Work Teams Manage Their Own Jobs at Frito-Lay." Reprinted with permission from *Industry Week*, February 23, 1987, pp. 15–16. Copyright, Penton Publishing, Inc., Cleveland, Ohio. **Section 4 integrative case:** Based on "Trips Pay Off for Panasonic and Apple," *Sales and Marketing Management*, July 2, 1984.

Chapter 16 **Introductory case:** From *Essentials of Management* by Harold Koontz, pp. 554–555. Copyright © 1978 by McGraw-Hill Book Company. Used with permission of McGraw-Hill Book Co. **Figure 16.1:** From Thomas L. Martin, *Malice in Blunderland* (New York: McGraw-Hill, 1973). Used with permission. Permission for newsletter format granted by the General Tire and Rubber Company, Akron, Ohio. **Management in Action:** Excerpted from Roger Lowenstein, "A Golfer Becomes an Executive: Jack Nicklaus's Business Education," *Wall Street Journal*, January 27, 1987, p. 37. Reprinted by permission of the *Wall Street Journal*, © Dow Jones & Company, Inc., 1987. All rights reserved. **Table 16.1:** Adapted from Y. K. Shetty, "Product Quality and Competitive Strategy," *Business Horizons* (May/June 1987): 47. Copyright, 1987, by the Foundation for the School of Business at Indiana University. Reprinted by permission. **Figure 16.4:** Reprinted by permission of the *Harvard Business Review*. An exhibit from "Better Reports for Better Control" by John G. McLean (May/June 1957): 98. Copyright © 1957 by the President and Fellows of Harvard College; all rights reserved. **Table 16.2:** Reprinted by permission from p. 13 of *Cost Accounting: A Managerial Approach*, 2e, by Cherrington, Hubbard, and Luthy. Copyright © 1988 by West Publishing Company. All rights reserved. **Concluding case:** The two block quotes are from Ed Magnuson, "A Serious Deficiency," *Time*, March 10, 1986, pp. 38–39, 42. Copyright 1986 Time Inc. All rights reserved. Reprinted by permission from *Time*. Other material adapted from Teresa M. Foley, "NASA Takes Action to Rebuild Safety, Quality Assurance," *Aviation Week & Space Technology*, November 17, 1986, p. 49. Courtesy *Aviation Week & Space Technology*. Copyright McGraw-Hill, Inc., 1986. All rights reserved.

Chapter 17 **Introductory case:** Based on Dennis Kneale, "Commodore Hits Production Snags in Its Hot-Selling Home Computer," *Wall Street Journal*, October 28, 1983. **Figure 17.1:** From *Accounting and Information Systems* by Joseph W. Wilkinson. Copyright © 1982 John Wiley & Sons, Inc. Reprinted by permission of John Wiley & Sons, Inc. **Table 17.1:** Based on Roger H. Mitchell and Vincent A. Mabert, "Robotics for Smaller Manufacturers: Myths and Realities," *Business Horizons* (July/August 1986): 9–16. **Table 17.2:** From *Plant Layout and Materials Handling* by James M. Apple. Copyright © 1977 John Wiley & Sons, Inc., New York. Reprinted by permission of John Wiley & Sons, Inc. **Figure 17.3:** From Richard B. Chase and Nicholas J. Aquilano, *Production and Operations Management: A Life Cycle Approach*, 4th ed., p. 5. © 1985 Richard D. Irwin, Inc. Reprinted by permission. **Figure 17.5:** Reprinted by permission of the *Harvard Business Review*. An exhibit from "Behind the Growth in Material Requirements Planning" by Jeffrey G. Miller and Linda G. Sprague (September/October 1975): 84. Copyright © 1975 by the President and Fellows of Harvard College; all rights reserved. **Management in Action:** Adapted from Allana Sullivan, "Mobil's New Chairman Acts Quickly to Shed Assets to Reduce Debt," *Wall Street Journal*, January 29, 1987, pp. 1, 13. Reprinted by permission of the *Wall Street Journal*, © Dow Jones & Company, Inc., 1987. All rights reserved. **Concluding case:** Compiled from Damon Darlin, "General Motors to Recall 750,000 Cars for Problems with Pollution Controls," *Wall Street Journal*, October 15, 1984; "GM Is Told by EPA to Recall 174,000 '80 Buicks, Pontiacs," *Wall Street Journal*, February 2, 1983; "GM Told to Recall '78 Cars Violating Clean-Air Rules," *Wall Street Journal*, March 25, 1983; "GM Cites Flaw in Converters, Begins a Recall," *Wall Street Journal*, July 8, 1983; "GM Is Ordered by EPA to Recall Some Chevettes," *Wall Street Journal*," October 21, 1983; "GM Is Told to Recall about 186,000 Autos," *Wall Street Journal*, March 20, 1984.

Chapter 18 **Introductory case:** From *The Management of Organizations*, p. 516, by Herbert G. Hicks and C. Ray Gullett. Copyright © 1976 by McGraw-Hill, Inc. Used with permission of McGraw-Hill Book Company. **Figure 18.1:** Reprinted by permission from G. Anthony Gorry and Michael S. Scott Morton, "A Framework for Management Information Systems," *Sloan Management Review*, vol. 13, no. 1 (Fall 1971): 59. **Figure**

18.2: From Roman R. Andrus, ''Approaches to Information Evaluation,'' p. 44, *MSU Business Topics* (Summer 1971). Reprinted by permission of the publisher, Division of Research, Graduate School of Business Administration, Michigan State University. **Table 18.1:** From Roman R. Andrus, ''Approaches to Information Evaluation,'' p. 44, *MSU Business Topics* (Summer 1971). Reprinted by permission of the publisher, Division of Research, Graduate School of Business Administration, Michigan State University. **Table 18.2:** Reprinted by permission from Alice M. Greene, ''Computers Big Pay-off for Small Companies,'' *Iron Age*, March 30, 1972, pp. 63–64. **Management in Action:** Excerpted from Amanda Bennett, ''CARE Makes a Comeback after Drive to Revamp Its Management Practices,'' *Wall Street Journal*, February 9, 1987, p. 21. Reprinted by permission of the *Wall Street Journal*, © Dow Jones & Company, Inc., 1987. All rights reserved. Figure courtesy of CARE Inc. **Table 18.3:** Reprinted by permission of *Harvard Business Review*. An exhibit from ''Manufacturing—Missing Link in Corporate Strategy'' by Wickham Skinner (May/June 1969): 141. Copyright © 1969 by the President and Fellows of Harvard College; all rights reserved. **Figure 18.5:** Adapted from Robert G. Murdick, ''MIS for MBO,'' *Journal of Systems Management* (March 1977): 34–40. Used with permission of *Journal of Systems Management*, 24587 Bagley Road, Cleveland, Ohio 44138. **Table 18.4:** Reprinted by permission of the *Harvard Business Review*, from ''Problems in Planning the Information System,'' by F. Warren McFarlan (March/April 1971): 82. Copyright © 1971 by the President and Fellows of Harvard College; all rights reserved. **Figure 18.6:** Reprinted by permission from R. E. Breen et al., *Management Information Systems: A Subcommittee Report on Definitions* (Schenectady, N.Y.: General Electric Co., 1969), p. 21. **Table 18.5:** Reprinted by permission of the Institute of Management Services from Bertram A. Colbert, ''The Management Information System,'' *Management Services* 4, no. 5 (September/October 1967): 18. **Table 18.6:** From Dickson/Simmons, ''The Behavioral Side of MIS,'' *Business Horizons* (August 1970): 68. Copyright, 1970, by the Foundation for the School of Business at Indiana University. Reprinted by permission. **Figure 18.7:** ''Parts of the Personal Computer and What They Do,'' *Time*, January 3, 1983, p. 39. Copyright 1983 Time Inc. All rights reserved. Reprinted by permission from *Time*. **Figure 18.8:** From Mark G. Simkin, *Computer Information Systems for Business*, p. 299. Copyright © 1987 Wm. C. Brown Publishers, Dubuque, Iowa. All rights reserved. Reprinted by permission. **Concluding case:** First block quotation from John Greenwald, ''Deadly Meltdown,'' *Time*, May 12, 1986, pp. 38–44, 49; second and third block quotations from Michael S. Serrill, ''Anatomy of a Catastrophe,'' *Time*, September 1, 1986, p. 26. Copyright 1986 Time Inc. All rights reserved. Reprinted by permission from *Time*. **Section 5 integrative case:** Based on Charles Anderson, ''Crackdown on Computer Capers,'' *Time*, February 8, 1982.

Chapter 19 **Figure 19.1:** Adapted from Terry W. McAdams, ''How to Put Corporate Responsibility into Practice.'' Reprinted by permission from *Business and Society Review* (Summer 1973): 12–13. Copyright 1973, Warren, Gorham and Lamont Inc., 210 South St., Boston, Mass. All rights reserved. **Management in Action:** Excerpted from Eric Morgenthaler, ''Ecology Effort: A Florida Utility Wins Naturalists' Praise for Guarding Wildlife,'' *Wall Street Journal*, May 7, 1987, pp. 1, 19. Reprinted by permission of the *Wall Street Journal*, © Dow Jones & Company, Inc., 1987. All rights reserved. **Table 19.1:** From R. Joseph Mansen, Jr., ''The Social Attitudes of Management,'' in Joseph W. McGuire, *Contemporary Management*, © 1974, p. 616.'' Reprinted by permission of Prentice-Hall, Inc., Englewood Cliffs, New Jersey. **Table 19.3:** From Sandra L. Holmes, ''Executive Perceptions of Social Responsibility,'' *Business Horizons* (June 1976). Copyright, 1976, by the Foundation for the School of Business at Indiana University. Reprinted by permission. **Figure 19.2:** From Ramon J. Aldag and Donald W. Jackson, Jr., ''A Managerial Framework for Social Decision Making,'' p. 34, *MSU Business Topics* (Winter 1975). Reprinted by permission of the publisher, Division of Research, Graduate School of Business Administration, Michigan State University. **Table 19.4:** © 1975 by the Regents of the University of California. Reprinted from S. Prakash Sethi, ''Dimensions of Corporate Social Performance: An Analytical Framework,'' *California Management Review*, Vol. 17, No. 3 (Spring 1975): 63, by permission of the Regents. **Figure 19.3:** From Kenneth E. Newgren, ''Social Forecasting: An Overview of Current Business Practices,'' in Archie B. Carroll, ed., *Managing Corporate Social Responsibility*. Copyright © 1977 by Little, Brown and Company (Inc.). Reprinted by permission of the author. **Figure 19.4:** Reprinted by permission of the *Harvard Business Review*, from ''How Companies Respond to Social Demands,'' by Robert W. Ackerman (July/August 1973): 96. Copyright © 1973 by the President and Fellows of Harvard College; all rights reserved. **Figure 19.5:** Reprinted by permission from John L. Paluszek, ''How Three Companies Organize for Social Responsibility,'' *Business and Society Review* (Summer 1973): 18, Warren, Gorham and Lamont, Inc., 210 South St., Boston, Mass. All rights reserved. **Figure 19.6:** Reprinted by permission from Bernard Butcher, ''Anatomy of a Social Performance Report,'' *Business and Society Review* (Autumn 1973): 29, War-

ren, Gorham and Lamont, Inc., 210 South St., Boston, Mass. All rights reserved. **Table 19.5:** Reprinted by permission from ''Code of Ethics and Standards of Conduct'' (Orlando, Fla.: Martin Marietta, n.d.), p. 3. **Table 19.6:** Reprinted by permission of Johnson & Johnson. **Concluding case:** Adapted from Richard Koenig, ''Medical Problems: As Liver Transplants Grow More Common, Ethical Issues Multiply,'' *Wall Street Journal*, October 14, 1986, pp. 1, 29. Reprinted by permission of the *Wall Street Journal*, © Dow Jones & Company, Inc., 1986. All rights reserved.

Chapter 20 **Introductory case:** Excerpts reprinted by permission of RJR Nabisco, Inc., from the 1987 Nabisco Brands Annual Report. **Figures 20.1, 20.2:** From U.S. Bureau of the Census, *Statistical Abstracts of the United States* (Washington, D.C.: Government Printing Office, 1987). **Table 20.1:** Excerpted from ''The FORBES Foreign Rankings,'' by permission of *Forbes* magazine, July 29, 1985. © Forbes Inc., 1985. **Figure 20.3:** Reprinted by permission of the author from Richard D. Robinson, *International Management* (Hinsdale, Ill.: Dryden Press, 1967). **Table 20.3:** From Stefan H. Robock and Kenneth Simmonds, *International Business and Multinational Enterprise*, 3d ed. Copyright © 1983 Richard D. Irwin, Inc. Reprinted by permission. **Table 20.4:** From Grant F. Winthrop, ''Can a Computer Tell the Ratio of Risk?'' *Fortune*, March 24, 1980, p. 95. © 1980 Time Inc. All rights reserved. **Table 20.5:** Reprinted with permission from Howard V. Perlmutter, ''The Tortuous Evolution of the Multinational Corporation,'' *Columbia Journal of World Business* 4 (January/February 1969): 12. **Table 20.6:** From Hugh E. Kramer, ''Concepts of Competition in America, Europe, and Japan,'' in *Business and Society* (Fall 1977). © 1977 Business and Society. Reprinted by permission. **Management in Action:** From Janice Castro, ''Mazda U.: American Workers Study Kaizen,'' *Time*, October 20, 1986, pp. 64–65. Copyright 1986 Time Inc. All rights reserved. Reprinted by permission from *Time*. **Figure 20.5:** From William Ouchi, *Theory Z*, © 1981, Addison-Wesley Publishing Co., Inc., Reading, Massachusetts. Page 58 (adapted figure). Reprinted with permission. **Concluding case:** Based on Rogers Worthington, ''Nissan's Tennessee Workers Adopt Japanese Way to a Happy Day,'' *Chicago Tribune*, January 9, 1983.

Chapter 21 **Figures 21.2, 21.3, 21.4:** From Bureau of Labor Statistics. **Table 21.1:** From Alma S. Baron and Robert L. Witte, ''The New Work Dynamic: Men and Women in the Work Force,'' *Business Horizons* (August 1980): 56–60. Copyright, 1980, by the Foundation for the School of Business at Indiana University. Reprinted by permission. **Figure 21.5:** From Bureau of Labor Statistics. **Management in Action:** Adapted from Helen Rogan, ''Top Women Executives Find Path to Power Strewn with Hurdles,'' *Wall Street Journal*, October 25, 1984, p. 35. Reprinted by permission of the *Wall Street Journal*, © Dow Jones & Company, Inc., 1984. All rights reserved. **Table 21.2:** Adapted from H. Igor Ansoff, ''Management in Transition,'' in Edward C. Bursk, ed., *Challenge to Leadership: Managing in a Changing World* (New York: The Free Press, 1973), p. 41. Copyright 1973 by the Conference Board, Inc. Used with permission. **Table 21.3:** © 1969 by the Regents of the University of California. Reprinted from H. Ansoff and R. Brandenburg, ''The General Manager of the Future,'' *California Management Review*, Vol. 11, No. 3, p. 69, by permission of the Regents. **Table 21.4:** From Presidential Address by Dr. George Steiner to American Academy of Management, Minneapolis, August 15, 1972. Courtesy of Dr. Steiner. **Concluding case:** Adapted from John Bussey, ''The Industrial Revolution: Manufacturing Concerns Begin Tapping Women for the Top Spots in Factories,'' *Wall Street Journal*, March 24, 1986, p. 14. Reprinted by permission of the *Wall Street Journal*, © Dow Jones & Company, Inc., 1986. All rights reserved. **Section 6 integrative case:** Based on Earl C. Gottschalk, Jr., ''Firms Hiring New Type of Manager to Study Issues, Emerging Troubles,'' *Wall Street Journal*, June 10, 1982.

Video Appendix **Video cases 1, 2, 4:** Synopses for ''Fired,'' ''Battle of the Blimps,'' and ''The Colonel Comes to Japan'' reprinted by permission of Coronet/MTI. Videos are available from Coronet/MTI Film & Video, Distributors of Disney Educational Productions and Learning Corp. of America, 108 Wilmot Road, Deerfield, IL 60015, 800/621–2131, 312/940–1260. **Video case 3:** Excerpt reprinted by permission of the *Harvard Business Review*. An excerpt from ''The Parable of the Sadhu'' by Bowen H. McCoy (September/October 1983): 104. Copyright © 1983 by the President and Fellows of Harvard College; all rights reserved.